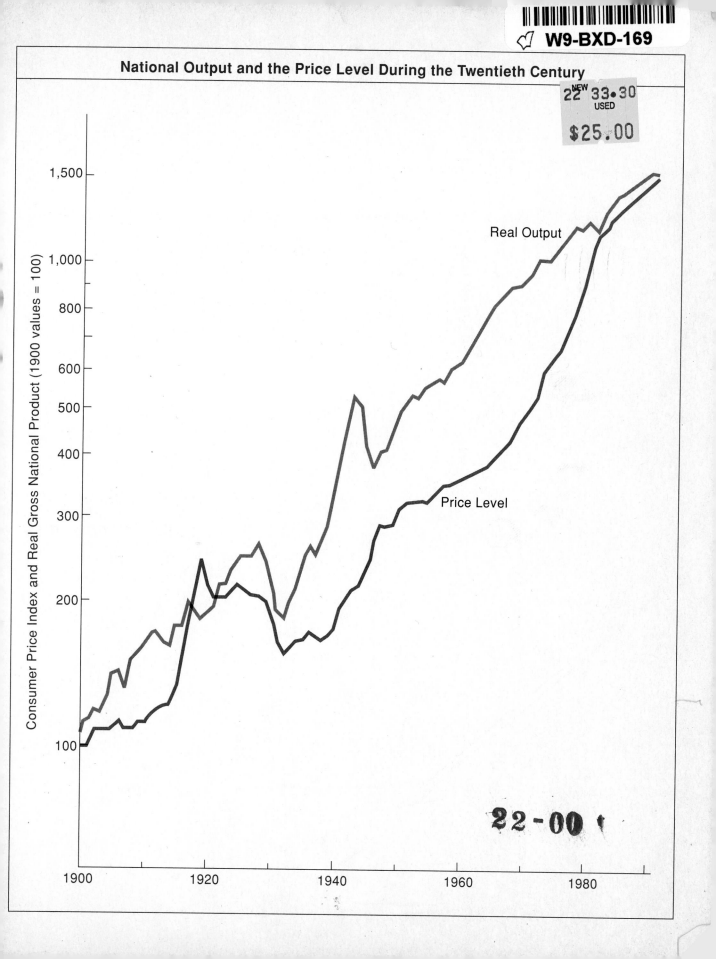

National Output and the Price Level During the Twentieth Century

MACRO-ECONOMICS

MACRO-ECONOMICS

FOURTEENTH EDITION

Paul A. Samuelson

INSTITUTE PROFESSOR EMERITUS

MASSACHUSETTS INSTITUTE

OF TECHNOLOGY

William D. Nordhaus

A. WHITNEY GRISWOLD PROFESSOR OF ECONOMICS

YALE UNIVERSITY

McGRAW-HILL, INC.

NEW YORK   ST. LOUIS   SAN FRANCISCO   AUCKLAND   BOGOTÁ   CARACAS   LISBON

LONDON   MADRID   MEXICO   MILAN   MONTREAL   NEW DELHI   PARIS

SAN JUAN   SINGAPORE   SYDNEY   TOKYO   TORONTO

MACROECONOMICS

2 3 4 5 6 7 8 9 0 DOC   DOC 9 0 9 8 7 6 5 4 3 2

ISBN 0-07-054892-7

This book was set in Zapf Book Light by York Graphic Services, Inc.
The editors were James A. Bittker and Larry Goldberg;
the production supervisor was Janelle S. Travers.
The cover was designed by Hermann Strobach.
New drawings were done by Vantage Art Studio.
R. R. Donnelley & Sons Company was printer and binder.

Library of Congress Cataloging-in-Publication Data

Samuelson, Paul Anthony, (date).
   Macroeconomics / Paul A. Samuelson, William D. Nordhaus. — 14th ed.
     p.   cm.
   "Derived from Economics, Fourteenth edition, by Paul A. Samuelson
and William D. Nordhaus, c1992"—T.p. verso.
   Includes index.
   ISBN 0-07-054892-7
   1. Macroeconomics.   I. Nordhaus, William D.   II. Samuelson, Paul
Anthony, (date).   Economics.   III. Title.
HB172.5.S255   1992
339—dc20   91-41624

THOMAS MOON

Paul A. Samuelson, founder of the renowned MIT graduate department of economics, was trained at the University of Chicago and Harvard. His many scientific writings brought him world fame at a young age, and he was the first American to receive a Nobel Prize in economics, in 1970. One of those rare scientists who can communicate with the lay public, Professor Samuelson long wrote an economics column for *Newsweek*. He testifies often before Congress and serves as academic consultant to the Federal Reserve, the U.S. Treasury, and various private, nonprofit organizations. He was economic adviser to President John F. Kennedy. Professor Samuelson plays tennis daily, and his family's size doubled when triplets arrived.

William D. Nordhaus is one of America's eminent economists. Born in New Mexico, he was an undergraduate at Yale, received his Ph.D. in economics at MIT, and is now the A. Whitney Griswold Professor of Economics at Yale University and on the staff of the Cowles Foundation for Research in Economics. His economic research has spanned a wide variety of topics—including the environment, inflation, energy, technological change, regulation, resource economics, and trends in profits and productivity. In addition, Professor Nordhaus takes a keen interest in economic policy. He served as a member of President Carter's Council of Economic Advisers from 1977 to 1979, was Provost of Yale University from 1986 to 1988, and writes occasionally for *The New York Times* and other periodicals. He regularly teaches the Principles of Economics course at Yale. Professor Nordhaus and his family live in New Haven, Connecticut, and share an enthusiasm for music, hiking, and skiing.

TO OUR CHILDREN AND STUDENTS

ECONOMICS
AND PERPETUAL YOUTH

It was never my idea to write an introductory economics textbook. My MIT department head, Ralph Freeman, came to me in 1945 and said:

> Paul, here's an offer you can't refuse. A year of economics is compulsory for our MIT students. And they find it dull.
>
> Take as much time off as you need. Write a book that people new to economics will like. It can be as short as you wish. Cover the topics *you* think important. I'm sure it will be a best seller.
>
> More importantly, you'll contribute to the education of a generation. Then you'll have two reputations. Paul Samuelson, the economic theorist who pioneers at the frontiers of high-falutin' mathematical economics. And Paul Samuelson, who has paid his dues to promoting economic literacy and rational understanding among the citizenry.

I laughed at first. I hesitated. Then I was lost. The die was cast. The rest, as they say, is history.

My publisher, McGraw-Hill, and my coauthor, Bill Nordhaus of Yale, have asked me to tell the story. So here goes.

Back to the Classroom

1945 was a crucial time. Germany and Japan were defeated, and American colleges were full to overflowing with returning service people and war workers. Economics was at a dynamic stage. The Great Depression of 1929–1935 had finally been licked by forceful programs that threw out the window the old orthodoxies of do-nothing monetary and fiscal policies. Britain and America had later mobilized their economies for a successful war in a way that Hitler, Mussolini, and the Emperor Hirohito's chieftains never dreamed of. And, though we could

not know it in 1945, a successful Marshall Plan and MacArthur occupation of Japan were about to set the stage for miracle decades of postwar growth in the "Age after Keynes."

College students deserved to understand all this. But, as teachers of my generation knew to our sorrow, the best-selling economics textbooks were seriously out of date. No wonder beginners were bored—and not only at MIT. My students at Harvard often had that glassy look.

This account must not be like the fictional work the humorist Mr. Dooley attributed to Teddy Roosevelt under the mythical title "Me and Cuba." If Newton had not invented the calculus when he did, Leibniz or someone named Smith would have done so. If my 1948 *Economics* had not brought guns-and-butter choices into elementary microeconomics, someone somewhere would soon have done so. At the time of my first edition, even the word "macroeconomics"—the study of what determines a society's unemployment, its price-level inflation rate, and its rate of real GNP growth—was not yet in the dictionary! Some scholar just had to come along and revolutionize the introductory textbooks of economics.

But why me? I was back from the MIT Radiation Laboratory, where I had worked at the mathematical job of designing automatic servomechanisms toward off enemy bombers. So to speak, I thirsted for a return to economic research and teaching. I was 30, the best age to write a text or innovate a treatise. By good chance, my advanced *Foundations of Economic Analysis*, which was to win me a Nobel Prize in economics 25 years later, was already in press. Now or never to author a textbook. But first I must tell a secret. Back in those days, a promising scholar was not supposed to write textbooks—certainly not basic texts for beginning sophomores and freshmen. Only hacks were supposed to do that. But because I had already published so many research articles, it seemed that my reputation and prospects for lifetime tenure could afford me the elbow room to respond positively to MIT's request for a new textbook. Being cocky and even brash in those good old days, it was myself I had to please.

What clinched the argument for me was this: Linus Pauling, so great a scholar and humanist that he was to win two Nobel Prizes, had already written a leading chemistry text—just as the great Richard Feynman was later to publish classic physics lectures. William James had long since published his great *Principles of Psychology*. Richard Courant, top dog at Göttingen in Germany, had not been too proud to author an accurate textbook on calculus. Who was Paul Samuelson to throw stones at scholars like these? And, working the other side of the street, I thought it was high time that we got the leaders in economics back in the trenches of general education. (Running ahead of the story, one can report that by the 1990s the innovators in undergraduate economic teaching have often been those who pierced farthest out into the frontiers of economics as a scholarly discipline.)

The Long Grind of Creation

Starting a baby is easy. Bringing it to full term involves labor and travail. As soon as each chapter was written, the mimeograph machine ground it out for testing on our MIT students. I found it demanding work, but pleasant.

Rome wasn't built in a day. And what I naively thought might be a year's job turned into 3 years of writing and rewriting. For once my tennis suffered, as weekends and summer vacations had to be devoted to the task of reducing to plain and understandable prose the fundamental complexities of economic science. Even the traditional diagrams of economics, I discovered, were overdue for redesigning if the "dismal science of economics" was to become the exciting subject it really is.

Of course, the word got out that a breakthrough was in the making. And soon publishers swarmed to my office like bees around flowers. "Pick us because we're big," some said. Or, "Pick us because we're small and we'll concentrate on your needs."

Or, "We have sales representatives in 48 states and 1500 colleges." I flipped a few coins and in the end decided to sign up with McGraw-Hill as publisher. Why? Because the firm was prestigious in science and business? Yes, in part. Because it had a magnificent marketing and selling staff? Yes, in part (but the other big publishers were no slouches when it came to selling college texts). What principally influenced my decision was this: (1) McGraw-Hill had published a magnificent multivolume series for the MIT Radiation Laboratory, a commercial success and a treasure house for radar and electronic sciences; and (2) McGraw-Hill had published, more for prestige than profit, the two-volume classic *Business Cycles* of Joseph Schumpeter, my famous master in the Harvard Graduate School.

The Moment of Truth

In the autumn of 1948 the first edition of *Economics* rolled off the press. No matter how hard the advance work or how optimistic the dreams, one can never be sure how the future will turn out. Fortunately, from the word "go" this novel approach to economics hit a responsive chord. Colleges big and little opted for the new. As each fresh printing was sold out, *Economics* was back again for new runs of the press.

Semester after semester our share of the market grew. In one year there was a clean sweep, with every school in the Ivy League adopting the text. As important to me were its successes at junior colleges and state universities across the map of the United States and Canada. International editions soon proliferated in English. When a Guggenheim Fellowship took me to Europe, I checked each city's main bookstore for the availability of translations into French, German, Italian, Swedish, and Portuguese.

My labor was more than rewarded. Aside from experiencing the natural vanity of an author, I was pleased as an educator to see that the citizenry, who would be deciding global policies in the last half of the century, was being exposed to the pros and cons of up-to-date mainstream economics.

Reviews of the book speeded up the bandwagon. The first one came from the pen of John Kenneth Galbraith, then an editor of the conservative business magazine *Fortune*. He predicted that the next generation would learn its economics from the

Samuelson *Economics.* Praise is sweet in authors' ears, but I must confess that it was the durability of the book's dominance that surprised me. As Andy Warhol put it: We live in a time when anyone can be a celebrity for about 15 minutes. Galbraith turned out to be more prescient than I. *Economics* did set a new and lasting pattern. Most of its successful rivals are written in its general mode, and it is heartwarming that much of the competition has come from the pens of good personal friends.

One summer the U.S. Chamber of Commerce put out over the Associated Press news wires the mock charge that McGraw-Hill's Samuelson, who writes about the need for antitrust control of monopolies, ought to be indicted for controlling a lopsided share of the total textbook market! When I attended the annual meetings of the American Economic Association, instructors frequently came up to me and said, "We use your book at Siwash" or "Winnsockie" or some other far-flung place. There was always an awkward pause, as I never knew quite what to say. My problem got solved when, one day, I heard myself saying, "Mrs. Samuelson will be pleased."

When success comes into an autobiography, the going gets boring. And Joseph Schumpeter, the great Harvard expert on innovations, will remind me from the grave how important *luck* was in all this. I happened to be there, at the right time in the right place. True, luck does favor the prepared mind. But the important minds that had become prepared for the new approach to economics were those of teachers who had been debating the cons and pros of the so-called Keynesian revolution and were thirsting for a "national income" approach in *macro*economics and a "general-equilibrium" approach in *micro*economics.

The Ever-Young Child

Actually, this account is not primarily about me as author. Just as a child takes on an individual identity distinct from the parent, so it was with the brainchild *Economics.* At first I was in command of it. But then it took over in its own right and came to be in charge of me.

The years passed. My hair turned from blond to brown. Then to gray. But like the portrait of Dorian Gray, which never grew old, the textbook *Economics* remained forever 21. Its cover turned from green

to blue, and then to brown and black, and to many-splendored hues. But helped by hundreds of letters and suggestions to the author from students and from professors with classroom experience, the economics inside the covers evolved and developed. A historian of mainstream-economic doctrines, like a paleontologist who studies the bones and fossils in different layers of earth, could date the ebb and flow of ideas by analyzing how Edition 1 was revised to Edition 2 and, eventually, to Edition 14.

And so it went. Hard, hard work—but ever so rewarding. Finally came the day when tennis beckoned. To McGraw-Hill I said: I've paid my dues. Let others carry on as I enjoy the good life of an emeritus professor, cultivating the researches that interest me most and letting revisions go hang.

McGraw-Hill had a ready answer: "Become a joint author. We'll make a list of congenial economists whose competence and views you admire." And so the search for the perfect William Nordhaus began. Yale is only 150 miles from MIT, and it was there that the real Nordhaus was to be found. It only helped that Bill had earned his Ph.D. at MIT. And in the days since then he has won his spurs serving on the President's Council of Economic Advisers and doing a tour of duty in Vienna with the International Institute for Applied Systems Analysis. Like Gilbert and Sullivan or Rogers and Hart, we turned out to form a congenial team.

And so, as in the classic tales, we have lived happily ever after. What matters is that the book stays young, pointing ahead to where the mainstream of economics will be flowing.

Rough Pebbles along the Way

Not always has it been fun and games. In the reactionary days of Senator Joseph McCarthy, when accusations of radicalism were being launched at the pulpit and in the classroom, my book got its share of condemnation. A conservative alumnus of MIT warned the university's president, Karl Compton, that Paul Samuelson would jeopardize his scholarly reputation if he were allowed to publish his apologetics for the "mixed economy." Dr. Compton replied that the day his faculty was subjected to censorship would be the day of his resignation from office. It all seems slightly comical four decades later, but it was no joke to be a teacher at a public university when many of the fashionable textbooks were at that time being denounced as subversive. (One excellent text, which came out a year before mine, was killed in its infancy by vicious charges of Marxism that were false on their face.) Nevertheless, if your cheek is smacked from the Right, the pain may be assuaged in part by a slap from the Left. *Anti-Samuelson*, a two-volume critique, was authored in the 1960s when student activism was boiling over on campuses here and abroad. Apparently I was an apologist for the laissez-faire world of markets where dog eats dog.

Each cold wind imparts a useful lesson. I learned to write with special care wherever controversial matters were concerned. It was not that I was a veritable Sir Galahad in all things. Rather, it was that I could only gain by leaning over backward to state fairly the arguments against the positions popular in mainstream economics. That is why conservative schools like my Chicago alma mater were motivated to assign *Economics* at the same time that prairie progressives found it an optimal choice. Even Soviet Russia felt a translation was mandatory, and within a month the entire supply of translated copies there had been exhausted. (Experts tell me that back in Stalin's day my book was kept on the special reserve shelf in the library, along with books on sex, forbidden to all but the specially licensed readers.) With the Gorbachev thaw, new translations are planned in Hungary, Czechoslovakia, Yugoslavia, Romania, and other Eastern European countries, as well as in China, Japan, Vietnam, and other Asian lands. All in all the number of translations, published or in the pipelines, involves more than 40 languages.

Tales, Tall but True

Legends abound concerning the saga of the textbook *Economics*. Here are a few from the dregs of memory.

Some years back one of MIT's graduate students, now a college president, went to a summer program at the London School of Economics. Attending were students from all over the world, from the jungles of Africa to the rice paddies of Asia. Only one thing did they have in common, he reported. All of them had begun their study of economics with the same textbook. He said his own stock went up because he could explain what some of the

American idioms meant and could pinpoint Fort Knox, Kentucky, as the place where the U.S. government stored its gold.

Japanese students are great buyers of books. *Economics* sells well there in English as well as Japanese. The erudite translator is my old Harvard classmate, Shigeto Tsuru, later to become president of Hitotsubashi University in Tokyo. With the royalties he received as translator, Dr. Tsuru purchased a luxurious condominium, and he invited various distinguished scholars to reside there during visits to Japan. As a special honor, he asked me to suggest a name for it. After some thought I came up with Royalty House, and thus it has been known ever since.

Once I received a letter from a diligent reader:

> Sir, in your textbook you say that the $24 that was paid to the Indians for the island of Manhattan—if invested at 6 percent compound interest—would have accumulated to about what all the real estate is worth today in Manhattan Island. I make that out, sir, to be several hundred billions of dollars. I don't think you can buy it for that little.

How was I to respond to her challenge? I asked my research assistant to look into the matter. The next day, Felicity Skidmore came back to say: "Tell her, boss, if 6 percent won't do it, try $6\frac{1}{2}$!"

Another time I received in the mail the following letter:

> I am a 10-year-old boy from Maine. When my Father and I were fishing last week in Lake Walden, I found a bottle floating. Inside it was the hand-printed message: If the finder of this bottle will get in touch with Professor Paul A. Samuelson of MIT, author of *Economics*, he will learn something to his advantage.
>
> Peter Quigley

Although I had not written the note (and all my department pals denied they had), I was on my mettle. But what to do? Finally, I sent this reply:

> Dear Mr. Quigley:
> Yes, I will tell you something worth knowing.
> *Don't believe everything you read in print.*
> Paul A. Samuelson, Ph.D., MIT

Rumors naturally proliferate. No, the beard I don't have is not white. No, I have not been dead since 1977. No, graduate students don't ghostwrite my book—nor do clever elderly females in white sneakers. Yes, I do admit to the vice of tennis.

Samuel Butler quipped: "While others polish their style, I perfect my handwriting." That is not my way. When I try to account for the textbook's durability, I suspect that its relaxed, almost colloquial style deserves some of the credit. That ease is not easily come by. Like Macaulay the historian, I write and rewrite in the hope that each sentence and clause will, at a first reading, reveal its meaning. I don't always succeed, but I do try. For this reason I take private pleasure in the fact that the book is used to teach English to foreigners; excerpts appear in anthologies for Japanese students and also in case materials used in teaching English as a second language to immigrants. Spread the gospel of economics anyway we can, I say.

Here is not the place to describe how the various editions have changed along with the evolution of modern mainstream economics. The first edition put much stress on what might be called "Model T Keynesian macro." With each new edition, the emphasis on monetary policy grew. And with the worst wastes of the Great Depression banished, the microeconomics of efficient market pricing has come to occupy more and more of the text's pages.

Science or Art?

Economics is not an exact science. Still, it is more than an art. We cannot predict with accuracy next year's national income—just as meteorologists cannot forecast next week's weather as precisely as they can guess the day after tomorrow's. But no bank or big business would be so rash as to consult astrologers rather than trained econometricians, or try to wing it by guess and by gosh.

Firms budget their machine replacements by microeconomic principles. Several of my former students earn a million dollars per year on Wall Street. Why? Because they know rich clients or are masters of slick sales techniques? Certainly not. It is because modern theories of finance, worked out intricately in seminar rooms at the business schools of Stanford, Wharton, Chicago, MIT, and Berkeley, really do stand up to statistical testing in the real world of markets.

A beginning textbook won't teach anyone to be an expert. Still, a journey of a thousand miles be-

gins with the first hundred yards. The great Winston Churchill, clever at writing history and heroic in leading nations, was color-blind all his life when it came to basic economic understanding. That kind of unnecessary illiteracy I and 10,000 teachers have vowed to fight.

Mine was the first generation of economists who were sought out by governments. I am the exception who never spent a full year in Washington. Still, I treasure in memory the many times I was called to testify before congressional committees or to serve as a Treasury and Federal Reserve academic consultant. Personally, most memorable were the years in which I had a chance to give economic counsel to John F. Kennedy (senator, presidential candidate, President-elect, and President in Camelot). Republican friends of mine—Fed Chairman Arthur F. Burns and Council of Economic Advisers Chairman Paul MacCracken—have similar stories to tell. Now that Eastern Europe has the need, in the "Age after Gorbachev," to move toward the market economy, Bill Nordhaus's generation is being drafted right and left.

A pseudoscience could not stand the Darwinian test of time. It was President Harry Truman who used to insist, "Give me a one-armed economist." Not for decisive Harry the adviser who says, "On the one hand this; on the other hand that." Well, I have advised legislators, candidates, and presidents. And this I have learned over a long lifetime: The prince or queen does not really want a one-armed economist. For in our profession, one-armed economists often come in two varieties: those with a Right arm only and those with only a Left arm. And then the sovereign must call in an eclectic economist like me to adjudicate between the rival zealots.

Economists are accused of not being able to make up their minds. In particular the brilliant John Maynard Keynes was accused of having volatile opinions. When a royal commission asked five economists for an opinion, it was said they would get six answers—two from Mr. Keynes. Keynes himself was quite unrepentant when pressed on the matter. He would say: "When my information changes, I change my opinion. What do you do, Sir?" He did not want to be the stopped clock that is right only twice a day.

The subject of economics is an ancient and honorable one, still growing and still having a long way to go before approaching the state of a tolerably accurate science. It began really with Adam Smith—our veritable Adam—who wrote in 1776 that great text called *The Wealth of Nations.* Then in 1848 John Stuart Mill, clocked with the highest IQ of all times, wrote *The Principles of Political Economy,* which served as the layperson's bible until 1890, when Alfred Marshall prepared his definitive *Principles of Economics.*

I would be an ingrate not to feel thrilled that, on my watch, the baton has been carried forward by this serendipitous brainchild. Science is a cooperative affair, a matter of public knowledge and never the product of one person's hand. Mostly I have been the mouthpiece of late-twentieth-century mainstream economics, but occasionally I have been able, so to speak, to get my own few licks in. Could any scholar lust for more?

Fortunately, as coauthors, William Nordhaus and I bring independent viewpoints to problems. But we are enough alike in our experiences and judgment to work the canoe forward on its steady course. The book has been lucky for the continuity plus change of its authors.

The future is longer than the present. You readers will look deep into the twenty-first century. William Nordhaus and I try to keep that ever in mind. We remember: Science progresses funeral by funeral. Science never stands still. What was great in Edition 1 is old hat by Edition 3; and maybe has ceased to be true by Edition 14. If scholars have been able to mark the evolution of economic knowledge decade by decade through study of this work's successive revisions, what never goes out of date is Respect for the Facts and for the Methods of cogent analysis and inference. If anywhere, therein resides economics' refusal to go stale and *Economics'* secret of perpetual youth.

The wood I chop warms me twice. I cannot close without remarking that the day Professor Freeman launched me on the adventure of writing a textbook for beginners in economics was the beginning of what has been sheer fun every mile of the way.

Paul A. Samuelson
Massachusetts Institute of Technology
Cambridge, Massachusetts
December 1991

PREFACE TO *MACROECONOMICS*

Books are the carriers of civilization. Without books, history is silent, literature dumb, science crippled, thought and speculation at a standstill. They are engines of change, windows on the world, lighthouses erected in a sea of time.

Barbara Tuchman

Economics has developed as a science over more than 200 years. For almost half a century, this book has served as the standard-bearer for the teaching of elementary economics in classrooms in America and throughout the world. Each new edition has distilled the best thinking of economists about how markets function and about what society can do to improve people's living standards.

But economics has changed profoundly since the first edition of this text appeared in 1948. Economics is above all a living and evolving subject. In every era, it must solve emerging mysteries and grapple with current dilemmas of public policy. Over the last decade, the United States grappled with new problems of slow growth in living standards and mounting poverty; with large government budget deficits and the need to make ends meet for both private and public households; with heightened foreign competition, trade deficits, and a large foreign debt; and with growing concern about international environmental problems and the need to forge agreements to preserve our natural heritage.

But all the news was not bad during the last few years. Many middle-income countries grew rapidly and slew the dragon of rapid population growth. And, in the most dramatic development of all, the nations of Eastern Europe threw off their socialist shackles and decided to cast their lot with market capitalism as a way of raising the living standards of their peoples. This was the *triumph of the market* as a way of organizing an advanced, technologically sophisticated economy.

All these and a host of other issues test the ingenuity of modern economics. The need to keep *Macroeconomics* at the forefront of modern economic analysis in the rapidly evolving world economy affords the authors an exciting opportunity to present the latest thinking of modern economists and to show how economics can contribute to a more prosperous world.

Our task in these pages is straightforward: to present a clear, accurate, and interesting introduction to the principles of modern macroeconomics and to the institutions of the American and world economy. Our primary goal is to survey macroeconomics. In doing this we emphasize the basic macroeconomic principles that will endure beyond today's headlines.

The Fourteenth Edition

Economics is a dynamic science—changing to reflect the shifting trends in economic affairs, in the environment, in the world economy, and in society at large. This book evolves along with the science it surveys. Every chapter has moved forward in time to keep pace with macroeconomic analysis and policy. What are the major changes?

1. Rediscovery of the Market. Running through the new edition of *Macroeconomics* is a leitmotif that we call "rediscovery of the market." All around the world, nations are discovering the power of the market as a tool for allocating resources. The most dramatic example of this, of course, occurred after the "velvet revolution" in Eastern Europe during 1989 and after the August 1991 putsch in the Soviet Union, when nation after nation threw out its communist leaders and rejected the command economy. In 1990, Poland undertook a grand experiment of undergoing "shock therapy" by introducing markets into much of its economy; other countries followed more gradually. These countries believed that only by introducing the discipline of markets—including the unemployment and inflation of a market economy—would they experience the rapid economic growth that has been enjoyed by Western Europe, North America, and Japan.

The rediscovery of the market was found in market economies as well. Many countries deregulated industries or "privatized" industries that had been in the public sectors. The results were generally favorable as productivity rose and prices fell. Economists the world around are analyzing the transition to the market in formerly socialist countries to see whether this new approach will boost economic growth in these depressed countries.

2. Weight Loss. Over the last few editions, *Macroeconomics* had gained bulk as new topics were added and new economic problems were analyzed. The time had come for a fierce weight-loss campaign to reduce the weight of the material, literally and figuratively. With this objective in mind, we surveyed teachers to determine which material was least used. In addition, we questioned leading scholars to ascertain which topics could be omitted at least cost to educating an informed citizenry and a new generation of economists. We drew up a list of deletions and said sad farewell to many appendices and sections. But at every stage, the question we asked was whether the material was central to modern macroeconomics. Only when a subject failed this test was it deleted.

3. Restructured Presentation. We have used the opportunity afforded by the radical change in the fourteenth edition to restructure its coverage. In the sections on macroeconomics, we have reoriented the chapters to focus more clearly upon the issues of short-run output determination and upon the issues of economic growth. The macroeconomics chapters begin with a complete development of the theory of aggregate demand, next develop the theory of aggregate supply, and then integrate the two parts. The chapters on macroeconomic policy are moved to the end so that the full analytical apparatus can be deployed to analyze the difficult issues the nation faces.

4. Incorporation of Growth Theory into Macroeconomics. One of the major recent developments in economics has been the resurgence of attention to the forces underlying long-run economic growth. Economists are increasingly examining the determinants of long-run economic growth, the sources of the slowdown in productivity growth, and the generation of new technological knowledge. The fourteenth edition reflects this revival by synthesizing growth theories and findings into the chapters on macroeconomics. We introduce growth theory as an integral part of aggregate supply and potential output. The advantage of this approach is that the controversies about the government deficit and debt can be better understood as affecting the growth of potential output.

5. Emphasis on the Open Economy. Americans are learning that no nation is an island. Our living standards are affected by technological developments in Japan and Europe; domestic producers must contend with competitors from Korea and Mexico. Similarly, no complete understanding of modern economics is possible without a thorough grounding in the world economy. The fourteenth edition continues to increase the material devoted to international economics and the interaction between international trade and domestic economic events.

The emphasis on international affairs is contained in this edition's revised treatment of macroeconomics. International-trade examples are woven through every chapter to highlight the importance of external events. The significance of international trade is underscored in both the overview of macroeconomics and in the chapter on output determination.

6. *Foundations of Macroeconomics.*

Some may feel that an analysis of the foundations of macroeconomics is too advanced for introductory textbooks. We disagree. Our fourteenth edition presents a straightforward survey of the economic underpinnings of modern mainstream macroeconomics. Reviewers of the last edition suggested that one area where more space was needed was in the explanation of aggregate supply and demand. We have therefore thoroughly overhauled the exposition of the analytical underpinnings of aggregate supply and demand. We have reorganized the development of macroeconomics so that the development of the material on aggregate demand is concentrated in Chapters 7 through 11, while the analysis of aggregate supply is more thoroughly developed in Chapters 8 and 12. In addition, we have streamlined the treatment of macroeconomics by shortening the analysis of rational-expectations macroeconomics and moving it from the appendix into Chapter 35.

7. *Balanced Treatment of Modern Macroeconomics.*

The fourteenth edition features all major schools of modern macroeconomics: Keynesian, classical, and monetarist. Each is clearly presented and compared with its competitors in a balanced and evenhanded way. For each, the empirical evidence is presented and evaluated.

Among the major revisions are Chapter 8's analysis of the fundamentals of aggregate supply and demand; the revised treatment of the role of money on economic activity, treated earlier in this edition in Chapters 10 and 11; integration of the rational-expectations approach into the text; and incorporation of issues of long-run economic growth into the discussion of macroeconomic policies and government deficits and debt.

8. *Emphasis on History and Policy.*

Economics is at its core an empirical science. It first aims to explain the world around us and then helps us devise economic policies, based on sound economic principles, that can enhance the living standards of people at home and abroad.

Drawing upon history, economic chronicles, and the authors' experience, the fourteenth edition continues to emphasize the use of case studies and empirical evidence to illustrate economic theories. Our comprehension of macroeconomic analysis increases when we see how government deficits in the 1980s lowered national saving and slowed capital accumulation in the United States. International economics comes to life when we study the reasons for the surging U.S. trade deficit of the 1980s or the successes of export-oriented countries.

This "hands-on" approach to economics allows students to understand better the relevance of economic analysis to real-world problems.

9. *Improved Exposition in Every Chapter.*

Although there are many new features in the fourteenth edition, the accent is upon improving the exposition of the core concepts of economics. We have labored over every page to improve this survey of introductory economics. We have received thousands of comments and suggestions from teachers, experts, and students and have incorporated their counsel in the fourteenth edition.

The attention to improved exposition will be seen in the redesign of this edition, with clearer figures and a new typeface. We have introduced scores of new end-of-chapter questions as well as new examples in the textual material. Above all, we believe that cutting out superfluous appendices, sections, and even chapters will lead to greater focus and ultimately to better understanding by the beginning student.

The glossary, which was first introduced in the twelfth edition, has been carefully tuned to meet the needs of this edition. All major terms now have a capsule definition that students can easily turn to. As a study aid, the most important terms are printed in **boldface** when first defined in the text; they all then appear again in the glossary to reinforce the indispensable vocabulary of economics in the student's mind.

One of the distinguishing features of *Macroeconomics* has been the presentation of central but somewhat advanced theories in understandable ways. For the fourteenth edition we have redrafted many chapters to make these topics understandable to beginning students.

Optional Matter

Economics courses range from one-quarter surveys to year-long intensive honors courses. This split edition on macroeconomics has been carefully designed to meet all situations. The more advanced materials have been put in separate appendices or specially designated sections. These will appeal to curious students and to those who teach demanding courses that survey the entire discipline thoroughly. We have included advanced problems to test the mettle of the most dedicated student.

If yours is a fast-paced course, you will appreciate the careful layering of the more advanced material. Hard-pressed courses can skip the advanced sections, covering the core of economic analysis without losing the thread of the economic reasoning. And for those who teach the bright honors students, this book will challenge the most advanced young scholar. Indeed, many of today's leading economists have written to say they have relied upon _Economics_ or its split volumes all along their pilgrimage to the Ph.D.

Format

The fourteenth edition has changed its format to improve the readability and to emphasize the major points. Special footnotes (in gray boxes) are reserved for important and useful illustrations of the core material in the chapter. Every figure has been redrawn with an eye to crystallizing the essential parts of the analysis.

New features in this edition include scores of fresh end-of-chapter questions, with a special accent upon short problems that reinforce the major concepts surveyed in the chapter. Terms printed in **boldface** mark the first occurrence and definition of the most important words that constitute the language of economics.

But these many changes have not altered one bit the central stylistic beacon that has guided _Economics_ and its split volumes since the first edition: to use simple sentences, clear explanations, and concise tables and graphs.

Alternative Formats

This textbook comes in three different formats. The standard hardcover text covers the entire subject.

In addition, for those courses that do not need to cover the entire subject, the fourteenth edition is available in two paperback volumes: this split edition, _Macroeconomics_, which covers Chapters 1 to 4 and 23 to 39 of the text; and another split edition, _Microeconomics_, which covers Chapters 1 to 22 and 36 to 39 of the text.

Auxiliary Teaching and Study Aids

Students of this edition will benefit greatly from the _Study Guide_. This carefully designed aid has been prepared by Professor Gary Yohe of Wesleyan University, who worked in close collaboration with us in our revision. Both when used alongside classroom discussions and when employed independently for self-study, the _Study Guide_ has proved to be an impressive success. There is a full-text _Study Guide_ and, for the first time, micro and macro versions are also available.

In addition, instructors will find the _Instructor's Manual and Test Bank_ useful for planning their courses and preparing multiple sets of test questions in both print and computerized formats. Moreover, McGraw-Hill has designed a beautiful set of two-color overhead transparencies for presenting the tabular and graphical material in the classroom. These items can all be obtained by contacting your local McGraw-Hill sales representative.

Economics in the Computer Age

This edition is accompanied by the _Interactive Economic Graphics Tutorial to accompany Samuelson/ Nordhaus_. IGT III is an upgraded version of McGraw-Hill's very successful economics software program developed by H. Scott Bierman at Carleton College and Todd Proebsting at the University of Wisconsin. Thousands of students have used the _Interactive Graphics Tutorial_ to learn, understand, and reinforce their study of economic graphics. This updated and technically advanced version includes microcomputer simulations, and is available for the IBM compatibles.

Acknowledgments

This book has two authors but a multitude of collaborators. We are profoundly grateful to colleagues, reviewers, students, and McGraw-Hill's staff for contributing to the timely completion of the fourteenth edition of *Economics*.

Colleagues at MIT, at Yale, and elsewhere who graciously contributed their comments and suggestions include William C. Brainard, E. Cary Brown, Robert J. Gordon, Lyle Gramley, Paul Joskow, Alfred Kahn, Richard Levin, Robert Litan, Barry Nalebuff, Merton J. Peck, Gustav Ranis, Paul Craig Roberts, Herbert Scarf, Robert M. Solow, James Tobin, Janet Yellen, and Gary Yohe.

In addition, we have benefitted from the tireless devotion of those whose experience in teaching elementary economics is embodied in this edition. We are particularly grateful to the reviewers of the Fourteenth Edition. They include:

John L. Adrian, Auburn University; **Lee J. Alston,** University of Illinois at Urbana-Champaign; **Marion S. Beaumont,** California State University, Long Beach; **Gerald Breger,** University of South Carolina; **Ernest Buchholz,** Santa Monica College; **J. S. Butler,** Vanderbilt University; **Richard Butler,** Trinity University; **Siddhartha Chib,** University of Missouri—Columbia; **Winston Chang,** S.U.N.Y. at Buffalo; **Philip Coelho,** Ball State University; **Ward Connolly,** Trinity University; **Paul Coomes,** University of Louisville; **Carl Davidson,** Michigan State University; **Edward J. Deak,** Fairfield University; **Catherine Eckel,** Virginia Polytechnic Institute and State University; **Wendy Eudy,** University of California at Berkeley; **Richard Gift,** University of Kentucky; **Jack Goddard,** Northeastern State University; **Fred Gottheil,** University of Illinois at Urbana-Champaign; **Jan M. Hansen,** University of Wisconsin-Eau Claire; **Suzanne Holt,** Cabrillo College; **James G. Ibe,** Calvin College; **Stephen Isbell,** Tennessee Technological University; **Dennis Jansen,** Texas A & M University; **Eric R. Jensen,** The College of William and Mary; **Kyoo H. Kim,** Bowling Green State University; **Felix Kwan,** Washington University; **Gary F. Langer,** Roosevelt University; **Stephen E. Lile,** Western Kentucky University; **David Loschky,** University of Missouri—Columbia; **Alfred Lubell,** State University of New York College at Oneonta; **Mark J. Machina,** University of California at San Diego; **John G. Marcis,** Illinois State University; **Thomas Mullen,** University of Wisconsin—Whitewater; **Kevin J. Murphy,** Oakland University; **Martha Paas,** Carleton College; **Andy Pienkos,** Cornell University; **James Price,** Syracuse University; **K. Ramagoapal,** University of Vermont; **Ed Shapiro,** University of Toledo; **Ben Slay,** Bates College; **John Solow,** Stanford University; **Frank Stafford,** University of Michigan; **Michael K. Taussig,** Rutgers University; **Joseph Turek,** Lynchburg College; **John Veitch,** University of Southern California; **Darwin Wassink,** University of Wisconsin—Eau Claire; **Janice Weaver,** Drake University; **David Weinberg,** Xavier University; **William C. Wood,** James Madison University; and **Gavin Wright,** Stanford University.

Students at MIT, Yale, and other colleges and universities have served as an "invisible college." They constantly challenge and test us, helping to make this edition less imperfect than its predecessor. Although they are too numerous to enumerate, their influence is woven through every chapter. The statistical and historical material was prepared and double-checked by Tan Yong Hui. Word processing assistance was provided by Glena Ames. As a sign of the changing times, the composition for this book was set for the first time directly from floppy disks.

This project would have been impossible without the skilled team from McGraw-Hill who nurtured the book at every stage. We particularly would like to thank, in chronological order of their appearance on the scene, Senior Editor Scott Stratford, Economics Editor Jim Bittker, Development Editors Judith Kromm and Becky Ryan, Editorial Assistant Lori Ambacher, Designer Hermann Strohbach, Editing Supervisors Larry Goldberg and Ira Roberts, Copy Editor Susan Gottfried, and Production Supervisor Janelle Travers. This group of skilled professionals turned a pile of floppy disks and a mountain of paper into a finely polished work of art.

A Word to the Beginning Student

Human history has witnessed waves of revolutions that shook civilizations to their roots—religious conflicts, wars for political liberation, struggles against colonialism, and nationalism. Today, the countries in Eastern Europe, in the Soviet Union, and elsewhere are wrenched by economic revolutions—people are battering down walls, overthrowing established authority, and agitating for a "market economy" because of discontent with their centralized socialist governments. Students like yourselves are marching to win the right to learn from Western textbooks like this one in hopes that they may enjoy the economic growth and living standards of market economies!

The Intellectual Marketplace

Just what is this market that Lithuanians and Poles and Russians are agitating for? In the pages that follow, you will learn about the markets for corn and wheat, stocks and bonds, French francs and Russian rubles, unskilled labor and highly trained neurosurgeons. You have probably read in the newspaper about the gross national product, the consumer price index, the stock market, and the unemployment rate. After you have completed a thorough study of the chapters in this textbook, you will know precisely what these words mean. Even more important, you will also understand the economic forces that influence and determine them.

There is also a marketplace of ideas, where contending schools of economists fashion their theories and try to persuade their scientific peers. You will find in the chapters that follow a fair and impartial review of the thinking of the intellectual giants of our profession—from the early economists like Adam Smith, David Ricardo, and Karl Marx to modern-day titans like John Maynard Keynes, Milton Friedman, and Robert Solow.

Skoal!

As you begin your journey into the land of markets and economic analysis, you may feel some apprehension. But take heart. The fact is that we envy you, the beginning student, as you set out to explore the exciting world of economics for the first time. This is a thrill that, alas, you can experience only once in a lifetime. So, as you embark, we wish you bon voyage!

Paul A. Samuelson
William D. Nordhaus

CONTENTS IN BRIEF

P A R T   T H R E E

AGGREGATE SUPPLY AND MACROECONOMIC POLICY

P A R T   F O U R

INTERNATIONAL TRADE AND THE WORLD ECONOMY

CONTENTS

PART ONE

BASIC CONCEPTS

P A R T   T W O
_____

FUNDAMENTAL CONCEPTS OF MACROECONOMICS

PART   THREE

AGGREGATE SUPPLY AND MACROECONOMIC POLICY

MACRO-ECONOMICS

BASIC CONCEPTS

The Road Ahead

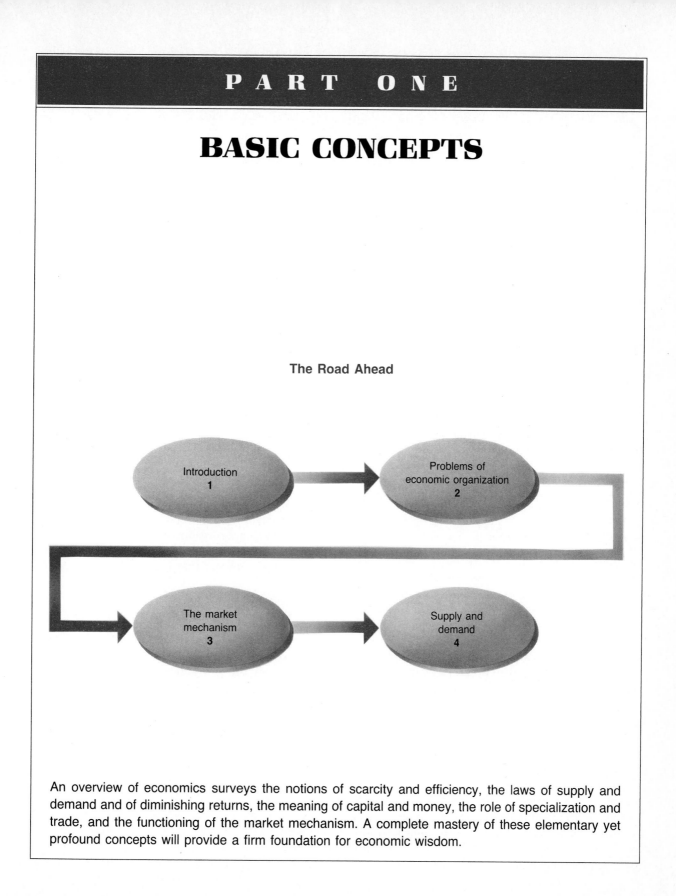

An overview of economics surveys the notions of scarcity and efficiency, the laws of supply and demand and of diminishing returns, the meaning of capital and money, the role of specialization and trade, and the functioning of the market mechanism. A complete mastery of these elementary yet profound concepts will provide a firm foundation for economic wisdom.

C H A P T E R   1

INTRODUCTION

The Age of Chivalry is gone; that of sophisters,
economists, and calculators has succeeded.
Edmund Burke

As you begin your reading, you are probably wondering, Why study economics? In fact, people do it for countless reasons.

Some study economics because they hope to make money.

Others worry that they will be illiterate if they cannot understand the laws of supply and demand.

People are also concerned to learn how recession or rising oil prices will affect their future.

For Whom the Bell Tolls

All these reasons, and many more, make good sense. Still, we have come to realize, there is one overriding reason to learn the basic lessons of economics.

All your life—from cradle to grave—you will run up against the brutal truths of economics. As a voter, you will make decisions on issues—on the government budget, regulating industries, taxes, and foreign trade—that cannot be understood until you have mastered the rudiments of this subject.

Choosing your life's occupation is the most important economic decision you will make. Your future depends not only on your own abilities but also upon how economic forces beyond your control affect your wages. Also, economics may help you invest the nest egg you have saved from your earnings. Of course, studying economics cannot make you a genius. But without economics the dice of life are simply loaded against you.

There is no need to belabor the point. We hope you will find that, in addition to being useful, economics is a fascinating field in its own right. Generations of students, often to their surprise, have discovered how stimulating economics can be.

What Is Economics?

Economics covers all kinds of topics. But at the core it is devoted to understanding how society allocates its scarce resources. Along the way to studying the implication of scarcity, economics tries to figure out the 1001 puzzles of everyday life.

Have You Ever Wondered . . .

You have undoubtedly asked a multitude of economic questions even before you picked up your first textbook on economics. You might come into your first class with questions like these:

Why do people worry about the government budget deficit? What are the effects of the budget deficit on inflation? For that matter, why do people worry about inflation? Why are some people rich and others poor? Why have the countries of Eastern Europe rejected socialism and why are they flocking to construct a market economy? What exactly is a market economy? What would happen if we kept foreign cars out of the United States to "protect" domestic workers and firms? Why is it sometimes hard to find a summer job? Sometimes easy? How much is it really costing me to go to college?

Rediscovery of the Market

As a scholarly discipline, economics is two centuries old. Adam Smith published his pathbreaking book *The Wealth of Nations* in 1776, a year also notable for the Declaration of Independence. It is no coincidence that both documents appeared in the same year. The movement for political freedom from the tyranny of European monarchies arose almost simultaneously with attempts to emancipate prices and wages from heavy-handed government regulation.

Adam Smith's contribution was to analyze the way that markets organized economic life and produced rapid economic growth. He showed that a system of prices and markets is able to coordinate people and businesses without any central direction. Almost a century later, as vibrant capitalist enterprises in railroads, textiles, and other sectors began to spread their influence into every region of the world, there appeared the massive critique of capitalism: Karl Marx's *Capital* (1867, 1885, 1894). Marx proclaimed that capitalism was doomed and would soon be followed by business depressions, revolutionary upheavals, and socialism.

In the decades that followed, events seemed to confirm Marx's predictions. Economic panics and deep depressions in the 1890s and 1930s led intellectuals of the twentieth century to question the viability of private-enterprise capitalism. Socialists began to apply their model in the Soviet Union in 1917 and by the 1980s almost one-third of the world was ruled by Marxian doctrines.

In 1936, in the trough of the Great Depression, however, John Maynard Keynes published *The General Theory of Employment, Interest and Money*. This landmark work described a new approach to economics, one that would help government monetary and fiscal policies tame the worst ravages of business cycles.

In the 1980s, the wheel turned full circle. The capitalist countries of the West and socialist countries of the East rediscovered the power of the market to produce rapid technological change and high living standards. In the West, governments reduced the regulatory burdens on industry and decontrolled prices. The most dramatic development occurred in Eastern Europe, where the peaceful revolution of 1989 forced the socialist countries to cast off their central-planning apparatus and allow market forces again to spring up. The fundamental insights of Adam Smith were rediscovered more than two centuries after he wrote *The Wealth of Nations*!

Definitions of Economics

What exactly is the subject that the economists from Smith to Marx to the present generation have analyzed? Here are a few definitions of economics:

- Economics asks *what* goods are produced, *how* these goods are produced, and *for whom* they are produced.
- Economics analyzes movements in the overall economy—trends in prices, output, unemployment, and foreign trade. Once such trends are understood, economics helps develop the policies by which governments can improve the performance of the economy.
- Economics is the study of commerce among nations. It helps explain why nations export some goods and import others, and analyzes the effects of putting economic barriers at national frontiers.
- Economics is the science of choice. It studies how people choose to use scarce or limited productive resources (labor, equipment, technical knowledge), to produce various commodities (such as wheat, overcoats, concerts, and missiles), and to distribute these goods for consumption.
- Economics is the study of money, banking, capital, and wealth.

The list is a good one, yet you could extend it many times over. But if we boil down all these definitions, we find a common theme:

Economics is the study of how societies use scarce resources to produce valuable commodities and distribute them among different people.

In our survey, we will distinguish between **macroeconomics,** which studies the functioning of the economy as a whole, and **microeconomics,** which analyzes the behavior of individual components like industries, firms, and households.

In the study of microeconomics, we examine the behavior of individual parts of the economy. We study, among other things, how individual prices are set, consider what determines the price of land, labor, and capital, and inquire into the strengths and weaknesses of the market mechanism. Microeconomics is economics through a microscope.

In macroeconomics, by contrast, we examine the economy through a wide-angle lens. Macroeconomics examines how the level and growth of output are determined, analyzes inflation and unemployment, asks about the total money supply, and investigates why some nations thrive while others stagnate.

The Scientific Approach

How, you might wonder, could Smith or Keynes or today's economists hope to answer the deep and difficult questions that economics addresses? How could anyone hope to know in a precise and scientific way why Japan has grown rapidly while the Soviet Union has stagnated. Can economists really explain why some people are fabulously rich while others can hardly afford one square meal a day?

Of course, economists have no monopoly on the truth about the important issues of the day. Indeed, many phenomena are poorly understood and highly controversial. But economists and other scientists have developed techniques—sometimes called the *scientific approach*—that give them a head start in understanding the complex forces that affect economic growth, prices and wages, income distribution, and foreign trade.

Observation. One of the major sources of economic knowledge is observation of economic affairs, especially drawing upon the historical record. As an example, consider inflation, which is a term meaning a rise in the general level of prices.[1] Citizens, bankers, and political leaders often worry about inflation and take painful steps, contracting output and increasing unemployment, to prevent or slow a threatening inflation.

How can we understand the damage done by in-

[1] Developing an understanding of economic issues requires a specialized vocabulary. If you are not familiar with a particular word or phrase, you should consult the Glossary at the back of this book. The Glossary contains most of the major technical economic terms used in this book. All terms printed in bold-face are also defined in the Glossary.

flation? One way is to study historical inflations. For example, we will later investigate the German inflation of the 1920s, during which prices rose 1,000,000,000,000 percent in 2 years. This destroyed much of the wealth of the middle class, led to social unrest, and, many people believe, abetted Hitler's rise to power. By examining the impacts of such virulent forms of inflation, we can gain insight into the more moderate inflations of the 1970s and 1980s.

The philosopher George Santayana wrote that those who forget the past are condemned to repeat it. Economists also can learn from the study of history, and the lessons are found on virtually every page of this textbook.

Economic Analysis. History and facts are central to an empirical science like economics, but facts cannot tell their own story. To recorded history we must add economic analysis, for only by developing and testing economic theories can we simplify and organize the jumble of data and facts into a coherent view of reality.

What do we mean by *economic analysis*? This is an approach that starts with a set of assumptions and then deduces logically certain predictions about the economic behavior of people, firms, or the overall economy.

For example, consider attempts to restrict the import of foreign goods in order to "protect" domestic workers and firms from foreign competition. In recent years, the United States has bought much more from abroad than it has sold to foreigners. As a result employment in American manufacturing industries has declined. Workers in the automobile, steel, machinery, and textile industries have complained that "cheap foreign labor" is costing them their jobs. They propose limiting imports of manufactured goods to preserve the jobs of American workers. An example of such a restriction is the tight quota limiting imports of textiles.

People can argue endlessly about the impacts of such import restraints. Economists prefer to use supply-and-demand analysis to determine the impact of trade restrictions, such as on textile imports. Such an analysis shows that import restraints on textiles will tend to increase the number of jobs in the domestic textile industry, but at the same time will raise clothing prices for consumers and lower the total national income. In fact, case study piled on case study confirms the validity of these predictions.

In the pages that follow, you will find a wide variety of analytical tools: supply and demand, cost schedules, and the like. Mastery of these tools is essential for understanding the controversial economic questions of the past, present, and future.

Statistical Analyses. A complete understanding of economic activity relies upon the use of economic data and statistical analysis. Governments and businesses issue volumes of data that can help us analyze economic behavior quantitatively. While the actual application of such information requires advanced tools in probability and econometrics, understanding the results requires only careful reading and common sense.

Where might we use statistics? Let's say that you are wondering why, on average, women earn only 60 percent as much as men. With millions of workers, you can hardly hope to compile a history of every person to explain the disparity. Instead, you collect representative data on wages of men and women, along with their personal characteristics (education, years of experience, occupation, and so forth). Using these data, you then employ statistical techniques to estimate what fraction of the difference in earnings of men and women is due to differences in characteristics. For example, studies have found that a significant part of the difference in earnings is associated with the fact that men have on average spent more time in the work force and have generally entered higher-paying occupations. But after all the statistical dust has settled, a significant part of the wage differential is unexplained, and some believe this remaining differential is due to discrimination.

Experiments. The economic world is enormously complicated, with millions of households and billions of prices. In an exciting new development, economists are turning to laboratory and other controlled experiments to study economic phenomena.

What are *controlled experiments*? A scientist sets up a controlled experiment by dividing a population into two or more groups, each of which is treated in exactly the same way except for a single factor. The scientist then measures the impact of the factor under study while *holding other influences constant*.

It is more difficult to perform experiments in economics than in the laboratory sciences. To begin with, economists cannot measure economic variables with the precision that physical scientists can apply in measuring mass, velocity, or distance. Moreover, it is difficult to replicate the real economy in a laboratory.

Notwithstanding these difficulties, economists are relying more and more on experiments to explain economic behavior. For example, in one group of controlled experiments over the last two decades, economists measured people's reactions to different kinds of government programs to raise the incomes of the poor. These experiments were extremely helpful in showing how changes in government programs might affect people's work habits and saving behavior. Other experiments today examine how markets behave with small numbers of producers.

These four techniques—observation, economic analysis, statistical analyses, and experiments—form the approach by which economic science progresses. Every day a new puzzle arises. In response, economists test new ideas and reject old ones, and economics evolves and changes. Textbooks embody both the established wisdom and the hot controversies of today. But in a decade or two, new facts will have toppled old theories, and the subject will evolve anew.

Pitfalls in Economic Reasoning

In all areas of economics, old and new, certain pitfalls lie in the path of the serious economist. This section reviews a few of them.

Failing to Keep "Other Things Equal"

Most economic problems involve several forces interacting at the same time. For example, the number of cars bought in a given year is determined by the price of cars, consumer incomes, gasoline prices, and so on. How can we isolate the impact on car sales of a single variable, such as the price of gasoline?

As we noted in our discussion of controlled experiments, the key step in isolating the impact of a single variable is to hold **other things equal.** This important phrase means that the variable under consideration is changed while all other variables are held constant. If we want to measure the impact of car prices on the number of cars purchased, we must examine the effect of changing car prices while ensuring that consumer incomes, gasoline prices, interest rates, and other variables are unchanged—that these "other things are held constant."

Say that you are interested in determining the impact on car sales of the big rise in gasoline prices that followed the Persian Gulf crisis in the fall of 1990. Your analysis will be complicated because the real incomes of consumers fell at the same time that gasoline prices rose. Nevertheless, you must try to isolate the effects of the higher gasoline prices by estimating what would happen if other things were equal. Unless you exclude the effects of other changing variables, you cannot accurately gauge the impact of changing gasoline prices.

The *Post Hoc* Fallacy

A common mistake in studies of cause-and-effect relationships is the *post hoc* fallacy. A classic example of the *post hoc* fallacy is the belief held by the medicine man in a primitive society that both witchcraft and a little arsenic were necessary to kill his enemy. Then there is the observation by Dr. Optimist that, after the government has cut tax rates, the government's total tax revenues began to rise. Dr. Optimist then claims, "Aha! If we lower tax rates, we will *raise* revenues and reduce the budget deficit." In this case, too, we have the ***post hoc* fallacy.**[2]

The fact that event A takes place before event B does not prove that event A caused event B. To conclude that "after the event" implies "because of the event" is to commit the *post hoc* fallacy.

The medicine man committed the *post hoc* fallacy because he concluded that witchcraft caused death because it preceded death. Dr. Optimist's fallacy was to assume that the tax cut was responsible for the increase in government revenues; overlooked was the fact that the growing economy was

[2] In logic, this is known as the *post hoc, ergo propter hoc* fallacy (translated from the Latin as "after this, therefore necessarily because of this").

raising people's incomes and might have increased tax revenues even more had taxes not been cut.

The Whole Is Not Always the Sum of the Parts

Have you ever seen people jump up at a football game to gain a better view? They usually find that, once everybody is standing up, the view has not improved at all. This example, in which what is true for an individual is not necessarily true for everyone, illustrates the "fallacy of composition," which is defined as follows:

The **fallacy of composition** is the misconception that what is true for a part is therefore true for the whole.

The following examples are true statements that might surprise people who have fallen into the fallacy of composition.

- Attempts of individuals to save more in a depression may reduce the community's total savings.
- If a single individual receives more money, that person will be better off; if everybody receives more money, no one will be better off.
- It may benefit the United States to reduce tariffs levied on imported goods, even if other countries refuse to lower their tariffs.
- If all farmers produce a big crop, total farm income will probably fall.

To see how the fallacy of composition works, take the last example. A corn farmer works from dawn to dusk to increase yields, apply the right amount of fertilizer, and so forth. If she is successful in increasing output, then her income will rise handsomely. But if *all* farmers succeed in raising their output, the price of corn may fall so sharply that the total sales of corn (price times quantity) actually fall. This shows how what holds for an individual does not necessarily hold for the group.

In the course of this book, all the apparent paradoxes listed above will be seen to be true. There are no magic formulas or hidden tricks. Rather, these are examples in which what seems to be true for individuals is not always true for society as a whole.

Subjectivity

Perhaps the greatest obstacle to mastering economics arises from the *subjectivity* we bring to studying the world around us. We sometimes believe that the task of our studies is to uncover an objective reality—to learn the facts and laws of nature or economics.

Alas, learning is not so simple. When we are young, our minds are open to new ideas. As we grow up, we begin to organize our ideas and to learn about the world from our family, friends, and teachers. But no sooner do we begin to understand our world than we become captives of our own knowledge. Growing up on planet Earth, it was natural for early scientists to believe that the rest of the universe revolved around them. Growing up in today's America, we may find it hard to understand economic revolutions taking place in Japan or in Eastern Europe. In the end, the way we perceive the observed facts depends on the theoretical spectacles we wear.

Scientists are just like other people; they are prisoners of their theoretical preconceptions. If physicists learned Newtonian physics well, this might actually hinder their grasp of Einstein's relativity theories.

That is why science belongs to the young. The old "know" too many things that are untrue but that they cannot unlearn. A striking illustration of this is given by Nobel-laureate Max Planck, the physicist renowned for his discovery of the revolutionary quantum theory. In his *Scientific Autobiography*, Planck reports what he observed in the development of physics:

This experience gave me also an opportunity to learn a fact—a remarkable one in my opinion: A new scientific truth does not triumph by convincing its opponents and making them see the light, but rather because its opponents eventually die, and a new generation grows up that is familiar with it.

This lesson applies as well to economics, where the giants like Smith, Marx, and Keynes—indeed, all whose names appear on the family tree of economics shown at the back of this book—transformed economic understanding by converting the young and open-minded.

Is It a Bird? A simple picture illustrates the subjectivity that exists in every science. Does picture (b) in Figure 1-1 show a bird looking to the left? Or is it an antelope looking to the right?

There is no right answer. Either may be correct depending upon the context. In the presence of the field of birds shown in Figure 1-1(a), most people think the shape in (b) is a bird. But next to the field of antelopes in (c), people see it as an antelope.

So it is with scientific facts and theories. After you have studied and learned a body of economic principles, you comprehend reality in a new and different way. This insight helps us understand why people who live on the same planet can have fundamentally different economic perceptions—why some believe markets are the best way to organize the economy while others cling to socialist central

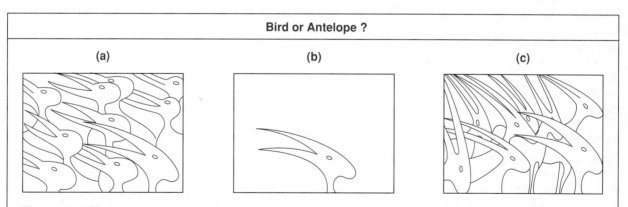

Bird or Antelope ?

(a)   (b)   (c)

Figure 1-1. The same facts may tell different stories to scientific observers who wear different theoretical spectacles

Is **(b)** a bird or an antelope? When **(c)** is covered up, most people think it is a bird. But when **(a)** is covered, most will see it as an antelope. Thus do differences in perception affect people's views on economic policy. [Source: N.R. Hanson, *Patterns of Discovery* (Cambridge University Press, London, 1961).]

planning, or why government welfare programs are admired by some and vilified by others.

So let us be forewarned to question the inevitable subjectivity of our own beliefs and philosophies and to be open-minded about views that differ from our own.

The Law of Scarcity

Now that we have seen how economics progresses and have learned about some of the pitfalls on the road to economic understanding, let's turn to one of the fundamental concepts of economics.

At the very core of economics lies the fact of **scarcity.** Economists study the way goods are produced and consumed because people want to consume far more than an economy can produce. If infinite quantities of every good could be produced or if human desires were fully satisfied, people would not worry about the efficient use of scarce resources. Businesses would not need to fret over the efficient use of labor and materials, and governments would not need to struggle over taxes or spending. Moreover, since all of us could have as much as we pleased, no one would care about the distribution of incomes among different people or classes.

In such an Eden of affluence, there would be no **economic goods**—goods that are scarce or limited in supply. There would be no need to economize on consumption, and indeed economics would no longer be a vital science. All goods would be free, like sand in the Saudi desert or water at the beach.

But no society has reached a utopia of limitless possibilities. Goods are limited while wants seem infinite. Even in the United States, the most productive economy ever known, production is not high enough to meet everyone's desires. An investigation of consumption patterns would reveal that people want and need central heating and cooling, movies and compact disks, autos and personal computers, concerts and recreation, leisure time and privacy, clean air and pure water, safe factories and clean streets, and innumerable other goods and services. If you add up all the wants, you quickly find that there are simply not enough goods and services to satisfy even a small fraction of everyone's consumption desires. Our national output would have to be

many times larger before the average American could live at the level of the average doctor or lawyer. And outside the United States, particularly in Africa and Asia, hundreds of millions of people suffer from hunger and material deprivation.

At the very core of economics is the undeniable truth that we call the **law of scarcity,** which states that goods are scarce because there are not enough resources to produce all the goods that people want to consume. All of economics flows from this central fact. Because resources are scarce, we need to study how society chooses from the menu of possible goods and services, how different commodities are produced and priced, and who gets to consume the goods that society produces.

The Uses of Economics

We suggested earlier that our economic knowledge serves us in managing our personal lives, in understanding society, and in improving the world around us. The ways that economics can help us individually will be as different as are our personal lives. Learning about the stock market may help people manage their own finances; knowledge about price theory and antitrust policy may improve the skills of a lawyer; better awareness of the determinants of cost and revenue will produce better business decisions. The doctor, the investor, and the farmer all need to know about accounting and regulation to get the most satisfaction and profit from their businesses.

Description and Policy in Economics

In addition to helping people cope with their personal concerns, economics improves knowledge of crucial national issues. People who have never made a systematic study of economics are handicapped in even thinking about national issues; they are like the illiterate trying to read.

Economics plays two distinct roles in promoting the analysis of national economic issues. It first helps to understand our society—to describe, explain, and predict economic behavior—for example, the causes of poverty. But for many people, the payoff comes when economic knowledge is applied to help design policies that will build a better society. This distinction between description and prescription is central to modern economics.

Normative vs. Positive Economics. In economics, we must be careful to distinguish between positive (or factual) statements and normative statements (or value judgments).

Positive economics describes the facts and behavior in the economy. What are the causes of poverty in the United States? What will be the effect of higher cigarette taxes on the number of smokers? How has the economic performance of socialist countries compared with that of capitalist countries? These questions can be resolved only by reference to facts—they may be easy or difficult questions, but they are all in the realm of positive economics.

Normative economics involves ethical precepts and value judgments. Should the government give money to poor people? Should the budget deficit be reduced by higher taxes or lower spending? Should the socialist countries introduce private property and stock markets? There are no right or wrong answers to these questions because they involve ethics and values rather than facts. These issues can be debated, but they can never be settled by science or by appeal to facts. There simply is no correct answer to how high inflation should be, whether society should help poor people, or how much the nation should spend on defense. These questions are resolved by political decisions, not by economic science.

Economics in Government

Economists have in recent years become the counselors of presidents and prime ministers. The political agenda is full of economic issues: Should we raise taxes to curb the budget deficit? Should the minimum wage be raised? Should the government regulate banks more closely? Political leaders need economic advisers to provide counsel on such complicated questions.

Increasingly, international aspects of economic activity concern policymakers. As the nation's trade deficit climbed in the 1980s, Congress labored to rewrite the rules of international commerce. People worry about whether the United States is losing its technological vitality and whether we will become a second-rate power behind Japan and Europe.

And scientific concerns about global warming have generated support for international measures to curb energy consumption.

Heads of government must constantly make vital decisions that involve economics. Naturally, national leaders need not themselves be experts in economics. Rather, they need to be literate "consumers" of the conflicting economic advice given them. Presidents who brought major economic changes to the United States— Franklin Roosevelt, John Kennedy, and Ronald Reagan— were not professional economists. Rather, they had brain trusts of advisers who were schooled in the major economic issues and could propose solutions to the problems of the day.

Similarly, few students will become professional economists. Many will study economics for only a term or two. This book will give a thorough introductory overview of the whole subject. Your view of the world will never be the same after a single semester of economics.

Why Economists Disagree

In recent years, economists have developed a reputation for being a crotchety lot who cannot agree on anything. One writer complained, "If you laid all economists end to end, they still wouldn't reach a conclusion."

A closer look reveals that economists agree much more than is generally supposed. A broad consensus exists on many questions of positive economics, particularly on issues in microeconomics such as the importance of the market in allocating resources, the harmful effects of many government regulations (such as rent control or tariffs), and the benefits of trade and specialization.

The major disagreements among economists lie in the normative arena. Economists differ as much as the rest of the population on questions concerning the appropriate size of government, the power of unions, the relative importance of inflation and unemployment, the fair distribution of income, and whether taxes should be raised or lowered. They are as divided as their brothers and sisters on the broad political and ethical issues of today.

● At the end of our overture, let us return briefly to our opening theme, Why study economics? Perhaps the best answer to the question is a famous one given by Lord Keynes in the final lines of his 1936 classic, *The General Theory of Employment, Interest and Money*:

> The ideas of economists and political philosophers, both when they are right and when they are wrong, are more powerful than is commonly understood. Indeed the world is ruled by little else. Practical men, who believe themselves to be quite exempt from any intellectual influences, are usually the slaves of some defunct economist. Madmen in authority, who hear voices in the air, are distilling their frenzy from some academic scribbler of a few years back. I am sure that the power of vested interests is vastly exaggerated compared with the gradual encroachment of ideas. Not, indeed, immediately, but after a certain interval; for in the field of economic and political philosophy there are not many who are influenced by new theories after they are twenty-five or thirty years of age, so that the ideas which civil servants and politicians and even agitators apply to current events are not likely to be the newest. But, soon or late, it is ideas, not vested interests, which are dangerous for good or evil.

To understand the ideas of generations of economists and how they apply to the problems of personal life and national issues—ultimately, this is why we study economics. ●

SUMMARY

1. What is economics? Economics is the study of how societies choose to use scarce productive resources that have alternative uses, to produce commodities of various kinds, and to distribute them among different groups.

2. Economics is studied for a variety of reasons: to understand problems facing the citizen and family, to help governments promote growth and improve the quality of life while avoiding depression and inflation, and to analyze fascinating patterns of social behavior. Because economic questions enter into both daily life and national issues, a basic understanding of economics is vital for sound decision making by individuals and nations.

3. Economists and other scientists have a variety of weapons that can be deployed to attack economic questions. Observation of economic history provides countless episodes from which to find patterns of behavior. Economic analysis allows the facts to be arrayed into general propositions. Often statistical studies permit understanding of complex situations. And experiments allow us to test different economic hypotheses.

4. In approaching economic questions, be careful to avoid the common pitfalls. Remember to hold other things equal; keep descriptions distinct from value judgments; avoid the *post hoc* fallacy and the fallacy of composition; and recognize the necessary subjectivity in our observations and theories.

5. Economics is grounded in the law of scarcity, which holds that goods are scarce because people desire much more than the economy can produce. Economic goods are scarce, not free, and society must choose among the limited goods that can be produced with its available resources.

CONCEPTS FOR REVIEW

Economics
definitions
normative vs. positive economics
macroeconomics vs. microeconomics

Approaching economics
other things equal
controlled experiment
fallacy of composition

post hoc fallacy

The law of scarcity
free goods, economic goods

QUESTIONS FOR DISCUSSION

1. Give five definitions of economics. Which is the most comprehensive one?
2. Define each term in your own words: *post hoc* fallacy; other things equal; normative and positive economics.
3. Define economic goods and free goods. Give some examples of each. Can you think of examples of goods that used to be free goods but are now economic goods?
4. Identify which of the following are normative and which are positive statements:
   (a) The 1990 Persian Gulf crisis raised oil prices, which led to lower consumption of gasoline.
   (b) The American economy has grown more rapidly than has the Soviet economy.
   (c) The deserving poor should pay no taxes.
   (d) The oil companies are making excessive profits and should be subject to a windfall-profits tax.
   (e) Rising food prices contributed to the French Revolution.
5. Give examples of the fallacy of composition and of the *post hoc* fallacy. Is the former involved in the debate over cigarette smoking and lung cancer? (Why not?) Might the latter be involved in this debate? (Why so?) Explain carefully the paradox of farm incomes (the fourth example in the section on the fallacy of composition).
6. The following table shows data on the top federal personal-tax rate, on federal personal-tax revenues, and on total personal income.

Year	Top tax rate (%)	Tax revenues ($, billion)	Personal income ($, billion)
1980	70	244	2259
1984	50	298	3109
1988	28	401	4646

Some might argue that lowering tax rates actually raises tax revenues. Analyze this argument. What fallacy is involved?

7. The gravestone of Karl Marx contains the following words he wrote at the age of 26:

> Up 'til now the philosophers have only interpreted the world in various ways. The point, though, is to change it!

Marx believed in violent revolution to overthrow the capitalist system, which he believed was exploiting workers. Are there any economic ills of society that you feel should be changed? How would you go about changing them?

HOW TO READ GRAPHS

A picture is worth a thousand words.
Chinese proverb

Before you can master economics, you must have a working knowledge of graphs. They are as indispensable to the economist as a hammer is to a carpenter. So if you are not familiar with the use of diagrams, invest some time in learning how to read them—it will be time well spent.

What is a *graph*? It is a diagram showing how two or more sets of data or variables are related to one another. Graphs are useful in economics because they pack a great deal of data into a small space.

You will encounter many different kinds of graphs in this book. Some graphs show how variables change over time (see, for example, the inside of the front cover); other graphs show the relationship between different variables (such as the example we will turn to in a moment). Each graph in the book will help you to understand an important economic law or trend.

The Production-Possibility Frontier

One of the first graphs you will encounter in this text is the production-possibility frontier. At any point in time, a country can produce only a certain quantity of goods and services with its limited resources: so much gasoline, so much heating oil, so many aircraft, and so forth. Moreover, more of one good cannot be produced without giving up some of another good: for example, the more gasoline produced, the less heating oil can be produced.

In economics, we represent this limitation on a country's productive potential by the **production-possibility frontier (*PPF*).** The *PPF* represents the maximum amounts of a pair of goods or services that can both be produced with an economy's given resources assuming that all resources are fully employed.

Let's look at a basic example using food and machines. The essential data for the *PPF* are shown in Table 1A-1. Of the two sets of data, one set gives possible outputs of food; the other set gives possible outputs of machines. Each output level of food is paired with the number of machines that could be produced at the same time. You can see that as the quantity of food produced increases, the production of machines falls. Thus, if the economy produced 10 units of food, it could produce a maximum of 140 machines, but when the output of food is 20 units, only 120 machines can be manufactured.

Alternative Production Possibilities		
Possibilities	Food	Machines
A	0	150
B	10	140
C	20	120
D	30	90
E	40	50
F	50	0

Table 1A-1. The pairs of possible outputs of food and machines
The table shows six potential pairs of outputs that can be produced with the given resources of a country. The country can choose one of the six possible combinations.

Production-Possibility Graph

The data shown in Table 1A-1 can also be presented as a graph. To construct the graph, we represent each of the pairs of data of Table 1A-1 by a single point on a two-dimensional plane. Figure 1A-1 displays in a graph the relationship between the food and machines outputs shown in Table

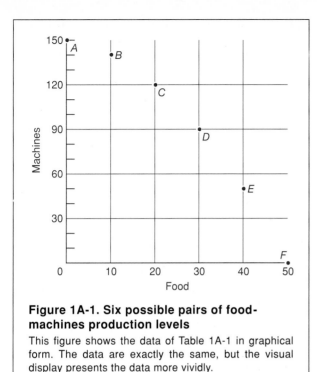

Figure 1A-1. Six possible pairs of food-machines production levels

This figure shows the data of Table 1A-1 in graphical form. The data are exactly the same, but the visual display presents the data more vividly.

1A-1. Each pair of numbers is represented by a single point in the graph. Thus the row labeled A in Table 1A-1 is graphed as point *A* in Figure 1A-1, and similarly for points *B, C,* and so on.

In Figure 1A-1, the vertical line at left and the horizontal line at bottom correspond to the two variables—food and machines. A *variable* is an item of interest that can be defined and measured and that takes on different values at different times or places. Important variables studied in economics are prices, quantities, hours of work, acres of land, dollars of income, and so forth.

The horizontal line on a graph is referred to as the *horizontal axis*, or sometimes the *X axis*. The horizontal axis is simply a convenient line for measuring the quantity of one of the variables. In Figure 1A-1, food output is measured on the black horizontal axis.

The vertical line at the left is known as the *vertical axis*, or *Y axis*. In Figure 1A-1, it measures the number of machines produced. Point *A* on the vertical axis stands for 150 machines.

The lower left-hand corner where the two axes meet is called the *origin*. It signifies 0 food and 0 machines in Figure 1A-1.

*A **Smooth Curve**.* In most economic relationships, variables can change by small amounts as well as by the large increments shown in Figure 1A-1. We therefore generally draw economic relationships as continuous curves. Figure 1A-2 shows the *PPF* as a smooth curve in which the points from *A* to *F* have been connected.

By comparing Table 1A-1 and Figure 1A-2 we can see why graphs are so often used in economics. The smooth *PPF* reflects the menu of choice for the economy. It is a visual device for showing what types of goods are available in what quantities. Your eye can see at a glance the relationship between machine and food production.

Slopes and Lines

In Figure 1A-2, we see a line depicting the relationship between food and machine production. One important way to describe the relationship between two variables is by the slope of the graph line.

The **slope** of a line represents the change in one variable that occurs when another variable changes. More precisely, it is the change in the variable *y* on the vertical axis per unit change in the

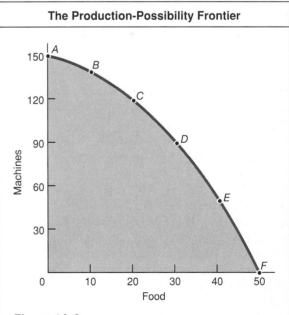

Figure 1A-2

A smooth curve fills in between the plotted pairs of points, creating the production-possibility frontier.

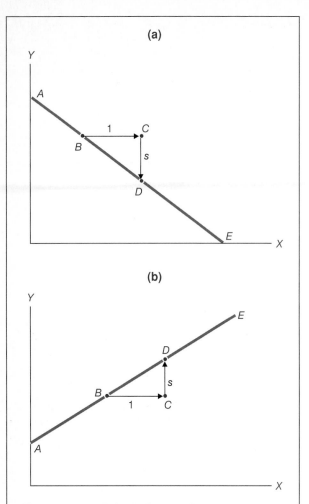

Figure 1A-3. Calculation of slope for straight lines

It is easy to calculate slopes for straight lines as "rise over run." Thus in both **(a)** and **(b)**, the numerical value of the slope is rise/run = CD/BC = s/1 = s. Note that in **(a)**, CD is negative, indicating a negative slope, or an inverse relationship between X and Y.

variable x on the horizontal axis. For example, in Figure 1A-2, say that food production rose from 25 to 26 units. The slope of the curve in Figure 1A-2 tells us the precise change in machinery production that would take place. *Slope is an exact numerical measure of the relationship between the change in* y *and the change in* x.

We can use Figure 1A-3 to show how to measure the slope of a straight line, say the slope of the line between points B and D. Think of the movement from B to D as occurring in two stages. First comes

a horizontal movement from B to C indicating a 1-unit increase in the x value (with no change in y). Second comes a compensating vertical movement up or down, shown as s in Figure 1A-3. (The movement of 1 horizontal unit is purely for convenience. The formula holds for movements of any size.) The two-step movement brings us from one point to another on the straight line.

Because the BC movement is a 1-unit increase in x, the length of CD (shown as s in Figure 1A-3) indicates the change in y per unit change in x. On a graph, this change is called the *slope* of the line $ABDE$.

Often slope is defined as "the rise over the run." The *rise* is the vertical distance; in Figure 1A-3, the rise is the distance from C to D. The *run* is the horizontal distance; it is BC in Figure 1A-3. The rise over the run in this instance would be CD over BC. Thus the slope of BD is CD/BC.

The key points to remember are:

1. The slope can be expressed as a number. It measures the change in y per unit change in x, or "the rise over the run."
2. If the line is straight, its slope is constant everywhere.
3. The slope of the line indicates whether the relationship between x and y is *direct* or *inverse*. Direct relationships occur when variables move in the same direction (that is, they increase or decrease together); inverse relationships occur when the variables move in opposite directions (that is, one increases as the other decreases). Thus a negative slope indicates the x-y relation is inverse, as it is in Figure 1A-3(a). Why? Because an increase in x calls for a decrease in y.

People sometimes confuse slope with the appearance of steepness. This conclusion is often valid—but not always. The steepness depends on the scale of the graph. Panels (a) and (b) in Figure 1A-4 both portray exactly the same relationship. But in (b), the horizontal scale has been stretched out compared to (a). If you calculate carefully, you will see that the slopes are exactly the same (and are equal to $\frac{1}{2}$).

Slope of a Curved Line. A curved or nonlinear line is one whose slope changes. Sometimes we want to know the slope *at a given point*, such as point B in Figure 1A-5. We see that the slope at point B is ris-

(a)

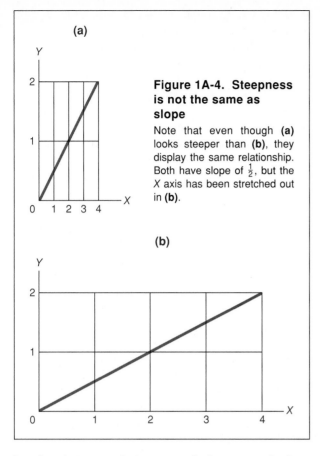

Figure 1A-4. Steepness is not the same as slope

Note that even though **(a)** looks steeper than **(b)**, they display the same relationship. Both have slope of $\frac{1}{2}$, but the X axis has been stretched out in **(b)**.

(b)

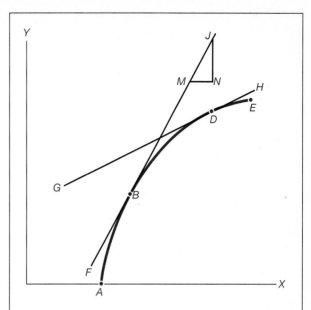

Figure 1A-5. Tangent as slope of curved line

By constructing a tangent line we can calculate the slope of a curved line at a given point. Thus the line *FBMJ* is tangent to smooth curve *ABD* at point *B*. The slope at *B* is calculated as the slope of the tangent line, i.e., as *NJ/MN*.

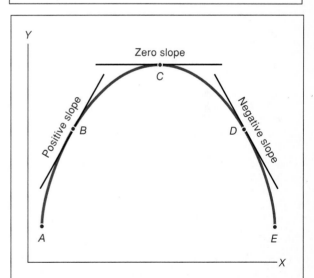

Figure 1A-6. Different slopes of nonlinear curves

Many curves in economics first rise, then reach a maximum, then fall. In the rising region from *A* to *C* the slope is positive (see point *B*). In the falling region from *C* to *E* the slope is negative (see point *D*). At the curve's maximum, point *C*, the slope is zero. (What about a U-shaped curve? What is the slope at its minimum?)

ing, but it is not obvious exactly how to calculate the slope.

To find the slope of a smooth curved line at a point, we calculate the slope of the straight line that just touches, but does not cross, the curved line at the point in question. Such a straight line is called a *tangent* to the curved line. Put differently, the slope of a curved line at a point is given by the slope of the straight line that is tangent to the curve at the given point. (Of course, we find the slope of the tangent line with the usual right-angle measuring technique discussed earlier.)

To find the slope at point *B* in Figure 1A-5, we simply construct straight line *FBJ* as a tangent to the curved line at point *B*. We then calculate the slope of the tangent as *NJ/MN*. Similarly, the tangent line *GH* gives the slope of the curved line at point *D*.

Another example of the slope of a nonlinear line is shown in Figure 1A-6. This shows a typical microeconomics curve, which is dome-shaped and has a maximum at point *C*. We can use our method of slopes-as-tangents to see that the slope of the curve is always positive in the region where the curve is rising and negative in the falling region. At the peak or maximum of the curve, the slope is exactly zero. A zero slope signifies that a tiny movement in the *x* variable around the maximum has no effect on the value of the *y* variable.[1]

Shifts of and Movement Along Curves

An important distinction in economics is between shifts of curves and movements along curves. We can examine the distinction in Figure 1A-7. The inner production-possibility frontier reproduces the *PPF* in Figure 1A-2. At point *D* society chooses

---

[1] For those who enjoy algebra, the slope of a line can be remembered as follows. A straight line (or linear relationship) is written as $y = a + bx$. For this line, the slope of the curve is b, which measures the change in y per unit change in x.

A curved line or nonlinear relationship is one involving terms other than constants and the x term. An example of a nonlinear relationship is the quadratic equation $y = (x - 2)^2$. You can easily verify that the slope of this equation is negative for $x < 2$ and positive for $x > 2$. What is its slope for $x = 2$?

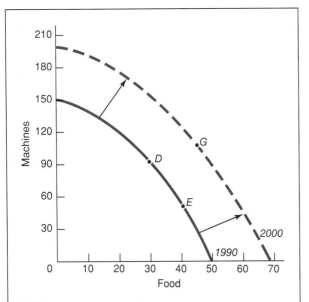

Figure 1A-7. Shift of curves versus movement along curves

In using graphs, it is essential to distinguish *movement along* a curve (such as from high-investment *D* to low-investment *E*) from a *shift* of a curve (as from *D* in an early year to *G* in a later year).

---

to produce 30 units of food and 90 units of machines. If society decides to consume more food *with a given PPF*, then it can *move along* the *PPF* to point *E*. This movement along the curve represents choosing more food and fewer machines.

Suppose that the inner *PPF* represents society's production possibilities for 1990. If we return to the same country in 2000, we see that the *PPF* has *shifted* from the inner 1990 curve to the outer 2000 curve. (This shift would occur because of technological change or because of an increase in labor or capital available.) In the later year, society might choose to be at point *G*, with more food and machines than at either *D* or *E*.

The point of this example is that in one case (moving from *D* to *E*) we see movement along a curve, while in the second case (from *D* to *G*) we see a shift of the curve.

Some Special Graphs

Figure 1A-2 shows one of the most important graphs of economics, one depicting the relationship between two economic variables (such as food and machines, or guns and butter). You will encounter other types of graphs in the pages that follow.

Time Series. Some graphs show how a particular variable has changed over time. Look, for example, at the graphs on the inside front cover of this text. The left-hand graph shows a time series since the American Revolution of a significant macroeconomic variable, the ratio of the federal government debt to total gross national product or GNP—this ratio is the "debt-GNP ratio." Time-series graphs have time on the horizontal axis and variables of interest (in this case, the debt-GNP ratio) on the vertical axis. This graph shows that the debt-GNP ratio has risen sharply during every major war.

Scatter Diagrams. Sometimes individual pairs of points will be plotted, as in Figure 1A-1. Often, combinations of variables for different years will be plotted. An important example of a scatter diagram from macroeconomics is the *consumption function*, shown in Figure 1A-8. This scatter diagram shows the nation's total disposable income on the horizontal axis and total consumption (spending by households on goods like food, clothing, and hous-

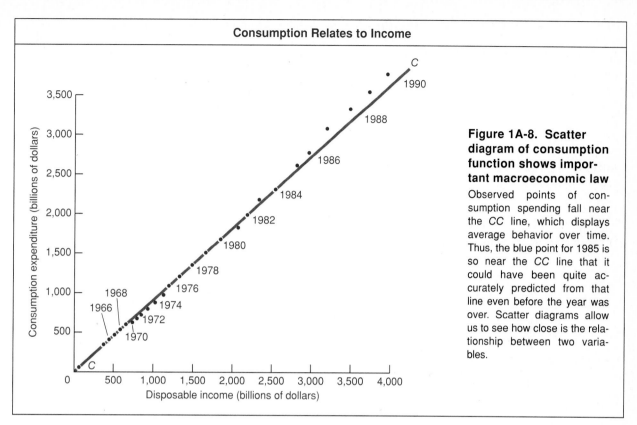

Consumption Relates to Income

Figure 1A-8. Scatter diagram of consumption function shows important macroeconomic law

Observed points of consumption spending fall near the CC line, which displays average behavior over time. Thus, the blue point for 1985 is so near the CC line that it could have been quite accurately predicted from that line even before the year was over. Scatter diagrams allow us to see how close is the relationship between two variables.

ing) on the vertical axis. Note that consumption is very closely linked to income, a vital clue for understanding changes in national income and output.

Diagrams with More Than One Curve. Often it is useful to put two curves in the same graph, thus obtaining a "multicurve diagram." The most important example is the supply-and-demand diagram, shown in Chapter 4 (see page 55). These graphs can show two different relationships simultaneously, such as how consumer purchases respond to price (demand) and how business production responds to price (supply). By graphing the two relationships together, we can determine the price and quantity that will hold in a market.

● This concludes our brief excursion into graphs. Once you have mastered these basic principles, the graphs in this book, and in other areas, can be both fun and instructive. ●

────────────── **SUMMARY TO APPENDIX** ──────────────

1. Graphs are an essential tool of modern economics. They provide a convenient presentation of data or of the relationship between two variables.

2. The important points to understand about a graph are: What is on each of two axes (horizontal and vertical)? What are the units on each axis? What kind of relationship is depicted in the curve or curves shown in the graph?

3. The relationship between the two variables in a curve is given by its slope. The slope is defined as "the rise over the run," or the increase in *y* per unit increase in *x*. If it is upward (or positively) sloping, the two variables are directly related; they move upward or downward together. If the graph has a downward (or negative) slope, then the two variables are inversely related.

4. In addition, we sometimes see special examples of graphs: time series, which show how a particular variable moves over time; scatter diagrams, which show the observations on a pair of variables; and multicurve diagrams, which show two or more relationships on a single figure.

CONCEPTS FOR REVIEW

Elements of graphs	slope as "rise over run"	**Examples of graphs**	multicurve graphs
horizontal, or *X*, axis	slope (negative, positive, zero)	time-series graphs	
vertical, or *Y*, axis	tangent as slope of curved line	scatter diagrams	

QUESTIONS FOR DISCUSSION

1. Consider the following problem for a student. After your 8 hours a day of sleep, you have 16 hours a day to divide between leisure and study. Let leisure be the x variable and study hours be the y variable. Plot the straight-line relationship between all combinations of x and y on a blank piece of graph paper. Be careful to label the axes and mark the origin.
2. In question 1, what is the slope of the line showing the relationship between study and leisure hours? Is it a straight line?
3. Let us say that you absolutely need 6 hours of leisure per day, no more, no less. On the graph, mark the point that corresponds to 6 hours of leisure. Now consider a *movement along the curve*: Assume that you decide that you need only 4 hours of leisure a day. Plot the new point.
4. Next show a *shift of the curve*: You find that you need less sleep, so that you have 18 hours a day to devote to leisure and study. Draw the new (shifted) curve.
5. Keep a record of your own leisure and study for a week. Plot a time-series graph of the hours of leisure and study each day. Next plot a scatter diagram of

hours of leisure and hours of study. Do you see any relationship between the two variables?

6. Reread footnote 1 on page 16. Plot the straight line or linear curve $y = 10 + 0.5x$. What is its slope? Next plot the quadratic equation $y = (x - 2)^2$. What is the slope of this curve at $y = (0, 1, 2, 10)$?
7. Consider the following data. Plot the relationship on a scatter diagram. Why can't you be sure which of the variables "causes" movement in the other variable? (Remember the *post hoc* fallacy.)

Year	Money supply ($, billion)	GNP ($, billion)
1965	168	705
1970	215	1,016
1975	288	1,598
1980	409	2,732
1985	620	4,015
1990	826	5,463

Source: *Economic Report of the President*, 1991.

CHAPTER 2

BASIC PROBLEMS OF ECONOMIC ORGANIZATION

Every gun that is made, every warship launched, every rocket fired signifies,
in the final sense, a theft from those who hunger and are not fed.

President Dwight D. Eisenhower

Whenever people gather into a community, they must necessarily confront a few universal economic problems. These fundamental questions are as crucial today as they were at the dawn of human civilization. And as long as goods are scarce, these questions will surely be faced by the brave new world of the future.

In this chapter we explore the central problems of economic organization. We will see that every economy must answer a triad of questions: *what*, *how*, and *for whom*. This is a shorthand list that reminds us that every society must determine *what* commodities shall be produced, *how* these goods should be made, and *for whom* they will be produced.

Having described the central economic problems, we then illustrate several important choices a society must make. Because an economy's production is limited by the amount of inputs available and by its technological knowledge, society must choose between necessities and luxuries, between public and private goods, and between consumption and investment. This insight leads to the important concept of opportunity cost—which signifies that when we choose to consume a good, something else must be given up. We also discuss how the features of a modern economy—specialization and trade, money, and capital—contribute to the enormous productivity of an advanced industrial country.

A. The Three Problems of Economic Organization

Every human society—whether it is an advanced industrial nation, a centrally planned economy, or an isolated tribal society—must confront and resolve three fundamental and interdependent economic problems.

- *What* commodities are to be produced and in what quantities? How much of each of the many possible goods and services should the economy

make? And when will they be produced? Should we produce pizzas or shirts today? A few high-quality shirts or many cheap shirts? Should we produce many consumption goods (like pizzas and concerts) or few consumption goods and many investment goods (like pizza factories and concert halls), allowing more consumption tomorrow?

- *How* shall goods be produced? By whom and

with what resources and in what technological manner are they to be produced? Who farms and who teaches? Is electricity to be generated from oil or from coal? With much air pollution or with little? Are goods produced by hand or with machines? In privately owned capitalist corporations or in state-owned socialist enterprises?

- *For whom* shall goods be produced? Who gets to eat the fruit of the economy's efforts? Or, to put it formally, how is the national product to be divided among different households? Are we to have a society in which a few are rich and many poor? Shall high incomes go to managers or workers or landlords? Shall the selfish inherit the earth? Shall the lazy eat well?

These three basic problems are common to all economies. But, as we will see later, different societies take different approaches in solving them.

Inputs and Outputs

In economic language, the three central economic tasks of every society are really about choices among an economy's inputs and outputs.

Inputs are commodities or services used by firms in their production processes. An economy uses its existing *technology* to combine inputs to produce outputs. **Outputs** are the various useful goods or services that are either consumed or employed in further production. Consider the "production" of an omelette. We say that the eggs, salt, heat, frying pan, and the chef's skilled labor are the inputs. The fluffy omelette is the output.

We classify inputs, also called *factors of production*, into three broad categories: land, labor, and capital.

- *Land*—or more generally natural resources—represents the gift of nature to our productive processes. It consists of the land used for farming or for underpinning houses, factories, and roads; energy resources to fuel our cars or heat our homes; and non-energy resources like copper and iron ore and sand. We should also view our physical environment—the air we breathe and the water we drink—as natural resources.
- *Labor* consists of the human time spent in production—working in automobile factories, tilling the land, teaching school, or cooking omelettes.

Thousands of occupations and tasks, at all skill levels, are performed by labor. It is at once the most familiar and the most crucial input for an advanced industrial economy.

- *Capital* resources form the durable goods of an economy, produced in order to produce yet other goods. Capital goods include machines, roads, computers, hammers, trucks, steel mills, automobiles, washing machines, and buildings. As we will later see, the accumulation of specialized capital goods is essential to the task of economic development.

Restating the three economic problems in terms of inputs and outputs, a society must decide: (1) *what* outputs to produce, and in what quantity; (2) *how* to produce them—that is, by what techniques inputs should be combined to produce the desired outputs; and (3) *for whom* the outputs should be produced and distributed.

Market, Command, and Mixed Economies

In the earliest societies, custom ruled every facet of behavior. *What, how,* and *for whom* were decided by traditions passed on from elders to youths. In ancient Egypt, a son unswervingly adopted the trade of his father. In a modern economy, however, custom cannot adapt quickly enough to keep up with the rapidly evolving production and consumption patterns. Different societies face the demands for change through *alternative economic systems*, and economics studies the different mechanisms that a society can use to allocate its scarce resources.

Today, societies are generally organized in one of two fashions. In some cases, government makes most economic decisions, with those on top of the hierarchy giving economic commands to those further down the ladder. In other cases, decisions are made in markets, where individuals or enterprises voluntarily agree to trade inputs and outputs, usually through payments of money. Let's examine each of these two forms of economic organization briefly.

A **command economy** is one in which the government makes all decisions about production and distribution. In a command economy, such as has operated in the Soviet Union during most of this century, the government owns a considerable fraction of the means of production (land and capital); it also owns and directs the operations of enterprises in most industries; it is the employer of most workers and tells them how to do their jobs; and the government in a command economy decides how the output of the society is to be divided among different goods and services. In short, in a command economy, the government answers the major economic questions through its ownership of resources and its power to enforce decisions.

In the United States and most democratic countries, by contrast, most economic questions are solved by the market. Hence their economic systems are called market economies. A **market economy** is one in which individuals and private firms make the major decisions about production and consumption. A system of prices, of markets, of profits and losses, of incentives and rewards determines *what, how,* and *for whom.* Firms produce the commodities that yield the highest profits (the *what*) by the techniques of production that are least costly (the *how*). Consumption is determined by individuals' decisions about how to spend the wages and property incomes generated by their labor and property ownership (the *for whom*).

No contemporary society falls completely into either of these polar categories. Rather, all societies are **mixed economies,** with elements of market and command. There has never been a 100 percent market economy (although nineteenth-century England came close). Today most decisions in the United States are made in the marketplace. But the government plays an important role in modifying the functioning of the market; government sets laws and rules that regulate economic life, produces educational and police services, and regulates pollution and business. And the Soviet Union and the countries of Eastern Europe, unhappy with the performance of their command economies, are searching for their own particular brands of the mixed economy.

B. Society's Technological Possibilities

Why are we concerned with the fundamental questions of *what, how,* and *for whom*? Because people want to consume far more than an economy can produce. Recall the law of scarcity stated in the last chapter: goods are scarce because there are not enough resources to produce all the goods that people want to consume.

Faced with the undeniable truth that goods are scarce relative to wants, an economy must decide how to cope with limited resources. It must choose among different potential bundles of goods (the *what*), select among different techniques of production (the *how*), and decide in the end who should consume the goods (the *for whom*). In this section, we use several examples to illustrate some of the key choices that every society must make.

The Production-Possibility Frontier

Consider an economy with only so much labor, so much technical knowledge, so many factories and tools, and so much land, water power, and natural resources. In deciding *what* shall be produced and *how,* the economy is deciding in reality just how to allocate its resources among the thousands of different possible commodities. How much land should go into wheat growing? Or into housing the population? How many factories will produce computers? How many will make pizzas?

These issues are complicated even to discuss, much less resolve. Therefore, we must simplify. Let us assume that only two economic goods (or classes of economic goods) are to be produced. For dramatic purposes we can select guns and butter to illustrate the problem of choosing between military spending and civilian goods. This example applies equally to America's massive mobilization during World War II, to the issue of how to pay for operation "Desert Storm" in Saudi Arabia in 1991, and to the choices of military versus civilian spending faced by any nation.

We can begin our study of guns and butter with a numerical example. Suppose that our economy throws all its energy into producing the civilian good, butter. There is still a maximum amount of butter that can be produced per year. The maximal amount of butter depends on the quantity and quality of resources of the economy in question and the productive efficiency with which they are used. Suppose 5 million pounds of butter is the maximum amount that can be produced with the existing technology and resources.

At the other extreme, imagine that all resources are instead devoted to the production of guns. Again, because of resource limitations, the economy can produce only a limited quantity of guns. For this example, assume that the economy can produce 15 thousand guns of a certain kind if no butter is produced.

These are two extreme possibilities. In between are many others. If we are willing to give up some butter, we can have some guns. If we are willing to give up still more butter, we can have still more guns.

A schedule of possibilities is given in Table 2-1. Combination *F* shows the extreme where all butter and no guns are produced, while *A* depicts the opposite extreme where all resources go into guns. In between—at *E*, *D*, *C*, and *B*—increasing amounts of butter are given up in return for more guns.

Butter is transformed into guns, not physically, but by the alchemy of diverting the economy's resources from one use to the other.

We can represent our economy's production possibilities more vividly in the diagram shown in Figure 2-1. This diagram measures butter along the horizontal axis and guns along the vertical one.

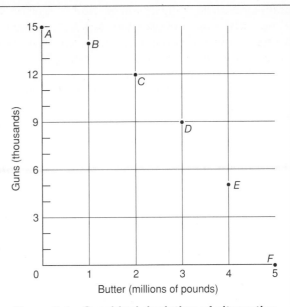

Figure 2-1. Graphical depiction of alternative production possibilities

This figure displays the alternative combinations of production pairs from Table 2-1.

Recalling the principles on using graphs outlined in Chapter 1's appendix, you should be able to go directly from the data in Table 2-1 to the figure: to *F*, by counting over 5 butter units to the right on the horizontal axis and going up 0 gun units on the vertical axis; to *E*, by going 4 butter units to the right and going up 5 gun units; and finally, to *A*, by going over 0 butter units and up 15 gun units.

If we fill in all intermediate positions with new blue points representing all the different combinations of guns and butter, we have the continuous blue curve shown as the **production-possibility frontier,** or *PPF*, in Figure 2-2.

The production-possibility frontier (or *PPF*) shows the maximum amounts of production that can be obtained by an economy, given the technological knowledge and quantity of inputs available. The *PPF* represents the menu of choices available to society.

Efficiency

Up to now, we have implicitly assumed that the economy was on, rather than inside, the production-possibility frontier. Operating on the frontier

Alternative Production Possibilities

Possibilities	Butter (millions of pounds)	Guns (thousands)
A	0	15
B	1	14
C	2	12
D	3	9
E	4	5
F	5	0

Table 2-1. Limitation of scarce resources implies the guns-butter tradeoff

As we go from *A* to *B* . . . to *F*, we are transferring labor, machines, and land from the gun industry to butter production.

implies that the economy is producing *efficiently*.

Efficiency is one of the central concepts of economics. **Efficiency** means absence of waste, or using the economy's resources as effectively as possible to satisfy people's needs and desires. More specifically, the economy is producing efficiently when it cannot produce more of one good without producing less of another good—when it is on the production-possibility frontier.

How do we know that any point on that frontier is efficient? Let us start in the situation shown by point *D* in Figure 2-2. Decree that we want another million pounds of butter. If we ignored the constraint shown by the *PPF*, we might think it possible to produce more butter without reducing gun production, say by moving to point *I*, due east of point *D*. But point *I* is outside the frontier in the "impossible" region. Starting from *D*, we cannot get more butter without giving up some guns. Hence point *D* is efficient, and point *I* is infeasible.

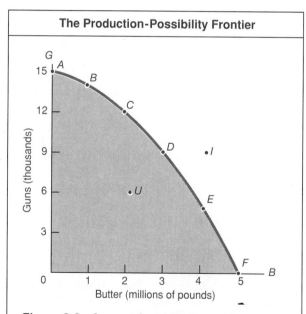

Figure 2-2. A smooth curve connects the plotted points of the numerical production possibilities

This frontier shows the schedule of choices along which society can choose to substitute guns for butter. It assumes a given state of technology and a given quantity of inputs. Points outside the frontier (such as point *I*) are infeasible or unattainable. Any point inside the curve, such as *U*, indicates that some resources are unemployed, or not used in the best possible way.

Productive efficiency occurs when society cannot increase the output of one good without cutting back on another good. An efficient economy is on its production-possibility frontier.

One further point about productive efficiency can be illustrated using the *PPF*: Being on the *PPF* means that producing more of one good inevitably requires sacrificing other goods. When we produce more guns, we are substituting guns for butter. Substitution is the law of life in a full-employment economy, and the production-possibility frontier depicts the menu of society's choices.

Unemployed Resources and Inefficiency. Even casual observers of modern life know that society has unemployed resources in the form of idle workers, idle factories, and idle land. Chapter 1 hinted that economic laws might be different when resources are less than fully employed. Being inside the *PPF* is one such instance.

When there are unemployed resources, the economy is not on its production-possibility frontier at all, but rather somewhere *inside* it. In Figure 2-2, point *U* represents a point inside the *PPF*; at *U*, society is producing only 2 units of butter and 6 units of guns. Some resources are unemployed, and by putting them to work we can have more butter and more guns. We can move from *U* to *D*, thereby producing more butter and more guns and improving the economy's efficiency.

Taking into account the possibility of unemployed resources throws light on the experience in World War II of two countries: the United States and the Soviet Union. After 1940, how was the United States able to become the "arsenal of democracy" and to enjoy civilian living standards higher than ever before? Largely by taking up the slack of unemployment from the Great Depression and moving toward the *PPF*.

The case of wartime U.S.S.R. was different. The Soviets had little unemployment before the war and were already on their rather low production-possibility frontier. To move northwest along their *PPF* the Soviets had no choice but to substitute war goods for civilian goods—with consequent privation.

Business-cycle depressions are not the only reason why an economy might be inside its *PPF*. An economy might suffer from inefficiency or dislocations because of strikes, political changes, or revolution. Such a case occurred during the early 1990s in Poland after that country substituted a free-market economy for its socialist command economy. Because of the dramatic changes in the economic system, output fell and unemployment rose as people attempted to adapt to the changed prices, laws, and incomes. A political and economic revolution pushed Poland temporarily inside its *PPF*.

Polish leaders hope that this inefficiency will be but a temporary setback. They foresee that a free market will boost incentives for efficient production. If they are right, Poland will soon move back toward its *PPF*, and indeed the *PPF* will begin to shift outward as the economy begins to grow rapidly.

Putting the *PPF* to Work

In addition to explaining efficiency, the production-possibility curve can help introduce many of the most basic concepts of economics.

1. Figure 2-2 illustrates our definition of economics as the science of choosing what goods to produce. Should we live in a fortress economy bristling with guns but with austere living habits, as at point *B* in Figure 2-2? Or should we reduce the military to a pittance and instead enjoy an economy with much bread and butter, as at point *E*?

    Such questions are debated in peacetime as well as in wartime. In the early 1980s, under the leadership of President Reagan, the United States increased real defense spending by around 50 percent. Then, following the revolutions in Eastern Europe in 1989, the Congress argued about who should receive a "peace dividend" from declining defense spending. After hostilities broke out in the Middle East in 1990, yet another debate occurred about how much to spend defending the vital oil fields of that region.

2. The production-possibility frontier provides a rigorous definition of scarcity. Economic scarcity describes the basic economic fact that—given our technical knowledge and endowment of land, labor, and capital—our economy can produce only certain maximum amounts of each economic good. The *PPF* shows the outer limit of producible goods dictated by the law of scarcity.

    Nowhere on the globe is the supply of goods so plentiful or are tastes so limited that the average family can have enough of everything it might fancy. Scarcity is a reflection of the limitation on our living standards imposed by the *PPF*.

3. The production-possibility schedule can also illustrate the three basic problems of economic life: *what*, *how*, and *for whom*.

    What goods are produced and consumed can be depicted by the point that ends up getting chosen on the *PPF*.

    How goods are to be produced involves an efficient choice of production techniques and a proper assignment of different quantities of different inputs to the various industries.

    For whom goods are to be produced cannot be discerned from the *PPF* alone, although you can sometimes make a guess from it. If you find a society on its *PPF* with many yachts and furs, but few houses and compact cars, you might suspect that it experiences considerable inequality of income and wealth among its people.

4. The production-possibility frontier can also illustrate the general point that we are always choosing among limited opportunities. People have limited time available to pursue different activities. For example, as a student, you might have 10 hours to study for upcoming tests in economics and history. If you study only history you will get a high grade there and do poorly in economics, and vice versa. Treating the grades on the two tests as the "output" of your studying, sketch out the *PPF* for grades, given your limited time resources.

    Alternatively, if the two student commodities are "grades" and "fun," how would you draw this *PPF*? Where are you on this frontier? Where are your lazier friends?

Pictures at an Exhibition

The same analysis that applies to choosing between the pair of goods—guns and butter—applies to any choice of goods. Thus the more resources the government uses to produce public goods (like weather forecasts), the less will be left to produce private goods (like houses); the more we choose to consume of food, the less we can consume of clothing; the more society decides to consume today, the less can be its production of capital goods (durable productive goods like equipment or factories) to turn out more consumption goods in the future.

The graphs of Figures 2-3 to 2-5 present some important applications of *PPF*s. Figure 2-3 shows the effect of economic growth on a country's production possibilities. As a result of increasing inputs of capital and labor and of improving technology, the *PPF* shifts out. A nation can have more of *all* goods as its economy grows. The figure also illustrates how poor countries must devote most of their resources to food production while rich countries can afford more luxuries as productive potential increases.

Figure 2-4 depicts how the electorate must choose between private goods (bought at a price) and public goods (paid for by taxes). Poor countries can afford little of public goods like public health and scientific research. But with economic growth, public goods as well as environmental quality take a larger share of output.

Figure 2-5 portrays how an economy chooses between (a) current consumption goods and (b) investment or capital goods (machines, factories, etc.). By sacrificing current consumption and producing more capital goods, a nation's economy can grow more rapidly, making possible more of *both* goods (consumption and capital) in the future.

These three diagrams introduce key themes of later chapters—how societies choose among different patterns of output, how they pay for their choice, how they benefit or lose in the future. A careful study of these diagrams is a good investment—just as a nation sometimes benefits from investing in capital goods for future enjoyment, so a few extra minutes spent here will bring you many rewards in your economic understanding.

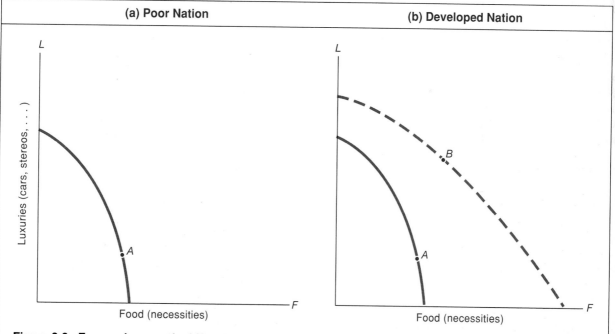

Figure 2-3. Economic growth shifts *PPF* outward

(**a**) Before development, the nation is poor. It must devote almost all its resources to food and enjoys few comforts. (**b**) Growth of inputs and technological change shift out the *PPF*. With economic growth, a nation moves from A to B, expanding its food consumption little compared with its increased consumption of luxuries. Note that it can increase its consumption of both goods if it desires.

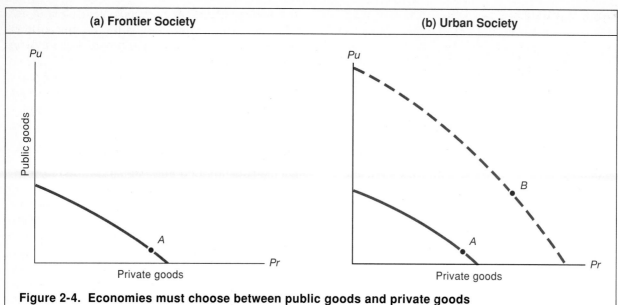

(a) Frontier Society

(b) Urban Society

Figure 2-4. Economies must choose between public goods and private goods

(**a**) A frontier economy is poor and dispersed, as in Thomas Jefferson's days. The proportion of resources going to public goods (defense, science, public health) is low.
(**b**) A modern industrial economy is more prosperous and chooses to spend more of its higher income on public goods or governmental services (roads, defense, antipollution programs, public health, education).

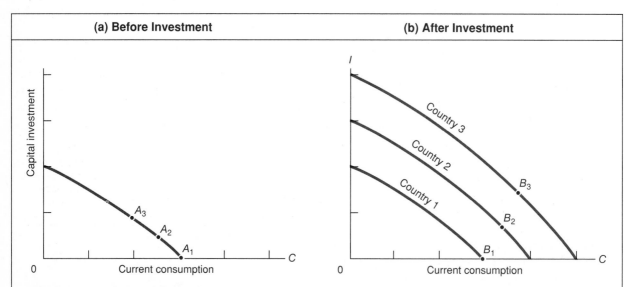

(a) Before Investment

(b) After Investment

Figure 2-5. Investment for future consumption requires sacrificing current consumption

A nation can produce either current consumption goods (pizzas and concerts) or investment goods (trucks and houses).
(**a**) Three countries start out even. They have the same *PPF* shown in the panel on the left, but they have different investment rates. Country 1 does no investment for the future and remains at A_1 (merely replacing machines). Country 2 abstains modestly from consumption and invests at A_2. Country 3 sacrifices a great deal of current consumption and invests heavily.
(**b**) In the following years, countries that invest more forge ahead. Thus thrifty Country 3 has shifted its *PPF* far out, while Country 1's *PPF* has not moved at all. In the future, thrifty Country 3 continues to invest heavily but has more current consumption as well.

Opportunity Cost

Life is full of choices. Because resources are scarce, we must constantly decide what to do with our limited time and income. Should we go to a movie or read a book? Should we travel in Europe or buy a car? Should we get postgraduate or professional training or begin work right after college? In each of these cases, making a choice in a world of scarcity requires us to give up something else, in effect costing us the opportunity to do something else. The alternative forgone is called the **opportunity cost.**

To take a simple example, say that, after necessary expenses, your income is $100. With that sum you can either take a trip to Chicago or buy a radio. If you decide to go to Chicago, we would say that the opportunity cost of your trip was the pleasure of enjoying the new radio.

The concept of opportunity cost can also be illustrated using the production-possibility frontier. Look back at the frontier in Figure 2-2 on page 23. Suppose the country has decided to step up its purchases of guns from 9000 guns at D to 12,000 guns at C. What is the opportunity cost of this decision? You might calculate it in dollar terms. But on the most fundamental level, the opportunity cost is the butter that must be given up to produce the extra guns. In this example the opportunity cost of the 3000 guns is easily seen to be 1 million pounds of butter.

The **opportunity cost** of a decision arises because choosing one thing in a world of scarcity means giving up something else. The opportunity cost is the value of the good or service forgone.

The concept of opportunity cost is a useful reminder that the actual dollar outlays are not always an accurate index of true costs. For example, if the government decides to run a highway through a national park, the needed land might look cheap in out-of-pocket or budget costs. But the opportunity cost of using parkland might be quite high because people could enjoy fewer picnics or hikes or camping trips.

Another important example of opportunity cost is the cost of going to college. If you went to a public university, you might calculate the total costs of tuition, room, board, books, and travel to be about $10,000 in 1990. Does this mean that $10,000 is your opportunity cost of going to school? Definitely not! You must include as well the opportunity cost of the *time* spent studying and going to classes. A full-time job for a 19-year-old high school graduate would on average pay around $16,000 in 1990. If we add up both the actual expenses and the earnings forgone, we find the opportunity cost of college to be $26,000 (equal to $10,000 + $16,000) rather than $10,000 per year.

The Law of Diminishing Returns

We can also use the production-possibility frontier to illustrate one of the most famous economic relationships: the law of diminishing returns. This law concerns the relationship between inputs and outputs in the productive process. More specifically, *the law of diminishing returns holds that we will get less and less extra output when we add successive doses of an input while holding other inputs fixed.*

As an example of diminishing returns, consider the following controlled experiment: Given a fixed amount of land, say 100 acres, assume that we use no labor inputs at all. With zero labor input there is no corn output. So, in Table 2-2, we record zero product when labor is zero.

Now we make another experiment. We add 1 unit of labor to the same fixed amount of land. We observe that 2000 bushels of corn are produced. In yet another controlled experiment, we continue to

Law of Diminishing Returns		
Units of labor (person-years)	Total output (bushels)	Extra output added by additional unit of labor (bushels per person-year)
0	0	
1	2,000	2,000
2	3,000	1,000
3	3,500	500
4	3,800	———
5	3,900	100

Table 2-2. Diminishing returns is a fundamental law of economics and technology

According to the law of diminishing returns, as additional units of labor are added, with land and other inputs held fixed, the extra output tends to decline. Fill in the extra output added by the fourth unit of labor.

hold land fixed and add exactly 1 extra unit of labor as before, going from 1 unit of labor to 2 units of labor.

What is the impact of the added labor on production? Do we have proportional returns, with an extra output of 2000 bushels added to the original output of 2000 bushels? Table 2-2 demonstrates the presence of diminishing returns. The second unit of labor adds only 1000 bushels of additional output, which is less than what the first unit of labor added. The third unit of labor adds even less output than does the second, and the fourth unit adds yet a bit less. The hypothetical experiment reported in Table 2-2 thus illustrates the law of diminishing returns.

The law of diminishing returns is an important and widely observed economic relationship. Be warned, however, that it is not universally valid for all technologies. Also, it may hold only after a few units of inputs have been added—that is, the first few units of inputs might yield increasing extra output, since a minimum amount of labor may be needed just to walk to the field and pick up a shovel. But, ultimately, diminishing returns will prevail for most technologies.

Some Examples

A little reflection suggests that the law of diminishing returns makes good sense. What happens as more and more labor cultivates the same 100-acre farm? For a while, output will increase sharply as we add labor—the fields will be more thoroughly seeded and weeded, irrigation ditches will be neater, scarecrows better oiled. At some point, however, the additional labor becomes less and less productive. The third hoeing of the day or the fourth oiling of the machinery adds little to output. Eventually, output grows very little as more people crowd onto the farm; too many tillers spoil the crop. Ultimately, output may even decline.

Diminishing returns are a key factor in explaining why many countries in Asia are so poor. Living standards in crowded China and India are low because there are so many workers per acre of land in these regions and not because land happens to be owned by the state or by absentee landlords.

We can also use the example of studying to illustrate the law of diminishing returns. You might find that the first hour of studying economics on a given day was productive—you learned new laws and facts, insights and history. The second hour might find your attention wandering a bit, with less learned. The third hour might show that diminishing returns had set in with a vengeance—so that by the next day you could remember nothing of what you had read during the third hour. Does the law of diminishing returns suggest why the hours devoted to studying should be spread out rather than crammed into the day before exams?

To summarize:

The law of diminishing returns holds that an increase in some input, with other inputs held constant, will increase total output. But after some point, the extra output resulting from additional doses of inputs will tend to become smaller and smaller.

C. Trade, Money, and Capital

No matter what system is used to organize economic activity, we will always find three distinguishing features in an advanced industrial economy: trade, money, and capital.

- An advanced economy is characterized by an elaborate network of *trade*, among individuals and countries, that depends on great specialization and an intricate division of labor.

- The economy today makes extensive use of *money*. The flow of money is the lifeblood of our system. Money provides the yardstick for measuring the economic value of things. But improper management of money by the central bank can cause inflation or depression.

- Modern industrial technologies rest on the use of vast amounts of *capital*: precision machinery, large-scale factories, and stocks of inventories. Capital goods leverage human labor power into a much more efficient factor of production and allow productivity many times greater than in an earlier age.

Trade, Specialization, and Division of Labor

One of the major differences between a modern economy and that of frontier days is found in the extensive network of trade and specialization of individuals and firms. Western economies have enjoyed rapid economic growth over the last two centuries as increasing specialization allowed each of us to become highly productive in a particular occupation and to trade our output for the other commodities we need.

Specialization occurs when people concentrate their efforts on a particular set of tasks—it permits each person and country to use to best advantage any peculiar skills and resources. One of the facts of economic life is that, rather than have everyone do everything in a mediocre way, it is better to establish a *division of labor*—dividing production into a number of small specialized steps or tasks. A division of labor permits slow people to fish and swift people to hunt, all exchanging what they make for what they need.

To illustrate the increased productivity of specialization, Adam Smith provided the classical example of pinmaking. One worker could at best make a few dozen imperfect pins per day. But when pinmaking is broken down into a number of simple repetitive operations, a few workers can turn out hundreds of thousands of perfect pins per day.

Perhaps the epitome of specialization is the modern automobile assembly line, where cars move down a conveyor belt and workers, or even robots, perform highly specialized functions. A worker might concentrate on putting left tires on Hondas. The result of such specialization is the enormous increase in labor productivity in many manufacturing industries.

The economies of specialization allow the intricate network of trade among people and nations that we see today. Very few of us produce a single finished good; we make but the tiniest fraction of what we consume. We might teach a small part of a college curriculum, or produce buttons or zippers, or assemble part of an automobile or computer. In exchange for this specialized labor, we will receive an income adequate to buy goods from all over the world.

What determines which goods we produce? Economists emphasize the *law of comparative advantage*. This law states that individuals or nations should specialize in producing and selling those commodities which they can produce at *relatively* low cost. Similarly, an individual or nation should buy rather than produce those goods which it could produce only at a relatively high cost. The surprising feature of the law of comparative advantage is that even people or countries that are absolutely more inefficient than others will find it beneficial to specialize in the production of some goods. Thus, even the low-productivity countries of Asia or Africa can find a niche for their products in the international marketplace because they are relatively efficient at producing some goods.

The idea of *gains from trade* forms one of the central insights of economics. Different people or countries tend to specialize in certain areas and then to engage in voluntary exchange of what they produce for what they need. Many countries in the Middle East produce and export oil for food and manufactures. Japan has grown enormously productive by specializing in manufacturing goods such as automobiles and consumer electronics; it exports much of its manufacturing output to pay for imports of raw materials. Trade enriches *all* nations and increases *everyone's* living standards.

To summarize:

Advanced economies engage in specialization and division of labor, which increases the productivity of their resources. Individuals and countries then voluntarily trade goods they specialize in for others' products, vastly increasing the range and quantity of consumption and raising everyone's living standards.

Money: The Lubricant of Exchange

If specialization permits people to concentrate on particular tasks, money then allows people to trade their specialized outputs for the vast array of goods produced by others. To be sure, we could imagine a state of *barter,* where people directly trade one commodity for another. In primitive economies, food might be traded for clothing, or help in building a house might be exchanged for help in clearing a field. But exchange today in all economies— market as well as command—takes place through the medium of money.

What is money? **Money** is the means of payment or the medium of exchange; in our economy, money consists of currency and checking accounts with which households and businesses pay for things. When you buy gum with a quarter, lunch with a $10 bill, or a stereo set with a check, in each case you are employing money.

Money is a lubricant that facilitates exchange. When everyone trusts and accepts money as payment for goods and debts, trade is facilitated. Just imagine how complicated economic life would be if you had to barter goods for goods every time you wanted to buy a pizza or go to a concert. What goods could you offer Sal's Pizza or the Rolling Stones? What do you have in abundance that they want to consume? Because everyone accepts money as the medium of exchange, the need to match supplies and demands is enormously simplified.

But like other lubricants, money can get gummed up. In a barter economy, if I am hungry and you are naked, I can always sew your clothes while you bake my bread. But trade can go haywire in a monetary economy. For example, in the Great Depression of the 1930s, the banks failed, money was hoarded, some people went hungry, and other people went in rags in the world's richest country. Poverty can prevail amid plenty when money is not properly managed by the central bank.

The problems of managing money—one of the most important tasks of government today—are taken up in our study of macroeconomics.

Capital

We have learned that the economy depends upon three major factors of production: labor, capital, and land. Land and labor are often called *primary factors of production.* A primary factor of production is one whose quantity is determined outside the economy (by social forces in the case of labor or geological history in the case of land).

Capital is a different kind of productive factor.

Capital (or capital goods) is a produced factor of production, a durable input which is itself an output of the economy. For example, we build a textile factory and use the factory to produce shirts; we assemble a computer and then employ the computer in educating students; and so forth.

Capital and Time

Capital has a special relationship to time. Why so? We will see that capital inherently involves time-consuming, indirect, roundabout methods of production. In fact, one of the paradoxes of capital is that the economy becomes enormously more productive by using indirect or roundabout methods.

If farmers had to work with their hands, without any capital in the form of tractors or shovels, farm productivity would be very low indeed. People learned long ago that direct methods of production are often less efficient than indirect or roundabout techniques. A direct method of catching fish would be to wade into the stream and catch fish with your hands, but this direct technique would yield few fish. Instead, people learned that by building nets and fishing boats (all these being capital equipment), fishing time becomes vastly more productive in terms of fish caught per day.

Other examples of efficient indirect or roundabout techniques are the following: A farmer spends time in clearing fields or digging ditches, so that the wheat yield will improve. A steelworker makes sheet steel, which will be used to manufacture a tractor, which will clear a field. A biologist injects DNA into a cell to produce a new and hardy seed. All these are roundabout ways of increasing the amount of wheat our economy can produce.

While we who toil inside the economy seldom stop to wonder about its roundaboutness, a moment's reflection will convince us that almost no one actually produces finished consumer goods. Almost everyone is doing work of a preparatory and roundabout nature, with the final consumption a distant future goal.

Growth from the Sacrifice of Current Consumption. If people are willing to *save*—to abstain from present consumption and wait for future consumption—then society can devote resources to new capital goods. A larger stock of capital helps the economy to grow faster by pushing out the *PPF.*

Look back at Figure 2-5 to see how forgoing current consumption in favor of investment adds to future production possibilities.

All this raises the question: If roundabout and indirect processes are so productive, why not replace *all* direct processes by more productive, roundabout ones, and all roundabout processes by still more roundabout processes? The advantage of using roundabout processes is offset by the initial disadvantage of having to forgo present consumption goods by diverting current consumption to investments in roundabout processes. The problem is that the roundabout processes bear fruit only after some time. We could invest time and resources in making our highways even wider and our railroad beds even flatter than they are, thereby reducing fuel and repair costs and driving time. Or students could go to school for 5 or 10 more years and acquire even greater specialized skills. We don't invest in even more roundabout investments because these would cause too great a reduction in today's consumption.

We summarize as follows:

Much of economic activity involves forgoing current consumption to increase our capital. Every time we invest—building a new factory or road, increasing the years or quality of education, or increasing the stock of useful technical knowledge—we are enhancing the future productivity of our economy.

Capital and Private Property

Physical capital goods are critical for any economy, market or command, because they help to increase productivity. But there is one significant difference between a capitalist and a socialist system: By and large, it is private firms and individuals who own the machines, buildings, and land in our market economy. What is the exception in our system—government ownership of the means of production—is the rule in a socialist state, where capital, land, and houses are collectively owned.

In a market economy, capital typically is privately owned, and the income from capital goes to individuals. Every patch of land has a deed, or title of ownership; almost every machine and building belongs to an individual or corporation. *Property rights* bestow on their owners the ability to use, exchange, paint, dig, drill, or exploit their capital goods. These capital goods also have market values, and people can buy and sell the capital goods for whatever price they will fetch. *The ability of individuals to own and profit from capital is what gives capitalism its name.*[1]

But while our society is one built on private property, property rights are limited. Society determines how much of "your" property you may bequeath to your heirs and how much must go in inheritance and estate taxes to the government. Society determines how much the owners of public utilities—such as electric and gas companies—can earn and how much pollution your car can emit. Even your home is not your castle. You must obey zoning laws and, if necessary, make way for a road.

Interestingly enough, the most valuable economic resource, labor, cannot be turned into a commodity that is bought and sold as private property. Since the abolition of slavery, it is against the law to treat human earning power like other capital assets. You are not free to sell yourself; you must rent yourself at a wage.

Property rights define the ability of individuals or firms to own, buy, sell, and use the capital goods and other property in a market economy.

● We now see how specialization, trade, money, and capital form a key to the productiveness of an advanced economy. But note as well that they are closely interrelated. Specialization creates enormous efficiencies, while increased production makes trade possible. Use of money allows trade to take place quickly and efficiently. Without the facility for trade and exchange that money provides, an elaborate division of labor would not be possible. Money and capital are related because the funds for buying capital goods are funneled through financial markets, where people's savings can be transformed into other people's capital.

Now that we have surveyed the central problems of economic organization, we can turn in the next chapter to an analysis of the way our own economy determines prices, quantities, and incomes. ●

---

[1] We must carefully distinguish *physical* capital from *financial* capital. Physical capital takes the form of factories, equipment, houses, and inventories; physical capital is an input or factor of production. Financial capital is "paper" assets or claims, like bonds, common stocks, checking and savings accounts, or home mortgages; financial capital is often the claim to physical capital, but it is never an input into the productive process.

——————————————————— **SUMMARY** ———————————————————

A. The Three Problems of Economic Organization

1. Every society must solve three fundamental problems: *what, how,* and *for whom? What* kinds and quantities shall be produced among the wide range of all possible goods and services? *How* shall resources be used in producing these goods? And *for whom* shall the goods be produced (that is, what shall be the distribution of income and consumption among different individuals and classes)?

2. Societies meet these problems in different ways. The most important forms of economic organization today are *command* and *market.* The command economy is directed by centralized control of governments; a market economy is guided by an informal system of prices and profits in which most decisions are taken by private individuals and firms. All societies have different combinations of command and market; all societies are *mixed* economies.

B. Society's Technological Possibilities

3. With given resources and technology, the production choices between two such goods as butter and guns can be summarized in the *production-possibility frontier (PPF).* The *PPF* shows how the production of one good (such as guns) is traded off against the production of another good (such as butter).

4. Productive efficiency occurs when production of one good cannot be increased without curtailing production of another good. This is illustrated by the *PPF.* When an economy is operating efficiently—on its *PPF*—it can produce more of one good only by producing less of another good.

   Societies are sometimes inside their frontier. When unemployment is high or when government regulation hampers firms' activities, the economy is inefficient and operates inside its *PPF.*

5. Production-possibility frontiers illustrate many basic economic processes: how economic growth pushes out the frontier, how a nation chooses relatively less food and other necessities as it develops, how a country chooses between private goods and public goods, and how societies choose between consumption goods and capital goods that enhance future consumption.

6. Dollar costs are not the same as true economic costs. When we measure the total cost of making choices in a world of scarcity, we calculate the opportunity cost, which measures the value of the things given up, or opportunities forgone.

7. The law of diminishing returns holds that, after a point, as we add equal extra doses of a variable input (such as labor) to a fixed input (such as land), the amount of extra output will decline.

C. Trade, Money, and Capital

8. As economies develop, they become more specialized. Division of labor allows a task to be broken into a number of smaller chores that can be mastered and performed more quickly by a single worker. Specialization arises from the increasing tendency to use roundabout methods of production that require many specialized skills.

9. As individuals and countries become increasingly specialized, they tend to concentrate on particular commodities and trade their surplus output for goods produced by others. Voluntary trade, based on specialization and comparative advantage, benefits all.

10. Trade in specialized goods and services today relies on money to lubricate the wheels of trade. Money is the universally acceptable medium of exchange—currency and checks. It is used to pay for everything from apple tarts to zebra skins. By accepting money, people and nations can specialize in producing a few goods and trade them for others; without money, we would waste much time constantly bartering one good for another.

11. Capital goods—produced inputs such as machinery, structures, and inventories of goods in process—permit roundabout methods of production that add much to a nation's output. These roundabout methods take time and resources to get started and therefore require a temporary sacrifice of present consumption. The rules that define how capital and other assets can be bought, sold, and used are the system of property rights. In no economic system are private-property rights unlimited.

CONCEPTS FOR REVIEW

Key problems of economic organization
what, how, and for whom
alternative economic systems:
    command vs. market
inputs and outputs

Choice among production possibilities
production-possibility frontier (PPF)
efficiency
opportunity cost
law of diminishing returns

Features of a modern economy
specialization and division of labor
money
factors of production (land, labor, capital)
capital and private property

QUESTIONS FOR DISCUSSION

1. Define each of the following terms carefully and give examples: PPF, efficiency, inputs, outputs, opportunity cost.
2. Assume Econoland produces haircuts and shirts with inputs of labor. Econoland has 1000 hours of labor available. A haircut requires $\frac{1}{2}$ hour of labor, while a shirt requires 5 hours of labor. Construct Econoland's production-possibility frontier.
3. Redraw society's production-possibility frontier in Figure 2-2 after scientific inventions have doubled the

productivity of its resources in butter production without any change in the productivity of gun manufacture.
4. Give three examples you know of specialization and division of labor. In what areas are you and your friends thinking of specializing? What might be the perils of overspecialization?
5. "Lincoln freed the slaves. With one pen stroke he destroyed much of the capital the South had accumulated over the years." Comment.

6. "Compulsory military service allows the government to fool itself and the people about the true cost of a big army." Compare the budget cost and the opportunity cost of a voluntary army (where army pay is high) and compulsory service (where pay is low). What does the concept of opportunity cost contribute to analyzing the quotation?

7. Many scientists believe that we are rapidly depleting our natural resources. Assume that there are only two inputs (labor and natural resources) producing two goods (haircuts and gasoline) with no improvement in society's technology over time. Show what would happen to the *PPF* over time as natural resources are exhausted. How would invention and technological improvement modify your answer? On the basis of this example, explain why it is said that "economic growth is a race between depletion and invention."

8. Say that Diligent has 10 hours to study for upcoming tests in economics and history. Draw a *PPF* for grades, given Diligent's limited time resources. If Diligent studies inefficiently by listening to loud music and chatting with friends, where will Diligent's grade "output" be relative to the *PPF*? What would happen to the grade *PPF* if Diligent increases study inputs from 10 hours to 15 hours?

9. From 1982 to 1990, the American economy grew rapidly as unemployment fell and capital equipment was utilized more intensively. Draw *PPF*s for 1982 and 1990 and put in two points to illustrate where the economy might have been in both those years.

MARKETS AND GOVERNMENT IN A MODERN ECONOMY

Every individual endeavors to employ his capital so that its produce may be of greatest value. He generally neither intends to promote the public interest, nor knows how much he is promoting it. He intends only his own security, only his own gain. And he is in this led by an invisible hand to promote an end which was no part of his intention. By pursuing his own interest he frequently promotes that of society more effectually than when he really intends to promote it.

Adam Smith, *The Wealth of Nations* (1776)

Both market and command economies have their roots in an earlier age. Centuries ago, government councils or town guilds directed much economic activity in regions of Europe and Asia. However, around the time of the American Revolution, governments began to exercise less and less direct control over prices and economic conditions. Feudal relationships gradually gave way to markets, or what is sometimes called "free enterprise" or "competitive capitalism."

This trend culminated in the nineteenth century, the age of **laissez-faire.** This doctrine, which translates as "leave us alone," holds that government should interfere as little as possible in economic affairs and leave economic decisions to the marketplace. Many governments followed this approach in the nineteenth century. But before full laissez-faire was achieved, the tide turned the other way.

Starting at the end of the last century, in almost all countries of North America and Europe, the economic functions of government expanded steadily. The welfare state increasingly displaced the market and family in capitalist economies, while socialist governments displaced the market in many countries of Europe and Asia.

In the 1980s, the tides shifted yet again. Conservative economic policies reduced government control of the economy in the market economies. Then, in 1990, many socialist governments cast off their hierarchical central planning systems and began to grope toward "the market."

What exactly is a market economy? How does government sometimes displace the market? The time has come to understand the principles that lie behind the market economy and to review government's role in economic life.

A. How Markets Solve the Basic Economic Problems

In a country like the United States, most economic questions are resolved through the market, so we begin our systematic study there. Who solves the three basic questions—*what, how,* and *for whom*—

in a market economy? You may be surprised to learn that *no one individual or organization is responsible for solving the economic problems in a market economy*. Instead, millions of businesses and consumers engage in voluntary trade, and their actions and purposes are invisibly coordinated by a system of prices and markets.

To see how remarkable this fact is, consider the city of New York. Without a constant flow of goods into and out of the city, New Yorkers would be on the verge of starvation within a week. For New York to thrive, many kinds of goods and services must be provided. From the surrounding counties, from 50 states, and from the far corners of the world, goods travel for days and months with New York as their destination.

How is it that 10 million people can sleep easily at night, without living in mortal terror of a breakdown in the elaborate economic processes upon which the city's existence depends? The surprising answer is that these economic activities are coordinated without coercion or centralized direction by anybody through the market.

Everyone in the United States notices how much the government does to control economic activity: it places tolls on bridges, legislates police protection, controls pollution, levies taxes, sends armies to the desert, prohibits drugs, and so forth. But we seldom think about how much of our ordinary economic life proceeds without government intervention. Thousands of commodities are produced by millions of people, willingly, without central direction or master plan.

Economic Order, Not Chaos

Before people study the way the market works, they see only a jumble of different firms and products. Few of us stop to wonder how it is that food is produced in suitable amounts, gets transported to the right place, and arrives in a palatable form at the dinner table. But a close look at New York is convincing proof that a market system does not produce chaos and anarchy. A market system contains an internal logic. It works.

A market economy is an elaborate mechanism for the unconscious coordination of people, activities, and businesses through a system of prices and markets. It is a communication device for pooling the knowledge and actions of millions of diverse individuals. Without central intelligence or computation, it solves a problem that the largest supercomputer could not solve today, involving millions of unknown variables and relations. Nobody designed the market; yet it functions remarkably well.

History's most dramatic example of the effectiveness of the market economy came in West Germany after World War II. In 1947, production and consumption had dropped to a low level. Neither bombing damage nor postwar reparation payments could account for this breakdown. Paralysis of the market mechanism was clearly to blame. Price controls and overarching government regulation hobbled markets. Money was worthless; factories closed down for lack of materials; trains could not run for lack of coal; coal could not be mined because miners were hungry; miners were hungry because peasants would not sell food for money and no goods were available for them to purchase in return. Markets were not functioning properly. People could not buy what they needed or sell what they produced at free-market prices.

Then in 1948, the government freed prices from controls and introduced a new currency, quickly putting the market mechanism back into effective operation. Very quickly production and consumption soared; once again *what*, *how*, and *for whom* were being resolved by markets and prices. People called it "an economic miracle," but the recovery was in fact largely the result of a smoothly running market mechanism.

The point to emphasize is that markets perform similar miracles around us all the time—if only we take care to observe our economy carefully. Moreover, history records that economic and political crises often occur when the market mechanism breaks down. Indeed, the socialist economies, having seen their living standards decline relative to their Western neighbors, are in the 1990s trying to duplicate the German miracle of 1948 by turning to the market to organize economic life in their countries.

The Market Mechanism

How does a market function? Exactly how does the market mechanism go about determining prices, wages, and outputs? Originally, a market was a *place* where goods were bought and sold. Economic histories of the Middle Ages record that market stalls—filled with slabs of butter, pyramids of cheese, wet fish, and heaps of vegetables—formed the commercial centers of villages and towns. Today, important markets include the Chicago Board of Trade, where oil, wheat, and other commodities are traded, and the New York Stock Exchange, where titles to ownership of the largest American firms are bought and sold.

More generally, markets are a mechanism by which buyers and sellers meet to exchange things. The market may be centralized (as for stocks, bonds, and wheat), or decentralized (as for houses or used cars), or may even be an electronic market (as occurs for many financial assets and services). The crucial characteristic of a market is that it brings buyers and sellers together to set prices and quantities.

A market is a mechanism by which buyers and sellers of a commodity interact to determine its price and quantity.

In a market system, everything has a price, which is the value of the good in terms of money. Prices represent the terms on which people and firms voluntarily exchange different commodities. When I agree to buy a used Honda from a dealer for $3150, this indicates that the Honda is worth more than $3150 to me and that the $3150 is worth more than the Honda to the dealer. I cannot find a better value for my money than the Honda; and the dealer cannot find anyone who will pay more than I will. The used-car market has determined the price of used Hondas and, through voluntary trading, has allocated cars to the people for whom they have highest value.

In addition, prices serve as *signals* to producers and consumers. If consumers want more of any good—say, gasoline to drive their cars—the demand for gasoline will rise. As oil companies find that their inventories of gasoline are reduced, they raise the price of gasoline to ration out the limited supply. And the higher price will encourage greater oil production.

On the other hand, what if a commodity such as cars becomes overstocked at the going market price? Sellers will lower car prices in their rush to unload unwanted models. At the lower price, more consumers will want cars, and producers will want to make fewer cars. As a result, a balance, or equilibrium, between buyers and sellers will be restored.

What is true of the markets for consumer goods is also true of markets for factors of production, such as labor. If computer programmers rather than typists are needed, job opportunities will be more favorable in the computing field. The price of computer programmers (their hourly wage) will tend to rise, and that of typists will tend to fall. The shift in relative wages will cause a shift of workers into the growing occupation.

Prices coordinate the decisions of producers and consumers in a market. Higher prices tend to reduce consumer purchases and encourage production. Lower prices encourage consumption and discourage production. Prices are the balance wheel in the market mechanism.

Market Equilibrium. At every moment, innumerable factors affect economic activity. Some people are buying while others are selling; firms are inventing new products while governments are passing laws to regulate pollution; foreigners are invading our markets while American firms are moving their plants abroad. Yet in the midst of all this turmoil, markets are constantly solving the *what, how,* and *for whom.* As they balance all the forces operating on the economy, markets are finding an **equilibrium of supply and demand.**

What is a market equilibrium? It represents a *balance among all the different buyers and sellers.* Households and firms all want to buy or sell certain quantities depending upon the price. The market finds the equilibrium price that just balances the desires of buyers and sellers. Too high a price would mean a glut of goods with too much output; too low a price would produce long lines in stores and a deficiency of goods. Those prices for which buyers desire to buy exactly the quantity that sellers desire to sell yield an equilibrium of supply and demand.

How a Market Solves the Three Economic Problems

We see how prices help balance consumption and production (or supply and demand) in an individual market. What happens when we put all the different markets together—gasoline, cars, land, labor, capital, and everything else? These form a market mechanism that grinds out a *general equilibrium* of prices and production.

By matching sellers and buyers (supply and demand) in each market, a market economy simultaneously solves the three problems of *what*, *how*, and *for whom*. Here is the bare outline of a market equilibrium.

1. *What* things will be produced is determined by the dollar votes of consumers—not every 2 or 4 years at the polls, but in their daily purchase decisions. The money that they pay into businesses' cash registers ultimately provides the payrolls, rents, and dividends that consumers, as employees, receive as income.

    Firms in turn are driven by the desire to maximize profits—**profits** being net revenues or the difference between total sales and total costs. Firms are lured by high profits into production of goods in high demand; by the same token, firms abandon areas where they are losing money.

    Relative costs also affect the production and trade of nations. Japan produces and exports consumer electronics and imports food, while America imports consumer electronics and exports food.

    Who makes these decisions? Is it Congress? Or the Japanese government planners? In fact, neither. The price system makes the decisions. Because land is plentiful in America, land is relatively inexpensive and food costs are relatively low. Because land is scarce and expensive in Japan while engineering talent is relatively plentiful, Japanese costs are relatively high for food and low for consumer electronics. By looking at price signals on land and labor, firms, farmers, and consumers can choose the most appropriate goods to produce, trade, and consume.

2. *How* things are produced is determined by the competition among different producers. The best way for producers to meet price competition and maximize profits is to keep costs at a minimum by adopting the most efficient methods of production. Because producers are spurred on by the lure of profit, inexpensive production methods will displace more costly ones.

    History is filled with examples of how efficient technologies replaced more expensive ones. Steam engines displaced horses because steam was cheaper per unit of useful work. Diesel and electric locomotives replaced coal-driven ones because of the higher efficiency of the new technologies. In the 1990s, glass fibers and lightwave communications will displace Alexander Graham Bell's traditional copper telephone lines.

3. *For whom* things are produced is determined by supply and demand in the markets for factors of production. Factor markets determine wage rates, land rents, interest rates, and profits—such prices are called *factor prices*. By adding up all the revenues from factors we can calculate people's incomes. The distribution of income among the population is thus determined by the *amounts* of factors (person-hours, acres, etc.) owned and the *prices* of the factors (wage rates, land rents, etc.).

    Be warned, however, that the distribution of income is also affected by many influences outside the marketplace. People's incomes depend significantly upon their ownership of property (such as land or stocks), upon acquired or inherited abilities, upon luck, and upon the extent of racial and gender discrimination.

Who Governs the Market?

Who is in charge of a market economy? Do monopolistic firms call the tune? Are consumers sovereign? If we examine the structure of a market economy carefully, we see a dual monarchy shared by *consumers and technology*. Consumers direct by their innate or acquired tastes—as expressed with their dollar votes—the ultimate uses to which society's resources are channeled. They pick the point on the production-possibility frontier.

But the available resources place a fundamental constraint on consumers. The economy cannot go outside its *PPF*. You can fly to London, but there are no flights to Mars. An economy's resources, along with the available science and technology, limit the places where consumers can put their dollar votes.

In other words, consumers alone cannot dictate *what* goods should be produced. Consumer demand has to dovetail with business supply of goods. So business cost and supply decisions, along with consumer demand, help to determine what is produced. *Just as a broker helps to match buyers and sellers, so do markets act as the go-betweens who reconcile the consumer's tastes with technology's limitations.*

It is important to see the role of profits in guiding the market mechanism. Profits provide the rewards and penalties for businesses. Profits induce firms to enter areas where consumers want more goods, to leave areas where consumers want fewer goods, and to use the most efficient (or least costly) techniques of production.

Like a master using carrots and kicks to coax a donkey forward, the market system deals out profits and losses to induce firms to produce desired goods efficiently.

A Picture of Prices and Markets

We can picture the circular flow of economic life in Figure 3-1. This provides an overview of how consumers and producers interact to determine prices and quantities for both inputs and outputs. Note the two different kinds of markets in the circular flow. At the top are the product markets, or flow of outputs like tea and shoes; at the bottom are the markets for inputs or factors of production like land and labor. Further see how decisions are

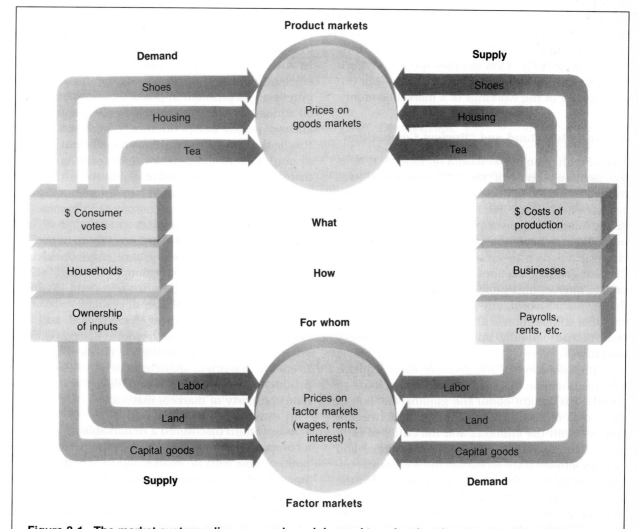

Figure 3-1. The market system relies on supply and demand to solve the trio of economic problems.

We see here the circular flow of a market economy. Dollar votes of households interact with what businesses supply in the goods markets at top, helping to determine *what* is produced. Further, business demand for inputs meets the public's supply of labor and other inputs in the factor markets below to help determine wage, rent, and interest payments. Business competition to buy factor inputs and sell goods most cheaply determines *how* goods are produced.

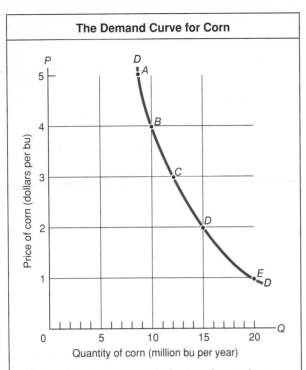

The Demand Curve for Corn

Figure 4-1. A downward-sloping demand curve relates quantity demanded to price

In the demand curve for corn, prices are measured on the vertical axis while quantity demanded is measured on the horizontal axis. Each pair of (P,Q) numbers from Table 4-1 is plotted as a point and then a smooth curve is passed through the points to give us a demand curve, DD. The negative slope of the demand curve illustrates the law of downward-sloping demand.

calculations by hand. Even today, in poor countries like India, only the richest businesses and banks own PCs.

But the prices of PCs have fallen sharply in the last decade. As more and more people could afford PCs, they came to be widely used for work, for school, and for fun. This history sheds light on one important reason for the law of downward-sloping demand: Lower prices entice new buyers.

In addition, a price reduction will induce extra purchases of goods by existing consumers. For example, when water is very expensive, we buy only enough of it to drink. Then when its price drops, we buy some to wash with. At still lower prices, we water flowers and use it lavishly for any possible purpose. Conversely, a rise in the price of a good will cause some of us to buy less.

Why does quantity demanded tend to fall as

price rises? For two reasons. First is the **substitution effect.** When the price of a good rises, I will substitute other similar goods for it (as the price of beef rises, I eat more chicken). A second element is the **income effect.** This comes into play because when a price goes up, I find myself somewhat poorer than I was before. If gasoline prices double, I have in effect less income, so I will naturally curb my consumption of gasoline and other goods.

Our discussion of demand has referred to "the" demand curve. But whose demand is it? Mine? Yours? Everybody's? The fundamental building block for demand is individual tastes and needs. However, when we analyze the price and quantity for a market, we will refer to the *market demand,* which represents the sum total of all individual demands. The market demand curve is found by adding together the quantities demanded by all individuals at each price. In this chapter, we will always focus on the market demand.

Behind the Demand Curve

What determines the market demand for corn or cars or computers? Up to now, we have ignored influences other than a commodity's own price. But other influences are significant: average levels of income, the size of the population, the prices and availability of related goods, individual tastes, and special influences.

The *average income* of consumers is a key determinant of demand. As people's incomes rise, individuals tend to buy more of almost everything—apples, boats, cars, etc.

The *size of the market*—measured say by the population—clearly affects the market demand curve. California's 30 million people tend to buy 30 times more apples and cars than do Rhode Island's 1 million people.

The prices and availability of *related goods* influence the demand for a commodity. A particularly important connection exists among substitute goods—ones that tend to perform the same function, such as pens and pencils, cotton and wool, or oil and natural gas. Demand for good A tends to be low if the price of substitute product B is low. (For example, if the price of natural gas is high in Boston, will the demand for oil tend to be low or high?)

In addition to these objective elements we must add a set of subjective elements called *tastes* or *preferences.* Tastes represent a variety of social and historical influences. They may reflect genuine psychological or physiological needs (for liquids, salt, warmth, or love). And they may include artificially contrived cravings (for cigarettes, drugs, or fancy sports cars). They may contain a large element of tradition or religion (eating beef is popular in America but taboo in India, while curried jellyfish is a delicacy in Japan).

Finally, individual goods generally have *special influences* behind their demand—rainfall contributes to the demand for umbrellas, snow depth affects ski sales, and ocean temperature influences the demand for surfboards. In addition, expectations about future economic conditions, particularly prices, may have an important impact on demand.

Much of our analysis will focus on price as the variable tending to balance supply and demand. As price changes, the quantity demanded changes and we move along the demand curve. But in addition to the importance of price, we must never lose sight of these other influences that ultimately determine the strength of demand and can shift the demand curve. The different elements behind the demand for a typical good, automobiles, are sketched in Table 4-2.

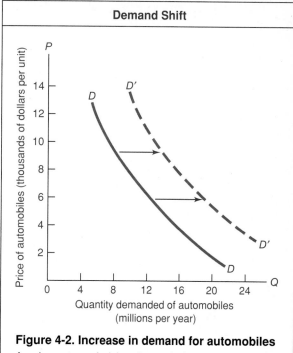

Figure 4-2. Increase in demand for automobiles
As elements underlying demand change, the demand for automobiles is affected. Here we see the effect of rising average income, increased population, and lower gasoline prices on the demand for automobiles. Why do these lead to an *increase* in demand?

Elements affecting demand	Example for automobiles
1. **The good's own price**	Higher own price reduces quantity demanded
2. **Average income**	As incomes rise, people increase car purchases
3. **Population**	Larger population increases car purchases
4. **Prices of related goods**	Lower gasoline prices raise the demand for cars
5. **Tastes**	Americans buy more cars than Europeans, other things equal
6. **Special influences**	Special influences include availability of subways, quality of road and rail network, dating patterns, expectation of future price increases, etc.

Table 4-2. Many elements, price and non-price, affect demand

A Change in Demand. As economic life evolves, demand changes incessantly. Demand curves sit still only in a textbook.

Why does the demand curve shift? Because the influences other than the good's price change. As an example, what were some possible reasons for the increase in the American demand for cars from 1950 to 1990? Many non-price influences were at work: the average real income of Americans almost doubled; the adult population rose by more than half; and there was a decline in the availability of alternative forms of transportation (bus, trolley, and rail). The result of all these changes was a rightward shift in the demand curve for cars.

The net effect of the changes in underlying influences is what we call an *increase in demand.* An increase in the demand for automobiles is illustrated in Figure 4-2 as a rightward shift in the demand curve. Note that the shift means that more cars will be bought at every price.

You can test yourself by answering the following

questions: Will a warm winter shift the demand curve for heating oil leftward or rightward? Why? What would happen to the demand for ski-lift tickets if snowfall were especially light? What will a sharp fall in the price of personal computers do to the demand for typewriters?

Supply Schedule and Supply Curve

Let us now turn from demand to supply. By "supply" we mean the quantity of a good that businesses willingly produce and sell. More precisely, we relate the quantity supplied of a good to its market price, holding equal other things such as costs of production, the prices of related goods, and the organization of the market.

The **supply schedule** (and **supply curve**) for a commodity shows the relationship between its market price and the amount of that commodity that producers are willing to produce and sell, other things held equal.

Table 4-3 shows a hypothetical supply schedule for corn, and Figure 4-3 plots the data from the table. These data show that at a corn price of $1 per bushel, no corn at all will be produced. At such a low price, farmers might devote their land to uses other than corn production. As the corn price rises (always holding constant things like the price of wheat), more land will be planted with corn. At ever-higher corn prices, farmers will find it profit-

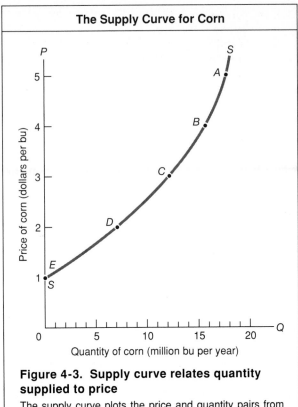

The Supply Curve for Corn

Figure 4-3. Supply curve relates quantity supplied to price

The supply curve plots the price and quantity pairs from Table 4-3. A smooth curve is passed through these points to give the upward-sloping supply curve, SS.

able to add even more land, labor, tractors, and fertilizer. All these will increase the output of corn at the higher market prices.

Note that the supply curve in Figure 4-3 slopes upward and to the right. Why do supply curves for individual commodities generally slope upward? One important reason is found in the law of diminishing returns. Take the case of wine. If society wants more wine, then more and more labor will have to be added to the same limited sites suitable for producing wine grapes. Each new worker will—according to the law of diminishing returns—be adding less and less extra product; hence, the price needed to coax out additional output will have to rise. By raising the price of wine, society can persuade wine producers to produce and sell more wine; the supply curve for wine is therefore upward-sloping. Similar reasoning applies to many other goods as well.

Supply Schedule for Corn		
	(1)	(2)
	Price ($ per bushel) P	Quantity supplied (millions of bushels per year) Q
A	5	18
B	4	16
C	3	12
D	2	7
E	1	0

Table 4-3. Supply schedule relates quantity supplied to price

The table shows, for each price, the quantity of corn that the country's farmers want to produce and sell. Note the direct or positive relation between price and quantity supplied.

Behind the Supply Curve

In examining the forces operating on supply, the fundamental point to grasp about businesses' supply behavior is that producers supply commodities for profit and not for fun or charity. For example, a farmer will supply more corn at higher corn prices because it is profitable to do so; conversely, when the corn price falls below the cost of production, as it did in the mid-1980s, farmers plant other crops, let the fields go to seed, or even sell their farms.

A key element underlying supply decisions, then, is the *cost of production*. When production costs for a good are low relative to the market price, it is profitable for producers to supply a great deal. When production costs are high relative to price, firms produce little or may simply go out of business.

Among the forces affecting production costs are technology and input costs. *Technological advances* certainly affect costs. A better computer program for crop rotation, genetically engineered seeds, and improved irrigation systems—all these would lower a farmer's production costs and increase supply.

Similarly, if technology did not change, but the *prices of inputs* changed, the costs of production would change and so would supply. For example, when oil prices rose in 1990, this raised production costs and lowered the supply of gasoline and diesel fuel.

Another major element influencing supply is the *prices of related goods*, particularly goods that can be readily substituted for one another in the production process. If the price of one production substitute rises, the supply of another substitute will decrease. For example, farmers can produce wheat as well as corn; an oil refinery can produce diesel fuel as well as gasoline. For each pair, as the price of one (e.g., diesel fuel) rises, this will tend to decrease the supply of the other (e.g., gasoline).

A further determinant of supply is the *market organization*. A reduction in tariffs and quotas on foreign goods will open up the market to foreign producers and will tend to increase supply. If a market becomes monopolized, the price at each level of output will increase. In general, a perfectly competitive market will produce the highest possible level of output at each price level.

Finally, *special influences* affect supply. The weather exerts an important influence on farming and on the ski industry. The computer industry has been marked by a keen spirit of innovation, which has led to a continuous flow of new products. In some industries, like railroads and telecommunications, government regulation has shunted supply decisions off the competitive track. And expectations about future prices often have an important impact upon supply decisions.

Table 4-4 highlights the important determinants of supply using automobiles as an example.

Shifts in Supply. A casual observer of markets knows that businesses are constantly changing their products and services. What lies behind changes in supply behavior?

Supply changes when any influences other than the commodity's own price changes. In terms of a supply curve, we say that supply increases (or decreases) when the amount supplied increases (or decreases) at each market price.

When automobile prices change, producers change their production and quantity supplied, but the supply and the supply curve do not shift. By contrast, when other influences affecting supply

Elements determining supply	Example for automobiles
1. **The good's own price**	Higher own price increases most profitable production level and raises quantity supplied
2. **Technology**	Computerized manufacturing lowers production cost and increases supply
3. **Input prices**	Autoworkers' wage cuts lower production costs and increase supply
4. **Prices of related goods**	If bus and truck prices fall, supply of cars increases
5. **Market organization**	Removal of quota on Japanese car imports increases supply
6. **Special influences**	If government lowers standards on pollution-control equipment, supply of cars may increase

Table 4-4. Supply is affected by price, production costs, and other influences

change, supply changes and the supply curve shifts.

We can illustrate a shift in supply for the automobile market. Supply would increase if the introduction of cost-saving computerized design and manufacturing reduced the labor required to produce cars, if autoworkers took a pay cut, if Japanese automakers were allowed to export more cars to the United States, or if the government removed some of the regulatory requirements on the industry. Any of these elements would increase the supply of automobiles in the United States at each price. Figure 4-4 illustrates an increase in supply of automobiles.

To test your understanding of supply shifts, think about the following: What happens to the supply curve for corn in Figure 4-3 after favorable weather produces a bumper crop? How does a Florida freeze affect the supply of orange juice? What would happen to the world supply of oil if political turmoil in the Soviet Union reduced its oil production?

Equilibrium of Supply and Demand

We have seen that consumers demand different amounts of corn, cars, and computers as a function of these goods' prices. Similarly, producers willingly supply different amounts of these and other goods depending on their prices. What happens when suppliers and demanders meet?

The answer is that the forces of supply and demand operate through the market to produce an equilibrium price and quantity, or a market equilibrium. The **market equilibrium** comes at that price and quantity where the supply and demand forces are in balance. At this point, the amount that buyers want to buy is just equal to the amount that sellers want to sell. At equilibrium, price and quantity tend to stay the same, as long as other things remain equal.

Let us work through the corn example in Table 4-5 to see how supply and demand determine a market equilibrium; the numbers in this table come from Tables 4-1 and 4-3. Up to this point we have been considering demand and supply in isolation. We know the amounts that are willingly bought and sold at each price. We now need to put supply and demand together to determine the actual price and quantity that the market will settle on.

To find the market price and quantity, we find a price at which the amounts desired to be bought and sold just match. If we try a price of $5 per bushel, will that prevail for long? Clearly not. As row A in Table 4-5 shows, at $5 producers would like to sell 18 million bushels per year while demanders want to buy only 9. The amount supplied at $5 exceeds the amount demanded, and stocks of corn pile up in the granary. Because too much corn is chasing too few consumers, the price of corn will tend to fall, as shown in column (5) of Table 4-5.

Say we try $2. Does that price clear the market? A quick look at row D shows that at $2 consumption exceeds production. The storehouses of corn begin to empty at that price. As people scramble around to find their desired quantity of corn, they will tend to bid up the price of corn, as is shown in column (5) of Table 4-5.

We could try other prices, but we can easily see that the equilibrium price is $3, or row C in Table

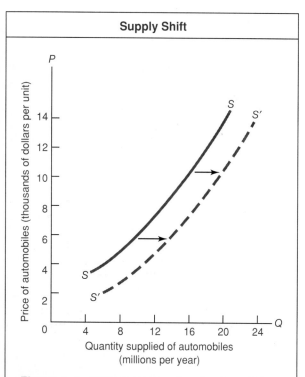

Figure 4-4. Increased supply of automobiles

As production costs fall or Japanese competition increases, the supply of automobiles increases. At each price, producers will supply more automobiles, and the supply curve therefore shifts to the right. (What would happen to the supply curve if autoworkers' wages increased sharply?)

Combining Demand and Supply for Corn				
(1)	(2)	(3)	(4)	(5)
Possible prices ($ per bushel)	Quantity demanded (millions of bushels per year)	Quantity supplied (millions of bushels per year)	State of market	Pressure on price
A 5	9	18	Surplus ↓	Downward
B 4	10	16	Surplus ↓	Downward
C 3	12	12	Equilibrium	Neutral
D 2	15	7	Shortage ↑	Upward
E 1	20	0	Shortage ↑	Upward

Table 4-5. Equilibrium price comes where quantity demanded equals quantity supplied

Only at the equilibrium price of $3 per bushel does amount supplied equal amount demanded. At too low a price there is a shortage and price tends to rise. Too high a price produces a surplus, which will depress price.

4-5. Only at $3 will consumers and suppliers *both* be making consistent decisions. At $3, consumers' desired demand exactly equals desired production, each of which is 12 units.

At the equilibrium price of $3, there is no tendency for price to rise or fall, and stockpiles of corn are neither growing nor declining. We also say that $3 is the market-clearing price. This denotes that all supply and demand orders are filled, the books are "cleared" of orders, and demanders and suppliers are satisfied.

Equilibrium with Supply and Demand Curves.
We show a market equilibrium graphically in Figure 4-5, which combines the supply curve from Figure 4-3 with the demand curve from Figure 4-1. Combining the two graphs is possible because they are drawn with exactly the same units on each axis.

We find the market equilibrium by looking for the price at which quantity demanded equals quantity supplied. *The equilibrium price comes at the intersection of the supply and demand curves, at point* C.

How do we know that the intersection of the supply and demand curves is the market equilibrium? Let us repeat our earlier experiment. Start with the initial high price of $5 per bushel, shown at the top of the price axis in Figure 4-5. At that price, suppliers want to sell more than demanders want to buy. The result is a *surplus*, or excess of quantity supplied over quantity demanded, shown in the figure by the black line labeled "Surplus." The arrows along the curves show the direction that price tends to move when a market is in surplus.

At a low price of $2 per bushel, the market shows a *shortage*, or excess of quantity demanded over

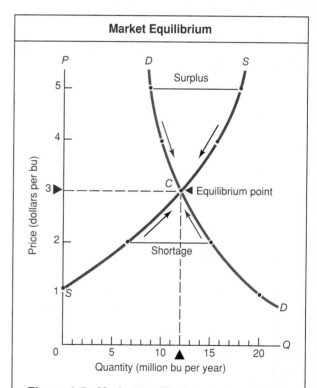

Figure 4-5. Market equilibrium comes at the intersection of supply and demand curves

The market equilibrium price and quantity come at the intersection of supply and demand curves. At a price of $3 at point C, firms willingly supply what consumers willingly demand. When price is too low (say at $2), quantity demanded exceeds quantity supplied, shortages occur, and prices are driven up to equilibrium. What occurs at a price of $4?

things equal can lead to erroneous reasoning. Say that Contrary is studying the market for pizzas. Contrary observes that in boom years, jobs are plentiful and people enjoy spending their high incomes in pizza parlors. When business activity is depressed and people are out of work, however, incomes are low and few pizzas are bought.

In Figure 4-7, Contrary records point E in prosperous years and E' in depression years. He takes a ruler, joins points E and E', and asserts, "I have disproved the law of downward-sloping demand. When price was lower, quantity was actually lower. My straight line joining E and E' produces an upward-sloping, not a downward-sloping, demand curve. So I have refuted a basic economic law."

Alas, poor Contrary is crestfallen to discover that he has broken one of the cardinal rules of economics: He did not hold other things equal. At the same time that price dropped, income declined. The tendency for a drop in price to raise purchases was more than masked by the countertendency of lowered income to decrease demand.

In addition, you might well be suspicious of the argument because it leads to nonsensical conclusions. Contrary would predict that corn prices will be high in years of large harvests because the demand curve is upward-sloping. Not only does such reasoning lead to absurd predictions, but it would also bankrupt the farmers or speculators who bought dear and sold cheap. Make sure, then, to hold other things equal when analyzing the impact of a change in supply or demand.

Movement along Curves vs. Shift of Curves

Great care must be taken not to confuse a *change in demand* (which denotes a shift of the demand curve) with a *change in the quantity demanded* (which means moving to a different point on the same demand curve after a price change). A similar distinction applies to supply and many other economic relationships.

A change in demand occurs when one of the elements underlying the demand curve shifts. Take the case of pizzas. If incomes increase, so will the number of pizzas that consumers want to buy at every price. In other words, higher incomes will increase demand and shift out the demand curve for pizzas.

In contrast, when the price of pizzas faced by consumers falls, and all other things remain constant, consumers will tend to purchase more pizzas. But the increased purchases result not from an increase in demand but from the price decrease. This change represents a *movement along* the demand curve, not a *shift in* the demand curve. A similar distinction applies to shifts in supply vs. changes in quantity supplied.

Figure 4-8 illustrates this crucial distinction. Figure 4-8(a) shows the case of an increase in demand or a shift in the demand curve. As a result of the shift, the equilibrium quantity demanded increases from 10 to 15 units.

The case of a movement along the demand curve is shown in Figure 4-8(b). In this case, a supply shift changes the market equilibrium from point E to point E''. As a result, the quantity demanded changes from 10 to 15 units. But demand does not change in this case; rather quantity demanded increases as consumers move along their demand curve from E to E''.

Let's put this distinction to work by analyzing the following incorrect argument: "A bad harvest need not raise price. The price might rise at first. But a higher price will diminish the demand. And a reduced demand will send the price down again. Therefore, a bad harvest might actually lower the price of corn!"

What is wrong with this statement? It errs because "demand" is used incorrectly in the third sentence; it uses the word "demand" in the sense of "quantity demanded," thus confusing a movement along a curve with a shift of the demand curve. The correct statement would run as follows:

"A bad harvest will raise price as the leftward shift in the supply curve raises the equilibrium price of corn. The higher equilibrium price will reduce the quantity demanded, as consumers move up the downward-sloping demand curve. But since no shift in the demand curve occurred, there is no reason to expect that price will fall as a result of a decrease in the quantity demanded."

Meaning of Equilibrium

The last hurdle concerns the meaning of the term "equilibrium." It is seen in the following challenge of a skeptic: "How can you say that supply and

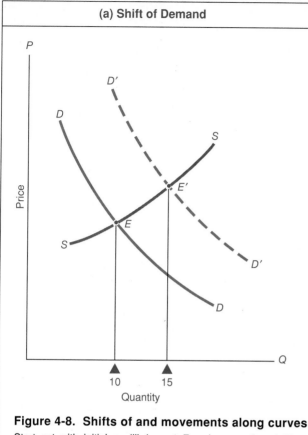

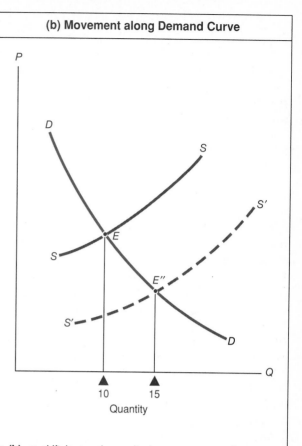

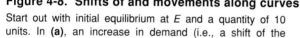

Figure 4-8. Shifts of and movements along curves

Start out with initial equilibrium at *E* and a quantity of 10 units. In **(a)**, an increase in demand (i.e., a shift of the demand curve) produces a new equilibrium of 15 units at *E'*.

In **(b)**, a shift in supply results in a movement along the demand curve from *E* to *E"*.

demand determine a particular equilibrium quantity? The quantity bought must always equal the quantity sold. This is true no matter what the price and whether or not the market is in equilibrium."

This challenge emphasizes the subtlety in the term "equilibrium." We might reply as follows: You are correct that the quantity bought must be identical to the quantity sold. But we are seeking that market equilibrium for which the supply and demand are in balance. At which price is the amount that consumers willingly buy just matched by the amount that producers willingly sell? Only at such a price will buyers and sellers be satisfied with their decisions; only at the equilibrium will price tend neither to rise nor fall.

At non-equilibrium prices, the measured amounts bought and sold are obviously equal. But at too high a price there is a surplus of goods, with producers eagerly trying to sell more goods than demanders will buy. This excess of desired supply over desired demand will put downward pressure on price until price finally reaches that equilibrium level where the two curves intersect.

At the equilibrium intersection of supply and demand, and there alone, everybody will be happy: the suppliers, the demanders, and the economist who seeks the price at which there are no surpluses or shortages.

Rationing by Prices

Let us now take stock of what the market mechanism accomplishes. By determining the equilibrium prices and quantities of all inputs and out-

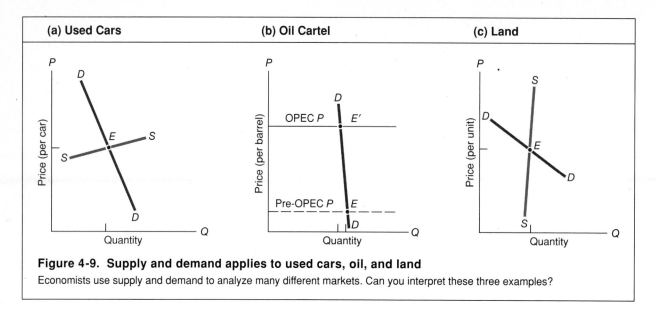

Figure 4-9. Supply and demand applies to used cars, oil, and land
Economists use supply and demand to analyze many different markets. Can you interpret these three examples?

puts, the market allocates or rations out the scarce goods of the society among the possible uses. Who does the rationing? A planning board or a legislature? No. The marketplace, through the interaction of supply and demand, does the rationing. This is rationing by the purse.

What goods are produced? This is answered by the signals of the market prices. High oil prices stimulate oil production, whereas low corn prices drive resources out of agriculture. Those who have the most dollar votes have the greatest influence on what goods are produced.

For whom are goods delivered? The power of the purse dictates the distribution of income and consumption. Those with higher incomes end up with larger houses, more clothing, and longer vacations. When backed up by cash, the most urgently felt needs get fulfilled through the demand curve.

Even the *how* question is decided by supply and demand. When corn prices are low, farmers cannot afford expensive tractors and fertilizers, and only the best land is cultivated. When oil prices are high, oil companies drill in deep offshore waters and employ novel seismic techniques to find oil.

A market economy solves the basic economic problems through the operation of supply and demand.

Three Markets

To conclude this introduction to supply and demand, let us look at three cases of markets where supply and demand can help explain how prices and quantities are determined. Figure 4-9(a) pictures a competitive market for used cars. What would happen to used-car prices in an economic boom when family incomes are high? Panel (b) shows how oil prices skyrocketed when OPEC (the Organization of Petroleum Exporting Countries) organized a price-fixing group (called a cartel). What would happen to the quantity of oil demanded if OPEC collapsed and oil prices fell sharply? The third case, in (c), shows the supply and demand for land in Manhattan. Note how little the supply of land responds to higher prices. Can you see why increased demand for land raises prices a great deal and hardly changes the quantity supplied of land?

These are but a small sample of the questions that supply-and-demand analysis can answer. Further study will deepen our understanding of the forces behind supply and demand and will show how this analysis can be applied to other important areas. But even this first survey will serve as an indispensable tool for interpreting the economic world in which we live.

———————————————————— **SUMMARY** ————————————————————

1. The analysis of supply and demand shows how a market mechanism grapples with the triad of economic problems, *what, how,* and *for whom.* It shows how dollar votes decide the prices and quantities of different goods.

2. A demand schedule represents the relationship between the quantity demanded and the price of a commodity, other things held constant. Such a demand schedule, represented graphically as a demand curve, holds equal other things like family incomes, tastes, and the prices of other goods. Almost all commodities obey the *law of downward-sloping demand,* which holds that quantity demanded falls as a good's price rises. This law is represented by a downward-sloping demand curve.

3. Many influences lie behind the demand schedule for the market as a whole: average family incomes, population, the prices of related goods, tastes, and special influences. When these influences change, the demand curve will shift.

4. The supply schedule (or supply curve) gives the relationship between the quantity of a good that producers desire to sell—other things equal—and that good's price. Quantity supplied generally responds positively to price, so that the supply curve rises upward and to the right.

5. Elements other than the good's price affect its supply. The most important influence is the commodity's production cost, determined by the state of technology and by input prices. Other elements in supply include the prices of related goods, the market organization, and special influences.

6. The equilibrium of supply and demand in a competitive market is attained at a price where the forces of supply and demand are in balance. The equilibrium price is that price at which the quantity demanded just equals the quantity supplied, which occurs graphically at the intersection of the supply and demand curves. At a price above the equilibrium, producers want to supply more than consumers want to buy, which results in a surplus of goods and exerts downward pressure on prices. Similarly, too low a price generates a shortage, and buyers will therefore tend to bid prices upward to the equilibrium.

7. Competitively determined prices ration the limited supply of goods among those with the demands and the necessary dollar votes.

8. To avoid pitfalls in the use of supply-and-demand analysis, we must observe certain strictures: (*a*) hold other things equal, which requires distinguishing the impact of a change in a commodity's price from the impact of changes in other elements; (*b*) distinguish a change in demand or supply (which produces a shift in a curve) from a change in the quantity demanded or supplied (which represents a movement along a curve); (*c*) recognize a supply-and-demand equilibrium, which is where buyers and sellers willingly engage in trades.

CONCEPTS FOR REVIEW

Supply-and-demand analysis
demand schedule or curve, *DD*
law of downward-sloping demand
supply schedule or curve, *SS*

influences affecting supply
  and demand curves
surplus, shortage
rationing by prices

Pitfalls in supply and demand
other things equal
shifts of curve versus movements along curve
equilibrium price and quantity

QUESTIONS FOR DISCUSSION

1. Define carefully what is meant by a demand schedule or curve. State the law of downward-sloping demand. Illustrate the law of downward-sloping demand with two cases from your own experience.

2. Define the concept of a supply schedule or curve. Show that an increase in supply means a rightward and downward shift of the supply curve. Contrast this with the rightward and upward shift in the demand curve implied by an increase in demand. Why the difference?

3. What might increase the demand for hamburgers? What would increase the supply? What would inexpensive frozen pizzas do to the market equilibrium for hamburgers? To the wages of teenagers who work at McDonald's?

4. Explain why the price in competitive markets settles down at the equilibrium intersection of supply and demand. Explain what happens if the market price started out too high or too low.

5. Explain why each of the following is false:
   (a) A freeze in Brazil's coffee-growing region will lower the price of coffee.
   (b) The high price of oil resulting from political disturbances in the Middle East will lower the demand for oil.
   (c) Concerns about the health effects of meat will lower the price of granola and raise the price of leather jackets.
   (d) The war against drugs, with increased interdiction of imported cocaine, will lower the price of domestically produced marijuana.

6. The four laws of supply and demand are the following:
   (a) An increase in demand generally raises price and raises quantity demanded.
   (b) A decrease in demand generally _____ price and _____ quantity demanded.
   (c) An increase in supply generally lowers price and raises quantity demanded.
   (d) A decrease in supply generally _____ price and _____ quantity demanded.
   Fill in the blanks. Demonstrate each law with a supply-and-demand diagram.

7. In each of the following, explain whether quantity demanded changes because of a demand shift or a price change, and draw a diagram to illustrate your answer.
   (a) As a result of increased military spending, the price of Army boots rises.
   (b) Fish prices fall after the Pope allows Catholics to eat meat on Friday.
   (c) A gasoline tax lowers the consumption of gasoline.
   (d) After a disastrous wheat blight, bread sales go down.
   (e) After a disastrous wheat blight, soybean sales go up.
   (f) After the Black Death struck Europe in the fourteenth century, wages rose.

8. "The government should protect the shoe industry from ruinous foreign competition. This will help consumers because the higher price of domestically produced shoes will lower demand and will ultimately end up lowering the price to consumers." Comment on the reasoning of this statement in terms of the discussion of "three hurdles" in the chapter. Write out a correct analysis of the impact of a restriction of foreign shoe supply on the market for shoes.

9. From the following data, plot the supply and demand curves and determine the equilibrium price and quantity.

Supply and Demand for Pizzas		
Price ($ per pizza)	Quantity demanded (pizzas per semester)	Quantity supplied (pizzas per semester)
10	0	40
8	10	30
6	20	20
4	30	10
2	40	0
0	125	0

What would happen if the demand for pizzas tripled at each price? What would occur if the price were initially set at $4 per pizza?

FUNDAMENTAL CONCEPTS OF MACROECONOMICS

The Road Ahead

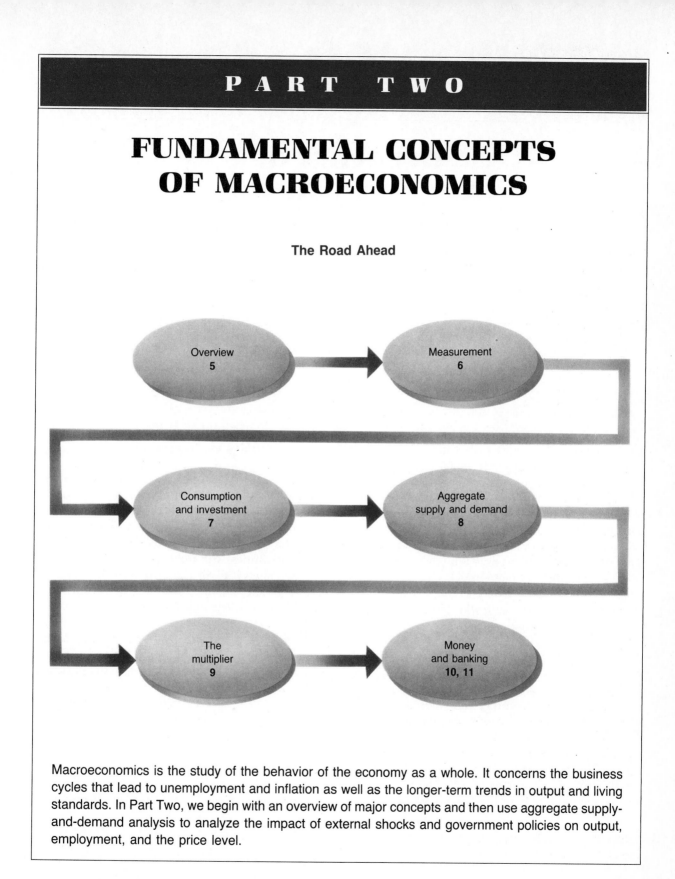

Macroeconomics is the study of the behavior of the economy as a whole. It concerns the business cycles that lead to unemployment and inflation as well as the longer-term trends in output and living standards. In Part Two, we begin with an overview of major concepts and then use aggregate supply-and-demand analysis to analyze the impact of external shocks and government policies on output, employment, and the price level.

C H A P T E R   5

OVERVIEW OF
MACROECONOMICS

The whole purpose of the economy is production of goods or services for consumption now or in the future. I think the burden of proof should always be on those who would produce less rather than more, on those who would leave idle men or machines or land that could be used. It is amazing how many reasons can be found to justify such waste: fear of inflation, balance-of-payments deficits, unbalanced budgets, excessive national debt, loss of confidence in the dollar.

James Tobin, *National Economic Policy*

Why did production and prices in America and much of the industrial world collapse during the Great Depression of the 1930s? Why was it during this period that millions of people were unable to find work and were living on the ragged edge of starvation? What forces propelled America into a sustained boom during World War II and then again during the Vietnam war? Why did unemployment rise to almost 11 percent of the labor force in 1982, only to decline steadily in the sustained expansion of the Reagan years? Why have prices risen a billionfold or more in some countries? And, most recently, why have sharp oil-price increases led to economic downturns three times in the last few years?

These vital questions are addressed by macroeconomics, which is introduced in this chapter. Section A examines the main macroeconomic concepts along with the central goals of macroeconomic policy. Section B then introduces the major tool of macroeconomic analysis—aggregate supply and demand—and applies this tool to analyze recent economic events in the United States.

Microeconomics vs. Macroeconomics

From Chapter 1 you will recall that **macroeconomics** is the study of the behavior of the economy as a whole. It examines the overall level of a nation's output, employment, prices, and foreign trade. By contrast, **microeconomics** studies individual prices, quantities, and markets.

A few examples will clarify this distinction. Microeconomics considers how an oil cartel might price its oil; macroeconomics asks why a sharp rise in the world price of oil causes inflation and unemployment. Microeconomics studies whether going to college is a good use of your time; macroeconomics examines the unemployment rate of young adults. Microeconomics examines the individual items of foreign trade, for example, why we import Toyotas and export heavy trucks. Macroeconomics examines overall trends in our imports and exports, asking questions such as why the exchange value of the dollar rose in the early 1980s and then fell in the late 1980s.

A. Macroeconomic Concepts and Goals

Goals and Instruments in Macroeconomics

The political, social, and military fate of nations depends greatly upon economic success, and no area of economics is today more vital to a nation's success than its macroeconomic performance. Countries like Japan, which has grown rapidly by winning export markets for its products, enjoy enhanced political power and higher living standards.

At the opposite extreme are countries that stagnate and suffer from rapid inflation, large trade deficits, and high foreign indebtedness. For example, although the Soviet Union is a vast country, well endowed with natural resources and human talent, its economic stagnation threatens to demote it to the rank of a second-rate power as its citizens scramble for bread.

A country's living standards depend crucially upon its macroeconomic policies. Before this century, countries had little understanding of how to combat periodic economic crises. But the revolutionary theory of John Maynard Keynes helped explain the forces producing economic fluctuations and devised an approach for controlling the worst excesses of business cycles. Thanks to Keynes and his modern successors, we know that in its choice of macroeconomic policies—those affecting the money supply, taxes, or government spending—a nation can speed or slow its economic growth, ignite a rapid inflation or slow price increases, produce a trade deficit or generate a trade surplus.

In analyzing macroeconomics, we always encounter a few key macroeconomic variables—the most important being gross national product (GNP), the unemployment rate, inflation, and net exports. These are the central measures by which we judge macroeconomic performance.

Table 5-1 lists the major goals and instruments of macroeconomic policy. We will now turn to a detailed discussion of each and examine some key

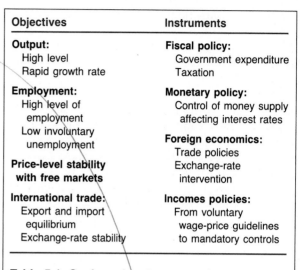

Objectives	Instruments
Output: High level Rapid growth rate	**Fiscal policy:** Government expenditure Taxation
Employment: High level of employment Low involuntary unemployment	**Monetary policy:** Control of money supply affecting interest rates
Price-level stability with free markets	**Foreign economics:** Trade policies Exchange-rate intervention
International trade: Export and import equilibrium Exchange-rate stability	**Incomes policies:** From voluntary wage-price guidelines to mandatory controls

Table 5-1. Goals and instruments of macroeconomic policy

The left-hand column displays the major goals of macroeconomic policy. These goals can be found in national laws and in the statements of political leaders. The right-hand column contains the major instruments or policy measures available to modern economies. These are the ways that policymakers can affect the pace and direction of economic activity.

questions that confront modern macroeconomics.

Goals

To evaluate the success of an economy's overall performance, economists look at four areas: output, employment, price stability, and international trade.

Output. The ultimate objective of economic activity is to provide the goods and services that the population desires. What could be more important for an economy than to produce ample shelter, food, education, and recreation for its people?

The most comprehensive measure of the total output in an economy is the **gross national product (GNP).** GNP is the measure of the market value of all final goods and services—apples, bananas, concerts, dog races, . . . , yak coats, and zithers—produced in a country during a year. There are two ways to measure GNP. *Nominal GNP* is measured in actual market prices. *Real GNP* is calculated in constant or invariant prices (say for the year 1982).

Movements in real GNP are the best widely available measure of the level and growth of output; they serve as the carefully monitored pulse of a nation's economy. Figure 5-1 shows the history of real GNP in the United States since 1929. Note the economic decline during the Great Depression of the 1930s, the boom during World War II, the rapid and stable growth during the 1960s, the recessions in 1975 and 1982, and the steady growth in the long expansion from 1982 to 1990.

A study of the patterns of output growth in capitalist economies shows periods of expansion and contraction in real GNP. The fluctuations in overall economic activity are known as *business cycles.*

During business-cycle downturns, millions of people lose their jobs, and the nation forgoes billions of dollars of goods and services because of depressed production. Business cycles have tended to be less violent since 1945 in part because progress in macroeconomics allowed policymakers to stabilize the economy after World War II.

Despite the short-term fluctuations in GNP seen in business cycles, advanced economies generally exhibit a steady long-term growth in real GNP and an improvement in living standards; this process is known as *economic growth.* The American economy has proven itself a powerful engine of progress over a period of more than a century, as shown by the growth in potential output.

Potential GNP is the long-run trend in real GNP. It represents the long-run productive capacity of the economy or the maximum amount the economy can produce while maintaining stable prices. Potential output is also sometimes called the high-

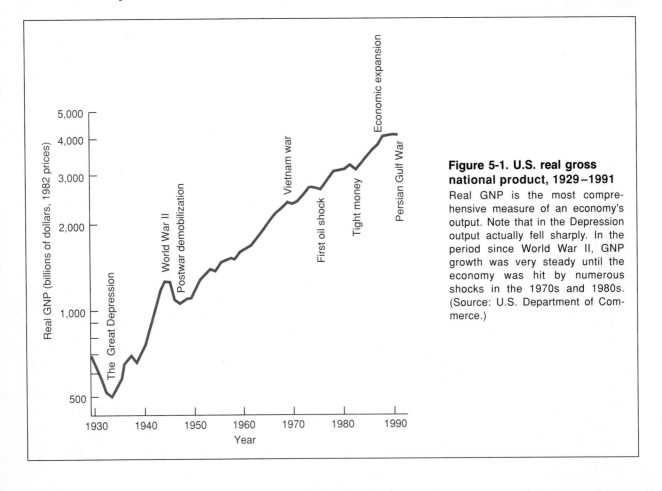

Figure 5-1. U.S. real gross national product, 1929–1991

Real GNP is the most comprehensive measure of an economy's output. Note that in the Depression output actually fell sharply. In the period since World War II, GNP growth was very steady until the economy was hit by numerous shocks in the 1970s and 1980s. (Source: U.S. Department of Commerce.)

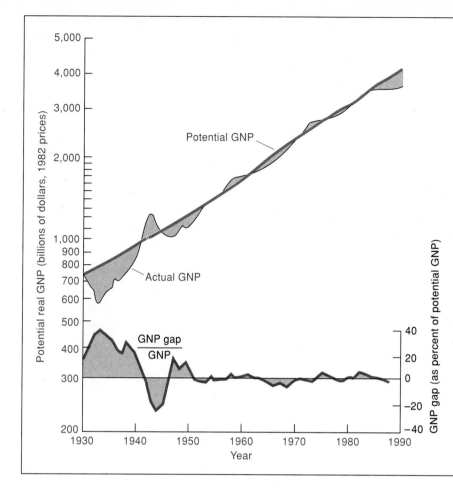

Figure 5-2. Actual and potential GNP and the GNP gap

Business cycles occur when actual output departs from its potential. The smooth blue line, with a scale at the left, shows potential or trend output over the period 1930–1990. Potential output has grown about 3 percent annually over the last half-century.

The lower curve, with its scale on the right-hand side, shows the GNP gap. This shows how much the actual output departed from its potential, as a percent of potential GNP. Note the large GNP gaps in the 1930s and 1980s. (Source: U.S. Department of Commerce and authors' estimates.)

employment level of output. When an economy is operating at its potential, unemployment is low and production is high.

During business cycles, actual GNP departs from its potential. In 1982 for example, the U.S. economy produced almost $300 billion less than potential output. This represented $5000 lost per family during a single year. The difference between potential and actual GNP is called the **GNP gap.** A large GNP gap means that the economy is in an economic downturn and is operating inside its production-possibility frontier. Economic downturns are called *recessions* when the gap is small and *depressions* when the gap is large. In years with large GNP gaps, goods are lost just as if they were dumped into the sea.

Figure 5-2 shows the estimated potential and actual output for the period 1930–1990. The gray areas between the two lines are the GNP gaps. Note

the large gaps in the 1930s and the early 1980s.

High Employment, Low Unemployment. The next major goal of macroeconomic policy is *high employment*, which is the counterpart of *low unemployment*. People want to be able to find good, high-paying jobs without searching or waiting too long. Figure 5-3 shows trends in unemployment over the last six decades. The **unemployment rate** on the vertical axis is the percentage of the labor force that is unemployed. The labor force includes all employed persons and those unemployed individuals who are seeking jobs. It excludes those without work who are not looking for jobs.

The unemployment rate tends to move with the business cycle: when output is depressed, the demand for labor falls and the unemployment rate increases. Unemployment reached epidemic proportions in the Great Depression of the 1930s, when

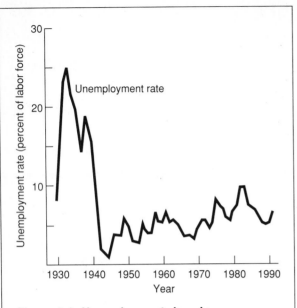

Figure 5-3. Unemployment rises in recessions, falls during expansions

The unemployment rate measures the fraction of the labor force that is looking for but cannot find work. Unemployment reached tragic proportions during the 1930s, peaking at 25 percent in 1933. Also note the upward creep of the unemployment rate since 1969, reaching a postwar high of 9.7 percent in 1982. (Source: U.S. Department of Labor.)

a quarter of the work force was idled. While the nation has avoided another Great Depression, over the last two decades there has been a marked upward drift in the fraction of the labor force that is unemployed. The goal of ensuring good jobs for all who want them has proven increasingly elusive.

Stable Prices. The third macroeconomic goal is to maintain *stable prices within free markets.* The desire to maintain free markets is a subtle concern, embodying the judgment that a smoothly functioning market economy is the most efficient way to organize most economic activity. In a free market, prices are determined by supply and demand to the maximum possible extent, and governments abstain from controlling the prices of individual goods. Only by allowing firms the ability to set prices freely can we ensure that the market will channel resources to their most effective use.

The second part of this goal is preventing the overall price level from rising or falling rapidly. Why

is price stability desirable? A market economy uses prices as a yardstick to measure economic values and as a way to conduct business. When the economic yardstick changes rapidly during periods of rising prices, people become confused, make mistakes, and spend much of their time worrying about the value of their money. Rapid price changes lead to economic inefficiency.

The most common measure of the overall price level is the **consumer price index,** popularly known as the CPI. The CPI monitors the cost of a fixed basket of goods (including items such as food, shelter, clothing, and medical care) bought by the typical urban consumer. The overall price level is often denoted by the letter *P.*

We call changes in the level of prices the **rate of inflation,** which denotes the rate of growth or decline of the price level from one year to the next.[1] Figure 5-4 illustrates the rate of inflation for the CPI from 1929 to 1991. Over this entire period, inflation averaged 3.4 percent per year. Note that price changes fluctuated greatly over the years, varying from *minus* 10 percent in 1932 to 14 percent in 1947.

A **deflation** occurs when prices decline (i.e., the rate of inflation is negative). At the other extreme is a *hyperinflation,* a rise in the price level of a thousand or a million percent a year. In such situations, as in Weimar Germany of the 1920s and Poland in the 1980s, prices are virtually meaningless and the price system breaks down.

Most nations seek a golden mean of price flexibility, often tolerating a gentle inflation, as the best way to allow the price system to function efficiently.

International Trade. Finally, most countries strive to participate fruitfully in international trade so as to raise the living standards of their citizens. They import and export goods, services, and capital. They borrow from or lend money to foreigners. They imitate foreign technologies or sell new products abroad. Their people travel to all parts of the world for business and pleasure. And so on. For the long term, nations generally strive to keep imports

---

[1] More precisely the rate of inflation of the CPI is:

$$\begin{array}{c} \text{Rate of inflation} \\ \text{of consumer prices} \\ \text{(in percent)} \end{array} = \frac{\text{CPI (this year)} - \text{CPI (last year)}}{\text{CPI (last year)}} \times 100$$

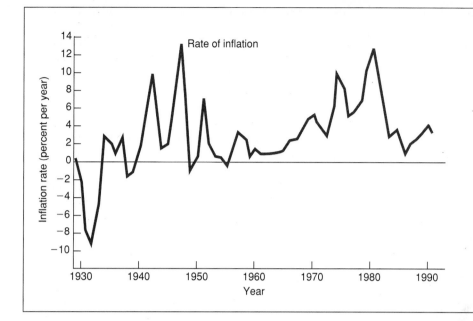

Figure 5-4. The rising trend of consumer price inflation 1929–1991
The rate of inflation measures the rate of change of prices from one year to the next; here we see the rate of inflation as measured by the consumer price index (CPI). Since World War II, prices have mainly moved upward, particularly after the oil shocks of 1973 and 1979. (Source: U.S. Department of Labor.)

and exports in balance. The numerical difference between the value of a country's exports and the value of its imports is called **net exports;** that is, net exports equal the value of exports minus the value of imports. When net exports are positive, a trade surplus exists. A trade deficit occurs when the value of imports is greater than the value of exports.

The goal of expanding international trade has become increasingly important as the nations of the globe have witnessed gains from international trade in spurring efficiency and raising economic growth. As the costs of transportation and communication links have declined, these international linkages have become tighter than they were a generation ago. International trade has replaced empire building and military conquest as the surest road to national wealth and influence. Some economies today trade over half their output.

One of the major developments of the 1980s was the change in pattern of U.S. international trade. For most of this century, the United States ran a trade surplus. That is, exports exceeded imports, yielding positive net exports. But in the 1980s, the value of imports exceeded exports and the United States incurred a trade deficit. Many Americans are concerned about the future impact of a large foreign debt.

The United States exports a variety of goods and services, including computers, grain, and aircraft, to other countries. We import oil, automobiles, electronic equipment, and a host of other commodities. Our consumption of foreign oil has been the cause of major economic disruptions in our economy over the past two decades. Most recently, when Iraq invaded the oil-rich nation of Kuwait, the sharp drop in oil supplies drove prices up, increased inflation, and contributed to an economic downturn in the United States.

Nations keep a close eye on their **foreign exchange rates,** which represent the price of their own currency in terms of the currencies of other nations. The foreign exchange rate of the U.S. dollar rose sharply against other currencies during the early 1980s and then fell sharply after 1985. For example, the U.S. dollar bought only 1.8 German marks in 1980, rose to 3.2 marks in 1985, and fell sharply to 1.8 marks in 1991.

When a nation's exchange rate rises, the prices of imported goods fall while exports become more expensive for foreigners. The result is that the nation becomes less competitive in world markets and net exports decline. Changes in exchange rates can also affect output, employment, and inflation. All these impacts make the exchange rate increasingly important for all nations.

We can summarize the goals of macroeconomic policy as follows:

1. A high and growing level of national output (i.e., real GNP)
2. High employment (with low unemployment)
3. A stable or gently rising price level, with prices and wages determined by supply and demand in free markets
4. Robust international trade in goods, services, and capital, with a stable foreign exchange rate and exports balancing imports

Policy Instruments

Put yourself in the shoes of the President or prime minister. Unemployment is rising and GNP is falling. Or, perhaps a recent rapid increase in oil prices has caused inflation to heat up, and the value of imports is rising much more rapidly than that of exports. What can your government do to improve economic performance? What policy tools can you use to reduce inflation or unemployment or to correct a trade imbalance?

Governments have certain instruments that they can use to affect macroeconomic activity. A *policy instrument* is an economic variable under the control of government that can affect one or more of the macroeconomic goals. That is, by changing monetary, fiscal, and other policies, governments can steer the economy toward a better mix of output, price stability, employment, and international trade. The four major sets of instruments of macroeconomic policy are listed on the right side of Table 5-1.

Fiscal Policy. Begin with *fiscal policy*, which denotes the use of taxes and government expenditures. The category of *government expenditure* includes government spending on goods and services—purchases of tanks and pencils, construction of dams and roads, salaries for judges and Army corporals, and so forth. Government spending determines the relative size of the public and private sectors, that is, how much of our GNP is consumed collectively rather than privately. From a macroeconomic perspective, government expenditure affects the overall level of spending in the economy and thereby influences the level of GNP.

The other part of fiscal policy, *taxation*, affects the overall economy in two ways. To begin with, taxes reduce people's incomes. By leaving house-holds with less disposable or spendable income, taxes tend to reduce the amount people spend on goods and services. This in turn lowers the demand for goods and services, which ultimately lowers the actual GNP.

In addition, taxes affect market prices, thereby influencing incentives and behavior. For example, the more heavily business profits are taxed, the more businesses are discouraged from investing in new capital goods. In 1991 President Bush lobbied to reduce the tax on capital gains, arguing that a lower tax rate would stimulate economic growth. Many other provisions of the tax code have an important effect on economic activity.

Monetary Policy. The second major instrument of macroeconomic policy is *monetary policy*, which government conducts through the management of the nation's money, credit, and banking system. You may have read how our central bank, the Federal Reserve System, operates to regulate the money supply. But what exactly is the money supply? **Money** consists of the means of exchange or method of payment. Today, people use currency and checking accounts to pay their bills. By engaging in central-bank operations, the Federal Reserve can regulate the amount of money available to the economy.

How does such a minor thing as the money supply have such a large impact on macroeconomic activity? By changing the money supply, the Federal Reserve can influence many financial and economic variables, such as interest rates, stock prices, housing prices, and exchange rates. Restricting the money supply leads to higher interest rates and reduced investment, which, in turn, causes a decline in GNP and lower inflation. If the central bank is faced with a business downturn, it can increase the money supply and lower interest rates to stimulate economic activity.

The exact nature of monetary policy—the way in which the central bank controls the money supply and the relationships among money, output, and inflation—is one of the most fascinating, important, and controversial areas of macroeconomics. A policy of tight money in the United States—lowering the rate of growth of the money supply—raised interest rates, slowed economic growth, and raised unemployment in the period 1979–1982. Then from 1982 until 1990, careful monetary management by the Federal Reserve supported the longest economic expansion in American history. Exactly how a central bank can control economic activity will be thoroughly analyzed in the chapters on monetary policy.

International Economic Policy. As economies become more closely linked, policymakers devote increasing attention to international economic policy. The major instruments fall into two categories. The first is *trade policies*, which consist of tariffs, quotas, and other devices that restrict or encourage imports and exports. Most trade policies have little effect on macroeconomic performance, but from time to time, as was the case in the 1930s, restrictions on international trade are so severe that they cause major economic dislocations, inflations, or recessions.

A second set of policies specifically aimed at the foreign sector is *exchange-market management.* A country's international trade is influenced by its exchange rate, which represents the price of its own currency in terms of the currencies of other nations. Nations adopt different systems to regulate their foreign exchange markets. Some systems allow exchange rates to be determined purely by supply and demand; others set a fixed exchange rate against other currencies. The United States today is in the first category, generally allowing the dollar's exchange rates to be determined by market forces.

In addition, central bankers and political leaders increasingly gather to *coordinate* their macroeconomic policies, for a nation's monetary and fiscal policies can spill over to affect its neighbors. Since 1975, the leaders of the major industrial countries have met annually at economic summit meetings to discuss joint economic issues and to take appropriate measures for attaining commonly agreed-upon goals. Such meetings have dealt with a wide variety of concerns ranging from coping with oil-price increases to studying global environmental problems. They are a reminder that economies cannot manage themselves and that governments must constantly keep alert to economic instability.

Incomes Policies. When inflation threatens to get out of control, governments grope for ways to stabilize prices. The traditional route for slowing inflation has been for governments to take fiscal or monetary steps to reduce output and raise unemployment. But this traditional strategy has proven extremely costly. It takes hundreds of billions of dollars in lost GNP (or in the GNP gap) to reduce inflation by a few percentage points. Faced with the need to take such unpleasant medicine, governments have often searched for other methods of containing inflation. These alternatives range from wage and price controls (used primarily in wartime) to less drastic measures like voluntary wage and price guidelines. Policies to control wages and prices are known as **incomes policies.**

Incomes policies are the most controversial of all macroeconomic policies. A generation ago, many economists advocated wage-price policies as an inexpensive way to reduce inflation. Evidence on the impact of incomes policies along with a more conservative attitude toward government intervention has led to a general disenchantment with wage-price policies. Many economists now believe they are simply ineffective. Others think they are worse than useless—that they interfere with free markets, gum up relative price movements, and fail to reduce inflation.

A nation has a wide variety of policy instruments that can be used to pursue its macroeconomic goals. The major ones are these:

1. Fiscal policy consists of government expenditure and taxation. Government expenditure influences the relative size of collective as opposed to private consumption. Taxation subtracts from incomes and reduces private spending; in addition, it affects investment and potential output. Fiscal policy affects total spending and thereby influences real GNP and inflation.
2. Monetary policy, conducted by the central bank, determines the money supply. Changes in the money supply move interest rates up or down and affect spending in sectors such as investment, housing, and net exports. Monetary policy has an important effect on both actual GNP and potential GNP.
3. Foreign economic policies—trade policies, exchange-rate setting, and monetary and fiscal policies—attempt to keep imports in line with exports and to stabilize foreign exchange rates. Governments work together to coordinate their macroeconomic goals and policies.
4. Incomes policies are government attempts to moderate inflation by direct steps, whether by verbal persuasion or by legislated wage and price controls.

Macroeconomic Policies and Goals in Practice

Now that we have examined the major goals and instruments of macroeconomic policy, we consider the economic policies that have been pursued in the United States. Before the Great Depression of the 1930s, understanding of macroeconomics was primitive. Aside from familiar homilies like "balance the budget," there was nothing resembling a coherent theory for managing the economy.

The 1930s marked the first stirrings of the science of macroeconomics, initiated by the contribution of John Maynard Keynes.[2] After World War II, reflecting both the increasing influence of Keynesian views and the fear of a depression, the U.S. Congress formally proclaimed federal responsibility for macroeconomic performance. It enacted the landmark Employment Act of 1946, which stated:

> The Congress hereby declares that it is the continuing policy and responsibility of the federal government to use all practicable means consistent with its needs and obligations . . . to promote maximum employment, production, and purchasing power.

For the first time Congress affirmed the government's role in promoting output growth and employment and maintaining price stability. In addition to setting forth these lofty but somewhat vague goals, the Employment Act established the Council of Economic Advisers (or CEA) to be part of the presidential staff.[3]

---

[2] John Maynard Keynes (1883–1946) was a many-sided genius who won eminence in the fields of mathematics, philosophy, and literature. In addition, he found time to run a large insurance company, advise the British treasury, help govern the Bank of England, edit a world-famous economics journal, collect modern art and rare books, and sponsor ballet and drama. He was also an economist who knew how to make money by shrewd speculation, both for himself and for his college, King's College, Cambridge. His 1936 book, *The General Theory of Employment, Interest and Money*, presented a profound challenge to macroeconomic thinking of the time and lay the foundation for the development of modern macroeconomics.

[3] In addition to advising the President, a major responsibility of the CEA is to prepare the *Economic Report of the President and the Council of Economic Advisers*, published annually along with the presidential budget. This document is required reading for macroeconomists. It contains a wealth of statistics and a diagnosis of current economic trends, along with analysis and defense of the administration's economic policies. Sometimes this dry document becomes controversial. A few

In the 1980s, the nation's priorities shifted. During the Reagan years, the government passed large tax cuts and undertook an extensive military buildup. These policies produced a sharp increase in the federal budget deficit, which is the difference between government expenditures and tax revenues. People became alarmed about the impact of large deficits on economic growth, and in response Congress passed the Balanced Budget Act of 1985 (known as the Gramm-Rudman Act, after its chief sponsors).

Gramm-Rudman imposed a stern fiscal discipline, requiring Congress to balance the budget by 1991. If the required decline in the deficit was not met, government expenditures were to be cut automatically and across the board. The goals of the Gramm-Rudman Act proved difficult to attain as deficits climbed to record levels in early 1990; Congress repeatedly postponed the deadline for balancing the budget. In 1990, Congress modified the Gramm-Rudman Act to impose expenditure limitations on major federal budget categories.

Why has it proved so difficult to attain full employment with stable prices or a balanced budget with rapid economic growth? The answer to this question lies in the nature of the *constraints* and *tradeoffs* that face the macroeconomy. The production-possibility curve showed that we cannot have maximum guns and maximum butter, or high consumption today and high consumption tomorrow, or much private and much collective consumption. You cannot eat your cake today and have it tomorrow.

There are similar tradeoffs in macroeconomics. Macroeconomic policy requires choice among competing objectives. A nation cannot simultaneously have high consumption and rapid growth. Lowering a high inflation rate requires either a period of high unemployment and low output or interference with free markets through incomes policies. Reducing a trade deficit requires that a nation reduce domestic consumption and investment.

Of all the macroeconomic goals, the most agonizing is maintaining full employment of labor and

---

years ago, President Reagan's Secretary of the Treasury said that the report of President Reagan's CEA was so bad that it should be "thrown in the wastebasket."

other resources. The electorate demands low unemployment and high output. But high levels of output and employment drive up prices and wages, and inflation tends to rise in periods of rapid economic growth. Policymakers are therefore forced to rein in the economy when it grows too fast, or when unemployment falls too far, in order to prevent runaway inflation.

An example of how policymakers reacted to inflation by slowing economic growth came during the oil-price shock of the late 1970s and early 1980s. After the Iranian revolution in 1978, oil production fell and oil prices jumped from $14 to $34 per barrel. Inflation in the United States rose from 6 percent in 1977 to 14 percent in 1980. Economic policymakers in the United States and abroad were frightened by the accelerating inflation. President Carter agonized: Should he slow down the economy, allow unemployment to rise, stifle economic growth, and face the wrath of the voters at the polls? Or should he introduce expansionary fiscal and monetary policies and risk igniting even greater inflation and even higher unemployment later on? Carter opted for an economic slowdown and a rise in unemployment. What would you have done?

Each country faced the same dilemma—and indeed the dilemma recurs again and again. It is impossible to escape the tradeoff between unemployment and inflation. Where prices and wages are determined in free markets, a policy to reduce inflation must pay the price in high unemployment and large GNP gaps. Conversely, if a nation wishes to grow rapidly and enjoy low unemployment, inflation will surely follow.

Other macroeconomic dilemmas confront policymakers. A country can temporarily curb inflation with wage and price controls, but the result is distorted prices and economic inefficiency. Increasing the rate of growth of potential GNP requires greater investment in knowledge and capital. This investment lowers current consumption of food, clothing, and recreation. These are the kinds of painful choices confronting macroeconomic policymakers in all market economies.

B. Aggregate Supply and Demand

We have seen that output, employment, and prices can change sharply under the influence of both economic policies and external shocks like rapid changes in oil prices. But we can go beyond description to diagnosis. What is the *economic mechanism* that transmits money or taxes or changing oil prices into output and retail prices? How can governments take steps to improve the economy's performance?

We begin our analysis of the forces determining overall economic activity by introducing a useful apparatus, aggregate supply and demand. This analysis allows us to understand how different forces affect the macroeconomy and to see how government policies can help counteract the slings and arrows of external shocks. After explaining this new tool, we conclude by using aggregate supply and demand to understand some important historical events.

Inside the Macroeconomy: Aggregate Supply and Demand

We begin with a simple picture of the forces operating on the macroeconomy, shown in Figure 5-5. This figure shows on the left the major variables affecting the macroeconomic system. First are the instruments or policy variables discussed in the last section: taxes, monetary policy, and so forth. In addition, we see a set of **external variables,** which influence economic activity but are unaffected by the economy. These variables include wars and revolutions, the weather, population growth, and many other factors.

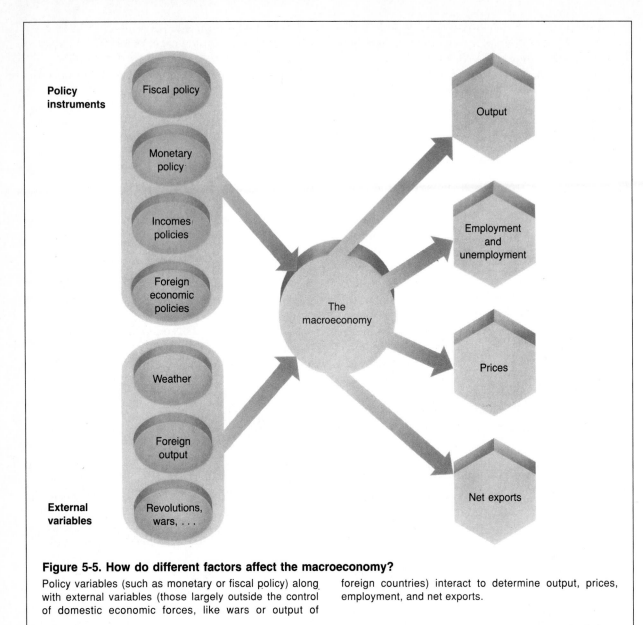

Figure 5-5. How do different factors affect the macroeconomy?

Policy variables (such as monetary or fiscal policy) along with external variables (those largely outside the control of domestic economic forces, like wars or output of foreign countries) interact to determine output, prices, employment, and net exports.

The policy and external variables interact to determine the key macroeconomic variables, shown on the right in Figure 5-5. Policy instruments and external variables determine national output, employment and unemployment, the price level, and net exports.

Definitions of Aggregate Supply and Demand

How do different forces interact to determine overall economic activity? Figure 5-6 shows the relationships among the different variables inside the macroeconomy. It separates policy and external variables into two categories: those affecting aggregate supply and those affecting aggregate demand. Dividing variables into these two categories is essential for our understanding of what determines the level of output, prices, and unemployment.

The lower part of Figure 5-6 shows the forces affecting aggregate supply. **Aggregate supply** refers to the total quantity of goods and services that the nation's businesses are willing to produce and sell in a given period. Aggregate supply (often written *AS*) depends upon the price level, the productive capacity of the economy, and the level of costs.

In general, businesses would like to produce at full capacity and sell all their output at high prices. However, in certain circumstances, prices and spending levels may be depressed, so businesses might find they have excess capacity. Under other conditions, such as during a wartime boom, factories may be operating at capacity as businesses scramble to produce to meet all their orders.

We see, then, that aggregate supply depends on the price level that businesses can charge as well as on the economy's capacity or potential output. But what determines potential output? Potential output is determined by the availability of productive inputs (labor and capital being the most important) and the efficiency with which those inputs are combined (that is, the technology of the society).

National output and the overall price level are determined by the twin blades of the scissors of aggregate supply and demand. The second blade of

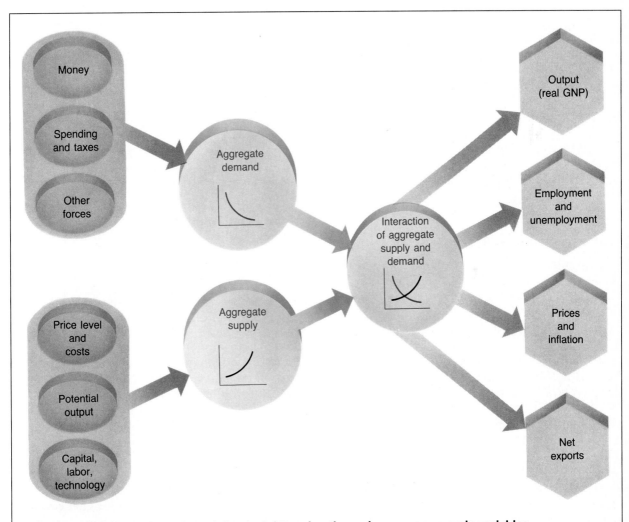

Figure 5-6. Aggregate supply and demand determine the major macroeconomic variables

This key diagram shows the major factors affecting overall economic activity. On the left are the major variables determining aggregate supply and demand: policy variables like monetary and fiscal policies along with stocks of capital and labor. In the center, aggregate supply and demand interact as the level of demand beats upon the available resources. The chief outcomes are shown on the right in hexagons: output, employment, prices, and net exports.

the scissors is **aggregate demand,** which refers to the total amount that different sectors in the economy willingly spend in a given period. Aggregate demand (often written *AD*) is the sum of spending by consumers, businesses, and other agents and depends on the level of prices, as well as on monetary policy, fiscal policy, and other factors.

In other words, aggregate demand measures total spending by all the different entities in the economy. It depends upon the cars, food, and other consumption goods bought by consumers; on plants and equipment bought by businesses; on smart bombs and computers bought by government; and on net exports. The total purchases are affected by the prices at which the goods are offered, by external forces, and by government policies.

Using both blades of the scissors of aggregate supply and demand, we can see the resulting equilibrium, as is shown in the right-hand circle of Figure 5-6. National output and the price level will move to that level where demanders willingly buy what businesses willingly sell. The resulting output and price level determine employment, unemployment, and net exports.

Aggregate Supply and Demand Curves

Supply and demand curves are often used to help analyze macroeconomic equilibrium. Recall that in Chapter 4 we used market supply and demand curves to analyze the prices and quantities of individual products. An analogous graphical apparatus can also help us understand the major macroeconomic issues of aggregate output and price determination. Using aggregate supply and demand, we can see how monetary expansion leads to rising prices and higher output. We can also see why increases in efficiency may lead to higher output and to a *lower* overall price level. Moreover, this powerful analysis will explain why a rise in world oil prices can lead to "stagflation," the unhappy circumstance where *stagnation* is combined with *inflation*.

Figure 5-7 shows the aggregate supply and demand schedules for the output of an entire economy. On the horizontal, or quantity, axis is the total output (real GNP) of the economy. On the vertical axis is the overall price level (say, as measured by the CPI).

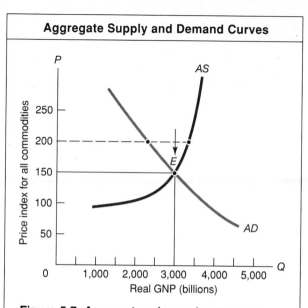

Figure 5-7. Aggregate price and output are determined by the interaction of aggregate supply and demand

National output and the overall price level are determined at the intersection of the aggregate demand and supply curves.

The *AD* curve represents the quantity of total spending at different price levels, with other factors held constant. The *AS* curve shows what firms will produce and sell at different price levels, other things equal.

The macroeconomic equilibrium lies at point *E*; this intersection occurs at an overall price level where firms willingly produce and sell an output of Q = 3000, and spenders willingly buy just that amount.

The downward-sloping curve is the **aggregate demand schedule,** or *AD* **curve.** It represents what all the entities in the economy—consumers, businesses, foreigners, and governments—would buy at different aggregate price levels (with other factors affecting aggregate demand held constant). From the curve, we see that at an overall price level of 150, total spending would be $3000 billion. If the price level were to rise to 200, total spending would fall to $2300 billion.

The upward-sloping curve is the **aggregate supply schedule,** or *AS* **curve.** This curve represents the quantity of goods and services that businesses are willing to produce and sell at each price level (with other determinants of aggregate supply held constant). According to the curve, businesses will want to sell $3000 billion at a price level of 150; they will want to sell a higher quantity, $3300 billion, if prices rise to 200. As the level of total output demanded rises, businesses will want to sell more goods and services at a higher price level.

It is necessary to mention one word of caution at this time: We must be careful not to confuse the macroeconomic *AD* or *AS* curves with the microeconomic *DD* or *SS* curves. The microeconomic supply and demand curves show the quantities and prices of *individual* commodities, with such things as national income and other goods' prices held as given. By contrast, the aggregate supply and demand curves show the determination of *total* output and the *overall* price level, with such things as the money supply, fiscal policy, and the capital stock held constant. The two sets of curves have a family resemblance, but they explain very different phenomena.

Macroeconomic Equilibrium. By looking at *AS* and *AD* together, we can also find the *equilibrium values of price and quantity*. That is, we can find the real GNP and the price level that would satisfy both buyers and sellers. For the *AS* and *AD* curves shown in Figure 5-7, the overall economy is in *equilibrium* at point *E*. Only at that point, where the level of output is $Q = 3000$ and $P = 150$, are spenders and sellers satisfied. Only at point *E* are demanders willing to buy exactly the amount that businesses are willing to produce and sell.

How does the economy reach its equilibrium? Indeed, what do we mean by equilibrium? A macroeconomic equilibrium is a combination of overall price and quantity at which neither buyers nor sellers wish to change their purchases, sales, or prices. Figure 5-7 illustrates the concept. If the price level were higher than equilibrium, say $P = 200$, then businesses would want to sell more than purchasers would want to buy. Goods would accumulate on the shelves as firms produce more than consumers buy. As the goods continue to pile up, firms would cut production and begin to shave their prices. As the price level declines from its original too-high level of 200, the gap between desired spending and desired sales would narrow until the equilibrium at $P = 150$ and $Q = 3000$ is reached. Once the equilibrium is reached, neither buyers nor sellers wish to change their quantities demanded or supplied, and there is no pressure on the price level to change.

Macroeconomic History: 1960–1991

We can use the aggregate supply-and-demand apparatus to analyze the recent macroeconomic history of the United States. This case study will focus on three major events: the economic expansion during the Vietnam war, the stagflation caused by the supply shocks of the 1970s, and the deep recession caused by the monetary contraction of the early 1980s.

Wartime Boom. The American economy entered the 1960s having experienced numerous recessions. John Kennedy took over the presidency hoping to resuscitate the economy. During this era the "New Economics," as the Keynesian approach was called, came to Washington. Economic advisers to Presidents Kennedy and Johnson recommended expansionary policies, and Congress enacted measures to stimulate the economy, including sharp cuts in personal and corporate taxes in 1964 and 1965. GNP grew 4 percent annually during the early 1960s, unemployment declined, and prices were stable. By 1965, the economy was at its potential output.

Unfortunately, the government underestimated the magnitude of the buildup for the Vietnam war; defense spending grew by 55 percent from 1965 to 1968. Even when it became clear that a major inflationary boom was under way, President Johnson postponed painful fiscal steps to slow the economy. Tax increases and civilian expenditure cuts came only in 1968, which was too late to prevent inflationary pressures from overheating the economy. The Federal Reserve accommodated the expansion with rapid money growth and low interest rates. As a result, for much of the period 1966–1970, the economy operated far above its potential output. Inflation gradually rose under the pressure of low unemployment and high factory utilization.

Figure 5-8 illustrates the events of this period. The tax cuts and defense expenditures increased aggregate demand, shifting the aggregate demand curve to the right from *AD* to *AD'*. Equilibrium moved from *E* to *E'*. Output and employment rose sharply, and prices began to creep upward as output exceeded capacity limits.

The lesson of this episode is that increasing aggregate demand produces higher output and employment. But if expansion takes the economy well

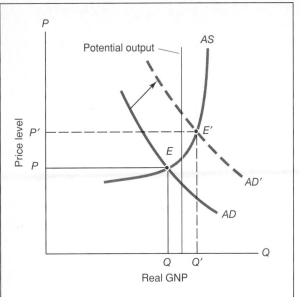

Figure 5-8. Wartime boom is propelled by increasing aggregate demand

During wartime, increased defense spending increases aggregate spending, moving aggregate demand from *AD* to *AD′*, with equilibrium output increasing from *E* to *E′*. When output rises far above potential output, the price level moves up sharply from *P* to *P′* and wartime inflation ensues.

beyond potential output, an overheated economy and price inflation will soon follow.

Supply Shocks and Stagflation. During the 1970s, the industrial world was struck by a new macroeconomic malady, supply shocks. A **supply shock** refers to a sudden change in conditions of cost or productivity that shifts aggregate supply sharply. Supply shocks occurred with particular virulence in 1973. Called the "year of the seven plagues," 1973 was marked by crop failures, shifting ocean currents, massive speculation on world commodity markets, turmoil in foreign exchange markets, and a quadrupling of the world price of crude oil.

This jolt to crude material and fuel supplies raised wholesale prices dramatically. The prices of crude materials and fuels rose more from 1972 to 1973 than they had in the entire period from the end of World War II to 1972. Shortly after the supply shock, inflation mounted sharply, and real output

fell as the United States experienced a period of stagflation.

How can we understand the combination of falling output and rising prices? The sudden rise in the cost of raw materials constituted a supply shock, which we can depict as a sharp upward shift in the aggregate supply curve. An upward shift in *AS* indicates that businesses will supply the same level of output only at substantially higher prices. Figure 5-9 illustrates a supply shift.

The results of a supply shock are startling:

A supply shock, seen as a sharp upward shift in the *AS* curve, results in higher prices along with a decline in output. Supply shocks thus lead to a deterioration of all the major goals of macroeconomic policy.

Tight Money, 1979–1982. By 1979 the economy had recovered from the 1973 supply shock. Output had returned to its potential. But unrest in the Mid-

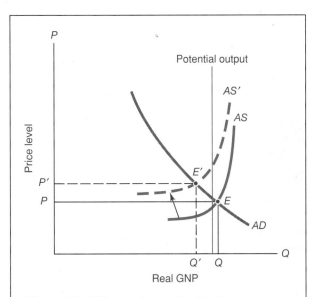

Figure 5-9. Effects of supply shocks

The effect of sharply higher oil, commodity, or labor costs is an increase in the costs of doing business. This leads to stagflation—stagnation combined with inflation.

As a result of the higher costs of oil and other inputs, businesses charge more for their products. The *AS* curve shifts up from *AS* to *AS′* and equilibrium shifts from *E* to *E′*. Output declines from *Q* to *Q′*, while prices rise. The economy thus suffers a double whammy—lower output *and* higher prices.

dle East led to another oil shock as the Iranian revolution produced a jump in oil prices from $14 per barrel in early 1978 to $34 per barrel in 1979. Inflation increased dramatically—averaging 12 percent per year from 1978 to 1980.

Double-digit inflation was unacceptable, and the Federal Reserve took steps to slow the inflation. Paul Volcker, then chairman of the Federal Reserve Board, used monetary policy to raise interest rates in 1979 (these steps constitute *tight money*). Interest rates rose sharply in 1979 and 1980, the stock market fell, and credit was hard to find. The Fed's tight-money policy slowed spending by consumers and businesses. Particularly hard-hit were interest-sensitive components of aggregate demand. After 1979, housing construction, automobile purchases, business investment, and net exports declined sharply.

Figure 5-10 shows how tight money raised interest rates and reduced aggregate demand. This result can be seen as a downward shift of the aggregate demand curve—exactly the opposite of the effect of the defense buildup during the 1960s. The decrease in aggregate demand reduced output almost 10 percent below its potential by the end of 1982, and the unemployment rate rose from below 6 percent in 1979 to more than 10 percent at the end of 1982.

The reward for these austere measures was a dramatic decline in inflation, from an average of 12 percent per year in the 1979–1980 period to 4 percent during the period from 1983 to 1988. High unemployment succeeded in wringing inflation out of the economy, but the cost was great in terms of lost output, income, and employment.

The low inflation and excess capacity of the early 1980s set the stage for the long economic expansion of the Reagan years and early part of the Bush administration. Real GNP grew steadily from 1982 to 1990, averaging $3\frac{1}{2}$ percent annually; unemployment fell from over 10 percent in 1982 to $5\frac{1}{2}$ percent in 1988–1990; and inflation remained in an acceptable region, averaging $3\frac{1}{2}$ percent from 1982 to 1990.

Economic Policy

We have seen some of the crucial forces that affect macroeconomic activity. Some factors operate on the spending side, changing aggregate demand

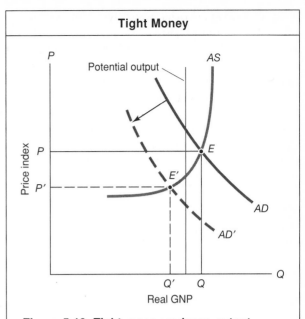

Figure 5-10. Tight money reduces output and inflation

From 1979 to 1982, the Federal Reserve slowed growth in money and credit, reducing aggregate demand, and producing a sharp downturn in economic activity. As a result, wage and price inflation slowed to a crawl for the rest of the 1980s.

because of shifts in consumer preferences or military expenditures. Other disturbances arise on the supply side, as when war or revolution leads to a doubling of oil prices or when bad harvests lead to major food-price increases.

The major task of macroeconomic policy today is to diagnose the different ailments affecting aggregate supply and demand and to prescribe the appropriate policies to remedy them. In some cases, policymakers face no dilemmas. For example, if the economy is heading into a recession when wartime spending begins to grow, as in early 1991, then no measures are immediately necessary to offset the higher spending. Or if the economy is operating at potential output, and the end of the cold war allows deep cuts in military spending, then the diagnosis is straightforward: the military cuts would tend to decrease aggregate demand, and most economists would agree that economic policy should offset the spending cuts by using monetary or fiscal policy to increase aggregate demand.

In the early 1970s, and again in 1990, adverse supply shocks led to an upward shift in aggregate supply. This led to stagflation, with a simultaneous rise in unemployment and inflation.

At the end of the 1970s, economic policymakers reacted to the rising inflation by tightening monetary policy and raising interest rates. The result was lower spending on interest-sensitive demands such as housing, investment, and net exports. The decline in aggregate demand caused a deep recession during the early 1980s, with the unemployment rate at its highest level in half a century.

CONCEPTS FOR REVIEW

Major macroeconomic concepts
macroeconomics vs.
  microeconomics
gross national product (GNP), actual
  and potential
employment, unemployment,
  unemployment rate

inflation, deflation
consumer price index (CPI)
incomes policy
net exports
fiscal policy (government
  expenditures, taxation)
money, monetary policy

Aggregate supply and demand
aggregate supply, aggregate demand
AS curve, AD curve
equilibrium of AS and AD
three macroeconomic shocks: wartime
  boom, supply shock, tight money
stagflation

QUESTIONS FOR DISCUSSION

1. What are the major goals of macroeconomics? Write a brief definition of each of the major goals. Explain why nations pursue each goal.
2. If a nation desires to have stable prices (or low inflation), why not simply pass a law that prohibits firms from changing prices?
3. If the CPI were 300 in 1993 and 315 in 1994, what would the inflation rate be for 1994? 5% $\frac{315-300}{300} \times 100$
4. What would be the effect of each of the following on aggregate demand or on aggregate supply, as indicated?
   (a) A large oil-price increase (on AS)
   (b) An arms-reduction agreement reducing defense spending (on AD)
   (c) An increase in potential output (on AS)
   (d) A monetary loosening that lowers interest rates (on AD)
5. For each of the events listed in question 4, use the AS-AD apparatus to show the effect on output and on the overall price level.
6. Put yourself in the shoes of an economic policymaker. The economy is in equilibrium with $P = 100$ and $Q = 3000 =$ potential GNP. You refuse to "accommodate" inflation; i.e., you want to keep prices absolutely stable at $P = 100$, no matter what happens to output. Finally, you can use monetary and fiscal policies to affect aggregate demand, but you cannot affect aggregate supply. How would you respond to:
   (a) A surprise increase in investment spending
   (b) A sharp food price increase following a major drought
   (c) A productivity decline that decreases potential output
   (d) An agreement to cut conventional military forces and associated expenditures by 20 percent
   (e) A sharp increase in net exports that followed a fall in the dollar's foreign exchange rate
7. In 1982–1983, the Reagan administration reduced taxes and increased government spending.
   (a) Explain why this policy would tend to increase aggregate demand; show the impact on output and prices assuming only an AD shift.
   (b) The "supply-side" school holds that tax cuts will affect aggregate supply mainly by increasing potential output. Assuming that the Reagan fiscal measures affected AS as well as AD, show the impact on output and the price level. Explain why the impact on output is unambiguous while the impact on prices is unclear.
8. After Iraq invaded Kuwait in 1990, oil prices rose sharply and the U.S. increased its defense spending. Review the impact of these two events on the econ-

omy. From what you know, write a short essay (like that under "Macroeconomic History," pages 77–79) describing the events and analyzing the period using *AS-AD* analysis.

9. Consider the data on real GNP and the price level in the table on the right.

    (a) For the years 1981 to 1985, calculate the rate of growth of real GNP and the rate of inflation. Can you guess in which year there was a steep recession?

    (b) In an *AS-AD* diagram like Figure 5-7, draw a set of *AS* and *AD* curves that would trace out the price and output equilibria shown in the table. How would you explain the recession that you have identified?

Year	Real GNP ($, billion, 1982 prices)	Price level* (1982 = 100)
1980	3,187	85.7
1981	3,249	94.0
1982	3,166	100.0
1983	3,279	103.9
1984	3,501	107.7
1985	3,619	110.9

*Note that the price index shown is the "GNP deflator," which is the price of all components of GNP.
(Source: *Economic Report of the President*, 1991.)

MEASURING NATIONAL OUTPUT AND INCOME

> When you can measure what you are speaking about, and express it in numbers, you know something about it; when you cannot measure it, when you cannot express it in numbers, your knowledge is of a meager and unsatisfactory kind; it may be the beginning of knowledge, but you have scarcely, in your thoughts, advanced to the stage of science.
>
> Lord Kelvin

Like other empirical sciences, economics focuses on concepts that can actually be measured—things such as prices of wheat, stock prices and interest rates, number of unemployed people, national output, or the price level. This chapter focuses on one of the most important sets of concepts in all economics, the national income and product accounts. We will learn here how to measure the gross national product (or GNP), which is the total dollar value of the national output.

Measuring national output is indispensable for macroeconomic theory and policy. It prepares us for tackling the central issues concerning economic growth, the business cycle, the relationship between economic activity and unemployment, and the measurement and determinants of inflation. Before the concept of GNP was invented, it was difficult to assess the state of the economy. Although the GNP has no patent and is not displayed in the Museum of Science and Technology, it is truly one of the great inventions of the twentieth century. Without measures of economic aggregates like GNP, macroeconomics would be adrift in a sea of unorganized data. The GNP data help policymakers steer the economy toward the nation's objectives.

In this chapter, we will also consider some of the criticisms of GNP. People do not live by bread alone, nor does society live on GNP alone. These days, we are increasingly concerned lest material growth be gained at the expense of the quality of the environment. Is it inevitable, people ask, that in driving our cars or air conditioning our houses we must also pollute the air and water and perhaps even change our climate? To answer this question, we must devise ways of converting the GNP concept into a more adequate measure of economic activity—hence the concept of *net economic welfare* or *NEW*.

Gross National Product: The Yardstick of an Economy's Performance

What is the **gross national product?** GNP is the name we give to the total dollar value of the final goods and services produced by a nation during a given year. It is the figure you arrive at when you apply the measuring rod of money to the diverse goods and services—from apples to zithers, from battleships to machine tools—that a country produces with its land, labor, and capital resources. GNP equals the sum of the money values of all consumption and investment goods, government purchases, and net exports to other lands.

GNP is used for many purposes, but the most important one is to measure the overall performance of an economy. If you ask an economic historian what happened during the Great Depression, the best short answer would be:

Between 1929 and 1933, GNP fell from $104 billion to $56 billion. This sharp decline in the money value of goods and services produced by the American economy caused hardship, bankruptcies, bank failures, riots, and political turmoil.

The gross national product (or GNP) is the most comprehensive measure of a nation's total output of goods and services. It is the sum of the dollar values of consumption, gross investment, government purchases of goods and services, and net exports.

We now discuss the elements of the national income and product accounts. We start by showing different ways of measuring GNP and distinguish-

ing real from nominal GNP. We then analyze the major components of GNP. Finally, we reflect on the shortcomings of GNP as an index of economic welfare and suggest an alternative approach to measuring national output.

Two Measures of National Product: Goods-Flow and Earnings-Flow

How do economists actually measure GNP? One of the major surprises is that we can measure GNP in two entirely independent ways. As Figure 6-1 shows, GNP can be measured either as a flow of products or as a sum of earnings.

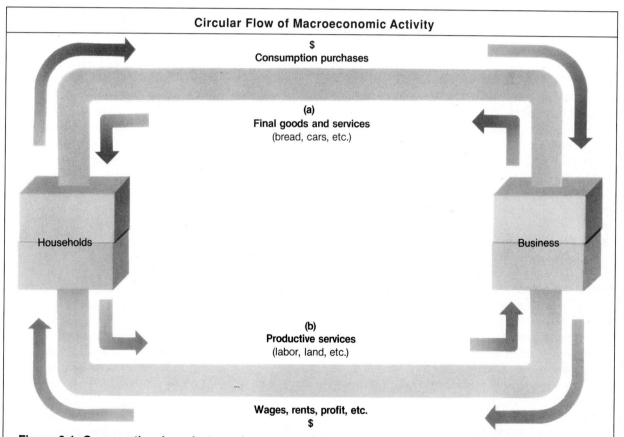

Figure 6-1. Gross national product can be measured either as (a) a flow of final products or, equally, as (b) a flow of costs

In the upper loop, people spend their money on final goods. The total dollar flow of these each year is one measure of gross national product.

The lower loop measures the annual flow of costs of output: the earnings that business pays out in wages, rent, interest, dividends, and business profits. The two measures of GNP must always be identical. Note that this figure is the *macroeconomic* counterpart of Fig. 3-1, which presented the circular flow of supply and demand.

To demonstrate the different ways of measuring GNP, we begin by considering an oversimplified world in which there is no government or foreign sector and in which no investment takes place. For the moment, our little economy produces only *consumption goods*, which are items that are purchased by households to satisfy their wants.

Flow-of-Product Approach. Each year the public consumes a wide variety of final goods and services: goods such as apples, oranges, and bread; services such as health care and haircuts. We include only *final goods*—goods ultimately bought and used by consumers. Households spend their incomes for these consumer goods, as is shown in the upper loop of Figure 6-1. Add together all the consumption dollars spent on these final goods, and you will arrive at this simplified economy's total GNP.

Thus, in our simple economy, you can easily calculate national income or product as the sum of the annual flow of *final* goods and services: (price of oranges × number of oranges) plus (price of apples × number of apples) plus. . . . The gross national product is defined as the total money value of the flow of final products produced by the nation.[1]

A crucial part of the calculation is the use of market prices as weights in valuing different commodities. Why use market prices rather than mass, volume, or labor-hours used in production? Economists use market prices because prices reflect the relative economic value of diverse goods and services. That is, the relative prices of different goods reflect how much consumers value their last (or marginal) units of consumption of these goods. Thus the choice of market prices as weights for different goods is not arbitrary; in a well-functioning market economy prices reflect the relative satisfactions that consumers receive from each good.

Earnings or Cost Approach. The second and equivalent way to calculate GNP is the earnings or cost approach. Go to the lower loop in Figure 6-1. Through it flow all the costs of doing business:

these costs include the wages paid to labor, the rents paid to land, the profits paid to capital, and so forth. But these business costs are also the earnings that households receive from the firm. By measuring the annual flow of these earnings or incomes, statisticians will again arrive at the GNP.[2]

Hence, a second way to calculate GNP is as the total of factor earnings (wages, interest, rents, and profits) that are the costs of producing society's final products.

Equivalence of the Two Approaches. Now we have calculated GNP by the upper-loop flow-of-product approach and by the lower-loop earnings-flow approach. Which of these two is greater? They are *exactly* the same.

We can understand the identity of the two approaches by examining a simple barbershop economy. Say the barbers have no expenses other than labor. If they sell 10 haircuts at $6 each, GNP is $60. But the barbers' earnings (in wages and profits) are also exactly $60. Hence, the GNP here is identical whether measured as flow of products ($60 of haircuts) or as cost and income ($60 of wages and profits).

In fact, the two approaches are identical because we have included "profit" in the lower loop—along with wages and rents. What exactly is profit? Profit is what remains from the sale of a product after you have paid the other factor costs—wages, interest, and rents. It is the residual that automatically adjusts to make the lower loop's costs or earnings exactly match the upper loop's value of goods.

To sum up:

GNP, or gross national product, can be measured in two different ways: (1) as the flow of final products, or (2) as the total costs or earnings of inputs producing output. Because profit is a residual, both approaches will yield exactly the same total GNP.

Business Accounts and GNP

The national income and product accounts can be built up from businesses' income statements. An *account* for a firm or nation is a numerical record of all flows (outputs, costs, etc.) during a given period.

---

[1] Our oversimplified example considers only consumption expenditures. A complete definition of GNP will include *all* final goods and services; that is, GNP is consumption, private investment, government spending on goods and services, and net exports to the rest of the world.

[2] When we leave our simple world in which GNP is only consumption, we will have to introduce government transfer payments and taxes into the calculations.

(a) Income Statement of Typical Farm			
Output in farming		**Earnings**	
Sales of goods (corn, apples, etc.)	$1,000	Costs of production:	
		Wages	$ 800
		Rents	100
		Interest	25
		Profit (residual)	75
Total	$1,000	Total	$1,000

(b) National Product Account (Millions of Dollars)			
Upper-loop flow of product		**Lower-loop flow of earnings**	
Final output (10 × 1,000)	$10,000	Costs or earnings:	
		Wages (10 × 800)	$ 8,000
		Rents (10 × 100)	1,000
		Interest (10 × 25)	250
		Profit (10 × 75)	750
GNP total	$10,000	GNP total	$10,000

Table 6-1. Construction of national product accounts from business accounts

Part **(a)** shows the income statement of a typical farm. The left side shows the value of production while the right side shows the firm's costs. Part **(b)** then adds up or aggregates the 10 million identical farms to obtain total GNP. Note that GNP from the product side exactly equals GNP from the earnings side.

The top half of Table 6-1 shows the results of a year's farming operations for a single, typical farm. We put sales of final products on the left-hand side and the various costs of production on the right. The bottom half of Table 6-1 shows how to construct the GNP accounts for a simple agrarian economy in which there is no government or investment and in which all final products are produced on 10 million identical farms. The national accounts simply add together the outputs and costs of the 10 million identical farms to get the two different measures of GNP.

The Problem of "Double Counting"

We defined GNP as the total production of final goods and services. A *final product* is one that is produced and sold for consumption or investment. GNP excludes *intermediate goods*—goods that are used up to produce other goods. GNP therefore includes bread but not wheat, and cars but not steel.

For the flow-of-product calculation of GNP, excluding intermediate products poses no major complications. We simply include the bread and cars in GNP but avoid including the wheat and dough that went into the bread or the steel and glass that went into the cars. If you look again at the upper loop in Figure 6-1, you will see that bread and cars appear in the flow of products, but you will not find any wheat, flour, or steel.

What has happened to products like wheat and steel? They are intermediate products and are simply cycling around inside the block marked "Business." They are never bought by consumers, and they never show up as final products in GNP.

"Value Added" in the Lower Loop. A new statistician who is being trained to make GNP measurements might be puzzled, saying:

> I can see that, if you are careful, your upper-loop product approach to GNP will avoid including intermediate products. But aren't you in some trouble when you use the lower-loop cost or earnings approach?

After all, when we gather income statements from the accounts of firms, won't we pick up what grain merchants pay to wheat farmers, what bakers pay to grain merchants, and what grocers pay to bakers? Won't this result in double counting or even triple counting of items going through several productive stages?

These are good questions, but there is an ingenious answer that will resolve the problem. In making lower-loop earnings measurements, statisticians are very careful to include in GNP only a firm's value added. **Value added** is the difference between a firm's sales and its purchases of materials and services from other firms.

In other words, in calculating the GNP earnings or value added by a firm, the statistician includes all costs that go to factors other than businesses and excludes all payments made to other businesses. Hence business costs in the form of wages, salaries, interest payments, and dividends are included in value added, but purchases of wheat or steel or electricity are excluded from value added. Why are all those purchases from other firms excluded from value added to obtain GNP? Because those purchases will get properly counted in GNP in the values added by other firms.

Table 6-2 uses the stages of bread production to illustrate how careful adherence to the value-added approach enables us to subtract the inter-mediate expenses that show up in the income statements of farmers, millers, bakers, and grocers. The final calculation shows the desired equality between (a) final sales of bread and (b) total earnings, calculated as the sum of all values added in all the different stages of bread production.

We can summarize as follows:

Value-added approach: To avoid double counting, we take care to include only final goods in GNP and to exclude the intermediate goods that are used up in making the final goods. By measuring the value added at each stage, taking care to subtract expenditures on the intermediate goods bought from other firms, the lower-loop earnings approach properly avoids all double counting and records wages, interest, rent, and profit exactly one time.

Details of the National Accounts

We have now studied the bare bones of the national income and product accounts. The rest of this chapter fleshes out how the various sectors fit together. Before we start on the journey to understanding the full national income and product accounts, look at Table 6-3 to get an idea of where we are going. This table shows a summary set of accounts for both the product and the income sides.

	Bread Receipts, Costs, and Value Added (Cents per Loaf)				
Stage of production	(1) Sales receipts	(2) Cost of intermediate materials or goods			(3) Value added (wages, profit, etc.) (3) = (1) − (2)
Wheat	24	−0	=		24
Flour	33	−24	=		9
Baked dough	60	−33	=		27
Delivered bread	90	−60	=		30
	207	−117	=		90 (sum of value added)

Table 6-2. GNP sums up value added at each production stage

To avoid double counting of intermediate products, we carefully calculate value added at each stage, subtracting all the costs of materials and intermediate products not produced in that stage but bought from other businesses. Note that every black intermediate-product item both appears in column (1) and is subtracted, as a negative element, in the next stage of production in column (2). (How much would we overestimate GNP if we counted all receipts, not just value added? The overestimate would be 117 cents per loaf.)

National Accounts Overview	
Product approach	**Earnings approach**
Components of gross national product: Consumption (*C*) + Gross private domestic investment (*I*) + Government (*G*) + Net exports (*X*)	**Earnings or costs as sources of gross national product:** Wages + Interest, rent, and other property income + Indirect taxes + Depreciation + Profits
Equals: Gross national product	**Equals: Gross national product**

Table 6-3. Overview of the national income and product accounts

This table shows the major components of the two sides of the national accounts. The left side shows the components of the product approach (or upper loop); the symbols *C*, *I*, *G*, and *X* are often used to represent these four items of GNP. The right side shows the components of the earnings or cost approach (or lower loop). Each approach will ultimately add up to exactly the same GNP.

If you know the structure of the table and the definitions of the terms in it, you will be well on your way to understanding GNP and its family of components.

Real vs. Nominal GNP: "Deflating" GNP by a Price Index

We define GNP as the dollar value of goods and services. In measuring the dollar value, we use the measuring rod of *market prices* for the different goods and services. But prices change over time, as inflation generally sends prices upward year after year. Who would want to measure things with a rubber yardstick—one that stretches in your hands from day to day—rather than a rigid and invariant yardstick?

The problem of changing prices is one of the problems economists have to solve when they use money as their measuring rod. Clearly, we want a measure of the nation's output and income that uses an invariant yardstick. Economists can repair most of the damage done by the elastic yardstick by using a *price index*, which is a measure of the average price of a bundle of goods.[3]

We can measure the GNP for a particular year

using the actual market prices of that year; this gives us the **nominal GNP,** or GNP at current prices. Usually we are more interested in determining what has happened to the **real GNP,** which measures GNP in a set of constant or invariant prices. To obtain real GNP, we divide nominal GNP by a price index known as the **GNP deflator.**

A simple example will illustrate the general idea. Say that a country produces 1000 bushels of corn in year 1 and 1010 bushels in year 2. The price of a bushel is $2 in year 1 and $2.50 in year 2. We can calculate nominal GNP (*PQ*) as $2 × 1000 = $2000 in year 1 and $2.50 × 1010 = $2525 in year 2. Nominal GNP therefore grew by $26\frac{1}{4}$ percent between the two years.

But the actual amount of output did not grow anywhere near that rapidly. To find real output, we need to use the GNP deflator. We use year 1 as the *base year,* or the year in which we measure prices. We set the price index, the GNP deflator, as $P_1 = 1$ in the first year. From the data in the last paragraph, we see that the price index is $P_2 = $2.50/$2 = 1.25/1 = 1.25$ in year 2. Real GNP (*Q*) is equal to nominal GNP (*PQ*) divided by the GNP deflator (*P*). Hence real GNP was equal to $2000/1 = $2000 in year 1 and $2525/1.25 = $2020 in year 2. Thus the growth in real GNP, which corrects for the change in prices, is 1 percent and equals the growth in the output of corn, as it should.

A 1929–1933 comparison will illustrate the deflation process for an actual historical episode. Table 6-4 gives nominal GNP figures of $104 billion for

---

[3] A price index is a weighted average of prices. The price index used to remove inflation (or "deflate" the GNP) is called the *GNP deflator*. It is defined as a weighted average of the prices of all commodities in the GNP, with each good's weight equal to its percentage importance in the total GNP. A full discussion will follow in Chapter 14.

1929 and $56 billion for 1933. This represents a 46 percent drop in nominal GNP from 1929 to 1933. But the government estimates that prices on average dropped about 23 percent over this period. If we choose 1929 as our base year, with the GNP deflator of 1 in that year, this means that the 1933 price index was about 0.77. So our $56 billion 1933 GNP was really worth much more than half the $104 billion GNP of 1929. Table 6-4 shows that real GNP fell to only seven-tenths of the 1929 level: in terms of 1929 prices, or dollars of 1929 purchasing power, real GNP fell to $73 billion. Hence, part of the near-halving shown by the nominal GNP was due to the optical illusion of the shrinking price yardstick.

The black line in Figure 6-2 shows the growth of nominal GNP since 1929, expressed in the actual dollars and prices that were current in each historical year. Then, for comparison, the real GNP, expressed in 1982 dollars, is shown in blue. Clearly, part of the increase in nominal GNP over the last half-century is due to inflation in the price units of our money yardstick.

To summarize:

Nominal GNP (PQ) represents the total money value of final goods and services produced in a given year, where the values are in terms of the market prices of each year. Real GNP (Q) removes price changes from nominal GNP and calculates GNP in constant prices. Because we define the GNP deflator (P) as the price of GNP, we have:

$$Q = \text{real GNP} = \frac{\text{nominal GNP}}{\text{GNP deflator}} = \frac{PQ}{P}$$

Investment and Capital Formation

So far, our analysis has banished all capital goods and instead talked of an economy of consumers buying bread, apples, and other things. In real life, however, nations devote part of their output to production of investment goods. **Investment** (or purchases of capital goods) consists of the additions to the nation's capital stock of buildings, equipment, and inventories during a year. Investment involves the sacrifice of current consumption to increase future consumption. Instead of eating more bread now, people build new ovens to make it possible to produce more bread for future consumption.

A warning is in order here: To economists, investment means production of durable capital goods. In common usage, investment often denotes using money to buy General Motors stock or to open a savings account. Try not to confuse these two different uses of the word "investment."

If I take $1000 from my safe and put it in the bank or buy a government bond, in economic terms, no investment has taken place. All that has happened is that I have exchanged one financial asset for another. Only when production of a physical capital good takes place is there what the economist calls investment.

How does investment fit into the national accounts? If people are using part of society's production possibilities for capital formation rather than for consumption, economic statisticians recognize that such outputs must be included in the upper-loop flow of GNP. Investments represent additions to the stock of durable capital goods that increase production possibilities in the future. So we must modify our original definition to read:

Gross national product is the sum of all final products. Along with consumption goods and services, we must also include gross investment.

Net vs. Gross Investment. Our revised definition included "gross investment" along with consump-

Sample Calculation of Real GNP		
(1)	(2)	(3)
Date	Nominal GNP (current $, billion)	Index number of prices (GNP deflator, 1929 = 1)	Real GNP ($, billion, 1929 prices) $(3) = \frac{(1)}{(2)}$
1929	104	1.00	$\frac{104}{1.00} = 104$
1933	56	0.77	$\frac{56}{0.77} = 73$

Table 6-4. Real (or inflation-corrected) GNP is obtained by dividing nominal GNP by a price index, the GNP deflator

Using price index of column (2), we deflate column (1) to get real GNP, column (3).

(Riddle: Can you show that 1929's real GNP was $80 billion in terms of 1933 prices? *Hint:* With 1933 as a base of 1, 1929's price index is 1.30.)

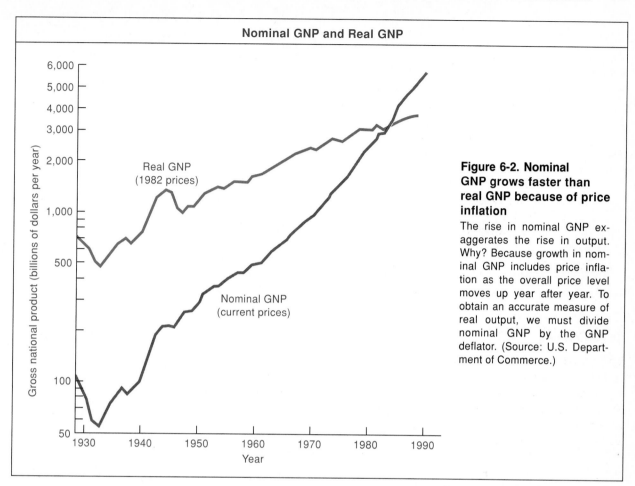

Nominal GNP and Real GNP

Gross national product (billions of dollars per year)

Real GNP
(1982 prices)

Nominal GNP
(current prices)

Year

Figure 6-2. Nominal GNP grows faster than real GNP because of price inflation

The rise in nominal GNP ex-aggerates the rise in output. Why? Because growth in nom-inal GNP includes price infla-tion as the overall price level moves up year after year. To obtain an accurate measure of real output, we must divide nominal GNP by the GNP deflator. (Source: U.S. Depart-ment of Commerce.)

tion. What does the word "gross" mean in this con-text? It indicates that investment includes all in-vestment goods produced. Gross investment is not adjusted for **depreciation,** which measures the amount of capital that has been used up in a year. Thus gross investment includes all the machines, factories, and houses built during a year—even though some were bought simply to replace some old capital goods that were thrown on the scrap heap.

If you want to get a measure of the increase in society's capital, gross investment is not a sensible measure. Because it excludes a necessary allow-ance for depreciation, it is too large—too gross.

An analogy to population will make clear the importance of considering depreciation. If you want to measure the increase in the size of the pop-ulation, you cannot simply count the number of births, for this would clearly exaggerate the net change in population. To get population growth, you must also subtract the number of deaths.

The same point holds for capital. To find the net increase in capital, you must start with gross in-vestment and subtract the deaths of capital in the form of depreciation, or the amount of capital used up.

Thus to estimate capital formation we measure net investment: net investment is always births of capital (gross investment) less deaths of capital (capital depreciation).

Net investment equals gross investment minus depreciation.

Table 6-5 provides data on both net investment and gross investment, which differ by the amount of depreciation. Typically net investment is sub-stantial. In the Great Depression, however, net in-vestment was *negative*, which indicates that the country was not investing enough to replace its capital stock.

Gross and Net Investment
(Billions of Dollars, 1982 Prices)

Investment components	1929	1933	1965	1990
Residential fixed	35.4	7.7	114.2	176.8
Business fixed	93.0	25.7	227.6	515.4
Change in business inventories	10.8	−10.7	25.2	−3.6
Gross private domestic investment	**139.2**	**22.7**	**367.0**	**688.7**
Allowances for depreciation or capital consumption (also = difference between GNP and NNP)	−86.8	−86.5	−183.6	−519.7
Net private domestic investment	**52.4**	**−63.8**	**183.4**	**169.0**

Table 6-5. To go from gross to net investment we subtract depreciation of capital

Gross births minus deaths equals any population's change. Similarly, net capital formation (or net investment) will equal gross capital formation (gross investment in all new capital goods) minus depreciation (or allowance for used-up capital goods). (Source: U.S. Department of Commerce.)

Government

Up to now we have talked about consumers but ignored the biggest consumer of all—federal, state, and local governments. Somehow GNP must take into account the billions of dollars of product a nation *collectively* consumes or invests. How do we do this?

After some debate, the income statisticians of the United States and the United Nations decided to use the simplest method of all. We simply add all government expenditures on goods and services to the flow of consumption, investment, and net exports.

These government expenditures include buying goods like roads and missiles and paying wages like those of marine colonels and weather forecasters. In short, all the government payroll expenditures on its employees plus the costs of goods (lasers, roads, and airplanes) it buys from private industry are included in this third great category of flow of products, called "government expenditure on goods and services." This category equals the contribution of federal, state, and local governments to GNP.

Exclusion of Transfer Payments. Does this mean that every dollar of government expenditure is included in GNP? Definitely not. GNP includes only government spending on goods and services; it excludes spending on transfer payments.

Government **transfer payments** are government payments to individuals that are not made in exchange for goods or services supplied. Examples of government transfers include unemployment insurance, veterans' benefits, and old-age or disability payments. They are intended to meet some form of need. Because transfers are not for purchase of a current good or service, they are omitted from GNP.

Thus if you receive a wage from the government because you are a substitute teacher, that is a factor payment and would be included in GNP. If you receive a welfare payment because you are poor, that payment is not in return for a service but is a transfer payment excluded from GNP.

One peculiar government transfer payment is the interest on the government debt. This is a return on debt incurred to pay for past wars or government programs and is not a payment for current government goods or services. Government interest payments are considered transfers and are therefore omitted from GNP.

Finally, do not confuse the way the national income accounts measure government spending on goods and services (G) with the official government budget. When the Treasury measures its expenditures, these include expenditures on goods and services (G) *plus* transfers.

Taxes. In using the flow-of-product approach to compute the GNP, we need not worry about how the government finances its spending. It does not matter whether the government pays for its goods and services by taxing, by printing money, or by borrowing. Wherever the dollars come from, the statistician computes the governmental component of GNP as the actual cost to the government of the goods and services.

It is fine to ignore taxes in the flow-of-product approach. But what about in the earnings or cost approach to GNP? Here we must account for taxes. Consider wages, for example. Part of my wages is turned over to the government through personal income taxes. These direct taxes definitely do get included in the wage component of business expenses and the same holds for direct taxes (personal or corporate) on interest, rent, and profit.

Or consider the sales tax and other indirect taxes that manufacturers and retailers have to pay on a loaf of bread (or on the wheat, flour, and dough stages). Suppose these indirect taxes total 10 cents per loaf, and suppose wages, profit, and other value-added items cost the bread industry 90 cents. What will the bread sell for in the product approach? For 90 cents? Surely not. The bread will sell for $1, equal to 90 cents of factor costs plus 10 cents of indirect taxes.

Thus the cost approach to GNP includes both indirect and direct taxes as elements of the cost of producing final output.

Net Exports

The United States is an open economy engaged in importing and exporting goods and services. The last component of GNP—increasingly important in recent years—is **net exports,** the difference between exports and imports of goods and services.

How do we draw the line between our GNP and other countries' GNPs? The U.S. GNP represents all goods and services produced by labor, capital, and other factors owned by U.S. residents. U.S. production differs from what is purchased by all sectors in the United States in two respects. First, some of our output (Iowa wheat and Boeing aircraft) is bought by foreigners and shipped abroad. Combining these sales abroad with earnings on American capital located abroad, we obtain *exports.* Second, some of what we consume (Mexican oil and Japanese cars) is produced abroad and shipped to the United States. Adding to these purchases the earn-

ings foreigners receive from foreign capital in the United States yields our *imports.*

For most of the last half-century, exports exceeded imports, and net exports were positive. During the 1980s, however, U.S. imports grew rapidly and net exports decreased sharply. As a result, the United States incurred a large trade deficit. We will study the sources and implications of the large trade deficit in the final four chapters of this text.

A Numerical Example. We can use a simple farming economy to understand how the national accounts work. Suppose that Agrovia produces 100 bushels of corn. Of these, 87 bushels are consumed (in C), 10 go for government purchases to feed the army (as G), and 6 go into domestic investment as increases in inventories (I). In addition, 4 bushels are exported while 7 bushels are imported, for net exports (X) of minus 3.

What then is the composition of the GNP of Agrovia? It is the following:

$$\text{GNP} = 87 \text{ of } C + 10 \text{ of } G + 6 \text{ of } I - 3 \text{ of } X$$
$$= 100 \text{ bushels}$$

A Simplification. In our survey of macroeconomics, we will sometimes simplify our discussion by combining domestic investment with net exports to get *total gross national investment,* which we will call I_n. Put differently, we measure total national investment as net exports plus domestic investment in new capital goods. Let us see why. When a nation exports more than it imports, it is investing the excess (the net exports) abroad. This component is called *net foreign investment.* This foreign investment should be added to domestic capital formation to obtain the total amount that the nation is setting aside for the future—that is, the total national investment.

Gross National Product, Net National Product, and Gross Domestic Product

Although GNP is the most widely used measure of national output in the United States, two other concepts are widely cited: net national product and gross domestic product.

Recall that GNP includes *gross* investment, which is net investment plus depreciation. A little thought suggests that including depreciation is rather like including wheat as well as bread. A better measure would include only *net* investment in total output. By subtracting depreciation from GNP we obtain **net national product (NNP).**

If NNP is a sounder measure of a nation's output than GNP, why do economists and journalists work with GNP? They do so because depreciation is somewhat difficult to estimate, whereas gross investment can be estimated fairly accurately.

An alternative measure of national output, widely used outside the United States, is **gross domestic product (GDP).** This is the total output produced inside a country during a given year. For example, Fords produced with U.S.-owned capital located in Britain are included in U.S. GNP but excluded from U.S. GDP. Can you see why these Fords are in Britain's GDP but not in its GNP?

To summarize:

Net national product (NNP) equals the total final output produced by a nation during a year, where output includes net investment or gross investment less depreciation:

$$\text{NNP} = \text{GNP} - \text{depreciation}$$

Gross domestic product (GDP) is the total final output produced within a country during a year.

We can now give a final comprehensive definition of important components of GNP:

- GNP from the product side is the sum of four major components, as listed below:
  1. Personal consumption expenditure on goods and services (*C*)
  2. Gross private domestic investment (*I*)
  3. Government expenditures on goods and services (*G*)
  4. Net exports (*X*), or exports minus imports
- GNP from the cost side is the sum of the following major components:
  1. Wages, interest, rents, and profit (always with the careful exclusion, by the value-added technique, of double counting of intermediate goods bought from other firms)
  2. Indirect business taxes that show up as an expense of producing the flow of products
  3. Depreciation
- The product and cost measures of GNP yield identical amounts by definition (i.e., by adher-

ence to the rules of value-added bookkeeping and the definition of profit as a residual).
- Net national product (NNP) equals GNP minus depreciation.

GNP and NNP: A Look at Numbers

Armed with an understanding of the concepts, we can turn to a look at the actual data in the important Table 6-6.

Flow-of-Product Approach. Look first at the left side of the table. It gives the upper-loop *flow-of-product* approach to GNP. Each of the four major components appears there, along with the production in each component for 1990. Of these, *C* and *G* and their obvious subclassifications require little discussion.

Gross private domestic investment does require one comment. Its total ($741 billion) includes all new business fixed investment in plant and equipment, residential construction, and increase in inventory of goods. This gross total excludes subtraction for depreciation of capital. After subtracting $520 billion of depreciation from gross investment, we obtain $169 billion of net investment.

Finally, note the large negative entry for *net exports*, −$31 billion. This negative entry represents the fact that in 1990 the United States imported $31 billion more in goods and services than it exported.

Adding up the four components on the left gives the total GNP of $5465 billion. This is the harvest we have been working for: the money measure of the American economy's overall performance for 1990.

Lower-Loop Flow-of-Cost Approach. Now turn to the right-hand side of the table. Here we have all *net costs of production* plus *taxes* and *depreciation*.

Wages and other employee supplements include all take-home pay, fringe benefits, and taxes on wages. *Net interest* is a similar item. Remember that interest on government debt is not included as part of *G* or of GNP but is treated as a transfer.

Rent income of persons includes rents received by landlords. In addition, if you own your own home, you are treated as *paying rent to yourself.* This is one of many "imputations" (or derived data) in the national accounts. It makes sense if we really want to measure the housing services the American

Gross National Product, 1990 (Billions of Current Dollars)					
Product approach			**Earnings or cost approach**		
1. Personal consumption expenditure		$3,657	1. Wages and other employee supplements		$3,244
Durable goods	$ 480		2. Net interest		467
Nondurable goods	1,194		3. Rental income of persons		7
Services	1,983		4. Indirect business taxes, adjustments, and statistical discrepancy		526
2. Gross private domestic investment		741	5. Depreciation		520
Residential fixed	222		6. Income of unincorporated enterprises		403
Business fixed	524		7. Corporate profits before taxes		298
Change in inventories	−5		Dividends	134	
3. Government purchases of goods and services		1,098	Undistributed profits	32	
			Corporate profit taxes	132	
4. Net exports		−31			
Exports	673				
Imports	704				
Gross national product		**$5,465**	**Gross national product**		**$5,465**

Table 6-6. Here are the two ways of looking at the GNP accounts in actual numbers

The left side measures flow of products (at market prices). The right side measures flow of costs (factor earnings and depreciation plus indirect taxes). (Source: U.S. Department of Commerce.)

people are enjoying and do not want the estimate to change when people decide to own a home rather than rent one.

Indirect business taxes, as we saw earlier, must be included as a separate item in the income approach if we are to match the product approach. Any direct taxes on wages, interests, or rents were already included directly in those items, so they must not be included again. We have included with indirect business taxes some adjustments: business transfer payments and the inevitable "statistical discrepancy," which reflects the fact that the officials never have every bit of needed data.[4]

[4] Statisticians must always work with incomplete reports and fill in data gaps by estimation. Just as measurements in a chemistry lab differ from the ideal, so, in fact, do errors creep into both upper- and lower-loop GNP estimates. These are reconnected by an item called the "statistical discrepancy." Along with the civil servants who are heads of units called "Wages," "Interest," and so forth, there actually used to be someone with the title "Head of the Statistical Discrepancy." If data were perfect, that individual would have been out of a job; but because real life is never perfect, that person's task of reconciliation was one of the hardest of all.

Depreciation on capital goods that were used up must appear as an expense in GNP, just like other expenses.

Profit comes last because it is the residual—what is left over after all other costs have been subtracted from total sales. There are two kinds of profits: profit of corporations and net earnings of unincorporated enterprises.

Income of unincorporated enterprises refers to earnings of partnerships and single-ownership businesses. This includes much farm and professional income.

Finally, *corporate profits before taxes* are shown. This entry's $298 billion includes corporate profit *taxes* of $132 billion. The remainder then goes to dividends or to undistributed corporate profits; the latter amount of $32 billion is what you leave or "plow back" into the business and is called *net corporate saving.*

On the right side, the flow-of-cost approach gives us the same $5465 billion of GNP as the flow-of-product approach. The right and left sides do agree.

tion of useless goods. As one dissenter said, "Don't speak to me of all your numbers and dollars, your gross national product. To me, GNP stands for gross national pollution!"

What are we to think? Isn't it true that GNP includes government purchases of bombs and missiles? Doesn't cutting our irreplaceable redwoods show up as a positive output in our national accounts? Does modern economics make a fetish of quantity of products at the expense of quality of life?

In recent years, economists have attempted to correct the defects of the official GNP numbers so that they better reflect the true satisfaction-producing products of our economy. One approach has been to construct a more meaningful measure of national output, called **net economic welfare,** or NEW. NEW is based upon GNP but makes two major changes.[6] First, NEW excludes many components of GNP that do not contribute to individual well-being; and second, some key consumption items that are omitted from GNP are included in NEW.

Net economic welfare (NEW) is an adjusted measure of total national output that includes only consumption and investment items that contribute directly to economic well-being.

We will describe the major elements of NEW.

Pluses: Value of Leisure Time. Suppose you decide, as you become more affluent, to work fewer hours, to get your psychic satisfactions from leisure as well as from goods and services. Then the measured GNP goes down even though welfare goes up. So, to correct for the psychic satisfaction of leisure, a positive correction must be added to get NEW from GNP.

Consider also do-it-yourself work done in the home—cooking meals or insulating walls. Because

[6] The discussion here is drawn from William Nordhaus and James Tobin, "Is Growth Obsolete?" in *Fiftieth Anniversary Colloquium V* (National Bureau of Economic Research, Columbia University Press, New York, 1972). We have replaced the earlier concept, a measure of economic welfare (MEW), by the more informative label "net economic welfare" (NEW). Further refinements have been undertaken by Japanese economists (who have constructed a series known as net national welfare) and by Robert Eisner, who estimates broader income and output measures in a total incomes system of accounts, or TISA [see Robert Eisner, "The Total Incomes System of Accounts," *Survey of Current Business* (January 1985), pp. 24–48].

the values added are not bought or sold in markets, they never enter into the goods and services of the GNP—neither in the upper loop nor in the lower loop. An estimate of NEW will need to include the value of similar do-it-yourself activities.

Pluses: The Underground Economy. In recent years, many economists claim to have detected an explosive growth in the underground economy. Underground activities are of two kinds: activities that are illegal (such as the drug trade or murder for hire), and activities that are legal but unrecorded for tax purposes (such as the work of a carpenter who builds your garage in the evenings in return for your personal advice about her finances).

In general, national accountants exclude illegal activities from a measure of national output—these are by social consensus "bads" and not "goods." A swelling cocaine trade will not enter into either GNP or NEW.

What about the second source of underground activity: the array of carpenters, doctors, babysitters, and farmers who produce valuable goods and services but might escape the net of national output statisticians? Several economists, led by Edward Feige and Peter Gutmann, claim that this sector is booming. They examine financial data (particularly the use of cash, which is the major means of payment in the underground economy) and conclude that real GNP growth in the last two decades was significantly understated because of the omission of underground activity. Some point to high tax rates as an incentive to work in the underground economy.

Some evidence confirms these views. Recent studies indicate that the overall level of compliance with the federal income-tax system has been falling in recent years. The result is that a larger fraction of national income escapes the tax collector's beady eye.

Others are skeptical. While not denying that between 5 and 10 percent of economic output is unreported to the Internal Revenue Service, these skeptics doubt whether the amount is growing. They point out that the national accounts already make imputations for unreported activities.

A careful examination by Edward Denison argues that the major source of error in the national accounts would arise from understatement of employment. But the reported employment data come from two completely independent sources (households and firms), and these two sources give much the same estimate of the growth of employment over the last two decades. Denison concludes that, given the consistency in the two different estimates of employment, "growth of national income and product is not being understated much as a result of growth of the underground economy."[7]

Minuses: Environmental Damage. Sometimes GNP counts the "goods" produced but ignores the "bads." For example, suppose the residents of Suburbia buy 10 million kilowatt-hours of electricity to cool their houses, paying Utility Co. 10 cents per kilowatt-hour. That $1 million covers the labor costs, plant costs, and fuel costs. But suppose the company damages the neighborhood with sulfur from fuel burned to produce electricity. It incurs no money costs for this externality. Our measure of output should not only add in the value of the electricity (which GNP does) but also subtract the environmental damage from the pollution (which GNP does not).[8]

To continue our example, suppose that in addition to paying 10 cents of direct costs, the surrounding neighborhood suffers 1 cent per kilowatt-hour of environmental damage. This is the cost of pollution (to trees, trout, streams, and people) not

paid by Utility Co. Then the total "external" cost is $100,000. To correct for these hidden costs and construct NEW, we must subtract $100,000 of "pollution bads" from the $1,000,000 flow of "electricity goods."

Economists have just begun the difficult task of constructing measures of national output that correct the GNP for pollution, congestion, depletion of natural resources, and other shortcomings. Preliminary studies suggest that NEW grows more slowly than does GNP. This difference may be inevitable in a world in which population and congestion are increasing and in which human interventions sometimes overwhelm the capacity of nature to absorb human wastes.

Having reviewed the measurement of national output and analyzed the shortcomings of the GNP, what should we conclude about the adequacy of our national accounts as measures of economic welfare? The answer was aptly stated in a review by Arthur Okun:

> It should be no surprise that national prosperity does not guarantee a happy society, any more than personal prosperity ensures a happy family. No growth of GNP can counter the tensions arising from an unpopular and unsuccessful war, a long overdue self-confrontation with conscience on racial injustice, a volcanic eruption of sexual mores, and an unprecedented assertion of independence by the young. Still, prosperity . . . is a precondition for success in achieving many of our aspirations.[9]

---

[7] Edward F. Denison, "Is U.S. Growth Understated Because of the Underground Economy? Employment Ratios Suggest Not," *Review of Income and Wealth* (October 1982).

[8] Why do the pollution costs not enter GNP? They are omitted because no one buys or sells the damage from the sulfur emissions. Recall our discussion of externalities in Chapter 3.

[9] *The Political Economy of Prosperity* (Norton, New York, 1970), p. 124.

SUMMARY
---

1. The gross national product (or GNP) is the most comprehensive measure of a nation's production of goods and services. It comprises the dollar value of consumption (C), gross private domestic investment (I), government purchases of goods and services (G), and net exports (X). Recall the formula:

$$GNP = C + I + G + X$$

This will sometimes be simplified by combining domestic investment and net exports into total gross national investment (I_n):

$$GNP = C + I_n + G$$

2. Because of the way we define residual profit, we can match the upper-loop flow-of-product measurement of GNP with the lower-loop flow-of-cost mea-

surement, as shown in Figure 6-1. The flow-of-cost approach uses factor earnings and carefully computes values added to eliminate double counting of intermediate products. And after summing up all (before-tax) wage, interest, rent, depreciation, and profit income, it adds to this total all indirect tax costs of business. GNP definitely does not include transfer items such as interest on government bonds or receipt of welfare payments.

3. By use of a price index, we can "deflate" nominal GNP (GNP in current dollars) to arrive at a more accurate measure of real GNP (GNP expressed in dollars of some base year's purchasing power). Use of such a price index corrects for the rubber yardstick implied by changing levels of prices.

4. Net investment is positive when the nation is producing more capital goods than are currently being used up in the form of depreciation. Since depreciation is hard to estimate accurately, statisticians have more confidence in their measures of gross investment than in those of net investment.

5. National income and disposable income are two additional official measurements. Disposable income (*DI*) is what people actually have left—after all tax payments, corporate saving of undistributed profits, and transfer adjustments have been made—to spend on consumption or to save.

6. Using the rules of the national accounts, measured saving must exactly equal measured investment. This is easily seen in a hypothetical economy with nothing but households. In a complete economy, the identity is

$$I_n = PS + GBS + GS$$

where total gross national investment (I_n, which equals both domestic and foreign investment) equals net personal saving (*PS*) plus gross business saving (*GBS*) plus net government saving (*GS*).

The identity between saving and investment is just that: saving must equal investment no matter whether the economy is in boom or recession, war or peace. It is a consequence of the definitions of national-income accounting.

7. Gross national product is an imperfect measure of genuine economic welfare. An alternative approach is net economic welfare (NEW). The calculation of NEW adds to NNP certain items—such as value of leisure, the services of homemakers, and do-it-yourself activities. It also subtracts from NNP such things as unmet costs of pollution and other disamenities of modern urbanization.

CONCEPTS FOR REVIEW

GNP
GNP deflator
GNP = $C + I + G + X$
GNP = $C + I_n + G$
GNP in two equivalent views:
 product (upper loop) and
 earnings (lower loop)

†intermediate goods, value added
 nominal and real GNP
 net investment = gross
  investment − depreciation
 NNP = GNP − depreciation
 gross domestic product (GDP)
 government transfers

disposable income (*DI*)
$I_n = S$
 = $PS + GBS + GS$
NEW = NNP + leisure and
  underground activity − pollution
  and disamenities

QUESTIONS FOR DISCUSSION

1. Define carefully the following and give an example of each:
   (a) Consumption
   (b) Gross private domestic investment
   (c) Government purchase of a good (in GNP)
   (d) Government transfer payment (not in GNP)
   (e) Export

2. "You can't add apples and oranges." Show that by using prices we do this in constructing GNP.

3. Consider the following data: Nominal GNP for 1990 was $5465 billion, as compared to $5201 for 1989. The GNP deflator for 1990 was 131.5, as compared to 126.3 for 1989. The GNP deflator was 100 in 1982.

   Calculate real GNP for 1989 and 1990, in 1982 prices. Calculate the rates of growth of nominal GNP and real GNP for 1990. What was the rate of inflation (as measured by the GNP deflator) for 1990?

4. Robinson Crusoe produces upper-loop product of $1000. He pays $750 in wages, $125 in interest, and $75 in rent. What *must* his profit be? If three-fourths of Crusoe's output is consumed and the rest invested, calculate Crusoeland's GNP in both the product and the income approaches and show that they must agree exactly.

5. Here are some brain teasers. Can you see why the following are *not* counted in GNP?
   (a) The home meals produced by a fine chef
   (b) Purchase of a plot of land
   (c) Purchase of an original Rembrandt painting
   (d) The value I get in 1992 from playing a 1985 Rolling Stones compact disk
   (e) Pollution damage to houses and crops from sulfur emitted by electric utilities

6. Consider the items listed in question 5. Analyze how each should be treated in NEW.

7. Consider the country of Agrovia, whose GNP is discussed in "A Numerical Example" on page 93. Construct a set of national accounts like that in Table 6-6 assuming that wheat costs $5 per bushel, there is no depreciation, wages are three-fourths of national output, indirect business taxes are used to finance government spending, and the balance of income goes as rent income to farmers.

CONSUMPTION AND INVESTMENT

There's many a slip 'twixt the cup and the lip.
Anonymous

Patterns of consumption and investment play a crucial role in a nation's economy. Nations that consume most of their incomes, such as the United States, tend to invest relatively little and show modest rates of economic growth. By contrast, those nations that consume a small fraction of their incomes tend to invest heavily; these countries—for example, Japan or Hong Kong—have rapidly growing output and productivity.

This chapter probes the reasons lying behind trends in consumption and investment. We will attempt to understand how people choose between saving and consumption and will see that poor people tend to save less than well-to-do people. In addition, we will study the determinants of investment, including such factors as taxes, interest rates, and expectations.

We study these topics not only for their intrinsic interest but also because consumption and investment are important determinants of the overall level of output and employment in the short run. When spending on investment and consumption grows rapidly, output as a whole tends to grow as well. Why is this? We will see in the next chapters that total output in the short run is significantly affected by the interplay of consumption and investment. When favorable tax treatment or growing markets give a spur to business investment—as was the case in the 1960s and the late 1980s—aggregate demand expands and output and employment grow rapidly. When business confidence withers or when the stock market declines—as happened during the 1930s and in the early 1980s—investment declines, aggregate demand falls, and output and employment fall.

This chapter begins the thorough study of the determination of aggregate demand by focusing upon the behavior of consumption and investment. Figure 7-1 shows how this chapter's analysis fits into the overall structure of the macroeconomy. Once we have surveyed consumption and investment, we can in the next chapter put these two components together into the simplest model of income determination—the multiplier model.

The tools introduced in the next few chapters form the intellectual core of what is called *Keynesian economics*. When introduced a half-century ago by the English economist John Maynard Keynes, these concepts were as foreign to the then practicing economists as "quarks" or "charm" are to freshmen in a modern college physics course. Today, many of the elements of Keynes' thinking—such as his theories about consumption and investment—are part of the language of modern economics.

A. Consumption and Saving

We begin our discussion with an analysis of consumption and savings behavior, first examining individual spending patterns and then looking at aggregate consumption behavior. Recall from

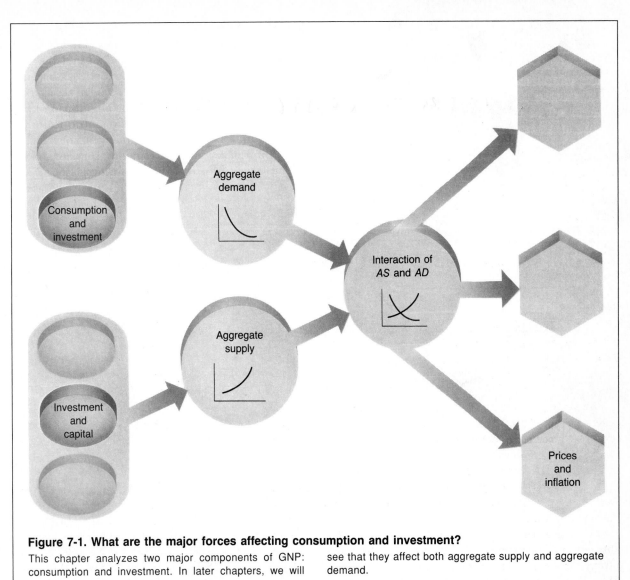

Figure 7-1. What are the major forces affecting consumption and investment?

This chapter analyzes two major components of GNP: consumption and investment. In later chapters, we will see that they affect both aggregate supply and aggregate demand.

Chapter 6 that household consumption is spending on final goods and services bought for the satisfaction gained or needs met by their use. Household saving, on the other hand, is by definition that part of income not spent on consumption.

Consumption is the largest single component of GNP, constituting 66 percent of total spending over the last decade. What are the major elements of consumption? Among the most important categories are housing, motor vehicles, food, and medical care. Table 7-1 displays the major elements, broken down into the three categories of durable goods, nondurable goods, and services. The items themselves are familiar, but their relative importance, particularly the increasing importance of services, is worth a moment's study.

Budgetary Expenditure Patterns

How do the patterns of consumption spending differ across different households in the United States?

No two families spend their disposable income in exactly the same way. Yet statistics show that there is a predictable regularity in the way people allocate their expenditures among food, clothing,

Consumption, 1990		
Category of consumption	Value of category ($, billion)	Percent of total
Durable goods	480	13
Motor vehicles	213	
Household equipment	177	
Other	90	
Nondurable goods	1,194	33
Food	625	
Clothing and apparel	213	
Energy	94	
Other	262	
Services	1,983	54
Housing	570	
Medical care	483	
Personal business	159	
Education	51	
Other	720	
Total, personal consumption expenditures	3,657	100

Table 7-1. The major components of consumption

Consumption is divided into three categories: durable goods, nondurable goods, and services. The size of the service sector is becoming increasingly large as basic needs for food are met and as health, recreation, and education claim a larger part of family budgets. (Source: U.S. Department of Commerce.)

and other major items. The thousands of budgetary investigations of household spending patterns show remarkable agreement on the general, qualitative patterns of behavior.[1] Figure 7-2 tells the story. Poor families must spend their incomes largely on the necessities of life: food and shelter. As income increases, expenditure on many food items goes up. People eat more and eat better. There are, however, limits to the extra money people will spend on food when their incomes rise. Consequently, the proportion of total spending devoted to food declines as income increases.

Expenditure on clothing, recreation, and auto-

---

[1] The spending patterns shown in Fig. 7-2 are called "Engel's Laws," after the nineteenth-century Prussian statistician Ernst Engel. The average behavior of consumption expenditure does change fairly regularly with income. But averages do not tell the whole story. Within each income class, there is a considerable spread of consumption around the average.

mobiles increases more than proportionately to after-tax income, until high incomes are reached. Spending on luxury items increases in greater proportion than income. Finally, as we look across families, note that saving rises very rapidly as income increases. Saving is the greatest luxury good of all.

Consumption, Income, and Saving

We suggested above that there is a close tie between income, consumption, and saving. What is the exact relationship?

Actually, the idea is simple. **Saving** is that part of income that is not consumed. That is, saving equals income minus consumption. The relationship between income, consumption, and saving for the United States in 1990 is shown in Table 7-2. Begin

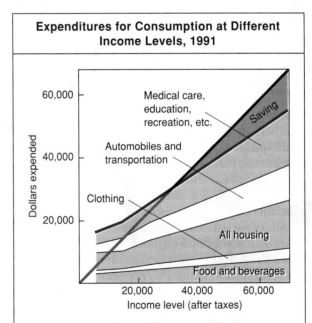

Figure 7-2. Family budget expenditures show regular patterns

Careful sampling of families and of individuals verifies the importance of disposable income as a determinant of consumption expenditure. Notice the drop in food as a percentage of higher incomes. Note also the rise in saving, from less than zero at very low incomes to substantial amounts at high incomes. [Source: U.S. Department of Labor, *Consumer Expenditure Survey: Interview Survey 1984* (August 1986), updated to 1991 prices by authors.]

Item	Amount, 1990 Billions of Dollars
Personal income	**4,646**
Less: Personal tax and nontax payments	700
Equals: Personal disposable income	**3,946**
Less: Personal consumption outlays (consumption and interest)	3,767
Equals: Personal saving	**179**
Memo: Saving as percent of personal disposable income	**4.5**

Source: U.S. Department of Commerce.

Table 7-2. Saving equals disposable income less consumption

with personal income (composed, as Chapter 6 showed, of wages, interest, rents, dividends, transfer payments, and so forth). In 1990, 15 percent of personal income went to personal tax and nontax payments. This left $3946 billion of personal disposable income. Household outlays for consumption (including interest) amounted to 95.5 percent of disposable income, or $3767 billion, leaving $179 billion as personal saving. The last item in the table shows the important **personal savings rate.** This is equal to personal saving as a percent of disposable income (4.5 percent in 1990).

Economic studies have shown that income is the primary determinant of consumption and saving. Rich people save more than poor people, both absolutely and also as a percent of income. The very poor are unable to save at all. Instead, as long as they can borrow or draw down their wealth, they tend to *dissave*. That is, they tend to spend more than they earn, reducing their accumulated saving or going deeper into debt.

Table 7-3 contains illustrative data on disposable income, saving, and consumption drawn from budget studies on American households. The first column shows seven different levels of disposable income. Column (2) indicates saving at each level of income, and the third column indicates consumption spending at each level of income.

The *break-even point*—where the representative household neither saves nor dissaves but consumes all its income—comes at around $25,000. Below the break-even point, say at $24,000, the household actually consumes more than its income; it dissaves (see the −$110 item). Above $25,000 it begins to show positive saving [see the +$150 and other positive items in column (2)].

Column (3) shows the consumption spending for each income level. Since each dollar of income is divided between the part consumed and the remaining part saved, columns (3) and (2) are not independent; they must always exactly add up to column (1).

	(1) Disposable income ($)	(2) Net saving (+) or dissaving (−) ($)	(3) Consumption ($)
A	24,000	−110	24,110
B	25,000	0	25,000
C	26,000	+150	25,850
D	27,000	+400	26,600
E	28,000	+760	27,240
F	29,000	+1,170	27,830
G	30,000	+1,640	28,360

Household Saving and Consumption

Table 7-3. Consumption and saving are primarily determined by income

This table shows average levels of consumption and saving at different levels of disposable income. The break-even point at which people cease to dissave and begin to do positive saving is shown here at $25,000. How much of each extra dollar do people devote to extra consumption at this income level? How much to extra saving? (Answer: About 85 cents and 15 cents, respectively, when we compare row B and row C.)

To understand the way consumption affects national output, we need to introduce some new tools. We need to understand how many *extra* dollars of consumption and saving are induced by each *extra* dollar of income. This relationship is shown by:

- The consumption function, relating consumption and income; and its twin,
- The savings function, relating saving and income

The Consumption Function

One of the most important relationships in all macroeconomics is the consumption function. The **consumption function** shows the relationship between the level of consumption expenditures and the level of disposable personal income. This concept, introduced by Keynes, is based on the hypothesis that there is a stable empirical relationship between consumption and income.

We can see the consumption function most vividly in the form of a graph. Figure 7-3 plots the seven levels of income listed in Table 7-3. Disposable income [column (1) of Table 7-3] is placed on the horizontal axis, and consumption [column (3)] is on the vertical axis. Each of the income-consumption combinations is represented by a single point, and the points are then connected by a smooth curve.

The relation between consumption and income shown in Figure 7-3 is called the consumption function.

The "Break-Even" Point. To understand the figure, it is helpful to look at the 45° line drawn northeast from the origin. Because the vertical and horizontal axes have exactly the same scale, the 45° line has a very special property. At any point on the 45° line, the distance up from the horizontal axis (consumption) exactly equals the distance across from the vertical axis (disposable income). You can use your eyes or a ruler to verify this fact.

The 45° line tells us immediately whether consumption spending is equal to, greater than, or less than the level of income. The point on the consumption schedule that intersects the 45° line represents the level of disposable income at which households just break even.

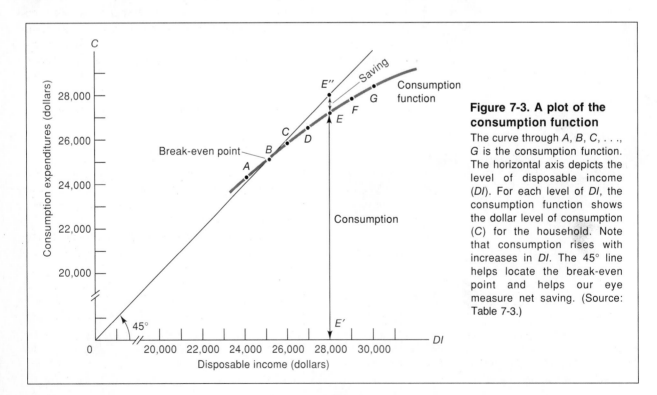

Figure 7-3. A plot of the consumption function

The curve through *A, B, C, . . ., G* is the consumption function. The horizontal axis depicts the level of disposable income (*DI*). For each level of *DI*, the consumption function shows the dollar level of consumption (*C*) for the household. Note that consumption rises with increases in *DI*. The 45° line helps locate the break-even point and helps our eye measure net saving. (Source: Table 7-3.)

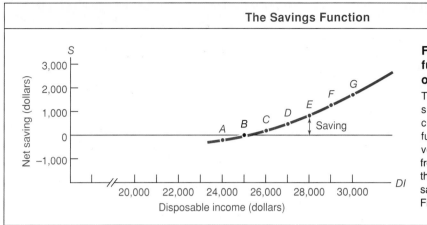

The Savings Function

Figure 7-4. The savings function is the mirror image of the consumption function

This savings schedule is derived by subtracting consumption from income. Graphically, the savings function is obtained by subtracting vertically the consumption function from the 45° line in Fig. 7-3. Note that the break-even point B is at the same $25,000 income level as in Fig. 7-3.

This break-even point is at B in Figure 7-3. Here, consumption expenditure is exactly equal to disposable income: the household is neither a borrower nor a saver. To the right of point B, the consumption function lies below the 45° line. The relationship between income and consumption can be seen by examining the thin black line from E' to E in Figure 7-3. At an income of $28,000 the level of consumption is $27,240 (see Table 7-3). We can see that consumption is less than income by the fact that the consumption function lies below the 45° line at point E.

What a household is not spending, it must be saving. The 45° line enables us to find how much the household is saving. Net saving is measured by the vertical distance from the consumption function up to the 45° line, as shown by the EE'' savings arrow in blue.

The 45° line tells us that to the left of point B the household is spending more than its income. The excess of consumption over income is "dissaving" and is measured by the vertical distance between the consumption function and the 45° line.

To review:

At any point on the 45° line, consumption exactly equals income and the household has zero saving. When the consumption function lies above the 45° line, the household is dissaving. When the consumption function lies below the 45° line, the household has positive saving. The amount of dissaving or saving is always measured by the vertical distance between the consumption function and the 45° line.

The Savings Function. The **savings function** shows the relationship between the level of saving and income. This is shown graphically in Figure 7-4. Again we show disposable income on the horizontal axis; but now saving, whether negative or positive in amount, is on the vertical axis.

This savings function comes directly from Figure 7-3. It is the vertical distance between the 45° line and the consumption function. For example, at point A in Figure 7-3, we see that the household's saving is negative because the consumption function lies above the 45° line. Figure 7-4 shows this dissaving directly—the savings function is below the zero-savings line at point A. Similarly, positive saving occurs to the right of point B because the savings function is above the zero-savings line.

The Marginal Propensity to Consume

Modern macroeconomics attaches much importance to the response of consumption to changes in income. This concept is called the marginal propensity to consume, or *MPC*.

The **marginal propensity to consume** is the extra amount that people consume when they receive an extra dollar of income.

The word "marginal" is used throughout economics to mean extra or additional. For example, "marginal cost" means the additional cost of producing an extra unit of output. "Propensity to consume" designates the desired level of consumption. *MPC*, then, is the additional or extra consumption that results from an extra dollar of income.

Table 7-4 rearranges Table 7-3's data in a more convenient form. First, verify its similarity to Table 7-3. Then, look at columns (1) and (2) to see how consumption expenditure goes up with higher levels of income.

Column (3) shows how we compute the marginal propensity to consume. From B to C, income rises by $1000, going from $25,000 to $26,000. How much does consumption rise? Consumption grows from $25,000 to $25,850, an increase of $850. The extra consumption is therefore 0.85 of the extra income. Out of each extra dollar of income, 85 cents goes to consumption and 15 cents goes to saving. As we move from point B to point C, we see that the marginal propensity to consume, or MPC, is 0.85.

You can compute MPC between other income levels. In Table 7-4, MPC begins at 0.89 for the poor and finally falls to 0.53 at higher incomes.

Marginal Propensity to Consume as Geometrical Slope. We now know how to calculate the MPC from data on income and consumption. We also want to understand how to calculate MPC graphically; we will see that the MPC is given by the slope of the consumption function.

Figure 7-5 shows how to calculate the MPC graphically. Near points B and C a little right triangle is drawn. As income increases by $1000 from point B to point C, the amount of consumption rises by $850. The MPC in this range is therefore $850/$1000 = 0.85. But, as the appendix to Chapter 1 showed, the slope of a line is "the rise over the

	Consumption and Saving				
	(1) Disposable income (after taxes) ($)	(2) Consumption expenditure ($)	(3) Marginal propensity to consume (MPC)	(4) Net saving ($) (4) = (1) − (2)	(5) Marginal propensity to save (MPS)
A	24,000	24,110		−110	
			$\frac{890}{1,000} = 0.89$		$\frac{110}{1,000} = 0.11$
B	25,000	25,000		0	
			$\frac{850}{1,000} = 0.85$		$\frac{150}{1,000} = 0.15$
C	26,000	25,850		+150	
			$\frac{750}{1,000} = 0.75$		$\frac{250}{1,000} = 0.25$
D	27,000	26,600		+400	
			$\frac{640}{1,000} = 0.64$		$\frac{360}{1,000} = 0.36$
E	28,000	27,240		+760	
			$\frac{590}{1,000} = 0.59$		$\frac{410}{1,000} = 0.41$
F	29,000	27,830		+1,170	
			$\frac{530}{1,000} = 0.53$		$\frac{470}{1,000} = 0.47$
G	30,000	28,360		+1,640	

Table 7-4. The marginal propensities to consume and to save

Each dollar of income not consumed is saved. Each dollar of extra income goes either into extra consumption or into extra saving. Combining these facts allows us to calculate the marginal propensity to consume (MPC) and the marginal propensity to save (MPS).

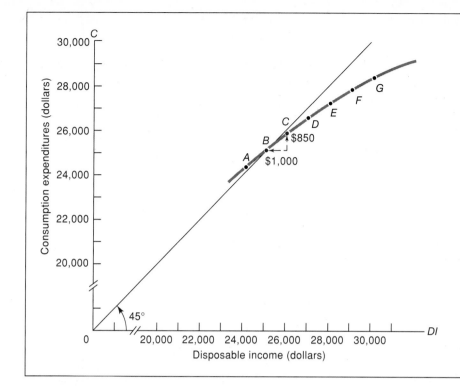

Figure 7-5. The slope of the consumption function is its MPC

To calculate the marginal propensity to consume (MPC), we measure the slope of the consumption function by forming a right triangle and relating height to base. From point B to point C, the increase in consumption is $850 while the change in disposable income is $1000. The slope, equal to the change in C divided by the change in DI, gives the MPC. If the consumption function is everywhere upward-sloping, what does this imply about the MPC?

run." We can therefore see that the slope of the consumption function between points B and C is 0.85.*

The slope of the consumption function, which measures the change in consumption per dollar change in income, is the marginal propensity to consume.

The Marginal Propensity to Save

Along with the marginal propensity to consume goes its mirror image, the marginal propensity to save, or MPS. The **marginal propensity to save** is defined as the fraction of an extra dollar of income that goes to extra saving.

Why are MPC and MPS related like mirror images? Recall that income equals consumption plus saving. This implies that each extra dollar of income must be divided between extra consumption and extra saving. Thus if MPC is 0.85, then MPS must be 0.15. (What would MPS be if MPC were 0.6? Or 0.99?) Comparing columns (3) and (5) of Table 7-4 confirms that at any income level, MPC and MPS must always add up to *exactly* 1, no more and

---

*The slope of lines was discussed in Chapter 1's appendix, but a brief review may be helpful. The numerical slope of a line can be illustrated with the help of the right triangle in Fig. 7-6. By the numerical slope of the line XW, we always mean the numerical ratio of the length of ZW to the length XZ. The slope is "the rise over the run."

If the line XW were not straight, as is the case of many curves in economics, then we would calculate the slope as the tangent.

That is, if you want to find the slope at point G in Fig. 7-5, you (1) first place a ruler tangent to the curve at point G, then (2) calculate the slope as the rise over the run of the tangent line created by the ruler.

In the case of the consumption function, its slope *is* the MPC, or the marginal propensity to consume. Similarly, if the curve is the savings function, its slope is defined as the marginal propensity to save, or the MPS.

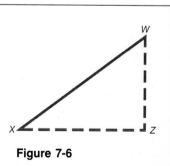

Figure 7-6

no less. Everywhere and always, $MPS \equiv 1 - MPC$.

Brief Review of Definitions

Let's review briefly the main definitions we have learned:

1. The consumption function relates the level of consumption to the level of disposable income.
2. The savings function relates saving to disposable income. Because what is saved equals what is not consumed, savings and consumption schedules are mirror images.
3. The marginal propensity to consume (*MPC*) is the amount of extra consumption generated by an extra dollar of income. Graphically, it is given by the slope of the consumption function.
4. The marginal propensity to save (*MPS*) is the extra saving generated by an extra dollar of income. Graphically, this is the slope of the savings schedule.
5. Because the part of each dollar of income that is not consumed is necessarily saved, $MPS \equiv 1 - MPC$.

National Consumption Behavior

Up to now we have examined the budget patterns and consumption behavior of typical families at different incomes. We now turn to a discussion of consumption for the nation as a whole. This transition from household behavior to national trends exemplifies the methodology of macroeconomics: we begin by examining economic activity on the individual level and then aggregate individuals to study the way the overall economy operates.

Why are we interested in national consumption trends? Consumption is important, first, because it is a major component of aggregate spending, and our task in these chapters is to understand the determination of aggregate demand. Second, what is not consumed—what is saved—is available to the nation for investment, and investment serves as a driving force behind long-term economic growth. Consumption and saving behavior are key to understanding economic growth and business cycles.

Determinants of Consumption

We begin by analyzing the major forces that affect consumer spending. What factors in a nation's life and livelihood set the pace of its consumption outlays?

Current Disposable Income. Figure 7-7 shows how closely consumption followed current disposable income over the period 1929–1991. The only period when income and consumption did not move in tandem was during World War II, when goods were scarce and rationed, and people were urged to save to help the war effort.

Informal observation and statistical studies show that the current level of disposable income is the central factor determining a nation's consumption.

Permanent Income. The simplest theory of consumption uses only the current year's income to predict consumption expenditures. Careful studies have shown that people base their consumption expenditures on long-run income trends as well as on current disposable income.

What are some examples? If bad weather destroys a crop, farmers will draw upon their previous saving. Because medical students can look forward to high professional earnings, they will borrow for consumption purposes while young. In these circumstances, consumers take the long view, asking, "Is this year's income temporarily high or low? Given my current and future income, how much can I consume today without incurring excessive debts?"

Evidence indicates that consumers generally choose their consumption levels with an eye to both current income and long-run income prospects. In order to understand how consumption depends on long-term income trends, economists have developed the *permanent-income theory* and the *life-cycle hypothesis*.

Permanent income is the level of income that households would receive when temporary or transient influences—such as the weather, a short business cycle, or a windfall gain or loss—are removed.[2] According to the permanent-income theory, consumption responds primarily to permanent income. This approach implies that

[2] The pathbreaking studies on longer-term influences were by Milton Friedman (on the permanent-income hypothesis) and Franco Modigliani (for the life-cycle model). Both received the Nobel Prize in economics for their accomplishments in these and other areas.

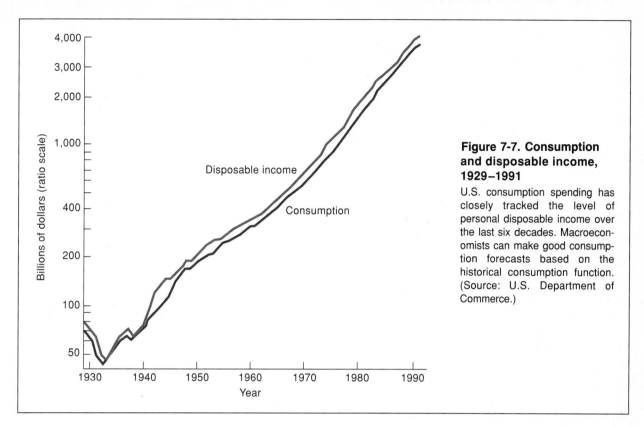

Figure 7-7. Consumption and disposable income, 1929–1991

U.S. consumption spending has closely tracked the level of personal disposable income over the last six decades. Macroeconomists can make good consumption forecasts based on the historical consumption function. (Source: U.S. Department of Commerce.)

consumers do not respond equally to all income shocks. If a change in income appears permanent (such as being promoted to a secure and high-paying job), then people are likely to consume a large fraction of the increase in income. On the other hand, if the income change is clearly transitory (for example, if it arises from a one-time bonus or a good harvest), then a significant fraction of the income change may be saved.

Wealth and Other Influences. A further important determinant of the amount of consumption is wealth. Consider two consumers, both earning $25,000 per year. One has $100,000 in the bank while the other has no saving at all. The first person may consume part of wealth, while the second has no wealth to draw down. The fact that higher wealth leads to higher consumption is called the *wealth effect*.

Normally, wealth does not change rapidly from year to year. Therefore, the wealth effect seldom causes sharp movements in consumption. From time to time, however, exceptions occur. When the stock market tumbled after 1929, fortunes collapsed

and paper-rich capitalists became paupers overnight. Many wealthy people were forced to curtail their consumption. Similarly, as stock prices soared in the mid-1980s, adding more than a trillion dollars to people's wealth after 1982, consumption was probably bolstered by the flush of wealth people felt.

Other factors are identified from time to time as important determinants of saving or consumption. Some economists believe that saving has been depressed by low rates of return to savings. Martin Feldstein, Harvard professor and the chairman of the Council of Economic Advisers under President Reagan, has argued that a generous social security system reduces personal saving; because we expect to get a large government pension when we retire, we save less for retirement today.

How important are influences other than current income in determining consumption? Few doubt the importance of permanent income, wealth, social factors, and expectations in affecting savings levels. But from year to year, the major determinant of changes in consumption is actual disposable income.

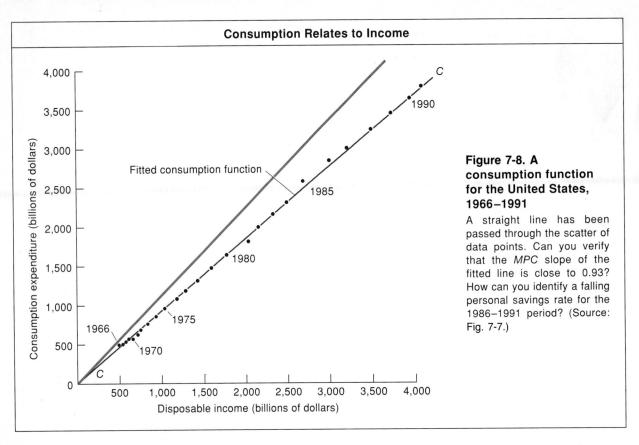

Consumption Relates to Income

(Vertical axis: Consumption expenditure (billions of dollars); *values 0, 500, 1,000, 1,500, 2,000, 2,500, 3,000, 3,500, 4,000)*

Fitted consumption function

Data points labeled: 1966, 1970, 1975, 1980, 1985, 1990; line labeled *C*

(Horizontal axis: Disposable income (billions of dollars); *values 500, 1,000, 1,500, 2,000, 2,500, 3,000, 3,500, 4,000)*

Figure 7-8. A consumption function for the United States, 1966–1991

A straight line has been passed through the scatter of data points. Can you verify that the *MPC* slope of the fitted line is close to 0.93? How can you identify a falling personal savings rate for the 1986–1991 period? (Source: Fig. 7-7.)

The National Consumption Function

Having reviewed the determinants of consumption, we may conclude that the level of disposable income is the primary determinant of the level of national consumption. Armed with this result, we can plot recent annual data on consumption and disposable income in Figure 7-8. The scatter diagram shows data for the period 1966-1991, with each point representing the level of consumption and income for a given year.

In addition, through the scatter points we have drawn a blue line—labeled *CC* and marked "Fitted consumption function." This fitted consumption function shows how closely consumption has followed disposable income over the last quarter-century. In fact, economic historians have found that a close relationship between disposable income and consumption holds back to the nineteenth century. This relationship—that consumers always save 7 percent of their disposable income—is among the most durable empirical regularities of

macroeconomics. Figure 7-8 shows that the fitted line tracks the actual data very closely.

The Declining U.S. Savings Rate

Over the long run, a nation's capital formation is determined by its national savings rate. When a nation saves a great deal, its capital stock grows rapidly and it enjoys rapid growth in its potential output. When a nation's savings rate is low, its equipment and factories become obsolete and its infrastructure begins to rot away. This close relationship between saving, investment, and economic growth is the major reason why economists worry about a nation's savings rate.

Table 7-5 lists the net savings rates of major countries for the period 1960–89. It shows that Japan leads the list in saving as a percent of national income while the United States lags behind other major countries. Moreover, the already low U.S. savings rate has declined even further over the

National Savings Rates, 1960–89	
Country	National savings rate (net private saving as % of GDP)
Japan	20.7
West Germany	14.0
France	13.6
Canada	9.9
United Kingdom	7.4
United States	7.2

Source: OECD, *National Accounts, 1960–89* (Paris, 1991) and U.S. Department of Commerce.

Table 7-5. U.S. savings rate trails that of other major industrial countries

The table shows net national private saving (equal to net saving of households and businesses at home and abroad) divided by GDP.

in the national savings rate? This is a highly controversial question today, but economists point to the following potential causes:

- *Federal budget deficits.* In the early 1980s, the federal government began to incur large budget deficits. The budget deficit grew from a few billion annually in the late 1970s to an average of around $150 billion annually by the late 1980s. Most economists believe that high budget deficits stimulate consumption and thereby lower national saving. Some have calculated that much of the recent decline in the national savings rate is due to the high budget deficits of the 1980s.[3]
- *Social security system.* Many economists have argued that the introduction of the social security system has removed some of the need for private saving. In earlier times, a family would

last decade. Figure 7-9 shows trends in net private saving (equal to the sum of net foreign investment and net private domestic saving) over recent decades. This measure of the national savings rate has declined from over 10 percent after World War II to around 2 percent in the late 1980s.

What are the reasons for the precipitous decline

[3] One school of thought, originating in studies of Harvard's Robert Barro, holds that government deficits will not stimulate consumption. The logic of Barro's theory is that, when the government borrows to cover its deficit, people know that the government will eventually have to raise taxes to pay back the interest and principal on the debt. Rational and farsighted consumers will accordingly save just enough to offset the stimulative effect of government deficits.

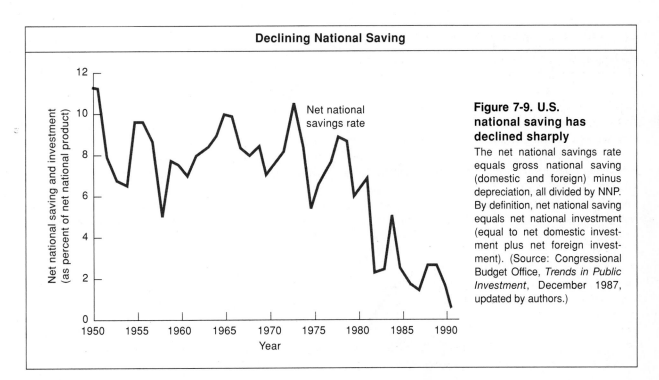

Figure 7-9. U.S. national saving has declined sharply

The net national savings rate equals gross national saving (domestic and foreign) minus depreciation, all divided by NNP. By definition, net national saving equals net national investment (equal to net domestic investment plus net foreign investment). (Source: Congressional Budget Office, *Trends in Public Investment*, December 1987, updated by authors.)

save during working years to build up a nest egg for retirement. Today, the government collects social security taxes and pays out social security benefits, displacing some of the need for private saving for retirement. Other income-support systems have a similar effect, reducing the need to save for a rainy day: crop insurance for farmers, unemployment insurance for workers, and medical care for the indigent all alleviate the precautionary motive for people to save.

- *Capital markets.* Until recently, capital markets had numerous imperfections. People found it hard to borrow funds for worthwhile purposes, whether for buying a house, financing an education, or starting a business. As capital markets developed, often with the help of government, new loan instruments allowed people to borrow more easily. One good example of this is student loans. Decades ago, college educations were financed either out of family saving or by students' working. Today, because the federal government guarantees many student loans, students can borrow to pay for their education and repay the loans from their own earnings later in life.
- *Other sources.* Many other culprits have been

indicted in the case of the declining national savings rate. Some analysts pointed to high inflation in the late 1970s and early 1980s, although this cause would seem to be acquitted given the continued decline of saving as inflation disappeared in the late 1980s. Others pointed to diluted incentives to save in recent years because of high tax rates and low post-tax returns to saving; here again, the argument is unconvincing because saving did not recover even after tax rates fell and real interest rates rose in the 1980s. Further suggestions include sociological hypotheses such as a perceived decline in the Protestant ethic (an ethic that Tawney and other historians thought was a major contributor to the rise of capitalism in earlier centuries).

The declining national savings rate remains a puzzling phenomenon testing the ingenuity of macroeconomists. While no one has demonstrated conclusively why the U.S. national savings rate has dropped so sharply in recent years, virtually all believe that the savings rate is too low to guarantee a vital and healthy rate of investment in the 1990s.

B. The Determinants of Investment

The second major component of private spending is investment.[4] Investment plays two roles in macroeconomics. First, because it is a large and volatile component of spending, sharp changes in investment can have a major impact on aggregate demand. This, in turn, affects output and employment. In addition, investment leads to capital accumulation. Adding to the stock of buildings and

equipment increases the nation's potential output and promotes economic growth in the long run.

Thus investment plays a dual role, affecting short-run output through its impact on aggregate demand and influencing long-run output growth through the impact of capital formation on potential output and aggregate supply.

What are the major determinants of investment? Recall from Table 6-5 that investment is broken down into three categories—purchases of residential structures, investment in business fixed plant and equipment, and additions to inventory. Of the total, about a quarter is residential housing, a twentieth normally is change in inventories, and the rest—averaging 70 percent of total investment in recent years—is investment in business plant and equipment.

Why do businesses invest? Ultimately, businesses

---

[4] Remember that macroeconomists use the term "investment" to mean additions to the stock of tangible capital goods—capital goods being equipment, structures, or inventories. When IBM builds a new factory or when the Smiths build a new house, these represent investments. Many people speak of "investing" when buying a piece of land, an old security, or any title to property. In economics, these purchases involve financial transactions or portfolio changes, because what one person is buying, someone else is selling. There is *investment* only when real capital is created.

buy capital goods when they expect that this action will earn them a profit—that is, will bring them revenues greater than the costs of the investment. This simple statement contains the three elements essential to understanding investment: revenues, costs, and expectations.

Revenues. An investment will bring the firm additional revenue if it helps the firm to sell more. This suggests that a very important determinant of investment is the overall level of output (or GNP). When factories are lying idle, firms have relatively little need for new factories, so investment is low. More generally, investment depends upon the revenues that will be generated by the state of overall economic activity. Some studies suggest that output fluctuations dominate the movement of investment over the business cycle. A recent example of a large output effect was seen during the business downturn of 1979–1982, when output fell sharply and investment declined by 22 percent.

Costs. A second important determinant of the level of investment is the costs of investing. Because investment goods last many years, reckoning the costs of investment is somewhat more complicated than doing so for other commodities like coal or wheat. When a purchased good lasts many years, we must calculate the cost of capital in terms of the interest rate on borrowings.

To understand this point, note that investors often raise the funds for buying capital goods by borrowing (say through a mortgage or in the bond market). What is the cost of borrowing? It is the *interest rate* on borrowed funds. Recall that the interest rate is the price paid for borrowing money for a period of time; for example, you might have to pay 13 percent to borrow $1000 for a year. In the case of a family buying a house, the interest rate is the mortgage interest rate.

The federal government sometimes uses fiscal policies to affect investment in specific sectors. In particular, *taxes* imposed by governments affect the cost of investment. The federal corporation income tax takes up to 34 cents of every dollar of corporate profits, thereby discouraging investment in the corporate sector. However, the government gives special tax breaks to oil and gas drilling, increasing activity in that sector. The tax treatment in different sectors, or even in different countries, will

have a profound effect upon the investment behavior of profit-seeking companies.[5]

Expectations. The third element in the determination of investment is expectations and business confidence. Investment is above all a gamble on the future, a bet that the revenue from an investment will exceed its costs. If businesses are concerned that future economic conditions in Germany will be depressed, they will be reluctant to invest in Germany. Conversely, when businesses see the likelihood of a sharp business recovery in the near future, they begin to plan for plant expansion.

Thus investment decisions hang by a thread on expectations and forecasts about future events. But, as one wit said, predicting is hazardous, especially about the future. Businesses spend much energy analyzing investments and trying to narrow the uncertainties about their investments.

We can sum up our review of the forces lying behind investment decisions as follows:

Businesses invest to earn profits. Because capital goods last many years, investment decisions depend on (a) the demand for the output produced by the new investment, (b) the interest rates and taxes that influence the costs of the investment, and (c) business expectations about the state of the economy.

The Investment Demand Curve

To analyze how different forces affect investment, we need to understand the relationship between interest rates and investment. This relationship is especially important because it is primarily through interest rates that governments influence investment. To show the relationship between interest rates and investment, economists use a schedule called the *investment demand* curve.

---

[5] In assessing the impact of taxation upon investment, economists examine the "marginal tax rate" on the return on investment. The marginal tax rate is the additional tax paid on an additional dollar of income. For 1990, the marginal tax rate on income from corporate investments, including taxes levied by all levels of government (federal, state, and local), is about 38 percent (see *Economic Report of the President*, 1987, for a discussion). This means that if an investment earns $100 of profit, the corporate investor keeps $62 and governments get $38. The high tax rate on corporate profits has led some to say that government is the largest single shareholder in American capitalism.

	**Interest Rates and Investment**						
(1)	(2)	(3)		(4) (5) Cost per $1,000 of project at annual interest rate of		colspan="2"	(6) (7) Annual net profit per $1,000 invested at annual interest rate of	
Project	Total investment in project ($, million)	Annual revenues per $1,000 invested ($)	10% ($)	5% ($)	10% ($) (6) = (3) − 4	5% ($) (7) = (3) − (5)
A	1	1,500	100	50	1,400	1,450
B	4	220	100	50	120	170
C	10	160	100	50	60	110
D	10	130	100	50	30	80
E	5	110	100	50	10	60
F	15	90	100	50	−10	40
G	10	60	100	50	−40	10
H	20	40	100	50	−60	−10

Table 7-6. The profitability of investment depends on the interest rate

The economy has eight investment projects, ranked in order of return. Column (2) shows the investment in each project. Column (3) calculates the perpetual return each year per $1000 invested.

Columns (4) and (5) then show the cost of the project, assuming all funds are borrowed, at interest rates of 10 and 5 percent; this is shown per $1000 of the project.

The last two columns calculate the annual net profit per $1000 invested in the project. If net profit is positive, then profit-maximizing firms will undertake the investment; if negative, the investment project will be rejected.

Note how the cutoff between profitable and unprofitable investments moves as the interest rate rises. (Where would the cutoff be if the interest rate rose to 15 percent per year?)

Consider a simplified economy where firms can invest in different projects: A, B, C, and so forth up to H. These investments are so durable (like power plants or buildings) that we can ignore the need for replacement. Further, they yield a constant stream of net income each year, and there is no inflation. Table 7-6 shows the financial data on each of the investment projects.

Consider project A. This project costs $1 million. It has a very high return—$1500 per year of revenues per $1000 invested (this is a rate of return of 150 percent per year). Columns (4) and (5) show the cost of investment. For simplicity, assume that the investment is financed purely by borrowing at the market interest rate, here taken alternatively as 10 percent per year in column (4) and 5 percent in column (5).

Thus at a 10 percent annual interest rate, the cost of borrowing $1000 is $100 a year, as is shown in all entries of column (4); at a 5 percent interest rate, the borrowing cost is $50 per $1000 borrowed per year.

Finally, the last two columns show the *annual net*

profit from each investment. For lucrative project A, the net annual profit is $1400 a year per $1000 invested at a 10 percent interest rate. Project H loses money.

To review our findings: In deciding among investment projects, firms compare the annual revenues from an investment with the annual cost of capital, which depends upon the interest rate. The difference between annual revenue and annual cost is the annual net profit. When annual net profit is positive, the investment makes money, while a negative net profit denotes that the investment loses money.[6]

The annual net profit on an investment is shown in the last two columns of Table 7-6. Examine the last column, corresponding to a 5 percent interest

---

[6] This example greatly simplifies the calculations businesses must make in actual investment analyses. Usually, investments involve an uneven stream of returns, depreciation of capital, inflation, taxes, and multiple interest rates on borrowed funds. Discussion of the economics of "discounting" and "present values" is found in analysis of capital theory and in advanced books on finance.

rate. Note that at this interest rate, investment projects A through G would be profitable. We would thus expect profit-maximizing firms to invest in all seven projects, which [from column (2)] total up to $55 million in investment. Thus at a 5 percent interest rate, investment demand would be $55 million.

However, suppose that the interest rate rises to 10 percent. Then the cost of financing these investments would double. We see from column (6) that investment projects F and G become unprofitable at an interest rate of 10 percent; investment demand would fall to $30 million.

We can show the results of this analysis in Figure 7-10. This figure shows the *demand-for-investment schedule*, which is here a downward-sloping step function of the interest rate. This schedule shows the amount of investment that would be undertaken at each interest rate; it is obtained by adding up all the investments that would be profitable at each level of the interest rate.

Hence, if the market interest rate is 5 percent, the desired level of investment will occur at point M, which shows investment of $55 million. At this interest rate, projects A through G are undertaken. If interest rates were to rise to 10 percent, projects F and G would be squeezed out; in this situation, investment demand would lie at point M' in Figure 7-10, with total investment of $30 million.

Shifts in the Investment Demand Curve

We have seen how interest rates affect the level of investment. Investment is affected by other forces as well. For example, an increase in the GNP will shift the investment demand curve out as is shown in Figure 7-11(a) on the following page.

An increase in business taxation would depress investment. Say that the government taxes away half the net yield in column (3) of Table 7-6, with interest costs in columns (4) and (5) not being deductible. The net profits in columns (6) and (7) would therefore decline. [Verify that at a 10 percent interest rate, a 50 percent tax on column (3) would raise the cutoff to between projects B and C, and the demand for investment would decline to $5 million.] The case of a tax increase on investment income is shown in Figure 7-11(b).

Finally, note the importance of expectations. What if investors become pessimistic and think that yields will soon halve? Or become optimistic and think yields will double? By working through these cases you can see how powerful an effect expectations can have on investment. Figure 7-11(c) displays how a bout of business pessimism would shift in the investment demand schedule, D_I.

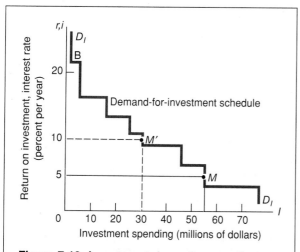

Figure 7-10. Investment depends upon the interest rate

The downward-stepping demand-for-investment schedule plots the amount that businesses would invest at each interest rate, as calculated from the data in Table 7-6. Each step represents a lump of investment project A has such a high rate that it is off the figure; the highest visible step is project B, shown at the upper left.

At each interest rate, all investments that have positive net profit will be undertaken. Thus at an interest rate of 5 percent, $55 million of investment will take place (in projects A through G), as shown by the intersection at point M of the demand-for-investment curve and the solid interest-rate line. If interest rates were to rise to 10 percent, the new equilibrium would be at M', with only $30 million of investment.

Real vs. Nominal Interest Rates

If you look at a newspaper from the late 1970s or early 1980s, you will see *nominal* (or money) *interest rates* of 8, 15, or even 18 percent per year. These compare with rates of 3 or 4 or 5 percent in the early 1960s. Does this comparison suggest that investment should have collapsed in recent years? Or take Brazil, where interest rates have been more than 100 percent per year. Wouldn't this dampen even the most robust entrepreneurial spirits?

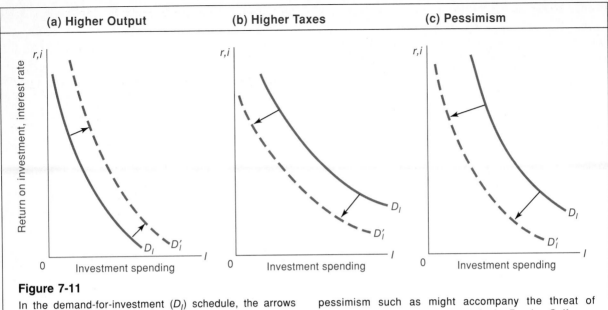

Figure 7-11

In the demand-for-investment (D_I) schedule, the arrows show the impact of **(a)** a higher level of GNP; **(b)** higher taxes on capital income; and **(c)** a burst of business pessimism such as might accompany the threat of recession, nationalization, or war in the Persian Gulf.

Surprisingly, the answer is no. Investment in the late 1970s and early 1980s in the United States was actually high by historical standards. And Brazil showed extremely high levels of real investment even though nominal interest rates were astronomical.

The key to this puzzle lies in the concept of the *real rate of interest*. In the United States and Brazil, the high money interest rates were matched by extremely high inflation rates. True, you had to pay a great deal to borrow, but when you repaid, it was in depreciated dollars or cruzados. The interest rates in terms of real goods were actually low or even negative.

An example will clarify the point. Say that the interest rate and the inflation rate are both 20 percent. If you borrow $1000 today, you have to pay back $1200 next year. But because of inflation the real value of the $1200 next year is exactly the same as the $1000 this year. So, in effect, you are repaying the exact same amount of real goods. In this case, the interest rate in terms of real goods (the *real interest rate*) is zero, not 20 percent. More generally:

The real interest rate is the interest that borrowers pay in terms of real goods and services. It is equal to the nominal (or money) interest rate less the rate of inflation.

How does this concept relate to investment? In our analysis of Table 7-6, we assumed no inflation, so the real and nominal rates of interest were equal. But if prices are rising, the income from investment is growing over time with inflation. The yield shown in column (3) is growing rather than remaining constant, and the investment would be more valuable than one with a constant yield over time.

In order to remove the distortionary effects of inflation on both revenues and on nominal interest rates, economists analyze investment in inflation-corrected terms. To do this, we examine a "real investment demand curve" that shows the effect of real output and real interest rates on real investment outlays (where "real" output and investment refer to the values of these variables in constant prices).

The concept of the real interest rate then resolves the paradox of high investment accompanying high interest rates found in Brazil and the United States in the 1970s. Although nominal interest rates were high, *real* interest rates were low. It was the low real interest rates that produced the high levels of investment.

FUN

More ge
understo
that mai
economy

Why did the American
a recession in 1990? Wh
sion mild while that of
and prolonged? How di
tary expenditure durin
major expansion of econ
three oil-price shocks o
to recessions in most i
how can governments us
cies to tame the excess
ployment?

The next few chapter
sues. This chapter begin
aggregate output and th
an examination of the
demand, building upon
tion and investment in
explain the foundations
examine the difference
price" and the "sticky-pr
Finally, we will sketch
tween the Keynesian and
to macroeconomics. We
the two views about bo
macroeconomy and the
inflation and unemployr

Volatile Investment

After learning about the factors affecting investment, you will not be surprised to discover that investment is extremely volatile. Investment behaves unpredictably because it depends on such uncertain factors as the success or failure of new and untried products, changes in tax rates and interest rates, political attitudes and approaches to stabilizing the economy, and similar changeable events of economic life.

Figure 7-12 presents a picture of the instability of investment. This shows investment as a percentage of potential GNP. Note the low levels of investment during the Great Depression of the 1930s and during World War II. We can also see how the investment incentives of the 1960s increased the share of investment in GNP. Business-cycle downturns, such as in 1975 and 1982, tend to produce a sharp decline in the investment-GNP ratio.

On to the Theory of Aggregate Demand

We have now completed our introduction to the basic concepts of macroeconomics and the major components of national output. We have seen that consumption and investment can fluctuate from year to year, and in the case of investment the fluctuations can be quite sharp. This suggests that the total flow of dollar spending (aggregate demand) is not guaranteed to grow smoothly from year to year.

The next four chapters investigate how the forces of spending and production interact to give an equilibrium level of national output. We will see

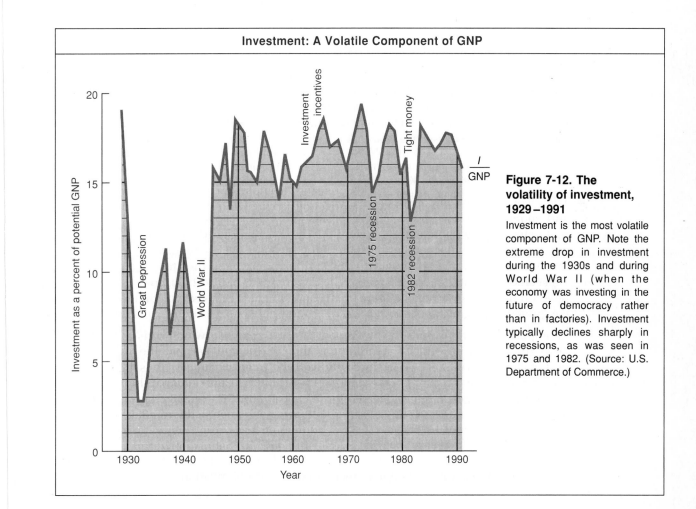

Investment: A Volatile Component of GNP

Figure 7-12. The volatility of investment, 1929–1991

Investment is the most volatile component of GNP. Note the extreme drop in investment during the 1930s and during World War II (when the economy was investing in the future of democracy rather than in factories). Investment typically declines sharply in recessions, as was seen in 1975 and 1982. (Source: U.S. Department of Commerce.)

upon their current inc¢
to receive future incor
cording to the followin

(1)	(2)	(3)
	Income	
Year	($)	Consump
1	30,000	_____
2	30,000	_____
3	25,000	_____
4	15,000	_____
5*	0	_____

* Retired.

consumption (that is, nominal or dollar consumption divided by the price index for consumption).

2. *Investment.* Investment (I) spending includes purchases of structures and equipment and accumulation of inventories. Our analysis in the last chapter showed that the major determinants of investment are the level of output, the cost of capital (as determined by tax policies along with interest rates and other financial conditions), and expectations about the future. The major channel by which economic policy can affect investment is through monetary policy.

3. *Government spending.* A third component of aggregate demand is government spending (G) on goods and services: purchases of goods like tanks or road-building equipment as well as the services of judges and public-school teachers. Unlike consumption and investment, this component of aggregate demand is determined directly by the government's spending decisions; when the Pentagon buys a new fighter aircraft, this output immediately adds to the GNP.

4. *Net exports.* A final component of aggregate demand is net exports (X), which equals the value of exports minus the value of imports. Imports are determined by domestic income and output, by the ratio of domestic to foreign prices, and by the foreign exchange rate of the dollar. Exports (which are imports of other countries) are the mirror image of imports, determined by foreign incomes and outputs, by relative prices, and by foreign exchange rates. Net exports, then, will be determined by domestic and foreign incomes, relative prices, and exchange rates.

Figure 8-1 shows the *AD* curve and its four major components. At price level *P*, we can read the level of consumption, investment, government spending, and net exports, which sum to *Q*. The sum of the four spending streams at the reference price level is aggregate spending, or aggregate demand, at that price level.

Behind the Aggregate Demand Curve

Figure 8-1 is a highly simplified illustration of the determinants of aggregate demand. It will aid our

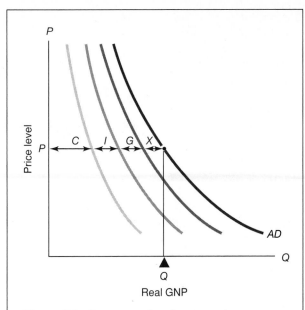

Figure 8-1. Components of aggregate demand

Aggregate demand (*AD*) consists of four streams—consumption (*C*), domestic private investment (*I*), government spending on goods and services (*G*), and net exports (*X*).

Aggregate demand shifts when there are changes in macroeconomic policies (such as monetary changes or changes in government expenditures or tax rates) or shifts in external events affecting spending (as would be the case with changes in foreign output, affecting *X*, or business confidence, affecting *I*).

understanding if we explore a number of questions about aggregate demand: Why does the *AD* curve slope downward? What factors would change aggregate demand (or shift the *AD* curve)? How does this macro demand curve differ from the micro demand curves used elsewhere in economics?

The Downward-Sloping AD Curve. The *AD* curve in Figure 8-1 shows the total real (or constant-price) expenditure for each price level, other things constant. Note that the level of real spending declines as the price level rises, so the *AD* curve is downward-sloping.

Why does *AD* slope downward? Although a number of factors lead real spending to decline as the price level rises, the most important is the **money-supply effect.** The money-supply effect means that, as prices rise with a fixed nominal quantity of money, the real demand for goods and services declines.

To understand the money-supply effect, we begin by emphasizing that when we draw an *AD* curve, we hold other things like the money supply constant. More concretely, we assume that the central bank manages the nation's monetary system so that the quantity of money is unchanged for different price levels. Hence, even though the consumer price index might rise from 100 to 150, the nation's money supply would remain at $600 billion.

But if the money supply is constant while the price level rises, the real money supply must fall. We define the *real money supply* as the nominal supply of money divided by the price level. In the example in the last paragraph, the real money supply was $600 billion in the first period and fell to $400 (= $600 × $\frac{100}{150}$) billion in the second period.

The decline in the real money supply will affect aggregate demand through the monetary mechanism to be discussed in detail in later chapters. In brief, what happens is that, as the real money supply falls, money becomes relatively scarce and a period of tight money ensues. What are the symptoms of tight money? Interest rates and mortgage payments rise, the stock market declines, the exchange rate on the dollar rises, and credit becomes harder to obtain. Tight money leads to a decline in investment, net exports, and even consumption. In short, a rise in prices with a fixed money supply, other things equal, leads to tight money and produces a decline in total real spending. The net effect is an upward movement along a given *AD* curve.

We can continue our example of a movement along the *AD* curve in Figure 8-2(*a*). Say that the economy is in equilibrium at point *B*, with a price level of 100 (in 1990 prices), a real GNP of $3000 billion, and a money supply of $600 billion. Next assume that as a result of a bad harvest, the price level increases to 150. Because the money supply is held constant, the real money supply (in 1990 prices) declines from $600 billion to $400 billion. With money now tight, interest rates rise. The result is a decline in spending on housing, plant and equipment, automobiles, and other interest-sensitive sectors. The net effect is that total real spending declines to $2000 billion, shown as point *C*.

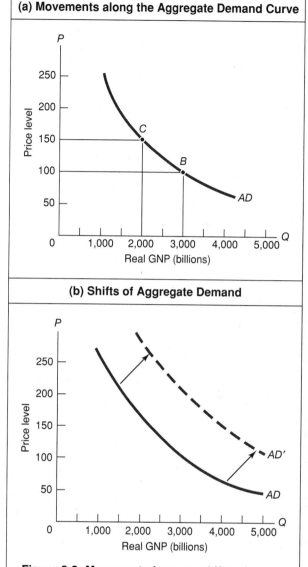

Figure 8-2. Movement along vs. shifts of aggregate demand

In **(a)**, a higher price level with a fixed money supply leads to tight money, higher interest rates, and declining spending on interest-sensitive investment and consumption. We see here a movement along the *AD* curve where other things are held constant.

In **(b)**, other things are no longer constant. Changes in variables underlying *AD*—such as money supply, tax policy, German political unification, or military spending—lead to changes in total spending at given price level.

Other factors also contribute to the relationship between real spending and the price level, although they are today quantitatively less significant than the money-supply effect.[1]

In summary:

We see that the *AD* curve slopes downward, indicating that the real output demanded declines as the price level rises. The primary reason for the downward-sloping *AD* curve is the money-supply effect, whereby higher prices operating on a fixed nominal money supply produce tight money and lower aggregate spending.

Shifts in Aggregate Demand. We have seen that total spending in the economy tends to decline as the price level rises, other things constant. But other things tend to change, and these produce changes in aggregate demand. What are the key variables that lead to shifts in aggregate demand?

We can separate the determinants of *AD* into two categories, as shown in Table 8-1. One set includes the major *policy variables* under government control. These are monetary policy—steps by which the central bank can affect the supply of money and other financial conditions—and fiscal policy—taxes and government expenditures. Table 8-1 illustrates how these government policies can affect different components of aggregate demand.

The second category is *external variables*, or variables that are determined outside the *AS-AD* framework. As Table 8-1 shows, some of these variables (such as wars or revolutions) are outside the scope of macroeconomic analysis proper, some (such as foreign economic activity) are outside the control of domestic policy, and others (such as the stock market) have significant independent movement.

What would be the effect of changes in the variables lying behind the *AD* curve? Suppose, for example, that the government increased its purchases of tanks, gas masks, and aircraft to fight in the Persian Gulf. The effect of this step would be to increase the spending on G. Unless some other

Variable	Impact on aggregate demand
Policy variables:	
Monetary policy	Increase in money supply lowers interest rates and improves credit conditions, inducing higher levels of investment and consumption of durable goods.
Fiscal policy	Increases in expenditures on goods and services directly increase spending; tax reductions or increases in transfers raise income and induce higher consumption.
External variables:	
Foreign output	Output growth abroad leads to an increase in net exports.
Asset values	Stock-price or housing-price rise produces greater household wealth and thereby increases consumption; also, this leads to lower cost of capital and increases business investment.
Oil-price decrease	Higher world oil production reduces world oil prices. Higher real incomes of consumers and higher business confidence increase consumption, automobile purchases, and investment

Table 8-1. Many factors can increase aggregate demand and shift out the *AD* curve

The simplest aggregate demand curve relates total spending to the price level. But numerous other influences affect aggregate demand—some policy variables, others external factors. The table illustrates changes that would tend to *increase* aggregate demand and shift out the *AD* curve.

component of spending offset the increase in G, the total *AD* curve would shift out and to the right as G increased. Similarly, an increase in the money supply, an oil-price decline, or an increase in the value of consumer wealth (say because of a stock-price increase) would lead to an increase in aggregate demand and an outward shift in the *AD* curve.

Figure 8-2(*b*) shows how the changes in the variables listed in Table 8-1 would affect the *AD* curve. To test your understanding, construct a similar table showing forces that would tend to *decrease* aggregate demand (see question 2 at the chapter's end).

Microeconomic vs. Macroeconomic Demand. Having explored the *AD* curve, we pause for a warn-

---

[1] One famous example is the *real-balance effect* or the "Pigou effect," named after the classical economist A. C. Pigou. This effect examines the wealth effect of a lower real quantity of money on consumption spending. The rationale behind the real-balance effect is that part of people's wealth consists of money balances. As the price level rises, the real value of your money balances declines and your wealth declines. As a result of the decline of the real value of your wealth, your consumption spending will tend to decline.

ing about the difference between macroeconomic and microeconomic demand curves. Recall from our study of supply and demand that the microeconomic demand curve has the price of an individual commodity on the vertical axis and production of that commodity on the horizontal axis, with all other prices and total consumer incomes held constant.

By contrast, in the aggregate demand curve, the general price level varies along the vertical axis. Moreover, total output and incomes vary along the *AD* curve, whereas incomes and output are held constant for the microeconomic demand curve.

Finally, the negative slope of the microeconomic demand curve comes from the ability of consumers to substitute other goods for the good in question. If the meat price rises, the quantity demanded falls because consumers substitute bread and potatoes for meat, using more of the relatively inexpensive commodities and less of the relatively expensive one. The aggregate demand curve is downward-sloping for quite a different reason: Total spending falls when the overall price level rises primarily because a fixed money supply must be rationed among money demanders by raising interest rates, tightening credit, and reducing spending.

To summarize:

Macroeconomic *AD* curves differ from their microeconomic cousins because the macro curve depicts changes in prices and output for the entire economy while the micro curve analyzes the behavior of an individual commodity. In addition, the *AD* curve slopes downward primarily because of the money-supply effect, while the micro demand curve slopes downward because of the substitution effect while incomes and other goods' prices are held constant.

Alternative Views of Aggregate Demand

Understanding the determination of aggregate demand is essential for analyzing the short-run movements of output and prices as well as the distribution of GNP among different components like consumption and investment. While economists generally agree on the factors influencing demand, they differ in the emphasis they place on different forces.

In analyzing movements in aggregate demand,

some economists concentrate primarily on monetary forces, especially on the role of the money supply. According to these economists, who are often called *monetarists*, the supply of money is the primary determinant of the total dollar value of spending. Monetarists hold that there is a strict relationship between the dollar value of all purchases and the amount of money available. If we identify total dollar spending with nominal GNP, then nominal GNP will be proportional to the money supply.

Other economists, on the other hand, hold that the major determinant of aggregate demand is *income and spending flows*. This approach focuses on changes in government spending and taxing, along with changes in investment and foreign economic conditions, for understanding the business cycle.

The majority of macroeconomists today adhere to an *eclectic approach*, holding that a wide variety of policy and external forces affect aggregate demand. The eclectic macroeconomists point to different forces moving the economy during different periods. For example, fiscal policy would be seen as the leading determinant of aggregate demand during World War II, when military spending was absorbing almost half of GNP. A similar analysis might have applied during the Korean and Vietnam wars. In recent years, however, as the Federal Reserve became more active in combating inflation and unemployment, monetary policy exercised the dominant influence over fluctuations in economic activity.

Often, external factors were decisive. From 1855 to 1875, investment opportunities opened up. Railroads were built all over the world, and the industrial economies enjoyed a sustained economic expansion. In the next two decades, nothing took the place of the railroads, and the United States suffered from a business depression. The early 1980s witnessed a massive decline in U.S. net exports, which deepened the economic downturn of that period.

This concludes our survey of the major elements of aggregate demand. These form one blade of the scissors that determine national output and the overall price level. We turn next to the other blade, aggregate supply, after which we will put aggregate supply and demand together and analyze today's schism between classical and Keynesian macroeconomics.

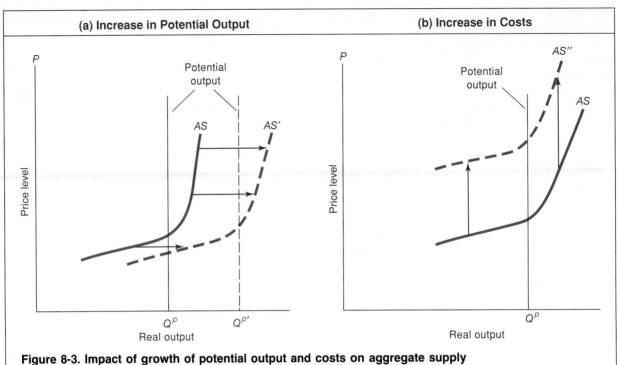

Figure 8-3. Impact of growth of potential output and costs on aggregate supply

In **(a)**, growth in potential output with no increase in production costs shifts aggregate supply curve rightward from *AS* to *AS'*. When costs increase (say because of rising wages) but potential output is unchanged, the aggregate supply curve shifts straight upward, as from *AS* to *AS''* in **(b)**.

shift was caused by the increase in potential output, say because of an increase in population and capital as well as technological change. The upward shift was caused by increases in the cost of production, as wages, energy prices, and other production costs rose. In sum, when costs increase over time along with growth in potential output, aggregate supply shifts from *AS* to *AS'* as shown in Figure 8-4.

Aggregate Supply in the Short Run and Long Run

One of the major controversies about modern macroeconomics involves the determination of aggregate supply. The major bone of contention is whether the aggregate supply curve is flat, or steep, or even vertical. Many economists of the Keynesian school hold that the *AS* curve is relatively flat. This implies that changes in aggregate demand have a significant and lasting effect on output. Economists who tend toward the classical approach hold that the *AS* curve is steep or even vertical; this group

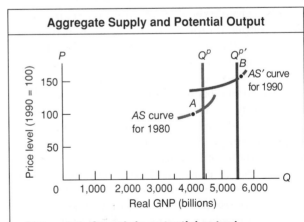

Aggregate Supply and Potential Output

Figure 8-4. Growth in potential output increases and shifts out aggregate supply

We show potential output for 1980 and 1990 as the vertical lines marked Q^P and $Q^{P'}$. This increase in potential output shifted aggregate supply (*AS*) to the right.

In addition, wages, energy prices, and other input costs increased, shifting the *AS* curve upward over time. The net impact of potential-output increase and cost increases was to shift *AS* upward and to the right.

believes that changes in aggregate demand have little lasting effect on output.

In fact, both views have some merit. Figure 8-5 depicts the two *AS* curves. The short-run *AS* curve on the left is upward-sloping or Keynesian. It indicates that firms are willing to increase their output levels in response to higher prices. In other words, as the level of aggregate demand rises, firms are willing to supply more output if they can also increase their prices as output rises.

Note, however, that the expansion of output cannot go on without limit in the short run. As output increases, labor shortages appear and factories operate close to capacity. In addition, firms can raise prices without losing customers to rivals. Therefore, as production rises above potential output, a larger fraction of the response to demand increases comes in the form of price increases and a smaller fraction comes in output increases. In terms of the aggregate supply curve, this implies that the short-run *AS* curve will be relatively flat to the left of the potential-output line, where output is less than potential output; but it will become steeper and steeper as output increases, that is, further and further to the right of the potential-output line.

Figure 8-5(*b*) illustrates the long-run response of aggregate supply to different price levels. We see there that the long-run *AS* curve is vertical or classical, with the output corresponding to potential

output. In a classical case, the level of output supplied is independent of the price level.

Why Do Short-Run and Long-Run *AS* Differ?

Why do short-run and long-run aggregate supply behaviors differ? Why do firms raise both prices and output in the short run as aggregate demand increases? Why, by contrast, do increases in demand lead to price changes but not to output changes in the long run?

The key to these puzzles lies in the way that wages and prices are determined in a modern market economy. Some elements of business costs are *inflexible* or *sticky* in the short run. As a result of this inflexibility, businesses will respond to higher levels of aggregate demand by producing and selling higher levels of output. Put differently, because some elements of cost are constant in the short run, firms find it profitable to raise prices and sell extra output as aggregate demand increases.

Suppose that a burst of extra spending occurs. Firms know that in the short run many of their production costs are fixed in dollar terms—workers are paid $15 per hour, rent is $1500 per month, and so forth. If firms can successfully raise their output prices in response to the extra burst of spending, they will also find it profitable to increase their output. Hence, in the short run, before wages and

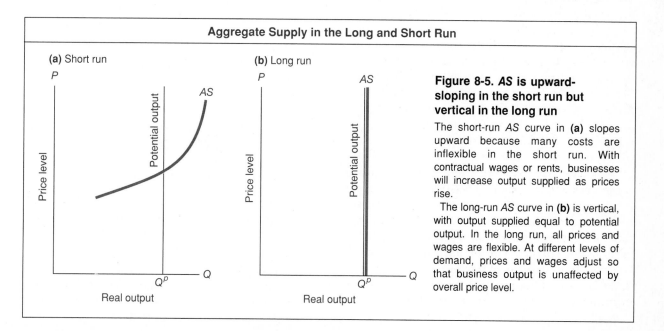

Aggregate Supply in the Long and Short Run

(a) Short run

P

Potential output

AS

Price level

Q

Q^P

Real output

(b) Long run

P

AS

Potential output

Price level

Q

Q^P

Real output

Figure 8-5. *AS* is upward-sloping in the short run but vertical in the long run

The short-run *AS* curve in **(a)** slopes upward because many costs are inflexible in the short run. With contractual wages or rents, businesses will increase output supplied as prices rise.

The long-run *AS* curve in **(b)** is vertical, with output supplied equal to potential output. In the long run, all prices and wages are flexible. At different levels of demand, prices and wages adjust so that business output is unaffected by overall price level.

rents and other dollar-fixed costs have adjusted, firms will react to aggregate demand increases by raising both prices and output. This positive association between prices and output is seen in the upward-sloping *AS* curve.

We have spoken repeatedly of "sticky" or "inflexible" costs. What are some examples? The most significant is wages. Almost half of all manufacturing workers are covered by long-term union contracts. In the United States, these contracts generally extend for 3 years and specify a dollar wage rate (with partial adjustment for price changes). Moreover, the contracts are staggered; they never expire and get renegotiated at the same time. For the life of the labor agreement, the wage rate faced by the firm will be largely fixed in dollar terms. Other prices and costs are similarly sticky in the short run. When a firm rents a building, the lease will often last for a year or more, and the rental is generally set in dollar terms. In addition, firms often sign contracts with their suppliers specifying the prices to be paid for materials or components. Some prices are fixed by government regulation, particularly those for utilities like electricity, gas, water, and local telephone service.

What happens in the long run? Eventually, the inflexible or sticky elements of cost—wage contracts, rent agreements, regulated prices, and so forth—become unstuck and negotiable. Firms cannot take advantage of fixed-money wage rates in their labor agreements forever; labor will soon recognize that prices have risen and insist on compensating increases in wages. Ultimately, all costs will adjust to the higher output prices. After the general price level has risen x percent because of the higher demand, money wages, rents, regulated prices, and other costs will in the end respond by moving up around x percent as well.

Once costs have adjusted upward as much as prices, firms will be unable to profit from the higher level of aggregate demand. The level of output will come back to its long-run equilibrium level at potential output. In the long run, after all elements of cost have fully adjusted, firms will face the same ratio of price to costs as they did before the change in demand. There will be no incentive for firms to increase their output. When we say that the *AS* curve is vertical, we mean that output supplied is independent of the level of prices and costs.

The aggregate supply for an economy will differ from potential output in the short run because of inflexible elements of cost. In the short run, firms will respond to higher demand by raising both production and prices. In the longer run, as costs respond to the higher level of prices, most or all of the response to increased demand takes the form of higher prices and little or none the form of higher output. The long-run *AS* curve is vertical because, given sufficient time, all costs adjust.

The Clash between Keynesian and Classical Views

Since the dawn of economics two centuries ago, one of the deepest controversies has concerned whether or not the economy has a tendency to move toward a long-run, full-employment equilibrium. Using modern language, we label as **classical theories** those approaches that emphasize the powerful self-correcting forces in an economy; classical macroeconomic thinking has its roots in Adam Smith, J. B. Say, and John Stuart Mill. The alternative approach, today called **Keynesian economics,** was not coherently expressed until J. M. Keynes' writings in this century.

The basic difference between classical and Keynesian approaches can be found in differing views about the behavior of aggregate supply. Keynesian economists believe that prices and wages adjust slowly, so any equilibrating forces may take many years or even decades to operate. The classical approach holds that prices and wages are flexible, so the economy moves to its long-run equilibrium very quickly. In the remainder of this chapter, we will use aggregate supply and demand analysis to explain the scientific foundations and the policy implications of these two fundamentally different approaches.[2]

The Classical Approach

Before Keynes wrote *The General Theory* in 1936, the major economic thinkers generally adhered to

---

[2] A brief and nontechnical survey of the debate between the new classical and Keynesian points of view can be found in N. Gregory Mankiw, "A Quick Refresher Course in Macroeconomics," *Journal of Economic Literature* (December 1990), pp. 1645–1660.

the classical view of the economy. Early economists were fascinated by the Industrial Revolution with its division of labor, accumulation of capital, and growing international trade.

Say's Law of Markets. Early economists knew about business cycles, but they viewed these as temporary and self-correcting aberrations. Their analysis revolved around *Say's Law of markets.* This theory was propounded in 1803 by the French economist J. B. Say and states that overproduction is impossible by its very nature. This is sometimes expressed today as "supply creates its own demand." What is the rationale for Say's Law? It rests on a view that there is no essential difference between a monetary economy and a barter economy—that if factories can produce more, workers will be there to buy the output.

A long line of the most distinguished economists, including D. Ricardo, J. S. Mill, and A. Marshall, subscribed to the classical macroeconomic view that overproduction is impossible. Even during the Great Depression, when a quarter of the American labor force was unemployed, the eminent economist A. C. Pigou wrote, "With perfectly free competition there will always be a strong tendency toward full employment. Such unemployment as exists at any time is due wholly to the frictional resistances [that] prevent the appropriate wage and price adjustments being made instantaneously."[3]

As the quote from Pigou suggests, the rationale behind the classical view is that wages and prices are sufficiently flexible that markets will "clear," or return to equilibrium, very quickly. If prices and wages adjust rapidly, then the short run in which prices are sticky will be so short that it can be neglected for all practical purposes. The classical macroeconomists conclude that the economy always operates at full employment or at its potential output.

The durable and valid core of Say's Law and of the classical approach is shown in Figure 8-6. This is an economy where prices and wages are determined in competitive markets, moving flexibly up and down to eliminate any excess demand or supply. In terms of our *AS-AD* analysis, it can be described by a standard, downward-sloping aggre-

[3] *The Theory of Unemployment* (1933).

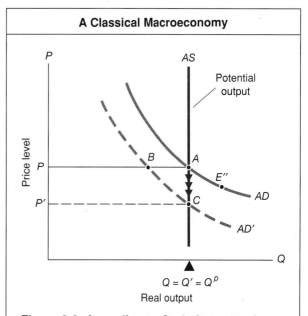

Figure 8-6. According to Say's Law, supply creates its own demand as prices move to balance demand with aggregate supply

Classical economists thought that persistent periods of glut could not occur. If *AS* or *AD* shifted, prices would react flexibly to ensure that full-employment output was sold. Here we see how flexible prices ensure that prices move down enough to increase spending to full-employment output. (What would happen if *AD* were unchanged, but potential output increased? What forces would move the economy to E″ ?)

gate demand curve along with a vertical aggregate supply curve.

Suppose that aggregate demand falls due to tight money or other external forces. As a result, the *AD* curve shifts leftward to *AD′* in Figure 8-6. Initially, at the original price of *P*, total spending falls to point *B*, and there might be a very brief period of falling output. But the demand shift is followed by a rapid adjustment of wages and prices, with the overall price level falling from *P* to *P′*. As the price level falls, total output returns to potential output, and full employment is reestablished at point *C*.

In the classical view, changes in aggregate demand affect the price level but have no impact upon output and employment. Price and wage flexibility ensures that the real level of spending is sufficient to maintain full employment.

Policy Consequences. The classical view has two conclusions that are vitally important for economic policy. First, the economy always enjoys full employment, and there are never any unutilized resources. The economy is always producing its potential output, and workers who want to work at the going wage rate can find jobs.

Does this proposition imply that there is no unemployment at all? Surely not, for there will always be *microeconomic* waste in any real-world economy. We would see unemployment of people who are moving between jobs or of unionized workers who have above-equilibrium wage rates. But in the classical view, an economy has no *macroeconomic* waste in the sense of underutilized resources due to insufficient aggregate demand.

The second element of the classical view is even more striking: Macroeconomic aggregate demand policies cannot influence the level of unemployment and output. Rather, monetary and fiscal policies can affect only the economy's price level, along with the composition of real GNP. This second classical proposition is easily seen in Figure 8-6. Consider an economy in equilibrium at point C, the intersection of the *AD'* and the vertical *AS* curves. Say that the government decides to undertake fiscal steps to expand the economy. What happens? For a brief instant, at the initial price level *P'*, there is excess demand. However, as prices and wages quickly begin to rise under the pressure of excess demand, the economy moves to the new equilibrium at point A. The net effect of the expansionary economic policy has been to inflate the overall price level sufficiently to restore the initial full-employment equilibrium without changing output and employment.

At the heart of the classical view is the belief that prices and wages are flexible and that price flexibility provides a self-correcting mechanism that quickly restores full employment and always maintains potential output. And, as we will see in later chapters, the classical approach is very much alive in the writings of today's new classical school. The new classical economists base their views on modern economic developments, including imperfect information, the existence of technological shocks, and frictions from shifts of resources among industries. Although dressed in modern clothing, their policy conclusions are closely linked to the classical economists of an earlier age.

The Keynesian Revolution

While the classical economists were preaching that persistent unemployment was impossible, economists of the 1930s could hardly ignore the vast army of unemployed workers—begging for work and selling pencils on street corners. How could economics explain such massive and persistent idleness?

Keynes' *General Theory* offered an alternative macroeconomic theory, a new set of theoretical spectacles for looking at the impact of economic policies as well as external shocks. In fact, the Keynesian revolution combined two different elements. First, Keynes presented the concept of aggregate demand that we have explained in this chapter. Second, Keynes argued that prices and wages were inflexible or sticky; this meant that the vertical classical *AS* curve would have to be replaced by the upward-sloping *AS* curve.

The Surprising Consequences. By combining these two new elements, Keynes brought a veritable revolution to macroeconomics. The essence of Keynes' argument is shown in Figure 8-7. This diagram combines an aggregate demand curve along with an upward-sloping aggregate supply curve.

The first observation is that a modern market economy can get trapped in an underemployment equilibrium—a balance of aggregate supply and demand in which output is far below potential and a substantial fraction of the work force is involuntarily unemployed. For example, if the *AD* curve intersects the *AS* curve far to the left, as is illustrated at point A, equilibrium output may lie far below potential output. Keynes emphasized that because wages and prices are inflexible, there is no economic mechanism to restore full employment and ensure that the economy produces its potential. A nation could remain in its low-output, high-misery condition for a long time because there is no self-correcting mechanism or invisible hand to guide the economy back to full employment.

Keynes' second observation follows from the first. Through monetary or fiscal policies, the government can stimulate the economy and help maintain high levels of output and employment. For example, if the government were to increase its purchases, aggregate demand would increase, say from *AD* to *AD'* in Figure 8-7. The impact would be

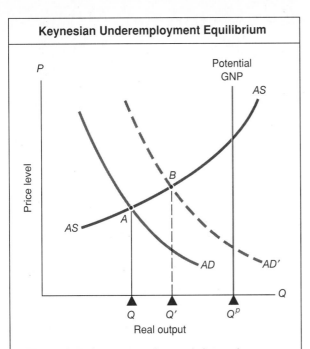

Keynesian Underemployment Equilibrium

Figure 8-7. Aggregate demand determines output in the Keynesian approach

In the Keynesian model, aggregate supply slopes upward, implying that output will increase with higher aggregate demand as long as there are unused resources. When AD is depressed, output will be in equilibrium at point A, with high unemployment.

If aggregate demand increases from AD to AD', the level of real output increases from A to B, with prices increasing as well. In this Keynesian paradigm, with AS upward-sloping in the short run, economic policies that increase aggregate demand succeed in increasing output and employment.

to increase output from Q to Q', reducing the gap between actual and potential GNP. In short, with appropriate use of economic policy, government can take steps to ensure high levels of national output and employment.

Keynes' analysis created a revolution in macroeconomics, particularly among young economists who were living through the Great Depression of the 1930s and sensed something was wrong with the classical model. Of course, the Great Depression was not the first event to reveal the untenability of the classical synthesis. But for the first time, the classical approach was confronted by a competing analysis. The Keynesian approach presented a new synthesis that swept through economics and changed fundamentally the way that

economists and governments think about business cycles and economic policy.

Theories and Policy

In economics, people's views on policy are often determined by the theoretical spectacles they wear. Does a President or a senator or an economist lean toward a classical or a Keynesian view? The answer to this question will often explain that person's view on many of the major economic-policy debates of the day.

Examples are legion. Economists who tend toward the classical view will often be skeptical about the need for government to stabilize business cycles. They argue that a government policy designed to increase aggregate demand will instead lead to escalating inflation. Moreover, classical economists would worry about government spending crowding out private production. By "crowding out," they mean that when the government increases its spending, production on private goods will be displaced. The higher production of guns will require resources that were previously used to produce butter.

Keynesian economists take a different tack. They think that the macroeconomy is prone to extended business cycles, with high levels of unemployed resources for long periods of time. They further hold that the government can stimulate the economy by taking monetary or fiscal steps to change aggregate demand. These policies might increase aggregate demand in periods of slow economic activity or curb spending in periods of boom with threatening inflation. The Keynesian economist might argue that government spending crowds out nothing at all because higher government spending increases output and allows private spending to continue. In essence, when the government takes a larger slice out of the pie, the pie actually becomes larger. Government spending, tax cuts, or more rapid money growth—all create more output and thus stimulate investment.

Which is the correct view—classical or Keynesian? The unalloyed truth is that both are oversimplified. In the chapters to come, we will see the strengths and weaknesses of both positions. For now, the key point to recognize is that many of the debates about economic policy arise because one participant has the classical model in mind while the other has the Keynesian view. The art of good macroeconomic judgment is to sense the strengths and weaknesses of each approach.

Toward a Better Understanding of Aggregate Demand

We have now completed our analysis of the foundations of aggregate supply and demand. The next three chapters explore the determinants of aggregate demand. We begin in the next chapter with a detailed analysis of the Keynesian multiplier model, which is the simplest example of a Keynesian approach to economic activity. We will also see how government fiscal policy and international trade feature in the multiplier framework. We then turn to an analysis of monetary economics, including the nature of money, the role of the central bank, and the way that money affects economic activity. By putting all these different elements together, we can acquire a full understanding of the forces affecting aggregate demand and of the impact of aggregate demand on the macroeconomy.

SUMMARY

1. Aggregate demand represents the total quantity of output willingly bought at a given price level, other things held constant. Components of spending include (a) consumption, which depends primarily upon disposable income; (b) investment, which depends upon present and expected future output and upon interest rates and taxes; (c) government spending on goods and services; and (d) net exports, which depend upon foreign and domestic outputs and prices and upon foreign exchange rates.

2. Aggregate demand curves differ from demand curves used in microeconomic analysis. The *AD* curves relate overall spending on all components of output to the overall price level, with policy and external variables held constant. The aggregate demand curve is downward-sloping primarily because of the money-supply effect, which occurs when a rise in the price level, with the nominal money supply constant, reduces the real money supply. A lower real money supply raises interest rates, tightens credit, and reduces total real spending. This represents a movement along an unchanged *AD* curve.

3. Factors that change aggregate demand include (a) macroeconomic policies, such as monetary and fiscal policies, and (b) external variables, such as foreign economic activity, changes in world oil prices, and shifts in asset markets. When these variables change, they shift the *AD* curve.

4. Aggregate supply describes the relationship between the output that businesses willingly produce and the overall price level, other things constant. The factors underlying aggregate supply are (a) potential output, determined by the inputs of labor, capital, and natural resources available to an economy along with the technology or efficiency with which these inputs are used, and (b) input costs, such as wages, oil and other energy prices, and import prices. Changes in these underlying factors will shift the *AS* curve.

5. In the long run, aggregate supply is closely tied to an economy's potential output. In the short run, price and wage relations will affect how production responds to different levels of aggregate demand. Accordingly, we generally treat the long-run *AS* curve as vertical or classical, indicating that

businesses will supply potential output whatever the level of prices. In the short run, because of the inflexibility of wages and prices, the *AS* curve is upward-sloping, showing that businesses will supply more output at a higher price level.

6. Two major approaches to output determination are the classical and Keynesian views:

   (*a*) The classical view is grounded in Say's Law, which states that "supply creates its own demand." In modern terms, the classical approach holds that flexible prices and wages quickly erase any excess supply or demand and reestablish full employment and full-capacity output. Moreover, macroeconomic policy can play no role in stabilizing the business cycle or reducing unemployment in a classical economy.

   (*b*) The Keynesian view holds that prices and wages are sticky in the short run due to contractual rigidities such as labor-union agreements. In this kind of economy, output responds positively to higher levels of aggregate demand because the *AS* curve is upward-sloping, particularly at low levels of output. In a Keynesian economy, the economy can experience long periods of persistent unemployment because the self-correcting mechanism of prices and wages is sluggish or absent. Monetary and fiscal policies can substitute for flexible wages and prices, stimulating the economy during depressions and helping to restore full employment or slowing the economy during booms to forestall inflationary tendencies.

7. A modern market economy combines elements of both the classical and the Keynesian models. In the short run, a period of a few months or years, the Keynesian model is most applicable. In the longer run of a decade or more, as prices and wages have time to adjust, the classical approach best describes the evolution of macroeconomic activity.

CONCEPTS FOR REVIEW

real variable
= nominal variable/price level
aggregate demand, *AD* curve
major components of aggregate demand: *C, I, G, X*
movement along vs. shift of *AD, AS* curves
aggregate supply, *AS* curve

downward-sloping *AD* curve:
   money-supply effect
   real-balance (Pigou) effect
factors underlying and shifting *AD* curve
aggregate supply: role of potential output and production costs
short-run vs. long run *AS*

flexible vs. sticky wages and prices
Say's Law of markets
classical and Keynesian economics:
   fundamental difference on price flexibility
   impact of demand shifts
   effectiveness of policy

QUESTIONS FOR DISCUSSION

1. Define carefully what is meant by the aggregate demand curve. Distinguish between movements along the curve and shifts of the curve. What might increase output by moving along the *AD* curve? What could increase output by shifting the *AD* curve?

2. Construct a table parallel to Table 8-1, illustrating events that would lead to a *decrease* in aggregate demand. (Your response should provide different examples rather than simply change the direction of the factors mentioned in Table 8-1.)

3. What, if anything, would be the effect of each of the following on the *AS* curve in both the short run and the long run, other things constant?
   (a) Potential output increases by 25 percent.
   (b) The money supply is reduced by the Federal Reserve.
   (c) A war in the Mideast leads to a doubling of world oil prices.
   (d) A nuclear accident leads regulators to shut down all nuclear power stations.
4. In regard to the events listed in question 3, what, if anything, would be the impact on the *AD* curve?
5. Again regarding the events listed in question 3, what would be the effect on output and prices in both the short run and the long run?
6. A noted macroeconomist has written, "For a couple of years, pumping up spending and money will produce many jobs and much output, although prices are likely to rise as well. But eventually, as the economy adjusts to the new policies, output and employment will return to their 'natural' levels. It simply is not possible to keep output above its potential for long." Evaluate this quotation using the *AS-AD* apparatus of this chapter. Do you agree with the quotation?
7. Answer the following questions from both the Keynesian and the classical viewpoints using the *AS-AD* analysis of this chapter.
   (a) What will be the effect of an increase in potential output on the level of actual output if aggregate demand is unchanged?
   (b) For a given level of potential output, what is the effect of a small increase in *AD*? Of a very, very large shift in *AD*?
8. State and explain Say's Law. Starting from an equilibrium, assume that potential output increases. Show in a graphical extension of Figure 8-6 and describe in words the sense in which supply creates its own demand.
9. Restate what is meant by the "real-balance effect" (see footnote 1 of this chapter). To estimate its quantitative importance on consumption, assume the following: At an initial price level of $P = 1$, household income is 1000, non-money wealth is 4800, and money wealth is 200. The marginal propensity to consume from income is 0.80 and the marginal propensity to consume from wealth is 0.03.

   Assume that the price level rises 10 percent, with money wealth constant in nominal terms and all other variables constant in real terms. Estimate the impact of the price increase on real money wealth, on total wealth, and on consumption. Draw an *AD* curve based upon the real-balance effect only. Compare the slope with the example depicted in Figure 8-2(a) and the text description accompanying Figure 8-2(a).
10. Explain the following statement: "Higher government spending increases output and allows private spending to continue; when the government takes a larger slice out of the pie, the pie actually becomes larger." Relate this quotation to the debate between Keynesian and classical economists.

THE MULTIPLIER MODEL

> If the propensity to consume and the rate of new investment result in
> a deficient effective demand, the actual level of employment will fall
> short of the supply of labour potentially available.
>
> J. M. Keynes, *General Theory* (1936)

All market economies experience swings in business activity when unemployment surges during depressions or when rapid increases in demand lead to inflation. Indeed, for the newborn postsocialist countries of Eastern Europe, the first taste of the market was of depression and unemployment. During the 1980s, the United States enjoyed rapid growth and falling unemployment. In 1990, under the pressure of tight money and temporarily rising oil prices, output growth slowed and unemployment began to rise.

How can we interpret these swings in economic activity? The aggregate demand-and-supply tools introduced in the last chapter can help explain the movements in output and the price level. But we also want to analyze exactly *why AS* or *AD* shifts and to predict how much output will change with changes of investment or government spending or net exports. For this task we develop the Keynesian multiplier model.

A. The Basic Multiplier Model

This chapter presents the **multiplier model,** which is a macroeconomic theory used to explain how output is determined in the short run. The name "multiplier" comes from the finding that each dollar change in certain expenditures (such as investment) leads to more than a dollar change (or a multiplied change) in GNP. The multiplier model explains how shocks to investment, foreign trade, and government tax and spending policies can affect output and employment in an economy with unemployed resources.

In this first section, we introduce the simplest multiplier model, one in which there is no government or international trade. With this background we will be able to analyze the impact of government and the foreign sector on economic activity. Figure 9-1 sketches the focus of the multiplier analysis.

As you begin your study of the multiplier, note that this approach in no way contradicts the *AS-AD* model of the last chapter. Rather, the multiplier *explains* the workings of aggregate demand by showing exactly how consumption, investment, and other variables interact to determine aggregate demand.

Chapter Overview

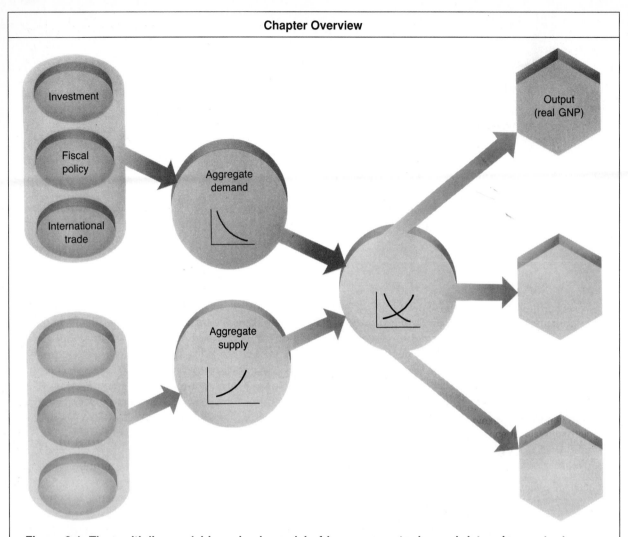

Figure 9-1. The multiplier model is a simple model of how aggregate demand determines output

This chapter develops the Keynesian multiplier model. It shows the interaction between induced consumption expenditure and autonomous variables like investment, government spending and taxation, and exports. In addition, it shows how these variables jointly determine aggregate output and employment.

Output Determination with Saving and Investment

Chapter 7 gave a simplified picture of the consumption and savings functions for the nation. These consumption and savings schedules are based on our knowledge of the budgets of different families, their wealth, and so forth. Here we shall initially simplify the picture by leaving out taxes, undistributed corporate profits, foreign trade, depreciation, and government fiscal policy. For the time being, we will assume that income is disposable income and equals GNP.

Figure 9-2 shows the national consumption and savings functions. Each point on the consumption function shows desired or planned consumption at that level of disposable income. Each point on the savings schedule shows desired or planned saving at that income level. Recall that the two schedules are closely related: since $C + S$ always equals income, the consumption and savings curves are mirror twins that will always add up to the 45° line.

We have seen that saving and investment are dependent on quite different factors: saving depends in a passive way on income, while investment depends on output and various other factors (such as expected future output, interest rates, tax policy, and business confidence).

(a) Consumption Function

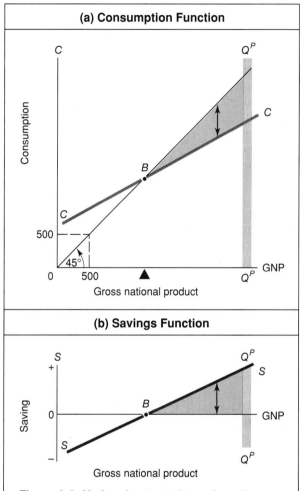

(b) Savings Function

Figure 9-2. National output determines the levels of consumption and saving

CC is the consumption function for the country, while SS is the savings function.

Recall that these are closely related in a mirror-image fashion. The break-even point is shown at point B—on the upper diagram where CC intersects the 45° line and on the lower diagram where SS intersects the horizontal axis. Can you explain why the vertically aligned arrows *must* be of equal length? The two points marked "500" emphasize the important property of the 45° line: Any point on it depicts a vertical distance exactly equal to the horizontal distance. The gray band marked $Q^P Q^P$ shows the level of potential GNP.

How Saving and Investment Determine Income

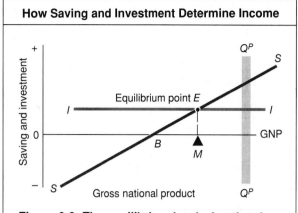

Figure 9-3. The equilibrium level of national output is determined by intersection of savings and investment schedules

The horizontal II line shows that investment is constant at the indicated level.

E marks the spot where investment and savings curves intersect. Equilibrium GNP comes at the intersection of the SS and II curves because this is the only level of GNP at which the desired saving of households exactly matches the desired investment of business.

For simplicity, we treat investment as an external or *autonomous* variable, one whose level is determined outside the model. Say that investment opportunities are such that investment would be exactly $200 billion per year regardless of the level of GNP. This means that, if we draw a schedule of investment against GNP, it will have to be a horizontal line—always the same distance above the horizontal axis. This case is shown in Figure 9-3, where the investment schedule is labeled II to distinguish it from the SS savings schedule. (Note that II does not mean Roman numeral 2.)

The savings and investment schedules intersect at point E in Figure 9-3. This point corresponds to a level of GNP equal to 0M and represents the equilibrium level of output in the multiplier model.

This intersection of the savings and investment schedules is the equilibrium level of GNP toward which national output will gravitate.

The Meaning of Equilibrium

Why is point E in Figure 9-3 an equilibrium? The reason is that at point E the desired saving of households equals the desired investment of firms. When desired saving and desired investment are not equal, output will tend to adjust up or down.

The savings and investment schedules shown in Figure 9-3 represent *desired* (or *planned*) *levels*. Thus at output level *M*, businesses will want their investment to be equal to the vertical distance *ME*. Also, households desire to save the amount *ME*. But there is no logical necessity for the actual saving (or investment) to be equal to the planned saving (or investment). People can make mistakes. Or they may forecast events incorrectly. When mistakes happen, saving or investment might deviate from planned levels.

To see how output adjusts until desired saving and desired investment are equated, we consider three cases. In the first case, the system is at *E*, where the schedule of what business firms want to invest intersects the savings schedule of what households want to save. When everyone's plans are satisfied, all will be content to go on doing just what they have been doing.

At equilibrium, firms will not find inventories piling up on their shelves; nor will their sales be so brisk as to force them to produce more goods. So production, employment, income, and spending will remain the same. In this case GNP stays at point *E*, and we can rightly call it an *equilibrium*.

The second case begins with a GNP higher than at *E*; say, GNP is to the right of *M*, at an income level where the savings schedule is higher than the investment schedule. Why can't the system stay there indefinitely? Because at this income level, families are saving more than business firms will be willing to go on investing. Firms will have too few customers and larger inventories of unsold goods than they want. What can businesses do about this situation? They can cut back production and lay off workers. This response moves GNP gradually downward, or leftward in Figure 9-3. The economy returns to equilibrium when it gets back to *E*. There the tendency to change has disappeared.

At this point, you should be able to analyze the third case. Show that if GNP were *below* its equilibrium level, strong forces would be set up to move it eastward back to *E*.

All three cases lead to the same conclusion:

The only equilibrium level of GNP occurs at *E*, where the savings and investment schedules intersect. At any other point, the desired saving of households does not coincide with the desired investment of business. This discrepancy will cause

businesses to change their production and employment levels, thereby returning the system to the equilibrium GNP.

Output Determination by Consumption and Investment

In addition to the saving-investment balance, there is a second way of showing how output is determined. The equilibrium is the same, but our understanding of output determination is deepened if we work through this second approach.

This second method is called the consumption-plus-investment (or *C + I*) approach. How does the *C + I* approach work? Figure 9-4 shows a curve of total spending graphed against total output or in-

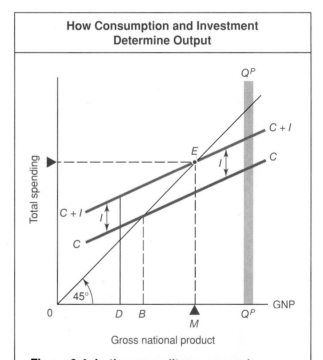

Figure 9-4. In the expenditure approach, equilibrium GNP level is found at the intersection of the *C + I* schedule with 45° line

Adding *I* to *CC* gives the *C + I* curve of total desired spending. At *E*, where this intersects the 45° line, we get the same equilibrium as in the savings-and-investment diagram. (Note the similarities between this figure and Fig. 9-3; the investment added to *CC* is the same as *II* of Fig. 9-3; break-even point *B* and potential-output band Q^P each come at the same GNP level on the two diagrams, and so must the *E* intersection.)

come. The black *CC* line is simply the consumption function, showing the level of desired consumption corresponding to each level of income. We then add desired investment (which is at fixed level *I*) to the consumption function. Thus the level of total desired spending is *C* + *I*, represented by the blue *C* + *I* curve in Figure 9-4.

We next put in a 45° line to help us identify the equilibrium. At any point on the 45° line, the total level of consumption plus investment spending (measured vertically) exactly equals the total level of output (measured horizontally).

We can now calculate the equilibrium level of output in Figure 9-4. Where the desired amount of spending, represented by the *C* + *I* curve, equals total output, the economy is in equilibrium. In summary:

The total spending (or *C* + *I*) curve shows the level of desired expenditure by consumers and businesses corresponding to each level of output. The economy is in equilibrium at the point where the *C* + *I* curve crosses the 45° line—at point *E* in Figure 9-4. At point *E* the economy is in equilibrium because at that level desired spending on consumption and investment exactly equals the level of total output.

The Adjustment Mechanism. It is essential to understand why point *E* is an equilibrium. Equilibrium occurs when planned spending (on *C* and *I*) equals planned output. If the system were to deviate from equilibrium, say, at output level *D* in Figure 9-4, what would happen? At this level of output, the *C* + *I* spending line is above the 45° line, so planned *C* + *I* spending would be greater than planned output. This means that consumers would be buying more cars and shoes than businesses were producing. Auto dealers would find their lots emptying, and shoe stores would be running low on many sizes.

In this disequilibrium situation, auto dealers and shoe stores would respond by increasing their orders. Automakers and shoe manufacturers would recall workers from layoff and gear up their production lines. *Thus, spending disequilibrium leads to a change in output.*

By following this chain of reasoning we see that only when firms are producing what households and firms plan to spend on *C* and *I*, precisely at point *E*, will the economy be in equilibrium. (You

should also work through what happens when output is above equilibrium.)

Planned vs. Actual Amounts. In this chapter, we repeatedly discuss "planned" or "desired" spending and output. These words call attention to the difference between (*a*) the amount of planned or desired consumption given by the consumption function or by the investment demand schedule and (*b*) the actual amount of consumption or investment measured after the fact.

This distinction emphasizes that GNP is at equilibrium only when firms and consumers are on their schedules of desired spending and investment. As measured by a national accounts statistician, saving and investment will always be exactly equal, in recession or boom. But *actual* investment will often differ from *planned* investment when actual sales are unequal to planned sales and firms consequently face an involuntary buildup or reduction of inventories. Only when the level of output is such that planned spending on *C* + *I* equals planned output will there be no tendency for output, income, or spending to change.

An Arithmetic Analysis

An arithmetic example may help show why the equilibrium level of output occurs where planned spending and planned output are equal.

Table 9-1 shows a simple example of consumption and savings functions. The break-even level of income, where the nation is too poor to do any net saving on balance, is assumed to be $3000 billion ($3 trillion). Each change of income of $300 billion is assumed to lead to a $100 billion change in saving and a $200 billion change in consumption; in other words, for simplicity *MPC* is assumed to be constant and exactly equal to $\frac{2}{3}$. Therefore, $MPS = \frac{1}{3}$.

Again, we assume that investment is autonomous. Suppose that the only level of investment that will be sustained indefinitely is exactly $200 billion, as shown in column (4) of Table 9-1. That is, at each level of GNP, businesses desire to purchase $200 billion of investment goods, no more and no less.

Columns (5) and (6) are the crucial ones. Column (5) shows the total GNP—this is simply column (1) copied once again into column (5). The figures in column (6) represent what business firms would

<div align="center">**GNP Determination Where Output Equals Planned Spending** (Billions of Dollars)</div>							
(1)	(2)	(3)	(4)	(5)		(6)	(7)
Levels of GNP and *DI*	Planned consumption	Planned saving (3) = (1) − (2)	Planned investment	Level of GNP (5) = (1)		Total planned spending on consumption and investment (6) = (2) + (4)	Resulting tendency of output
4,200	3,800	400	200	4,200	>	4,000	↓ Contraction
3,900	3,600	300	200	3,900	>	3,800	↓ Contraction
3,600	3,400	200	200	3,600	=	3,600	Equilibrium
3,300	3,200	100	200	3,300	<	3,400	↑ Expansion
3,000	3,000	0	200	3,000	<	3,200	↑ Expansion
2,700	2,800	−100	200	2,700	<	3,000	↑ Expansion

Table 9-1. Equilibrium output can be found arithmetically as the level where planned spending equals GNP

The blue row depicts the equilibrium GNP level, where the $3600 that is being produced is just matched by the $3600 that households plan to consume and that firms plan to invest. In upper rows, firms will be forced into unintended inventory investment and will respond by cutting back production until equilibrium GNP is reached. Interpret the lower rows' tendency toward expansion of GNP toward equilibrium.

actually be selling year in and year out; this is the planned consumption spending plus planned investment. It is the *C* + *I* schedule from Figure 9-4 in numbers.

When businesses as a whole are producing too high a level of total product (higher than the sum of what consumers and businesses want to purchase), they will be involuntarily piling up inventories of unsalable goods.

Reading the top row of Table 9-1, we see that if firms are temporarily producing $4200 billion of GNP, planned or desired spending [shown in column (6)] is only $4000 billion. In this situation, excess inventories will be accumulating. Firms will respond by contracting their operations, and GNP will fall. In the opposite case, represented by the bottom row of Table 9-1, total spending is $3000 billion and output is $2700 billion. Inventories are being depleted and firms will expand operations, raising output.

We see, then, that when business firms as a whole are temporarily producing more than they can profitably sell, they will want to contract their operations, and GNP will tend to fall. When they are selling more than their current production, they increase their output and GNP rises.

Only when the level of output in column (5) exactly equals planned spending in column (6) will

business firms be in equilibrium. Their sales will then be just enough to justify continuing their current level of aggregate output. GNP will neither expand nor contract.

● Let us summarize. GNP is one of the major indicators of a nation's economic health. What determines the level of GNP? In the very long run, potential output limits the amount a country can produce. But in the short run, the multiplier model suggests that aggregate demand, influenced by investment spending and the consumption function, determines GNP. Moreover, as the Keynes' quotation at the beginning of this chapter suggests, consumption and investment spending help us to understand high unemployment. While the relationships presented here have been simplified, their essence will remain valid even when extended to situations involving government fiscal policy, monetary policy, and foreign trade. ●

The Multiplier

Where is the multiplier in all this? To answer this question, we need to examine how a change in autonomous investment spending affects GNP. It is logical that an increase in investment will raise the level of output and employment. But by how much? The Keynesian multiplier model shows that an increase in investment will increase GNP by an amplified or multiplied amount—by an amount greater than itself.

The **multiplier** is the number by which the change in investment must be multiplied in order to determine the resulting change in total output.

For example, suppose investment increases by $100 billion. If this causes an increase in output of $300 billion, the multiplier is 3. If, instead, the resulting increase in output were $400 billion, the multiplier would be 4.

Woodsheds and Carpenters. Why is it that the multiplier is greater than 1? Let's suppose that I hire unemployed resources to build a $1000 woodshed. My carpenters and lumber producers will get an extra $1000 of income. But, that is not the end of the story. If they all have a marginal propensity to consume of $\frac{2}{3}$, they will now spend $666.67 on new consumption goods. The producers of these goods will now have extra incomes of $666.67. If their *MPC* is also $\frac{2}{3}$, they in turn will spend $444.44, or $\frac{2}{3}$ of $666.67 (or $\frac{2}{3}$ of $\frac{2}{3}$ of $1000). The process will go on, with each new round of spending being $\frac{2}{3}$ of the previous round.

Thus an endless chain of *secondary consumption responding* is set in motion by my *primary* investment of $1000. But, although an endless chain, it is an ever-diminishing one. Eventually it adds up to a finite amount.

Using straightforward arithmetic, we can find the total increase in spending in the following manner:

$1000.00	$1 \times \$1000$
+	+
666.67	$\frac{2}{3} \times \$1000$
+	+
444.44	$(\frac{2}{3})^2 \times \$1000$
+ $=$	+
296.30	$(\frac{2}{3})^3 \times \$1000$
+	+
197.53	$(\frac{2}{3})^4 \times \$1000$
+	+
$\vdots$	$\vdots$
$3000	$\frac{1}{1-\frac{2}{3}} \times \$1000$, or $3 \times \$1000$

This shows that, with an *MPC* of $\frac{2}{3}$, the multiplier is

3; it consists of the 1 of primary investment plus 2 extra of secondary consumption responding.

The same arithmetic would give a multiplier of 4 for an *MPC* of $\frac{3}{4}$, because $1 + \frac{3}{4} + (\frac{3}{4})^2 + (\frac{3}{4})^3 + \cdots$ finally adds up to 4. For an *MPC* of $\frac{1}{2}$, the multiplier would be 2.

The size of the multiplier thus depends upon how large the *MPC* is. It can also be expressed in terms of the twin concept, the *MPS*. For an *MPS* of $\frac{1}{4}$, the *MPC* is $\frac{3}{4}$, and the multiplier would be 4. For an *MPS* of $\frac{1}{3}$, the multiplier is 3. If the *MPS* were $1/x$, the multiplier would be x.

By this time it should be clear that the simple multiplier is always the inverse, or "reciprocal," of the marginal propensity to save.[1] It is equal to $1/(1 - MPC)$. Our simple multiplier formula is:

$$\text{Change in output} = \frac{1}{MPS} \times \text{change in investment}$$

$$= \frac{1}{1 - MPC} \times \text{change in investment}$$

In other words, the greater the extra consumption responding, the greater the multiplier.

Up to now, we have discussed the multiplier as relating to the extra consumption and saving. This is only part of the picture. Later in this chapter, we will see that the multiplier applies to changes in total spending and changes in total leakages from spending.

Graphical Picture of the Multiplier

Our discussion of the multiplier has relied up to now largely on common sense and arithmetic. Can we get the same result using our graphical analysis of saving and investment? The answer is yes.

Suppose, as back in Table 9-1, the *MPS* is $\frac{1}{3}$ and a burst of inventions gives rise to an extra $100 billion of continuing investment opportunities. What will be the new equilibrium GNP? If the multiplier is indeed 3, the answer is $3900 billion.

A look at Figure 9-5 can confirm this result. Our

---

[1] The formula for an infinite geometric progression is

$$1 + r + r^2 + r^3 + \cdots + r^n + \cdots = \frac{1}{1 - r}$$

as long as the *MPC* (r) is less than 1 in absolute value.

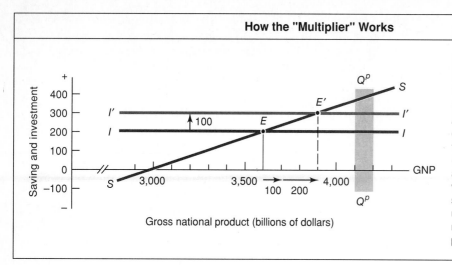

How the "Multiplier" Works

Figure 9-5. Each dollar of investment is "multiplied" into 3 dollars of output

New investment shifts *II* up to *I'I'*. *E'* gives the new equilibrium output, with output increasing by 3 for each 1 increase in investment. (*Note*: The broken horizontal blue arrow is 3 times the length of the vertical blue arrow of investment shift, and is broken to show 2 units of secondary consumption responding for each 1 unit of primary investment.)

old investment schedule *II* is shifted upward by $100 billion to the new level *I'I'*. The new intersection point is *E'*; the increase in income is exactly 3 times the increase in investment. As the blue arrows show, the horizontal output distance is 3 times as great as the upward shift in the investment schedule. We know that desired saving must rise to equal the new and higher level of investment. The only way that saving can rise is for national income to rise. With an *MPS* of $\frac{1}{3}$, and an increase in investment of $100, income must rise by $300 to bring forth $100 of additional saving to match the new investment. Hence, at equilibrium, $100 of additional investment induces $300 of additional income, verifying our multiplier arithmetic.[2]

The Multiplier in the *AS-AD* Framework

The multiplier model has been enormously influential in macroeconomic analysis over the last half-century. How does it fit into the broader macroeconomic conception of *AS* and *AD* analysis?

The relationship between the multiplier analysis and the *AS-AD* approach is shown in Figure 9-6. Part (*b*) displays an upward-sloping short-run *AS*

curve that becomes relatively steep as output exceeds potential output. In the region where there are unused resources, to the left of potential output, output is determined primarily by the strength of aggregate demand. As investment increases, this increases *AD*, and equilibrium output rises.

The same economy can be described by the multiplier diagram in the top panel of Figure 9-6. The multiplier equilibrium gives the same level of output as the *AS-AD* equilibrium—both lead to a real GNP of *Q*. They simply stress different features of output determination.

These two diagrams make a key point that lies behind the multiplier diagram: The multiplier analysis applies to situations where output is less than its potential, that is, where there are unemployed resources. When there are unemployed resources, an increase in aggregate demand can raise output levels. By contrast, if an economy is producing at its maximum potential, there is simply no room for expansion when aggregate demand expands. In conditions of full employment, then, demand increases lead to higher prices rather than output increases.

Putting this in plain English, when investment or other autonomous spending increases in an economy with excess capacity and unemployed workers, most of the increments to total spending will end up in extra real output, with only small increases in the price level. However, as the economy reaches and surpasses potential output, it is not

---

[2] Alter Table 9-1, on p. 144, to verify this answer. In column (4), we now put $300 billion instead of $200 billion of investment. Show that the new equilibrium output now shifts one row up from the old blue equilibrium row. Can you also show that the multiplier works downward?

Output Determination in Two Approaches

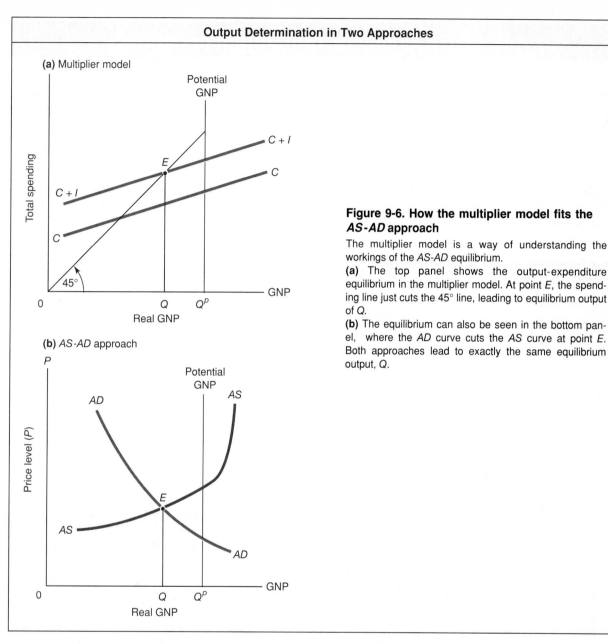

(a) Multiplier model

(b) *AS-AD* approach

Figure 9-6. How the multiplier model fits the *AS-AD* approach

The multiplier model is a way of understanding the workings of the *AS-AD* equilibrium.

(a) The top panel shows the output-expenditure equilibrium in the multiplier model. At point *E*, the spending line just cuts the 45° line, leading to equilibrium output of *Q*.

(b) The equilibrium can also be seen in the bottom panel, where the *AD* curve cuts the *AS* curve at point *E*. Both approaches lead to exactly the same equilibrium output, *Q*.

possible to coax out more production at the going level of prices. Hence, at high levels of output, higher spending [upward shifts in the *AD* curve of Figure 9-6(*b*)] will simply result in higher price levels and little or none of the *AD* increase will end up in higher real output or employment.

This discussion points to a crucial limitation of the multiplier model. While it may be a highly use-

ful approach to describe depressions or even recessions, it cannot apply to periods of full employment, when real GNP exceeds potential output. Once factories are operating at full capacity and when all the workers are employed, the economy simply cannot produce more output. This fact reinforces the point that the multiplier model applies only in an economy with unemployed resources.

Why do we simply add G on the top? Because spending on government buildings (G) has the same macroeconomic impact as spending on private buildings (I); the collective consumption expenditure involved in maintaining a public library (G) has the same effect on jobs as private consumption expenditure for newspapers or books (C).

We end up with the three-layered cake of $C + I + G$, calculating the amount of total spending forthcoming at each level of GNP. We now must go to its point of intersection with the 45° line to find the equilibrium level of GNP. At this equilibrium GNP level, denoted by point E in Figure 9-8, total planned spending exactly equals total planned output. Point E is thus the equilibrium level of output when we add government purchases to the multiplier model.

Impact of Taxation on Aggregate Demand

How does government taxation tend to reduce aggregate demand and the level of GNP? We do not need graphs to tell us what happens when the government increases our taxes while at the same time holding its expenditures constant.

Extra taxes lower our disposable incomes, and lower disposable incomes tend to reduce our consumption spending. Clearly, if investment and government expenditure remain the same, a reduction in consumption spending will then reduce GNP and employment. Thus, in the multiplier model, higher taxes without increases in government spending will tend to reduce real GNP.

A look back at Figure 9-7 confirms this reasoning. In this figure, the upper CC curve represents the level of the consumption function with no taxes. The CC curve is unrealistic, of course, because consumers must pay taxes on their incomes. For simplicity, we assume that consumers pay $300 billion in taxes at every level of income; thus DI is exactly $300 billion less than GNP at every level of output. As is shown in Figure 9-7, this level of taxes can be represented by a rightward shift in the consumption function of $300 billion. This rightward shift will also appear as a downward shift; if the MPC is $\frac{2}{3}$, then the rightward shift of $300 billion will be seen as a downward shift of $200 billion.

Without a doubt, taxes lower output in our multiplier model. Another glance at Figure 9-8 will show why. When taxes increase, $I + G$ do not change, but the increase in taxes will lower disposable income,

thereby shifting the CC consumption schedule downward. Hence, the $C + I + G$ schedule shifts downward. You can pencil in a new, lower $C' + I + G$ schedule in Figure 9-8. Confirm that its new intersection with the 45° line must be at a lower equilibrium level of GNP.

Keep in mind that G is government outlays on goods and services. It excludes spending on transfers such as unemployment insurance or social security payments. These transfers are treated as *negative taxes*, so that the taxes (T) considered here can best be thought of as taxes less transfers. Therefore, if direct and indirect taxes total $400 billion, while all transfer payments are $100 billion, then net taxes, T, equal $400 − $100 = $300 billion.

A Numerical Example

The points made up to now can be illustrated by Table 9-2. This table is very similar to Table 9-1, which illustrated output determination in the simplest multiplier model. The first column shows a reference level of GNP, while the second shows a fixed level of taxes, $300 billion. Disposable income in column (3) is GNP less taxes. Consumption, taken as a function of DI, is shown in column (4). Column (5) shows the fixed level of investment, while column (6) exhibits the level of government spending. To find total aggregate demand in column (7), we add together the $C + I + G$ in columns (4) through (6).

Finally, we compare total spending in column (7) with the initial level of GNP in column (1). If spending is above GNP, output rises; if spending is below GNP, output falls. This tendency, shown in the last column, assures us that output will tend toward equilibrium at $3600 billion.

Fiscal-Policy Multipliers

Investment, taxes, and government spending represent autonomous spending streams that interact with induced consumption spending to determine the equilibrium level of national output. We have discovered that government fiscal policy is high-powered spending much akin to investment. The parallel between investment and fiscal policy suggests that fiscal policy should also have multiplier effects upon output. And this is exactly right.

The **government expenditure multiplier** is the

Output Determination with Government
(Billions of Dollars)

(1) Initial level of GNP	(2) Taxes (T)	(3) Disposable income (DI)	(4) Planned consumption (C)	(5) Planned investment (I)	(6) Government expenditure (G)	(7) Total spending (C + I + G)	(8) Resulting tendency of economy
4,200	300	3,900	3,600	200	200	4,000	Contraction
3,900	300	3,600	3,400	200	200	3,800	Contraction
3,600	300	3,300	3,200	200	200	3,600	Equilibrium
3,300	300	3,000	3,000	200	200	3,400	Expansion
3,000	300	2,700	2,800	200	200	3,200	Expansion

Table 9-2. Government spending, taxes, and investment determine equilibrium GNP

This table shows how output is determined when government spending on goods and services is added to the multiplier model. In this example, taxes are "lump sum" or independent of the level of income. Disposable income is thus GNP minus $300 billion. Total spending is I + G + (the consumption determined by the consumption function).

At levels of output less than $3600 billion, spending is greater than output, so output expands. Levels of output greater than $3600 are unsustainable and lead to contraction. Only at output of $3600 is output in equilibrium—that is, planned spending equals output.

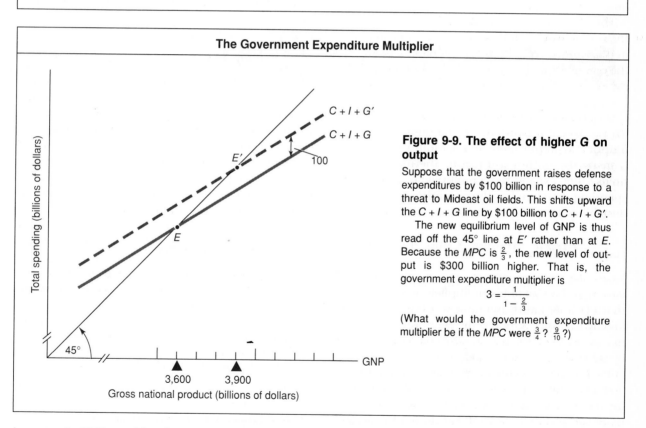

The Government Expenditure Multiplier

Figure 9-9. The effect of higher G on output

Suppose that the government raises defense expenditures by $100 billion in response to a threat to Mideast oil fields. This shifts upward the C + I + G line by $100 billion to C + I + G'.

The new equilibrium level of GNP is thus read off the 45° line at E' rather than at E. Because the MPC is $\frac{2}{3}$, the new level of output is $300 billion higher. That is, the government expenditure multiplier is

$$3 = \frac{1}{1 - \frac{2}{3}}$$

(What would the government expenditure multiplier be if the MPC were $\frac{3}{4}$? $\frac{9}{10}$?)

increase in GNP resulting from an increase of $1 in government expenditures on goods and services. An initial government purchase of a good or service will set in motion a chain of respending: if the government builds a road, the road-builders will spend some of their incomes on consumption goods, which in turn will generate additional incomes, some of which will be respent. In the simple model examined here, the ultimate effect on GNP of an extra dollar of G will be the same as an extra dollar of I: the multipliers are equal to 1/(1 − MPC). Figure 9-9 shows how a change in G will result in a

Output Determination with Foreign Trade
(Billions of Dollars)

(1) Initial level of GNP	(2) Domestic demand (C + I + G)	(3) Exports (e)	(4) Imports (m)	(5) Net exports (X = e − m)	(6) Total spending (C + I + G + X)	(7) Resulting tendency of economy
4,200	4,000	360	420	−60	3,940	Contraction
3,900	3,800	360	390	−30	3,770	Contraction
3,600	**3,600**	**360**	**360**	**0**	**3,600**	**Equilibrium**
3,300	3,400	360	330	30	3,430	Expansion
3,000	3,200	360	300	60	3,260	Expansion

Table 9-3. Net exports add to aggregate demand of economy

To the domestic demand of C + I + G, we must add net exports of X = e − m to obtain total aggregate demand for a country. Note that higher net exports have the same multiplier as do investment and government expenditure increases.

mestic incomes and output, which clearly change in the different rows of Table 9-3. For simplicity, we assume that the country always imports 10 percent of its total output, so imports in column (4) are 10 percent of column (1).

Subtracting column (4) from column (3) gives net exports in column (5). This is a negative number when imports exceed exports and a positive number when exports are greater than imports. Net exports in column (5) are the net addition to the spending stream contributed by foreigners. Equilibrium output in an open economy comes at the

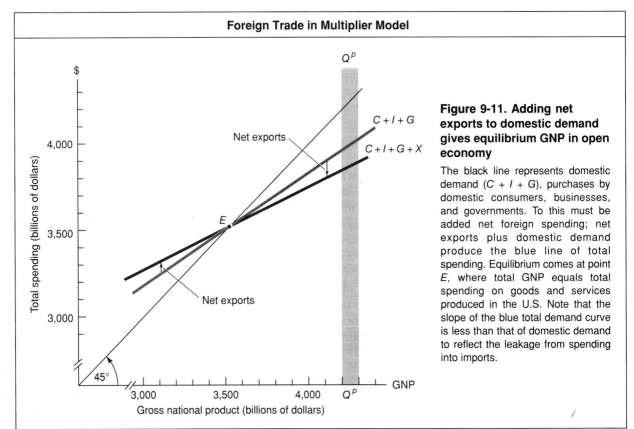

Foreign Trade in Multiplier Model

Figure 9-11. Adding net exports to domestic demand gives equilibrium GNP in open economy

The black line represents domestic demand (C + I + G), purchases by domestic consumers, businesses, and governments. To this must be added net foreign spending; net exports plus domestic demand produce the blue line of total spending. Equilibrium comes at point E, where total GNP equals total spending on goods and services produced in the U.S. Note that the slope of the blue total demand curve is less than that of domestic demand to reflect the leakage from spending into imports.

point where total spending in column (6) exactly equals total output. In this case, equilibrium comes with net exports of exactly zero, although generally the net export position would differ from zero. (Make sure that you can explain why the economy is not in equilibrium when spending does not equal output.)

Figure 9-11 shows the open-economy equilibrium graphically. The upward-sloping black line marked $C + I + G$ is the same curve used in Figure 9-8 to illustrate output determination with government spending. To this line we must add the level of net exports that is forthcoming at each level of GNP. Net exports from column (5) of Table 9-3 are added to get the blue line of total aggregate demand or total spending. To the left of point E in the figure, net exports are positive so the blue line lies above the black curve; at the right, imports exceed exports and net exports are negative so the total spending line lies below the line for domestic demand.

Equilibrium GNP occurs where the blue line of total spending intersects the 45° line. This intersection comes at exactly the same point, at $3600 billion, that is shown as equilibrium GNP in Table 9-3. Only at $3600 billion does GNP exactly equal what consumers, businesses, governments, and foreigners want to spend on goods and services produced in the United States.[5]

The Marginal Propensity to Import and the Spending Line

Note that the aggregate demand curve, the blue $C + I + G + X$ curve in Figure 9-11, has a slightly smaller slope than the black curve of domestic demand. The explanation of this is that there is an additional leakage from spending, into imports. This new leakage arises from our assumption that 10 cents of every dollar of income is spent on imports. To handle this requires introducing a new term, the marginal propensity to import. The **marginal propensity to import,** which we will denote MPm, is the increase in the dollar value of imports for each $1 increase in GNP.

Recall that we labeled the increase in consumption per unit increase of income the "marginal propensity to consume." The marginal propensity to import is closely related. It tells how much is imported for each dollar increase in total GNP. What marginal propensity to import is assumed to hold in Table 9-3? Clearly, the answer is $MPm = 0.10$, for every $300 billion of increased income leads to $30 billion of increased imports. (What is the marginal propensity to import in an economy with no foreign trade? Zero.)

Returning to Figure 9-11, let us examine the slope of the total spending line (that is, the line showing total spending on $C + I + G + X$). Note that the slope of the total spending line is less than the slope of the domestic demand line of $C + I + G$. As GNP and total incomes rise by $300, spending on consumption rises by the income change times the MPC (assumed to be two-thirds), or by $200. At the same time, spending on imports, or foreign goods, also rises by $30. Hence spending on domestic goods rises by only $170 (= $200 − $30), and the slope of the total spending line falls from 0.667 in our closed economy to 0.567 in our open economy.[6]

The Open-Economy Multiplier

You might suspect that the leakage of spending outside the economy into imports would change the multiplier in an open economy, especially because the import leakage changes the slope of the spending line. You would be correct. Let us see why.

One way of understanding the expenditure multiplier in an open economy is to calculate the

---

[5] Note that the two lines in Fig. 9-11 cross where net exports are zero, but the fact that equilibrium comes at zero net exports is purely coincidental. Change the export column to 460 in Table 9-3, recalculate the new equilibrium, and redraw the equilibrium in Fig. 9-11.

[6] Our analysis has considered only leakages from income into saving and into imports. A complete account of the economy would include two further important *leakages:* (a) those into taxes, because some taxes (such as income or sales taxes) rise with higher levels of income and output, and (b) those into business saving when businesses earn higher profits but do not pay those profits out to individuals.

In addition, a complete model would include one further item of *induced* spending: as Chapter 7 hinted, private investment tends to respond positively as output rises, for businesses tend to spend more on investment to increase capacity at higher levels of output.

These further leakages and induced-spending streams will change the slope of the aggregate spending curve and will also change the economy's multiplier.

rounds of spending and responding generated by an additional dollar of government spending, investment, or exports. For example, say that Germany needs to buy American computers to modernize antiquated facilities in what used to be East Germany. Each extra dollar of U.S. computers will generate $1 of income in the United States, of which $\$\frac{2}{3} = \$0.667$ will be spent by Americans on consumption. However, because the marginal propensity to import is 0.10, one-tenth of the extra dollar of income or $0.10 will be spent on foreign goods and services, leaving only $0.567 of spending on domestically produced goods. That $0.567 of domestic spending will generate $0.567 of U.S. income, from which $0.567 \times (\$0.567) = \$0.321$ will be spent on consumption of domestic goods and services in the next round. Hence the total increase in output, or the **open-economy multiplier,** will be

$$\begin{aligned} \text{Open-economy} \atop \text{multiplier} &= 1 + 0.567 + (0.567)^2 + \cdots \\ &= 1 + (\tfrac{2}{3} - \tfrac{1}{10}) + (\tfrac{2}{3} - \tfrac{1}{10})^2 + \cdots \\ &= \frac{1}{1 - \tfrac{2}{3} + \tfrac{1}{10}} = \frac{1}{\tfrac{13}{30}} = 2.3 \end{aligned}$$

This compares with a closed-economy multiplier of $1/(1 - 0.667) = 3$.

Another way of calculating the multiplier is as follows: Recall that the multiplier in our simplest model was $1/MPS$, where MPS = the marginal propensity to save. This result can be extended by noting that the analog to the MPS in an open economy is the *total leakage* per dollar of extra income—the dollars leaking into saving (the MPS) plus the dollars leaking into imports (the MPm). Hence, the open-economy multiplier should be $1/(MPS + MPm) = 1/(0.333 + 0.1) = 1/0.433 = 2.3$. Note that both the leakage analysis and the rounds analysis provide exactly the same answer.

To summarize:

Because a fraction of any income increase leaks into imports in an open economy, the open-economy multiplier is somewhat smaller than that of a closed economy. The exact relationship is

$$\text{Open-economy multiplier} = \frac{1}{MPS + MPm}$$

where MPS = marginal propensity to save and MPm = marginal propensity to import.

The U.S. Trade Deficit and Economic Activity

In a world where nations are increasingly linked by trade and commerce, countries must pay close attention to events abroad. If a country's policies are out of step with those of its trading partners, the roof can fall in, with recession, inflation, or major trade imbalances.

A good example of the influence of trade is shown in Figure 9-10, which depicts one of the major economic events of the last decade—the deterioration of the U.S. net export position during the early 1980s. To get a rough measure of the size of the shift, we can compare 1980 and 1986, years in which the overall utilization of resources was approximately the same. From 1980 to 1986, real net exports in 1982 prices moved from a surplus of $57 billion to a deficit of $130 billion. This decline of $187 billion in real net exports is 6 percent of the average real GNP for this period.

Unless offset by other items, this sharp decline in net exports would exert a severe contractionary effect upon the American economy. The change would be the approximate equivalent of a $187 billion decrease in government spending on goods and services. From 1980 to 1982, the decline in net exports was reinforced by monetary and fiscal policies. The result was a steep decline in U.S. aggregate demand and the deepest recession in 50 years. However, after 1982, the decrease in net exports was counteracted because the federal government budget was shifting in an *expansionary* direction. From 1982 to 1986, the federal government deficit increased by $146 billion. The fiscal expansion, along with a loosening of monetary policies, more than offset the decline in net exports; the economy pulled out of its slump.

This example serves as a warning that international conditions can have a major impact upon domestic economic activity.

How Large Are Multipliers?

In order to understand the impact of fiscal policy or of investment decisions or of changes in foreign trade, economists must be able to estimate the size of fiscal, investment, or foreign-trade multipliers. Just as a physician prescribing a pain-killer must know the effect of different dosages, so an economist must know the quantitative magnitude of expenditure and tax multipliers.

One of the recent developments in economics has been techniques for estimating econometric models of national economies. An *econometric model* is a set of equations, representing the behavior of the economy, that has been estimated using historical data. Early work in this area began with pioneers like Jan Tinbergen of the Netherlands and Lawrence Klein of the University of Pennsylvania—both winners of the Nobel Prize for constructing empirical macroeconomic models. Today, there is an entire industry of econometricians estimating macroeconomic models, determining multipliers, and forecasting the future of the economy.

Estimates of Multipliers. Textbook models give a highly simplified picture of the structure of the macroeconomy. For a more realistic picture of the response of output to changes in government expenditures, economists estimate large-scale econometric models and then perform numerical experiments by calculating the impact of a change in government expenditures on the economy. Such models serve as the basis for policy recommendations.

A recent comprehensive survey of econometric models of the United States provides a representative sample of multiplier estimates. The models surveyed include equations to predict the behavior of all major sectors of the economy (including both monetary and financial sectors, along with investment demand schedules and consumption functions) and they incorporate a full set of links with the rest of the world. In the experiments, the level of real government purchases of goods and services is permanently increased by $1 billion. The models then calculate the impact on real GNP. The change in real GNP resulting from the increase in government spending provides an estimate of the size of the government expenditure multiplier.

Figure 9-12 shows the results of this survey. The heavy blue line shows the average government expenditure multiplier estimated by eight models, while the light gray lines show the range of estimates of the individual models. The average multiplier for the first and second years is around 1.4, but after the second year the multiplier tends to decline slightly as monetary forces and international impacts come into play. (The monetary forces represent the impact of higher GNP on interest rates, which leads to a crowding out of investment, as we will explain in later chapters.)

One interesting feature of these estimates is that the different models (represented by the light gray

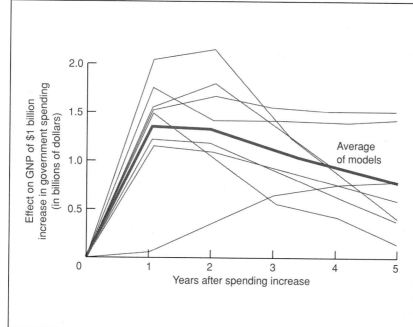

Figure 9-12. Expenditure multipliers in macroeconomic models

A recent study shows the estimated government expenditure multipliers in different macroeconomic models. These experiments show the estimated impact of a permanent $1 billion increase in the real value of government purchases of goods and services on real GNP at different intervals following the spending increase. That is, they show the impact of a $1 billion change in *G* on *Q*. The heavy blue line shows the average multiplier for the different models while the gray lines represent the multipliers for each individual model. [Source: Ralph C. Bryant, Gerald Holtham, and Peter Hooper, "Consensus and Diversity in Model Simulations," in *Empirical Macroeconomics for Interdependent Economies* (Brookings, Washington, D.C., 1988).]

lines in Figure 9-12) show considerable disagreement about the size of multipliers. Why do the estimates differ? To begin with, there is inherent uncertainty about the nature of economic relationships. Of course, uncertainty is the essence of the scientific enterprise, in both natural and social sciences. Research in economics is particularly challenging because economists cannot make controlled experiments in a laboratory. Even more perplexing is the fact that the economy itself evolves over time, so the "correct" model for 1960 is different from the "correct" model for 1990.

In addition, economists have fundamental disagreements about the underlying nature of the macroeconomy. Some economists believe that a classical approach best explains macroeconomic behavior while others are convinced that the Keynesian multiplier approach is the best starting point. Given all these hurdles, it is not surprising that there is no clear consensus about the actual multipliers for the U.S. economy.

Qualifications

We have completed our survey of the most important applications of the Keynesian multiplier model. This approach is an indispensable aid in understanding business fluctuations and the linkage between international trade and national output. It shows how government fiscal policy can be used to fight unemployment and inflation.

But it would be a mistake to believe you can make a macroeconomist out of a parrot by simply teaching it to say "$C + I + G + X$" or "Polly has a multiplier." Behind such concepts are important assumptions and qualifications.

First, recall that the multiplier model assumes that investment is fixed and prices are inflexible. A more realistic approach takes into account that investment responds to monetary conditions and to the level of output and that prices will rise more rapidly as output and employment increase. Only after we have mastered elements of monetary theory and policy, along with the essentials of inflation analysis, can the full impact of fiscal policy and trade flows be understood. When all these elements of reality are included in the analysis, the multiplier for government purchases, taxes, or foreign trade may be attenuated; in some cases it may even approach zero.

These qualifications will concern us for the rest of the chapters on macroeconomics. We now turn to an analysis of one of the most fascinating parts of all economics, the study of money. Once we understand how the central bank determines the money supply, we will have a fuller appreciation of how governments can tame the business cycles that have run wild through much of the history of capitalism.

SUMMARY

A. The Basic Multiplier Model

1. The multiplier model provides a simple way to understand the impact of aggregate demand on the level of output. In this approach, household consumption is a function of disposable income and investment is fixed. People's desires to consume and the willingness of businesses to invest are brought into line with each other by means of changes in output. The equilibrium level of national output must be at the intersection of savings and investment schedules SS and II. Or, to put it another way, equilibrium output comes at the intersection of the consumption-plus-investment schedule $C + I$ with the 45° line.

2. If output were temporarily above its equilibrium level, businesses would find output higher than sales, with inventories piling up involuntarily and profits plummeting. Firms would therefore cut production and employ-

ment back toward the equilibrium level. The only equilibrium path of output that can be maintained is at the output level where households will voluntarily continue to save exactly as much as businesses will voluntarily continue to invest.

3. Thus for the simplified Keynesian model of this chapter, investment calls the tune, and consumption dances to the music. Investment determines output, while saving responds passively to income changes. Output rises or falls until planned saving has adjusted to the level of planned investment.

4. Investment has a *multiplier effect* on output. When investment changes, output will at first rise by an equal amount. But as the income receivers in the capital-goods industries get more income, they set into motion a whole chain of additional secondary consumption spending and employment.

    If people always spend about $\frac{2}{3}$ of each extra dollar of income on consumption, the total of the multiplier chain will be

$$1 + \tfrac{2}{3} + (\tfrac{2}{3})^2 + \cdots = \frac{1}{1 - \tfrac{2}{3}} = 3$$

The multiplier works in either direction, amplifying either increases or decreases in investment. The simplest multiplier is numerically equal to the reciprocal of the *MPS* or, equivalently, to $1/(1 - MPC)$. This result occurs because it always takes more than a dollar of increased income to increase saving by a dollar.

B. Fiscal Policy in the Multiplier Model

5. Ancient societies suffered famines due to harvest failures. The modern market economy can suffer from poverty amidst plenty when business conditions deteriorate and unemployment soars. Or, excessive spending may lead to inflation. But fiscal steps, analyzed here, and monetary policies, studied later, can help smooth out the cycle of boom and bust.

6. The analysis of fiscal policy presented here elaborates the Keynesian multiplier model. For clarity, we assume a world in which prices and wages are inflexible, so that the aggregate supply curve is relatively flat for output levels below potential GNP.

7. An increase in government expenditure—taken by itself with taxes and investment unchanged—has an expansionary effect on national output much like that of investment. The schedule of $C + I + G$ shifts upward to a higher equilibrium intersection with the 45° line.

8. A decrease in taxes—taken by itself with investment and government expenditure unchanged—raises the equilibrium level of national output. The *CC* schedule of consumption plotted against GNP is shifted upward and leftward by a tax cut, but since extra dollars of disposable income go partly into saving, the dollar increase in consumption will not be quite so great as the dollars of new disposable income. Therefore, the tax multiplier is smaller than the government expenditure multiplier.

C. Output Determination in Open Economies

9. An open economy is one that engages in foreign trade, exporting goods to other countries and importing goods produced abroad. The difference between exports and imports of goods and services is called net exports. For most of the twentieth century, the United States had net exports near zero, but in the 1980s net exports moved sharply into deficit.

10. When foreign trade is introduced, domestic demand can differ from national output. Domestic demand comprises consumption, investment, and government purchases $(C + I + G)$. To obtain GNP, exports (e) must be added and imports (m) subtracted, so that

$$\text{GNP} = C + I + G + X$$

where X = net exports = $e - m$. Imports are determined by domestic income and output along with the prices of domestic goods relative to those of foreign goods; exports are the mirror image, determined by foreign income and output along with relative prices. The dollar increase of imports for each dollar increase in GNP is called the marginal propensity to import (MPm).

11. Foreign trade has an effect on GNP similar to that of investment or government purchases. As net exports rise, there is an increase in aggregate demand for domestic output. Net exports hence have a multiplier effect on output. But the expenditure multiplier in an open economy will be smaller than that in a closed economy because of leakages from spending into imports. The multiplier is

$$\text{Open-economy multiplier} = \frac{1}{MPS + MPm}$$

where MPS = marginal propensity to save and MPm = marginal propensity to import. Clearly, other things equal, the open-economy multiplier is smaller than the closed-economy multiplier, where $MPm = 0$.

12. Using statistical techniques and macroeconomic models, economists have built realistic models to estimate expenditure multipliers. For mainstream models, these tend to show multipliers of between 1 and $1\frac{1}{2}$ for periods of up to 4 years.

CONCEPTS FOR REVIEW

The basic multiplier model
$C + I$ schedule
two ways of viewing GNP
  determination:
    planned saving = planned
      investment
    planned C + planned I
      = GNP

investment equals saving: planned
  vs. actual levels
multiplier effect of investment
multiplier
  $= 1 + MPC + (MPC)^2 + \cdots$
  $= \dfrac{1}{1 - MPC} = \dfrac{1}{MPS}$

Government expenditures and taxation
fiscal policy:
  G effect on equilibrium GNP
  T effect on CC and on GNP
multiplier effects of government
  spending (G) and taxes (T)
$C + I + G$ curve for closed economy

Open-economy macroeconomics
$C + I + G + X$ curve for open
  economy
net exports $= X = e - m$
domestic demand vs. spending on
  GNP

marginal propensity to import
  (MPm)
multiplier:
  in closed economy $= 1/MPS$
  in open economy $=$
    $1/(MPS + MPm)$

impact of trade flows,
  exchange rates
  on GNP

QUESTIONS FOR DISCUSSION

1. In the simple multiplier model, assume that investment is always zero. Show that equilibrium output in this special case would come at the break-even point of the consumption function. Why would equilibrium output *not* occur at the break-even point when investment is not zero?

2. The savings-and-investment diagram and the 45° line $C + I$ diagram are two different ways of showing how national output is determined in the multiplier model. Describe each. Show their equivalence.

3. Reconstruct Table 9-2 assuming that net investment is equal to (*a*) $300 billion, (*b*) $400 billion. What is the resulting difference in GNP? Is this difference greater or smaller than the change in I? Why? When I drops from $200 billion to $100 billion, how much must GNP drop?

4. Give (*a*) the common sense, (*b*) the arithmetic, (*c*) the geometry of the multiplier. What are the multipliers for $MPC = 0.9$? 0.8? 0.5? For $MPS = 0.1$? 0.8?

5. Work out the explosive(!) chain of spending and respending when $MPC = 2$. Try to explain the economics of the arithmetic of the divergent infinite geometric series.

6. Explain the following concepts: government expenditure multiplier, marginal propensity to consume, marginal propensity to import, open-economy multiplier.

7. Explain in words and using the notion of expenditure rounds why the tax multiplier is smaller than the expenditure multiplier.

8. During most of the 1980s, many political leaders have argued for lowering government deficits. Analyze the impact of lower government purchases of goods and services on the government deficit and on output.

9. Explain why governments might use fiscal policy to stabilize the economy. Why would fiscal policy be effective in raising output in a Keynesian economy but not in a classical economy?

10. Explain the impact upon net exports and GNP of the following, using Table 9-3 where possible:
    (a) An increase in investment (I) of $100 billion
    (b) A decrease in government purchases (G) of $50 billion
    (c) An increase of foreign output which increased exports by $10 billion
    (d) A depreciation of the exchange rate that raised exports by $30 billion and lowered imports by $20 billion at every level of GNP

11. What would the expenditure multiplier be in an economy without government spending or taxes where the MPC is 0.80 and where the MPm is 0? Where the MPm is 0.1? Where the MPm is 0.9? Explain why the multiplier might even be less than 1.

12. "Even if the government spends billions on wasteful military armaments, this action can create jobs in a recession and will be socially worthwhile." Discuss.

unthinkable without the introduction of the great social invention of money.

As economies develop, people do not directly exchange one good for another. Instead, they sell goods for money, and then use money to buy other goods they most wish to have. At first glance this seems to complicate rather than simplify matters, to replace one transaction by two. After all, you have apples and want nuts; would it not be simpler to trade one for the other rather than to sell the apples for money and then use the money to buy nuts?

Actually, the reverse is true: two monetary transactions are simpler than one barter transaction. For example, some people may want to buy apples, and some may want to sell nuts. But it would be a most unusual circumstance to find a person with trading desires that exactly complement your own—eager to sell nuts and buy apples. To use a classical economic phrase, instead of there being a "double coincidence of wants," there is likely to be a "want of coincidence." So, unless a hungry tailor happens to find an undraped farmer who has both food and a desire for a pair of pants, under barter neither can make a direct trade.

Societies that traded extensively simply could not overcome the overwhelming handicaps of barter. The use of a commonly accepted medium of exchange, money, permitted the farmer to buy pants from the tailor, who buys shoes from the cobbler, who buys leather from the farmer.

Commodity Money. Money as a medium of exchange first came into human history in the form of commodities. A great variety of items have served as money at one time or another: cattle, olive oil, beer or wine, copper, iron, gold, silver, rings, diamonds, and cigarettes.

Each of the above has advantages and disadvantages. Cattle are not divisible into small change. Beer does not improve with keeping, although wine may. Olive oil provides a nice liquid currency that is as minutely divisible as one wishes, but it is a bit messy to handle. And so forth.

By the nineteenth century, commodity money was almost exclusively limited to metals like silver and gold. These forms of money had *intrinsic value,* denoting that they had use value in themselves. Because money had intrinsic value, there was no need for the government to guarantee its value, and the quantity of money was regulated by the market through the supply and demand for gold or silver. The disadvantages of metallic money are that scarce resources are required to dig it out of the ground and that it might become scarce or abundant simply because of accidental discoveries of ore deposits.

The advent of monetary control by central banks has led to a much more stable currency system. The intrinsic value of money is now the least important thing about it.

Paper Money. The age of commodity money gave way to the age of paper money. The essence of money is now laid bare. Money is wanted not for its own sake but for the things it will buy. We do not wish to consume money directly; rather we use it by getting rid of it. Even when we choose to keep money, its value comes from the fact that we can spend it later on.

The use of paper currency has become widespread because it is a convenient medium of exchange. Currency is easily carried and stored. With careful engraving, the value of money can be protected from counterfeiting. The fact that private individuals cannot legally create money keeps it scarce.

Given this limitation in supply, currency has value. It can buy things. As long as people can pay their bills with currency, as long as it is accepted as a means of payment, it serves the function of money.

Bank Money. Today is the age of bank money—checks written on funds deposited in a bank or other financial institution. Checks are accepted in place of cash payment for many goods and services. In fact, if we calculate the total dollar amount of transactions, nine-tenths take place by bank money, the rest by currency.

Continued Evolution. Today there is extremely rapid innovation in the different forms of money. For example, some financial institutions will now link a checking account to a savings account or even to a stock portfolio, allowing customers to write checks on the value of their stock. Credit cards and traveler's checks can be used for many transactions. The fast-changing nature of money causes difficult problems for central banks, which are charged with measuring and controlling the nation's money supply.

Components of the Money Supply

Let us now look more carefully at the different kinds of money that Americans employ. The major *monetary aggregates* are the quantitative measures of the supply of money. They are known today as M_1 and M_2, and you can read about their week-to-week movements in the newspaper, along with sage commentaries on the significance of the latest wiggle. Here we will delve into the exact definitions as of 1991.

Transactions Money. One important and closely watched measure of money is *transactions money*, or M_1, which consists of items that are actually used for transactions. The following are the components of M_1:

• *Coins.* M_1 includes coins not held by banks.
• *Paper currency.* More significant is *paper currency*. Most of us know little more about a $1 or $5 bill than that it is inscribed with the picture of an American statesman, that it bears some official signatures, and that each has a numeral showing its face value.

  Examine a $10 bill or some other paper bill. You will probably find it says "Federal Reserve Note." Also, it announces itself as "legal tender for all debts, public and private." But what "backs" our paper currency? Many years ago, paper money was backed by gold or silver. There is no such pretense today. Today, all U.S. coins and paper currency are *fiat money.* This term signifies that something is money because the government decrees it is money. More precisely, the government states that coins and paper currency are *legal tender*, which must be accepted for all debts, public and private.

  Coins and paper currency (the sum known as "currency") add up to about one-fourth of total transactions money, M_1.
• *Checking accounts.* There is a third component of transactions money—checking deposits or bank money. These are funds, deposited in banks and other financial institutions, that you can write checks on. These are technically known as "demand deposits and other checkable deposits." [1]

If I have $1000 in my checking account at the Albuquerque National Bank, that deposit can be regarded as money. Why? For the simple reason that I can pay for purchases with checks drawn on it. The deposit is like any other medium of exchange. Possessing the essential properties of money, bank checking-account deposits are counted as transactions money, as part of M_1.

Table 10-1 shows the dollar values of the different components of transactions money, M_1.

Broad Money. Although M_1 is strictly speaking the most appropriate measure of money as a means of payment, a second closely watched aggregate is *broad money*, or M_2. Sometimes called "asset money" or "near-money," M_2 includes M_1 as well as savings accounts in banks and similar assets that are very close substitutes for transactions money.

Examples of such near-monies in M_2 include deposits in a savings account in your bank; a money market mutual fund account operated by your stockbroker; a deposit in a money market deposit account run by a commercial bank. And so on.

Why are these not transactions money? Because they cannot be used as means of exchange for all purchases; they are forms of near-money, however, because you can convert them into cash very quickly with no loss of value.

Over the last decade, M_2 has been a useful indicator of trends in money-supply growth. It showed

---

[1] Until the late 1970s, virtually all checking accounts were "demand deposits" at commercial banks and earned no interest. Under the pressure of advancing technology and high interest rates, the sharp difference between demand deposits and other assets gradually eroded. In 1980 and 1982, Congress passed laws allowing other financial institutions to offer checking accounts (called "negotiable orders of withdrawal," or NOW accounts), and allowed payment of interest on checking accounts. By the late 1980s, interest-rate ceilings on almost all assets were removed. The result of this dismantling of regulatory restrictions between different institutions and assets is a blurring of the distinction between money and other financial assets. One of the side effects of the deregulated financial markets was the savings and loan fiasco of the late 1980s and early 1990s.

Kinds of money	Billions of dollars		
	1959	1971	1990
Currency (outside of financial institutions)	28.8	52.0	245.9
Demand deposits (excludes government deposits and certain foreign deposits)	110.8	175.1	277.5
NOW accounts and other checkable deposits	0.4	1.3	302.1
Total transactions money (M_1)	140.0	228.4	825.5
Savings accounts and small time deposits (includes money market funds)	157.8	484.3	2,497.8
Broad money (M_2)	297.8	712.7	3,323.3

Table 10-1. Components of the money supply of the United States

Two widely used definitions of the money supply are transactions money (M_1) and broad money (M_2). M_1 consists of currency and checking accounts. M_2 adds to these certain "near-monies" such as savings accounts and time deposits. (Source: Federal Reserve Board.)

greater stability than M_1, because when new kinds of checking accounts were introduced in the 1980s, M_1 behaved very erratically. At that time M_2 proved to be a better barometer of economic activity.

There are many other technical definitions of money that are used by specialists in monetary economics. But for our purposes, we need master only the two major definitions of money.

The major monetary concept is **transactions money,** or M_1, which is the sum of coins and paper currency in circulation outside the banks, plus checkable deposits. Less often we will also refer to **broad money** (called M_2), which includes assets such as savings accounts in addition to coins, paper currency, and checkable deposits.

The Nature of Interest Rates

In analyzing the supply and demand for money in later sections, we will need to consider the price of money, which is the interest rate:

Interest is the payment made for the use of money. The **interest rate** is the amount of interest paid per unit of time. In other words, people must pay for the opportunity to borrow money. The cost of borrowing money, measured in dollars per year per dollar borrowed, is the interest rate.

Some examples will illustrate how interest works.

• When you graduate from college you have $500 to your name. You decide to keep it in currency. If you spend none of your funds, at the end of a year you still have $500 because currency has a zero interest rate.

• You place $2000 in a savings account in your local bank, where the interest rate on savings accounts is 5 percent per year. At the end of 1 year, the bank will have paid $100 in interest into your account, so the account is now worth $2100.

• You start your first job and decide to buy a $10,000 car. You will be able to pay for it in a year. Your employer offers you a short-term loan at 12 percent per year. The loan requires you to pay interest of $100 per month (or $1200 per year) and repay the principal of $10,000 at the end of the year.

• After a few months in your new job, you find a small house to purchase and settle on a price of $100,000. You go to your local bank and find that 30-year, fixed-interest-rate mortgages have an interest rate of 10 percent per year. Each month you make a mortgage payment of $877.58. Note that this payment is a little bit more than the pro-rated monthly interest charge of $\frac{10}{12}$ percent per month. Why? Because it includes not only interest but also *amortization.* This is repayments of *principal,* the amount borrowed. By the time you have made your 360 monthly payments, you will have completely paid off the loan.

From these examples we see that interest rates have the dimension of a pure number, in percent per year. Interest is the price paid to borrow money, which allows the borrower to obtain real resources over the time of the loan.

An Array of Interest Rates

Textbooks often speak of "*the* interest rate," but a glance at a newspaper like the *Wall Street Journal* reveals a bewildering array of interest rates in today's complex financial system. Interest rates differ mainly in terms of the characteristics of the loan or of the borrower. Let us review the major differences.

1. *Term or maturity.* Loans differ in their term or maturity—the length of time until they must be paid off. The shortest loans are overnight. For example, a bank may lend funds to a firm that is expecting payment the next day. Short-term securities are for periods up to a year. Companies often issue bonds that have maturities of 10 to 30 years, and mortgages are typically up to 30 years in maturity. Longer-term securities generally command a higher interest rate than do short-term issues because people are willing to sacrifice quick access to their funds only if they can increase their yield.

2. *Risk.* Some loans are virtually riskless while others are highly speculative. Investors require that a premium be paid when they invest in risky ventures. At the safe end of the spectrum lie the securities of the U.S. government. These bonds and bills are backed by the full faith, credit, and taxing powers of the government. These items are safe because interest on the government debt will almost certainly be paid. Intermediate in risk are borrowings of creditworthy corporations, states, and localities. Risky investments, which bear a significant chance of default or nonpayment, include those in companies close to bankruptcy, cities with shrinking tax bases, or Latin American countries with large overseas debts and little import income.

   The U.S. government pays what is called the "riskless" interest rate; over the last decade this has ranged from 5 to 15 percent per year for short-term loans. Riskier securities might pay 1, 2, or 5 percent per year more than the riskless rate; this premium reflects the amount necessary to compensate the lender for losses in case of default.

3. *Liquidity.* An asset is said to be "liquid" if it can be converted into cash quickly and with little loss in value. Most marketable securities, including common stocks and corporate and govern-ment bonds, can be turned into cash quickly for close to their current value. Illiquid assets include unique assets for which no well-established market exists. For example, if you own a house in a depressed region, you might find it difficult to sell the house quickly or at a price near its replacement cost. Similarly, it might be difficult to cash in on the full value of a small, privately owned company. The house and the small company are illiquid assets. Because of the higher risk and the difficulty of extracting the borrower's investment, illiquid assets or loans usually command considerably higher interest rates than do liquid, riskless ones.

4. *Administrative costs.* Loans differ in terms of the time and diligence needed for their oversight and administration. Some loans simply require cashing interest checks periodically. Others, such as student loans, mortgages, or credit-card advances, require ensuring timely payments. Sometimes lenders hire detectives and lawyers to track down debtors. Loans with high administrative costs may command interest rates from 5 to 10 percent per year higher than other interest rates.

When these four factors are put together, it is not surprising that we see so many different financial instruments and so many different interest rates. Figure 10-2 shows the behavior of a few important interest rates over the last three decades. In the discussion that follows, when we speak of "the interest rate" we are referring to the interest rate on short-term government securities, such as the 90-day Treasury-bill rate. As Figure 10-2 shows, most other interest rates rise and fall in step with the 3-month Treasury-bill rate.

Real vs. Nominal Interest Rates

Interest is measured in dollar terms, not in terms of fish or cars or goods in general. The *nominal interest rate* measures the yield in dollars per year per dollar invested. But dollars can become distorted yardsticks. The prices of fish, or cars, and goods in general change from year to year—these days prices generally rise due to inflation. Put differently, the interest rate on dollars does not measure what a lender really earns in terms of goods and services. Let us say that you lend $100 today at 5 percent per

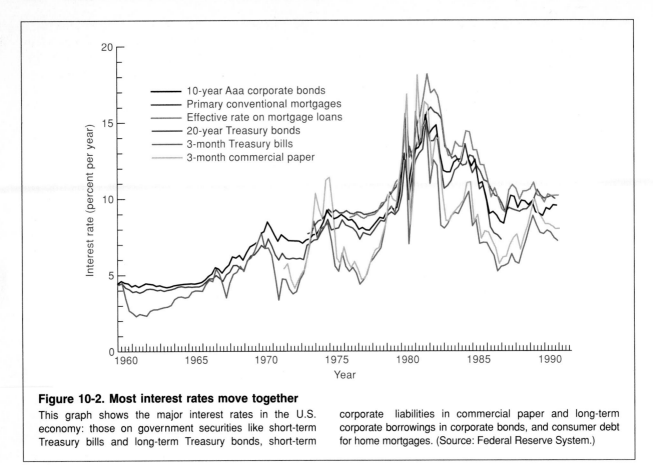

Figure 10-2. Most interest rates move together

This graph shows the major interest rates in the U.S. economy: those on government securities like short-term Treasury bills and long-term Treasury bonds, short-term corporate liabilities in commercial paper and long-term corporate borrowings in corporate bonds, and consumer debt for home mortgages. (Source: Federal Reserve System.)

year interest. You would get back $105 at the end of a year. But because prices changed over the year, you would not be able to obtain the same quantity of goods that you could have bought at the beginning of the year with the original $100.

Clearly, we need another concept of interest that measures the return on investments in terms of real goods and services rather than the return in terms of dollars. This alternative concept is the *real interest rate,* which measures the quantity of goods we get tomorrow for goods forgone today. The real interest rate is obtained by correcting nominal or dollar interest rates for the rate of inflation.

The **nominal interest rate** (sometimes also called the "money interest rate") is the interest rate on money in terms of money. When you read about interest rates in the newspaper, or examine the interest rates in Figure 10-2, you are looking at nominal interest rates; they give the dollar return per dollar of investment.

In contrast, **real interest rates** are corrected for inflation and are defined as the nominal interest rate minus the rate of inflation. As an example, suppose the nominal interest rate is 13 percent per year and the inflation rate is 7 percent per year; we can calculate the real interest rate as 13 − 7 = 6 percent per year. In other words, if you lend out 100 market baskets of goods today, you will next year get back only 106 (and not 113) market baskets of goods as principal and real interest payments.

During inflationary periods, we must use real interest rates, not nominal or money interest rates, to calculate the yield on investments in terms of goods earned per year on goods invested. The real interest rate is the nominal interest rate less the rate of inflation.

Recent Interest-Rate Movements. The difference between nominal and real interest rates is illustrated in Figure 10-3. It shows that most of the rise in nominal interest rates from 1960 to 1980 was purely illusory, for nominal interest rates were just keeping up with inflation during those years. After 1980, however, real interest rates rose sharply.

What was the reason for the jump in real interest rates? Most macroeconomists believe that the real interest rates increased because the Federal Reserve tightened monetary policy in reaction to the high inflation of that period. (The next chapter will illustrate the mechanism by which this tightening occurs.)

The Demand for Money

The demand for money is different from the demand for ice cream or movies. Money is not desired for its own sake; you cannot eat nickels, and we seldom hang $100 bills on the wall for the artistic quality of their engraving. Rather, money is held because it serves us indirectly, as a lubricant to trade and exchange. The need to hold money to buy things is the essence of the demand for money.

Money's Functions

Before we analyze the demand for money, let's review money's functions.

1. By far the most important function of money is to serve as a *medium of exchange*. Without money we would be constantly roving around

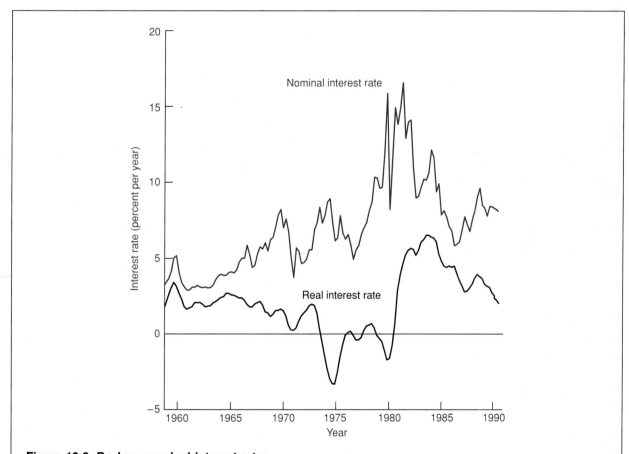

Figure 10-3. Real vs. nominal interest rates
This figure shows in blue the nominal interest rates on safe short-term securities (1-year Treasury notes). Note their upward trend over the last 25 years. Most of the upward movement can be seen as the reflection of the increase in inflation. The black curve shows the real interest rate, equal to the nominal or money rate less the realized inflation rate over the prior year. Note that real interest rates drifted downward until 1980. After 1980, however, real interest rates moved up sharply. (Source: Federal Reserve Board, U.S. Department of Labor.)

looking for someone to barter with. We are often reminded of money's utility when it does not work properly, as in the Soviet Union in the early 1990s, when people spent hours in line waiting for goods and tried to get dollars or other foreign currencies because the ruble ceased functioning as an acceptable means of exchange.

2. Money is also used as the *unit of account*, the unit by which we measure the *value* of things. Just as we measure weight in kilograms, we measure value in money. The use of a common unit of account simplifies economic life enormously.

3. Money is sometimes used as a *store of value*; it allows value to be held over time. In comparison with risky assets like stocks or real estate or gold, money is relatively riskless. In earlier days, people held currency as a safe form of wealth. Today, more and more people are holding high-yield money (such as NOW accounts) as a safe asset. But the vast preponderance of wealth is held in other assets, such as savings accounts, stocks, bonds, and real estate.

The Costs of Holding Money

These three functions of money are extremely important to people, so important that they are willing to incur a cost to hold currency or low-yielding checking accounts. What is the *cost of holding money?* It is the sacrifice in interest that you must incur by holding money rather than a riskier, less liquid asset or investment.

Say that you put $1000 in a savings account at the beginning of 1990; you would earn about 8 percent interest and would end with $1080 at the end of 1990. This represents an 8 percent money or nominal interest rate. By contrast, suppose that you had left your $1000 in currency rather than in the money fund for 1990. You would end up with only $1000, for currency pays no interest. The cost of holding money as currency in this case would be $80.

Money allows easy and quick transactions, unambiguous determination of price, plus storage of value over time. These services are not free, however. If wealth were held in stocks, bonds, or savings accounts rather than money, it would yield a higher interest rate.

Let's consider yet another example. You have $1000 in your checking account, or bank money

(M_1). The bank pays 5 percent per year on your checking account, or $50 per year. Alternatively, you can earn 8 percent in a savings account. Thus the net cost (or opportunity cost) of keeping your $1000 in bank money is $30 (=$80 − $50).

Why might you sacrifice the $30? Because it is worthwhile to keep the money in your checking account to pay for food or a new bike. You are getting "money services" that are worth at least $30 a year.

Two Sources of Money Demand

Transactions Demand. People and firms use money as a medium of exchange: households need money to buy groceries, and firms need money to pay for materials and labor. These needs constitute the *transactions demand for money.*

Figure 10-4 illustrates the mechanics of the transactions demand for money. This figure shows the average money holdings of a family that earns $3000 per month, keeps it in money, and spends it during the month. Calculation will show that the family holds $1500 on average in money balances.

This example can help us see how the demand for money responds to different economic influences. If all prices and incomes double, then the vertical axis in Figure 10-4 is simply relabeled by doubling all the dollar values. Clearly the nominal demand for M doubles. Thus the transactions demand for money doubles if nominal GNP doubles with no change in real GNP or other real variables.

An extremely important question is, How does the demand for money vary with interest rates? Recall that our family is paying an opportunity cost for its checking account—the interest rate on M is less than that on other assets. As interest rates rise, the family might say:

> Let's put only half of our money in the checking account at the beginning of the month, and put the other half in a savings account earning 8 percent per annum. Then on day 15, we'll take that $1500 out of the money fund and put it in our checking account to pay the next 2 weeks' bills.

Note the net effect: As interest rates rose, and the family decided to put half its earnings in a savings account, the average money balance of our family fell from $1500 to $750. This shows how money holdings (or the demand for money) may be sensi-

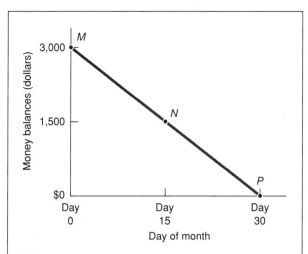

Figure 10-4. The transactions demand for money

How much money might a typical family hold? Assume that the family is paid $3000 at the beginning of the month, and spends the whole amount over the course of the month at a constant rate of $100 per day. Moreover, the family does not put any of its money in another asset during the month. Thus the family has $3000 on day 0, $1500 on day 15, and nothing at the end of the month. This is illustrated by the line *MNP*.

How much money does the family hold on average? Answer: $\frac{1}{2}$ of $3000 = $1500.

To understand the way the demand for money behaves, consider how this figure would change if all prices and incomes doubled. If real incomes doubled. If interest rates on savings accounts went to 20 percent.

tive to interest rates: *other things equal, as interest rates rise, the quantity of money demanded declines.*

You might think that the economic gain from a constant reshuffling of portfolios is so small that household money holdings are not likely to be affected by interest-rate fluctuations. Average bank balances change very little when people find they can earn 2 or 4 percent more on their money funds.

In fact, the major impact of interest rates on the demand for money comes in the business sector. Firms often find themselves with bank balances of $100 million one day, $250 million the next day, and so forth. If they do nothing, they could easily lose $20 to $50 million a year in interest payments. Since the 1970s the era of high interest rates has ushered in corporate "cash management," in which banks help their corporate customers keep their cash

constantly invested in high-yield assets rather than lying fallow in zero-yield checking accounts. And with higher interest rates, corporations work a little harder to keep their cash balances at a minimum.

Asset Demand. In addition to holding money for transactions needs, people may also hold money as a store of value. As we noted in the discussion of consumption in Chapter 7, people save for retirement, for hard times, and for their children's educations. At the end of 1988, households owned about $12 trillion of financial assets of various kinds. Shouldn't money be one of these assets?

One of the most important topics of modern economics is **portfolio theory,** which describes how rational investors put their wealth into a "portfolio" (or group of securities). For example, your portfolio might consist of $10,000 worth of Treasury bonds, $5000 in a money market fund, and $14,000 in the stock market.

Portfolio theory begins with the fundamental assumption that people seek high returns on their investments but are averse to risky investments. In other words, people will generally hold risky investments only if their returns are sufficiently high. (*Returns* consist of the annual return per dollar of investment.) Given two assets with equal returns, people seek the safer investment. To draw people away from low-risk assets into risky stocks or real estate, the high-risk asset must offer a higher return.

Portfolio theory analyzes how a risk-averse investor should allocate wealth. One important rule is to diversify the portfolio among different assets. "Don't put all your eggs in one basket" is one way of expressing this rule.

In addition, advanced studies of portfolio theory show that an optimal portfolio would generally contain a mixture of low-risk and high-risk assets. The low-risk assets might well include interest-bearing checking accounts. We should not be surprised, therefore, that in today's world many households will hold money as part of their strategy for investing their wealth and not only for transactions purposes.

What of the rest of the portfolio? Calculations show (as we will see in this chapter's appendix) that by diversifying their wealth among a broad group of investments—different common stocks, different kinds of bonds, perhaps real estate—

people can attain a good return on their wealth without incurring unacceptable risks.*

We summarize as follows:

The demand for money is grounded in the need for a medium of exchange, the transactions demand. We hold currency and checking accounts to buy goods and pay our bills. As our incomes rise, the value of the goods we buy goes up, and we therefore need more money for transactions, raising our demand for money.

The transactions demand for M will be sensitive to the cost of holding money. When interest rates on alternative assets rise relative to the interest rate on money, people and businesses tend to reduce their money holdings.

In addition, people sometimes hold money as an asset. They want to protect some of their wealth against the vicissitudes of economic life, avoiding the folly of putting all their eggs in one basket. And one basket that many investors will want to use is that of an ultra-safe asset. This asset may be a high-yield checking account, part of M_1, or it may be a near-money in M_2, perhaps a savings account or a money fund.

B. Banking and the Supply of Money

Section A showed that transactions money, M_1, has two major components: currency and checking accounts. To understand the way that money affects the economy, we need to master the process by which money is created. We begin by surveying some historical and institutional aspects of commercial banking. We will then analyze the process by which banks "create" money.

Banking as a Business

Bank money and many other financial services are today provided by financial intermediaries. **Financial intermediaries** are institutions like banks, insurance companies, and a dwindling number of savings and loan associations that take deposits or funds from one group and lend these funds to another group. For example, financial intermediaries accept savings deposits from households or firms or foreigners. They then lend these funds to households and businesses for a variety of purposes.

What are the major financial intermediaries today? The largest class consists of commercial banks, which are financial institutions in which most of the nation's checkable deposits are housed; these banks have about 30 percent of the assets of financial institutions. Savings and loan associations and mutual savings banks rank second, with about 17 percent of the assets. Other important groups are life-insurance companies, pension funds, and money market mutual funds. Altogether, at the end of 1988, all such firms had a total of $9.7 trillion of assets and liabilities.

In what follows we will focus on commercial banks, or "banks" for short. We do so because these institutions are still the main source of checking accounts, or the bank-money component of M_1.

In summary:

Financial institutions transfer funds from lenders to borrowers. In doing this, they create financial instruments (like checking and savings accounts).

---

*The theory of portfolio choice is at the center of one of the most exciting and popular fields of intermediate economics: money and banking. This analysis uses a framework similar to that of the utility theory used in microeconomics. It assumes that people like high yields on assets but dislike risky assets. Work of Nobel-laureates Harry Marko- witz and James Tobin showed that utility-maximizing consumers would spread their wealth (i.e., diversify their portfolios) among many different risky assets.

This line of research has become extremely important in modern finance theory and takes its modern form in the "capital asset pricing model," for which William Sharpe won the 1990 Nobel Prize in economics. Every good portfolio manager on Wall Street uses these techniques to bolster his or her intuition in choosing stocks and bonds.

For his contribution to portfolio theory and other aspects of monetary and macroeconomic theory, Tobin was awarded the Nobel Prize in economics in 1981.

Balance Sheet of All Commercial Banking Institutions, 1991 (Billions of Dollars)			
Assets		**Liabilities**	
Reserves	$ 54	Checking accounts	$ 602
Loans	2,259	Savings and time deposits	1,780
Investments and securities	628	Other liabilities	998
Other assets	439		
Total	$3,380	Total	$3,380

Table 10-2. Reserves and checking deposits are major balance sheet entries of commercial banks

Reserves and checking accounts are key to bank creation of money. Checking accounts are payable on demand and thus can be drawn on quickly when customers write checks. Reserves are large primarily to meet legal requirements, not to provide against possible unexpected withdrawals. [Source: *Federal Reserve Bulletin* (June 1991).]

But from a macroeconomic vantage point the most important instrument is bank money (or checking accounts) primarily provided today by commercial banks.

A Business Venture

Banks and other financial intermediaries are much like other businesses. They are organized to earn profits for their owners. A commercial bank is a relatively simple business concern. It provides certain services for customers and in return receives payments from them.

Table 10-2 shows the consolidated balance sheet of all U.S. commercial banks. A *balance sheet* is a statement of a firm's financial position at a point in time. It lists *assets* (items that a firm owns) and *liabilities* (items the firm owes). The difference between assets and liabilities is called *net worth*. Each entry in a balance sheet is valued at its actual market value or its historical cost.

Except for minor rearrangements, a bank's balance sheet looks much like the balance sheet of any business. The unique feature of the bank balance sheet is an item called "reserves," which appears on the asset side. **Reserves** are funds or assets banks hold in the form of cash on hand or of funds deposited by the bank with the central bank. A small fraction of reserves is for day-to-day business needs, but the bulk is held to meet legal reserve requirements.

How Banks Developed from Goldsmith Establishments

Commercial banking in England began with the goldsmiths, who developed the practice of storing people's gold and valuables for safekeeping. At first, such establishments were simply like baggage checkrooms or warehouses. Depositors left gold for safekeeping and were given a receipt. Later they presented their receipt, paid a small fee for the safekeeping, and got back their gold.

The goldsmiths soon found it more convenient not to worry about returning exactly the same piece of gold that each customer had left. Customers were quite willing to accept any gold as long as it was equivalent in value to what they had deposited. This "anonymity" was important for it freed goldsmiths to relend the gold.

What would balance sheets of a typical goldsmith establishment look like? Perhaps like Table 10-3. We assume that First Goldsmith Bank no longer hammers gold bars but is occupied solely with storing people's money for safekeeping. A total of $1 million has been deposited in its vaults, and this whole sum is held as a cash asset (this is the item "cash reserves" in the balance sheet). To balance this asset, there is a demand deposit of the same amount. Cash reserves are therefore 100 percent of deposits.

The bank money would just offset the amount of ordinary money (gold or currency) placed in the bank's safe and withdrawn from active circulation.

Goldsmith Balance Sheet			
Assets		**Liabilities**	
Cash reserves	$1,000,000	Demand deposits	$1,000,000
Total	$1,000,000	Total	$1,000,000

Table 10-3. First Goldsmith Bank held 100 percent cash reserves against demand deposits
In a primitive banking system, with 100 percent backing of demand deposits, no creation of money out of new reserves is possible.

No money creation has taken place. The process would be of no more interest than if the public decided to convert nickels into dimes. We say that a 100 percent reserve banking system has a neutral effect on money, spending, and prices—not adding or subtracting from total *M*.

Modern Fractional-Reserve Banking

As profit maximizers, the goldsmith-bankers recognized that, although deposits are payable on demand, they are not all withdrawn together. Reserves equal to total deposits are necessary if all depositors suddenly had to be paid off in full at the same time, but this almost never occurred. On a given day, some people make withdrawals while others make deposits. These two kinds of transactions generally balanced out.

Funds held as reserves are sterile—sitting in a vault they do not earn interest. Early banks hit upon the idea of using the money entrusted to them to buy bonds or other earning assets. They soon found that investing their deposits was beneficial because depositors could still be paid on demand while the bank could make some extra earnings.

By putting most of the money deposited with them in earning assets and keeping only *fractional* cash reserves against deposits, banks maximize their profits. With these profits they can provide extra services or lower fees to depositors.

The decision to hold fractional rather than 100 percent reserves against deposits was revolutionary. It enabled banks to create money. That is, banks could turn 1 dollar of reserves into several dollars of deposits. In the next section we will see how this process works.

Legal Reserve Requirements

In banking, reserves are that part of a bank's assets held either as cash on hand or as deposits with the central bank. A prudent banker, concerned only with assuring customers that the bank has enough cash for daily transactions, might choose to keep 1 or 2 percent of the bank's assets in reserves. In fact, banks today set aside more than 10 percent of their checking deposits in reserves. These are held in deposits with our central bank, the Federal Reserve System, often called "the Fed."

Why are reserves in fact so high? All financial institutions are required by law and Federal Reserve regulations to keep a fraction of their deposits as reserves. Reserve requirements apply to all types of checking and savings deposits, independent of the actual need for cash on hand.

The regulatory structure that determines the legal reserve requirements is explored in the next chapter. The key point here is the following:

The main function of legal reserve requirements is to enable the Federal Reserve to control the amount of checking deposits that banks can create. By imposing high fixed legal reserve requirements, the Fed can better control the money supply.

The Process of Deposit Creation

In our simplified discussion of goldsmith banks, we suggested that banks turn reserves into bank money. There are, in fact, two steps in the process:

- The central bank (the Fed) determines the quantity of reserves of the banking system. The detailed process by which the central bank does this is discussed in the next chapter.

• Using those reserves as an input, the banking system transforms them into a much larger amount of bank money. The currency plus this bank money then is the money supply, M_1. This process is called the *multiple expansion of bank deposits.*

How Deposits Are Created: First-Generation Banks

Let us consider what happens when new reserves are injected into the banking system. Assume that the Federal Reserve buys a $1000 government bond from Ms. Bondholder, and she deposits the $1000 in her checking account at Bank 1.

The change in the balance sheet of Bank 1, as far as the new demand deposit is concerned, is shown in Table 28-4(a).[2] When Ms. Bondholder made the deposit, $1000 of bank money, or checking deposits, was created. Now, if the bank were to keep 100 percent of deposits in reserves, like the old goldsmiths, no extra money would be created from the new deposit of $1000. The depositor's $1000 checking deposit would just match the $1000 of reserves. But modern banks do not keep 100 percent reserves for their deposits. In our example we will assume a reserve requirement of 10 percent, for simplicity of calculations. Therefore Bank 1 must set aside as reserves $100 of the $1000 deposit.

---

[2] For simplicity, our tables will show only the *changes* in balance sheet items, and we use reserve ratios of 10 percent. Note that when bankers refer to their loans and investments, by "investments" they mean their holdings of bonds and other financial assets. They don't mean what economists mean by "investment," which is capital formation.

What can Bank 1 now do? It has $900 more in reserves than it needs to meet the reserve requirement. Because reserves earn no interest, our profit-minded bank will loan or invest the excess $900. The loan might be for a car, or the investment might be a purchase of a Treasury bond.

Let's say the bank makes a loan or buys a bond. The person who borrows the money or sells the bond takes the $900 (in cash or check) and deposits it in her account in another bank. Very quickly, then, the $900 will be paid out by Bank 1.

What does the bank's balance sheet look like after all transactions and investments have been made? After it has loaned or invested $900, Bank 1's legal reserves are just enough to meet its legal reserve requirements. There is nothing more it can do until someone deposits more money. The balance sheet of Bank 1, after it has made all possible loans or investments (but still meets its reserve requirement), is shown in Table 10-4(b).

Note that Bank 1 has created money. How? To the original $1000 of deposits shown on the right of Table 10-4(b) it has added $900 of demand deposits in another account (i.e., in the checking account of the person who got the $900). Hence, the total amount of M is now $1900. *Bank 1's activity has created $900 of new money.*

Chain Repercussions on Other Banks

What happens after the $900 created by Bank 1 leaves the bank? It will soon be deposited in another bank, and at that point it starts up a chain of expansion whereby still more bank money is created.

Bank 1 in Initial Position			
Assets		**Liabilities**	
Reserves	+$1,000	Deposits	+$1,000
Total	+$1,000	Total	+$1,000

Table 10-4(a). Multiple-bank deposit creation is a story with many successive stages. At the start, $1000 of newly created reserves are deposited in original first-generation bank

Bank 1 in Final Position			
Assets		**Liabilities**	
Reserves	+$ 100	Deposits	+$1,000
Loans and investments	+ 900		
Total	+$1,000	Total	+$1,000

Table 10-4(b). A profit-maximizing bank will lend or invest any excess reserves. Thus Bank 1 has kept only $100 of the original cash deposit (as required reserves) and has lent or invested the other $900

Second-Generation Banks. To see what happens to the $900, let's call all the banks that receive the $900 "second-generation banks" (or Bank 2). Their combined balance sheets now appear as shown in Table 10-4(c). To these banks, the dollars deposited function just like our original $1000 deposit. These banks do not know, and do not care, that they are second in a chain of deposits. Their only concern is that they are holding too much non-earning cash, or excess reserves. Only one-tenth of $900, or $90, is legally needed against the $900 deposit. They will use the other nine-tenths to acquire $810 worth of loans and investments. Hence, their balance sheets will soon reach the equilibrium shown in Table 10-4(d).

Second-Generation Banks in Initial Position			
Assets		**Liabilities**	
Reserves	+$900	Deposits	+$900
Total	+$900	Total	+$900

Table 10-4(c)

At this point, the original $1000 taken out of hand-to-hand circulation has produced a total of $2710 of money. The total of M has increased, and the process continues.

Later-Generation Banks. The $810 spent by the second-generation banks in acquiring loans and investments will go to a new set of banks called "third-generation banks."

You can create the balance sheets (initial and final) for third-generation banks. Evidently, the third-generation banks will lend out their excess reserves and will thereby create $729 of new money. A fourth generation of banks will clearly end up with nine-tenths of $810 in deposits, or $729, and so on.

Final System Equilibrium

What will be the final sum: $1000 + $900 + $810 + $729 + · · ·? Table 10-5 shows that the complete effect of the chain of money creation is $10,000. We can get the answer by arithmetic, by common sense, and by elementary algebra.

Common sense tells us that the process of de-

Final Position of Second-Generation Banks			
Assets		**Liabilities**	
Reserves	+$ 90	Deposits	+$900
Loans and investments	+ 810		
Total	+$900	Total	+$900

Table 10-4(d). Next, the money lent out by Bank 1 soon goes to new banks, which in turn lend out nine-tenths of it

Multiple Expansion of Bank Deposits Through the Banking System			
Position of bank	New deposits ($)	New loans and investments ($)	New reserves ($)
Original banks	1,000.00	900.00	100.00
2d-generation banks	900.00	810.00	90.00
3d-generation banks	810.00	729.00	81.00
4th-generation banks	729.00	656.10	72.90
5th-generation banks	656.10	590.49	65.61
6th-generation banks	590.49	531.44	59.05
7th-generation banks	531.44	478.30	53.14
8th-generation banks	478.30	430.47	47.83
9th-generation banks	430.47	387.42	43.05
10th-generation banks	387.42	348.68	38.74
Sum of first 10 generations of banks	6,513.22	5,861.90	651.32
Sum of remaining generations of banks	3,486.78	3,138.10	348.68
Total for banking system as a whole	10,000.00	9,000.00	1,000.00

Table 10-5. Finally, through this long chain, all banks create new deposits of 10 times new reserves

All banks together do accomplish what no one small bank can—multiple expansion of reserves into M. The final equilibrium is reached when every dollar of original new reserves supports $10 of demand deposits. Note that in every genera-tion each bank has "created" new money in the following sense: It ends up with a final bank deposit 10 times the reserve it finally retains.

posit creation must come to an end only when no bank anywhere in the system has reserves in excess of the 10 percent reserve requirement. In all our examples, no cash reserves ever leaked out of the banking system; the money simply went from one set of banks to another set of banks. The banking system will reach equilibrium when the $1000 of new reserves is all used up as required reserves on new deposits. In other words, the final equilibrium of the banking system will be the point at which 10 percent of new deposits (D) equals the new reserves of $1000. What level of D satisfies this condition? The answer is $D = \$10,000$.

We can also see the answer intuitively by looking at a consolidated balance sheet for all banks together—first, second, and hundredth generation. This is shown in Table 10-6. If total new deposits were less than $10,000, the 10 percent reserve ratio would not yet be reached, and full equilibrium would not yet be attained.[3]

[3] The algebraic solution can be shown as follows:

$$\$1000 + \$900 + \$810 + \cdots$$
$$= \$1000 \times [1 + \tfrac{9}{10} + (\tfrac{9}{10})^2 + (\tfrac{9}{10})^3 + \cdots]$$
$$= \$1000\left(\frac{1}{1 - \tfrac{9}{10}}\right) = \$1000 \times \left(\frac{1}{0.1}\right) = \$10,000$$

Consolidated Balance Sheet Showing Final Position			
Assets		**Liabilities**	
Reserves	+$ 1,000	Deposits	+$10,000
Loans and investments	+ 9,000		
Total	+$10,000	Total	+$10,000

Table 10-6. All banks together ultimately increase deposits and M by a multiple of the original injection of reserves

money supply is transactions money (M_1)—made up of currency and checking deposits. Another important concept is broad money (M_2), which includes M_1 plus highly liquid "near-monies" like savings accounts.

4. The definitions of the M's have changed over the last decade as a result of rapid innovation in financial markets. This development makes the conduct of monetary policy more difficult because monetary definitions (and thus targets for money growth) are ambiguous when new assets appear.

5. Interest rates are the price paid for borrowing money and are measured in dollars per year paid back per dollar borrowed, or in percent per year. People willingly pay interest because borrowed funds allow them to buy goods and services to satisfy consumption needs or make profitable investments.

6. Markets produce a wide array of interest rates. These rates vary because of the term or maturity of loans, because of the risk and liquidity of investments, and because of the associated administrative costs.

7. Interest rates generally rise during inflationary periods, reflecting the fact that the purchasing power of money declines as prices rise. To calculate the interest yield in terms of real goods and services, we use the real interest rate, which equals the nominal or money interest rate minus the rate of inflation.

8. The demand for money differs from that for other commodities. Money is held for its indirect rather than its direct value. But money holdings are limited because keeping assets in money rather than in other forms has an opportunity cost: we sacrifice interest earnings when we hold money.

9. The demand for money is grounded in the need to make transactions and the desire to hold assets for the future. The most important—the transactions demand—comes because people need cash or checking deposits to pay bills or buy goods. Such transactions needs are met by M_1 and are chiefly related to the value of transactions, or to nominal GNP. Other assets are held in high-yield, interest-bearing checking accounts as a supersafe part of investors' portfolios.

   Economic theory predicts, and empirical studies confirm, that the demand for money is sensitive to interest rates; higher interest rates lead to a lower demand for M.

B. Banking and the Supply of Money

10. Banks are commercial enterprises that seek to earn profits for their owners. One major function of banks is to provide checking accounts to customers. Modern banks gradually evolved from the old goldsmith establishments in which money and valuables were stored. Eventually it became general practice for goldsmiths to hold less than 100 percent reserves against deposits; this was the beginning of fractional-reserve banking.

11. If banks kept 100 percent cash reserves against all deposits, there would be no multiple creation of money when new reserves were injected by the

central bank into the system. There would be only a 1-to-1 exchange of one kind of money for another kind of money.

12. Today, banks are legally required to keep reserves on their checking deposits. These can be in the form of cash on hand or of non-interest-bearing deposits at the Federal Reserve. For illustrative purposes, we examined a required reserve ratio of 10 percent. In this case, the banking system as a whole—together with public or private borrowers and the depositing public—does create bank money 10 to 1 for each new dollar of reserves created by the Fed and deposited somewhere in the banking system.

13. Each small bank is limited in its ability to expand its loans and investments. It cannot lend or invest more than it has received from depositors; it can lend only about nine-tenths as much.

14. Although no bank alone can expand its reserves 10 to 1, the banking system as a whole can. The first individual bank receiving a new $1000 of deposits lends nine-tenths of its newly acquired cash on loans and investments. This gives a second group of banks nine-tenths of $1000 in new deposits. They, in turn, keep one-tenth in reserves and lend the other nine-tenths on new earning assets; this causes them to lose cash to a third set of banks, whose deposits have gone up by nine-tenths of nine-tenths of $1000. If we follow through the successive groups of banks in the dwindling, never-ending chain, we find for the system as a whole new deposits of

$$\$1000 + \$900 + \$810 + \$729 + \cdots = \$1000 \times [1 + \tfrac{9}{10} + (\tfrac{9}{10})^2 + (\tfrac{9}{10})^3 + \cdots]$$

$$= \$1000\left(\frac{1}{1 - \tfrac{9}{10}}\right) = \$1000\left(\frac{1}{0.1}\right)$$

$$= \$10{,}000$$

15. Only when each $1 of the new reserves retained in the banking system ends up supporting $10 of deposits somewhere in the system will the limits to deposit expansion be reached. Then the system is loaned up; it can create no further deposits until it acquires more reserves. The 10-to-1 ratio of increased bank money to increased reserves is called the money-supply multiplier.

16. There will be some leakage of new cash reserves of the banking system into circulation outside the banks and into assets other than checking accounts. Therefore, instead of $10,000 of new checking deposits created, as in the previous examples, there may be something less than that—the difference being due to what is withdrawn from the system.

   Moreover, a bank may keep excess reserves above the legally required reserves. Excess reserves crop up when the interest rate on reserves is close to the rate on safe investments.

   When some of the new reserves leak into assets other than checking deposits, the relationship of money creation to new reserves may depart from the 10-to-1 formula given by the money-supply multiplier.

STOCK MARKET FLUCTUATIONS

The stock market is but a mirror which provides an image
of the underlying or fundamental economic situation.
John Kenneth Galbraith, *The Great Crash* (1955)

This chapter concentrated on monetary economics, which is crucial to an understanding of macroeconomic policy. But, as Table 10A-1 shows, households invest in many assets other than money.

Among the most fascinating assets owned by households are common stocks (or corporate equities). These are volatile securities through which people's fortunes are made and lost overnight. The

Financial Assets of Households		
	Percent of total assets in each class	
Class of asset	1963	1988
Dollar-denominated:		
Currency and checking deposits (M_1)	4.6	4.2
Savings accounts	14.3	21.0
Government securities	6.4	8.5
Other	3.3	2.2
Equity in businesses:		
Corporate	31.3	18.4
Noncorporate	25.7	19.8
Pension fund and life-insurance reserves	13.4	23.9
Other	1.0	1.9
Total	100.0	100.0
Item: Total assets of households (billions)	$1,641	$12,139

Table 10A-1. Pension assets and savings accounts are largest component of household assets

This table shows how the holdings of households were divided among different assets in 1963 and 1988. Note that the share of equities fell sharply, while pension funds and savings accounts rose markedly. (Source: Federal Reserve System.)

1980s illustrate the perils of "playing the market." Beginning in 1982, the stock market surged upward steadily for 5 years, gaining almost 300 percent. Those who had the luck or vision to put all their assets into stocks made a lot of money. The market peaked in the summer of 1987. On October 19, 1987—"black Monday"—the stock market lost 22 percent of its value in 6 hours. The shock to securities markets was a vivid reminder of the risks you take when you buy stocks. Nevertheless, 35 million Americans own stocks; 3 million of them are people with incomes under $10,000. Only a small fraction of shares are held by low-income households, but the fact that so many people are willing to invest their wealth this way attests to the lure of prospective gains from stock ownership.

In this appendix we explore modern theories of the behavior of the stock market. A **stock market** is a place where the shares in publicly owned companies, the titles to business firms, are bought and sold. In 1990, the value of these titles was estimated at $3 trillion in the United States. Sales in a single year might total $2 trillion. The stock market is the hub of our corporate economy.

The New York Stock Exchange is the main stock market, listing more than a thousand securities. The smaller American Stock Exchange began when brokers met on the street to buy and sell, giving hand signals to the clerks hanging out the windows to record the transactions. Only in the twentieth century did the American Stock Exchange move indoors.

Every large financial center has a stock exchange. Major ones are located in Tokyo, London, Frankfurt, Hong Kong, Toronto, Zurich, and, of course, New York. A stock exchange is the essence of a market economy. When the countries of Eastern Europe decided to scrap their centrally planned, so-cialist systems, one of their first acts was to introduce a stock market to buy and sell ownership rights in companies.

The Great Crash

A study of stock exchanges and financial markets relies upon both economic analysis and a careful reading of the lessons of history. One traumatic event has cast a shadow over stock markets for dec-ades—the 1929 panic and crash. This event ush-ered in the long and painful Great Depression of the 1930s.

The "roaring twenties" saw a fabulous stock mar-ket boom, when everyone bought and sold stocks. Most purchases in this wild *bull* market (one with rising prices) were *on margin*. This means a buyer of $10,000 worth of stocks put up only part of the price in cash and borrowed the difference, pledg-ing the newly bought stocks as collateral for the purchase. What did it matter that you had to pay the broker 6, 10, or 15 percent per year on the bor-rowings when, in one day, Auburn Motors or Beth-lehem Steel might jump 10 percent in value!

A speculative mania fulfills its own promises. If people buy because they think stocks will rise, their act of buying sends up the price of stocks. This causes people to buy even more and sends the dizzy dance off on another round. But, unlike peo-ple who play cards or dice, no one apparently loses what the winners gain. Of course, the prizes are all on paper and would disappear if everyone tried to cash them in. But why should anyone want to sell such lucrative securities?

The great stock market boom of the 1920s was a classic *speculative bubble*. Prices rose because of hopes and dreams, not because the profits and div-idends of companies were soaring. The crash came in "black October" of 1929. Everyone was caught, the big-league professionals as well as the piddling amateurs—Andrew Mellon, John D. Rockefeller, the engineer-turned-President in the White House, and Yale's great economics professor Irving Fisher.

When the bottom fell out of the market in 1929, investors, big and small, who bought on margin could not put up funds to cover their holdings and the market fell still further. The bull market turned into a *bear* (or declining) market. By the trough of

the Depression in 1933, the market had lost 85 per-cent of its 1929 value.

Trends in the stock market are tracked using stock-price indexes, which are weighted averages of the prices of a basket of company stocks. Com-monly followed averages include the Dow-Jones Industrial Average ("DJIA") of 30 large companies, and Standard and Poor's index of 500 companies (the "S&P 500"), which is a weighted average of the stock prices of the largest 500 American corpora-tions.

Figure 10A-1 on the following page shows the history since 1920 of the Standard and Poor 500. The lower curve shows the "nominal" stock price average, which records the actual average during a particular year. The upper line shows the "real" price of stocks; this equals the nominal price di-vided by an index of consumer prices that equals 1 in 1991.

Figure 10A-1 shows that, after the banking crisis of 1933, the stock market began to recover. Accord-ing to this index, real stock prices did not recover their 1929 level until 1955. Moreover, the 1991 level was just slightly shy of the all-time high of real stock prices in 1968.[1]

Where will it all end? Is there a crystal ball that will foretell the movement of stock prices? This is the subject of modern finance theory.

The Efficient-Market Theory

Economists and finance professors have long stud-ied prices in speculative markets, like the stock market, and markets for commodities such as corn. Their findings have stirred great controversy and have even angered many financial analysts. Yet this is an area in which the facts have largely corrobo-rated the theories.

Modern economic theories of stock prices are grouped under the heading of **efficient-market theory**.[2] One way of expressing the fundamental theory is: *You can't outguess the market.*

---

[1] A detailed account of the role of the stock market in the Great Depression is provided in John Kenneth Galbraith, *The Great Crash of 1929* (Avon, New York, 1988); and C. P. Kindleberger, *Manias, Panics, and Crashes* (Basic Books, New York, rev., 1989).

[2] "Efficiency" in finance theory is used differently than in other parts of economics. Here, "efficiency" means that information is quickly absorbed, not that resources produce the maximal outputs.

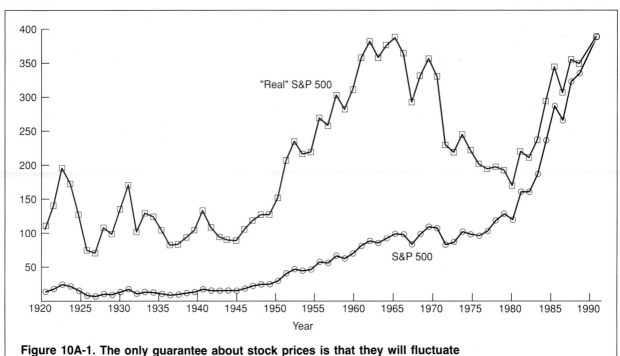

Figure 10A-1. The only guarantee about stock prices is that they will fluctuate

Stock prices in nominal terms, shown in the bottom line, tend to rise with inflation. The Standard and Poor's index (the "S&P 500") shown here tracks the value-weighted average of the stock prices of the 500 largest American companies.

The top line shows the "real S&P 500" which is the S&P 500 corrected for movements in the consumer price index. The all-time high came in 1968, and by 1991 real stock prices were only two times the pre-Depression peak of 1929.

We'll see in a minute *why* this proposition is plausible. First, let's consider its factual basis. There have been numerous studies over the years about rules or formulas for making money. Typical rules are "buy after 2 days of increases" or "buy on the bad news and sell on the good news." An early study by Alfred Cowles investigated the recommendations of stockbrokers. He examined how well different brokers performed by looking at the return (in dollars of total income per year per dollar invested) on the stocks they selected. He found that, on average, a stockbroker's choices did no better than a random portfolio (or combination) of stocks. This observation led to the *dart-board theory* of stock selection:

You can throw a dart at the *Wall Street Journal* as a way of selecting stocks. Better still, buy a little of everything in the market, so that you hold a diversified "index" portfolio of the stock market. This would probably leave you better off than your cousin who follows a broker's advice. Why? Because he would have to pay more broker's commis-

sions and his stocks, on average, would not outperform yours.

This bleak view has been generally confirmed in hundreds of studies over the last four decades. Their lesson is not that you will never become rich by following a rule or formula, but that, in general, such rules cannot outperform a randomly selected and diversified portfolio of stocks.

Rationale for the Efficient-Market View

Finance theorists have spent many years analyzing stock and bond markets in order to understand why the dart-board theory might hold. Why do well-functioning financial markets rule out persistent excess profits? The theory of efficient markets explains this.

An **efficient market** is one where all new information is quickly understood by market participants and becomes immediately incorporated into market prices. For example, say that Lazy-T Oil Company has just struck oil in the Gulf of Alaska.

This event is announced at 11:30 A.M. on Tuesday. When will the price of Lazy-T's shares rise? The efficient-market theory holds that the news will be incorporated into prices immediately. The market participants will react at once, bidding the price of Lazy-T up by the correct amount. In short, at every point in time, markets have already digested and included in stock prices or corn prices or other speculative prices all the latest available information.

This means that if you read about a heavy frost in Florida you can't enrich yourself by buying frozen orange juice futures during your lunch break: the orange juice price went up the minute the news was reported, or even earlier.[3]

The theory of efficient markets holds that market prices contain all available information. It is not possible to make profits by looking at old information or at patterns of past price changes.

A Random Walk

The efficient-market view provides an important way of analyzing price movements in organized markets. Under this approach, the price movements of stocks should look highly erratic, like a random walk, when charted over a period of time.

A price follows a *random walk* when its movements over time are completely unpredictable. For example, toss a coin for heads or tails. Call a head "plus 1" and a tail "minus 1." Then keep track of the running score of 100 coin tosses. Draw it on graph paper. This curve is a random walk. Now for comparison also graph 100 days' movement of IBM stock and of Standard and Poor's 500 index. Note how similar all three figures appear.

Why do speculative prices resemble a random walk? Economists, on reflection, have arrived at the following truths: In an efficient market all predictable things have already been built into the price. It is the arrival of *new* information—a freeze in Florida, war in the Persian Gulf, a report that the Federal Reserve has tightened the money supply—that

---

[3] Scholars have attempted to measure the speed of price adjustment in such efficient markets. One study found that, if you were willing to put up $100,000, you could make a profit only if you bought stocks within 30 seconds after new information became public.

affects stock or commodity prices. Moreover, the news must be random and unpredictable (or else it would be predictable and therefore not truly news).

To summarize: The efficient-market theory explains why movements in stock prices look so erratic. Prices respond to news, to surprises. But surprises are unpredictable events—like the flip of a coin or next month's rainstorm—that may move in any direction. Because stock prices move in response to erratic events, stock prices themselves move erratically, like a random walk.

Objections

There are four major objections to the efficient-market view of markets.

1. Suppose everybody accepts the efficient-market philosophy and stops trying to digest information quickly. If everyone assumes that stock prices are correctly valued, then will those prices *stop* being accurate?

   This is a good question, but it is unlikely that everyone will quit. Indeed, the minute too many people stopped looking ahead, the market would cease being efficient. We could then make profits by acting on old information. So the efficient market is a stable, self-monitoring equilibrium state.

2. Some people are quicker and smarter than others. Some have much money to spend on information to narrow down the odds on the uncertain future. Doesn't it stand to reason that they will make higher profits?

   There are many such people competing against each other. The Rockefellers can buy the best financial counsel there is. But so can a number of other people and institutions. Competition provides the checks and balances of efficiency and ensures minimal excess profits.

   Moreover, the efficient-market theory does suggest that a few people with special flair and skills will permanently earn high returns on their skills—just as great quarterbacks and sopranos do.

3. Economists who look at the historical record ask whether it is plausible that sharp movements in stock prices could actually reflect new information. Consider the sharp percent drop in the

stock market from October 15 to October 19, 1987. The efficient-market view would hold that this drop was caused by economic events that depressed the value of future corporate earnings. What were those events? James Tobin, Yale's Nobel Prize–winning economist, commented, "There are no visible factors that could make a 30 percent difference in the value of stock [prices over these four days]." Efficient-market theorists fall silent before this criticism.

4. Finally, the efficient-market view applies to individual stocks but not necessarily to the entire market. Some economists have found evidence of long, self-reversing swings in stock market prices. Others believe that these swings reflect changes in the general mood of the financial community. These long-term swings may lie behind the boom psychology of the 1920s and 1980s or the depression mentality of the 1930s.

Let us say that we believed that the whole stock market was too high in 1991 or too low in 1931. What could we do? We could not individually buy or sell enough stocks to overcome the entire national mood. So, from a macroeconomic perspective, speculative markets *can* exhibit waves of pessimism or optimism without powerful economic forces moving in to correct these swings of mood.

Financial Strategies

Only a few financial analysts are willing to accept the view that "passive" financial strategies, simply buying an indexed share of the market, are the best approach. A growing number of institutions, however, follow a passive approach, and some banks, such as Wells Fargo in San Francisco, have adopted this philosophy and now invest billions of dollars in passive accounts.

What are the lessons of the many studies of the behavior of financial markets and financial advisers?

- Be skeptical of approaches that claim to have found the quick route to success. You can't get rich by consulting the stars (although, unbelievably, some financial advisers push astrology to their clients). Hunches work out to nothing in the long run.

- The best brains on Wall Street do not, on average, beat the averages (Dow-Jones, Standard & Poor's, etc.). This is not so surprising. True, the big money managers have all the money needed for any kind of research and digging. But they are all competing with one another.

- Investors who want to achieve a good return with the least possible risk buy a broadly diversified portfolio of common stocks. They might buy an "index fund," which is a fixed portfolio of stocks with minimal management and brokerage fees. They might combine this with some diversified bonds or savings accounts. Over the longer run, such a strategy will probably earn a return of a few percentage points per year above inflation.

- Investors can also increase their expected return if they are willing to bear greater risks. Some stocks are inherently riskier than others. By investing in more cyclical stocks, in stocks that move up and down relatively more than the market as a whole, and in small companies, investors, on average, can probably beat the market. But buyer beware: When the market goes down, you will generally suffer worse-than-average losses in these riskier stocks.

If, after reading all this, you still want to try your hand in the stock market, do not be daunted. But take to heart the caution of one of America's great financiers, Bernard Baruch:

If you are ready to give up everything else—to study the whole history and background of the market and all the principal companies whose stocks are on the board as carefully as a medical student studies anatomy—if you can do all that, and, in addition, you have the cool nerves of a great gambler, the sixth sense of a kind of clairvoyant, and the courage of a lion, you have a ghost of a chance.

SUMMARY TO APPENDIX
---

1. Stock markets, of which the New York Stock Exchange is the most important, are places where titles of ownership to the largest companies are bought and sold. The history of stock prices is filled with violent gyrations, such as the Great Crash of 1929. Trends are tracked by the use of stock-price indexes, such as Standard and Poor's 500 or the familiar Dow-Jones Industrial Average.

2. Modern economic theories of stock prices generally focus on the role of efficient markets. An efficient market is one in which all information is quickly absorbed by speculators and is immediately built into market prices. In efficient markets, there are no easy profits; looking at yesterday's news or past patterns of prices or elections or business cycles will not help predict future price movements.

3. Thus, in efficient markets, prices respond to surprises. Because surprises are inherently random, stock prices and other speculative prices move erratically, as in a random walk.

CONCEPTS FOR REVIEW

New York Stock Exchange	efficient market	new news, old information, and
common stocks (corporate equities)	random walk of stock prices	speculative prices
Standard and Poor's 500	index fund, passive strategies	

QUESTIONS FOR DISCUSSION

1. According to the efficient-market theory, what effect would the following events have on the price of GM's stock?
   (a) A surprise announcement that the government was going to undertake a new program to contract the economy by raising corporation taxes on next July 1
   (b) An increase in tax rates on July 1, six months after Congress had passed the enabling legislation
   (c) An announcement, unexpected by experts, that the United States was imposing quotas on imports of Japanese cars for the coming year
   (d) Implementation of (c) by issuing regulations on December 31
2. One economist commented as follows on the sharp drop in stock prices during October 1987: "There have been no events over the last few days that can rationally explain the selling frenzy during 'black October.'

News about inflation, the trade balance, the budget deficit, or events in the Persian Gulf can be indicted for no more than a few dozen points of the 509 point decline in the Dow-Jones." Explain how this quotation relates to the efficient-market hypothesis. If you agree with this quotation, what would you conclude about the validity of that hypothesis?

3. Flip a coin 100 times. Count a head as "plus 1" and a tail as "minus 1." Keep a running score of the total. Plot it on a graph paper. This is a random walk. (Those with access to a computer can do this using a computer program, a random-number generator, and a plotter.)

   Next, keep track of the closing price of the stock of your favorite company for a few weeks (or get it from past issues of the newspaper). Plot the price against time. Can you see any difference in the pattern of changes? Do both look like random walks?

C H A P T E R   1 1

CENTRAL BANKING
AND MONETARY POLICY

There have been three great inventions since the
beginning of time: fire, the wheel, and central banking.

Will Rogers

We learned in the last chapter about the unique properties of money. As the French economist Frederic Bastiat put it, "People are not nourished by money. They do not clothe themselves with gold; they do not warm themselves with silver." Money is held because it facilitates trade and exchange.

This chapter continues the discussion of the money supply by analyzing the tasks of central banking. The Federal Reserve System, which is the central bank of the United States, is a banker's bank. Its primary function is to control the supply of bank reserves. This activity regulates the nation's money supply and credit conditions and determines the level of interest rates. Every country has a central bank that is responsible for managing its monetary affairs.

The Federal Reserve's goals are steady growth in national output and low unemployment. Its sworn enemy is inflation. If aggregate demand is excessive and prices are being bid up, the Federal Reserve Board may reduce the growth of the money supply, thereby slowing aggregate demand and output growth. If unemployment is high and business languishing, the Fed may consider increasing the money supply, thereby raising aggregate demand and augmenting output growth. In the second half of this chapter, we will see exactly how the Federal Reserve can use its powers to pursue these goals.

A. Central Banking and the Federal Reserve System

The Federal Reserve System

Figure 11-1 shows the role of central banking in the economy and depicts its relationship to the banks and the capital markets in which interest rates and credit availability are determined. In this section we analyze how the Fed manipulates its instruments—bank reserves, the discount rate, and other tools—to determine the money supply.

Structure of the Federal Reserve

History. During the nineteenth century, the United States was plagued by banking panics. Panics occurred when people suddenly attempted to turn their bank deposits into currency. When they arrived at the banks, they found that the banks had an inadequate supply of currency because the supply of currency was fixed and smaller than the

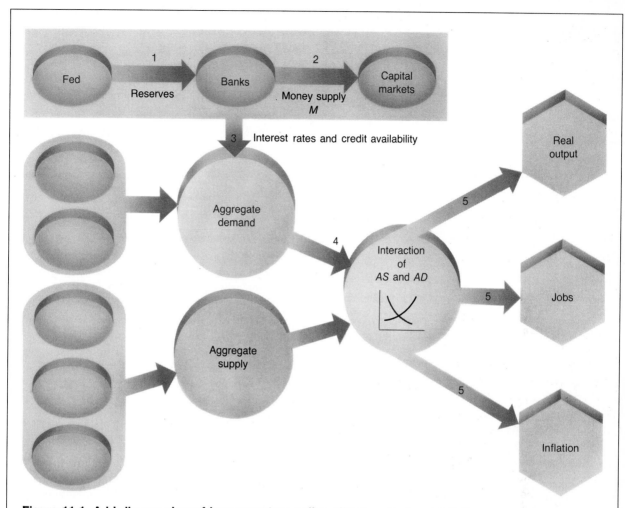

Figure 11-1. A bird's-eye view of how monetary policy affects output and inflation

This diagram shows graphically the steps by which Fed policy affects economic activity. (1) is a change in reserves; leading to (2), a change in *M*; leading to (3), changes in interest rates and credit conditions. In (4), *AD* is changed by a response of investment and other interest-sensitive spending. In (5), changes in output, employment, and inflation follow.

Remember, however, that monetary policy is not the only influence: Entering in crucial step 4, fiscal policy feeds into the aggregate demand circle.

amount of bank deposits. Bank failures and economic downturns ensued. After the severe panic of 1907, agitation and discussion led to the creation of the Federal Reserve System in 1913.

The Federal Reserve System consists of 12 regional Federal Reserve Banks, located in New York, Chicago, Richmond, Dallas, San Francisco, and other major cities. The sprawling regional structure was originally designed in a populist age to ensure that different areas would have a voice in banking matters and to avoid too great a concentration of central-banking powers in Washington or in the hands of the bankers of the eastern establishment. Each Federal Reserve Bank today manages bank operations and oversees banks in its region.

Who's in Charge? The core of the Federal Reserve is the *Board of Governors* of the Federal Reserve System, which consists of seven members nominated by the President and confirmed by the Senate to serve overlapping terms of 14 years. Members of the board are generally bankers or economists

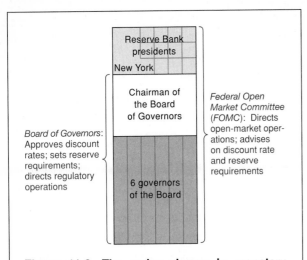

Figure 11-2. The major players in monetary policy

The powers of the Federal Reserve are lodged in two bodies. The seven-member Board of Governors approves changes in discount rates and sets reserve requirements. The 19-member FOMC directs the setting of bank reserves. The Chairman of the Board of Governors steers both committees.

The size of each box indicates that person's or group's relative power; note the size of the Chairman's box. The relative importance of different people is drawn on the basis of the study by former Fed governor Sherman Maisel, *Managing the Dollar* (Norton, New York, 1973.)

who work full-time at the job.

The key decision-making body in the Federal Reserve System is the *Federal Open Market Committee (FOMC)*. The 12 voting members of the FOMC include the seven governors plus five of the presidents of the regional Federal Reserve Banks. This key group controls the single most important and frequently used tool of modern monetary policy—the supply of bank reserves.

At the pinnacle of the entire system is the *Chairman of the Board of Governors*, currently an economist, Alan Greenspan. He chairs the board and the FOMC, acts as public spokesman for the Fed, and exercises enormous power over monetary policy. He is often, and accurately, called the "second most powerful man in America," reflecting the extent to which he can influence the entire economy through his impact on monetary policy.

In spite of the formally dispersed structure of the Fed, close observers think that power is quite centralized. The Federal Reserve Board, joined at meet-

ings by presidents of the 12 regional Federal Reserve Banks, operates under the Fed Chairman to formulate and carry out monetary policy. The informal structure of the Federal Reserve System is shown in Figure 11-2.

Independence. On examining the structure of the Fed, one might ask, "In which of the three branches of government does the Fed lie?" The answer is, "None. Legally, the 12 regional banks are private. In reality, the Fed as a whole behaves as an independent government agency."

Although nominally a corporation owned by the commercial banks that are members of the Federal Reserve System, the Federal Reserve is in fact a public agency. It is directly responsible to Congress; it listens carefully to the advice of the President; and whenever any conflict arises between its making a profit and promoting the public interest, it acts unswervingly in the public interest. The Fed is allowed to print currency, in return for which it holds interest-bearing government securities. Through this activity, it earns billions of dollars of profits each year. But, to reflect its public mission, profits above a certain return go to the U.S. government.

Above all, the Federal Reserve is an *independent* agency. While they listen carefully to Congress and the President, and even to the election returns, in the end the members of the Board of Governors and the FOMC decide monetary policy according to their views about the nation's economic interests. As a result, the Fed sometimes comes into conflict with the executive branch. The Roosevelt, Johnson, Carter, Reagan, and Bush administrations all had occasional harsh words for Fed policy. The Fed listened politely, but the President could not force the Fed to bend to his wishes.

From time to time, people argue that the Fed is too independent. "How can a democracy allow a group of private bankers to control monetary policy?" ask critics. Who, they ask, gave the Federal Reserve the authority to raise interest rates to 20 percent in 1980? Where can we read that the Fed is authorized to tighten money and create recessions? Shouldn't monetary policy be set by elected representatives in Congress or by the executive branch?

There is no right answer to these questions. On the one hand, an independent central bank is the guardian of the value of a nation's currency and the best protector against rampant inflation. Moreover, independence ensures that monetary policy is not subverted to partisan political objectives; the Fed's independence allows it.the leeway to undertake policies, such as fighting inflation, that have little popular support. The elected branches will not always sacrifice their offices for long-run economic welfare.

At the same time, because they are so far removed from the political process, monetary managers at the Fed may lose touch with social and economic realities. Members of Congress are routinely forced to confront unemployed autoworkers and bankrupt farmers—groups seldom encountered in the Federal Reserve building in Washington.

The debate about the Fed's independence is neither new nor frivolous. Proposals to change the composition of the board, to put representatives of Congress or the executive branch on the FOMC or to let each new President appoint his own Chairman of the Board of Governors, are perennial topics for debate.

We can summarize the structure of the Federal Reserve System this way:

The Federal Reserve Board in Washington, together with the 12 Federal Reserve Banks, constitutes our American central bank. Every modern country has a central bank. Its primary mission is to control the nation's money supply and credit conditions.

Overview of the Fed's Operations

How does the Fed actually manage the money supply? In answering this question, it is useful to start by viewing the world as seen by the Fed. Figure 11-3 shows the various stages of Federal Reserve operations. The Federal Reserve has at its disposal a number of policy instruments that can affect certain intermediate targets (such as reserves, the money supply, and interest rates). All its operations through these instruments are intended to help achieve the ultimate objectives of a healthy economy—low inflation, rapid growth in output, and low employment. It is important to keep these three sets of variables distinct in our analysis.

The three major instruments of monetary policy are:

- *Open-market operations*—buying or selling government bonds
- *Discount-rate policy*—setting the interest rate, called the discount rate, at which member banks can borrow reserves from the Fed
- *Reserve-requirements policy*—Changing the legal reserve ratio requirements on deposits with banks and other financial institutions

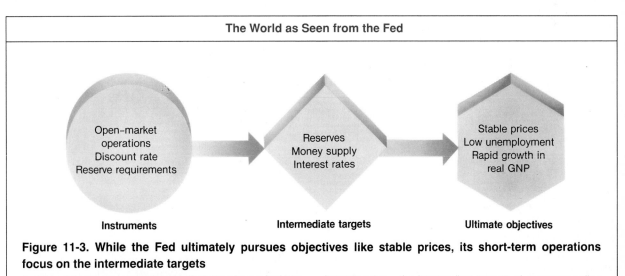

The World as Seen from the Fed

Open-market operations
Discount rate
Reserve requirements

Reserves
Money supply
Interest rates

Stable prices
Low unemployment
Rapid growth in
real GNP

Instruments   **Intermediate targets**   **Ultimate objectives**

Figure 11-3. While the Fed ultimately pursues objectives like stable prices, its short-term operations focus on the intermediate targets

In determining monetary policy, the Fed directly manipulates the instruments or policy variables under its control—open-market operations, discount rate, and reserve requirements. These help determine bank reserves, the money supply, and interest rates—the intermediate targets of monetary policy. Ultimately, the Fed is a partner with fiscal policy in pursuing the major objectives of rapid growth, low unemployment, and stable prices.

In managing money, the Federal Reserve must keep its eye on a set of variables known as *intermediate targets*. These are economic variables that are neither Fed policy instruments nor true policy objectives but stand as intermediates in the transmission mechanism between Fed instruments and goals. When the Fed wants to affect its ultimate objectives, it first changes one of its instruments. This change affects an intermediate variable like interest rates, credit conditions, or the money supply. Much as a doctor interested in the health of a patient will monitor pulse and blood pressure, so will the Federal Reserve keep a careful watch on its intermediate targets.

Balance Sheet of the Federal Reserve Banks

Before analyzing the way the Fed determines the money supply, we need to describe the consolidated balance sheet of the Federal Reserve System, shown in Table 11-1. The first asset consists mostly of gold certificates, i.e., warehouse receipts from the Treasury for official gold. U.S. government securities (e.g., bonds) make up most of the rest of the assets. The small items, loans and acceptances, are primarily loans or advances to commercial banks. The interest rate the Fed charges banks for such loans, or "discounts," is called the discount rate, which is another of the Fed's tools.

Liabilities include the usual capital accounts: original capital paid in by the member banks plus retained earnings or accumulated surplus. Federal Reserve notes are the Fed's principal liabilities. This is the paper currency we use every day.

Of vital importance are the bank reserves, or balances kept on deposit by commercial banks with the Federal Reserve Banks and shown as Fed liabilities. Taken along with small amounts of the banks' vault cash, these are the reserves we have been talking about. They provide the basis for multiple deposit creation by the nation's banking system.

By altering its holding of government securities, the Fed can change bank reserves and thereby trigger the sequence of events that ultimately determines the total supply of money.

The Nuts and Bolts of Monetary Policy

Open-Market Operations

The Fed's most useful tool is "open-market operations."

By selling or buying government securities in the open market, the Fed can lower or raise bank reserves. These so-called open-market operations are a central bank's most important stabilizing instrument.

Every month the FOMC meets to decide whether to pump more reserves into the banking system by

Combined Balance Sheet of 12 Federal Reserve Banks, 1991
(Billions of Dollars)

Assets		Liabilities and net worth	
Gold certificates and other cash	$ 11.7	Capital accounts	$ 3.2
U.S. government securities	247.4	Federal Reserve notes	267.4
Loans and acceptances	0.2	Deposits:	
Miscellaneous other assets	56.0	Bank reserves	24.1
		U.S. Treasury	10.9
		Miscellaneous liabilities	9.7
Total	$315.3	Total	$315.3

Table 11-1. Federal Reserve notes and deposits underlie our money supply
By controlling its earning assets (government securities and loans), the Fed controls its liabilities (deposits and Federal Reserve notes). It determines the economy's money supply (currency and demand deposits, M_1), and thereby affects GNP, unemployment, and inflation. (Source: *Federal Reserve Bulletin.*)

Federal Reserve assets (billions)		Federal Reserve liabilities (billions)	
U.S. securities	−$1	Bank reserves	−$1
Total	−$1	Total	−$1

Commercial bank assets (billions)		Commercial bank liabilities (billions)	
Reserves	−$ 1	Checking deposits	−$10
Loans and investments	− 9		
Total	−$10	Total	−$10

Table 11-2(a). Open-market sale by Fed cuts reserves initially

This crucial set of tables shows how open-market operations affect the Fed's balance sheet and the balance sheet of banks.

In Table 11-2(a), the Fed has sold $1 billion of securities. The funds used to pay for the securities are deposited in the Fed, reducing bank reserves by $1 billion. Bank reserves thus decline by $1 billion as a result of the open-market operation.

Then in Table 11-2(b), we see the effect on the balance

Table 11-2(b). . . . and ultimately cuts deposits 10 to 1

sheet of banks. With a required reserve ratio of 10 percent of deposits, the banks will be content only when they have no excess or deficit reserves. The reserve contraction cascades through the banking system. Thus deposits must fall by $10 billion for the banking system to be back in equilibrium.

In the end, an open-market operation in which the Fed sells $1 billion of securities leads to an eventual decline of $10 billion in bank money and in the money supply.

buying Treasury bills (i.e., short-term bonds) and longer-term government bonds, or whether to tighten monetary policy by selling government securities.

To see how an open-market operation changes reserves, let us suppose that the Fed thinks the economic winds are blowing up a little inflation. The FOMC holds its meeting in Washington and hears presentations and projections from its talented staff of economists. The committee decides, "Let's sell $1 billion of Treasury bills from our portfolio to contract reserves and tighten overall money and credit." The motion is unanimously approved by vote of the seven Washington governors and five regional Bank presidents.

To whom are the bonds sold? To the open market; this includes dealers in government bonds, who then resell them to commercial banks, big corporations, and other financial institutions.

The purchasers usually buy the bonds by writing checks to the Fed, drawn from an account in a commercial bank. For example, if the Fed sells $10,000 worth of bonds to Ms. Smith, she writes a check on the Farmers' Bank of Seattle. The Fed presents the check at the Farmers' Bank. When the Farmers' Bank pays the check, it will reduce its balance with the Fed by $10,000. At the end, the Farmers' Bank, and the entire commercial banking system, will lose $10,000 in reserves at the Federal

Reserve System.

Table 11-2(a) shows the ultimate effect of a $1 billion open-market operation on the Federal Reserve balance sheet. The open-market sale changes the Federal Reserve balance sheet by reducing both assets and liabilities by $1 billion: the Fed has sold $1 billion of government bonds, and its liabilities have declined by exactly the same amount, $1 billion of bank reserves.

Effects on Money. To understand the effect of the reserve change on the money supply, we must consider the banks' response. In this chapter, we continue the algebraic convenience of assuming that banks are assumed to hold 10 percent of their deposits as reserves with the central bank; the legal reason for this practice is discussed in greater detail later in this chapter.

What happens to the money supply? Reserves go down by $1 billion, and that tends to set off a contraction of deposits. If the legal reserve requirement is 10 percent, the $1 billion sale of government bonds will result in a $10 billion cut in the community's money supply. (We saw in the last chapter how a change in bank reserves would lead to a multiplied change in total bank deposits.) Table 11-2(b) shows the banks' ultimate position after $1 billion of reserves have been extinguished by the open-market operation. In the end, the Fed's open-market sale has caused a $10 billion contraction in the money supply.

Operating Procedures

The FOMC meets eight times a year to give instructions to its operating arm, the Federal Reserve Bank of New York. The instructions are contained in an "FOMC policy directive." The directive has two parts: a general assessment of economic conditions and a review of the objectives of monetary policy. As an example, consider the August 1982 directive. In the midst of the deepest recession of the post-war period, the FOMC began with its review of the economy:[1]

> The information reviewed at this meeting suggests only a little further advance in real GNP in the current quarter, following a relatively small increase in the second quarter, while prices on the average are continuing to rise more slowly than in 1981.

What objectives did the Fed establish for monetary policy? It stated:

> The Federal Open Market Committee seeks to foster monetary and financial conditions that will help to reduce inflation, promote a resumption of growth in output on a sustainable basis, and contribute to a sustainable pattern of international transactions.

The most important part of the procedure is instructing the front-line troops at the New York Fed about how to manage financial markets on a day-to-day basis. The operating procedures have changed over time. Before the 1970s, the FOMC used to give such vague instructions as, "Keep credit conditions and interest rates as tight as they have been." Or, "Loosen credit a little to help expand GNP." Because the Fed acted cautiously, it was sometimes slow to react to changing business-cycle conditions.

In the late 1970s, the Federal Reserve altered its operating procedures to pay closer attention to movements in the money supply. It was accused of helping to reelect President Nixon in 1972; shortly afterward, the Fed was charged with overreacting to the sharp recession of 1974–1975 and with allowing unemployment to rise too sharply. To rein in the Fed, Congress directed it to set explicit growth-

---

[1] The FOMC quotations are from the *Federal Reserve Bulletin*, which contains monthly reports on Federal Reserve activities and other important financial developments.

rate targets for the major monetary aggregates.

From October 1979 until late 1982, the Federal Reserve undertook a major experiment, concentrating almost exclusively on the growth of M_1, M_2, and bank reserves. It hoped that a clear and decisive strategy of targeting the monetary aggregates would help reduce an annual inflation rate that was surging beyond 10 percent. An example of the operational directive given by the FOMC dates from August 1982:

> In the short run, the Committee continues to seek behavior of reserve aggregates consistent with growth of M_1 and M_2 from June to September [1982] at annual rates of about 5 percent and about 9 percent respectively.

The shift to targeting reserves and the money supply in 1979 was highly controversial. The immediate result was a major reduction in the growth of the money supply and a consequent tightening of monetary policy. This led to an increase of market interest rates to levels not seen since the Civil War. It was followed shortly thereafter by the deepest recession since the 1930s. The policy was definitely successful in reducing inflation to 3 to 4 percent per year by the mid-1980s.

In the political hue and cry surrounding the sharp recession of 1982, the Fed concluded that its monetary policy had become overly restrictive. In addition, the definitions of the monetary aggregates became confused at this time because of the addition of a number of new assets (such as interest-bearing checking accounts) to M_1 and M_2. The Fed therefore retreated from its strict reserve and monetary targeting in the fall of 1982.

After 1982, the Fed began to downplay the use of monetary aggregates in its decisions about monetary policy. In 1987, it ceased stating explicit targets in terms of M_1, although it continued to publish monitoring ranges for other aggregates.

Choice of Policies. How does the Federal Reserve choose its money and interest-rate targets today? The process is shrouded in mystery, but firsthand accounts and memoirs of Fed governors and staff members boil down to something like the following.

The Fed staff and the FOMC have certain macro-economic objectives, including goals for inflation, the foreign exchange rate of the dollar, real GNP, unemployment, and the trade balance. The Fed makes regular projections on variables outside its control (such as fiscal policy, oil prices, foreign economic growth, and so forth) and then forecasts the behavior of the economy using a number of different assumptions about monetary policy.

The FOMC then debates the proper course for monetary policy. If the economy is performing satisfactorily, it might decide to leave interest rates and money-supply growth at their current levels. Or, if the FOMC thought that the current setting was encouraging inflation, it might choose to tighten monetary policy a notch. Alternatively, if the Fed thought that a recession loomed ahead, it might inject reserves into the system, increasing the money supply and consequently lowering interest rates.

It is not always easy to understand the exact chain of reasoning that led to a particular monetary-policy step. Nonetheless, historians who sift through the decisions usually find that the Fed is ultimately concerned with preserving the integrity of our financial institutions, combating inflation, defending the exchange rate of the dollar, and preventing excessive unemployment.[2]

Discount-Rate Policy: A Second Instrument

When commercial banks are short of reserves, they are allowed to borrow from the Federal Reserve Banks. Their loans were included under the asset heading "Loans and acceptances" in the Fed balance sheet in Table 11-1. We will call these loans *borrowed reserves.* When borrowed reserves are growing, the banks are borrowing from the Fed, thereby increasing total bank reserves (borrowed plus unborrowed reserves). Conversely, a drop in borrowed reserves promotes a contraction in total bank reserves.

Although borrowed reserves get multiplied into bank money just like the unborrowed reserves we discussed in the last section, they are not a precise instrument under the control of the Fed. It's like the old saying, "You can lead a horse to water, but you can't make him drink." The Fed can encourage or discourage bank borrowings, but it cannot set a precise level of borrowed reserves.

If the Fed thinks that the money supply is growing too slowly and needs to be boosted, it does not send sales agents out to drum up more borrowing. Instead, it might lower the **discount rate,** which represents the interest rate charged on bank borrowings from the 12 regional Federal Reserve Banks. But the relationship between the discount rate and bank borrowings is not very precise. In recent years, borrowed reserves have not played a major role in monetary policy.[3]

Changing the Discount Rate. For many years, the discount rate was the bellwether of monetary policy. For example, in 1965 when the Fed wanted to send a signal to markets that the Vietnam war boom threatened to become inflationary, it raised the discount rate. So powerful was this signal that Fed Chairman Martin was called to the LBJ ranch for a dressing down by President Johnson, who was afraid the higher discount rate would slow the economy. More recently, as the U.S. economy has become more integrated with other countries, the discount rate has occasionally been used to signal major changes in economic policy or to coordinate monetary policies with other countries.

Some economists would like the Federal Reserve to make the discount rate a market-based interest rate. One reform proposal would tie the discount rate directly to short-term interest rates—in principle removing any need for the Fed to ration borrowing by banks. Other economists fear that such a move would make the money supply more unpredictable. It is unlikely that such a change is in the wind today.

Changing Reserve Requirements

We noted above that, but for government rules, banks would probably keep only about 1 percent of their deposits in the form of reserves. In fact, today American banks are required to keep substantially

---

[2] For a careful analysis of political and economic forces operating on the Federal Reserve, see Donald Kettl, *Leadership at the Fed* (Yale University Press, New Haven, Conn., 1986).

[3] When the Federal Reserve System was started, it was thought that discount policy would be most important of all. The idea was to have banks buy their customers' promissory notes at a "discount," sending them over to the Reserve Banks in return for new cash. That way, the neighborhood banks would never run out of money to accommodate worthy farm and business borrowers. It did not work out that way. Why not? Largely because the last thing a healthy economy wants is an elastic money supply that will *automatically* expand when business is good and contract when it is bad. That way lies disastrous reinforcement of business cycles and inflation.

more reserves than are necessary for meeting customers' needs. These legal reserve requirements are a crucial part of the mechanism by which the Fed controls the supply of bank money. This section describes the nature of legal reserve requirements and shows how they affect the money supply.

Legal Reserve Requirements. We have mentioned that banks are required to hold a minimum amount as non-interest-bearing reserves. Table 11-3 shows current reserve requirements along with the Fed's discretionary power to change reserve requirements. The key concept is the level of *required reserve ratios*.[4] They range from 12 percent against checkable deposits down to zero for personal sav-

---

[4] The legislation that set out the rules for today's financial intermediaries was contained in the Depository Institutions Deregulation and Monetary Control Act of 1980 and the Garn–St Germain Depository Institutions Act of 1982. For brevity, we call these the 1980 and 1982 Banking Acts.

Type of deposit	Reserve ratio (%)	Range in which Fed can vary (%)
Checking (transaction) accounts:		
First $41 million	3	No change allowed
Above $41 million	12	8 to 14
Time and savings deposits:		
Personal	0	
Nonpersonal		
Up to $1\frac{1}{2}$ years' maturity	0	0 to 9
More than $1\frac{1}{2}$ years' maturity	0	0 to 9

Table 11-3. Required reserves for financial institutions

This table shows the pattern of reserve requirements for financial institutions under the 1980 Banking Act (known as the Depository Institutions Deregulation and Monetary Control Act of 1980). The reserve ratio column shows the percent of deposits in each category that must be held in non-interest-bearing deposits at the Fed or in cash on hand.

There are three classes of deposits. Checking-type accounts in large banks face required reserves of 12 percent. Checking accounts in small banks face a small reserve requirement of 3 percent. Other deposits will have no reserve requirements.

Note as well that the Fed has power to alter the reserve ratio within a given range. It does so only on the rare occasion when economic conditions warrant a sharp change in monetary policy. (Source: *Federal Reserve Bulletin*, June 1991.)

ings accounts. For convenience in our numerical examples, we use 10 percent reserve ratios, with the understanding that the actual ratio required is slightly different from 10 percent.

Bankers often complain that they are required to hold non-interest-bearing, barren reserve assets beyond what is needed to meet the ebb and flow of withdrawals and receipts. While this view has merit from the point of view of bankers, it misses the macroeconomic point: *Legal reserve requirements are set high in order to allow the central bank to control the money supply.* That is, by setting reserve requirements well above the level that banks themselves desire, the central bank can determine the exact level of reserves and can thereby control the money supply more precisely.

Put differently, by setting reserve requirements so high, the central bank can be confident that banks will generally want to hold no more than the legal minimum. The supply of bank money will then be determined by the supply of bank reserves (determined by the Fed through open-market operations) and by the money-supply multiplier (determined by the required reserve ratio). Because the Fed controls both bank reserves and the required reserve ratio, it has (within a small margin of error) control over the money supply.

Impacts of Changes in Required Reserves. In addition, the Fed can change reserve requirements if it wants to change the money supply quickly. For instance, if the Fed wants to tighten money overnight, it can raise the required reserve ratio for the big banks to the 14 percent statutory limit. It might even raise reserve requirements on time deposits. On the other hand, if the Fed wants to ease credit conditions, it can do the reverse and cut legal reserve ratios.

Exactly how does an increase in required ratios operate to tighten credit? Suppose the required reserve ratio is 10 percent and banks had built up their reserves to meet this requirement. Now suppose the Fed decides to tighten credit and Congress allows it to raise the required reserve ratio to 20 percent. (This fantastic figure is for algebraic simplicity. The Fed cannot and would not take such a drastic step today.)

Even if the Fed does nothing by way of open-market operations or discount policy to change bank reserves, banks now have to contract their loans and investments greatly—and their deposits as well. Why? Because (as Chapter 10 showed) bank deposits can now be only 5 times reserves, not 10 times reserves. So there must be a drop by one-half in all deposits!

This painful cut will start to take place quickly. As soon as the Federal Reserve Board signs the new rule raising the requirement to 20 percent, banks will find that they have insufficient reserves. They will have to sell some bonds and call in some loans. The bond buyers and borrowers will drain their checking accounts. The process ends only after banks have brought down their deposits to 5 rather than 10 times their reserves.

Such an enormous change in so short a time would lead to very high interest rates, credit rationing, large declines in investment, and great reductions in GNP and employment. So this extreme example warns that this powerful tool of changing reserve requirements has to be used with great caution. Changes in reserve requirements are made extremely sparingly because they present too large and abrupt a change in policy. Open-market operations can achieve the same results in a less disruptive way.

Interest-Rate Regulation

In addition to the three major instruments discussed above, the Federal Reserve (with the help of Congress and other government agencies) has historically regulated financial markets by limiting interest rates. Until the 1980s, most interest rates paid by commercial banks were controlled. Banks were not allowed to pay interest on checking accounts, and there were ceilings on interest rates on savings accounts and time deposits.

Regulated interest rates could not survive in competitive markets. Financial institutions devised new types of instruments which lured funds from low-yield deposits. The high interest rates of the late 1970s and early 1980s put further pressure on the system, because banks (which paid 5 percent per year on their savings accounts) had to compete with money market mutual funds (which paid 10 or 15 percent on their deposits). Eventually the regulatory edifice constructed during the Great Depression began to crumble. Congress reacted with the Banking Acts of 1980 and 1982, which largely deregulated interest rates.

The New Regulatory Structure. The Banking Acts of 1980 and 1982 created a new regulatory structure that has largely decontrolled interest rates in financial markets. The analytical basis of the new approach was to separate transactions accounts from non-transactions accounts. A *transactions account* is one whose primary purpose is to serve as a means of payment; these include currency and checking accounts. A *non-transactions account* is an asset whose primary purpose is to put aside funds for the future, not to pay bills (a savings account is an example of a non-transactions account).

Once this distinction had been made, the 1980 and 1982 Acts effectively deregulated non-transactions accounts. This legislation phased out interest-rate ceilings for non-transactions accounts in 1986 and set reserve requirements on these deposits at zero for personal accounts and at minimal levels for business accounts. As of the late 1980s, non-transactions accounts earn market interest rates and are effectively outside the regulatory structure of the Federal Reserve.

The remaining assets—transactions assets like checking accounts—have been largely deregulated. These accounts are subject to substantial reserve requirements (currently amounting to 12 percent of transactions deposits for large banks). However, personal transactions accounts are no longer subject to interest-rate ceilings. The result is a financial sector that has been largely removed from regulation over the last two decades.

International Reserve Movements

The dollar is today used extensively in world trade and as a safe asset by many foreign investors. Consequently, dollars are widely held abroad by those who export and import with the United States, by foreign and American investors, by those who finance trade and investments between other countries, by speculators and dealers in foreign financial markets, by foreign governments, by central banks, and by international agencies like the International Monetary Fund. Foreigners own hundreds of billions of dollars in U.S. dollar-denominated assets. Because currency itself yields no interest return, foreigners prefer to hold interest-bearing assets (bonds, stocks, etc.). However, to have a medium for buying and selling such earning assets, foreigners do hold some transactions dollars in M_1.

Why are we concerned about international money holdings at this point? The reason is that deposits by foreigners in the banking system increase the total amount of bank reserves in the same way that deposits of domestic residents do. Thus changes in foreigners' dollar money holdings can set off a chain of expansion or contraction of the U.S. money supply.

For example, say the Japanese decide to deposit $1 billion of U.S. currency in U.S. banks. What happens? There is a $1 billion increase in reserves in the domestic banking system, as illustrated in Table 10-4(a) in the last chapter. As a result, the banking system can expand deposits tenfold, in this case to $10 billion.

Thus the Fed's control of the nation's M is modified by international disturbances to bank reserves. But the Fed has the power to offset any change in reserves coming from abroad. It effects this by engaging in what is called sterilization. *Sterilization* refers to actions by a central bank that insulate the domestic money supply from international reserve flows. Sterilization usually is accomplished when the central bank implements an open-market operation that reverses the international reserve movement.

To summarize:

The central bank's control over bank reserves is subject to disturbances from abroad. These disturbances can, however, be offset if the central bank sterilizes the international flows.

In practice, the Fed routinely sterilizes international disturbances to reserves. Other countries, with less well developed financial markets and central-banking systems, sometimes have trouble fully sterilizing international reserve flows.

Other Activities

At this point, you probably have concluded that the Fed is pretty busy. But we have described only the money market functions of the Fed—those relating to control of the money supply. There are, in addition, a number of subsidiary tasks delegated to the Fed and other federal agencies:

- *Managing exchange markets.* The Fed buys and sells different currencies on foreign exchange markets on behalf of the government. While this task is generally easy, from time to time foreign exchange markets become disorderly, and the Fed, under orders from the Treasury, steps in. A full discussion of the way that central banks can intervene to affect currency values is given in Chapter 21.

- *Coordinating international finances.* The Federal Reserve took the lead during the 1980s in working with foreign countries and with international agencies to alleviate the problems of large debt burdens. The debt crisis, which surfaced in 1981, found many middle-income and poor countries, such as Mexico and Brazil, burdened with extremely high levels of interest payments relative to their export earnings. The Fed understood that the debt crisis could lead to a crisis of confidence in the financial system, because many large American banks had worthless foreign loans that were as large as their net worth. Working together with other agencies, the Fed helped manage the crisis, so that by 1991 the debt burdens of most countries, along with the risks to the international financial system, had been significantly reduced.

- *Regulating banks and insuring deposits.* Since the Great Depression, the federal government has stood behind the banks. To instill confidence in banks, the government insures bank deposits, inspects the books of banks, and takes over insolvent banks. One important function of government is the insurance of bank deposits. The government insures up to $100,000 per deposit at banks that are members of the Federal Deposit Insurance Corporation (the F.D.I.C.).

The deregulation in financial markets over the last decade, along with the structural changes in financial markets and the real economy, led to a major fiasco in the U.S. deposit insurance system. Savings and loan associations (S&Ls) were allowed to undertake risky investments with very little regulatory supervision. As a result, they paid high interest rates on insured deposits and put those funds into real estate, energy projects, and high salaries for the directors. These were "Heads I win, tails the government loses" situations. When the real estate and energy markets went sour in the late 1980s, hundreds of savings and loan associations, along with a score of commercial banks, became insolvent.

The result was that the federal government was forced to bail out banks whose insured deposits exceeded their assets by an amount estimated to be between $150 and $250 billion. Taxpayers were ultimately being forced to pay the bill. Many economists believe that the deposit insurance system must be drastically overhauled if this sad episode is not to be repeated in the future.

We have completed our analysis of the money supply. It can be summarized as follows:

The money supply is ultimately determined by the policies of the Fed. By setting reserve require-ments and the discount rate, and especially by undertaking open-market operations, the Fed de-termines the level of reserves and the money sup-ply.

Banks and the public are cooperating partners in this process. Banks create money by multiple ex-pansion of reserves; the public agrees to hold money in depository institutions.

Putting these together, the Fed can determine the money supply on a medium-term basis.

B. The Effects of Money on Output and Prices

It is only in this interval between the acquisition of money and the rise of prices that the increasing quantity of gold and silver is favor-able to industry.

David Hume, *Essays*, "Of Money"

Having examined the building blocks of monetary theory, we now describe the *monetary transmis-sion mechanism*, the route by which changes in the supply of money are translated into changes in out-put, employment, prices, and inflation.

How Monetary Policy Works to Control Spending

We begin with an overview of the steps in the pro-cess by which the Federal Reserve affects output and prices. For concreteness, assume that the Fed-eral Reserve is concerned about rising prices and has decided to slow down the economy. There are five steps in the process.

1. *To start the process, the Fed takes steps to re-duce bank reserves.* As we saw in the first part of this chapter, the Fed reduces bank reserves pri-marily by selling government securities in the open market. This changes the balance sheet of the banking system by reducing total bank re-serves.
2. *Each dollar reduction in bank reserves produces a multiple contraction in checking deposits, thereby reducing the money supply.* This step was described in the last chapter, where it was shown that changes in reserves lead to a multi-plied change in deposits. Since the money sup-ply equals currency plus checking deposits, the reduction in checking deposits reduces the money supply.
3. *The reduction in the money supply will tend to increase interest rates and tighten credit condi-tions.* With an unchanged demand for money, a reduced supply of money will raise interest rates. In addition, the amount of credit (loans and borrowing) available to people will decline. Interest rates will rise for mortgage borrowers and for businesses that want to build factories, buy new equipment, or add to inventory. Higher interest rates will also lower the values of peo-ple's assets, depressing the prices of bonds, stocks, land, and houses.
4. *With higher interest rates and lower wealth, in-terest-sensitive spending—especially investment —will tend to fall.* The combination of higher in-terest rates, tighter credit, and reduced wealth will tend to discourage investment and con-sumption spending. Businesses will scale down their investment plans, as will state and local governments. When a town finds it cannot float its bonds at any reasonable rate, the new road is not built and the new school is postponed. Simi-larly, consumers decide to buy a smaller house, or to renovate their existing one, when rising mortgage interest rates make monthly payments high relative to monthly income. And in an econ-

omy increasingly open to international trade, higher interest rates may raise the foreign exchange rate of the dollar, depressing net exports. Hence, tight money will raise interest rates and reduce spending on interest-sensitive components of aggregate demand.

5. *Finally, the pressures of tight money, by reducing aggregate demand, will reduce income, output, jobs, and inflation.* The aggregate supply-and-demand (or, equivalently, the multiplier) analysis showed how such a drop in investment and other autonomous spending may depress output and employment sharply. Furthermore, as output and employment fall below the levels that would otherwise occur, prices tend to rise less rapidly or even to fall. Inflationary forces subside. If the Fed's diagnosis of inflationary conditions was on target, the drop in output and the rise in unemployment will help relieve inflationary forces.

We can summarize the steps as follows:

$$R \text{ down} \rightarrow M \text{ down} \rightarrow i \text{ up} \rightarrow I, C, X \text{ down} \rightarrow$$
$$AD \text{ down} \rightarrow \text{real GNP down and } P \text{ down}$$

This five-step sequence—from the Fed's changes in commercial bank reserves, to a multiple change in total M, to changes in interest rates and credit availability, to changes in investment spending that shift aggregate demand, and finally to the response of output, employment, and inflation—is vital to the determination of output and prices. If you look back at Figure 11-1, you will see how each of the five steps fits into our thematic flow chart. We have already explained the first two steps; the balance of this chapter is devoted to analyzing steps 3 through 5.

The Money Market

Step three in the transmission mechanism is the response of interest rates and credit conditions to changes in the supply of money. Recall from the last chapter that the *demand for money* depends primarily on the need to undertake transactions. Households, businesses, and governments hold money so they may buy goods, services, and other items. In addition, some part of the demand for M derives from the need for a supersafe and highly liquid asset.

The *supply of money* is jointly determined by the private banking system and the nation's central bank. The central bank, through open-market operations and other instruments, provides reserves to the banking system. Commercial banks then create deposits out of the central-bank reserves. By manipulating reserves, the central bank can determine the money supply within a narrow margin of error.

Supply and Demand for Money

The supply and demand for money jointly determine the market interest rates. Figure 11-4 shows the total quantity of money (M) on the horizontal axis and the nominal interest rate (i) on the vertical axis. The supply curve is drawn as a vertical line on the assumption that the Federal Reserve manipulates its instruments to keep the money supply at a given level, shown as M^* in Figure 11-4.

In addition, we show the money demand schedule as a downward-sloping curve because the holdings of money decline as the level of interest rates rises. At higher interest rates, people and busi-

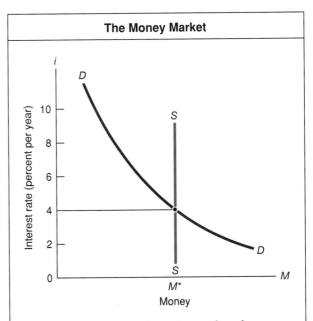

Figure 11-4. Demand and supply of money determine the interest rate

The Fed has a money target at M^*, represented by the vertical supply-of-money schedule, *SS*. The public (households and businesses) has a downward-sloping money demand schedule. In this example, the money market is in equilibrium with a nominal interest rate of 4 percent per year.

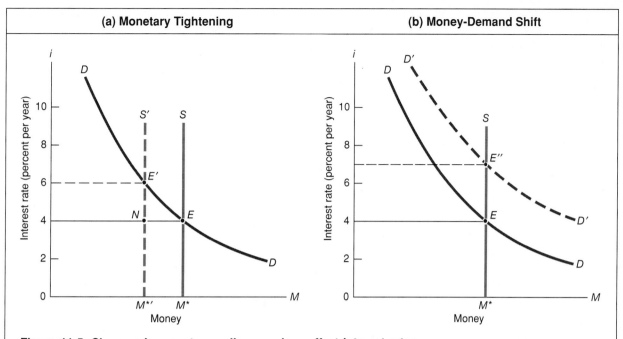

(a) Monetary Tightening

(b) Money-Demand Shift

Figure 11-5. Changes in monetary policy or prices affect interest rates

In **(a)**, the Federal Reserve contracts bank reserves and the money supply in response to fears of rising prices. The lower money supply produces an excess demand for money shown by the gap *NE*. As the public attempts to attain the desired money stock, interest rates rise to the new equilibrium at *E'*.

In **(b)**, the demand for money has increased because of a run-up in the price level with real output held constant. The higher demand for money forces market interest rates upward until they in turn force the quantity of money demanded back down to *M**.

nesses shift more of their assets to higher-yield assets and away from low-yield or no-yield money. This is accomplished by shifting funds to high-interest assets more often, by holding less currency on average and replenishing cash more often, by trying to synchronize income and expenditures, and by engaging in similar cash-management schemes.

The intersection of the supply and demand schedules in Figure 11-4 determines the market interest rate. Recall that interest rates are the prices paid for the use of money. Interest rates are determined in the **money markets,** which are the markets where short-term funds are lent and borrowed. Important interest rates include short-term rates such as the rates on 3-month Treasury bills, short-term commercial paper (notes issued by large corporations), and the Federal Funds rate that banks pay each other for the overnight use of bank reserves. Longer-term interest rates include 10-year or 20-year government and corporate bonds and mortgages on real estate. (See Figure 10-2 for a graph of recent trends in interest rates.)

In Figure 11-4, the equilibrium interest rate is 4 percent per year. Only at 4 percent is the level of the money supply that the Fed has targeted consistent with the desired money holdings of the public. At a higher interest rate, there would be excessive money balances, and people would be unwilling to hold all the *M**. People would get rid of their excessive money holdings by buying bonds and other financial instruments, thereby lowering market interest rates toward the equilibrium 4 percent rate. What would happen at an interest rate of 2 percent?

We are concerned with the effects of changes in the supply or demand for money in the money market. First consider a change in monetary policy. Suppose that the Federal Reserve becomes worried about inflation and tightens monetary policy by selling securities and reducing the money supply.

The impact of a monetary tightening is shown in Figure 11-5(*a*). The leftward shift of the money supply schedule means that at the going 4 percent interest rate, money balances will not meet people's transactions and asset needs. The gap between E and N shows the extent of excess demand for money at the old interest rate. People start to sell off some of their assets and increase their money holdings. Interest rates rise until the new equilibrium is attained, shown in Figure 11-5(a) at point E' with a new and higher interest rate of 6 percent per year.

Another disturbance might come from higher prices. Suppose the money supply is held constant by the Fed. However, due to an increase in oil prices, the general price level rises and the money desired to finance transactions increases with no change in real GNP. In this case, shown in Figure 11-5(b), the demand for money would increase, shifting the money demand curve to the right from DD to $D'D'$, and leading to an increase in equilibrium interest rates.

The opposite cases would occur with Federal Reserve concern about a recession, a contraction in the demand for money because of a fall in prices, a decline in real output, and a shift in the public's desire to hold money.

To check your understanding, make sure you can work through the following cases using Figure 11-4: (1) The Federal Reserve has decided that unemployment is rising too sharply and wants to reverse this trend by expanding the money supply. What steps must the Fed take to expand money? What will be the impact on the money supply curve? What is the reaction in money markets? (2) As a result of a falling foreign exchange rate on the dollar, exports rise and real GNP increases. What happens to the demand for money? What is the impact upon the market interest rate? (3) As banks introduce new interest-bearing checking accounts, people decide to put more of their assets into these accounts and less into savings accounts at every level of GNP and of interest rates. The Fed is uncertain about the significance of this behavior and therefore keeps the money supply constant. What will be the impact of the asset switch on money supply and demand? On market interest rates?

To summarize our findings about the money market:

The money market is affected by a combination of (1) the public's desire to hold money (represented by the demand-for-money DD curve) and (2) the Fed's monetary policy (which is shown in Figure 11-4 as a fixed money supply or a vertical SS curve at point M^*). Their interaction determines the market interest rate, i. A tighter monetary policy shifts the SS curve to the left, raising market interest rates. An increase in the nation's output or price level shifts the DD curve to the right and raises interest rates. Monetary easing or a money-demand decline has the opposite effects.

The Monetary Mechanism

Every day, the newspapers and television feature reports on money markets and monetary policy, analyzing how monetary affairs affect interest rates, foreign exchange rates, the trade and budget deficits, output, employment, inflation, and virtually every macroeconomic variable. If you read the news recently, you might have seen the following statements:

A big question is whether the Federal Reserve will react to the budget pact between Congress and the White House by cutting short-term interest rates. The Fed's policy-making committee faces intense pressure from White House officials to reduce short-term interest rates to help bolster the sagging economy.

(Wall Street Journal)

The Federal Reserve Board warned that passage of protectionist trade legislation or a higher minimum wage bill would unleash inflationary forces that the Fed would have to counter by tightening credit, perhaps severely.

(New York Times)

Earlier, Washington had been pressing officials to cut Japanese interest rates to enable the Federal Reserve to lower U.S. rates without risking flows of capital out of the U.S. With American's recession ending, the Fed may be less eager to trim U.S. rates. However, it is still worried that slowing growth abroad may eventually crimp American exports.

(Wall Street Journal)

Underlying these statements are views about the way the Federal Reserve operates, the way money affects the economy, and the way political leaders and the populace want to shape monetary policy. Let us look at the impact of changing monetary conditions by using the multiplier model. We then will examine the transmission mechanism by using the aggregate demand-and-supply framework.

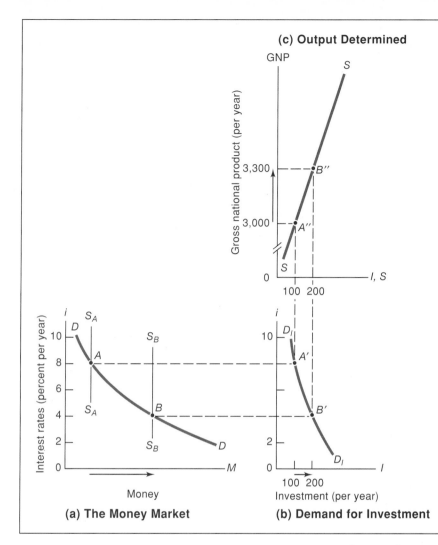

(c) Output Determined

Figure 11-6. Central bank determines the money supply, changing interest rates and investment, thereby affecting GNP

When the Fed raises the money supply, from S_A to S_B, interest rates fall as people increase their money balances. That is, the economy moves down the money demand schedule in **(a)**.

Lower interest rates reduce the cost of investment, thus encouraging business purchases of plant and equipment and consumer purchases of houses. The economy moves down the demand-for-investment schedule $D_I D_I$ from A' to B' in **(b)**.

By the multiplier mechanism in **(c)**, the higher investment raises aggregate demand and GNP from A'' to B''.

Can you trace the reverse process in which open-market sales by the Fed will contract M, I, and GNP?

(a) The Money Market

(b) Demand for Investment

Graphical Analysis of Monetary Policy

Figure 11-6 shows the effects of a monetary expansion upon economic activity. Part (a) shows the money market in the lower left, (b) the determination of investment in the lower right, and (c) the determination of aggregate demand and GNP by the multiplier mechanism in the upper right. We can think of the causality as moving counterclockwise from the money market through investment to the determination of aggregate demand and GNP as a whole.

Starting at the lower left in Figure 11-6(a), we see the demand and supply for money that were depicted in Figures 11-4 and 11-5. For purposes of the present discussion, assume that in the initial state the money supply schedule was S_A and the interest

rate was 8 percent per year. If the Fed was concerned about a looming recession, it might increase the money supply by making open-market purchases, shifting the curve to S_B. In the case shown in Figure 11-6(a), market interest rates would thereby fall to 4 percent.

Figure 11-6(b) picks up the story to show how lower interest rates increase spending on interest-sensitive components of aggregate demand. We saw in Chapter 7 that a decline in interest rates would induce businesses to increase their spending on plant, equipment, and inventories. The effects of eased monetary policy are rapidly seen in the housing market, where lower interest rates mean lower monthly mortgage payments on the typical house, thus encouraging households to purchase more and larger houses.

In addition, consumption spending increases, both because lower interest rates generally increase the value of wealth—as stock, bond, and housing prices tend to rise—and because consumers tend to spend more on automobiles and other big-ticket consumer durables when interest rates are low and credit is plentiful. Moreover, as we have seen in Chapter 9, lower interest rates tend to lower the foreign exchange rate on the dollar, thereby increasing the level of net exports. We see then how lower interest rates lead to increased spending in many different areas of the economy.

These consequences are evident in Figure 11-6(*b*), where the drop in interest rates (caused by the increase in the money supply) leads to a rise in investment from A' to B'. In this case, we should construe "investment" in the very broad sense sketched a moment ago: it includes not only business investment but also consumer durables and residences, as well as net foreign investment in the form of net exports.

Finally, Figure 11-6(*c*) shows the impact of changes in investment in the multiplier model. This diagram is simply Figure 9-5 turned on its side. Recall from Chapter 9 that, in the simplest multiplier model, equilibrium output is attained when desired saving equals desired investment. In Figure 11-6(*c*), we have shown this relationship by drawing the savings schedule as the SS schedule; this line represents the desired level of saving (measured along the horizontal axis) as a function of GNP on the vertical axis. Equilibrium GNP is attained at that level where the investment demand from panel (*b*) equals the desired saving from the SS schedule.

The initial level of investment was 100, as read off at A' in panel (*b*), producing a level of GNP of 3000. After easier money has lowered the interest rate from 8 to 4 percent, investment rises to 200 at point B'. This higher level of investment raises aggregate spending to the new equilibrium at B'' in panel (*c*) with a new equilibrium GNP of 3300.

What has occurred? The rise in the money supply from S_A to S_B lowered the interest rate from A to B; this caused investment to rise from A' to B'; and this in turn, acting through the multiplier, led to a rise in GNP from A'' to B''.

Such is the route by which monetary policy acts through intermediate targets like the money supply and interest rates to affect its ultimate targets.

Monetary Policy in the *AD-AS* Framework

The three-part diagram in Figure 11-6 illustrates how an increase in the money supply would lead to an increase in aggregate demand. We can now show the effect on the overall macroeconomic equilibrium by using aggregate supply and demand curves.

The increase in aggregate demand produced by an increase in the supply of money causes a rightward shift of the *AD* curve as drawn in Figure 11-7. This shift illustrates a monetary expansion in the presence of unemployed resources, with a relatively flat *AS* curve. Here, the monetary expansion

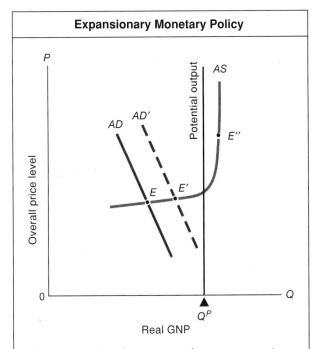

Figure 11-7. An expansionary monetary policy shifts *AD* curve to the right, raising output and prices

Earlier discussion and Figure 11-6 showed how an increase in the money supply would lead to an increase in investment and thereby to a multiplied increase in aggregate demand. This results in a rightward shift of the *AD* curve.

In the Keynesian region where the *AS* curve is relatively flat, a monetary expansion has its primary effect on real output, with only a small effect on prices.

In the classical region, the *AS* curve is near-vertical (shown at point *E''*), and a monetary expansion will primarily raise prices and nominal GNP with little effect on real GNP. Can you see why in the long run money may have little impact on real output?

shifts aggregate demand from *AD* to *AD'*, and the overall equilibrium moves from *E* to *E'*. This case demonstrates how monetary expansion can increase aggregate demand and have a powerful impact on real output.

The sequence therefore runs as follows:

Monetary expansion bids down market interest rates. This stimulates interest-sensitive spending on business investment, housing, consumer durables, and the like. Via the multiplier mechanism, aggregate demand increases, raising output and prices above the levels they would otherwise attain. Therefore, the basic sequence is:

$$M \text{ up} \rightarrow i \text{ down} \rightarrow I, C, X \text{ up} \rightarrow AD \text{ up} \rightarrow$$
$$\text{GNP up and } P \text{ up}$$

But what would happen if the economy were operating near its capacity? This is illustrated by point *E''* on the steeply sloping (or classical) segment of the *AS* curve in Figure 11-7. In this case, monetary changes would have little impact on real output. Rather, in the classical region of the *AS* curve, the higher money stock, chasing the same amount of output, would primarily end up raising prices.

To clinch your understanding of this vital sequence, work through the opposite case of a monetary contraction. Say that the Federal Reserve decides, as it did in 1979, to contract reserves, slow the economy, and reduce inflation. You can trace this sequence in Figure 11-6 by reversing the direction of the monetary policy, thereby seeing how money, interest rates, investment, and aggregate demand interact when monetary policy is tightened. Then see how a leftward shift of the *AD* curve in Figure 11-7 would reduce both output and prices.

Monetary Effects in the Long Run

Many economists believe that changes in the supply of money in the long run will mainly increase the price level with little or no impact upon real output. We can understand this point by analyzing the effects of monetary changes with different-shaped *AS* curves. As shown in Figure 11-7, monetary changes will affect aggregate demand and will tend to change real GNP in the short run when there are unemployed resources and the *AS* curve is relatively flat.

However, we emphasized in Chapter 8 that as prices and wages adjust over the longer run, the output effects of *AD* shifts will diminish, and the price effects will tend to dominate. Recall that the *AS* curve tends to be vertical or near-vertical in the long run as all sticky or contractual elements of wages and prices adapt to the higher expected levels of prices and wages. This means that in the long run, as prices and wages become more flexible, more and more of the effect of the money-supply change turns up in prices and less and less shows up in real output.

What is the intuition behind this difference between the short run and the long run? We can construct a highly simplified example to see the difference. Suppose we start out as in Figure 11-6 with a nominal GNP of 3000 and stable prices; then a monetary expansion that increases the money supply by 10 percent might increase nominal GNP by 10 percent to 3300. Studies by Robert J. Gordon and others indicate that, in the short run, "nominal GNP changes have been divided consistently, with two-thirds taking the form of output change and the remaining one-third the form of price change." Consequently, in the first year, the money-supply expansion might increase real GNP around 7 percent and increase prices around 3 percent.

As time passes, however, wages and prices begin to adjust more completely to the higher price and output levels. Demand inflation in both labor and product markets would raise wages and prices; wages would be adjusted to reflect the higher cost of living; cost-of-living provisions in contracts would raise wages and prices even further. After a second year, prices might rise another 1 or 2 percent, with output then being only 5 or 6 percent above its original level. In the third year, prices might rise again while output falls somewhat. Where would it end? It might continue over a period of years and decades until prices had risen by fully 10 percent and output was back to the original level. Thus, the monetary policy would have raised prices and wages by about 10 percent but would have left real output unchanged.

In this example, finally, all nominal magnitudes are increased by 10 percent, while all real magnitudes are unchanged. Nominal magnitudes like the GNP deflator, the CPI, nominal GNP, wages, the money supply, currency, checking deposits, dollar consumption, dollar imports, the dollar value of wealth, and so forth are 10 percent higher. But real GNP, real consumption, the real money supply (equal to the money supply divided by the price level), real wages, real incomes, and the real value of wealth are all unchanged by the monetary policy. In the long run, then, we say that money is *neutral*.

A word of caution is in order: The scenario that money changes lead to proportionate changes in all nominal magnitudes but no changes in real variables is intuitively plausible and supported by certain empirical evidence. But it is not a universal law. The long run may be a period of many decades; intervening events may throw the economy off the idealized long-run trajectory; and interest-rate changes along the path might have an irreversible impact upon the ultimate outcome.[5] The long-run neutrality of money is therefore only a tendency and not a universal law.

As we near the end of this chapter, we note that the discussion of the role of monetary policy has taken place without reference to fiscal policy. In reality, whatever the philosophical predilections of the government, every advanced economy simultaneously conducts both fiscal and monetary policies. Each policy has strengths and weaknesses. In the chapters that follow, we return to an integrated consideration of the roles of monetary and fiscal policies both in combating the business cycle and in promoting economic growth.

[5] An example will show how interest-rate changes might knock the economy off a neutral trajectory. When the Federal Reserve contracted the money supply and raised interest rates in 1979, the intention was to push the economy onto a low-inflation path by slowing the economy. The dramatic rise of interest rates, with short-term Treasury securities rising from 7 percent in 1978 to 14 percent in 1981, led to an appreciation of the dollar, to a massive foreign-trade deficit by the mid-1980s, and to a "debt crisis" among middle-income countries. By 1990, the United States was saddled with a foreign debt of around $400 billion, which will affect its economy for the foreseeable future.

From Aggregate Demand to Aggregate Supply

We have completed our introductory analysis of the determinants of aggregate demand. To recapitulate our findings: We examined the foundations of aggregate demand and saw that *AD* is determined by external or autonomous factors, such as investment and net exports, along with government policies, such as monetary and fiscal policies. In the short run, changes in these factors lead to an increase in spending and to increases in both output and prices.

In today's volatile world, economies are exposed to shocks from both inside and outside their borders. Wars, revolutions, debt crises, oil shocks, and government miscalculations have led to periods of high inflation or high unemployment or both in times of stagflation. Because there is no automatic self-correcting mechanism to eliminate macroeconomic fluctuations, governments today have a responsibility to moderate the swings of the business cycle. But even the wisest governments cannot eliminate unemployment and inflation in the face of all the shocks to which an economy is exposed.

Our next task is to examine more carefully issues of aggregate supply. We begin with an analysis of the process of long-run economic growth, which will deepen our understanding of the determinants of potential output and aggregate supply. We then tackle the interrelated topics of inflation and unemployment and see how modern market economies are severely constrained by the need to maintain stable prices. Finally, we return to the pressing dilemmas of macroeconomic policy today: fiscal policy and the government debt, the interrelation between fiscal policy and monetary policy, the need to promote long-term economic growth, and the new issues that arise because the United States is increasingly an open economy, exposed to the winds of international trade and finance.

SUMMARY

A. Central Banking and the Federal Reserve System

1. The Federal Reserve System is a central bank, a bank for bankers. Its function is to control the amount of bank reserves, thereby determining the nation's supply of money and affecting credit conditions and interest rates.

2. The Federal Reserve System (or "Fed" as it is often called) was created in 1913 to control the nation's money and credit. It is run by the Board of

Governors and the Federal Open Market Committee (or FOMC). The Fed acts as an independent government agency and has great discretion in determining monetary policy.

3. The Fed has three major policy instruments: (a) open-market operations, (b) the discount rate on bank borrowing, and (c) legal reserve requirements on depository institutions. Using these instruments, the Fed sets intermediate targets, such as the level of bank reserves, market interest rates, and the money supply. All these operations aim to improve the economy's performance with respect to the ultimate objectives of monetary policy: achieving the best combination of low inflation, low unemployment, rapid GNP growth, a sustainable trade balance, and orderly financial markets. In addition, the Fed along with other federal agencies must backstop the domestic and international financial system in times of crisis.

4. The most important instrument of monetary policy is the Fed's open-market operations. Sales by the Fed of government securities in the open market reduce the Fed's assets and liabilities and thereby reduce the reserves of banks. The effect is to decrease banks' reserve base for deposits. People end up with less M and more government bonds. Open-market purchases do the opposite, ultimately expanding M by increasing bank reserves.

5. Outflows of international reserves can reduce reserves and M unless offset by central-market purchases of bonds. Inflows have opposite effects unless offset. The process of offsetting international flows is sterilization. In recent years, the Fed has routinely sterilized international reserve movements.

B. The Effects of Money on Output and Prices

6. If the Fed desires to slow the growth of output, the five-step sequence goes thus:
   (a) The Fed reduces bank reserves through open-market operations.
   (b) Each dollar reduction of bank reserves produces a multiple contraction of bank money and the money supply.
   (c) In the money market, a reduction in the money supply moves along an unchanged money demand schedule, raising interest rates, restricting the amount and terms of credit, and tightening money.
   (d) Tight money reduces investment and other interest-sensitive items of spending like consumer durables or net exports.
   (e) The reduction in investment and other spending reduces aggregate demand by the familiar multiplier mechanism. The lower level of aggregate demand lowers output and the price level or inflation.
   The sequence is summarized by:

$$R \text{ down} \rightarrow M \text{ down} \rightarrow i \text{ up} \rightarrow I, C, X \text{ down} \rightarrow$$
$$AD \text{ down} \rightarrow \text{real GNP down and } P \text{ down}$$

7. Although the monetary mechanism is often explained in terms of money affecting "investment," in fact the monetary mechanism is an extremely rich and complex process whereby changes in interest rates and asset prices influence a wide variety of elements of spending. These sectors include housing, affected by changing mortgage interest rates and housing prices; business investment, affected by changing interest rates and stock prices;

We begin our inquiry with a historical review of *theories of economic growth*—the factors that allow some nations to grow rapidly, some slowly, and others not at all. Our theories should help us to answer such questions as: Why have living standards risen since the Industrial Revolution? Can we discern patterns of economic growth in industrial countries? Has the period since the early 1970s witnessed a change in the patterns of economic growth?

We also want to know the sources of economic growth. Did our living standards rise because of more capital or because of technological progress? And what can a nation do to improve its economic performance?

The Magnificent Dynamics of Smith and Malthus

Even the earliest economists searched for an explanation of the evolution of output and wages. In *The Wealth of Nations* (1776), Adam Smith provided a handbook of economic development. He began with a hypothetical golden age: "that original state of things, which precedes both the appropriation of land and the accumulation of [capital] stock." This was a time when labor alone counted, when land was freely available to all, and before there was any capital to speak of.

What determines pricing and distribution in this simple and timeless dawn? Prices and outputs depend on labor alone. Every commodity trades at prices proportional to the amount of work required to produce it. If it takes twice the time to find and trap beavers than it does deer, then beavers will cost twice as much as deer. An economy in which prices are determined by the amount of labor that goes into the production of each commodity is governed by the **labor theory of value.**

In an economy such as Smith described, average labor cost would determine price no matter how many goods there were. Supply and demand are operating in this golden age, but the situation is so simple that we do not need an elaborate theory to explain it. The long-run supply curves for the different goods are simply horizontal lines at average costs, and average labor costs therefore determine prices.

Now consider the dynamics of such an economy. Population might be growing swiftly. Because land is freely available, people simply spread out onto more acres. National output exactly doubles as population doubles. The price ratio of deer to beaver remains exactly as before.

What about real wages? Wages still earn the entire national income because there is no subtraction for land rent or interest on capital. Output expands in step with population, and land is not a drag on output, so diminishing returns do not set in. The real wage per worker is therefore constant over time.

That would be the end of the story until, say, some clever hunter found a better way to catch deer or beavers. This innovation would raise the national product per capita. A balanced improvement in the productivity of labor would leave the price ratio of beaver to deer unchanged, but it would raise the real wage rate. In this world of the labor theory of value, inventions can only raise wages and speed the pace of economic growth.[1]

Scarce Land and Diminishing Returns

Eventually, as population continues to grow, all the land will be occupied, and the golden age in which only labor counts will come to an end. As we saw in Chapter 2, once the frontier of free land disappears, balanced growth of land, labor, and output is no longer possible. New laborers begin to crowd onto existing soils. Now land is scarce, and a rent is charged to ration it among different uses.

Population still grows, and so does national product. But output must grow more slowly than does population. Why? With new laborers added to fixed land, each worker now has less land to work with, and the law of diminishing returns comes

---

[1] Question 6 at the end of this chapter will apply the production-possibility frontier to Smith's beaver-deer economy.

into operation. The increasing labor-land ratio leads to a declining marginal product of labor and hence to declining real wage rates.[2] The classical economists believed that a clash of interests arises between classes. More people create a higher labor-land ratio, which produces lower wage rates and lower per capita incomes. At the same time, scarcer land produces higher rent rates per acre of land. Landlords gain at the expense of labor. This gloomy picture led Thomas Carlyle to criticize economics as "the dismal science."

Paradise Lost and Regained

How bad can things get? The dour Reverend T. R. Malthus thought that population pressures would drive the economy to a point where workers were at the minimum level of subsistence. Malthus reasoned that whenever wages were above the subsistence level, population would expand; below-subsistence wages would lead to high mortality and population decline. Only at subsistence wages could there be a stable equilibrium of population. He believed the working classes to be destined to a life that is brutish, nasty, and short.

But Malthus' forecast was wide of the mark, for

[2] The theory in this chapter relies on an important finding from microeconomics. In analysis of the determination of wages under simplified conditions, including perfect competition, it is shown that the wage rate of labor will be equal to the extra or marginal product of the last worker hired. For example, if the last worker contributes goods worth $12.50 per hour to the firm's output, then under competitive conditions the firm will be willing to pay up to $12.50 per hour in wages to that worker. Similarly, the rent on land is the marginal product of the last unit of land and the real interest rate will be determined as the marginal product of the least productive piece of capital.

he overlooked the future contribution of invention and technology. He failed to recognize that technological innovation could overcome the law of diminishing returns. He stood at the brink of a new era and failed to anticipate that the succeeding two centuries would show the greatest scientific and economic gains in history.

Economic Growth with Capital Accumulation: The Neoclassical Model

Whereas the classical economists stressed the role of scarce land in economic growth, history records how entrepreneurs and capital—not landowners and land—have called the tune since the early nineteenth century. Land did not become increasingly scarce. Instead, the Industrial Revolution brought forth power-driven machinery that increased production, factories that gathered teams of workers into giant firms, railroads and steamships that linked together the far points of the world, and iron and steel that made possible stronger machines and faster locomotives. As market economies entered the twentieth century, important new industries grew up around the telephone, the automobile, and electric power. Capital accumulation and new technologies became the dominant force affecting economic development.

To understand how capital accumulation and technological change affect the economy, we must consider the **neoclassical model of economic growth.** This approach was pioneered by Robert Solow of MIT, who was awarded the 1987 Nobel Prize for this and other contributions to economic-growth theory.* The neoclassical growth model

---

*Robert M. Solow was born in Brooklyn and educated at Harvard, and then moved to MIT in 1950. In the next few years he developed the neoclassical growth model and applied it in a number of studies using the growth-accounting framework discussed in the second half of this chapter. According to the committee that awards the Nobel Prize, "The increased interest of government to expand education and research and development was inspired by these studies. Every long-term report . . . for any country has used a Solow-type analysis."

Solow is known for his enthusiasm for economics as well as for his humor. He worries that the hunger for publicity has led some economists to exaggerate their knowledge. He criticized economists for "an apparently irresistible urge to push their science further than it will go, to answer questions more delicate than our limited understanding of a complicated question will allow. Nobody likes to say 'I don't know.'"

A lively writer, Solow worries that economics is terrifically difficult to explain to the public. At his news conference after winning the Nobel Prize, Solow quipped, "The attention span of the people you write for is shorter than the length of one true sentence." Nonetheless, Solow continues to labor for his brand of economics, and the world increasingly listens to the apostle of economic growth at MIT.

serves as the basic tool for understanding the growth process in advanced countries and has been applied to empirical studies of the sources of economic growth.

Basic Assumptions

The neoclassical growth model describes an economy in which a single homogeneous output is produced by two types of inputs, capital and labor. In contrast to the Malthusian analysis, labor growth is determined by forces outside the economy and is unaffected by economic variables. In addition, we assume that the economy is competitive and always operates at full employment, so we can analyze the growth of potential output.

The major new ingredients in the neoclassical growth model are capital and technological change. For the moment, assume that technology remains constant and focus on the role of capital in the growth process. What do we mean by capital? Capital consists of durable produced goods that are used to make other goods. Capital goods include structures like factories and houses, equipment like computers and machine tools, and inventories of finished goods and goods-in-process.

For convenience, we will assume that there is a single versatile kind of capital good (call it K). We then measure the aggregate stock of capital as the total quantity of capital goods. In our real-world calculations, we approximate the universal capital good as the total dollar value of capital goods (i.e., the constant-dollar value of equipment, structures, and inventories). Under perfect competition and without risk or inflation, the rate of return on capital is also equal to the real interest rate on bonds and other financial assets.

Turning now to the economic-growth process, economists stress the need for **capital deepening,** which is the process by which the quantity of capital per worker increases over time. Examples of capital deepening include the multiplication of farm machinery and irrigation systems in farming, of railroads and highways in transportation, and of computers and communication systems in banking. In each of these industries, societies have invested heavily in capital goods, increasing the amount of capital per worker. As a result, the output per worker has grown enormously in farming, transportation, and banking.

What happens to the return on capital in the process of capital deepening? For a given state of technology, a rapid rate of investment in plant and equipment tends to depress the return on capital (the real interest rate). This occurs because the most worthwhile investment projects get constructed first, after which the investments become less and less valuable. Once a full railroad network or telephone system has been constructed, new investments will branch into more sparsely populated regions or duplicate existing lines. The rates of return on these late investments will be lower than the high returns on the first lines between densely populated regions.

In addition, the wage rate paid to workers will tend to rise as capital deepening takes place. Why? Each worker has more capital to work with and his or her marginal product therefore rises. As a result, the competitive wage rate rises along with the marginal product of labor. We will see the wage rate rise for farm laborers, transport workers, or bank tellers as increases in capital per worker raise marginal products in those sectors.

We can summarize the impact of capital deepening in the neoclassical growth model as follows:

Capital deepening occurs when the stock of capital grows more rapidly than the labor force. In the absence of technological change, capital deepening will produce a growth of output per worker, of the marginal product of labor, and of wages; it also will lead to diminishing returns on capital and a consequent decline in the real interest rate.

Geometrical Analysis of the Neoclassical Model

We can analyze the effects of capital accumulation using Figure 12-2. The left-hand panel shows the relationship between the capital-per-worker ratio on the horizontal axis and the rate of return on capital, or the real interest rate, on the vertical axis. This *DD* curve is downward-sloping to reflect the fact that, for given inputs of labor, capital accumulation forces the marginal product of capital to decline. This diminishing marginal productivity of capital is just the principle of diminishing returns applied to capital rather than to labor.

Figure 12-2(*b*) displays a new graph, called the *factor-price frontier.* This frontier shows the relationship between the competitively determined

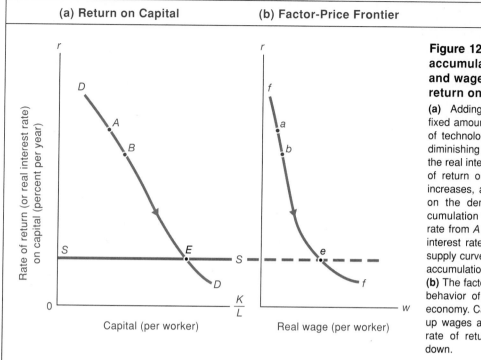

(a) Return on Capital   **(b) Factor-Price Frontier**

Figure 12-2. Capital accumulation raises output and wages, but depresses the return on capital

(a) Adding more capital goods to a fixed amount of labor (in the absence of technological change) will lead to diminishing returns on capital. Thus the real interest rate (which is the rate of return on capital) falls as capital increases, as is shown by the arrow on the demand curve. Capital accumulation drives the real interest rate from A to B to E. Eventually, the interest rate reaches a point (on the supply curve) where no further capital accumulation takes place.

(b) The factor-price frontier shows the behavior of wages in a competitive economy. Capital accumulation drives up wages at the same time that the rate of return on capital is beaten down.

wage rate and the competitive real interest rate. As capital deepens, the economy moves down and to the right on the factor-price frontier; that is, the real interest rate falls as the wage rate rises. Conversely, if a great war were to destroy much of a nation's capital, the capital-labor ratio would fall, the real interest rate would rise, and the wage rate would fall—this would represent a movement up and to the left along the factor-price frontier.

Let's use Figure 12-2 to analyze the process of economic growth with capital accumulation. Assume we have a low-income country, poorly endowed with capital per worker, shown at point A.

In the absence of technological change, capital accumulation takes us down the blue DD curve from A to B. Indeed, at some point the real interest rate might decline so far that people would feel it no longer pays them to save anything for enhanced future consumption. The SS line in Figure 12-2 shows the level of interest rates at which the economy's net saving is zero. At point E, the diminished desire for saving snuffs out further capital accumulation.

The process of capital accumulation is also shown by the factor-price frontier *ff* in Figure 12-2(b). In that graph, economic growth begins at an

initial low-wage, high-interest equilibrium at point a. Then capital deepening moves the economy to point b with a higher wage rate and a lower real interest rate. Finally, the economy comes into equilibrium at point e with a still higher capital-output and capital-labor ratio.

Note that our earlier verbal summary of the impact of capital deepening is verified by the analysis in Figure 12-2.

Long-Run Steady State. What is the long-run equilibrium in the neoclassical growth model without technological change? We see a *steady state* in which capital deepening has ceased, real wages are no longer growing, and real interest rates are constant. The steady state might arrive with high wages and per capita income if a great deal of capital has been accumulated. Although there is no longer constant improvement in incomes and output, the picture of stagnation is nevertheless more optimistic than the dismal view held by Malthus.

Technological Change and Continued Growth

A glance at economic history will reveal that the pessimistic view of stagnant wages and profits was not in history's script. Rather, a never-ending stream of inventions and technological change led to a vast improvement in the production possibilities of Europe, North America, and Japan. **Technological change** denotes changes in the processes of production or introduction of new products such that more or improved output can be obtained from the same bundle of inputs. Process inventions that have greatly increased productivity were the steam engine, the Bessemer process for producing steel, the internal-combustion engine, and the wide-body jet. Fundamental technological changes include product inventions such as the telephone, the radio, the airplane, the phonograph, and television. The most dramatic technological developments of the modern era occur in electronics and computers, where today's tiny notebook computers can outperform the fastest computer of the 1960s. These inventions provide the most spectacular examples of technological change, but technological change is in fact a continuous process of small and large improvements, as witnessed by the fact that the United States has issued over 3 million patents and there are further millions of small refinements that are part of the routine progress of an economy.

For the most part, technology advances in a quiet, unnoticed fashion as small improvements increase the quality of products or the quantity of output. Occasionally, however, changes in technology create headlines and produce unforgettable visual images. During the war in the Persian Gulf in 1991, the world was stunned by the tremendous advantage that high-technology weapons—Stealth aircraft, "smart" bombs, antimissile missiles—gave to the United States and its allies against an opponent armed with a technology that was but a few years behind. Civilian technological advances are less dramatic but no less impressive in contributing to the increase in living standards of market economies.

How can we represent technological change in our neoclassical growth model? Technological change means that more output can be produced with the same inputs of capital and labor. Technological change shifts out the *PPF*.

In terms of our growth diagram, technological change shifts outward and upward the marginal product curve on the left of Figure 12-2, and it shifts out the factor-price frontier on the right side of Figure 12-2.

Figure 12-3 presents an important interpretation of economic growth. These graphs show that, instead of moving an economy to a steady state with

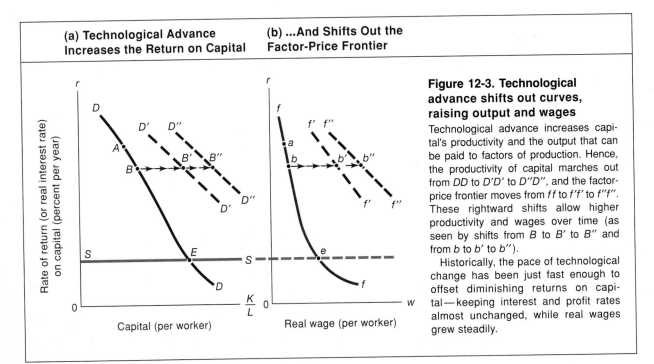

(a) Technological Advance Increases the Return on Capital

(b) ...And Shifts Out the Factor-Price Frontier

Figure 12-3. Technological advance shifts out curves, raising output and wages

Technological advance increases capital's productivity and the output that can be paid to factors of production. Hence, the productivity of capital marches out from *DD* to *D'D'* to *D"D"*, and the factor-price frontier moves from *ff* to *f'f'* to *f"f"*. These rightward shifts allow higher productivity and wages over time (as seen by shifts from *B* to *B'* to *B"* and from *b* to *b'* to *b"*).

Historically, the pace of technological change has been just fast enough to offset diminishing returns on capital—keeping interest and profit rates almost unchanged, while real wages grew steadily.

constant output, wage rates, and interest rates, inventions increase the amount of output that each unit of input can produce. As a result of technological progress, capital per worker, output per worker, and wages per worker grow over time, yet the real interest rate need not fall. Invention increases the productivity of capital and repeals the law of the falling rate of profit. In the race between diminishing returns and advancing technology, technology has won by several lengths.

Bias of Invention. Not all inventions are even-handed. Some inventions favor capital, others

labor. For example, machines and tractors reduce the need for labor and increase the demand for capital. These are thus called "labor-saving inventions," and they increase profits relative to wages. An invention that reduces the capital requirement more than the labor requirement (such as the introduction of multiple-shift workdays) is "capital-saving" and raises wages relative to profits. Between the two are "neutral inventions," which have no major effect on the relative demands of or returns to different factors. Since the Industrial Revolution, inventions appear to have been labor-saving on balance.[3]

B. The Trends and Sources of Economic Growth

We have now completed our survey of the primary theoretical approaches to economic growth. In advanced market economies, economic growth is largely determined by the growth of inputs (particularly labor and capital) and by technological change. But what are the relative contributions of labor, capital, and technology? To answer this question, we turn to an analysis of the quantitative aspects of growth and of the useful approach known as growth accounting.

The Facts of Economic Growth

Thanks to the painstaking gathering of data and construction and analysis of national accounts by Simon Kuznets, Edward Denison, Dale Jorgenson, and many others, we can discern several patterns of economic development in the United States and other advanced nations. Figure 12-4 depicts the key trends of economic development for the United States in this century. Similar patterns have been found in most of the major industrial countries.

Figure 12-4(*a*) shows the trends in real GNP, the capital stock, and population. Population and employment have more than tripled since 1900. At the same time, the stock of physical capital has risen almost tenfold. Thus the amount of capital per worker (the *K/L* ratio) has increased by a factor of almost 3. Clearly, a great deal of capital deepening

has occurred.

What about the growth in output? Has output grown less rapidly than capital, as would occur in a model that ignored technological change? No. The fact that the output curve in Figure 12-4(*a*) is not in between the two factor curves, but actually lies above the capital curve, demonstrates that technological progress must have increased the productivity of capital and labor.

Indeed, the capital-output ratio—shown in Figure 12-4(*b*)—has fallen over time, rather than rising as would be expected in the capital-accumulation model without technological progress.

The average person judges an economy by the wage rate earned for working, shown in Figure 12-4(*c*) in terms of real wages (or wages corrected for inflation). Wages have shown an impressive growth

---

[3] The impact of invention on human society has concerned economists since the Industrial Revolution. The tools of this chapter will allow us to analyze patterns of invention and growth in a competitive economy. A vital example for humanity is the following: Some people today argue that robots and computers will make humans economically obsolete. In their view, human labor will follow the horse's role in history—from being a central economic factor to being a mere luxury.

To analyze this view, recall that robots are a different kind of capital good. The robotization of the economy suggests, then, that inventions will be highly labor-saving, and that as a result the real interest rate will rise drastically and wages will decline drastically. Hence the key variable to watch in the robotization of America is movements in the rate of return on capital.

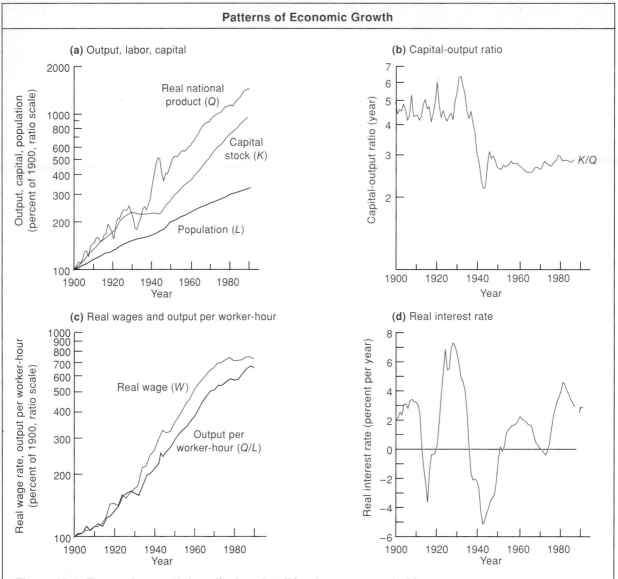

Figure 12-4. Economic growth has displayed striking long-run regularities

(a) Capital stock has grown faster than population and labor supply. Nonetheless, total output has grown even more rapidly than capital.

(b) Capital-output ratio declined sharply during the first half of the twentieth century, but has remained steady over the last four decades.

(c) Real wages have grown steadily and somewhat faster than average product per worker-hour. Note the slowdown of growth in output, real wages, and productivity since 1973. Does the productivity slowdown augur the end of the Industrial Revolution?

(d) Real interest rate has been trendless over this century, suggesting that technological change has offset diminishing returns to capital accumulation. (Source: U.S. Departments of Commerce and Labor, Federal Reserve Board, Bureau of the Census, and historical studies by John Kendrick.)

for most of this century, as we would expect from the growth in the capital-labor ratio and from steady technological advance.

The real interest rate (i.e., the money interest rate minus the rate of inflation) is shown in Figure 12-4(d). Interest rates and profit rates fluctuate greatly in business cycles and wars but display no strong trend upward or downward for the whole period.

Either by coincidence, or because of an economic mechanism inducing this pattern, technological change has just about offset diminishing returns.

Output per worker-hour is the solid black curve in Figure 12-4(c). As could be expected from the deepening of capital and from technological advance, Q/L has risen steadily.

The fact that wages rise at the same rate as output per worker does not mean that labor has captured all the fruits of productivity advance. Rather, it means that labor has kept about the same share of total product, with capital also earning about the same relative share throughout the period. Actually, a close look at Figure 12-4(c) shows that real wages have grown slightly faster than has output per worker-hour over the last nine decades. This trend implies a slow upward creep in the share of labor in GNP, with capital's share declining gently.

Seven Basic Trends of Economic Development

The economic history of the advanced nations can be summarized approximately by the following trends:

Trend 1. Population and the labor force have grown, but at a much more modest rate than the capital stock, resulting in capital deepening.

Trend 2. There has been a strong upward trend in real wage rates.

Trend 3. The share of wages and salaries in national income has edged up very slightly over the long run.

Trend 4. There have been major oscillations in real interest rates and the rate of profit, particularly during business cycles, but there has been no strong upward or downward trend in this century.

Trend 5. Instead of steadily rising, which would be predicted by the law of diminishing returns, the capital-output ratio has actually declined since 1900. However, it has changed little since 1950.

Trend 6. For most of the twentieth century, the ratios of national saving and of investment to GNP have been stable. Since 1980, however, the large federal budget deficit has led to a sharp decline of the national savings rate.

Trend 7. After effects of the business cycle are removed, national product has grown at an average

rate of close to 3 percent per year. Output growth has been much higher than a weighted average of the growth of capital, labor, and resource inputs, suggesting that technological innovation must have played a key role in economic growth.

We must issue one warning about the trends of economic growth. The persistence of these trends might suggest that they have taken on a certain inevitability—that we can forever expect our economy to generate rapid growth in output per worker, real wages, and real output.

But this view of constant growth should be resisted, for it misreads the lessons of history and economic theory. While trends have been persistent, a closer examination shows major waves or deviations during periods of a decade or more. Moreover, there is no theoretical reason why technological innovation should remain high, forever raising living standards. Eventually, diminishing returns may become more significant, or perhaps the need to combat pollution or global environmental threats may overwhelm technological change. The period since 1973—with a marked slowdown in growth of output, real wages, and output per worker—is a reminder that there is no economic or technological reason why the future must continue the robust growth experience of the prior century.

The Economic Growth of the Mixed Economy

While the seven trends of economic history are not like the immutable laws of chemistry, they do portray fundamental facts about economic growth. How do they fit into our economic-growth theories?

Trends 2 and 1—higher wage rates when capital deepens—fit nicely together with classical and neoclassical theories of production and distribution. Trend 3—that the wage share has grown only very slowly—is an interesting coincidence that is consistent with a wide variety of production functions relating Q to L and K.

Trends 4 and 5, however, warn us that neoclassical theory cannot hold in static form. A steady profit rate and a declining, or steady, capital-output ratio cannot hold if the K/L ratio rises in a world with unchanging technology; taken together, they contradict the basic law of diminishing returns under deepening of capital. We must therefore recognize the key role of technological progress in explaining the seven trends of modern economic growth. Indeed, given the ample evidence of the contribution of science, technology, and engineering to the economy, it would be difficult to ignore advancing technology.

The trends confirm the hypothesis of technological progress shown in Figure 12-3. That figure shows an economic evolution consistent with trends 1 through 7. The tendency toward diminishing returns has been offset by technological change, with the real interest rate changing little and the wage rate rising somewhat more rapidly than output per head.

The Sources of Economic Growth

Economists have not rested contentedly with trends and theories. Under the leadership of Robert Solow, John Kendrick, and Edward Denison, economic archaeologists have begun to ferret out the sources of economic growth. Looking at theories alongside the trends shown in Figure 12-4, we now have a much better understanding of why nations grow.

The Growth-Accounting Approach[4]

Detailed studies of economic growth rely on what is called **growth accounting.** This technique is not a balance sheet or national product account of the kind we met in earlier chapters. Rather, it is a way of exhaustively accounting for the ingredients that lead to observed growth trends.

In our simple model shown in Figure 12-3, growth in output (Q) can be decomposed into three separate sources: growth in labor (L), growth in capital (K), and technological innovation itself. Momentarily ignoring technological change, an assumption of constant returns to scale means that a 1 percent growth in L together with a 1 percent growth in K will lead to a 1 percent growth in output.

But suppose L grows at 1 percent and K at 5 percent. It is tempting, but wrong, to guess that Q will then grow at 3 percent, the simple average of 1 and

5. Why wrong? Because the two factors do not necessarily contribute equally to output. Rather, the fact that three-fourths of national income goes to labor while only one-fourth goes to capital suggests that labor growth will contribute more to output than will capital growth.

If labor's growth rate gets 3 times the weight of K's, then we can calculate the answer as follows: Q will grow at 2 percent per year ($= \frac{3}{4}$ of 1% $+ \frac{1}{4}$ of 5%). To growth of inputs, we also add technological change and thereby obtain all the sources of growth.

Hence, output growth per year follows the *fundamental equation of growth accounting:*

% Q growth
$$= \tfrac{3}{4}(\% \ L \text{ growth}) + \tfrac{1}{4}(\% \ K \text{ growth}) + \text{T. C.} \quad (1)$$

where T. C. represents technological change (or total factor productivity) that raises productivity, and where $\frac{3}{4}$ and $\frac{1}{4}$ are the relative contributions of each input to economic growth, given by their relative shares of national income (of course, these fractions would be replaced by new fractions if the relative shares of the factors were to change).

To explain per capita growth, we can eliminate L as a separate growth source. Now, using the fact that capital gets one-fourth share of output, we have from equation (1):

$$\% \ \frac{Q}{L} \text{ growth} = \% \ Q \text{ growth} - \% \ L \text{ growth}$$

$$= \tfrac{1}{4}(\% \ \frac{K}{L} \text{ growth}) + \text{T. C.} \quad (2)$$

This relation shows clearly how capital deepening would affect per capita output if technological advance were zero. Output per worker would grow only one-fourth as fast as capital per worker, reflecting diminishing returns.

One final point remains: We can measure Q growth, K growth, L growth, as well as the shares of K and L. But how can we measure T. C. (technological change)? We cannot. Rather, we must *infer* T. C. as the residual or leftover after the other components of output and inputs are calculated. Thus if we examine the equation above, T. C. is calculated by subtraction from equation (1) as:

$$\begin{aligned} \text{T. C.} = \ & \% \ Q \text{ growth} \\ & - \tfrac{3}{4}(\% \ L \text{ growth}) - \tfrac{1}{4}(\% \ K \text{ growth}) \quad (3) \end{aligned}$$

[4] This discussion covers advanced materials, so short courses may skip right to the next topic, "Detailed Studies."

This equation allows us to answer critically important questions about economic growth. What part of per capita output growth is due to capital deepening and what part is due to technological advance? Does society progress chiefly by dint of thrift and the forgoing of current consumption? Or is our rising living standard the reward for the ingenuity of inventors and the daring of innovator-entrepreneurs?

Numerical Example. To determine the contributions of labor, capital, and other factors in output growth, we substitute representative numbers for the period 1900–1991 into equation (2) for the growth of Q/L above. Since 1900, L has grown 1.3 percent per year, and K has grown 2.5 percent per year, while Q has grown 3.1 percent per year. Thus, by arithmetic, we find that

$$\% \, \frac{Q}{L} \text{ growth} = \tfrac{1}{4}(\% \, \frac{K}{L} \text{ growth}) + \text{T. C.}$$

becomes

$$1.8 = \tfrac{1}{4}(1.2) + \text{T. C.} = 0.3 + 1.5$$

Thus of the 1.8 percent-per-year increase in output per worker, about 0.3 percentage point is due to capital deepening, while an astounding 1.5 percent per year stems from T. C.

Detailed Studies

More thorough studies refine the simple calculation but show quite similar conclusions. Table 12-1 presents the results of studies by Edward Denison and the Department of Labor analyzing the sources of growth over the 1948–1989 period. Over this period, output (measured as gross output of the private business sector) grew at an average rate of 3.3 percent per year. Input growth (of capital, labor, and land) contributed 1.9 percentage points per year, while **total factor productivity**—the growth of output less the growth of the weighted sum of all inputs—averaged 1.4 percent annually.

Somewhat more than one-half of the growth in output in the United States can be accounted for by the growth in labor and capital. The remaining growth is a residual factor that can be attributed to education, innovation, economies of scale, scientific advances, and other factors.

Growth accounting yields many dividends in

Contribution of Different Elements to Growth in Real GNP, United States, 1948–1989		
	In percent per year	As percent of total
Real GNP growth	3.3	100
Contribution of inputs	1.9	58
Capital	1.2	37
Labor	0.7	21
Land	0.0	0
Total factor productivity growth	1.4	42
Education	0.4	12
Advances in knowledge and other	1.0	30

Table 12-1. Education and advances in knowledge outweigh capital in contributing to economic growth

Studies using the techniques of growth accounting break down the growth of GNP in the private business sector into its contributing factors. These studies find that capital growth accounts for 37 percent of output growth. Education, technological change, and other sources make up 42 percent of total GNP growth and more than half of the growth of output per worker. [Source: Edward F. Denison, *Trends in American Economic Growth, 1929–1982* (Brookings, Washington, D.C., 1985); U.S. Department of Labor, "Multifactor Productivity Measures, 1988 and 1989," March 1991.]

understanding economic growth. For example, many people have wondered about the sources of growth in countries like Japan and the Soviet Union during much of this century.

Using growth accounting, scholars have uncovered some surprising answers to this puzzle. Over much of the period since World War II, Japan's GNP grew at an amazing 10 percent per year. Empirical analysis indicates that this was partly due to very rapid growth in inputs. In addition, Japan had extremely rapid technological change over this period compared to other industrial countries.

Analyses of Soviet growth show a different pattern. According to most studies, the Soviet Union grew rapidly during the period from 1930 until the mid-1960s. It appears, however, that the high growth rate came primarily from forced-draft increases in capital and labor inputs. The estimated pace of growth in total factor productivity for the Soviet Union over the last half-century has been slower than that for the United States. In the period of perestroika over the last decade, studies indicate there has been a *decline* in total factor productivity in the Soviet Union.

The Productivity Slowdown

We noted earlier that the rapid growth of output and productivity in the United States slowed abruptly around 1973. This break in the trend, which is called the **productivity slowdown,** is seen in Figure 12-4(*c*), in which labor productivity (*Q/L*) begins to flatten out in the early 1970s. What caused the abrupt slowdown in productivity growth?

The basic facts are shown in Table 12-2, which provides data on the growth of productivity in the U.S. economy both for the entire business sector and for different subsectors. This table shows **labor productivity,** which measures total output produced in a sector divided by the number of person-hours worked in that sector. As you can see, labor productivity slowed in all sectors in the 1970s with nonmanufacturing showing the sharpest decline. Among the areas showing the biggest deterioration in productivity were mining, construction, and services. Similar patterns, with a slowdown of productivity growth in the aggregate and in most sectors after 1973, characterize all major industrial countries.

The decline in productivity growth remains a mystery to economists. Most studies point to a number of unfavorable factors converging on the American economy at about the same time, including the following:

- In the late 1960s and early 1970s, environmental regulations required firms to spend money on plant and operations to improve health and safety, yet these improvements did not show up as measured output increases. One of the most dramatic cases was in underground mining, in which productivity declined sharply.
- The increase in energy prices in the early 1970s led firms to substitute other inputs (labor and capital) for energy. As a result, the productivity of labor and capital declined relative to earlier growth rates.
- The 1970s witnessed an infusion of inexperienced, low-wage workers into many nonmanufacturing sectors, particularly into service industries like fast-food outlets. This rapid growth increased the share of employment in the low-productivity sectors and thereby lowered overall productivity growth.

Other factors mentioned in studies of the productivity slowdown were a lower level of expenditure on civilian research and development, declining investment in plant and equipment, and higher inflation. All told, however, these factors explain only a fraction of the slowdown.

Speeding Economic Growth

In response to the lagging productivity growth, many people have called for policies to restore the earlier pace of productivity improvement. What steps can be taken to speed growth? A study by Edward Denison investigated this subject in detail, and the results appear in Table 12-3.

Labor Productivity Growth by Business Sector, 1948–1989 (Average Annual Percent Change)			Nonfarm	
Period	Total business	Farm	Manufacturing	Nonmanufacturing
1948–1973	3.0	6.5	2.9	1.9
1973–1979	0.8	4.6	1.4	−0.1
1979–1989	1.3	3.3	3.6	0.4

Table 12-2. Labor productivity growth by sector

Labor productivity in the total business sector slowed sharply after 1973 with the most dramatic decline occurring in non-manufacturing areas like services. Manufacturing productivity growth regained ground in the 1980s. (Source: Council of Economic Advisers, *Economic Report of the President*, 1987; U.S. Department of Agriculture; U.S. Department of Labor, Bureau of Labor Statistics.)

A Menu for Growth	
Growth-encouraging steps	Estimated potential for increasing real economic growth, 1990–2000 (% per year)
1. Increase net national investment and savings rate by one-third (i.e., from 6 to 8% of GNP)	0.16
2. Increase civilian research and development by one-fifth (i.e., from 2 to 2.4% of GNP)	0.18
3. Lower the average rate of unemployment by 1% of the labor force	0.20
4. Eliminate all strikes	0.01
5. Reach an arms-control agreement that allows government to reduce strategic programs and increase government investment	0.10
Total	0.65

Table 12-3. How can the United States grow faster?
This menu of growth shows the kinds of steps that might be taken to speed the growth of potential output and labor productivity. Economists have concluded that a major increase in the growth of potential output is difficult to accomplish.

[Source: Edward Denison, *Sources of Growth in the United States* (Committee for Economic Development, New York, 1961); updated with further calculations by authors.]

These figures show that raising the growth rate of potential output or of productivity per worker is possible but difficult. The most obvious way to grow more rapidly is to increase the national savings-and-investment rate. As our discussion of fiscal and monetary policies in later chapters will show, an increase in the national savings rate could be accomplished by changing the mix of fiscal and monetary policy; for example, reducing the budget deficit and easing money would tend to increase national savings. An ambitious program might succeed in raising national net investment by 2 percent of GNP. This would lead to an increase of slightly less than two-tenths of a percentage point in the annual growth rate of potential GNP and of labor productivity over the following decade.

One cannot help but be impressed by the small magnitude of the numbers shown in Table 12-3. Increasing productivity growth is not impossible, but no easy paths have yet been found.

C. Supply-Side Economics[5]

One approach to stimulating economic growth enjoyed a meteoric rise in popularity during the 1980s. This approach, known as *supply-side economics*, motivated the fiscal policies of the Reagan administration (1981–1989). Looking back at that period, we can use our macroeconomic analysis to appraise the contribution of supply-side prescriptions for reviving the U.S. economy.

During most of the period from World War II until 1980, economic policy focused on the need to counter the evils of inflation and unemployment. Whenever unemployment rose, liberals would call for tax cuts or expenditure increases; whenever inflation threatened, conservatives would prescribe the unpleasant medicine of tight monetary or fiscal policies.

Toward the end of the 1970s, critics of the con-

[5] An excellent set of readings on the political and social debate over supply-side economics is contained in Thomas R. Swartz, Frank J. Bonello, and Andrew F. Kozak, *The Supply Side: Debating Economic Issues* (Dushkin, Guilford, Conn., 1983).

ventional approach to macroeconomics argued that economic policy had become too oriented toward the management of aggregate demand. They claimed that excessive concerns with short-run actions tended to threaten the long-run vitality of the economy. Some critics, including orthodox conservative economists, pressed for a return to more traditional policies of balancing the budget and squeezing inflation out of the economy.

At the same time, a new phalanx of theorists joined the debate. Their school of **supply-side economics** emphasized incentives for people to work and to save, downplayed the role of demand management, and proposed large tax cuts to reverse slow economic growth and slumping productivity growth. Among the proponents of this approach were economists Arthur Laffer, Paul Craig Roberts, and Norman Ture. Supply-side economics was espoused forcefully by President Reagan in the United States and by Margaret Thatcher, prime minister of Great Britain from 1979 to 1990.

Although these economists and political leaders have embraced a wide variety of positions, three central features of supply-side economics emerge: retreat from Keynesian demand-management policies, emphasis on incentives and supply effects, and advocacy of large tax cuts.

Retreat from Keynes.
Keynesian economics holds that, in the short run, national output and employment are primarily determined by aggregate demand. Further, the Keynesians believe that monetary and fiscal policies should be used to combat unemployment or inflation.

Toward the end of the 1970s, disenchantment with the Keynesian approach became widespread within the economics profession. An influential article by Harvard's Martin Feldstein laid out the case against demand-oriented policies.[6] Feldstein argued for greater emphasis on factors that would increase the growth in potential output—factors such as increased saving and investment, regulatory reform, and reduced taxation of capital income. In his view, macroeconomic policies should focus primarily on increasing long-run economic growth rather than on short-run economic stabilization.

What was the basis of this *volte face* in economic philosophy? Although the theory was not clearly presented, it appears to be grounded in a classical view of the economy and asserts that output responds more to incentives, taxes, and post-tax factor returns than to changes in aggregate demand. In terms of the *AS-AD* framework, supply siders believe that the *AS* curve is near-vertical, so that adverse shocks to aggregate demand would have small and short-lived impacts on output and most of the effect of tight money would be on the price level.

A New Emphasis on Incentives.
A second theme of supply-side economics was the key role played by *incentives*, which denote adequate returns to working, saving, and entrepreneurship. Supply siders emphasized the loss of incentives that occurs when tax rates are excessively high and argued that Keynesians, in their excessive concern with demand management, had ignored the impact of tax rates and incentives on aggregate supply. A paraphrase of the argument by a spokesman is as follows:

> Supply-side economics emphasizes the role of fiscal policy in the determination of economic growth and aggregate supply. Our analysis relies upon straight classical price theory. According to supply-side economics, tax changes affect the economy through their effect on post-tax factor rewards rather than on dollar flows of incomes and spending; tax rates affect the relative prices of goods and thereby affect supplies of labor and capital. We seek to raise the after-tax rewards to growth activities such as labor, saving, and investment relative to leisure and consumption.
>
> It is far more important to analyze the impact of a tax change on the rate of return to labor or saving or investment than to look at the dollar amount of the tax change on disposable income. By lowering tax rates on labor or interest or dividends, we can increase saving, investment, and economic growth.[7]

[7] This excerpt is a paraphrase of Stephen J. Entin, "Comments on the Critics" in a symposium, "Supply Side Economics: What Remains?" American Economic Association Annual Meeting, December 1985, *Treasury News*.

A favorable account is contained in Paul Craig Roberts, *The Supply-Side Revolution: An Insider's Account of Policymaking in Washington* (Harvard University Press, Cambridge, Mass., 1984). For a critical analysis, see the papers by Martin Feldstein, Lawrence Chimerene and Richard Young, and George von Furstenberg and F. Jeffrey Green in *American Economic Review* (May 1986).

[6] See Martin Feldstein, "The Retreat from Keynesian Economics," *The Public Interest* (Summer 1981), pp. 92–105.

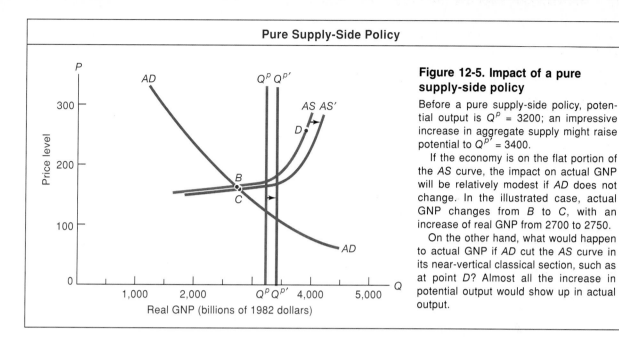

Pure Supply-Side Policy

Figure 12-5. Impact of a pure supply-side policy

Before a pure supply-side policy, potential output is $Q^P = 3200$; an impressive increase in aggregate supply might raise potential to $Q^{P'} = 3400$.

If the economy is on the flat portion of the AS curve, the impact on actual GNP will be relatively modest if AD does not change. In the illustrated case, actual GNP changes from B to C, with an increase of real GNP from 2700 to 2750.

On the other hand, what would happen to actual GNP if AD cut the AS curve in its near-vertical classical section, such as at point D? Almost all the increase in potential output would show up in actual output.

What is the hypothesized relationship between tax policy and overall economic activity? In the context of aggregate supply-and-demand analysis, lowering tax rates would raise the post-tax return to capital and labor; higher post-tax returns would induce greater labor and capital supply, along with higher rates of innovation and productivity growth; and the increase of inputs and innovation would increase the growth of potential output and thereby shift aggregate supply to the right.

Figure 12-5 illustrates the effects of a hypothetical supply-side program. Suppose that the supply-side program has the net effect of increasing the total supply of inputs like labor and capital. This increase of inputs increases potential output and shifts the AS curve outward as shown in the figure.

What is the impact of this supply-side measure? The answer depends upon the shape of the aggregate supply curve. If the economy is Keynesian, or in a recession, with a relatively flat AS curve as shown at point B in Figure 12-5, the impact of the supply shift on actual output will be relatively modest. In the hypothetical case, the equilibrium moves from point B to point C, with a small increase of output and a tiny decrease in the overall price level.

On the other hand, let's consider a classical economy, such as the one shown at point D on the AS curve in Figure 12-5. In this case, the increase in potential output from Q^P to $Q^{P'}$ would translate into a substantial increase in actual output, with each 1 percent increase in potential output producing almost 1 percent increase in actual output. We therefore conclude that supply-side policies are likely to be most effective when the economy behaves in a near-classical fashion.

How large an impact are supply-side policies likely to have in reality? At the beginning of the Reagan administration, supply-side enthusiasts predicted that the program would lead to rapid economic recovery, with an anticipated growth in real GNP of 4.8 percent per year over the next 4 years. In fact, the actual growth rate fell far short of the forecast, averaging only 2.5 percent per year. Given the difficulty of increasing the growth of potential output shown in the last section (see Table 12-3), we should not be surprised to learn that the supply-side policies had little impact on potential-output growth in the 1980s. The wheels of supply-side policies grind exceedingly slowly.

Tax Cuts. The final strand of supply-side thinking emerged in its advocacy of large tax cuts. We saw in our analysis of the multiplier model how taxes could affect aggregate demand and output. Supply-side economists believe that the role of taxes in affecting aggregate demand has been overemphasized. They argue that government in the 1960s and 1970s used taxes to raise revenues or stimulate demand while ignoring the impacts of the rising tax burden on incentives. The high taxes, in their view, lead people to reduce their labor and capital supply. Indeed, some supply-side economists, particularly Arthur Laffer, suggested that high tax rates might actually lower tax revenues. This "Laffer-curve" proposition held that high tax rates shrink the tax base because of a lower level of economic activity. Many mainstream economists and even some supply-side economists scoffed at the Laffer proposition.[8]

To counter earlier approaches to taxation, supply-side economists proposed a radical restructuring of the tax system, sometimes called the "supply-side tax cuts." The philosophy underlying supply-side tax cuts was that the reforms should improve incentives by lowering tax rates on the last dollar of income (or marginal tax rates); that the tax system should be less progressive (that is, it should lower the tax burden on high-income individuals); and that the system should be designed to encourage productivity or supply rather than to manipulate aggregate demand.

Figure 12-6 uses AS-AD analysis to illustrate the impact of a supply-side tax cut. We know from our multiplier analysis that, other things equal, tax cuts will increase consumption and increase aggregate demand. A large permanent tax cut—such as the 25 percent cut in personal taxes enacted in 1981—produces the large shift in AD as shown in Figure 12-6. In addition, such a tax cut might increase potential output if labor or capital supply increased. However, as the last section indicated, the size of the potential-output increase would be extremely modest in the short run. We therefore show the tax cut as shifting the AS curve only slightly to the right.

Just as the supply siders predict, the net effect of a massive supply-side tax cut is to increase output significantly. This change is shown by the movement from point A to point B in Figure 12-6. In the short run, the major source of the economic expansion from supply-side tax cuts is through its impact on aggregate demand rather than the effect on potential output and aggregate supply. Some

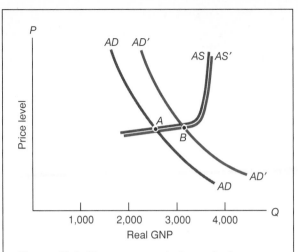

Figure 12-6. Macroeconomic impact of a supply-side tax cut

Supply-side economists recommend massive tax cuts as a measure for combating economic ailments. Tax cuts have two effects: They shift out the AD curve (from AD to AD') as shown by multiplier analysis. And they may increase potential output if lower taxes induce larger quantities of labor or capital—thus shifting out the AS curve from AS to AS'. Such tax cuts do, as supply siders suggest, increase real GNP. But statistical studies suggest that for periods up to a decade the major impact on actual output comes through the effect upon aggregate demand.

---

economists have argued that the Reagan economic expansion of the mid-1980s was indeed a demand-side recovery dressed up in a supply-side cloak.

Appraisal. The radical supply-side approach to economics gradually faded after Reagan left office. What, it can be asked, is the preliminary verdict on this experiment? While many questions remain, economists generally have found that many of the supply-side propositions were not supported by economic experience in the 1980s. Among the key findings are the following:

- The supply siders predicted that the deep cuts in tax rates would stimulate economic activity and incomes so much that tax revenues would hardly fall and might even rise. In fact, tax revenues fell sharply relative to trend after the tax cuts, leading to an increase in the federal budget deficit that has persisted into the 1990s.
- Inflation was brought down sharply in the early 1980s. But the decline was, as the Keynesians had

---

[8] Say that R = total tax revenues, t = tax rate, and B = the tax base. For capital, R would be the total taxes on capital income, t the tax rate on capital income, and B total capital income. The Laffer proposition holds that, after a point, as t rises toward 100 percent, B shrinks so rapidly that $R = tB$ actually declines.

predicted, bought at a high price in terms of unemployment during the deep recession and high unemployment in 1981–1983.

- Supply-side economists predicted that the lower tax rates, increasing incentives for saving and investing, would increase national saving. All the supply-side encouragement of saving appears to have had no net positive effect on the national savings rate. Indeed, the national savings rate fell sharply over the 1980s and reached its lowest level since World War II in 1987.

- The fundamental goal of supply-side policies was to increase the rate of growth of potential output. The average rate of growth of potential output is estimated to have fallen from 3.6 percent per year in 1960–1970 to 3.1 percent per year in 1970–1980 to 2.3 percent per year in 1980–1990. While the fall in potential growth in the 1980s cannot be entirely attributed to macroeconomic policies, the decline does suggest that there was no sea change in economic performance in the supply-side years.

SUMMARY

A. The Theory of Economic Growth

1. Aggregate supply is derived from the economy's capability to produce—that is, from its potential output. The analysis of economic growth examines the factors that lead to the growth of potential output over the long run.

2. The classical models of Smith and Malthus describe economic development in terms of fixed land and growing population.

   In the absence of technological change, increasing population ultimately exhausts the supply of free land. The resulting increase in population density triggers the law of diminishing returns. With less and less land to work, each new worker adds less and less extra product; as a result, competitive wages fall while land rents go up. The Malthusian equilibrium is attained when the wage has fallen to the subsistence level, below which population cannot sustain itself. In reality, however, technological change has kept economic development progressing in industrial countries by continually shifting the productivity curve of labor upward.

3. Growth theories incorporating capital accumulation form the core of modern analysis. This approach examines a world in which labor grows for non-economic reasons while capital is accumulated in response to profit opportunities. In the beginning, there is a gradual increase of the amount of capital per worker, or "capital deepening." In the absence of technological change and innovation, an increase in capital per worker would not be matched by a proportional increase in output per worker because of diminishing returns. Hence, capital deepening would lower the rate of return on capital (equal to the real interest rate under risk-free competition).

4. The fundamental factor-price frontier depicts how wages must rise when the return on capital or the real interest rate falls. In a world with capital deepening, the downward trend in the real interest rate leads to a rise in real wages along the factor-price frontier.

5. Technological change, by increasing the output produced for a given bundle of inputs, pushes outward and rightward both the capital-productivity curve and the factor-price frontier, allowing output to rise even more rapidly than capital and labor inputs.

B. The Trends and Sources of Economic Growth

6. Numerous trends of economic growth are seen in data for this century. Among the key findings are that real wages and output per hour have risen steadily, although there has been some slowdown since the 1970s; the real interest rate has shown no major trend; and the capital-output ratio has declined.

7. The major trends are consistent with the simple model of capital accumulation augmented by technological advance. Thus economic theory confirms what common sense tells us—that technological advance increases the productivity of inputs and shifts out both the productivity-of-capital curve and factor-price frontiers.

8. The last trend—relatively stable growth in potential output over the last nine decades—raises the important question of the sources of economic growth. Applying quantitative techniques, economists have used growth accounting to determine that "residual" sources—such as innovation and education—outweigh capital deepening in their impact on GNP growth or labor productivity. This technique also shows the great effort required to add even a few tenths of a percentage point to the underlying potential GNP growth rate.

C. Supply-Side Economics

9. Until the 1980s, most economists focused on Keynesian remedies for stabilizing the economy; this approach emphasized changing monetary and fiscal policy to stabilize the economy. In the 1980s, supply-side economists proposed a new approach to macroeconomic policy-making: (*a*) a non-Keynesian approach to fiscal policy, focusing on the medium run, avoiding fine-tuning of the economy, and downplaying the importance of changes in aggregate demand; (*b*) a new emphasis on economic incentives—with particular attention to the impact of tax policy on post-tax returns to labor and capital as determining saving, investment, and labor supply; and (*c*) advocacy of large tax cuts, sometimes holding that these might actually pay for themselves by generating larger revenues.

10. The historical record of the 1980s suggests that supply-side policies were not successful in improving the performance of the U.S. economy. The legacy of this approach was stubborn federal budget deficits, slow growth in potential output, and a low national savings rate.

CONCEPTS FOR REVIEW

Economic-growth theory
Smith's golden age
Malthus' limited land
neoclassical growth model
K/L rise as capital deepens
capital-output ratio, K/Q

factor-price frontier
seven trends of economic growth
growth accounting
   % Q growth = $\frac{3}{4}$(% L growth) + $\cdots$
   % Q/L growth = $\frac{1}{4}$(% K/L
     growth) + T. C.

Supply-side economics
tenets of supply-side economics
impact of policies on economic
   performance

QUESTIONS FOR DISCUSSION

1. According to economic data, the living standards of a family in 1990 were about 7 times that of a family in 1900. What does this mean in terms of actual consumption patterns? Discuss with your parents or older relatives how your living standards today compare with those of their parents; make a comparison of the differences.

2. "If the government subsidizes science and invention and controls stagflation and cycles, we will see economic growth that would astound the classical economists." Evaluate critically.

3. "Without either population growth or technological change, persistent capital accumulation would ultimately destroy the capitalist class." Explain why such a scenario might lead to a zero interest rate and to a disappearance of profits.

4. Given that labor's share shows a slight uptrend and the capital-output ratio a slight downtrend, that the interest rate fluctuates considerably, and that the ratio of private net investment to private GNP is volatile, would you be much surprised if the basic trends on page 223 were to fluctuate sharply in the future?

5. Recall the growth-accounting equation (1) on page 224. Calculate the rate of growth of output if labor grows at 1 percent per year, capital grows at 4 percent per year, and technological change is $1\frac{1}{2}$ percent per year.

    How would your answer change if:

    (a) Labor growth slowed to 0 percent per year.

    (b) Capital growth increased to 5 percent per year.

    (c) Labor and capital had equal shares in GNP.

    Also, calculate for each of these conditions the rate of growth of output per worker.

6. Using the *PPF* discussed in Chapter 2, analyze Adam Smith's beaver-deer economy as follows.

    Assume that catching a deer takes 2 hours, while trapping a beaver requires 4 hours. For a society with 100 hours of labor, first draw the *PPF* as a straight line—going from the intercept on the vertical axis of the 50 deer producible with that much labor, to the intercept on the horizontal axis of 25 beavers. The absolute slope of this *PPF* gives the 2-to-1 price ratio prevailing at any point where both goods are being produced and consumed. (Demand curves are still needed to tell where society ends up on the *PPF*.)

    What would happen to the *PPF* if the amount of labor doubled with exactly the same technology? Also, show the effect of a doubling of labor productivity in both industries.

7. Political candidates have proposed the following policies to speed economic growth for the 1990s. For each, explain qualitatively the impact upon the growth of potential output and of per capita potential output. If possible, give a quantitative estimate of the increase in the growth of potential output and per capita potential output over the next decade:

    (a) Cut the federal budget deficit by 2 percent of GNP, increasing the ratio of investment to GNP by the same amount.

    (b) Increase the federal subsidy to research and development (R&D) by $\frac{1}{4}$ percent of GNP, assuming that this subsidy will increase private R&D by the same amount and that R&D has a social rate of return that is 3 times that of private investment.

    (c) Decrease defense spending by 1 percent of GNP, with a multiplier of 2.

    (d) Increase the labor-force participation rate of females so that total labor inputs increase by 1 percent.

    (e) Increase investments in "human capital" (or education and on-the-job training) by 1 percent of GNP.

8. A brooding pessimist might argue that 1973 marked the end of the great expansion that began with the Industrial Revolution. Assume that all the features of the earlier era were still present today *except* that technological change and innovation were to cease. What would the new seven trends look like for coming decades? What would happen to the important real wage? What steps could be taken to counteract the new trends and to put the economy back on the earlier path?

9. A supply-side economist might recommend a large tax cut to revive the economy. How might such a measure affect the *AS* curve? The *AD* curve? The resulting levels of price and real output?

10. **Advanced problem:** Many fear that robots will do to humans what tractors and cars did to horses—the horse population declined precipitously early in this century after technological change made horses obsolete. If we treat robots as a particularly productive kind of K, what would their introduction do to the *DD* and *ff* curves in Figure 12-2? Can total output go down with a fixed labor force? Under what conditions would the real wage decline? Can you see why the horse analogy might not apply?

BUSINESS CYCLES AND UNEMPLOYMENT

The fault, dear Brutus, is not in our stars—but in ourselves.
William Shakespeare, *Julius Caesar*

Business conditions never stand still. Prosperity may be followed by a panic or a crash. Economic expansion gives way to recession. GNP, employment, and real incomes fall. Inflation and profits decline, and people are thrown out of work.

Eventually the bottom is reached, and recovery begins. The recovery may be slow or fast. It may be incomplete, or it may be so strong as to lead to a new boom. Prosperity may mean a long, sustained plateau of brisk demand, plentiful jobs, and rising living standards. Or it may be marked by a quick, inflationary flaring up of prices and speculation, to be followed by another slump.

Upward and downward movements in output, prices, interest rates, and employment form the business cycle that has characterized market economies for the last two centuries—ever since an elaborate, interdependent money economy began

to replace the relatively self-sufficient precommercial society. In the first section of this chapter, we survey the history of business cycles and sort through the different interpretations put forth by macroeconomists over the years.

The second half of this chapter examines one of the most important features of business cycles: unemployment. We will see that changes in unemployment tend to mirror business-cycle fluctuations. The social costs of high unemployment, reflected in idle time and lost income, continue to haunt market economies and even threaten the newly emerging market economies of Eastern Europe and the Soviet Union.

Figure 13-1 shows the themes discussed in this chapter and indicates that it integrates many of the different elements of aggregate supply and demand.

A. Business Cycles

Features of the Business Cycle

Business cycles occur when economic activity speeds up or slows down. More precisely, we define a business cycle as follows:

A **business cycle** is a swing in total national output, income, and employment, usually lasting for a period of 2 to 10 years, marked by widespread expansion or contraction in many sectors of the economy.

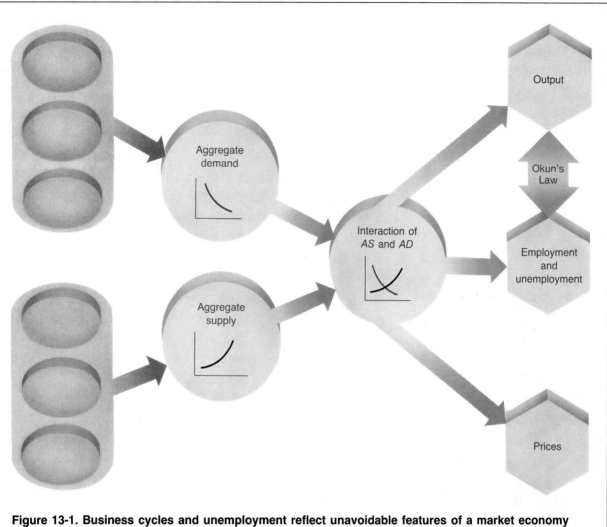

Figure 13-1. Business cycles and unemployment reflect unavoidable features of a market economy

We begin with an analysis of theories and facts of the business cycle, which combine elements of both aggregate supply and demand. Then we examine how unemployment is measured and why it fluctuates over the business cycle.

What are the common features of the business cycle? Modern analysts divide business cycles into phases. "Peaks" and "troughs" mark the turning points of the cycles, while "recession" and "expansion" are the major phases. Figure 13-2 shows the successive phases of the business cycle. The downturn of a business cycle is called a **recession,** which is defined as a period in which real GNP declines for at least 2 consecutive quarter-years. The recession begins at a peak and ends at a trough. According to the unofficial dater of business cycles, the National Bureau of Economic Research, the United States enjoyed a long expansion from late 1982 until a peak in the summer of 1990, at which time a shallow recession began.

Note that the pattern of cycles is irregular. No two business cycles are quite the same. No exact formula, such as might apply to the motions of the moon or of a pendulum, can be used to predict the duration and timing of business cycles. Rather, in their irregularities, business cycles more closely resemble the fluctuations of the weather. Figure 13-3 shows how the American economy has been battered by the business cycle throughout our re-

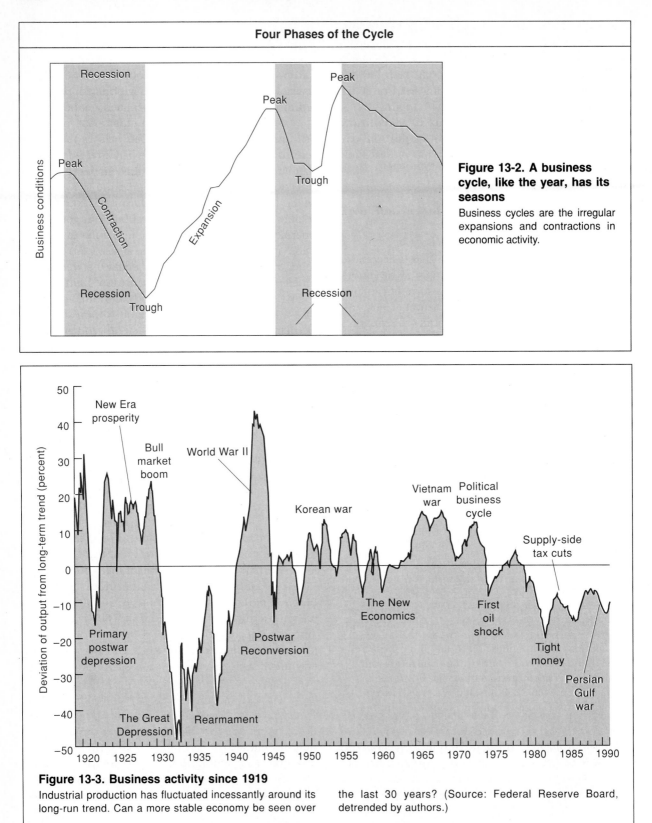

Four Phases of the Cycle

Figure 13-2. A business cycle, like the year, has its seasons

Business cycles are the irregular expansions and contractions in economic activity.

Figure 13-3. Business activity since 1919

Industrial production has fluctuated incessantly around its long-run trend. Can a more stable economy be seen over the last 30 years? (Source: Federal Reserve Board, detrended by authors.)

cent history. You can see that cycles are like mountain ranges, with different levels of heights and valleys. Some valleys are very deep and broad—as in the Great Depression; others are shallow and narrow, as was that of 1970.

While business cycles are not identical twins, they often have a familial similarity. If a reliable economic forecaster announces that a recession is about to arrive, are there any typical phenomena that you should expect to accompany the recession? The following are a few of the relationships that characterize a recession:

- Often, consumer purchases decline sharply while business inventories of automobiles and other durable goods increase unexpectedly. As businesses react by curbing production, real GNP falls. Shortly afterward, business investment in plant and equipment also falls sharply.
- The demand for labor falls—first seen in a drop in the average workweek, followed by layoffs and higher unemployment.
- As output falls, demand and supplies of crude materials decline, and the prices of many commodities tumble. Wages and manufacturing prices are less likely to decline, but they tend to rise less rapidly in economic downturns.
- Business profits fall sharply in recessions. In anticipation of this, common-stock prices usually tumble as investors sniff the scent of a business downturn. However, because the demand for credit falls, interest rates generally also fall in recessions.

We have spoken in terms of recessions. Booms are the mirror image of recessions, with each of the above factors operating in the opposite direction.

Business-Cycle Theories

Business Cycles as Shifts in Aggregate Demand

What causes business cycles? Although there is no single answer, business cycles generally occur as a result of shifts in aggregate demand. A typical cycle is illustrated in Figure 13-4, which shows how a decline in aggregate demand lowers output.

Say that the economy is originally in short-run equilibrium at point B. Then, as a result of a shift in

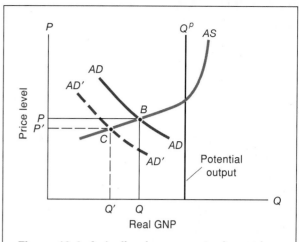

Figure 13-4. A decline in aggregate demand leads to an economic downturn

A downward shift in the *AD* curve along a relatively flat and unchanging *AS* curve leads to lower levels of output as well as lower prices or inflation. Note that as a result of the downward shift in the *AD* curve, the gap between actual and potential GNP becomes greater during a recession.

consumer, government, or business spending, there is a shift to the left in the curve of aggregate spending to AD'. If there is no change in aggregate supply, the economy will reach a new equilibrium at point C. Note that output declines from Q to Q' and that prices are lower (or in a more realistic situation, the rate of inflation falls).

The case of a boom is, naturally, just the opposite. Here, the *AD* curve shifts to the right, output approaches potential GNP or perhaps even overshoots it, and prices (and inflation) rise.

Alternative Approaches

Although the main interpretation of business cycles looks to changes in aggregate demand, we want to know more about the mechanism by which the cycle is generated. We may classify the different theories into two categories, external and primarily internal. The *external* theories find the root of the business cycle in the fluctuations of something outside the economic system—in wars, revolutions, and elections; in gold discoveries, rates of growth of population, and migrations; in discoveries of new lands and resources; in scientific breakthroughs and technological innovations; even in sunspots or the weather.

The *internal* theories look for mechanisms within the economic system itself that will give rise to self-generating business cycles. In this approach, every expansion breeds recession and contraction, and every contraction breeds revival and expansion—in a quasi-regular, repeating chain.

Here are some of the most important business-cycle theories along with their proponents:

1. *Monetary* theories attribute the business cycle to the expansion and contraction of money and credit (Hawtrey, Friedman).
2. *Innovation* theories attribute the cycle to the clustering of important inventions such as those surrounding the railroad or the automobile (Schumpeter, Hansen).
3. The *multiplier-accelerator model* proposes that external shocks are propagated by the multiplier along with an investment theory known as the accelerator, thereby generating regular, cyclical fluctuations in output (Samuelson).
4. *Political* theories of business cycles attribute fluctuations to politicians who manipulate fiscal and monetary policies in order to be reelected (Kalecki, Nordhaus, Tufte).
5. *Equilibrium-business-cycle* theories claim that misperceptions about price and wage movements lead people to supply too much or too little labor, which leads to cycles of output and employment (Lucas, Barro, Sargent).
6. *Real-business-cycle* proponents hold that productivity shocks spread through the economy and cause fluctuations (Prescott, Long, Plosser).

This list just hints at the variety of explanations of movements in output, unemployment, and prices. In looking at different business-cycle theories, however, we would want to check to see whether they correspond to the salient features described above. One important pattern, noted above, is that purchases of investment and other durable goods tend to move sharply up in expansions and down in recessions; another feature is the cyclical movement of profits. A comparison of the theories with the business-cycle facts reveals that all have elements of validity, but none is universally valid in all times and places.

Forecasting Business Cycles

Given the wide swings in economic activity, economic forecasting is one of the most important tasks of economists. Like bright headlights on a car, a good forecast illuminates the economic terrain ahead and helps decision makers adapt their actions to economic conditions.

Econometric Modeling and Forecasting

In an earlier era, economists forecasted the business cycle by looking at a wide variety of data on things like money, boxcar loadings, and steel production. Sometimes the numbers were added together to form an "index of leading indicators" which, it was hoped, would be a barometer of future economic conditions.

As economics entered the age of statistics and computers, macroeconomic forecasting has made great progress. Thanks to the pioneering work of Holland's Nobel-laureate Jan Tinbergen, today we have dozens of macroeconomic models. Lawrence Klein of the Wharton School, who won the 1980 Nobel Prize for his contribution to economic modeling, has built a number of forecasting systems over the last three decades. Commercial consulting firms, such as Data Resources Inc. (DRI), have developed models that are widely used by firms and policymakers.

How are computer models of the economy constructed? Generally modelers start with an analytical framework containing equations representing both aggregate demand and aggregate supply. Using the techniques of modern econometrics, each equation is "fitted" to the data to obtain parameter estimates (such as the *MPC*, the shape of the money-demand equation, the growth of potential GNP, etc.). Of course, at each stage modelers use their own experience and judgment to assess whether the results are reasonable.[1]

Finally, the whole "model" is put together and run as a system of equations. In small models there are one or two dozen equations. Today, large sys-

---

[1] The process by which forecasts are generated is somewhat mysterious to their users. The mixture of art and science has led one observer to ask: "What does an economic forecast have in common with a dog's breakfast? Simple: You never know what's in it."

tems forecast from a few hundred to 10,000 variables. Once the external and policy variables are specified (population, government spending and tax rates, monetary policy, etc.), the system of equations projects important economic variables into the future.

Often the forecasts are accurate. For example, the 1990–1991 recession was foreseen by a large number of economic forecasters. At other times, particularly when there are major policy shifts, forecasting is a hazardous profession. Table 13-1 shows the projections made by DRI, one of the nation's most influential forecasters, right after the Reagan supply-side policies were announced. With major changes in fiscal and monetary policy underway, along with dramatic movements in the dollar's exchange rate and a foreign debt crisis brewing, DRI and other forecasters missed both the deep recession and the growing federal deficit that lay over the horizon. This experience emphasizes that forecasting is as much art as science in our uncertain world. Still, the strength of economic forecasting is that, year in and year out, professional forecasters provide more accurate forecasts than do those who use unsystematic or unscientific approaches.

Is the Business Cycle Avoidable?

Just as there are waves of prosperity and recession, there also follow swings in popular views about the necessity of business cycles. From time to time, an economist or President will proclaim, "I do not believe recessions are inevitable."

Such pronouncements are overly sanguine. A more balanced view was taken by Arthur Okun:

> Recessions are now generally considered to be fundamentally preventable, like airplane crashes and unlike hurricanes. But we have not banished air crashes from the land, and it is not clear that we have the wisdom or the ability to eliminate recessions. The danger has not disappeared. The forces that produce recurrent recessions are still in the wings, merely waiting for their cue.[2]

Over the two decades since Okun wrote these words, the United States has experienced numerous cyclical ups and downs. At the same time, we have avoided *depressions*—the prolonged, cumulative slumps like those of the 1870s, 1890s, or 1930s. What has changed in the last 50 years? Pri-

[2] Arthur M. Okun, *The Political Economy of Prosperity* (Norton, New York, 1970), pp. 33 ff.

Forecasting Turbulent Times—and Results			
	(1) DRI forecast of April 1981 for 4th quarter of 1982	(2) Actual data for 4th quarter of 1982	(3) Percentage error
GNP ($, billion):			
Real	1,582	1,477	7
Nominal	3,482	3,108	11
Inflation rate (% per year, GNP deflator)	10.1	3.7	63
Unemployment rate (%)	6.6	10.7	−62
Interest rates (% per year):			
3-month Treasury bills	13.8	7.9	43
Long-term bonds (AAA)	13.1	11.1	15
Federal deficit ($, billion)	24	203	−746
Stock prices (S&P 500)	146	137	6

Table 13-1. A forecast of the economy 18 months in advance
This shows the macroeconomic forecast of the performance of the U.S. economy made in spring 1981 for economic conditions 18 months later. The recession was not foreseen, nor was the accompanying reduction in inflation. Most other forecasters (including the government) did even worse. According to DRI's Otto Eckstein, "[1982] proved to be the most difficult for forecasting that has been experienced in modern memory." [Source: *The Data Resources Review of the U.S. Economy* (April 1981 and February 1983).]

labor quantity L^* when wage levels are high. We will call L^* the labor force.

Voluntary Unemployment. The left-hand panel of Figure 13-7 shows the usual picture of competitive supply and demand, with a market equilibrium at point E and a wage of W. At the competitive, market-clearing equilibrium, firms willingly hire all qualified workers who want to work at the market wage. The number of employed is represented by the line from A to E. Some members of the labor force, shown by the segment EF, would like to work, but only at a higher wage rate. *The unemployed workers, represented by the segment from* E *to* F, *are* **voluntarily unemployed** *in the sense that they do not want to work at the going market wage rate.*

The existence of voluntary unemployment points to an important misconception about unemployment. An economy may well be performing at the peak of efficiency even though it generates a certain amount of unemployment. The voluntarily unemployed workers might prefer leisure or other activities to jobs at the going wage rate. Or they may be frictionally unemployed, perhaps moving from college to their first job. Or they might be low-productivity workers who prefer leisure to low-paid work. There are countless reasons why people might voluntarily choose not to work at the going wage rate, yet some of these people would be officially counted as unemployed.

It is important to note that voluntary unemployment might well be economically efficient even though a philosopher or politician might bemoan the fact that everybody cannot obtain a high-paying job. Just as a factory needs spare parts in case a critical piece of machinery breaks down, maybe an economy needs spare, unemployed workers, willing to go to work immediately when a critical job vacancy arises. This example shows why a complex modern economy, operating at the peak of its productivity, may generate unemployment.

In summary, a labor market characterized by perfectly flexible wages will not contain involuntary unemployment. Prices and wages simply float up or down until the markets are cleared. In any economy with perfectly flexible wages, widespread unemployment such as that in the 1930s or 1980s would simply not exist.

Involuntary Unemployment. Reread the quotations from unemployed workers on page 243. Who would seriously argue that these workers are voluntarily unemployed? They surely do not sound like consumers carefully balancing the value of work against the value of leisure. Nor do they resemble people choosing unemployment as they search for a better job. To understand cyclical unemployment we need to construct a theory of involuntary unemployment. Keynes' great breakthrough was to let the facts oust a beautiful but irrelevant theory. He explained why we see occasional bouts of *involuntary unemployment*, periods in which qualified workers are unable to get jobs at the going wage rates.

The key to his approach was to note that wages do not adjust to clear labor markets. Rather, wages tend to respond sluggishly to economic shocks. If wages do not move to clear markets, a mismatch between job seekers and job vacancies can arise. This mismatch may lead to the patterns of unemployment that we see today.

We can understand how inflexible wages lead to involuntary unemployment with an analysis of *a non-clearing labor market*, shown in Figure 13-7(*b*). This example assumes that in the wake of an economic disturbance the labor market finds itself with too high a wage rate. Labor's price is at W' rather than at the equilibrium or market-clearing wage of W.

At the too-high wage rate, there are more qualified workers looking for work than there are jobs looking for workers. The number of workers willing to work at wage W' is at point G on the supply curve, but firms only want to hire H workers, as shown by the demand curve. Because the wage exceeds the market-clearing level, there is a surplus of workers. The unemployed workers represented by the dashed line segment HG are said to be **involuntarily unemployed**, signifying that they are qualified workers who want to work at the prevailing wage but cannot find jobs. When there is a surplus of workers, firms will ration out the jobs by setting more stringent skill requirements, adding to the workload, and hiring the most qualified or most experienced workers.

The opposite case occurs when the wage is too low. Here, in a labor-shortage economy, employers cannot find enough workers to fill the existing vacancies. Firms put "Help Wanted" signs in their windows, advertise in the newspaper, and even recruit people from other towns.

Sources of Inflexibility. The theory of involuntary unemployment assumes that wages are inflexible. But this raises a further question: Why do wages not move up or down to clear markets? Why are labor markets not like the auction markets for grain, corn, and common stocks?

These questions are among the deepest unresolved mysteries of modern economics. Few economists today would argue that wages move quickly to erase labor shortages and surpluses. Yet no one completely understands the reasons for the sluggish behavior of wages and salaries. We can therefore provide no more than a tentative assessment of the sources of wage inflexibility.

A helpful distinction is that between auction markets and administered markets. An *auction market* is a highly organized and competitive market where the price floats up or down to balance supply and demand. At the Chicago Board of Trade, for example, the prices of "number 2 stiff red wheat delivered in St. Louis" or "dressed 'A' broiler chickens delivered in New York" change every minute to reflect market conditions—market conditions that are seen in frantic buy and sell orders of farmers, millers, packers, merchants, and speculators.

But 90 percent of all goods, as well as 100 percent of all labor, is sold in administered markets and not in competitive auction markets. Nobody grades labor into "number 2 subcompact-automobile tire assembler" or "class 'AAA' assistant professor of economics." No specialist burns the midnight oil trying to make sure that steelworkers' wages or professors' salaries are set at just the level where all qualified workers are placed into jobs.

Rather, most firms *administer* their wages and salaries, setting fixed pay scales and hiring people at an entry-level wage or salary. These wage scales are generally fixed for a year or so, and when they are adjusted, the pay for almost all categories goes up by the same percentage. For example, a bank might have 15 different categories of staff: three grades of secretaries, two grades of tellers, and so forth. Each year, the bank managers will decide how much to increase wages and salaries—say 5.5 percent in 1993—and the compensation in each category will then move up by that percentage. On infrequent occasions the bank might decide to move one category up or down more than the average. Given the procedure by which wages and salaries are determined, there is little room for major adjustments when the firm finds shortages or gluts in a particular area. Except in extreme cases, the firm will tend to adjust the minimum qualifications required for a job rather than its wages when it finds labor market disequilibrium.[9]

For unionized labor markets, the wage patterns are even more rigid. Wage scales are typically set for a 3-year contract period; during that period, wages are not adjusted for excess supply or demand in particular areas. Moreover, unionized workers seldom accept wage cuts even when many of their workers are unemployed.

To summarize, a careful look at wage setting in America and other market economies today reveals a highly administered process. Wages and salaries are generally set infrequently (usually no more than once a year), and relative wages tend to change very slowly.

Wages and salaries adjust to reflect shortages or surpluses in a particular market only over an extended period of time.

Let's go a step further and ask, What is the economic reason for the sluggishness of wages and salaries? Most economists believe that the inflexibility arises because of the costs of administering compensation. To take the example of union wages, negotiating a contract is a long process that requires much worker and management time and produces no output. It is because collective bargaining is so costly that such agreements are generally negotiated only once every 3 years.

Setting compensation for nonunion workers is less costly, but it nevertheless requires considerable scarce management time and has important effects on worker morale. Every time wages or sala-

---

[9] The example of college admissions illustrates the kind of adjustment that takes place when shortages or gluts occur. Many colleges found that applications for places soared in the 1980s. How did they react? Did they raise their tuition enough to choke off the excess demand? No. Instead, they raised their admission standards, requiring better grades in high schools and higher average SAT scores. Upgrading the requirements rather than changing wages and prices is exactly what happens in the short run when firms experience excess supply of labor.

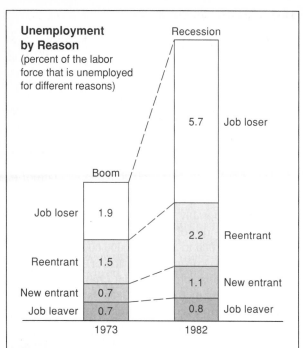

Unemployment by Reason
(percent of the labor force that is unemployed for different reasons)

Recession	
5.7	Job loser

Boom		
Job loser	1.9	
	2.2	Reentrant
Reentrant	1.5	
	1.1	New entrant
New entrant	0.7	
Job leaver	0.7	0.8	Job leaver

1973   1982

Figure 13-9.   Distribution of unemployment by reason

Why did people become unemployed? Less than 1 percent of those in the labor force are unemployed because they left their jobs, and another 2 to 3 percent are new entrants into the labor force (say, because they just graduated from college) or reentrants (people who earlier left the labor force and are back looking for a job). The major change from boom to recession, however, is found in the number of job losers. From 1973 to 1982 the fraction of those in the labor force unemployed because they lost their jobs rose by a factor of 3. (Source: U.S. Department of Labor, *Employment and Earnings*.)

	Unemployment rate (% of labor force)	
Age	White	Black
16–17	15.7	36.7
18–19	12.0	28.0
20–24	7.2	19.9
25–34	4.6	11.7
35–44	3.6	7.8
45–54	3.3	5.3
55–64	3.2	4.6
65 and over	2.8	5.3

Table 13-4. Unemployment rate at different ages, 1990

As workers search for jobs and gain training, they settle on a particular occupation; they tend to stay in the labor force; and they find a preferred employer. As a result, the unemployment rates of older people fall to a fraction of that of teenagers. (Source: U.S. Department of Labor, *Employment and Earnings,* January 1991.)

the labor force very frequently. They get jobs quickly and change jobs often. The average duration of teenage unemployment is only half that of adults; by contrast, the average length of a typical job is 12 times greater for adults than teenagers. In most years, half the unemployed teenagers are "new entrants" who have never had a paying job before. All these factors suggest that teenage unemployment is largely frictional; that is, it represents the job search and turnover necessary for young people to discover their personal skills and to learn what working is all about.

But teenagers do eventually learn the skills and work habits of experienced workers. Table 13-4 shows the unemployment rate at different ages for blacks and whites in 1990. The acquisition of experience and training, along with a greater desire and need for full-time work, is the reason middle-aged workers have much lower unemployment rates than teenagers.

Black Teenage Unemployment. While most evidence suggests that unemployment is largely frictional for white teenagers, the labor market for young black workers has behaved quite differently. After World War II, the labor market data for black teenagers was virtually identical to that for white teenagers. The labor-force participation rates and unemployment rates of black and white teenagers were virtually identical until 1955. Since that time, however, unemployment rates for black teenagers have risen relative to those of other groups while their labor-force participation rates fell. By 1990, 31 percent of black teenagers (16 to 19 years of age) were unemployed, compared to 13 percent of white teenagers. The employment rate (equal to the ratio of total employment to total population) was only 27 percent for black teenagers as opposed to 50 percent for white teenagers.

What accounts for this extraordinary divergence in the experience of the two groups? One explanation might be that labor market forces (such as the composition or location of jobs) have worked against black workers in general. This explanation does not tell the whole story. While adult black workers have always suffered higher unemployment rates than adult white workers—because of lower education levels, fewer contacts with people who can provide jobs, less on-the-job training, and racial discrimination—the ratio of black to white adult unemployment rates has not increased since World War II.

Numerous studies of the sources of the rising black teenage unemployment rate have turned up no clear explanations for the trend. One possible source is discrimination, but a rise in the black-white unemployment differential would require an increase in racial discrimination—for which there is no evidence.

Another theory holds that a high minimum wage tends to drive low-productivity black teenagers into unemployment. The change in the relation of the minimum wage to average wages allows a test of this hypothesis. From 1981 to 1989, the ratio of the minimum wage to average wages in nonfarm establishments fell from 46 percent to 34 percent, yet no improvement in the relative unemployment situation of black teenagers occurred. That no improvement took place casts doubt on the minimum wage as the prime suspect. Some conservative critics of the modern welfare state blame high unemployment of blacks on the culture of dependency that is nurtured by government aid to the poor, although there is little firm data to support these propositions.

Does high teenage unemployment lead to long-lasting labor market damage, with permanently lower levels of skills and wage rates? This question is a topic of intensive ongoing research, and the tentative answer is, Yes, particularly for minority teenagers. It appears that when youths are unable to develop on-the-job skills and work attitudes, they earn lower wages and experience higher unemployment when they are older. To the extent that this research is validated, it suggests that public policy has an important stake in devising programs to reduce teenage unemployment among minority groups.

SUMMARY

A. Business Cycles

1. Business cycles are swings in total national output, income, and employment, marked by widespread expansion or contraction in many sectors of the economy. They occur in all advanced market economies. We distinguish the phases of expansion, peak, recession, and trough.

2. Most modern business-cycle theories stress the role of shifts in aggregate demand in causing business fluctuations. In recent years, supply shocks (such as oil-price changes) have added to the list of factors affecting cycles.

3. Economists have suggested a wide variety of reasons for business cycles. Theories differ in their emphasis on external and internal factors. Importance is often attached to fluctuations in such external factors as population growth, gold discoveries, and political events or wars leading to oil-price shocks. Most theories emphasize that these external shocks interact with internal mechanisms, such as the multiplier and investment-demand shifts, to produce cyclical behavior.

4. Economic forecasting is still inexact. The most successful forecasters use computer models, based on statistical estimates, to forecast changes in the economy.

B. Unemployment

5. There is a clear connection between movements in output and the unemployment rate over the business cycle. According to Okun's Law, for every 1 percent that actual GNP declines relative to potential GNP, the unemployment rate rises $\frac{1}{2}$ percentage point. This rule is useful in translating cyclical movements of GNP into their effects on unemployment.

6. Although unemployment has plagued capitalism since the Industrial Revolution, understanding its causes and costs has been possible only with the rise of modern macroeconomic theory. It is now apparent that recessions and the associated high unemployment are extremely costly to the economy. Major periods of slack like the 1970s and 1980s cost the nation hundreds of billions of dollars and have great social costs as well.

7. The government gathers monthly statistics on unemployment, employment, and the labor force in a sample survey of the population. People with jobs are categorized as employed; people without jobs who are looking for work are said to be unemployed; people without jobs who are not looking for work are considered outside the labor force. Over the last decade, 65 percent of the population over 16 was in the labor force, while 7 percent of the labor force was unemployed.

8. Economists classify unemployment into three groups: (a) frictional unemployment, workers who are between jobs; (b) structural unemployment, workers who are in regions or industries that are in a persistent slump; and (c) cyclical unemployment, workers laid off when the overall economy suffers a downturn.

9. A careful look at the unemployment statistics reveals several regularities:
   (a) Recessions hit all groups in roughly proportional fashion—that is, all groups see their unemployment rates go up and down in proportion to the overall unemployment rate.
   (b) A very substantial part of unemployment is short-term. In low-unemployment years (such as 1973) more than 90 percent of unemployed workers are unemployed less than 26 weeks. The average duration of unemployment rises sharply in deep and prolonged recessions.
   (c) In most years, a substantial amount of unemployment is due to simple turnover, or frictional causes as people enter the labor force for the first time or reenter. Only during recessions is the pool of unemployed composed primarily of job losers.

10. Understanding the causes of unemployment has proved one of the major challenges of modern macroeconomics. Some unemployment (often called voluntary) would occur in a flexible-wage, perfectly competitive economy when qualified people chose not to work at the going wage rate. Voluntary unemployment might be the efficient outcome of competitive markets.

11. Most economists believe that some unemployment, particularly the high cyclical unemployment that occurs during recessions, does not reflect voluntary decisions of qualified workers not to work at going wages. Rather, cyclical unemployment occurs because wages are inflexible, failing to adjust quickly to labor surpluses or shortages. If a wage is above the market-

clearing level, some workers are employed, but other qualified workers cannot find jobs. Such unemployment is involuntary and also inefficient in that both workers and firms could benefit from an appropriate use of monetary and fiscal policies.

12. The key element to understanding involuntary unemployment is the inflexibility of wages in the face of economic shocks. Inflexibility arises because of costs involved in administering the compensation system. These costs are seen in the long duration of union contracts—which typically last 3 years. In nonunion settings, wages and salaries are generally set no more than once a year. Frequent adjustment of compensation would command too large a share of management time, would upset workers' perceptions of fairness, and would undermine worker morale and productivity.

CONCEPTS FOR REVIEW

Business cycles
business cycle
business-cycle phases: peak, trough
  expansion, contraction
recession
external and internal cycle theories
macroeconomic models

Unemployment
Okun's Law
unemployed, employed, labor force,
  not in labor force, unemployment
  rate
frictional, structural, and cyclical
  unemployment

flexible-wage (market-clearing)
  unemployment vs. rigid-wage
  (non-market-clearing)
  unemployment
voluntary vs. involuntary
  unemployment

QUESTIONS FOR DISCUSSION

1. Describe the different phases of the business cycle. In which phase is the economy now?

2. Assume that the unemployment rate is 8 percent and GNP is $4000. What is a rough estimate of potential GNP if the natural rate of unemployment is 6 percent? Assume that potential GNP is growing at 3 percent annually. What will potential GNP be in 2 years? How fast will GNP have to grow to reach potential GNP in 2 years?

3. Some business cycles originate from the demand side, while others arise from supply shocks.
   (a) Give examples of each. Explain the observable differences between the two kinds of shocks for output, prices, and unemployment.
   (b) State whether each of the following would lead to a supply-side business cycle or a demand-side cycle and illustrate the impact using the AS-AD diagram: a wartime increase in defense spending; devastation from wartime bombing of factories and power plants; a decrease in net exports from a debt-induced recession in Latin America; an oil-price increase following a Mideast revolution; a sharp slowdown in the rate of productivity growth.

4. What is the labor-force status of each of the following?
   (a) A teenager who is searching for a first job
   (b) An autoworker who has been dismissed and has given up hope of finding work but would like to work
   (c) A retired person who moved to Florida but reads the want ads to find a part-time job
   (d) A parent who works part-time, wants a full-time job, but doesn't have time to look
   (e) A teacher who has a job but is too ill to work

5. Think about your work status during the last 2 or 3 years. For each month, decide what your labor-force status was (employed, unemployed, not in labor force). Then for the periods you were unemployed, classify your unemployment as frictional, structural, or cyclical. What has been your personal unemployment rate? What does your experience tell you about the sources of teenage unemployment? Compare notes with your classmates.

6. Assume that Congress is considering a minimum-wage law that sets the minimum wage above the market-clearing wages for teenagers but below that for adult workers. Using supply-and-demand diagrams, show the impact of the minimum wage on the

employment, unemployment, and incomes of both sets of workers. Is the unemployment voluntary or involuntary? What would you recommend if you were called to testify about the wisdom of this measure?

7. Do you think that the economic costs or stress of a teenager unemployed for 1 month of the summer might be less or more than a head-of-household unemployed for a year? Do you think that this suggests that public policy should have a different stance with respect to these two groups?

8. **Advanced problem:** In recent years, a new theory of "equilibrium business cycles" has been proposed. This suggests that workers work harder or firms produce more as a result of misperceptions about relative prices. Thus firms are thought to move up their supply curves because they think their prices have risen in booms, when in fact the economywide price level P has risen. Such a view also holds that people have "rational" expectations—being excellent forecasters of future events.

   Could such a theory explain: (a) why output may rise above potential output (and unemployment may fall below its natural rate) when prices rise unexpectedly, and (b) how business downturns may persist for many years, as in the 1930s?

9. **Advanced problem:** Find two dice and use the following technique to see if you can generate something that looks like a business cycle. Record the numbers from 20 or more rolls of the dice. Take five-period moving averages of the successive numbers. Then plot these. They will look very much like movements in GNP, unemployment, or inflation.

   One sequence thus obtained was 7, 4, 10, 3, 7, 11, 7, 2, 9, 10 . . . . The averages were $(7 + 4 + 10 + 3 + 7)/5 = 6.2$, $(4 + 10 + 3 + 7 + 11)/5 = 7$, . . . and so forth.

   Why does this look like a business cycle? [*Hint:* The random numbers generated by the dice are like exogenous shocks of investment or wars. The moving average is like the economic system's (or a rocking chair's) internal multiplier or smoothing mechanism. Taken together, they produce what looks like a cycle.]

10. **Advanced problem:** An eminent macroeconomist, George Perry of Brookings, wrote the following after the Persian Gulf war of 1990–1991:

   Wars have usually been good for the U.S. economy. Traditionally they bring with them rising output, low unemployment, and full use of industrial capacity as military demands add to normal economic activity. This time, for the first time, war and recession occurred together. What does this anomaly tell us about the recession? (*Brookings Review*, Spring 1991)

   Go to the library and find data on the major determinants of aggregate demand during the 1990–1991 period as well as during earlier wars (World War II, Korean war, Vietnam war). Examine particularly government spending on goods and services (especially defense spending), taxes, and interest rates. Can you explain the anomaly that Perry describes?

THE COST OF INFLATION

Lenin is said to have declared that the best way to destroy the capitalist system was to debauch the currency. By a continuing process of inflation, governments can confiscate, secretly and unobserved, an important part of the wealth of their citizens.

J. M. Keynes

In the last chapter, we reviewed the characteristics of business cycles, with particular attention to the cyclical nature of unemployment. But to understand why society tolerates high unemployment, we need also to grasp the tradeoff between unemployment and inflation. This dilemma was aptly described by Arthur Okun:

The task of combining prosperity with price stability now stands as the major unsolved problem of aggregative economic performance. [W]e must find a satisfactory compromise that yields growth and unemployment rates that we can be proud of, on the one hand, and a price performance that we can be comfortable with, on the other.[1]

Inflation is a major problem in many developing countries and has been the hallmark of socialist countries making the transition to the market, such as Poland and Yugoslavia. Many observers fear that the Soviet Union is on the verge of a major inflation in 1991.

It is time to analyze questions of aggregate price behavior and inflation. Why are nations so concerned about galloping inflation? What steps can be taken to keep inflation in the barn rather than running wild? Answers to these questions must be found if we are to understand why nations take stern measures and tolerate high unemployment to beat down high inflation rates.

[1] Arthur M. Okun, *The Political Economy of Prosperity* (Norton, New York, 1970), p. 130.

Figure 14-1 provides an overview of this chapter, which is concerned with the definition, measurement, and history of the price level and inflation.

What Is Inflation?

Inflation is widespread but widely misunderstood. Let us begin with a careful definition:

Inflation denotes a rise in the general level of prices. The **rate of inflation** is the rate of change of the general price level and is measured as follows:

Rate of inflation (year t)

$$= \frac{\begin{array}{c} \text{price level} \\ (\text{year } t) \end{array} - \begin{array}{c} \text{price level} \\ (\text{year } t-1) \end{array}}{\text{price level (year } t-1)} \times 100$$

But how do we measure the "price level" that is involved in the definition of inflation? Conceptually, the *price level* is measured as the weighted average of the goods and services in an economy. In practice, we measure the overall price level by constructing *price indexes*, which are averages of consumer or producer prices.

As an example, take the year 1990, when consumer prices rose 5.4 percent. In that year, the prices of all major product groups rose: food, beverages, shelter, apparel, transportation, medical care, and so forth. It is this general upward trend in prices that we call inflation.

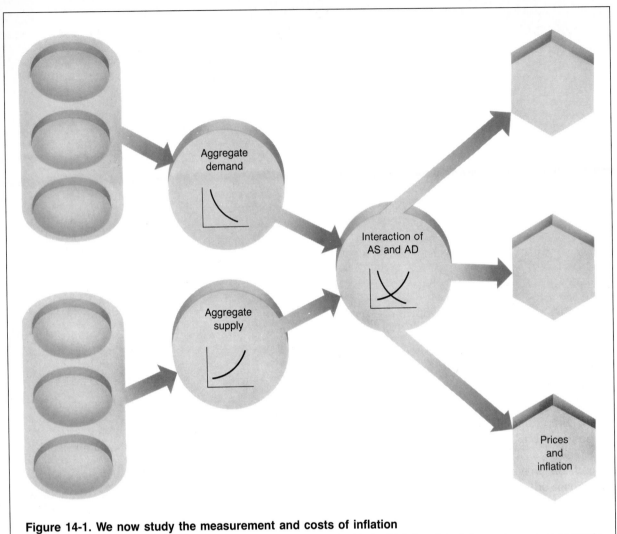

Figure 14-1. We now study the measurement and costs of inflation

Having analyzed the fundamentals of aggregate demand and unemployment, we now examine the determination of changes in the overall price level. How do we measure the overall price level and the rate of inflation? What are the major kinds of inflations? And do people react so adversely to high and variable inflation rates? These questions will be addressed in this chapter.

Not all prices rise by the same amount during inflationary periods, however. During 1990, for example, energy prices rose more than 5.4 percent while food prices rose less; but the increase in the *average price level* was 5.4 percent.

Deflation. The opposite of inflation is **deflation,** which occurs when the general level of prices is falling. Deflations have been rare in the late twentieth century. In the United States, the last time consumer prices actually fell from one year to the next was 1955. Sustained deflations, where prices fall steadily over a period of several years, are associated with depressions, such as the 1930s or the 1890s. The advent of active government stabilization policies, which have eradicated deep depressions in most advanced industrial market countries, has also eliminated deflations from the economic scene.

A related term is **disinflation,** which denotes a decline in the rate of inflation. The most recent period of disinflation occurred in the early 1980s, when the high inflation rate, reaching double-digit levels, was reduced through a policy of tight money.

Price Indexes

When newspapers tell us "Inflation is rising" or "The Federal Reserve reacted to increased inflationary tendencies," they are really reporting the movement of a price index. A **price index** is a weighted average of the prices of a number of goods and services; in constructing price indexes, economists weight individual prices by the economic importance of each good. The most important price indexes are the consumer price index, the GNP deflator, and the producer price index.

The Consumer Price Index (CPI). The most widely used measure of inflation is the consumer price index, also known as the CPI. The CPI measures the cost of a market basket of consumer goods and services, including prices of food, clothing, shelter, fuels, transportation, medical care, college tuition, and other commodities purchased for day-to-day living. Prices on 364 separate classes of commodities are collected from over 21,000 establishments in 91 areas of the country.

How are the different prices weighted in constructing price indexes? It would clearly be silly merely to add up the different prices or to weight them by their mass or volume. Rather, a price index is constructed by *weighting each price according to the economic importance of the commodity in question.*

In the case of the CPI, each item is assigned a *fixed* weight proportional to its relative importance in consumer expenditure budgets; the most recent weights for each item are proportional to the total spending by consumers on that item as determined by a survey of consumer expenditures in the 1982–1984 period.

Numerical Example. We can use a numerical example to help clarify the idea of how inflation is measured. Assume that consumers buy three commodities: food, shelter, and medical care. A hypothetical budget survey finds that consumers spend 20 percent of their budgets on food, 50 percent on shelter, and 30 percent on medical care.

Using 1995 as the *base year*, we reset the price of

each commodity at 100 so that differences in the units of commodities will not affect the price index. This implies that the CPI is also 100 in the base year [= $(0.20 \times 100) + (0.50 \times 100) + (0.30 \times 100)$]. Next, we calculate the consumer price index and the rate of inflation for 1996. In 1996, food prices rise 2 percent to 102, shelter prices rise 6 percent to 106, and medical care prices are up 10 percent to 110. We recalculate the CPI for 1996 as follows:

CPI (1996)
$$= (0.20 \times 102) + (0.50 \times 106) + (0.30 \times 110)$$
$$= 106.4$$

In other words, if 1995 is the base year in which the CPI is 100, then in 1996 the CPI is 106.4. The rate of inflation in 1996 is then [$(106.4 - 100)/100] \times 100 = 6.4$ percent per year. Note that in a fixed-weight index like the CPI, the *prices* change from year to year but the *weights* remain the same.

This example captures the essence of how inflation is measured. The only difference between this simplified calculation and the real one is that the CPI in fact contains many more commodities. Otherwise, the concepts are exactly the same.

GNP Deflator. We met the GNP deflator in the discussion of national income and output accounting in Chapter 6. Recall that the GNP deflator is the ratio of nominal GNP to real GNP and can thus be interpreted as the price of *all* components of GNP (consumption, investment, government purchases, and net exports) rather than of a single sector. This index differs from the CPI also because it is a variable-weight index, weighting prices by the current-period quantities. In addition, there are deflators for components of GNP, such as for investment goods, personal consumption, and so forth, and these are sometimes used to supplement the CPI.

The Producer Price Index (PPI). This index, dating from 1890, is the oldest continuous statistical series published by the Labor Department. It measures the level of prices at the wholesale or producer stage. It is based on approximately 3400 commodity prices, including prices of foods, manufactured products, and mining products. The fixed weights used to calculate the PPI are the net sales of the commodity. Because of its great detail, this index is widely used by businesses.

Index-Number Problems. While price indexes like the CPI are enormously useful, they are not without their faults. Some problems are intrinsic to price indexes. One issue is the *index-number problem,* which concerns the choice of an appropriate period for the base year. Recall that the CPI uses a fixed weight for each good. As a result, the cost of living is overestimated compared to the situation where consumers substitute relatively inexpensive for relatively expensive goods. For example, the weighting in the CPI neglects the fact that the amount of gasoline bought by consumers declined after gasoline prices rose sharply in the early 1970s. One could change the base year, or devise more elaborate weighting methods, but there is no way of solving the index-number problem perfectly.

Another difficulty arises because the CPI does not accurately capture changes in the quality of goods. For example, the CPI is not corrected for quality improvements such as better sound reproduction in phonographic equipment, safer air travel, or more accurate watches. Studies indicate

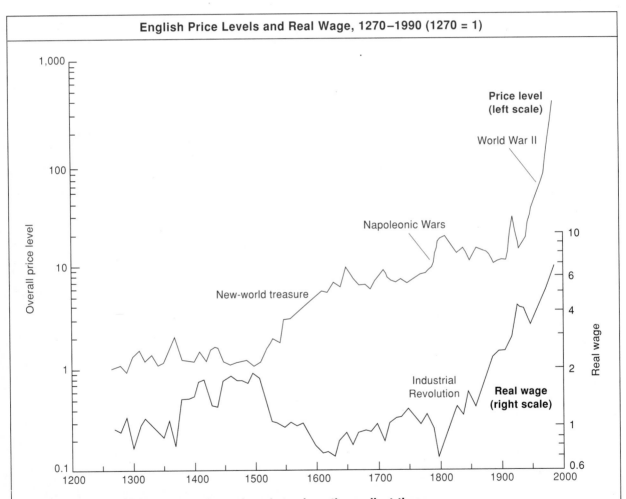

Figure 14-2. Price inflation has dogged markets since the earliest times

The graph shows England's history of prices and real wages since the Middle Ages. Note that the price of a market basket of goods has risen almost 400-fold since 1270. In early years, price increases were associated with increases in the money supply, such as from discoveries of new-world treasure and the printing of money during the Napoleonic Wars.

Note the meandering of the real wage (money wage divided by the price level) prior to the Industrial Revolution. Since then real wages have risen sharply and steadily. (Source: E. H. Phelps Brown and S. V. Hopkins, *Economica*, 1956, updated by authors.)

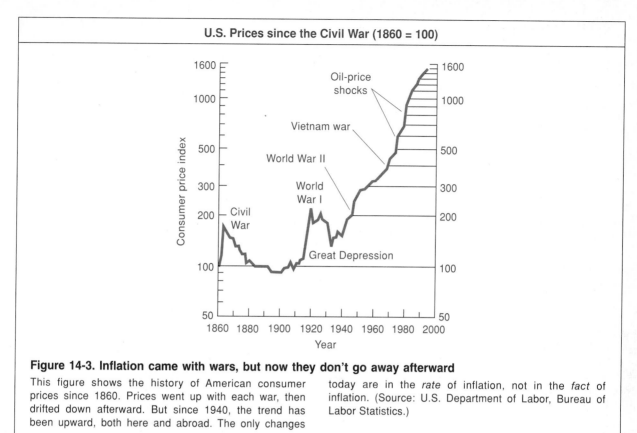

U.S. Prices since the Civil War (1860 = 100)

Figure 14-3. Inflation came with wars, but now they don't go away afterward

This figure shows the history of American consumer prices since 1860. Prices went up with each war, then drifted down afterward. But since 1940, the trend has been upward, both here and abroad. The only changes today are in the *rate* of inflation, not in the *fact* of inflation. (Source: U.S. Department of Labor, Bureau of Labor Statistics.)

that if quality change were properly incorporated into price indexes, the CPI would have risen less rapidly in recent years.

Misconceptions. People often get confused about inflation. Here are some questions that reflect common misconceptions along with the correct answers.

Does inflation mean that goods are expensive? No, inflation means that the average price level is rising.

Does inflation mean that we are getting poorer? Not necessarily. Our nominal incomes tend to rise rapidly during inflationary periods, so our real incomes (incomes corrected for the cost of living) may go up or down during inflationary times.

Do companies get rich at workers' expense during inflationary times? Not necessarily. The effect of inflation on the distribution of income depends on the cause of the inflation.

You will hear many more misconceptions about inflation, but you can avoid adopting them if you remember the definition of inflation given above.

The Long History of Inflation

Inflation is as old as market economies. Figure 14-2 depicts the history of English inflation since the thirteenth century. Over the long haul, prices have generally risen, as the blue line reveals. But examine also the black line, which plots the path of *real wages* (the wage rate divided by consumer prices). Real wages meandered along until the Industrial Revolution. Comparing the two lines shows that inflation is not necessarily accompanied by a decline in real income. You can see, too, that real wages have climbed steadily since around 1800, rising more than tenfold.

Figure 14-3 focuses on the behavior of consumer prices in the United States since the Civil War. Until

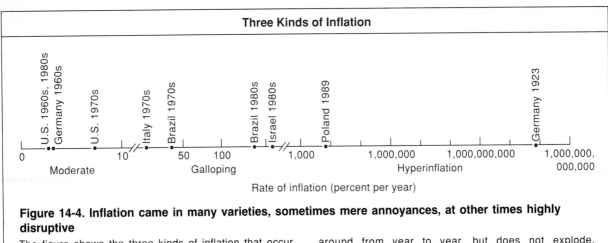

Figure 14-4. Inflation came in many varieties, sometimes mere annoyances, at other times highly disruptive

The figure shows the three kinds of inflation that occur. Moderate inflation is typical today in most industrialized countries. In galloping inflation, such as that seen in Brazil and Israel during recent years, inflation jumps around from year to year, but does not explode. Hyperinflation occurs when prices rise at a thousand, million, or trillion percent annually.

1945, the pattern was regular: prices would soar during wartime, then fall back during the postwar slump. But the pattern changed ominously after World War II. Prices and wages now travel on a one-way street upward. They rise rapidly in periods of economic expansion; in recessions they do not fall but merely rise less rapidly. In other words, price and wage behavior has undergone a major structural change since 1940: it is now inflexible downward.

Three Strains of Inflation

Like diseases, inflations exhibit different levels of severity. It is useful to classify them into three categories: moderate inflation, galloping inflation, and hyperinflation. A pictorial description is shown in Figure 14-4.

Moderate Inflation. Moderate inflation is characterized by slowly rising prices. We might arbitrarily classify this as single-digit annual inflation rates. When prices are relatively stable, *people trust money.* They are willing to hold on to money because it will be almost as valuable in a month or a year as it is today. People are willing to write long-term contracts in money terms because they are confident that the price level will not get too far out of line for the good they are selling or buying. People do not waste time or resources trying to put

their wealth into "real" assets rather than "money" or "paper" assets because they believe their money assets will retain their real value.

Galloping Inflation. Inflation in the double- or triple-digit range of 20, 100, or 200 percent a year is labeled "galloping inflation." At the low end of this spectrum we sometimes find advanced industrial countries like Italy. Many Latin American countries, such as Argentina and Brazil, had inflation rates of 50 to 700 percent per year in the 1970s and 1980s.

Once galloping inflation becomes entrenched, serious economic distortions arise. Generally, most contracts get indexed to a price index or to a foreign currency, like the dollar. In these conditions, money loses its value very quickly; real interest rates can be minus 50 or 100 percent per year. Consequently, people hold only the bare minimum amount of money needed for daily transactions. Financial markets wither away, and funds are generally allocated by rationing rather than by interest rates. People hoard goods, buy houses, and never, never lend money at low nominal interest rates.

The surprise is that economies with 200 percent annual inflation manage to survive even though the price system is behaving so badly. These economies tend to develop major economic distortions, however, as people send their investment funds abroad and domestic investment withers away.

Hyperinflation. While economies seem to survive under galloping inflation, a third and deadly strain takes hold when the cancer of hyperinflation strikes. Nothing good can be said about a market economy in which prices are rising a million or even a trillion percent per year.

Hyperinflations are particularly interesting to students of inflation because they highlight its effects. Consider this description of hyperinflation in the Confederacy during the Civil War:

> We used to go to the stores with money in our pockets and come back with food in our baskets. Now we go with money in baskets and return with food in our pockets. Everything is scarce except money! Prices are chaotic and production disorganized. A meal that used to cost the same amount as an opera ticket now costs twenty times as much. Everybody tends to hoard "things" and to try to get rid of the "bad" paper money, which drives the "good" metal money out of circulation. A partial return to barter inconvenience is the result.

The most thoroughly documented case of hyperinflation took place in the Weimar Republic of Germany in the 1920s. Figure 14-5 shows how the government unleashed the monetary printing presses, driving both money and prices to astronomical levels. From January 1922 to November 1923, the price index rose from 1 to 10,000,000,000. If a person had owned $300 million worth of bonds in early 1922, this amount would not have bought a piece of candy 2 years later.

Studies have found several common features in hyperinflations. First, the real demand for money (measured by the money stock divided by the price level) falls drastically. By the end of the German hyperinflation, real money demand was only one-thirtieth of its level 2 years earlier. People are in effect rushing around, dumping their money like hot potatoes before they get burned by money's loss of value. Second, relative prices become highly unstable. Under normal conditions, the real wages of a person move only a percent or less from month to month. During 1923, German real wages changed on average one-third (up or down) each month. This enormous variation in relative prices and real wages—and the inequities and distortions caused by these fluctuations—illustrates the major cost of inflation.

Perhaps the most profound effect of a hyperinfla-

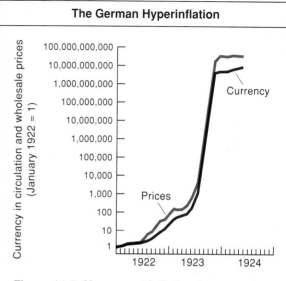

Figure 14-5. Money and inflation in Germany

In the early 1920s, the young Weimar Republic of Germany was struggling to meet harsh reparations payments and satisfy creditors. It could not borrow or raise enough taxes to pay for government spending, so it turned to the printing press. The stock of currency rose astronomically from early 1922 to December 1923, and prices spiraled upward as people frantically tried to dump their money before it lost all value. If you held a billion marks in January 1922, what would be left of your riches at the end of this hyperinflation?

tion is on wealth distribution. The British economist Lionel Robbins summarized the impact:

> The depreciation of the mark . . . destroyed the wealth of the more solid elements in German society; and it left behind a moral and economic disequilibrium, apt breeding ground for the disasters which have followed. Hitler is the foster-child of the inflation.[2]

Do Inflations Accelerate?

Many people fear inflation, even moderate inflation rates of 6 or 9 percent, because they worry that prices will begin to gallop upward, or perhaps that the moderate inflation will degenerate into a hyper-

[2] The history of the German hyperinflation is told in detail in C. Bresciani-Turroni, *The Economics of Inflation: A Study of Currency Depreciation in Post-War Germany*, 3d ed. (Augustus M. Kelley, London, 1968). The quotation from Professor Robbins is from the introduction to the book.

inflation. Does creeping inflation inevitably become a trot? A trot become a canter? A canter become a gallop?

The history of inflations suggests that there is no such inevitable sequence. Hyperinflations are extremely rare. They occur mainly during wartime or in the backwash of war and revolution. The most recent hyperinflations occurred in countries making the revolutionary transition from socialism to market economy; in Poland, prices rose over 1000 percent a year in 1989–1990.

Galloping inflation, on the other hand, is not rare. Like periods of prolonged unemployment, galloping inflation breaks out occasionally even in advanced economies. Since the oil shock of 1973, France, Italy, and Britain have experienced bouts of galloping inflation. In general, however, nations are able to use macroeconomic policies to keep inflation at a moderate creep and hold its costs down to tolerable levels.

The Impact of Inflation

Politicians and central bankers pronounce daily on the dangers of inflationary expectations. Public-opinion polls often find that inflation is economic enemy number one. What is so dangerous and costly about inflation?

Identifying the costs of inflation has proven a difficult task. We noted above that during periods of inflation all prices and wages do not move at the same rate; that is, changes in *relative prices* occur. As a result of the diverging relative prices, two definite effects of inflation are:

- A *redistribution* of income and wealth among different classes
- *Distortions* in the relative prices and outputs of different goods, or sometimes in output and employment for the economy as a whole

Impacts on Income and Wealth Distribution

The major distributional impact of inflation arises from differences in the kinds of assets and liabilities that people hold.[3] When people owe money, a

sharp rise in prices is a windfall gain for them. Suppose you borrow $100,000 to buy a house and your annual mortgage payments are $10,000. Suddenly, a great inflation doubles all wages and prices. Your dollar income doubles although the amount of goods that your income can buy is unchanged. But what has happened to the real cost of your mortgage? Your mortgage payment is still $10,000 per year, but you will need to work only half as long as before to make your mortgage payment. The great inflation has increased your wealth $50,000 by halving the real value of your mortgage debt.

This kind of thinking may encourage people to borrow heavily to buy houses or farmland. Then, when inflation slows and recession hits, the mortgage payments are so burdensome that thousands of people end up in bankruptcy court.

If you are a lender and have assets in mortgages or long-term bonds, the shoe is on the other foot. A sudden rise in prices will leave you the poorer because the dollars repaid to you are worth less than you originally expected.

Real-Interest-Rate Adjustment. If an inflation persists for a long time, people come to anticipate it and markets begin to adapt. An allowance for inflation will gradually be built into the market interest rate. Say the economy starts out with interest rates of 3 percent and stable prices. Once people expect prices to rise at 9 percent per year, bonds and mortgages will tend to pay 12 percent rather than 3 percent. The 12 percent nominal interest rate reflects a 3 percent real interest rate plus a 9 percent inflation premium. There are no further major redistributions of income and wealth once interest rates have so adjusted.

Adjustment of interest rates to chronic inflation has been observed in Brazil, Chile, and other countries with a long history of rising prices. In the 1980s, we saw a similar inflation premium built into American and European interest rates.[4]

The major redistributive impact of inflation occurs through its effect on the real value of people's wealth. In general, unanticipated inflation redistributes wealth from creditors to debtors (that is, unanticipated or unforeseen inflation helps those who have borrowed money and hurts those who

---

[3] The important elements of balance sheets were described in Chapter 10.

[4] Figure 10-3 shows movements in nominal and real interest rates for the United States in recent years.

have lent money). An unanticipated decline in inflation has the opposite effect.

Special Cases. Governments find that the burden of their debt shrinks during inflation. Someone who invests money in real estate or gold will make a large profit during unforeseen inflation. It used to be thought that common stocks were also a good inflation hedge, but their performance was disappointing in recent years. When inflation jumped in 1990, stock prices fell sharply all around the world as investors anticipated that central banks would tighten money.

Because of institutional changes, some old myths are no longer applicable. It used to be said that widows and orphans were hurt by inflation; today, they receive social security pensions that are "indexed" to the CPI so they are insulated from inflation because benefits automatically increase as the CPI increases. Also, many kinds of debt (like "floating-rate" mortgages) have interest rates that move up and down with market interest rates, so unanticipated inflation benefits debtors and hurts lenders less than before.

There have been volumes of research on the redistributional impacts of inflation. The summary wisdom of these studies indicates that the overall impact is highly unpredictable. Those who live on capital income tend to lose from inflation, while wage earners tend to gain. Contrary to stereotypes, statistics indicate that poor families often gain from inflation at the expense of the affluent.

But the main conclusion is that inflation mainly churns income and assets, randomly redistributing wealth around the population with little significant impact on any single group.

Effects on Output and Economic Efficiency

In addition to redistributing incomes, inflation affects the real economy in two specific areas: it affects total output and it influences economic efficiency.

Macroeconomic Impacts. The first impact is on the level of *output as a whole*. Until the 1970s, high inflation usually went hand in hand with high employment and output. Rising inflation occurred when investment was brisk and jobs were plentiful. Periods of unanticipated declines in inflation—the

1930s, 1954, 1958, and 1982—were times of high unemployment of labor and capital. Indeed, periods where declining inflation supposedly left banks and other creditors "better off" actually left them with uncollectible debts—whether owed by farmers in the 1930s or by Latin Americans in the mid-1980s.

In analyzing this experience, we must be cautious in interpreting the causality. In the observed association between inflation and output, which was cause and which effect? Was the rising output caused by the rising prices? Or were the rising prices the result of rising output? Or were both the result of a third factor that moved prices and output?

Today, macroeconomists believe that there is no necessary relationship between prices and output. An increase in aggregate demand will increase both prices and output; but a supply shock, shifting up the aggregate supply curve, will raise prices and *lower* output.[5]

We conclude with the surprising result that inflation may be associated with either a higher or a lower level of output and employment.

Microeconomic Impacts. Another, more subtle effect of inflation is the microeconomic impact on *economic efficiency*. Generally the higher the inflation rate, the greater are the distortions of relative prices.

What do we mean by price distortions? These occur when prices get out of line relative to costs and demands. A humorous example of a distortion is found in many Eastern European countries where bread prices are held far below costs. Often, bread prices are lower than fodder, and farmers have been seen feeding bread to pigs. Little wonder that there are bread lines when the price distortion is so severe.

A less humorous example concerns the distortions in the use of money, whose return is severely distorted by inflation. Currency does not receive interest. But recall that the real interest rate (the interest rate in terms of real goods) is defined as the nominal interest rate minus the rate of inflation. Thus, the real interest rate on currency is equal to

---

[5] These two cases were shown in our overview of macroeconomics, in Figures 5-8 and 5-9 respectively.

minus the inflation rate. For example, those who held currency in 1980 earned a real return equal to minus 13 percent (since 13 percent was the inflation rate). The upshot here is that the real interest rate on currency is dramatically affected by inflation; people will tend to unload their currency and acquire other assets when prices begin to rise rapidly. People expend real resources trying to economize on their paper money holdings.

Also, the prices of inputs or goods that are priced under long-term arrangements (labor contracts and prices in regulated or state-owned industries) tend to become more out of line with the general price level during inflationary periods. We will analyze these and other inefficiencies below.

Analysis of Inflation's Costs

As we have seen, inflation distorts relative prices and reduces economic efficiency. In addition, the severity of inflation's effects depends on whether or not the inflation is anticipated. The impact of inflation will be analyzed first by considering what happens in an idealized inflation that is both anticipated and balanced. By a "balanced" inflation, we mean one in which relative prices do not change.

Balanced, Anticipated Inflation

Suppose that all prices are rising at 10 percent each year. Nobody is surprised by the price changes. Food and clothing, wages and rents are all rising at 10 percent each year, and all real interest rates (that is, interest rates corrected for inflation) are just the same as they would be if all prices were stable.

Would anyone be concerned about such an inflation? Would the efficiency of resource use or real GNP be any smaller or larger? The answer to both questions is, No. *There is no effect on real output, efficiency, or income distribution of an inflation that is both balanced and anticipated.* My income is rising 10 percent faster than it would be with stable prices but the cost of living is also rising 10 percent faster. There is no gain or loss to different kinds of assets. Prices are, in this case, simply a changing yardstick to which people completely adjust their behavior.

This idealized case raises an unsettling thought:

Is the social cost of inflation an illusion? Do people overestimate the economic costs of inflation. Do people dislike inflation because they see their living costs rise but forget that their incomes are rising in step with costs?

There is no correct answer to these questions. Economists believe that people often misunderstand the nature of inflation, confusing high *inflation* with high *prices*. In fact, the low cost of balanced and anticipated inflation suggests that popular perceptions about the ills of inflation may sometimes be inaccurate.

Unbalanced Inflation: Inflation-Induced Distortions

Let us take a step toward realism by recognizing that inflation affects relative prices, costs, and tax burdens. For the moment, let us stay with the case of anticipated inflation.

One inefficiency resulting from unbalanced inflation occurs because some prices do not adjust to reflect inflationary trends; money and taxes are two important examples. Currency is money that bears a zero nominal interest rate. If the inflation rate rises from 0 to 10 percent annually, then the real interest rate on currency falls from 0 to −10 percent per year. There is no easy way for a central bank or government to correct this distortion.

How does the negative real interest rate on currency or other kinds of money lead to inefficiency? Studies show that when inflation rises, people devote real resources to reducing their money holdings. They go to the bank more often—using up "shoe leather" and valuable time. Corporations set up elaborate "cash management" schemes. Real resources are thereby consumed to cope with the changing monetary yardstick. Empirical studies indicate, however, that this cost is modest.

The impact of inflation on taxes is potentially more significant. Under a tax system in which people pay higher taxes as their nominal incomes rise, inflation automatically raises people's average tax rates. It thus allows the government to raise taxes without passing laws. Such "taxation without legislation" has led many countries to index their tax laws to prevent inflation-induced tax increases. Parts of the U.S. tax code were indexed during the 1980s.

Indexing alone will not purge the tax system of the impacts of inflation because inflation distorts the measurement of income. For example, if you earned an interest rate of 10 percent on your funds in 1990, half of this simply replaced your loss in the purchasing power of your funds from a 5 percent inflation rate. Yet the tax code does not distinguish between real return and the interest that just compensates for inflation. Many similar distortions of income and taxes are present in the tax code today.

Some economists point to "menu costs" of inflation. The idea is that when prices are changed, restaurants will have to reprint their menus, and that task uses real resources. Other examples of menu costs are the cost of reprinting catalogues, of remetering taxis, or of changing the price tags of goods in stores.

Inflation causes many similar distortions in the economy. Often governments let the real value of their programs erode as prices rise. A recent study shows that government payments for medical care for poor people have declined in real terms as governments failed to increase their budgets in line with the rising cost of medical care. Regulated industries sometimes find that their requests for price increases are trimmed or rejected during inflationary periods. Many company pension plans provide benefits that are fixed in nominal terms so that the real benefits decline if inflation strikes. These are among the many examples of how inflation can affect people's incomes in unexpected ways.

Inflation Destroys Information. A final point to stress is that prices contain information that is valuable to consumers. We may remember that Elm City sells gas for $1.20 a gallon; with this in mind, it is easy to compare Elm City's prices with those of Exxon or Arco.

Inflation can destroy information. In rapid inflations, price tags are changed frequently and consumers have difficulty comparing prices. Consequently, consumers may mistakenly pay more than necessary for goods.

An analogy shows how a rapid change in prices destroys valuable information. Imagine that every year telephone numbers were increased a bit as we experience "telephone-number inflation." Think of how much trouble it would cause you if telephone-number inflation were rapid, and you had to find out the number for your home every day. What if the number for the operator and directory assistance also changed daily?

Unanticipated Inflation

We turn next to unanticipated inflations. Changes in inflation are usually a big surprise, even to professional forecasters. Generally, unanticipated moderate inflation has a more significant effect on the distribution of income and wealth than on the efficiency of the system. An unexpected jump in prices will impoverish some and enrich others, but will have little impact on how effectively farms and factories are run.

How costly is this redistribution? Perhaps "cost" does not describe the problem. The effects may be more social than economic. An epidemic of burglaries may not lower GNP, but it causes great distress. Similarly, randomly redistributing wealth by inflation is like forcing people to play a lottery they would prefer to avoid.

Moreover, the effect of a redistribution due to inflation depends on how big the inflation is. There is no doubt that galloping inflation or hyperinflation saps the morale and vitality of an economy. On the other hand, an inflation rate of 3 to 5 percent, such as that in the United States in the early 1990s, probably has but a minor impact on the distribution of income and wealth.

Unbalanced and Unanticipated Inflation

In reality, most inflations are both unbalanced and unanticipated. The most recent surge of inflation came in the fall of 1990, when a surprise attack on Kuwait led to an unanticipated temporary doubling of oil-prices. Like the earlier oil-price increases of 1973 and 1979, a certain amount of redistribution occurred. Fortune smiled on those lucky enough to own oil wells, oil-bearing land, or oil companies. By contrast, people who owned gas-guzzling cars, airplanes, or airline companies suffered economic losses.

The history of these oil-price shocks and the accompanying inflation is an instructive lesson on the impact of inflation. Much of the perceived cost of inflation did not stem from the inflation per se. Rather, social frictions arose from the changes in relative prices. Real incomes fell because people had to pay more for oil products, not because the general price level rose. Even if the inflation rate had been zero, the rising relative price of oil would still have hurt oil-consuming households and nations.

Recapitulation

Table 14-1 summarizes this discussion. In addition to the size of the inflation, two facets of inflation will determine its severity: whether it is balanced and whether it is anticipated. The mildest effects will be found when inflations are at a low rate. Such inflations are shown in the upper left corner of this table—small, anticipated, and balanced. Galloping inflations and hyperinflations lead to major economic and social dislocations; in these cases, high inflation rates are unanticipated and unbalanced.

The Macroeconomic Reaction

Whatever the real or perceived costs of inflation, most nations today will not tolerate high inflation rates for long. Sooner or later, they take steps to reduce inflation—by restraining the growth of real output and raising unemployment, or sometimes by putting controls on prices and wages. The result is almost always a painful period of stagnation, as workers are pinched by layoffs, short hours, and poor job prospects. Indeed, the decision by governments to contain inflation was the prime cause of the long period of stagnation in Europe and North America that followed the 1979 oil-price increase and lasted until the end of the 1980s in Europe.

Thus, whatever economists may conclude about the "menu costs" or other microeconomic costs of inflation, the reaction of monetary and fiscal policy must be counted as one of the costs of inflation. And that reaction has generally been to contain inflation by high unemployment and low GNP growth; as the next chapter shows, the amount of output and jobs that must be lost to curb inflation is very large.

Two Dimensions of Inflation's Costs		
	Balanced inflation	**Unbalanced inflation**
Anticipated inflation	Inflation has no cost	Efficiency losses
Unanticipated inflation	Income and wealth redistribution	Efficiency losses and redistribution

Table 14-1. The impacts of inflation are governed by two main factors: whether it is balanced and whether it is anticipated

The costs of inflation depend on two different factors. First, is it a balanced inflation, where no relative prices are being changed and there are no inflation-induced distortions? Second, is it anticipated?

Final Appraisal

Inflation is a complex phenomenon, with many different kinds of costs. Can we make a final estimate of inflation's burdens? Does inflation markedly lower a nation's real output? Are the measurable costs to GNP or the unmeasured costs to morale and social stability great or small?

A careful sifting of the evidence suggests that moderate inflation like that seen recently in the United States has only a modest impact on productivity and real output. It is difficult to find studies that can point to yearly effects of more than a few billion dollars in a $6 trillion economy. Even during the German hyperinflation, output and employment fell less than in the Great Depression. On the other hand, the consequences of sudden inflation-induced distortions or changes in income and wealth undoubtedly are severe and unpleasant for many individuals, not unlike the experience of being robbed.

And, finally, even though the costs of inflation appear modest, the electorate responds forcefully to an upsurge in prices. People vote for leaders who promise to take measures to reduce inflation, and the leaders in turn take measures to curb inflation by slowing output growth and raising unemployment. This reaction is the most visible and dramatic effect of inflation in a modern economy.

SUMMARY

1. Changes in aggregate demand lead to changes in prices as well as output. Indeed, because of the inflexibility of wages, prices may be rising even though the economy still has high unemployment and unutilized capacity.

2. Inflation occurs when the general level of prices is rising (and deflation occurs when they are generally falling). Today, we calculate inflation by using price indexes—weighted averages of the prices of thousands of individual products. The consumer price index (CPI) measures the cost of a market basket of consumer goods and services relative to the cost of that bundle during a particular base year. The GNP deflator is the price of GNP.

3. Until World War II, prices rose during wartime and fell afterward. These days, we see that inflation rises during booms and subsides during recessions. But the overall price level almost never declines.

4. Like diseases, inflations come in different strains. We generally see moderate inflation in the United States (a few percentage points annually). Sometimes, galloping inflation produces price rises of 50 or 100 or 200 percent each year. Hyperinflation takes over when the printing presses spew out currency and prices start rising many times each month. Historically, hyperinflations have almost always been associated with war and revolution.

5. Inflation affects the economy by redistributing income and wealth and by changing the level and efficiency of production. When inflations and deflations are balanced and anticipated, all prices and wages are expected to move by the same percentage, with no one helped and no one hurt by the process. This type of inflation is rare. Unforeseen inflation usually favors debtors, profit seekers, and risk-taking speculators. It hurts creditors, fixed-income classes, and timid investors.

6. Because of the costs of inflation, containing inflation is one of the prime targets of macroeconomic policy. Unbalanced inflations distort relative prices, tax rates, and real interest rates. People take more trips to the bank, taxes may creep up, and measured income may become distorted. Also, unanticipated inflations lead to mistaken investments and to demoralizing and random income redistributions. And when society determines to take steps to lower inflation, the real costs of such steps in terms of lower output and employment can be painful.

CONCEPTS FOR REVIEW

inflation, deflation, disinflation
price index (CPI, GNP deflator, PPI)
strains of inflation (moderate, galloping, hyperinflation)
balanced and unbalanced inflation

impacts of inflation (redistributional, on output and employment)
costs of inflation: "shoe leather," "menu costs," income and tax distortions, loss of information

anticipated and unanticipated inflation
macroeconomic reaction to inflation

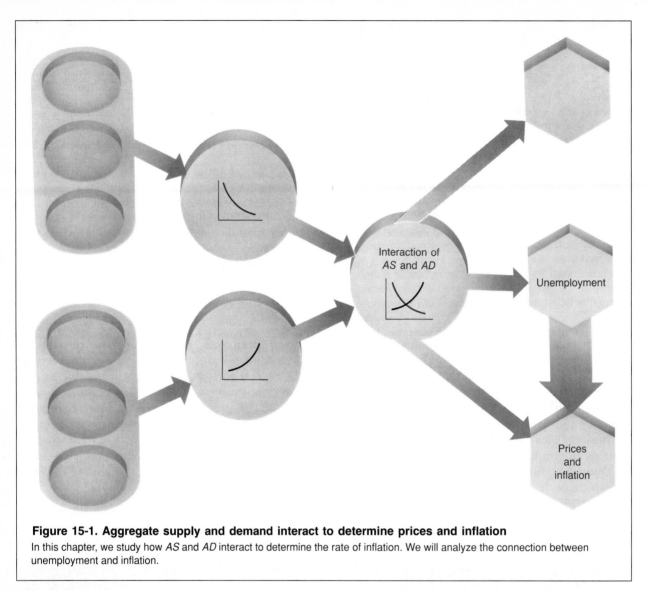

Figure 15-1. Aggregate supply and demand interact to determine prices and inflation

In this chapter, we study how AS and AD interact to determine the rate of inflation. We will analyze the connection between unemployment and inflation.

percent inflation rate; government monetary and fiscal plans assumed a 4 percent rate. Nominal GNP could grow at 7 percent (3 percent growth of output and 4 percent inflation) without any major surprises. During this period, the *inertial rate of inflation* was 4 percent per year. Other names sometimes heard for this concept are the core, underlying, or expected inflation rate.

The rate of inflation that is expected and built into contracts and informal arrangements is the inertial or core rate of inflation.

Inertial inflation can persist for a long time—as long as most people expect the inflation rate to remain the same. Under this condition, inflation is built into the system. A fully built-in inflation represents a *neutral* equilibrium, one which is able to sustain itself at a particular rate for an indefinite period of time.

But history shows that inflation does not remain undisturbed for long. Frequent shocks from changes in aggregate demand, sharp oil-price changes, poor harvests, movements in the foreign exchange rate, productivity changes, and countless other economic events move inflation above or below its inertial rate. The major kinds of shocks are demand-pull and cost-push. In summary:

At a given time, the economy has an ongoing rate of inflation to which people's expectations have adapted. This built-in inertial inflation rate tends to persist until a shock causes it to move up or down.

Demand-Pull Inflation

One of the major shocks to inflation is a change in aggregate demand. In earlier chapters we saw that changes in investment, government spending, or net exports can change aggregate demand and propel output beyond its potential. We also saw how a nation's central bank can affect economic activity. Whatever the reason, **demand-pull inflation** occurs when aggregate demand rises more rapidly than the economy's productive potential, pulling prices up to equilibrate aggregate supply and demand. In effect, demand dollars are competing for the limited supply of commodities and bid up their prices. As unemployment falls and workers become scarce, wages are bid up and the inflationary process accelerates.

One influential demand-pull theory holds the supply of money to be a prime determinant of inflation. The reasoning behind this approach is that money-supply growth increases aggregate demand which in turn increases the price level. In this example, the direction of causation is clear-cut. It proceeds from the money supply through aggregate demand to inflation. Thus, when the German central bank printed billions and billions of paper marks in 1922–1923 and these came into the marketplace in search of bread or housing, it was no wonder that the German price level rose a billionfold, making the currency worthless. This was demand-pull inflation with a vengeance. This scene was replayed when the Soviet government financed its budget deficit by printing rubles in the early 1990s.

Demand-pull inflation can arise from other sources as well; for example, during the Vietnam war, excessive fiscal deficits raised the demand for output well above its potential and ignited a rapid inflation.

Figure 15-2 illustrates the process of demand-pull inflation in terms of aggregate supply and demand. Starting from an initial equilibrium at

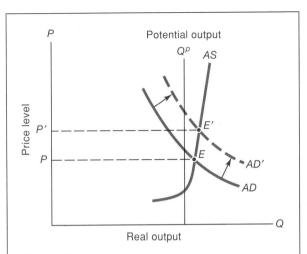

Figure 15-2. Demand-pull inflation occurs when too much spending chases too few goods

At high output levels, when aggregate demand increases, the rising spending is competing for limited goods. With a steep AS curve, much of the higher aggregate spending ends up in higher prices. Prices rise from P to P'. Hence, it is higher demand that pulls up the prices—demand-pull inflation. How would cost-push inflation be analyzed in this framework?

point E, suppose there is an expansion of spending that pushes the AD curve up and to the right. The economy's equilibrium moves from E to E'. At this higher level of demand, prices have risen from P to P'. Demand-pull inflation has taken place.

Cost-Push Inflation

The rudiments of demand-pull inflation were understood by the classical economists and used by them to explain historical price movements. But during the last half-century, the inflation process changed, as a glance back at the history of prices on page 259 reminds us. Prices today travel a one-way street—up in recession, up faster in boom. And this is true for all the market economies of the world. What differentiates modern inflation from the simple demand-pull variety is that prices and wages begin to rise before full employment is reached. They rise even when 30 percent of factory capacity lies idle and 10 percent of the labor force is unemployed. This phenomenon is known as "cost-push" or "supply-shock" inflation.

c
o
li
fl
Per
tl
p
r
b

N
pec
rate
rio
sup
ers
ecc
un
tho
nal
did
of i

V
cu
flat
the
om
the
thi
Ca
198

Th

We
div
the
pe
rat
tha
un
gar
Inf
cei
an

to
un
dif

The Costs of Disinflation, 1980–1984

Inertial rate of inflation:

1979	9%
1984	4%

Change: –5 percentage points

Difference between potential and actual GNP (1990 prices):

1980	$ 128 billion
1981	144
1982	356
1983	311
1984	136

Total: $1075 billion

Cost of disinflation = $1075 billion/5 percentage points
= $215 billion per percentage point

Table 15-1. Illustration of the cost of disinflation

This table illustrates the cost of reducing the inertial rate of inflation from around 9 percent in 1979 to around 4 percent in 1984. Over that period the inertial rate declined 5 percentage points, while the economy produced $1075 billion less than its potential GNP. Dividing these two figures provides an estimate of $215 billion of output lost per percentage-point reduction in inflation. This figure has been confirmed by numerous statistical studies of the American economy. (Source: Authors' estimates.)

tant issue. In the last decade, many economists argued that the Phillips-curve approach was too pessimistic. The dissenters held that *credible* and publicly announced policies—for example, adopting fixed monetary rules or the gold standard—would lead to a rapid and inexpensive reduction in inflation. These economists backed up their recommendations by citing "regime changes," such as monetary and fiscal reforms, that ended Austrian and Bolivian hyperinflations at relatively low cost in terms of unemployment or lost GNP. Other economists argued that, while such policies might work in countries torn by hyperinflation, war, or revolution, no realistic policy could hope to work miracles in the United States.

The bold experiment of 1980–1984 provided a good laboratory to test the credibility view against the mainstream approach. During this period, monetary policy was tightened in a clear and forceful manner. Yet the price tag was extremely high, as Table 15-1 shows. Using tough, preannounced policies to enhance credibility did not appear effective in lowering the cost.

The finding that it costs the nation $100 to $300 billion per point of inflation reduction provokes different responses from people. Some people ask whether the costs are worth the benefits of lower inflation. Others ask if there are not cheaper ways to lower inflation. These are questions that arise in the design of anti-inflation policies, to which we turn next.

Can We Lower the Natural Rate of Unemployment?

When considering the predicament raised by the conflict between high employment and stable prices, we should first analyze potential labor market policies. This raises the important question: Is the natural rate the optimal level of unemployment? If not, what can we do to lower it toward a more desirable level?

To begin with, we observe that, although it has become common parlance among macroeconomists, the term "natural rate" is misleading. The natural rate is in no way natural; it is influenced by the pattern of demographic change, by the kinds of shocks the economy experiences, by government's labor market policies, and perhaps even by the past history of unemployment itself. Some economists prefer more neutral terms such as the "inflation-safe unemployment rate" or the "non-accelerating-inflation rate of unemployment" or "NAIRU."

Moreover, the natural rate is not necessarily the optimal unemployment rate. The optimal level of unemployment for an economy would come where net economic welfare was maximized. Those who have studied the relationship of unemployment to economic welfare believe that the optimal unemployment rate is lower than the natural rate. They note that there are many spillovers or externalities in the labor market. For example, workers who have been laid off suffer from a variety of social and economic hardships. Yet employers do not pay the costs of unemployment; most of the costs (unemployment insurance, health costs, family distress, etc.) spill over as external costs and are absorbed by the worker or by the government. To the extent that unemployment has external costs, the natural unemployment rate is likely to be higher than the optimal rate.

The natural rate of unemployment is likely to be above the optimal unemployment rate, that is, above that level of unemployment where net economic welfare is maximized.

If the natural rate is neither natural nor optimal, why not simply aim for a lower level of unemployment? The reason is, as we have stressed above, that such a step would lead to rising, and unacceptable, inflation. An enormous social dividend, therefore, would reward the society that discovers how to reduce the natural unemployment rate significantly.

What measures might lower the natural rate? Some important suggestions include the following:

- *Improve labor market services.* Some unemployment occurs because job vacancies are not matched up with unemployed workers. Through better information, such as computerized job lists, the amount of frictional and structural unemployment can be reduced.
- *Bolster government training programs.* If you read the "help wanted" section of your Sunday newspaper, you will find that most of the job vacancies call for skills held by few people. Conversely, most of the unemployed are unskilled or semiskilled workers, or find themselves in the wrong job or in a depressed industry. Many believe that government training programs can help unemployed workers retool for better jobs in growing sectors. If successful, such programs provide the double bonus of allowing people to lead productive lives and of reducing the burden on government transfer programs.
- *Remove government obstacles.* We noted above that, in protecting people from the hardships of unemployment and poverty, the government has at the same time removed the sting of unemployment and reduced incentives to seek work. Some economists call for reforming the unemployment-insurance system; reducing the disincentives for work in welfare, disability, and social security programs; and strengthening work requirements in welfare programs.

Having reviewed the options for reducing the natural unemployment rate, we must add a cautionary note. Three decades of research and labor market experiments on this subject have led objective analysts to be extremely modest in their claims. Short of solutions that force the unemployed to go hungry in the cold, most proposals would probably have minimal effect on the natural rate.

Elimination or Adaptation?

Given the costs of eliminating inflation, and the difficulty of reducing the natural unemployment rate, people often ask whether it is really desirable to eliminate inflation through recession and high unemployment. Wouldn't it be better to learn to live with inflation as the lesser evil as has been done by many countries in Latin America and elsewhere?

One technique for adaptation is to "index" the economy. **Indexing** is a mechanism by which wages, prices, and contracts are partially or wholly compensated for changes in the general price level. Examples of partial indexation are found in many labor contracts which guarantee workers cost-of-living adjustments (or *COLAs*). A typical example would run as follows: Next year a firm will give a worker a 2 percent wage increase if there is no inflation. However, if prices rise 10 percent over the next 12 months, the firm will add another 4 percent as a cost-of-living adjustment. Other sectors that are sometimes indexed include the tax system, rents, and long-term industrial contracts.

Why not index the entire economy? In such a world, inflation would not matter for anything "real," and we could ignore inflation and concentrate on reducing unemployment. This sounds like a good idea, but in practice it has serious drawbacks. Full indexation is impossible because it guarantees a certain level of *real* incomes that may simply not be producible. Moreover, the greater the indexation, the more an inflationary shock will rage through the economy like an epidemic.

A high rate of indexation is like a big multiplier—it amplifies outside price shocks. Full indexation is an invitation to galloping inflation. Adaptation to inflation thus contains a paradox: the more a society insulates its members from inflation, the more unstable inflation is likely to become. Countries that have thoroughly indexed their economies (such as Brazil) have found it virtually impossible to eradicate inflation even through draconian measures.

Wanted: A Low-Cost Anti-inflation Policy

How can nations resolve the dilemma of inflation versus unemployment? Policies that attempt to lower inflation without raising unemployment are sometimes called "incomes policies." **Incomes**

policies are government actions that attempt to moderate inflation by direct steps, whether by verbal persuasion, legal controls, or other incentives. In terms of our economic analysis, they are attempts to shift the Phillips curve inward.

What are some approaches to anti-inflation policies? How successful have they been? Here are some examples:

- *Peacetime wage-price controls* have been used in Scandinavia, the Netherlands, and elsewhere. Although they have sometimes been effective for a short time, in the longer run controls have either blown up or become ineffective because people evaded them. In some cases, such as the United States during 1971–1974, price and wage controls appear to have been totally ineffective in the struggle to slow the wage-price spiral.

- *Voluntary wage-price guidelines* showed some modest success in the Netherlands, and also in the United States during the Kennedy, Johnson, and Carter years. But with time they tended to become ineffective and inequitable—particularly when accompanied by excessively stimulative fiscal and monetary policies that ignited demand-pull price pressures.

- A *market strategy* has been urged by many economists. This approach would rely on the natural discipline of markets to restrain price and wage increases. Advocates emphasize strengthening market forces by deregulation of regulated industries; removing market impediments to competition in perverse antitrust laws and in retail-price maintenance; repealing government laws that inhibit competition such as foreign-trade quotas and minimum-wage laws; banning labor-union monopolies; and above all encouraging international competition. Policies that strengthen market forces may increase the resistance to price and wage increases, particularly in imperfectly competitive labor and product markets.

- *Tax-based incomes policies* (sometimes dubbed "TIP") have been proposed as a way of using the market mechanism to attain macroeconomic objectives. TIP would use fiscal carrots and sticks to encourage anti-inflationary actions by taxing those whose wages and prices are rising rapidly and subsidizing those whose wages and prices are rising slowly. TIP has been used in socialist countries such as Hungary and Poland with some success, and has sometimes been proposed for the United States. Even the enthusiasts of TIP stress, however, that it is a complement and not a substitute for the discipline of the market mechanism and tight fiscal and monetary policies to contain inflation.

The search for an effective and durable incomes policy has not found the Holy Grail. As a thorough study of the subject by Lloyd Ulman and Robert Flanagan summarized:

> Incomes policy, to generalize from the experience of the [seven] countries studied in this account, has not been very successful. [Experience] suggests that in none of the variations so far turned up has incomes policy succeeded in its fundamental objective, as stated, of making full employment consistent with a reasonable degree of price stability.

The Cruel Dilemma

Many economists today think that there is a natural rate of unemployment below which our economies can go only at the risk of spiraling inflation. Moreover, the natural rate of unemployment is often thought to be excessively high. Critics of capitalism find the high unemployment that prevails in North America and Europe to be the central flaw in modern capitalism. The search for a way to resolve the cruel dilemma of needing high unemployment to contain inflation continues to be one of the most pressing concerns of modern macroeconomics.

--------------------- SUMMARY ---------------------

A. Sources of Inflation

1. At any time, an economy has a given *inertial* or expected inflation rate. This is the rate that people have come to anticipate and that is built into labor contracts and other agreements. The inertial rate of inflation can chug along at the same rate each year without a strong tendency to rise or fall.

The inertial rate of inflation is a short-run equilibrium, and persists until the economy is shocked.

2. In reality, the economy receives incessant price shocks. The major kinds of shocks that propel inflation away from its inertial rate are demand-pull and cost-push.

   Demand-pull inflation results from too much spending chasing too few goods, causing the aggregate demand curve to shift up and to the right. Wages and prices then are bid up in markets. *Cost-push* inflation is a new phenomenon of modern industrial economies. It arises when the costs of production rise even in periods of high unemployment and idle capacity. Cost-push pressures dominate when labor unions or businesses exercise market power by raising wages or prices despite high unemployment or excess capacity, or when external factors drive up commodity prices unexpectedly.

B. Modern Inflation Theory

3. The Phillips curve shows the inverse relationship between inflation and unemployment. In the short run, lowering one rate means raising the other. Suppose in a given year the inertial inflation rate is 4 percent and the natural rate of unemployment is 6 percent. If output growth drives unemployment below the natural rate, inflation will rise above the inertial rate, perhaps to an inflation rate of 5 or 6 percent or more. Similarly, if unemployment rises above the natural rate, inflation tends to fall below the inertial rate.

4. But the short-run Phillips curve tends to shift over time as expected inflation and other factors change. If inflation persists above the expected or inertial inflation rate, the expected inflation rate itself rises. If policymakers attempt to hold unemployment below the natural rate for long periods, inflation will tend to spiral upward.

5. Modern inflation theory relies on the concept of the natural rate of unemployment. The natural unemployment rate is the lowest sustainable rate that the nation can enjoy without risking an upward spiral of inflation. It represents the level of unemployment of resources at which labor and product markets are in inflationary balance.

6. Under the natural-rate theory, there is no permanent tradeoff between unemployment and inflation, and the long-run Phillips curve is vertical.

7. While many macroeconomists accept the natural-rate theory, it leaves many questions unanswered, such as the reasons for the upward drift in unemployment rates in Europe over the last two decades. The natural rate of unemployment is estimated to be between $5\frac{1}{2}$ and 6 percent in the United States today. The upward creep in the natural rate came from a mixture of demographic trends, changes in social policies, and increases in structural unemployment.

C. Dilemmas of Anti-inflation Policy

8. A central concern for policymakers is the cost of reducing inertial inflation—i.e., what are the costs of disinflation? Current estimates indicate that a substantial recession—reducing GNP by \$100 to \$300 billion below

its potential for 1 year—is necessary to slow inertial inflation by 1 percentage point.

9. Economists have put forth many proposals for lowering the natural unemployment rate; notable proposals include improving labor market information, improving education and training programs, and refashioning government programs so that workers have greater incentives to work. Sober analysis of politically viable proposals leads most economists to expect only small improvements from such labor market reforms.

10. Because of the high costs of reducing inflation through recessions, nations have often looked for other approaches. These are incomes policies such as wage-price controls and voluntary guidelines, tax-based approaches, and market-strengthening strategies. In the end, no economy has succeeded in maintaining full employment, stable prices, and free markets. The dilemma of anti-inflation policy remains.

CONCEPTS FOR REVIEW

Causes and theories of inflation
inertial inflation
sources of shock to inflation
   (demand-pull and cost-push)
short-run and long-run Phillips curves
natural rate of unemployment and
   the long-run Phillips curve

boom cycle, austerity cycle,
   Phillips-curve loops
natural vs. optimal rate of
   unemployment

Anti-inflation policy
costs of disinflation

indexing, COLA adjustments
measures to lower the natural
   rate of unemployment
incomes policies: wage-price
   controls and guidelines,
   competition, TIP

QUESTIONS FOR DISCUSSION

1. "Unemployment in the steel industry is 9 percent in 1991, yet wage rates in the steel industry are rising at 6 percent per year." Show that this is cost-push and not demand-pull inflation in the labor market. What reasons might exist for this phenomenon?

2. What is a short-run Phillips curve? What is on its horizontal axis? On its vertical axis? What can cause the short-run Phillips curve to shift up or down?

3. The data on the right describe inflation and unemployment in the United States in the 1980s.

    Note that the economy started out near the natural rate of unemployment in 1979 and ended near the natural rate in 1990. Can you explain the decline of inflation over these years? Do so by drawing the short-run and long-run Phillips curves for each of the years from 1979 to 1990.

4. Many economists argue as follows: "Because there is no long-run tradeoff between unemployment and inflation, there is no point in trying to shave the peaks and troughs from the business cycle." Does this view suggest that we should not care whether

Year	Unemployment rate (%)	Inflation rate, CPI (% per year)
1979	5.8	11.3
1980	7.1	13.5
1981	7.6	10.3
1982	9.7	6.2
1983	9.6	3.2
1984	7.5	4.3
1985	7.2	3.6
1986	7.0	1.9
1987	6.2	3.6
1988	5.5	4.1
1989	5.3	4.8
1990	5.5	5.4

Source: *Economic Report of the President*, 1991.

the economy is stable or fluctuating widely as long as the average level of unemployment is the same? Would you agree?

5. Is unemployment above or below the natural rate

today? What are the arguments for leaving the unemployment rate where it is? For moving it toward the natural rate? How do you resolve these two views?

6. A leading economist has written: "If you think back to our discussion of the social costs of inflation, at least of moderate inflation, it is hard to avoid coming away with the impression that they are minor compared with the costs of unemployment and depressed production." Write a short essay describing your views on this issue.

7. What is the natural rate of unemployment? Why is it not zero? Why is it so high in the United States? What would you expect the natural rate to be in a country like Japan, which has a "lifetime employment system," a kind of job tenure for most of its workers?

8. Can the government set policies that will put the actual unemployment rate below the natural rate for a year or two? For several decades?

9. The following policies and phenomena affected labor markets during the 1980s. Explain the likely effect of each on the natural rate of unemployment:

(a) The minimum wage fell 40 percent relative to the average wage rate.

(b) Unemployment insurance became subject to taxation.

(c) Funds for training programs for unemployed workers were cut sharply by the federal government.

(d) Because of high cyclical unemployment, many minority-group teenagers received little on-the-job training.

(e) Because of the decline of labor unions, a smaller fraction of the work force operated under 3-year collective bargaining agreements.

10. Examine the data on inflation and unemployment in question 3. Plot a series of short-run Phillips curves along with a long-run Phillips curve that might be consistent with that data.

11. Incomes policies are attempts to shift the Phillips curve in a favorable direction. Choose two examples of incomes policies given in the text. For each, describe the policy and show how it might affect the short-run and the long-run Phillips curves.

12. Consider the following anti-inflation policies: high unemployment, wage and price controls, and tax-based incomes policies. For each, list the advantages and disadvantages in terms of inflation control and other economic objectives. Which would you choose if the President asked for your recommendation?

CHAPTER   16

FISCAL POLICY, DEFICITS,
AND THE GOVERNMENT DEBT

The only good budget is a balanced budget.

Adam Smith of Glasgow (1776)

The only good rule is that the budget should never be balanced—
except for an instant when a surplus to curb inflation is being
altered to a deficit to fight recession.

Warren Smith of Ann Arbor (1965)

Since the American Revolution, the federal government of the United States has generally balanced its fiscal budget. Heavy military spending during wartime has customarily been financed by borrowing, so the government debt tended to soar in wartime. In peacetime, the government would pay off some of the debt, and the debt burden would shrink.

This pattern changed during the 1980s. The Reagan administration pursued a new economic philosophy that emphasized reducing taxes while sharply increasing America's military spending. Balancing the budget was sacrificed for other objectives, and the federal budget deficit soared to over $200 billion a year in the mid-1980s. The government debt grew from $660 billion when President Reagan was inaugurated to nearly $2000 bil-

lion when he left office in 1989. The policies of the Reagan period marked a turning point in America's fiscal history, leading to a struggle to contain the deficit that has lasted well into the 1990s.

What were the causes of the surging deficits in the 1980s? How did the large deficits affect the economy's pattern of investing and saving? Did government deficits "crowd out" investment? And what will be the long-lasting impact of the government debt upon economic growth? We will consider these crucial questions in this chapter.

Figure 16-1 shows the topics to be analyzed in this chapter. We begin with an analysis of the major institutional features of government budgeting and then survey the economic effects of deficits and the government debt.

A. Budgets and Fiscal Policy

Basic Definitions

Governments use budgets to control and record their fiscal affairs. A **budget** shows, for a given year, the planned expenditures of government programs and the expected revenues from tax systems. The budget typically contains a list of specific programs (education, welfare, defense, etc.), as well as tax sources (individual income tax, social-insurance taxes, etc.).

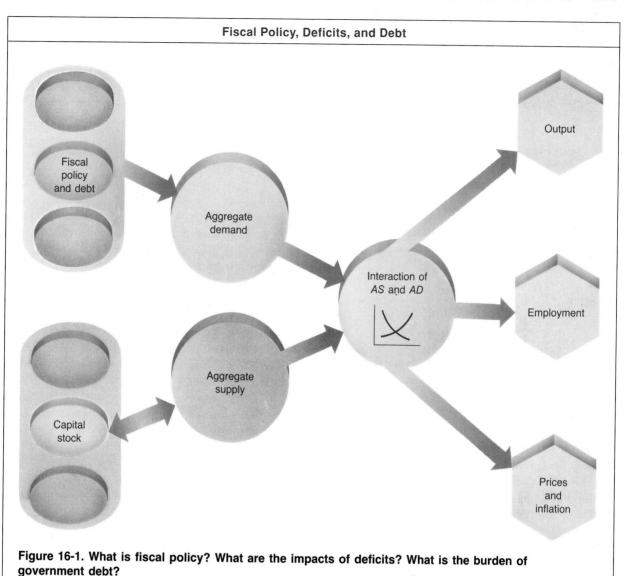

Figure 16-1. What is fiscal policy? What are the impacts of deficits? What is the burden of government debt?

This chapter explores the economic impact of fiscal policy, deficits, and government debt. Note how the causal arrows point both toward and away from the capital stock, reminding us that fiscal policies leave a significant mark on investment, capital, and economic growth.

In a given year, budgets are generally out of balance. A **budget surplus** occurs when all taxes and other revenues exceed government expenditures. A **budget deficit** is incurred when expenditures exceed taxes. When revenues and expenditures are equal during a given period, the government has a **balanced budget.**

As an example, consider President Bush's budget for fiscal year 1992. Submitted to Congress in February 1991, the proposal outlines taxes and expen-

ditures for the 1992 fiscal year (October 1, 1991, to September 30, 1992). Bush's budget called for receipts of $1165 billion and expenditures of $1446 billion. The planned deficit was $281 billion.

When the government incurs a budget deficit, it must borrow from the public to pay its bills. To borrow, the government issues bonds, which are IOUs that promise to pay money at some time in the future. The **government debt** (sometimes called the public debt) consists of the total or accumulated borrowings by the government; it is the total dollar value of government bonds owned by the public (households, banks, businesses, foreigners, and other non-federal entities). In the pages that follow, we will study the impact of government deficits and debt upon the economy.

The Making of Fiscal Policy

Many early enthusiasts of the simple Keynesian multiplier analysis believed that fiscal policy was the philosopher's stone, the answer to prayers for curbing business cycles. If unemployment strikes, simply raise spending or cut taxes; if inflation threatens, do the opposite. Today, no one holds such naively optimistic views about banishing the business cycle to the history books. Business cycles are still with us, and fiscal policy works better in theory than in practice.

By *fiscal policy*, we mean the process of shaping taxation and public expenditure in order (a) to help dampen the swings of the business cycle, and (b) to contribute to the maintenance of a growing, high-employment economy, free from high or volatile inflation.

Suppose the economic system in a particular year is threatened with a deep and prolonged recession. What action might people call for? The Federal Reserve might use monetary policy to try to stimulate investment. Additionally, Congress and the President might alter fiscal policy, changing tax and public expenditure programs to help reach their output and inflation targets. Alternatively, if inflation is unacceptably high, Congress might raise tax rates and trim expenditure programs, or the Federal Reserve might reduce the growth of the money supply and raise interest rates.

In summary:

Fiscal policies dealing with taxes and public expenditure, in cooperation with monetary policies, have as their goals rapid economic growth with high employment and stable prices.

Automatic Stabilizers

You might get the impression that fiscal policy requires round-the-clock vigilance by the government. In fact, the modern fiscal system has inherent *automatic stabilizing properties.* All through the day and night, whether or not Congress is in session, taxes and spending are stabilizing the economy. If a recession gets under way, powerful automatic forces will instantly begin to counter the economic slowdown.

What are these automatic stabilizers? They are primarily the following:

- *Automatic changes in tax receipts.* Our federal tax system depends on progressive personal and corporate income taxes. (Progressive taxes are those for which the average tax rate rises as income rises.) How does progressive taxation ensure stability? As soon as income begins to fall off, even if Congress makes no change in tax rates, the government tax receipts decline. Today, for each $10 billion drop in GNP, total federal tax receipts drop by about $3\frac{1}{2}$ billion.

Why are such tax changes useful? They may be the right medicine for an unexpected change in the economy. If output drops, tax receipts will automatically fall so that personal incomes and spending will be cushioned; output will not fall as much as it otherwise would have. In inflationary times, an increase in tax revenues will lower personal income, dampen consumption spending, reduce aggregate demand, and slow the upward spiral of prices and wages.

A century ago, economists thought that stability of tax revenue was a good thing; they felt that taxes should be invariant to business conditions. From a macroeconomic point of view, exactly the opposite is true. We are fortunate, therefore, that our present tax system possesses a high degree of automatic flexibility, with receipts tending to rise in inflationary times and to fall in times of recession. This is a powerful factor stabilizing the economy and moderating the business cycle.

- *Unemployment insurance, welfare, and other transfers.* The modern welfare state has an elaborate system of transfer payments that are designed to supplement incomes and relieve economic hardship. An important example is unemployment insurance (UI). Soon after employees are laid off, they begin to receive UI; when they go back to work, the payments cease. Thus UI pumps funds into or out of the economy in a countercyclical, stabilizing way. Similar features are seen in other income-support programs such as food stamps, aid to families with dependent children, and Medicaid.

Limitations of Automatic Stabilizers

Automatic stabilizers are a first line of defense but are not by themselves sufficient to maintain full stability. To see why, consider the example of taxes.

Recall that in the multiplier model, a shock to spending (in, say, investment, net exports, or government spending) will have a multiplied impact on output. However, the automatic tendency for taxes to take away a fraction of each extra dollar of income reduces the size of the multiplier. But the impact of the shock will be *reduced*, not completely eliminated. Say the *MPC* in the economy without taxes is 0.9; here the multiplier would be 10. If taxes took one-third of all income, then the multiplier would be reduced to $2\frac{1}{2}$. Instead of disturbances having their effects on GNP multiplied 10 times, because of the automatic stabilizing effect of taxes, the impact would be much smaller.[1]

Automatic stabilizers act to reduce business-cycle fluctuations in part, but they cannot wipe out 100 percent of the disturbance. Whether to reduce the balance of a disturbance, and how, remains the task of discretionary monetary and fiscal policy.

Discretionary Stabilization Policy

Even after automatic stabilizers have done their job, fluctuations in economic activity remain. In the United States today, short-run economic stabilization is handled primarily through monetary policy. (Recall our discussion in Chapter 11 of how money affects economic activity.)

In addition, at certain times, governments use discretionary fiscal policy to combat business cycles. A *discretionary fiscal policy* is one in which the government changes tax rates or spending programs. In contrast to automatic stabilizers, discretionary policies generally involve passing legislation to change the structure of the fiscal system. The principal weapons of discretionary fiscal policy are public works, other capital programs, public-employment projects, and changes in tax rates.

---

[1] The partial stabilizing effect can be illustrated as follows: Assume that without any taxes, government, foreign sector, etc., the *MPC* is $\frac{9}{10}$; this implies that the multiplier is 10. Now assume that $33\frac{1}{3}$ percent of any additional income is taxed away, so for every dollar of increase in GNP, $\$\frac{1}{3}$ goes to taxes and $\$\frac{2}{3}$ goes to disposable income (*DI*). And of the $\$\frac{2}{3}$ going to *DI*, 90 percent (or 60 cents of the original dollar) is spent. The multiplier is now only 2.5.

Public Works. When governments first searched for ways to counteract depressions, they often relied on public investment projects to create jobs for the unemployed. Some public-works investments, such as rural electrification, proved enormously beneficial to underdeveloped areas. Others, such as raking leaves, were no more than inefficient "make-work" projects that produced little of value.

Planners realize that it takes a long time to start a post office or implement a road-building or pollution-abatement program. Plans must be made; blueprints drawn; land acquired by purchase or court condemnation; buildings razed; new structures built.

It may be years before a significant part of the funds is spent and people are employed. Given the difficulty of forecasting more than a year or two into the future, we might find that the antirecession public-works project is just coming on stream as the economy is recovering from the recession and inflation is heating up. Today, the economic impacts of countercyclical programs are well understood and seldom relied upon to combat recessions.

Public-Employment Projects. At the other extreme from highly capital-intensive, long-duration public-works projects are public-employment projects. These programs are designed to hire unemployed workers for periods of a year or so, after which people can move to regular jobs in the private sector. Public jobs avoid one of the major shortcomings of public-works projects; they can be started up and phased out very quickly. Critics find them wasteful, citing that the projects are often of secondary importance. In addition, the transition from special public jobs to regular jobs has been a rocky one; most studies indicate that getting a public-employment job does not markedly improve one's chances of holding a regular private-sector job later.

Variation of Tax Rates. A third approach to discretionary fiscal policy is to cut income-tax rates temporarily in order to keep disposable incomes from falling and to prevent a decline from snowballing into a deep recession. Varying tax rates can be used to either stimulate or restrain an economy.

Many advocates of discretionary stabilization policy see varying tax rates as the ideal weapon. Once taxes have been changed, consumers react

and tightening of credit will tend to choke off or "crowd out" investment and other interest-sensitive spending.[5]

How does this chain of events relate to deficits? Our example assumes that there is a discretionary increase in G or cut in T, implying that the structural deficit is increased. This analysis shows that budget deficits may crowd out investment through the workings of monetary policy and financial markets.

Crowding out occurs in the short run when the effectiveness of fiscal policy is reduced by money market reactions. An increase in the structural deficit, through tax cuts or higher government spending, will tend to raise interest rates and therefore lower investment. Thus some of the induced increase in GNP may be offset as the higher structural deficit crowds out investment.

Crowding Out from Structural Deficits. Crowding out is primarily concerned with the effects of structural rather than cyclical deficits. If the deficit rises because of a recession (a cyclical deficit), the logic of crowding out simply does not apply. Why not? Because a recession causes a *decline* in the demand for money and leads to *lower* interest rates. The relationship between deficits, interest rates, and investment during recessions shows why there is no automatic crowding out of investment by higher deficits.

Impact of Structural Deficits

What is the impact of higher structural deficits on investment? Most macroeconomists agree that at least some investment is crowded out by government deficits. However, they debate about *how much* investment is reduced. Is investment reduced by only a small fraction of the government deficit? Or by virtually the whole amount?

Complete Crowding Out. At one extreme is a case of complete crowding out of investment by govern-

[5] Recall that tight money will lead to a reduction in spending in a wide variety of interest-sensitive sectors, including business investment, housing, consumption spending on consumer durables, net exports, and capital items of state and local governments. In the discussion that follows, we will examine the impact on "investment," but keep in mind that these other components of spending are just as important.

ment spending when the monetary reaction is powerful. Suppose that the Federal Reserve determines that any rise in output would be inflationary. The Fed therefore boosts interest rates to curb investment. If the Fed has an output target, then the effect will be to crowd out investment 100 percent.[6]

This case is illustrated in Figure 16-3, which employs a Keynesian-cross diagram. The solid $C + I + G + X$ line shows the situation before any government spending increase, with an equilibrium at E. Next the government enacts a spending program, increasing government spending on goods and services from G to G'. As a result, we have the new $C + I + G' + X$ line. If there were no monetary reaction, GNP would rise from Q to Q'.

However, because of the monetary reaction, in-

[6] The next chapter will show that this case also holds for the strict "monetarist" world where the demand for money is completely inelastic with respect to interest rates.

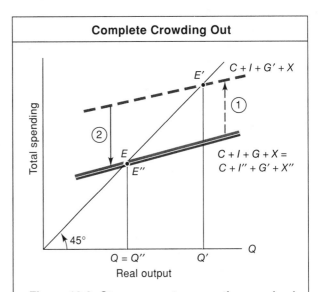

Complete Crowding Out

Figure 16-3. Strong monetary reaction can lead to complete crowding out

Crowding out can occur when the Federal Reserve moves to offset the impact of fiscal expansions through monetary tightening. In step **1**, an increase in government spending on goods and services shifts upward the $C + I + G + X$ line to $C + I + G' + X$. The monetary reaction in step **2** raises interest rates and lowers interest-sensitive components, leading to $C + I'' + G' + X''$ and a new equilibrium at E'', which is identical to the initial equilibrium at E. In this case, investment and net exports have been 100 percent crowded out by government spending.

terest rates rise and reduce investment and net exports. Indeed, the reaction is so powerful that the new spending line is $C + I'' + G' + X''$, with a new equilibrium (E''), which is exactly at the old equilibrium (E).

What has happened? As the fiscal policy stimulated the economy, monetary policy tightened and interest rates rose; business cut back on capital projects, and the rising exchange rate on the dollar reduced exports and increased imports. In the end interest rates had to rise by enough to reduce investment and net exports by just the amount of the G increase. *Hence, in the polar case of a strong monetary response, investment is 100 percent crowded out by an increase in government spending.*

Investment Encouragement. At the other extreme is a situation where, in the short run, investment is actually *encouraged* (or "crowded in") by larger deficits. This point of view runs as follows: We have seen that high interest rates discourage investment. On the other hand, investment is boosted by higher GNP because businesses need to buy more plant and equipment as their current plant and equipment are more intensively used. This reasoning suggests that investment might actually increase if output is stimulated by fiscal policy when productive capacity is underutilized.

This case is illustrated in Figure 16-4. This diagram differs from our earlier analyses because the investment curve is drawn as *upward-sloping* rather than horizontal. The positive slope signifies that investment rises with higher GNP because of the capacity effect. In addition, we assume that there is no monetary effect, so there is no interest-rate impact of the kind shown in Figure 16-3. In this example, equilibrium occurs where the total spending line (the $C + I + G + X$ line) intersects the 45° line.

What is the effect of higher G in this case? As fiscal policy raises spending from G to G', the spending line shifts upward to the new aggregate spending line, and the equilibrium level of output increases from Q to Q'. But the higher level of output induces higher investment, and investment increases from I to I' in Figure 16-4, so the final equilibrium is shown by $C + I' + G' + X$. *Investment is encouraged and ends up higher than it was before the fiscal expansion.* We conclude that in an underemployed economy a fiscal expansion with accom-

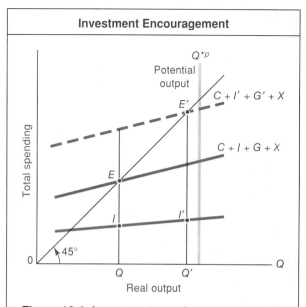

Figure 16-4. Investment may be encouraged if there are unemployed resources

Investment may be encouraged by higher deficits when there are unutilized resources and when investment responds to higher output. An increase in G shifts up the $C + I + G + X$ curve. Equilibrium output rises from Q to Q'. But because investment responds positively to the higher level of output, I increases as a result of the higher government spending.

modating monetary policy may actually raise investment.

Empirical Evidence

Such are the theories. Which of these extremes is closer to actual experience? History provides no clear-cut answer. During the 1960s, fiscal expansions appear to have encouraged investment, partly because there were ample unutilized resources and partly because the Federal Reserve allowed the economy to expand without raising interest rates.

The earlier pattern reversed during the 1980s as higher government deficits brought about a sharp monetary response, which led to a decline in net exports and private investment. The actual pattern of saving and investment for the 1980s is given in Table 16-3. The historical record shows two major conclusions. First, personal saving did not rise to offset the lower public saving; personal saving fell despite lower tax rates and higher post-tax real returns on saving.

Impact of Deficits on Saving and Investment, 1979–1986			
Sector	1979	1986	Change
Gross saving (as % of GNP):			
Personal	4.7	2.9	−1.8
Business	13.1	13.9	0.8
Government			
Federal	−0.6	−4.9	−4.3
State and local	1.1	1.3	0.2
Gross investment (as % of GNP):			
Private investment			
Residential housing	5.5	5.1	−0.4
Business	12.6	10.6	−2.0
Net foreign investment			
(net exports)	0.1	−2.5	−2.6

Table 16-3. Increase in fiscal deficit produced surprising results

The increase in deficits of the 1980s provided a laboratory for different macroeconomic theories. From 1979 to 1986, the federal government deficits (or dissaving) increased from 0.6 percent to 4.9 percent of GNP. What was the impact upon private saving and investment? The public dissaving was, surprisingly, reinforced rather than offset by lower personal saving.

In terms of investment, a small part of the decline in total saving was reflected in residential housing; the share of business investment declined modestly. The largest part of the investment decline came in net foreign investment. (Source: U.S. Department of Commerce.)

The second and surprising result came when there was a sharp decline in net exports (or net foreign investment). The higher interest rates after 1979 led to an appreciation of the dollar, which in turn led to higher imports and lower exports and depressed real net exports from a surplus of $4 billion in 1979 to a deficit of $130 billion in 1986.[7]

What can we conclude about the extent of crowding out? The events of the last decade con-

[7] We cannot say, however, that the increase in the federal deficit *caused* the changes in personal saving, business investment, and net foreign investment. To make that claim without showing the causal linkage would be to commit the *post hoc, ergo propter hoc* fallacy. While many analysts believe that the change in the federal deficit was the major force causing the changes shown in Table 16-3, other forces—such as the tight monetary policies of 1979–1982 and the debt crisis after 1982— also exerted important influences on saving and investment during this period.

firm the views of those who argue that monetary policy and financial-market reactions tend largely to offset or crowd out the impact of government spending. It is important to note, however, that the extent of the crowding out depends on the stance of the Federal Reserve; an aggressive anti-inflation Fed will produce more crowding out than a complacent and accommodative central bank. Because the link between deficits and investment is so complex—involving savings behavior, the foreign sector, financial markets, and monetary policy—it is difficult to predict which route crowding out will follow in the next fiscal expansion.

Government Debt and Economic Growth

We turn now from the short-run impact of government deficits to the longer-run issue of how government debt affects economic growth. Will the high public debt lower future living standards for the average American? This question raises three specific issues: the difficulties of servicing a large external debt, the inefficiencies of levying taxes to pay interest on the debt, and the diminished economic growth that occurs when a large debt displaces capital accumulation.

External vs. Internal Debt

The first distinction to be made is between an internal and an external debt. An *internal debt* is owed by a nation to its own citizens. Many argue that an internal debt poses no burden because "we owe it all to ourselves." While this statement is oversimplified, it does represent a genuine insight. If every citizen owned $10,000 of government bonds and all were equally liable for the taxes to service that debt, it would not make sense to think of a heavy load of debt that each citizen must carry; the citizens simply owe the debt to themselves.

An *external debt* is owed by a nation to foreigners. This debt does involve a net subtraction from the resources available to people in the debtor nation. In the 1980s, many nations experienced severe economic hardships after they incurred large external debts. They were forced to export more than they imported—to run trade surpluses—in order to "service their external debts," that is, to pay the interest and principal on their past borrowings. In the late 1980s, countries like Brazil and Mexico needed to set aside one-fourth to one-third of export earnings to service their external debts. The debt-service burden on an external debt represents a reduction in the consumption possibilities of a nation.

In the late 1980s, the United States joined the list of debtor countries. Its large external deficit (large negative net exports) turned the United States from a creditor nation to a debtor nation. By 1990, the United States owed over $400 billion to foreigners. How will this affect the U.S. economy? The United States must eventually generate positive net exports, or run a trade surplus, to pay the interest on its foreign loans; it will need to export many billions of dollars more in aircraft, food, and other goods than it imports. The difficulties of making this adjustment will be studied in the final chapters of this text.

Efficiency Losses from Taxation

An internal debt requires payments of interest to bondholders, and taxes must be levied for this purpose. But even if the same people were taxed to pay the same amounts they receive in interest, there would still be the *distorting effects on incentives* that are inescapably present in the case of any taxes. Taxing Paula's interest income or wages to pay Paula interest would introduce microeconomic distortions. Paula might work less and save less; either of these outcomes must be reckoned a distortion of efficiency and well-being.

Displacement of Capital

Perhaps the most serious consequence of a large public debt is that it displaces capital from the nation's stock of wealth. As a result, the pace of economic growth slows and future living standards will decline.

What is the mechanism by which debt affects capital? Recall from our earlier discussion that people accumulate wealth for a variety of purposes such as retirement, education, and housing. People save by purchasing different assets, such as houses, stocks and bonds of corporations, savings accounts, and government bonds. We can separate the assets into two piles: (*a*) government debt and (*b*) assets that ultimately represent ownership of

the stock of private capital and other durable goods. The effect of government debt is this:

As the government debt grows, people will accumulate government debt instead of private capital, and the nation's private capital stock will be displaced by public debt.

To illustrate this point, suppose that people desire to hold exactly 1000 units of wealth for retirement and other purposes. As the government debt increases, people's holdings of other assets will be reduced dollar for dollar. This occurs because as the government sells its bonds, other assets must be reduced since total desired wealth holdings are fixed. But these other assets ultimately represent the stock of private capital; stocks, bonds, and mortgages are the counterpart of factories, equipment, and houses. In this example, if the government debt goes up 100 units, we would see that people's holdings of capital and other private assets fall by 100 units. This is the case of 100 percent displacement (which is the long-run analog of 100 percent crowding out).

Full displacement is unlikely to hold in practice. In the discussion below, we will use supply-and-demand analysis to demonstrate that a higher government debt will produce higher interest rates and may stimulate higher levels of accumulation to accommodate part of the higher debt. In an open economy, the country may borrow abroad rather than reduce its domestic capital stock. The exact amount of displacement will depend on the conditions of production and on the savings behavior of domestic households and foreigners.

A Geometric Analysis.[8] The process by which the stock of capital is displaced in the long run is illustrated in Figure 16-5. In the left panel we show the supply and demand for capital as a function of the real interest rate or return on capital. As interest rates rise, firms demand less capital, while individuals may want to supply more. The equilibrium shown is for a capital stock of 4000 units with a real interest rate of 4 percent.

Now say that the government debt rises from 0 to 1000—because of war, recession, supply-side fiscal policies, or some other reason. We can analyze the impact of the increase in debt in the right-hand

---

[8] The balance of the discussion of displacement is somewhat more technical and can be omitted in short courses.

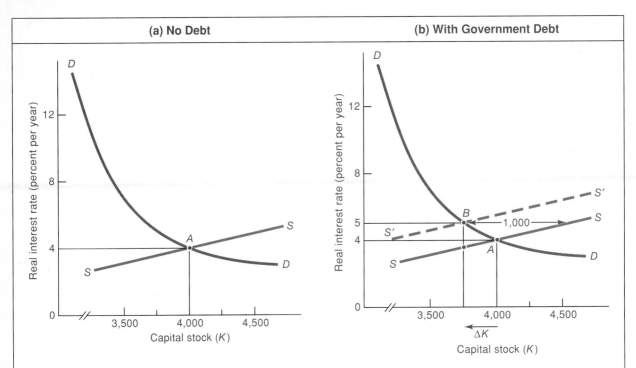

Figure 16-5. Government debt displaces private capital

Firms demand capital, while households supply capital by saving in private and public assets. The demand curve is the downward-sloping business demand for *K*, while the supply curve is the upward-sloping household supply of *K*.

Panel **(a)** shows the equilibrium without government debt. *K* is 4000 and the real interest rate is 4 percent.

Panel **(b)** shows the impact of 1000 units of government debt. The government debt will be sold off for what it will yield, so government securities are the bedrock of households' portfolios. Thus the curve showing the *net*

supply of *K* shifts to the left by the 1000 units of the government debt. The new equilibrium arises northwest along the demand-for-*K* curve, moving from point *A* to point *B*. The interest rate is higher, firms are discouraged from holding *K*, and the capital stock falls.

In the long run, the 1000 units of government debt displace 250 units of society's capital stock, and output is therefore smaller. (These numbers are hypothetical for we do not know the extent to which public debt displaces private capital.)

diagram of Figure 16-5. This figure shows the 1000-unit increase in debt as a shift in the supply-of-capital (or *SS*) curve. As depicted, the households' supply-of-capital schedule shifts 1000 units to the left, to *S′S′*.

We represent an increase in government debt as a leftward shift in the households' supply-of-capital schedule. To see why, note that, because the *SS* curve represents the amount of capital that people willingly hold at each interest rate, the capital holdings are equal to the total wealth holdings minus the holdings of government debt. Since the amount of government debt (or assets other than capital) rises by 1000 and the government debt must be sold, the amount of private capital that people can buy after they own the 1000 units of government debt is 1000 less than total wealth at each interest

rate. Therefore, if *SS* represents the total wealth held by people, *S′S′* (equal to *SS* less 1000) represents the total amount of capital held by people. In short, after 1000 units of government debt are sold, the new supply-of-capital schedule is *S′S′*.[9]

What is the net impact of a 1000-unit increase in government debt? As the supply of capital dries up—with national saving going into government

---

[9] An argument by Robert Barro of Harvard suggests that because of future taxes, government bonds may not be net wealth for the nation. For every dollar of government bonds there is an equal present value of taxes for which taxpayers are liable now or in the future. If people are very farsighted and take their heirs' well-being into account, then they may reduce their consumption by just the present value of taxes—completely offsetting the wealth effect of the bonds. In such a case, there will be no shift in the supply curve of Fig. 16-5(b).

bonds rather than into housing or into companies' stocks and bonds—the market equilibrium moves northwest along the demand-for-K curve. Interest rates rise. Firms slow their purchases of new factories, trucks, and computers.

In the new long-run equilibrium, the capital stock falls from 4000 to 3750. Thus, in this example, 1000 units of government debt have displaced 250 units of private capital. Such a reduction has significant economic effects, of course. With less capital, potential output, wages, and the nation's income are lower than they would otherwise be.

The diagram shown in Figure 16-5 is purely hypothetical. How large is the displacement effect in reality? Does the $2484 billion of government debt at the beginning of fiscal 1992 displace $2484 billion of capital? Or $1000 billion? Or none? And what fraction of the additional government debt will be held by foreigners?

In fact, there are no accurate estimates of the displacement effect. Looking at historical trends, particularly in the United States since World War II, the best evidence suggests that capital is partially displaced by government debt. It is clear, however, that the possibility of capital displacement is extraordinarily important for the United States as the debt continues to climb in the next few years.

Debt and Growth

If we consider all the effects of government debt on the economy, we see that a large public debt can be detrimental to long-run economic growth. Figure 16-6 illustrates this connection. Say that an economy were to operate over time with no debt. According to the principles of economic growth outlined in Chapter 12, the capital stock and potential output would follow the hypothetical path indicated by the solid lines in Figure 16-6.

Next consider policies that incur a large government deficit and debt. As the debt accumulates over time, more and more capital is displaced, as shown by the dashed capital line in the bottom of Figure 16-6. As taxes are raised to pay interest on the debt, inefficiencies further lower output. Also, an increase in external debt lowers national income and raises the fraction of national output that has to be set aside for servicing the external debt. Taking all the effects together, output and consumption will grow more slowly than they would had there been no large government debt and defi-

cit, as is shown by comparing the top lines in Figure 16-6.

This is the major point about the long-run impact of a large government debt on economic growth:

A large government debt tends to reduce a nation's growth in potential output because it displaces private capital, increases the inefficiency from taxation, and forces a nation to service the external portion of the debt.

A New Discipline?

We have seen that modern macroeconomics has destroyed the shibboleth of the balanced budget. But this does not mean that government can go wild and let legislators' pet projects gobble up an ever-increasing portion of the national pie. Resources are limited, so some new discipline must replace the budget-balancing maxim.

Many people, particularly conservatives, believe that Congress lacks the self-control to prevent the continued growth of transfer programs and public

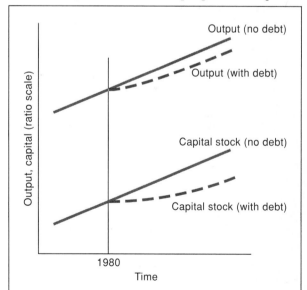

Figure 16-6. Impact of government debt on economic growth

Solid lines show the path of capital and output if the government balances its books and has no debt.

A more realistic case occurs when the government incurs a large debt. As private capital is displaced by public debt, the nation's capital stock stagnates, and the nation must pay interest on foreign holdings of its external debt. The dashed lines illustrate the impact on capital and output of the higher government debt.

works. Fiscal conservatives called for a constitutional amendment to balance the budget and contain the growth in federal spending. A dramatic turn came when Congress passed the *Gramm-Rudman Act*, which mandated a decline in the budget deficit. This bill required Congress to reduce the deficit to no more than a specified dollar amount each year and targeted a balanced budget by 1991. If Congress was unable to meet the quantitative Gramm-Rudman target, expenditures would be automatically cut across the board.

The Gramm-Rudman bill went into effect in late 1985 but the ambitious targets were not met. Congress responded by amending the bill in 1987, and in 1990 replaced the deficit targets with spending limitations in different parts of the budget. Under the 1990 amendments, Congress must find the revenues to pay for new spending programs or tax cuts; otherwise, automatic spending cuts will be imposed to offset the increased deficit.[10]

What has been the impact of the Gramm-Rudman approach? It does provide a kind of "budget constraint" on the federal government. Moreover, the process has imposed a new budgetary discipline, albeit a somewhat imperfect one, on the federal budget. While the budget is not balanced, the ratio of the federal deficit to GNP has declined. Moreover, new programs cannot be introduced without budgeting new taxes or spending cuts. But any rule legislated by Congress can be changed by Congress, so the future of this self-imposed discipline is uncertain.

Valediction

As we end our discussion of the government debt and its impact on economic growth, we should

[10] The budget procedures appear in the 1990 Omnibus Budget Reconciliation Act. A description of new procedures along with an analysis in terms of modern public finance theory is contained in the *Economic Report of the President*, 1991.

pause to reflect upon the fiscal difficulties faced by the United States. Those who study economics or make economic policies in the 1990s will confront the need to service a large external debt and the possibility of sluggish economic growth. But in the midst of today's tempest, keep in mind the observations on growth and debt of the English historian Lord Macaulay, written more than a century ago:

> At every stage in the growth of that debt, the nation has set up the same cry of anguish and despair. At every stage in the growth of that debt, it has been seriously asserted by wise men that bankruptcy and ruin were at hand. Yet still the debt went on growing; and still bankruptcy and ruin were as remote as ever. . . .
>
> The prophets of evil were under a double delusion. They erroneously imagined that there was an exact analogy between the case of an individual who is in debt to another individual and the case of a society which is in debt to a part of itself. . . . They made no allowance for the effect produced by the incessant progress of every experimental science, and by the incessant efforts of every man to get on in life. They saw that the debt grew; and they forgot that other things grew as well.

What can Macaulay teach us for the 1990s? We can hardly doubt that high fiscal deficits are producing an unprecedented growth in peacetime debt in the United States. Because much of the debt is flowing abroad to finance a large trade deficit, the nation will face rising interest payments, debt burdens, and taxes to service the debt. At some point, the trade deficit will have to turn to a surplus as we export our future production to pay for current consumption. It is possible that the transition from today's low-saving economy to a high-saving economy may be accompanied by reductions in living standards for consumers.

But it would be unwise to forecast economic collapse. The specter of national bankruptcy or financial ruin is remote for the United States in the 1990s.

SUMMARY

A. Budgets and Fiscal Policy

1. Budgets are systems used by governments and organizations to indicate planned expenditures and revenues for a given year. Budgets are in surplus or deficit depending on whether the government has revenues greater or less than its expenditures.

2. Fiscal policy refers to taxation and expenditure policies. In this connection, the modern economy is blessed with important "built-in stabilizers." Requiring no discretionary action, tax receipts change automatically when income changes, reducing the multiplier and offsetting part of any disturbance. The same stabilizing effect is produced by unemployment compensation and other welfare transfers that grow automatically as income falls.

3. Automatic stabilizers never fully offset the instabilities of an economy. They reduce the multiplier, but do not make it zero. Scope is left for discretionary programs. Discretionary policies include public works, jobs programs, and various tax programs. Public works involve such long time lags in getting under way as to make their use for combating short recessions impractical. Discretionary variations in tax rates offer greater short-run flexibility but suffer from severe political complications in the United States. Most macroeconomists believe that monetary policy is more useful than fiscal policy for combating the short-term fluctuations of the business cycle.

4. When people began to drop the notion that the government's budget had to be balanced in every year or month, they first thought it would be in balance over the business cycle—with boom-time surpluses matching depression deficits. Today, we realize that only by coincidence would the surpluses in prosperous years just balance deficits in recession years.

5. To get a better measure of changes in discretionary fiscal policy, economists supplement knowledge of the budget by separating the actual budget into its structural and cyclical components. The structural budget calculates how much the government would collect and spend if the economy were operating at potential output. The cyclical budget accounts for the impact of the business cycle on tax revenues, expenditures, and the deficit. To assess the impact of fiscal policy on the economy, we should pay close attention to the structural deficit; changes in the cyclical deficit are a result of changes in the economy rather than a cause of changes in the economy.

B. The Economic Consequences of the Deficit

6. The government debt represents the accumulated borrowings from the public. It is the sum of past deficits. A useful measure of the size of the debt is the debt-GNP ratio, which for the United States has tended to rise during wartime and fall during peacetime. The decade of the 1980s was an exception, for the debt-GNP ratio rose sharply during this period.

7. In analyzing fiscal impacts, it is useful to separate the short-run and long-run effects of deficits and debts. For the short run, a pervasive concern has been that government deficits crowd out investment. This statement makes sense only for policies that raise the structural deficit.

8. The extent to which active fiscal policy will crowd out investment also depends upon financial markets, the determinants of investment, and how deficits are financed. Investment is likely to be largely crowded out when the central bank and financial markets react to higher output with tight money. In this case, investment and other interest-sensitive sectors may decline by the entire increase in government spending.

9. Active fiscal policy, if introduced during deep recessions with accommodative monetary policies, may instead encourage investment. An increase in investment occurs when output rises and businesses are induced to spend on plant and equipment because capacity utilization increases. This encouragement effect can outweigh interest-rate, crowding-out effects until the system begins to approach high employment.

10. There is mixed evidence on the extent of crowding out. Evidence from the high-deficit era of the 1980s points to a complex set of reactions to deficits, including lower domestic and foreign investment. In other periods, crowding out appears to have been minimal. The best bet today is that, outside of deep recessions, investment will be significantly crowded out by government spending.

11. The public debt need not burden the shoulders of a nation as if its citizens were forced to carry rocks on their backs. To the degree that we borrow from abroad for consumption and pledge posterity to pay back the interest and principal on such external debt, our descendants will indeed find themselves sacrificing consumption to service this debt.

12. To the degree that we leave future generations an internal debt but no change in capital stock, there are various internal effects. The process of taxing Peter to pay Paula, or taxing Paula to pay Paula, can involve various distortions of production and efficiency but should not be confused with owing money to another country.

13. In addition, economic growth may slow if the public debt displaces capital in people's portfolios. This syndrome occurs because firms' bonds and common stocks are good substitutes for government bonds. Hence, an increase in government debt may reduce the economy's capital stock.

14. In the long run, a larger government debt may slow the growth of potential output and consumption because of the costs of servicing an external debt, the inefficiencies that arise from taxing to pay the interest on the debt, and the diminished capital accumulation that comes from capital displacement.

CONCEPTS FOR REVIEW

Budgets and fiscal policy
government budget
budget deficit, surplus, and
  balance
discretionary policies vs.
  automatic stabilizers
automatic stabilization and
  the reduced multiplier

tools of discretionary policy
budget: actual, structural,
  cyclical

Economics of debt and deficits
relation of debt to past deficits
ratios of debt to GNP over space
  and time

short-run impact: crowding out vs.
  investment encouragement
long-run impacts on economic:
  growth
  internal vs. external debt
  distortions from taxation
  displacement of capital
Gramm-Rudman Act

QUESTIONS FOR DISCUSSION

1. Define automatic and discretionary stabilizers. What would be your preferred discretionary stabilizer for fighting inflation? For fighting recessions? Which dis-

cretionary stabilizers seem least useful? Why?

2. Recall the definitions of structural and cyclical deficits. For each of the following, analyze the effects on

the actual, structural, and cyclical deficits:

(a) A permanent tax cut
(b) A sharp decrease in private investment
(c) A tightening of monetary policy
(d) An increase in exports
(e) An increase in welfare benefit levels

3. In year 0, GNP is 1000, taxes are 200, and government spending is 250. Output is equal to potential output. In year 1, the government increases G to 270. If revenues are "lump-sum" taxes that are unaffected by changes in income, and if the expenditure multiplier is 2, what is the impact of the fiscal expansion upon the structural and cyclical budgets? How would your answer change if tax revenues rise 20 cents for every dollar increase in GNP?

4. J. M. Keynes wrote, "If the Treasury were to fill old bottles with banknotes, bury them in disused coal mines, and leave it to private enterprise to dig the notes up again, there need be no more unemployment and the real income of the community would probably become a good deal greater than it actually is." (*The General Theory*, p. 129, edited from the original). Explain why Keynes' analysis of the utility of a discretionary public-works program might be correct during a depression. How could well-designed fiscal or monetary policies have the same macroeconomic impacts while producing a larger quantity of useful goods and services?

5. Is it possible that government *promises* might have a displacement effect along with government debt? Thus, if the government were to promise large future social security benefits to workers, would workers feel richer? Might they reduce saving as a result? Could the capital stock end up smaller? Illustrate using Figure 16-5.

6. Trace the impact upon the government debt, the nation's capital stock, and real output of a government program that borrows abroad and spends the money on the following:

(a) Capital to drill for oil, which is exported (as did Mexico in the 1970s)
(b) Grain to feed its population (as did the Soviet Union in the early 1990s)

7. Professor Robert Eisner of Northwestern University wrote: "Significant cuts in our budget deficits, whether by slashing expenditures or raising taxes, pose a serious danger. They will hold down consumption, but in the process they are likely to drag down investments and along with them GNP, employment, and profits." Analyze the reasoning behind this statement in terms of the crowding-out debate. What do the lessons of history suggest about Eisner's contention?

8. Construct a graph like that in Figure 16-6 showing the path of consumption and net exports with and without a large government debt.

9. **Advanced problem:** Figure 16-7 shows a recent estimate of the accumulation of assets by the social security trust fund (which is, in effect, the opposite of government debt) over the next seven decades, as a percent of GNP. Assuming that the rest of the budget is balanced after 1995, what would be the impact of the buildup of the trust fund on the capital stock and national output:

(a) Assuming that the trust fund retires government debt
(b) Assuming that the Barro hypothesis (in footnote 9, page 302) is correct
(c) Assuming that people change their private pension contributions to offset payments to social security on a dollar-for-dollar basis

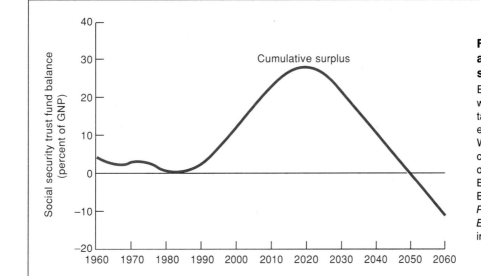

Figure 16-7. Estimated accumulation of assets in social security trust fund

Estimates show the extent to which cumulative social security taxes plus interest on balances exceed cumulative benefits. What will be the effect on the capital stock and national output? [Source: Henry Aaron, Barry Bosworth, and Gary Burtless, *OASDI Trust Fund Policy, National Saving, and the Economy* (Brookings, Washington, D.C., 1988).]

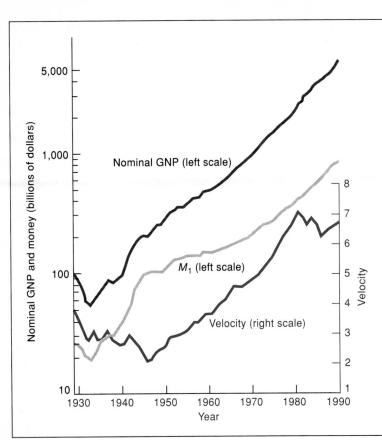

Figure 17-1. Velocity and its components, 1929–1990

Income velocity for transactions money is the ratio of nominal GNP to M_1. Over the period since 1929, money has grown 32-fold while nominal GNP has grown 53-fold.

One of the tenets of monetarism is that V is relatively stable and predictable. How stable does V appear? Can you think of some reasons why V has grown over time? *Hint*: Think of the determinants of the demand for money. (Source: V constructed by the authors from data of the Federal Reserve Board and the Department of Commerce.)

$$P \equiv \frac{MV}{Q} \equiv \left(\frac{V}{Q}\right)M \equiv kM$$

This equation is obtained from the earlier definition of velocity by substituting the variable k as a shorthand for V/Q. We write the equation this way because many classical economists believed that, if transactions patterns were stable, k would be constant. In addition, they generally assumed full employment, which meant real output would grow smoothly and would equal potential GNP. Putting these two assumptions together, k ($= V/Q$) would be near-constant in the short run and a smoothly growing trend in the long run.

What are the implications of the quantity theory? As we can see from the equation, if k were constant, the price level would then move proportionally with the supply of money. A stable money supply would produce stable prices; if the money supply grew rapidly, so would prices. Similarly, if the money supply was multiplied by 10 or 100, the economy would experience galloping inflation or hyperinflation. Indeed, the most vivid demonstra-

tions of the quantity theory of prices can be seen in hyperinflations. Turning back to Figure 14-5, page 261, note how prices rose a billionfold in Weimar Germany after the central bank unleashed the monetary printing presses.

This is the quantity theory with a vengeance. It can also usefully be applied to countries like Poland and the Soviet Union which are moving toward a market system. By applying the quantity theory, we can make a rough estimate of the impact of price decontrols on the price level.

To understand the quantity theory of prices, it is essential to recall that money differs fundamentally from ordinary goods like bread or cars. We want bread to eat and cars to drive. But we want money only for the work it does in buying us bread or cars. If prices in Brazil today are 50 times what they were a decade ago, then it is natural that people will need about 50 times as much money to buy things as they did 10 years ago. Here lies the core of the quantity theory of money: the demand for money rises proportionally with the price level.

The quantity theory of prices holds that prices move proportionally with the supply of money. Although the quantity theory of prices is only a rough approximation, it does help explain why countries with low money growth have moderate inflation while others with rapid money growth find their prices galloping along.

Modern Monetarism

Modern monetary economics was developed after World War II by Chicago's Milton Friedman and his numerous colleagues and followers. Under Friedman's leadership, monetarists challenged the Keynesian approach to macroeconomics and emphasized the importance of monetary policy in macroeconomic stabilization. About two decades ago, the monetarist approach branched. One fork continued the older tradition that we will now describe. The younger offshoot became the influential rational-expectations school that is analyzed later in this chapter.

The monetarist approach postulates that the growth of money determines nominal GNP in the short run and prices in the long run. This analysis operates in the framework of the quantity theory of prices and relies on the analysis of trends in velocity. Monetarists argue that the velocity of money is relatively stable (or in extreme cases constant). If correct, this is an important insight, for the quantity equation shows that, if V is constant, then movements in M will affect PQ (or nominal GNP) proportionally.

The Essence of Monetarism

Like all serious schools of thought, monetarism has differing emphases and degrees. The following points are central to monetarist thinking:

1. *Money-supply growth is the prime systematic determinant of nominal GNP growth.* Monetarism, like Keynesian multiplier theory, is basically a theory of the determinants of aggregate demand. It holds that nominal aggregate demand is affected primarily by changes in the money supply. Fiscal policy is important for some things (like the fraction of GNP devoted to defense or private consumption), but the major

macroeconomic variables (aggregate output, employment, and prices) are affected mainly by money. This was put neatly in the following oversimplified way: "Only money matters."

What is the basis for monetarist belief in the primacy of money? It is based on two central propositions. First, as Friedman has stated, "There is an extraordinary empirical stability and regularity to such magnitudes as income velocity that cannot but impress anyone who works extensively with monetary data." Second, many monetarists used to argue that the demand for money is completely insensitive to interest rates.[3]

Why do these two assumptions lead to the monetarist view? From the quantity equation of exchange, if velocity V is stable, then M will determine $PQ \equiv$ nominal GNP. Similarly, fiscal policy is irrelevant according to the monetarists because, if V is stable, the only force that can affect PQ is M. With constant V, there is simply no door by which taxes or government expenditures can enter the stage.

2. *Prices and wages are relatively flexible.* Recall that one of the precepts of Keynesian economics is that prices and wages are "sticky." While generally accepting the view that there is *some* inertia in wage-price setting, monetarists argue that the Phillips curve is relatively steep even in the short run and insist that the long-run Phillips curve is vertical. In the *AS-AD* framework, monetarists hold that the short-run *AS* curve is quite steep.

The monetarists put points 1 and 2 together. Because (1) money is the prime determinant of nominal GNP and (2) prices and wages are fairly flexible around potential output, this implies that money moves real output only modestly and for a short time. M mainly affects P.

Accordingly, money can affect both output and prices in the short run. But in the long run, because the economy tends to operate near full employment, money's main impact is on the price level. Fiscal policy affects output and prices negligibly in both the short run and the long run. This is the essence of monetarist doctrine.

[3] The proposition that the demand for money is insensitive to the interest rate has been discredited and has generally fallen out of favor in recent years.

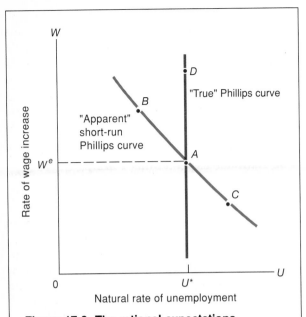

Figure 17-3. The rational-expectations Phillips curve

According to rational-expectations macroeconomics, the true Phillips curve is vertical. But we may observe an "apparent" short-run Phillips curve, drawn through points B, A, and C.

Point B arises when an inflationary shock raises money wages above their expected levels. Workers are confused, thinking that their real wages have increased, they decide to work more, and unemployment falls. Thus the economy moves from point A to point B. (Trace through the opposite pathway to C.)

As a result, economic historians see a scatter of points that look like A, B, and C and erroneously conclude that a stable short-run Phillips curve exists.

parent short-run Phillips curve arises from misperceptions of real wages or relative prices.

Policy Implications

Policy Ineffectiveness

Rational-expectations theory has important implications for the conduct of macroeconomics. The first concerns the effect of economic policy. Given the RE view of labor markets, you might say to yourself: "Okay, so RE economists believe that the Phillips curve is downward-sloping because people are fooled about what is happening to their real wages. But it's no tragedy if the people are fooled off the

vertical Phillips curve. It's all for their own benefit anyway, because unemployment will be lower."

Not so, say the rational-expectations theorists. They demonstrate that, under their assumptions, government attempts to affect output and employment through monetary and fiscal policies would be fruitless. To understand the argument, imagine the government saying, "Election time is coming. Let's pump up the money supply a little." But people would say to themselves, "Yes, elections are coming. From past experience, I know that the government always pumps up the money supply before elections. They can't fool *me* and get me to work any harder." In terms of the Phillips curve of Figure 17-3, the government tries to stimulate the economy and move it from point C to point B. But as people anticipate the government's economic stimulation, the economy ends up at point D, with unemployment equal to the natural rate, but with higher inflation.

This is the *policy ineffectiveness theorem:*

With rational expectations and flexible prices and wages, anticipated government policy cannot affect real output or unemployment.

The policy ineffectiveness theorem depends on both rational expectations and flexible prices. The assumption of flexible prices implies that the only way that economic policy can affect output and unemployment is by surprising people and causing misperceptions. But you can hardly surprise people if your policies are predictable. Hence predictable policies cannot affect output and unemployment.

Fixed Rules Optimal

Earlier, we described the monetarist case for fixed rules. The RE approach put this argument on a much firmer footing. An economic policy can be divided into two parts, a predictable part (the "rule") and an unpredictable part ("discretion"). RE macroeconomists argue that discretion should be avoided like the plague.

Why so? They reason that policymakers cannot forecast the economy any better than the private sector can. Therefore, by the time policymakers act on the news—a war in the desert sands, a declining dollar, a corn blight—flexibly moving prices in markets populated by well-informed buyers and sellers have already incorporated the news. Markets have attained their efficient supply-and-demand equilibria. Unemployment has gravitated to its natural rate. There are simply no discretionary steps the government can take to improve the outcome or prevent the brief spells of involuntary unemployment that are caused by transient misperceptions.

Government policy can make things worse, however, with unpredictable discretionary policies that give misleading economic signals, confuse people, distort their economic behavior, and cause waste. Rather than risk such confusing "noise," say the RE economists, governments should completely avoid any discretionary macroeconomic policies.

Monetarist Rules and the Lucas Critique

The rational-expectations revolution has provided support for the monetarist advocacy of fixed rules. But at the same time it levied a devastating argument against a key monetarist assumption. Monetarists note that the velocity of money has shown a remarkable stability. Thus, they conclude, we can stabilize $MV \equiv PQ \equiv$ nominal GNP by imposing a fixed-money rule.

. But the *Lucas critique*, named after RE economist Robert Lucas, argues that people may change their behavior when policy changes. Just as the apparent short-run Phillips curve might shift when Keynesian governments attempt to manipulate it, so might the apparently constant velocity change if the central bank adopts a fixed-money-growth rule.

This insight was borne out in the period from 1979 to 1982, when the United States conducted the monetarist experiment described in the last section. Velocity became extremely unstable, and 1982 showed the biggest decrease in velocity since the Federal Reserve began collecting the data.

The Lucas critique is a stern warning that economic behavior can change when policymakers rely too heavily upon past regularities.

State of the Debate

The RE theory has not been favorably received by mainstream macroeconomists. Criticisms have centered principally on the issue of flexible prices and wages. Much evidence suggests that prices often move slowly in response to shocks, and few economists believe that labor markets are in constant supply-demand equilibrium. What happens to the rational-expectations theory when the assumption of perfectly flexible wages and prices is abandoned? In general, policy will regain its power to affect the real economy in the short run.[6]

A second set of criticisms aims at the rational-expectations assumption, taking issue with the assertion that humans incorporate the latest forecast or data into their behavior like supercomputers. Empirical studies of behavior have uncovered significant elements of non-rational expectations, even among the most sophisticated professional economic forecasters.

Finally, critics argue that the predictions of the RE theory are inaccurate. The theory forecasts that misperceptions lie behind business-cycle fluctuations. But can misperceptions about wages and prices really explain deep depressions and persistent bouts of unemployment? Did it really take people a full decade to learn how hard times were in the Great Depression? Most mainstream economists believe that these implications tend to discredit the theory.

A New Synthesis?

After two decades of analysis and econometric testing of the RE approach to macroeconomics, elements of a synthesis of old and new theories are beginning to appear. What are some of the lessons? To begin with, economists now must pay careful attention to expectations in economic activity. Approaches that assume that expectations react mechanically will no longer survive careful scrutiny, particularly in auction markets like those in the financial sector.

Some macroeconomists have begun to fuse the

---

[6] Perhaps the best example is work that maintains the rational-expectations framework except for one modest change. Studies of "overlapping wage contracts," particularly by John Taylor (Stanford), a member of the Council of Economic Advisers under President Bush, recognize that a substantial part of the labor force works under long-term contracts that are written in *nominal* (rather than real) terms. A typical labor contract will specify a fixed money wage rate. During the period of the contract, anticipated macroeconomic policy can affect unemployment. Put in terms of the expectational view, the macroeconomic policymakers can use information that comes available *after* the contract is written but was unavailable when workers agreed to a particular money-wage path.

new view of expectations with the modern mainstream (or neo-Keynesian) view of product and labor markets. This synthesis is embodied in macroeconomic models that assume (a) labor and goods markets display inflexible wages and prices, (b) the prices and quantities in financial auction markets adjust rapidly to economic shocks and expectations, and (c) the expectations in auction markets are formed in a forward-looking way.

A recent survey compares the behavior of macroeconomic models that incorporate the adaptive ("backward-looking") approach to expectations with models that incorporate the rational ("forward-looking") approach. The adaptive assumption holds that people form their expectations simply and mechanically on the basis of past information. The forward-looking or rational approach is as described above.

A model comparison finds a number of important differences. One salient feature is that forward-looking models tend to have large "jumps" or discontinuous changes in interest rates, stock prices, or exchange rates when major changes in policy or external events occur. For example, an election of an expansionist President or prime minister might lead people to think that inflation was on the horizon. This perception could result in a sharp jump in interest rates along with a fall in the stock market and exchange rates. The prediction of "jumpy" prices replicates one realistic feature of auction markets and thus suggests where forward-looking expectations might be important in the real world.

Figure 17-4 compares the predictions of different models. It shows the expenditure multipliers of four forward-looking models and of seven adaptive-expectations models. Note that the multipliers of the forward-looking models are significantly smaller than those of the adaptive models.

The smaller multipliers in the forward-looking models occur for two reasons: First, after a fiscal expansion, interest rates generally rise more rapidly in forward-looking than in adaptive models. This occurs because forward-looking market participants predict a future expansion of output after an increase in government spending. A higher expected future output tends to increase interest rates *today*, and crowding out therefore occurs rapidly in forward-looking models.

Second, as interest rates rise quickly in response

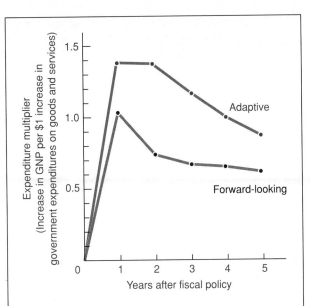

Figure 17-4. Comparison of multipliers in forward-looking and adaptive models

This graph shows the difference in expenditure multipliers of models that are adaptive (or backward-looking) and forward-looking (or rational).

Because interest rates crowd out domestic investment and exchange rates affect net exports, adjustment takes place more rapidly in forward-looking models. Forward-looking expenditure multipliers are considerably smaller than those in adaptive models. [Source: Ralph C. Bryant, Gerald Holtham, and Peter Hooper, "Consensus and Diversity in the Model Simulations," in Ralph C. Bryant et al. (eds.), *Empirical Macroeconomics for Interdependent Economies* (Brookings, Washington, D.C., 1988), Fig. 3-33.]

to a fiscal stimulus in forward-looking models, the flexible exchange rate on the dollar tends to jump upward. A rise in the exchange rate of the dollar leads to a reduction in net exports and tends to reduce the size of the fiscal stimulus.

Although this discussion touches on only two of many differences between the rational-expectations approach and more traditional macroeconomics, it does point to an important set of results that every serious macroeconomist must study carefully. Economic relationships with rational expectations may differ from those with adaptive expectations. The reaction of markets to external events, and even to policies and policymakers themselves, cannot be ignored.

Although academic scribblers will wrangle end-lessly about the best macroeconomic model, poli-cymakers cannot wait for the final scientific verdict. They must cope with this year's inflation or reces-sion and confront the big macroeconomic trade-offs. In this section, we evaluate the principles that lie behind monetary and fiscal policies today.

The Interaction of Monetary and Fiscal Policies

A government can use either monetary or fiscal pol-icy to stabilize the economy. But what should be the division of labor between monetary and fiscal policies? There is no simple answer to this ques-tion. Rather, the best setting for monetary and fiscal policy will depend upon two factors: the need for demand management and the desired fiscal-monetary mix.

Demand Management

The first consideration in determining the appro-priate combination of monetary and fiscal policies is the overall state of the economy and the need for adjusting aggregate demand. When the economy is stagnating, fiscal and monetary policies can be used to stimulate the economy and promote eco-nomic recovery. When inflation threatens, mone-tary and fiscal policies can help to slow the econ-omy and dampen inflationary fires. These are examples of *demand management*, which refers to the use of monetary and fiscal policies to set aggre-gate demand at the desired level.

Suppose, for example, that the economy is enter-ing a severe recession. Aggregate demand is de-pressed relative to potential output. What can the government do to revive the lagging economy? It can manage aggregate demand by raising money growth, or increasing the structural budget deficit, or both. After the economy has responded to the monetary and fiscal stimulus, output growth and employment would increase and unemployment would fall. (What steps could the government take during inflationary periods?)

The first consideration in setting monetary and fiscal policies is the state of the business cycle and the requirements of demand management.

The Policy Mix

The second factor affecting fiscal and monetary policy is the desired **fiscal-monetary mix,** which refers to the relative strength of fiscal and monetary policies and their effect on different components of output. In other words, monetary and fiscal poli-cies can be used to affect not only the *level* of GNP but also the *composition* of GNP. By varying the mix of taxes, government spending, and monetary pol-icy, the government can change the fraction of GNP devoted to business investment, consumption, net exports, and government purchases of goods and services.

Example 1. Let's say that the people empower a President to start a big defense buildup, leaving overall output unchanged, by having housing and other investment contract to provide the necessary resources. What could be done? The President could increase defense spending, leave taxes alone, and tighten money, thereby raising interest rates enough to squeeze investment and net exports to make room for the added government purchases. This policy would also lead to an increase in the structural budget deficit and higher real interest rates. Such a fiscal course was followed in the United States from 1981 to 1988.

Example 2. Suppose that a country became con-cerned about a low national savings rate and de-sires to raise investment so as to increase the capi-tal stock and boost the growth rate of potential output. Moreover, this step should not change the overall level of GNP; rather, higher investment should come at the expense of private consump-tion. What policy mix should be pursued?

Undertake an expansionary monetary policy to lower interest rates and raise investment; keep gov-ernment spending on goods and services un-

The imprint of economic openness on policy is clearest for monetary policy. Let's review briefly the route by which monetary policy affects trade and then output. Suppose the Federal Reserve decides to slow money growth to fight inflation, as occurred in the 1979–1982 period. This process drives up interest rates on assets denominated in U.S. dollars. Attracted by higher dollar interest rates, investors will buy dollar securities, driving up the foreign exchange rate on the dollar. The high exchange rate on the dollar encourages the United States to import and hurts U.S. exports. Net exports fall, decreasing aggregate demand. This has the impact of both lowering real GNP and lowering prices or the rate of inflation.

Note that the direction of the effect of monetary policy is the same for the trade impact as for the impact on domestic investment: tight money lowers output and prices. *The trade impact reinforces the domestic-economy impact.* But the open-economy issues pose additional complications for policymakers.

The first complication arises because the quantitative relationships between monetary policy, the exchange rate, foreign trade, and output and prices are intricate and imperfectly understood. The weak point in our understanding comes at the very first link. Current economic models cannot accurately predict the impact of monetary-policy changes on exchange rates. Further, even if we knew the money–exchange-rate relationship, the impact of exchange rates on net exports is complicated and difficult to predict. On balance, confidence in our ability to determine the best timing and likely effects of monetary policies has eroded in recent years.

Foreign economic relations add another dimension to economic policy. Domestic policymakers must concern themselves with foreign repercussions of domestic policies. Rising interest rates at home change interest rates, exchange rates, and trade balances abroad, and these changes may be unwelcome. In heavily indebted countries, such as Brazil and Mexico, higher interest rates increase debt-service burdens. In the 1980s, skyrocketing interest rates caused severe hardships for these countries. To complicate matters, these countries owe billions of dollars to American banks, and loan defaults could cause untold damage to the U.S. financial system. Finally, the nation cares not only about the total of its GNP; the composition of output matters as well. Because of shifting patterns of foreign trade, the United States has witnessed stagnation in its "tradable" sectors (manufactures, mining, and agriculture) since the early 1980s.

Open-economy macroeconomics is one of the most exciting areas of modern economics. Economists clearly have much to learn about the interactions between monetary policy and economic performance in a world increasingly open to foreign trade and financial flows.

SUMMARY

A. Velocity and Monetarism

1. Monetarism relies upon the analysis of trends in the velocity of money to understand the impact of money on the economy. The income velocity of circulation of money (V) is defined as the ratio of the dollar GNP flow to the stock of M:

$$V \equiv \frac{GNP}{M} \equiv \frac{PQ}{M}$$

While V is definitely not a constant—if only because it rises with interest rates—its movements are somewhat regular and predictable.

2. From velocity's definition comes the quantity theory of prices:

$$P \equiv kM \qquad \text{where } k \equiv \frac{V}{Q}$$

The quantity theory of prices regards P as almost strictly proportional to M. This view is useful for understanding hyperinflations and certain long-term trends, but it should not be taken literally.

3. Monetarism has grown into a major economic school. It rests on three propositions:
   (a) The growth of the money supply is the major systematic determinant of nominal GNP growth.
   (b) Prices and wages are relatively flexible.
   (c) The private economy is stable.
   These propositions suggest that macroeconomic fluctuations arise primarily from erratic money-supply growth.

4. Monetarism is generally associated with a laissez-faire and anti-big-government political philosophy. Because of a desire to avoid active government and a belief in the inherent stability of the private sector, monetarists often propose that the money supply grow at a fixed rate of 3 or 5 percent annually. Some monetarists believe that this will produce steady growth with stable prices in the long run.

5. The Federal Reserve conducted a full-scale monetarist experiment from 1979 to 1982. The experience from this period convinced most observers that:
   (a) Money is a powerful determinant of aggregate demand.
   (b) Most of the short-run effects of money changes are on output rather than on prices.
   (c) A firm and credible monetary policy does not appear to reduce inflation at lower cost than other anti-inflation policies.
   (d) Velocity may become quite unstable when a monetarist approach is followed.

B. Rational Expectations in Macroeconomics

6. Rational-expectations (RE) macroeconomics rests on two fundamental hypotheses: People's expectations are formed efficiently and rationally, and prices and wages are flexible. In the RE economy, all unemployment is voluntary, and the Phillips curve is vertical in the short run, even though it may appear otherwise.

7. The policy ineffectiveness theorem holds that predictable government policies cannot affect real output and unemployment. The RE theory states that, while we may *observe* a downward-sloping short-run Phillips curve, we cannot *exploit* the slope for the purposes of lowering unemployment. If economic policymakers systematically attempt to increase output and decrease unemployment, people will soon come to understand and to anticipate the policy. When such a policy is anticipated, prices and wages will adjust in advance. People will remain on their supply and demand

that a prohibitive tariff or quota (one stringent enough to shut off all foreign trade) will unambiguously hurt a country:

A prohibitive tariff or quota, far from helping consumers in a country, reduces their real incomes by making imports too expensive and by making the whole world less productive. Countries lose from protectionism because reduced international trade eliminates the efficiency inherent in specialization and division of labor.

Extensions to Many Commodities and Countries

The world of international trade consists of more than two countries and two commodities. However the principles we explained in the example above are essentially unchanged in more realistic situations.

Many Commodities

When two countries produce many commodities at constant costs, they can be arranged in order according to the comparative advantage or cost of each. For example, the commodities might be wheat, aircraft, computers, automobiles, wine, and shoes—all arranged in the comparative-advantage sequence shown in Figure 18-3. As you can see from the figure, of all the commodities, wheat is least expensive in America relative to the costs in Europe. Europe has its greatest comparative advantage in shoes, while its advantage in wine is somewhat less than that in shoes.

We can be virtually sure that the introduction of trade will cause America to produce and export wheat, and Europe will produce and export shoes. But where will the dividing line fall? Between automobiles and computers? Or wine and shoes? Or will the dividing line fall on one of the commodities

rather than between them—so that, say, automobiles might be produced in both places?

You will not be surprised to find that the answer depends upon the comparative strength of international demands for the different goods. We can think of the commodities as beads arranged on a string according to their comparative advantage; the strength of supply and demand will determine where the dividing line between American and European production will fall. An increased demand for aircraft and wheat, for example, would tend to shift prices in the direction of American goods. The shift might lead America to specialize so much more in areas of its comparative advantage that it would no longer be profitable to produce in areas of comparative disadvantage, like wine.

Many Countries

What about the case of many countries? Introducing many countries need not change our analysis. As far as a single country is concerned, all the other nations with which it trades can be lumped together into one group as "the rest of the world." The advantages of trade have no special relationship to national boundaries. The principles already developed apply between groups of countries and, indeed, between regions within the same country. In fact, they are just as applicable to trade between our northern and southern states as to trade between the United States and Canada.

Triangular and Multilateral Trade

With many countries brought into the picture, all will find it beneficial to engage in *triangular* or *multilateral trade* with a multitude of other countries. Generally *bilateral* trade between two countries is unbalanced.

A simple example of triangular trade flows is illustrated in Figure 18-4, where the arrows show the

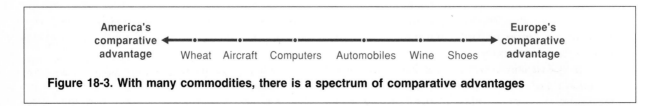

Figure 18-3. With many commodities, there is a spectrum of comparative advantages

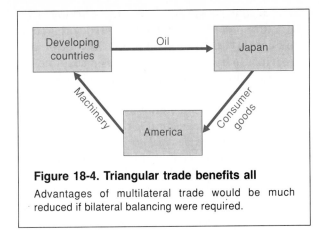

Figure 18-4. Triangular trade benefits all

Advantages of multilateral trade would be much reduced if bilateral balancing were required.

direction of exports. America buys consumer goods from Japan, Japan buys oil and primary commodities from developing countries, and developing countries buy machinery and computers from America. In reality, trade patterns are even more complex than this triangular example.

The multilateral nature of trade should give caution to those who argue for bilateral balance between particular countries, as was the case in recent proposals in the United States. What would happen if all nations signed bilateral trade agreements that balanced trade between each pair of countries? Trade would be sharply curbed; imports would balance exports, but at the level of whichever was the smaller. The gains from trade would be severely reduced.

Graphical Analysis of Comparative Advantage

We can use the production-possibility frontier (*PPF*) to expand our analysis of comparative advantage. We will continue the numerical example based upon labor costs, but the theory is equally valid in a competitive world with many different inputs.

America without Trade

Chapter 2 introduced the *PPF*, which shows the combinations of commodities that can be produced with a society's given resources and technology. Using the simple production data shown in Table 18-2, and assuming that both Europe and

America have 600 units of labor, we can easily derive each region's *PPF*. The table that accompanies Figure 18-5 shows the possible levels of food and clothing that America can produce with its inputs and technology. Figure 18-5 plots the production possibilities; the blue line *DA* shows America's *PPF*. The *PPF* has a slope of $-\frac{1}{2}$, for this represents the terms on which food and clothing can be substituted in production; in competitive markets with no international trade, the price ratio of food to clothing will also be one-half.

So far we have concentrated on production and ignored consumption. However, if America is isolated from all international trade, then what it can produce is also what it can consume. Say that, for the incomes and demands in the marketplace, point B in Figure 18-5 marks America's production

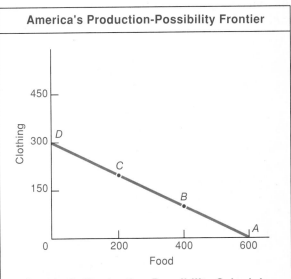

America's Production-Possibility Frontier

America's Production-Possibility Schedule
(1-to-2 Constant-Cost Ratio)

Possibilities	Food (units)	Clothing (units)
A	600	0
B	400	100
C	200	200
D	0	300

Figure 18-5. American production data

The constant-cost line *DA* represents America's domestic production-possibility frontier. America will produce and consume at *B* in the absence of trade.

bilities at the world price ratio of $\frac{2}{3}$. The blue arrows show the amounts exported and imported. America ends up at the point B'. Through trade it moves onto the black line $D'A$ just as if a fruitful new invention had pushed out its *PPF*.

The lessons of this analysis are summarized in Figure 18-8. This figure shows the *world* production-possibility frontier. How is the world *PPF* obtained? It represents the maximum output that can be obtained from the world's resources when goods are produced in the most efficient manner, that is, with the most efficient division of labor and regional specialization.

The world *PPF* is built up from the two regional *PPF*s (see Figure 18-6) by determining the maximum level of world output that can be obtained from the individual region *PPF*s. For example, the maximum quantity of food that can be produced (with no clothing production) is seen in Figure 18-6 to be 600 units in America and 200 units in Europe, for a world maximum of 800 units. This same point (800 food, 0 clothing) is then plotted in the world *PPF* in Figure 18-8. Additionally, we can plot the point (0 food, 450 clothing) in the world *PPF* by in-

spection of the regional *PPF*s. All the individual points in between can be constructed by a careful calculation of the maximum world outputs that can be produced if the two regions are efficiently specializing in the two goods.

Before opening up borders to trade, the world is at point B. This is an inefficient point—inside the world *PPF*—because regions have different levels of *relative* efficiency in different goods.

After opening the borders to trade, the world moves out to point E, the free-trade equilibrium. At E, countries are specializing in areas of comparative advantage. With free trade in competitive markets, the world is on its production-possibility frontier.

Qualifications and Conclusions

We have now completed our look at the elegant theory of comparative advantage. Its conclusions apply for any number of countries and commodities. Moreover, it can be generalized to handle many inputs, changing factor proportions, and diminishing returns.

But comparative advantage has its limitations. The major defect lies in its classical assumptions, for it assumes a smoothly working economy with flexible prices and wages and no involuntary unemployment. Would the theory still hold if autoworkers, laid off when the share of Japanese cars sold in the American market rises rapidly, cannot easily find new jobs? What if an overvalued foreign exchange rate reduces the demand for manufacturing workers and these workers cannot find comparable jobs in other sectors? In such cases, trade might well push a nation *inside* its *PPF* as unemployment rose and GNP fell, and the gains from trade along with the theory of comparative advantage would fail.

Given this reservation, there can be little wonder that the theory of comparative advantage sells at a big discount during periods of major macroeconomic dislocations. During the Great Depression of the 1930s, as unemployment soared and real outputs fell, nations built high tariff walls at their borders and the volume of foreign trade shrank sharply. Comparative advantage gained prestige in the period after World War II as economic integration among the world's industrial nations led to a

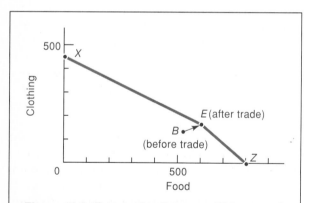

Figure 18-8. Free trade allows world to move to its production-possibility frontier

We here show the effect of free trade from the viewpoint of the world as a whole.

Before trade is allowed, each region is on its own national *PPF*. Without trade, regions are producing goods in which they are relatively inefficient, so the world is *inside* the world *PPF*, shown as the blue line *XEZ*.

Free trade allows each region to specialize in the goods in which it has comparative advantage. As a result of the specialization, the world as a whole moves out to point E, which is on the world *PPF*.

period of unprecedented economic growth. But, in every recession, underutilized labor and capital lobby to protect their markets from foreign competition. These epochs of history remind us that the classical theory of comparative advantage is strictly valid only when exchange rates, prices, and wages are at appropriate levels and when macroeconomic policies banish major business cycles or trade dislocations from the economic scene.

Notwithstanding its limitations, the theory of comparative advantage provides a most important glimpse of truth. A nation that neglects comparative advantage may pay a heavy price in terms of living standards and economic growth.

B. The Balance of International Payments

Balance-of-Payments Accounts

The affairs of nations today are heavily involved in their trade deficits and foreign debts or credits. The press is full of stories about the trade deficit or growing indebtedness of the United States, or the need for balance-of-payments adjustments in Latin American countries. In order to master the elements of international trade, a general understanding of the nature of balance-of-payments accounting is essential.

Up to now we have treated international trade as if nations simply barter goods—oil for aircraft or bananas for computers. In fact, international exchange, like domestic exchange, takes place through the medium of money, and the monetary flows into and out of a country are measured in a nation's balance of payments.

A country's **balance of international payments** is a systematic statement of all economic transactions between that country and the rest of the world; it forms an overall measure of the flows of goods, services, and capital between a country and the rest of the world. The U.S. Department of Commerce keeps records of U.S. transactions, makes official estimates of all international transactions, and publishes the U.S. balance-of-payments statistics. These include data on merchandise exports and imports, money lent or borrowed abroad, tourist expenditures, interest and dividends paid or received, and so forth.

The balance of international payments is listed in four sections:

I. Current account
       Private:
           Merchandise (or "trade balance")
           Invisibles (services and net investment income)
           Governmental exports or imports and grants
II. Capital account
       Private
       Government
III. Statistical discrepancy
IV. Official settlements

We will now explain each of these major components of the balance of payments.

Debits and Credits

Like other accounts, balance-of-payments accounts record pluses and minuses. A plus item is called a *credit*, while a minus item is called a *debit*.

In general, exports are **credits** and imports are **debits.** A good rule to use in deciding how any item should be treated is to ask whether it earns foreign currencies for the country. *Foreign currencies* are other countries' monies.

Remember the following rule:

If an item provides us with more foreign currency, as exports do, it is called a "credit." If the item is like imports and draws down our stock of foreign currencies, it is called a "debit."

How is the U.S. import of a Japanese camera recorded? It is clearly a debit, for it depletes our stock of Japanese yen. How shall we treat interest and dividend income on investments received by Americans from abroad? Clearly, they are credit items like exports because they provide us with foreign currencies.

Details of the Balance of Payments

Balance on Current Account. The totality of items under section I is usually referred to as the **balance on current account.** This summarizes the difference between our total exports and imports of goods and services. It is almost identical to net exports in the national output accounts.

In the past, many writers concentrated on the **trade balance,** which consists of merchandise imports or exports. The composition of merchandise imports and exports was shown in Table 18-1; it consists mainly of primary commodities (like food and fuels) and manufactured goods. In an earlier era, the mercantilists strove for a trade surplus (an excess of exports over imports), calling this a "favorable balance of trade." They hoped to avoid an "unfavorable trade balance," by which they meant a trade deficit (an excess of imports over

exports). This choice of terms has carried over to today as many nations seek trade surpluses; economics teaches, however, that trade deficits are sometimes economically advantageous for countries that need an infusion of foreign capital.

In addition to the trade balance, we must not forget the increasing role played by *invisibles*, which include services and investment income. Services consist of such items as shipping, financial services, and foreign travel. Investment income includes the net earnings on investment abroad (that is, earnings on U.S. assets abroad less payments on foreign assets in the U.S.). The invisibles component was an important positive or credit item for the United States from World War II until the 1980s, although the U.S. international debt position has reduced this surplus item in the early 1990s.

Table 18-3 presents a summary of the U.S. balance of international payments for 1990. Note its four main divisions: current account, capital account, statistical discrepancy, and official settlements. (Each row is numbered to make reference easy.) Each item is listed by name in column (a). Credits are listed in column (b) while column (c) shows the debits. Column (d) then lists the net

		(b) Credits (+)	(c) Debits (−)	(d) Net credits (+) or debits (−)
Section	Items (a)			
I.	**Current account**			
	1. Merchandise trade balance	390	−498	−108
	2. Invisibles (services, investment income, other)			9
	3. **Balance on current account**			**−99**
II.	**Capital account**			
	[lending (−) or borrowing (+)]			
	4. Capital flows	88	−59	
	5. **Balance on capital account**			29
III.	**Statistical discrepancy**			73
	6. **Total needing to be offset**			2
	(line 3 + line 5 + statistical discrepancy)			
IV.	**Official settlements**			
	7. Official settlements balance			−2
	(net change in U.S. official assets)			
	8. Formal overall net total			0

U.S. Balance of Payments, 1990
(Billions of Dollars)

Table 18-3. By definition, current account plus capital account plus statistical discrepancy must be offset by official government settlements
(Source: Adapted from U.S. Department of Commerce.)

credits or debits; it shows a credit if the item added to our stock of foreign currencies or a debit if, on balance, it subtracted from our foreign currency supply.

In 1990 our merchandise exports gave us credits of $390 billion. But our merchandise imports gave us debits of $498 billion. The *net* difference between credits and debits was a debit of $108 billion. This "trade deficit" is listed in column (d), on the first row. (Be sure you know why the algebraic sign is shown as − rather than as +.) From the table we see that services or invisible items plus transfers were slightly in surplus. Our current account deficit was thus $99 billion for 1990.

Capital Account. We have now completed analysis of the current account. But how did the United States "finance" its $99 billion current account deficit in 1990? The United States must have either borrowed or reduced its foreign assets. For it is definitional that what you buy you must either pay for or owe for. This means that the balance of international payments as a whole must by definition show a final zero balance.

Capital movements are loans private citizens or governments make to or receive from foreign private citizens or governments. Capital movements occur, for example, when a Japanese pension fund buys U.S. government securities or when an American buys stock in a British firm.

It is easy to decide which are credit and which are debit items in the capital account if you use the following rule: Always think of the United States as exporting and importing stocks, bonds, or other securities—or, for short, exporting and importing IOUs in return for foreign currencies. Then you can treat these exports and imports like any other exports and imports. When we borrow abroad to finance a current account deficit, we are sending IOUs (like Treasury bills) abroad and gaining foreign currencies. Is this a credit or a debit? Clearly this transaction gives rise to a credit.

Similarly, if our banks lend abroad to finance a steel mill in Brazil, this means the U.S. banks are importing IOUs from Brazilians and losing foreign currencies; this is clearly a debit item.

Line 5 shows that in 1990 the United States was a net *borrower:* we borrowed abroad more than we lent to foreigners. The United States was a net exporter of IOUs (a net borrower) in the amount of $29 billion.

Part III shows that there was a huge statistical discrepancy (the net sum of all unrecorded transactions) accounting for $73 billion. This indicates that $73 billion of unrecorded funds entered the United States.

Adding all current and capital account items to the statistical discrepancy, we find a net surplus of $2 billion.

Official Settlements. When the United States was on the gold standard and the government followed a strict laissez-faire policy, any amount remaining on line 6 had to be settled by exporting or importing gold. Now that countries are no longer on the gold standard, they balance their books with government payments or receipts of foreign currencies. These balancing flows provided by governments are called "official settlements." The most common way of providing official settlements today is for countries to buy or sell U.S. government securities. Note that in line 7 there was a small addition ($2 billion) to U.S. official assets in 1990.

Stages of the Balance of Payments

A review of the economic history of advanced industrial countries reveals that they go through four stages in their balance of payments as they grow from young debtor to mature creditor. This sequence is found, with variations related to their particular histories, in the advanced economies of North America, Europe, and Southeast Asia. We can illustrate the stages by recounting briefly the history of the balance of payments of the United States.

- *Young and growing debtor nation.* From the Revolutionary War until after the Civil War, the United States imported on current account more than it exported. Europe lent the difference, which allowed the country to build up its capital stock. The United States was a typical young and growing debtor nation.
- *Mature debtor nation.* From about 1873 to 1914, the U.S. balance of trade moved into surplus. But growth of the dividends and interest that were owed abroad on past borrowing kept the current account more or less in balance. Capital movements were also nearly in balance as lending just offset borrowing.
- *New creditor nation.* During World War I, the

United States expanded its exports tremendously. American citizens and the government lent money to allies England and France for war equipment and postwar relief needs. The United States emerged from the war a creditor nation.

• *Mature creditor nation.* In the fourth stage, earnings on foreign capital and investments provided a large surplus on invisibles that was matched by a deficit on merchandise trade. This pattern was followed by the United States until the early 1980s. Countries like Japan and West Germany today play the role of mature creditor nation as they enjoy large current account surpluses which they in turn invest abroad.

The United States, surprisingly, has moved out of the mature creditor nation stage, as the balance-of-payments data in Table 18-3 shows. The United States is once again a debtor nation, borrowing large amounts from stage-4 countries. The difference between this new situation and stage 1 is that the borrowings are now for consumption rather than for investment.

Some economists wonder whether the United States has entered a fifth stage, that of *senile debtor nation.* They note that the macroeconomic policy mix of tight money and high government deficits of the 1980s has lowered national saving. The United States is now unable to generate a volume of saving sufficient to provide its capital requirements, and we must turn to thriftier nations to do our saving for us. The counterpart of American dissaving is that foreigners, particularly Japanese investors, are purchasing substantial American assets for their portfolios.

Is this new stage of the U.S. balance of payments a transient period? Or does it mark the beginning of a long period of "structural" trade deficits that will last for decades to come? No one can answer this question with certainty. Corrective forces in the early 1990s appear to be returning the U.S. current account back toward balance, but with a heavy foreign debt to service. When that occurs, the United States will once again be a mature debtor nation, going back to stage 2 above.

SUMMARY

A. Economic Basis for International Trade

1. As soon as differences in productivities arise within a country, specialization and exchange become beneficial. The same holds across nations. International exchange allows an efficient degree of specialization and division of labor—one that is more efficient than relying only on domestic production.

2. Diversity is the fundamental reason that nations engage in international trade. Within this general principle, we see that trade occurs: (a) because of differences in the conditions of production; (b) because of decreasing costs (or economies of scale); and (c) because of diversity in tastes.

3. The most profound reason for international trade is the Ricardian principle of comparative advantage. This principle holds that trade between two regions is advantageous even if one region is absolutely more or less productive than the other in all commodities. As long as there are differences in *relative* or *comparative* efficiencies among countries, every country must enjoy a comparative advantage or a comparative disadvantage in some goods. Powerful benefits arise when countries specialize in the production of goods in their areas of comparative advantage, exporting those goods and trading them for goods in which other nations have a comparative advantage.

4. The law of comparative advantage predicts more than just the geographical pattern of specialization and direction of trade. It also demonstrates that countries are made better off and that the real wages (or, more generally,

returns to the factors of production taken as a whole) are improved by trade and the resulting enlarged totals of world production. Prohibitive quotas and tariffs, designed to "protect" workers or industries, will lower a nation's total income and consumption possibilities.

5. When there are many goods or many countries, the same principles of comparative advantage apply. With many commodities, we can arrange products along a continuum of comparative advantage, from relatively more efficient to relatively less efficient. With many countries, trade may be "triangular" or multilateral, with countries having large bilateral (or two-sided) surpluses or deficits with other individual countries. Triangular trade allows imbalances in bilateral trade, but this reflects the fact that a nation's accounts must balance only multilaterally—between a nation and the rest of the world. Imposing bilateral balance would hamper economic efficiency.

B. The Balance of International Payments

6. The balance of international payments is the set of accounts that measures all the economic transactions between a nation and the rest of the world. It includes exports and imports of goods, services, and financial capital. Exports are credit items, while imports are debits. More generally, a country's credit items are transactions that make foreign currencies available to it; debit items are ones that reduce its holdings of foreign currencies.

7. The major components of the balance of payments are:
   I.   Current account (including the merchandise or trade balance along with invisibles like services and investment income)
   II. Capital account (private and government purchases and sales of assets like stocks, bonds, and real estate)
   III. Statistical discrepancy
   IV. Official settlements

   The rule of balance-of-payments accounting is that the sum of all items must equal zero: $I + II + III + IV = 0$.

8. Historically, countries tend to go through stages of the balance of payments: from the young debtor borrowing for economic development, through mature debtor and young creditor, to mature creditor nation living off earnings from past investments. In the 1980s, the United States moved to yet a different stage where low domestic saving again led it to borrow heavily abroad and become a debtor nation.

CONCEPTS FOR REVIEW

Principles of international trade
open economy
sources of trade: cost differences, decreasing costs, differences in tastes, comparative advantage
absolute and comparative advantage (or disadvantage)
principle of comparative advantage

economic gains from trade
effects of tariffs and quotas
spectrum of comparative advantage
triangular and multilateral trade
terms of trade
consumption vs. production possibilities with trade
world vs. national *PPF*s

Balance of payments
balance of payments (current account, capital account, official settlements)
balance of payments must total zero: $I + II + III + IV = 0$
debits and credits
stages of balance of payments

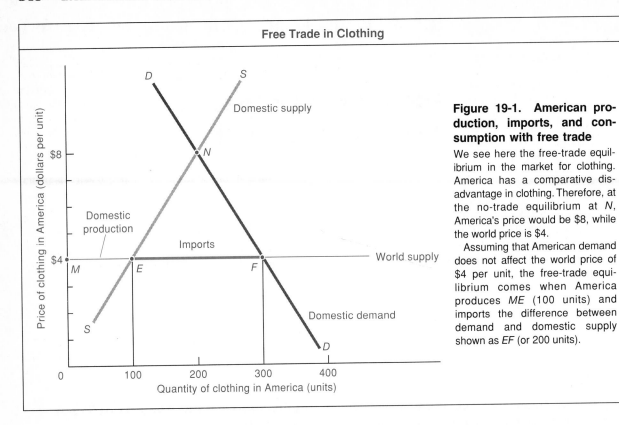

Free Trade in Clothing

Figure 19-1. American production, imports, and consumption with free trade

We see here the free-trade equilibrium in the market for clothing. America has a comparative disadvantage in clothing. Therefore, at the no-trade equilibrium at *N*, America's price would be $8, while the world price is $4.

Assuming that American demand does not affect the world price of $4 per unit, the free-trade equilibrium comes when America produces *ME* (100 units) and imports the difference between demand and domestic supply shown as *EF* (or 200 units).

the world market (assumed to be much larger than the American market) and is equal to $4 per unit.

Later, we will take into account that transactions in international trade are carried out in different currencies. But for now we can simplify by translating each of those foreign currencies into dollars. For example, although French suppliers want to be paid in francs, we can convert the French supply schedule into a dollar supply curve by using the current exchange rate.

No-Trade Equilibrium. Suppose that transportation costs or tariffs for clothing were prohibitive (say, $100 per unit of clothing). Where would the no-trade equilibrium lie? In this case, the American market for clothing would be at the intersection of domestic supply and demand, shown at point *N* in Figure 19-1. At this no-trade point, prices would be relatively high at $8 per unit, and domestic producers would be meeting all the demand.

Free Trade. Next open up trade in clothing. In the absence of transport costs, tariffs, and quotas, the price in America must be equal to the world price.

Why? Because if the American price were above the European price, sharp-eyed entrepreneurs would buy where clothing was cheap (Europe) and sell where clothing was expensive (America)—Europe would export clothing to America. Once trade flows fully adapted to supplies and demands, the price in America would equal the world price level. (In a world *with* transportation and tariff costs, the price in America would equal the world price adjusted for these costs.)

Figure 19-1 illustrates how prices, quantities, and trade flows will be determined under free trade in our clothing example. The horizontal line at $4 represents the supply curve for imports; it is horizontal, or perfectly price elastic, because American demand is assumed to be too small to affect the world price of clothing.

Once trade opens up, imports flow into America, lowering the price of clothing to the world price of $4 per unit. At that level, domestic producers will supply the amount *ME*, or 100 units while at that price consumers will want to buy 300 units. The difference, shown by the heavy line *EF*, is the amount of imports.

Who decided that we would import just this amount of clothing and that domestic producers would supply only 100 units? A European planning agency? A cartel of clothing firms? No, the amount of trade was determined by supply and demand.

Moreover, we can say that the level of prices in the no-trade equilibrium determined the direction of the trade flows. America's no-trade prices were higher than Europe's, so goods flowed into America. Remember this paradoxical rule: *Under free trade, goods flow uphill from low-price regions to high-price regions.* Clothing flows uphill from the low-price European market to the higher-price American market when markets are opened to free trade.

The supply and demand curves are highly useful in understanding the forces operating on a single industry, but they are incomplete. What determines the world price of clothing? Why is the no-trade equilibrium clothing price higher in America than in Europe? To answer these questions we have to analyze the supplies and demands for all industries. In the last chapter, we used general-equilibrium analysis to look at an economy's comparative advantage. The same principles of comparative advantage explain why Europe would export clothing and import food.[1]

Tariffs and Quotas

For centuries, governments have used tariffs and quotas to raise revenues and influence the development of individual industries. Since the eighteenth century—when the British Parliament attempted to impose tariffs on tea, sugar, and other commodities on its American colonies—tariff policy has proved fertile soil for revolution and political struggle.

We can use supply-and-demand analysis to understand the economic effects of tariffs and quotas. To begin with, note that a **tariff** is a tax levied on imports. Table 19-1 shows some representative tariff rates for the United States and Japan in the 1980s. To take an example, the United States today has a 2.5 percent tariff on automobiles. If a foreign

---

[1] Economists explain that these supply and demand curves depict only "partial equilibrium." They must be anchored in general-equilibrium analysis, of which the Ricardian theory of comparative advantage described in Chapter 18 is a special case.

Commodity class	Average tariff rate, 1987 (%)	
	United States	Japan
Agricultural products	1.8	18.4
Food products	4.7	25.4
Wearing apparel	22.7	13.8
Printing and publishing	0.7	0.1
Iron and steel	3.6	2.8
Transport equipment	2.5	1.5
Average, industrial products	4.4	2.8

Table 19-1. Average tariff rates for United States and Japan

Tariff rates for industrial countries like the United States and Japan are generally low today. High tariffs or import quotas are found in politically sensitive sectors like agriculture in Japan and clothing in the United States. [Source: Congressional Budget Office, *The GATT Negotiations and U.S. Trade Policy* (U.S. Government Printing Office, Washington, June 1987).]

car costs $10,000, then the domestic price including the tariff would be $10,250. A **quota** is a limit on the quantity of imports. The United States has quotas on many products, including peanuts, textiles, and beef.

Prohibitive Tariff. The easiest case to analyze is a *prohibitive tariff*—one that is so high as to completely discourage any imports. Looking back at Figure 19-1, what would happen if the tariff on clothing is more than $4 per unit (that is, more than the difference between America's no-trade price of $8 and the world price of $4)? This would be a prohibitive tariff, shutting off all clothing trade. Any importer who buys clothing at the world price of $4 can sell it in America for at most the no-trade price of $8. But the tariff the importer has to pay would come to more than the difference between the U.S. price and the world price. Prohibitive tariffs thus kill off all trade.

Nonprohibitive Tariff. More moderate tariffs (less than $4 per unit of clothing) would injure but not kill off trade. Figure 19-2 shows the equilibrium in the clothing market with a $2 tariff. Again assuming no transportation costs, a $2 tariff means that foreign clothing will sell in America for $6 per unit (equal to the $4 world price plus the $2 tariff).

The equilibrium result of a $2 tariff is to lower

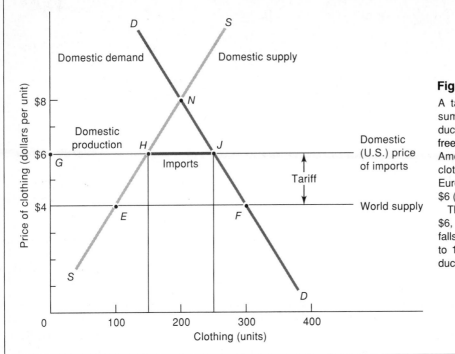

Figure 19-2. Effect of tariff

A tariff lowers imports and consumption, raises domestic production and price. Starting from the free-trade equilibrium in Fig. 19-1, America now puts a $2 tariff on clothing imports. The price of European clothing imports rises to $6 (including the tariff).

The market price rises from $4 to $6, so the total amount demanded falls. Imports shrink from 200 units to 100 units, while domestic production rises from 100 to 150 units.

domestic consumption (or quantity demanded) from 300 units in the free-trade equilibrium to 250 units after the tariff is imposed, to raise the amount of domestic production by 50 units, and to lower the quantity of imports by 100 units. This example summarizes the economic impact of tariffs:

A tariff will tend to raise price, lower the amounts consumed and imported, and raise domestic production.

Quotas. Quotas have the same qualitative effect as tariffs. A prohibitive quota (one that prevents all imports) would achieve the same result as a prohibitive tariff. The price and quantity would move back to the no-trade equilibrium at N in Figure 19-2. A less stringent quota might limit imports to 100 clothing units; this quota would equal the heavy line HJ in Figure 19-2. A quota of 100 units would lead to the same equilibrium price and output as did the $2 tariff.

Although there is no essential difference between tariffs and quotas, some subtle differences do exist. A quota makes an industry more prone to supply shocks. Moreover, a tariff gives revenue to the government, perhaps allowing other taxes to be re-

duced and thereby offsetting some of the harm done to customers in the importing country. A quota, on the other hand, puts the profit from the resulting price difference into the pocket of the importers lucky enough to get a permit or license to import. They can afford to wine and dine, or even bribe, the officials who give out import licenses.

Because of these differences, economists generally regard tariffs as the lesser evil. They advise that, if a government is determined to impose quotas, it should auction off the scarce import-quota licenses. An auction will ensure that the government rather than the importer or the exporter gets the revenue from the scarce right to import; and in addition, the bureaucracy will not be tempted to allocate quota rights by bribery, friendship, or nepotism.

Transportation Costs. What of transportation costs? The cost of moving bulky and perishable goods has the same effect as tariffs, reducing the extent of beneficial regional specialization. For example, if it costs $2 per unit to transport clothing from Europe to the United States, the supply-and-demand equilibrium would look just like Figure 19-2, with the American price $2 above the European price.

But there is one difference between protection and transportation costs: transport costs are imposed by nature—by distances, mountains, and rivers. Restrictive tariffs are squarely the responsibility of nations. Indeed, one economist called tariffs "negative railroads." Imposing a tariff has the same economic impact as throwing sand in the engines of vessels that transport goods to our shores from other lands.

The Economic Costs of Tariffs

In the last chapter, we saw that all countries would benefit by opening up their borders to international trade. We can also use our supply-and-demand apparatus to analyze the economic costs of tariffs.

What happens when America puts a tariff on clothing, such as the $2 tariff shown in Figure 19-2? We have seen that there are three effects: (a) The domestic producers, operating under a price umbrella provided by the tariff, can now expand production; (b) consumers are faced with higher prices and therefore reduce their consumption; and (c) the government gains tariff revenue. What is the net economic impact of the tariff?

Tariffs create economic inefficiency. More precisely, when tariffs are imposed, the economic loss to consumers exceeds the revenue gained by the government plus the extra profits earned by producers.

Diagrammatic Analysis

Figure 19-3 shows the economic cost of a tariff. The supply and demand curves are identical to those in Figure 19-2, but three areas are highlighted.

A. A tariff raises the price in domestic markets from $4 to $6. Businesses are thereby induced to increase their domestic production using relatively costly capacity. They produce output up to the point where marginal cost is $6 per unit (instead of up to $4 per unit under free trade). Firms reopen inefficient old factories or work existing factories extra shifts. From an economic point of view, using these high-cost plants is inefficient, for the new clothing produced by these factories

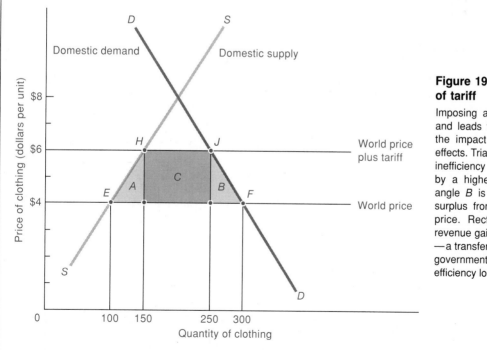

Figure 19-3. Economic cost of tariff

Imposing a tariff raises revenues and leads to inefficiency. We see the impact of the tariff as three effects. Triangle *A* is the cost of the inefficiency in production induced by a higher domestic price. Triangle *B* is the loss in consumer surplus from the inefficiently high price. Rectangle *C* is the tariff revenue gained by the government —a transfer from consumers to the government but not necessarily an efficiency loss.

at costs between $4 and $6 could be bought from abroad at $4.

We can easily depict the amount of this waste as area A in Figure 19-3. This area is the sum of the marginal costs of domestic producers (represented by the domestic supply curve) minus the marginal costs of foreign producers ($4). The total loss in A is $50 (which, by geometry, is equal to $\frac{1}{2}$ times the tariff times the induced domestic production).

B. In addition, there is a loss of consumer surplus from the too high price. Recall that the demand curve represents the marginal utilities of consumers, or the value of the different units of clothing. The resource cost of each unit of clothing is the world price, $4. Hence, triangle B measures the loss in consumer satisfaction from having to cut back on consumption. It is also equal to $50 (which is calculated as equal to one-half the price difference times the consumption reduction).

C. Area C is simply the tariff revenue, equal to the amount of the tariff times the units of imports. Revenues in Figure 19-3 are $200. Note that, unlike triangles A and B, revenue rectangle C need not be an efficiency cost or a deadweight loss. The government revenues raised by tariffs can be employed to finance useful government programs or can be returned to consumers.

Figure 19-3 illustrates one feature that is important in understanding the politics and history of tariffs. When a tariff is imposed, part of the impact is upon economic efficiency but the largest effect is often redistributive. In the example shown in Figure 19-3, areas A and B represent efficiency losses from inefficiently high domestic production and inefficiently low consumption, respectively. Under the simplifying assumptions used above, the efficiency losses are equal to the two little triangles and sum up to $100. The redistribution involved and shown as area C is much larger, however, equaling $200 raised in tariff revenues levied upon consumers of the commodity. Consumers will be unhappy about the higher product cost, and producers may attempt to capture the potential revenues by shifting from tariffs to quotas. We can see why battles over import restrictions generally center more on the redistributive gains and losses than on the issues of economic efficiency.

Imposing a tariff has three effects. It encourages inefficient domestic production; it induces consumers to reduce their purchases of the tariffed good below efficient levels; and it raises revenues for the government. Only the first two of these necessarily impose efficiency costs on the economy.

An Example of Tariffs on Textiles

Let's put some flesh on this analysis with the example of a particular tariff, such as a tariff on clothing. Today, tariffs on imported textiles and apparel are among the highest levied by the United States (see Table 19-1). How do these high tariffs affect consumers and producers?

To begin with, the tariff raises domestic clothing prices; it costs more to buy a suit or dress than it would under free trade. Because of the higher prices, many factories, which would otherwise be bankrupt in the face of a declining comparative advantage in textiles, remain open. They are just barely profitable, but they somehow manage to eke out enough sales to continue domestic production. A few more workers are employed in textiles than would otherwise be the case although, because of pressure from foreign competition, textile wages remain among the lowest of any manufacturing industry.

From a national point of view, we are wasting resources in textiles. These workers, materials, and capital would be more productively used in other sectors—perhaps in producing computers or corn or aircraft. The nation's productive potential is lower because it keeps factors of production in an industry in which it has lost its comparative advantage.

Consumers, of course, pay for this protection of the textile industry with higher prices. They get less satisfaction from their incomes than they would if they could buy textiles from Hong Kong, Korea, or China at prices that exclude the high tariffs. Consumers are induced to cut back on their clothing purchases, channeling funds into food, transportation, or recreation, whose relative prices are lowered by the tariff.

In addition, the government gets a few million dollars of revenues from tariffs on textiles. These revenues can be used to buy public goods or to reduce other taxes, so (unlike the consumer loss or the productive inefficiency) this effect is not a real social burden.

Now that we have completed our examination of the way that tariffs affect the price and quantity of a good, we turn to an analysis of the arguments for and against protecting a nation's industries from foreign trade.

The Economics of Protectionism

The arguments for tariff or quota protection against the competition of foreign imports take many different forms. Here are the main categories:

- Non-economic arguments that suggest it is desirable to sacrifice economic welfare in order to subsidize other national objectives
- Arguments that are economically false: some that are clearly defective and some whose falsity can be detected only by subtle and sophisticated economic reasoning
- A few analyses that are invalid in a perfectly competitive full-employment world, but that contain kernels of truth for a nation large enough to affect its import or export prices or for a nation suffering from unemployment

Many of these arguments are a century old; others have been devised by a school known as the "new international economics."[2]

Non-Economic Goals

The first category is most easily considered. If you ever are on a debating team given the assignment of defending free trade, you will strengthen your case at the beginning by conceding that economic welfare is not the only goal in life. A nation surely should not sacrifice its liberty and national security for a few dollars of extra real income gained in trade.

Consider the example of oil. If foreign supplies of oil are insecure, subject to sabotage and monopolization, then it would surely be reasonable for a nation to attempt to reduce its dependence on imported oils.

In some cases, a nation might not produce enough of a product for its essential military needs. This might be true for cobalt or copper. The domestic copper industry might come before Congress and lobby for a high tariff on copper, arguing that only by this means can the nation guarantee an adequate supply in wartime. A careful analysis of this contention reveals that there are often more efficient ways of ensuring the needed amount of strategic materials than by raising tariffs—a particularly useful policy being the storage of such materials in a strategic stockpile.

Yet another argument is that the nation's scientific resources (in aircraft, microelectronics, or computers) will wither away if they are not kept hard at work, protected from foreign competition. Tariffs are sometimes seen as part of a social strategy—to preserve the family farm or the centuries-old tradition of Swiss watchmaking.

A thoughtful analyst cannot dismiss such objectives out of hand. But most economists prefer the use of subsidies rather than quotas or tariffs as a way of attaining non-economic goals. A *subsidy* is a direct payment to a person or a firm that performs a desired service. For example, if the United States wants to maintain its peanut-farming tradition, subsidizing peanut farms would be more efficient than imposing a prohibitive quota on peanuts. Subsidies are preferable because they are more visible and can be debated openly; they prevent sky-high prices that are sometimes produced when supply shocks occur; they do not raise all prices, but affect only the returns of the subsidized firms or workers; and they are subject to periodic review by legislatures.

There are many non-economic goals in a humane society. But attaining them by economic protectionism is usually inefficient and costly.

Grounds for Tariffs Not Based on Sound Economics

Mercantilism. To Abraham Lincoln has been attributed the remark, "I don't know much about the tariff. I do know that when I buy a coat from England, I have the coat and England has the money. But when I buy a coat in America, I have the coat and America has the money."

This reasoning represents an age-old fallacy typi-

[2] An official statement on trade policy is contained in the *Economic Report of the President*, 1991 (Goverment Printing Office, Washington, 1991). For a nontechnical account of the sources of the trade deficit and an account of the "new international economics" as told by one of its leading practitioners, see Paul Krugman, *The Age of Diminished Expectations: U.S. Economic Policy in the 1990s* (MIT Press, Cambridge, Mass., 1990).

an advanced country; already two of your brothers and sisters have died before reaching adulthood.

Most people in your country work on farms. Few can be spared from food production to work in factories. You work with but one-sixtieth the horsepower of a prosperous North American worker. You know little about science, but much about your village traditions.

You and your fellow citizens in the 40 poorest countries constitute 55 percent of the world population, but must divide among each other only 5 percent of world income. You are often hungry, and the food you eat is mainly roughage or rice. While you were among those who got some primary schooling, like most of your friends you did not go on to high school, and only the wealthiest go to a university. You work long hours in the fields without the benefit of machinery. At night you sleep on a mat. You have little household furniture, perhaps a table and a radio. Your only mode of transportation is an old pair of boots.

Such is the way of life in the poorest countries of the world.

Population: The Legacy of Malthus

Some nations are endowed with few people, enjoying a vast continent teeming with minerals and fertile land; others see their people crowded into small plots, leaving no tillable corner untouched. The theory of population can help to explain such disparities among countries.

One of the earliest writers to analyze the relation between population and the economy was T. R. Malthus. He first developed his views while arguing at breakfast against his father's perfectionist view that the human race was always improving. Finally the son became so agitated that he wrote *An Essay on the Principle of Population* (1798). This was an instantaneous best-seller and since then has influenced the thinking of people all over the world about population and economic growth.

Malthus began with the observation of Benjamin Franklin that, in the American colonies where resources were abundant, population tended to double every 25 years or so. He then postulated a universal tendency for population—unless checked by limited food supply—to grow exponentially, or by a

geometric progression.[1] Eventually, a population which doubles every generation—1, 2, 4, 8, 16, 32, 64, 128, 256, 512, 1024, . . . —becomes so large that there is not enough space in the world for all the people to stand.

But Malthus had one further card to play. At this point he unleashed the devil of diminishing returns.He argued that because land is fixed while labor inputs keep growing, food would tend to grow by an arithmetic progression and not by a geometric progression. (Compare 1, 2, 3, 4, . . . , with 1, 2, 4, 8, ...) Malthus concluded:

As population doubles and redoubles, it is as if the globe were halving and halving again in size— until finally it has shrunk so much that the supply of food falls below the level necessary for life.

When the law of diminishing returns is applied to a fixed supply of land, food production tends not to keep up with a population's geometric-progression rate of growth.

Now, Malthus did not say that population necessarily would increase at a geometric rate. This was only its tendency if unchecked. He described the checks that operate, in all times and places, to hold population down. And in his later, little-read editions, Malthus retreated from his gloomy doctrine, holding out hope that population growth could be slowed by birth prevention, rather than by pestilence, famine, and war.

This important application of diminishing returns illustrates the profound effects a simple theory can have. Malthus' ideas had wide repercussions. His book was used to support a stern revision of the English poor laws. Under the influence of Malthus' writings, people argued that poverty should be made as uncomfortable as possible. His opinions also bolstered the argument that trade unions could not improve the welfare of workers— since any increase in their wages would allegedly

---

[1] Exponential (or geometric) growth occurs when a variable increases at a constant proportional rate from period to period. Thus, if a population of 200 is growing at 3 percent per year, it would equal 200 in year 0, 200×1.03 in year 1, $200 \times 1.03 \times 1.03$ in year 2, $200 \times (1.03)^3$ in year 3, . . . , $200 \times (1.03)^{10}$ in year 10, and so on. Money earning compound interest grows geometrically. For example, at 6 percent compound interest, money doubles in value every 12 years. It has been estimated that the $24 received by the Indians for Manhattan Island would, if deposited at compound interest, be worth as much today as all property on the island.

only cause workers to reproduce until all were reduced to a bare subsistence.

Flawed Prophecies of Malthus. Despite his careful statistical studies, demographers today think
that Malthus' views were oversimplified. In his discussion of diminishing returns, Malthus never fully
anticipated the technological miracle of the Industrial Revolution. Nor did he foresee that after 1870
population growth in most Western nations would
begin to decline just as living standards and real
wages grew most rapidly.

In the century following Malthus, technological
advance shifted out the production-possibility
frontiers of countries in Europe and North America.
This rapid technological change allowed output to
far outstrip population, resulting in a rapid rise in
real wages.

Nevertheless, the germs of truth in Malthus' doctrines are still important for understanding the
population behavior of India, Ethiopia, China, and
other parts of the globe where the balance of numbers and food supply is a vital consideration.

Modern Views on Population

The history of population in developed countries
did not follow Malthus' script. In fact, populations
stabilized in most advanced countries as these
countries made the transition from high birth and
death rates in preindustrial times to low birth and
death rates today. Before we can fully understand
this important shift, we must master some of the
concepts of modern **demography,** the study of the
behavior of population.[2]

Birth and Death Rates

Basic to understanding population are the concepts of *crude birth and death rates.* These are simply the number of births or deaths per year per
1000 people. If we subtract the death rate from the

---

[2] An informative summary of the relationship between population and the overall economy is contained in Gary Becker's
presidential address to the American Economic Association,
"Family Economics and Macro Behavior," *American Economic
Review* (March 1988), pp. 1–13.

Sources of Population Growth, 1988 (Rates per 1,000 of Population per Year)			
	Birth rate	Death rate	Natural growth rate
Low-income countries:			
Zambia	49	13	36
Malawi	54	19	35
India	31	11	20
Middle-income countries:			
Venezuela	29	5	24
Brazil	27	8	19
Thailand	22	7	15
High-income countries:			
United States	15	9	6
France	14	10	4
Germany	10	11	−1

**Table 20-2. Birth, death, and population growth
rates**

Data for three groups of countries illustrate how patterns of
population growth change with levels of development. Poor
countries have high birth and death rates. When health conditions improve in the course of economic development, countries experience a fall in death rates. In the richest countries,
birth rates fall, population growth declines, and population
stabilizes. (Source: World Bank, *World Development Report,*
1991.)

birth rate, we get the rate of population growth.[3]
Birth, death, and population growth rates for representative countries are shown in Table 20-2.

The Demographic Transition

We are now in a position to understand the demographic transition that occurs during the course of
economic development. An idealized picture of the
stages is shown in Figure 20-1. Here, population
growth proceeds through four stages:

1. Traditional, preindustrial societies, in which
high birth and death rates lead to low population growth. These societies are today found
only in remote and isolated populations.

---

[3] When applied to a specific country, this calculation assumes
no migration. If there is net immigration (or emigration), then
this figure would have to be added to (or subtracted from)
births minus deaths to get net increase in population.

Capital Formation

While the hands of people are much the same the world around, workers in advanced countries have their hands on a great deal more capital—and are therefore much more productive.

Accumulating capital, as we have seen, requires a sacrifice of current consumption over many decades. But there's the rub, for the poorest countries are near a subsistence standard of living. When you are poor to begin with, reducing current consumption to provide for future consumption seems impossible.

In advanced economies, 10 to 20 percent of income may go into capital formation. By contrast, the poorest agrarian countries are often able to save only 5 percent of national income. Moreover, much of the low level of saving goes to provide the growing population with housing and simple tools. Little is left over for development.

But let's say a country has succeeded in hiking up its rate of saving. Even so, it takes many decades to accumulate the railroads, electricity-generating plants, equipment, factories, and other capital goods that underpin a productive economic structure.

In many developing countries, the single most pressing problem is too little saving. Particularly in the poorest regions, urgent current consumption competes with investment for scarce resources. The result is too little investment in the productive capital so indispensable for rapid economic progress.

Social Overhead Capital. When we think of capital, we must not concentrate only on trucks and steel mills. Many large social investments must precede industrialization, or even the efficient marketing of farm products.

To develop, a private economy must have **social overhead capital.** This consists of the large-scale projects that precede trade and commerce—roads, railroads, irrigation projects, public-health measures, etc. All these involve large investments that tend to be "indivisible," or lumpy, and sometimes have increasing returns to scale. No small farm or family can profitably undertake to build a railroad system; no pioneering private enterprise can hope to make a profit from a telephone or irrigation sys-

tem before the markets have been developed. These large-scale investment projects spread their benefits widely across the economy.

Often these projects involve external economies, or spillovers that private firms cannot capture. For example, a regional agricultural adviser can help all farmers in an area; or a public-health program inoculating people against typhoid or diphtheria protects the population beyond those inoculated. In each of these cases it would be impossible for an enterprising firm to capture the social benefits because the firm cannot collect fees from the thousands or even millions of beneficiaries. Because of the large indivisibilities and external effects, the government must step in, provide the necessary funds and initiative, and ensure that these social overhead investments are undertaken.

Foreign Borrowing and the Debt Crisis

If there are so many obstacles to finding domestic saving for capital formation, why not rely more heavily on foreign sources? Does not economic theory tell us that a rich country, which has tapped its own high-yield investment projects, can benefit both itself and the recipient by investing in high-yield projects abroad?

Actually, prior to 1914, economic development did proceed in this fashion. Britain in the last century saved about 15 percent of its GNP and invested fully half this amount abroad. And during most of the period after World War II, the United States and other advanced countries lent large sums to developing countries. The figures on foreign investment in low- and middle-income countries show an impressive record of capital transfer: foreign loans averaged $112 billion annually in the period 1980–1982. Investors in wealthy countries sent their funds abroad in search of higher returns than were available at home; poor countries, hungry for funds to finance investment projects or even consumption, welcomed this flow of foreign capital.

By the end of the 1970s, however, the extent of foreign borrowing by developing countries had become unsustainably large. Total outstanding debt grew almost 20 percent per year and increased by almost $500 billion from 1973 to 1982. Some of these loans were put to good use in investments in oil drilling, textile factories, and coal-mining equipment, but others simply raised consumption levels.

As long as the exports of these countries grew at the same rate as borrowings, all was well. But with the rise in world interest rates and the slowdown in the world economy after 1980, many countries found that their borrow-and-invest strategy had led them to the brink of financial crisis. Some countries (such as Bolivia and Peru) needed all their export earnings simply to pay the interest on their foreign debt. Others found themselves unable to meet debt-repayment schedules. Almost all indebted developing countries were staggering under heavy debt-service burdens (i.e., the need to repay the interest and principal on their loans). As a result, country after country, particularly in Latin America, failed to make interest payments and had their debts "rescheduled," or postponed.

By the early 1990s, the debt crisis continued to pose serious problems for heavily indebted countries. What does economic history suggest will be the future course of events in the area of foreign debt? If no severe shocks hit the world economy, indebted countries can probably move back toward lower levels of foreign debt. However, a severe shock to output, interest rates, or confidence might weaken the international financial system so much that loans to poor countries would once again be severely restricted.

Technological Change and Innovations

In addition to the fundamental factors of population, natural resources, and capital formation, development depends on the vital fourth factor, technology. Here developing countries have one potential advantage: they can hope to benefit by relying on the technological progress of more advanced nations.

Imitating Technology. Poor countries do not need to find modern Newtons to discover the law of gravity; they can read about it in any physics book. They don't have to repeat the slow, meandering climb of the Industrial Revolution; they can buy tractors, computers, and power looms undreamed of by the great merchants of the past.

Japan and the United States clearly illustrate this in their historical developments. Japan joined the industrial race late and only at the end of the nineteenth century sent students abroad to learn Western technology. The Japanese government took an active role in stimulating the pace of development and in building railroads and utilities. Relying on the adaptation of foreign technologies, Japan moved into its position today as the world's second-largest industrial economy.

The case of the United States itself provides a hopeful example to the rest of the world. Only in the 1930s did America reach the front rank in the field of pure science. Yet for a century its applied technology was outstanding. The key inventions involved in the automobile originated almost exclusively abroad. Nevertheless, Henry Ford and General Motors applied foreign inventions and outproduced the rest of the world. The examples of the United States and Japan show how countries can thrive by adapting foreign science and technology to local market conditions.

Entrepreneurship and Innovation. From the histories of Japan and the United States, it might appear that adaptation of foreign technology is an easy recipe for development. You might say: "Just go abroad; copy more efficient methods; put them into effect at home; then sit back and wait for the extra output to roll in."

In fact, technological change is not that simple. You can send a textbook on chemical engineering to Poorovia, but without skilled scientists, engineers, and entrepreneurs and without adequate capital, Poorovia couldn't even think about building a working petrochemical plant. Remember, the advanced technology was itself developed to meet the special conditions of the advanced countries—including high wages, plentiful capital relative to labor, and ample skilled engineers. These conditions do not prevail in poorer countries.

One of the key tasks of economic development is the fostering of an entrepreneurial spirit. A country cannot thrive without a group of owners or managers willing to undertake risks, open new plants, adopt new technologies, confront strife, and import new ways of doing business. Government can help entrepreneurship by setting up extension services for farmers, educating and training the work force, establishing management schools, and making sure that government itself maintains a healthy re-spect for the role of private initiative.

Vicious Cycle

We have emphasized that poor countries face great obstacles in combining the four elements of prog-ress—labor, capital, resources, and entrepreneur-ship. In addition, countries find that the difficulties reinforce each other in a *vicious cycle of poverty.*

Figure 20-2 illustrates how one hurdle raises yet other hurdles. Low incomes lead to low saving; low saving retards the growth of capital; inadequate capital prevents introduction of machinery and rapid growth in productivity; low productivity leads to low incomes. Other elements in poverty are also self-reinforcing. Poverty is accompanied by low levels of skill and literacy; these in turn prevent the adaptation of new and improved technologies.

Overcoming the barriers of poverty often requires a concerted effort on many fronts, and some devel-opment economists recommend a "big push" for-ward to break the vicious cycle. If a country is fortu-nate, simultaneous steps to invest more, develop skills, and curb population growth can break the vicious cycle of poverty and stimulate a virtuous cycle of rapid economic development.

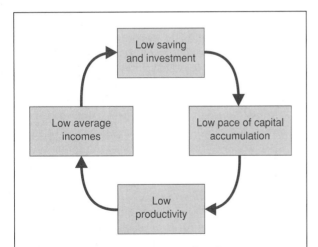

Figure 20-2. The vicious cycle of underdevelopment

Many obstacles to development are reinforcing. Low levels of income prevent saving, retard capital growth, hinder productivity growth, and keep income low. Successful development may require taking steps to break the chain at many points.

Strategies of Economic Development

We see how countries must combine labor, re-sources, capital, and technology in order to grow rapidly. But this is no real formula; it is the equiva-lent of saying that an Olympic sprinter must run like the wind. Why do some countries succeed in running faster than others? How do poor countries ever get started down the road of economic devel-opment?

Comprehensive Theories

Historians and social scientists have long been fas-cinated by the differences in the pace of economic growth among nations. Some early theories stressed climate, noting that all advanced countries lie in the earth's temperate zone. Others have pointed to the importance of custom, culture, or religion as a key factor. Max Weber emphasized the "Protestant ethic" as a driving force behind capital-ism. More recently, Mancur Olson has argued that nations begin to decline when their decision struc-ture becomes brittle and when interest groups or oligarchies prevent social and economic change.

No doubt each of these theories has some valid-ity for a particular time and place. But they do not hold up as universal explanations of economic de-velopment. Weber's theory leaves unexplained why the cradle of civilization appeared in the Near East and Greece while the later-dominant Europeans lived in caves, worshiped trolls, and wore bear-skins. Where is the Protestant ethic in a sleek Japa-nese factory in which workers gather to pay hom-age to Buddha? How can we explain that a country like Japan, with a rigid social structure and power-ful lobbies, has become the world's most produc-tive economy?

To understand the diversity of economic experi-ence, we must turn to broader explanations.

Recent Approaches to Development

For decades economists have been intensely inter-ested in economic development. The following ac-count represents a montage of important ideas developed in recent years. Each theory attempts to describe how countries break out of the vicious cycle of poverty and begin to mobilize the four wheels of economic development.

The Takeoff. Human history is long, and the era of economic development has come only recently. During most of history, life was nasty, brutish, and short. But, in a few places over a brief period, superior production techniques were introduced. Great inequality of income allowed a few to funnel saving into capital formation. Economic development could take place.

So dramatic was the discontinuity between earlier periods and the Industrial Revolution that scholars like W. W. Rostow developed a theory stressing stages of economic growth. One of Rostow's stages is called the *takeoff,* the analogy being with an airplane, which can fly only after attaining a critical speed.

Different countries had their takeoffs in different periods: England at the beginning of the eighteenth century, the United States around 1850, Japan in 1910, and Mexico after 1940.

The takeoff is impelled by "leading sectors," such as a rapidly growing export market or an industry displaying large economies of scale. Once these leading sectors begin to flourish, a process of *self-sustaining growth* (the takeoff) occurs. Growth leads to profits; profits are reinvested; capital, productivity, and per capita incomes spurt ahead. The virtuous cycle of economic development is under way.

The Backwardness Hypothesis. A second view emphasizes the international context of development. We saw above that poorer countries have important advantages that the first pioneers along the path of industrialization did not. Developing nations can now draw upon the capital, skills, and technology of more advanced countries. This hypothesis, advanced by Alexander Gerschenkron of Harvard, suggests that *relative backwardness* itself may aid development. Countries can buy modern textile machinery, efficient pumps, miracle seeds, chemical fertilizers, and medical supplies. Because they can lean on the technologies of advanced countries, today's developing countries can grow more rapidly than did Britain or Western Europe in the period 1780–1850.

Balanced Growth. The takeoff and backwardness hypotheses have caught the attention of scholars and experts. But we must step back and assess history to see whether they fit the facts. Some writers suggest that growth is a *balanced* process with

countries progressing steadily ahead. In their view, economic development resembles the tortoise, making continual progress, rather than the hare, who runs in spurts and then rests when exhausted.

The three alternatives can be seen graphically in Figure 20-3. Here we see how the takeoff, the backwardness hypothesis, and the balanced-growth views would appear over time for three countries—advanced A, middle-income B, and low-income C.

Which of these three views appears most closely to explain history? In one outstanding study, Nobel-laureate Simon Kuznets examined the history of 13 advanced countries, going back as far as 1800.[4] He concluded that the balanced-growth model is most consistent with the countries he studied. He saw no significant rise or fall in economic growth as development progressed.

Note one further important difference between the three theories. The takeoff theory suggests that there will be increasing *divergence* among countries (some flying rapidly, while others are unable to leave the ground). The backwardness hypothesis suggests *convergence,* while the Kuznets view suggests roughly constant differentials. Empirical evidence shown in Table 20-3 indicates that there has

---

[4] Simon Kuznets, *Economic Growth of Nations* (Harvard University Press, Cambridge, Mass., 1971).

Recent Growth Trends		
	Rate of growth of real GNP (% per year)	
Country group	1965–1980	1980–1989
Low-income:		
China and India	5.0	7.6
Other	4.6	3.4
Middle-income:		
Lower-middle	5.5	2.5
Upper-middle	6.8	3.2
Industrial market economies	3.8	3.0

Table 20-3. Poorer countries are slowly closing the income gap

Data on the growth in total output show that poor countries were unable to close the gap between themselves and the industrial market economies during the 1960s, but middle-income or newly industrializing countries grew rapidly. Stagnation in high-income market economies during the 1970s allowed the relative output gaps to close by 10 to 25 percent. (Source: World Bank, *World Development Report, 1991.*)

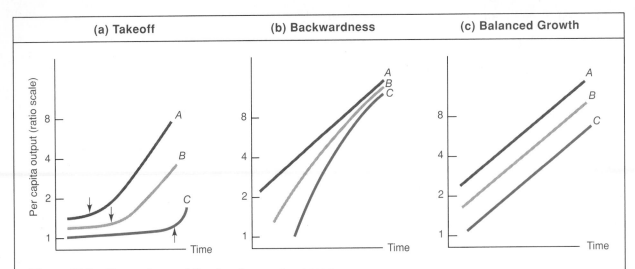

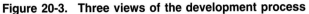

Figure 20-3.   Three views of the development process

Consider advanced Country A, middle-income Country B, and low-income Country C. In part **(a)**, leading sectors such as exports promote a takeoff (shown by arrows) into rapid self-sustaining growth. In part **(b)**, backward countries rely on and adopt technologies invented by richer countries. They thus grow rapidly and gradually catch up with advanced countries. In the final scheme, **(c)**, countries grow at the same rate, and the relative gap between countries is roughly constant.

Note that output is shown on a ratio scale, meaning that the *slope* of each line represents the *growth* rate of output. Thus a constant slope, as in part **(c)**, indicates a constant annual growth rate of output; while an increasing slope, as in part **(a)**, indicates an increasing growth rate of output. What is occurring in part **(b)**? [Adapted from Bruce Herrick and Charles P. Kindleberger, *Economic Development* (McGraw-Hill, New York, 1983)].

been little convergence between advanced and developing countries in the last quarter-century (although the performance of individual countries has varied greatly from the average)—a pattern of growth rates most consistent with the balanced-growth view.

Issues in Economic Development

To say that countries must encourage rapid growth in capital and technology does not answer *how* these key ingredients are to be deployed. Among the vast array of issues that arise in development planning, we focus here on four recurrent themes: the balance between industry and agriculture, the role of outward orientation, the risks of overspecialization, and the role of the market.

Industrialization vs. Agriculture. In most countries, incomes in urban areas are almost double those in rural agriculture. And in affluent nations, much of the economy is in industry, particularly manufacturing. Hence, many nations jump to the

conclusion that industrialization is the cause rather than the effect of affluence.

We must be wary of such inferences, which often fall into the *post hoc* fallacy. You sometimes hear, "Rich men smoke cigars, but smoking a cigar will not make you a rich man." Similarly, there is no economic justification for a poor country to insist upon having its own national airline and large steel mill. These are not the fundamental necessities of economic growth.

The lesson of decades of attempts to accelerate industrialization at the expense of agriculture has led many analysts to rethink the role of farming. Industrialization tends to be capital-intensive, attracts workers into crowded cities, and often produces high levels of unemployment. Raising productivity on farms may require less capital, while providing productive employment for surplus labor.

Indeed, if Bangladesh could increase the productivity of its farming by 20 percent, that would do more to release resources for the production of comforts than would trying to construct a domestic steel industry that would displace imported metals.

Inward vs. Outward Orientation. A fundamental issue of economic development concerns a country's stance toward international trade. Should developing countries attempt to be self-sufficient, replacing most imports with domestic production? (This is known as a strategy of *import substitution.*) Or should a country strive to pay for the imports it needs by improving efficiency and competitiveness, developing foreign markets, and giving incentives for exports? (This is called a strategy of *outward orientation.*)

Policies of import substitution have often been popular in Latin America. The policy most frequently used toward this end has been to build high tariff walls around manufacturing industries so that local firms can produce and sell goods that would otherwise be imported. For example, Brazil has placed high tariffs on automobiles to encourage firms to assemble autos at home rather than import much less expensive cars from North America or Japan.

Critics observe that such subsidized import substitution generally limits competition, dampens innovation and productivity growth, and keeps the country's real income low. This approach ignores the benefits of specialization and comparative advantage. The consumers and the entire economy might be better off if the emphasis on import substitution were replaced by an emphasis on outward orientation. Outward expansion sets up a system of incentives that stimulates exports. Key features of this approach are maintaining a competitive foreign exchange rate, choosing foreign-trade policies that encourage firms to produce for export, and minimizing unnecessary government regulation of businesses, especially of small firms.

The success of outward-expansion policies is best illustrated by the East Asian NICs. A generation ago, countries like Taiwan, South Korea, and Singapore had per capita incomes one-quarter to one-third of those in the wealthiest Latin American countries. Yet, by saving large fractions of their national incomes and channeling these to high-return export industries, the East Asian NICs overtook every Latin American country by the late 1980s. The secret to success was not a complete laissez-faire policy, for the governments in fact en-

gaged in some planning and intervention. Rather, the outward orientation allowed the countries to reap economies of scale and the benefits of international specialization and thus to increase employment, effectively use domestic resources, enjoy rapid productivity growth, and provide enormous gains in living standards.

A recent study of the economic prospects of Latin America concludes with the following assessment of the effects of outward expansion:

> Outward orientation is the keystone of the strategies of virtually all the "success stories" [of economic development]—in East and southeast Asia, in Latin America in certain periods, in Turkey, and elsewhere. Even where success has been limited, as in Africa, relatively outward-oriented countries have done much better than inward-oriented.[5]

The Dangers of Overspecialization. We have repeatedly emphasized the economic gains from specialization, whether within a nation or among nations, because division of labor allows a vast increase in the quantity and variety of producible goods and services. But can a nation become dangerously overspecialized? Imagine the fate of a nation with big cost advantages that specialized completely in horseshoe manufacture in 1900, in production of vacuum tubes in 1945, or in construction of nuclear reactors in 1975?

Some degree of diversification is essential. If Venezuela exports mainly oil and Zambia mainly copper, price fluctuations in these markets will have a large effect on their foreign-trade balances and real incomes. Table 20-4 shows the degree to which some economies engage in "monoculture"—that is, have most of their exports concentrated in a single product. The oil-exporting countries are the most vulnerable to the dangers of overspecialization, followed by producers of other primary commodities.

[5] Bela Belassa et al., *Toward Renewed Economic Growth in Latin America* (Institute for International Economics, Washington, D.C., 1986), p. 24. This study points out that microeconomic government regulations may be as important as macroeconomic policies, with the following example: "The state as regulator has stifled much entrepreneurial initiative throughout [Latin America]. In several countries, numerous licenses are needed even to begin exporting—hardly an auspicious framework within which to promote outward expansion. In Peru, it recently took 289 days to register a new corporation—compared with four hours in Miami" (p. 30).

ery. It offers much hope to the developing nations inasmuch as they can adapt the more productive technologies of advanced nations. This requires entrepreneurship. One task of development is to spur internal growth of the scarce entrepreneurial spirit.

8. Numerous theories of economic development help explain why the four fundamental factors are present or absent at a particular time. Geography and climate, custom, religious and business attitudes, class conflicts and colonialism—each affects economic development. But none does so in a simple and invariable way.

   More convincing are the takeoff theory (whereby increasing returns and social overhead capital combine to allow rapid growth in a short period); the backwardness hypothesis (in which less advanced countries can converge quickly toward the more advanced by borrowing their technology and technologists); and the balanced-growth view (in which countries tend to grow at pretty much the same rate whether advanced or backward).

CONCEPTS FOR REVIEW

Basic concepts
developing country, LDC
indicators of development
Malthusian population theory
demographic transition
   (stages 1, 2, 3, 4)

social overhead capital, externalities

Development strategies
four elements in development:
   human resources, natural
      resources, capital, technology

   and innovation
takeoff, backwardness, and balanced-
   growth hypotheses
inward vs. outward orientation
overspecialization in exports

QUESTIONS FOR DISCUSSION

1. Examine each of the countries in Table 20-2. Can you say where each is in its demographic transition?

2. Many economists believe that the state should not interfere in a market where there are no important externalities—this being the "liberal" or laissez-faire tradition. Are there externalities in population growth that would lead to positive or negative spillovers? Consider such items as education, national defense, roads, pollution, and the creation of geniuses like Mozart or Einstein.

3. A *geometric progression* is a sequence of terms $(g_1, g_2, \ldots, g_t, g_{t+1}, \ldots)$ in which each term is the same multiple of its predecessor, $g_2/g_1 = g_3/g_2 = \cdots = g_{t+1}/g_t = \beta$. If $\beta = 1 + i > 1$ the terms grow exponentially like compound interest. An *arithmetic progression* is a sequence $(a_1, a_2, a_3, \ldots, a_t, a_{t+1}, \ldots)$ in which the difference between each term and its predecessor is the same constant: $a_2 - a_1 = a_3 - a_2 = \cdots = a_{t+1} - a_t = \alpha$. Give examples of each. Satisfy yourself that any geometric progression with $\beta > 1$ must even-

tually surpass any arithmetic progression. Relate this to Malthus' theory.

4. Recall that Malthus asserted that unchecked population would grow geometrically, while food supply—constrained by diminishing returns—would grow only arithmetically. Use a numerical example to show why per capita food production must decline if population is unchecked while diminishing returns lead food production to grow more slowly than labor inputs.

5. Would you expect everyone to agree with the praise of material well-being expressed in the chapter's opening quotation?

6. Delineate each of the four important factors driving economic development. With respect to these, how was it that the high-income oil-exporting countries became rich? What hope is there for a country like Bangladesh, which has very low per capita resources of capital, land, and technology?

7. Some fear the "vicious cycle of underdevelopment."

Rapid population growth eats into whatever improvements in technology occur and lowers living standards. With a low per capita income, the country cannot save and invest and mainly engages in subsistence farming. With most of the population on the farm, there is little hope for education, decline in fertility, or industrialization. If you were to advise such a country, how would you break through the vicious cycle?

8. Compare the situation a developing country faces today with that it might have faced (at an equivalent level of per capita income) 200 years ago. Considering the four wheels of economic development, explain the advantages and disadvantages that today's developing country might experience.

9. **Advanced problem** (for those who have also studied economic-growth theory in Chapter 12): We can extend our growth-accounting equation to include three factors and write the following equation:

$$g_Q = s_L g_L + s_K g_K + s_R g_R + \text{T. C.}$$

where g_Q = the growth rate of output, g_i = the growth rate of inputs (i = inputs to production = L for labor, K for capital, and R for land and other natural resources), and s_i = the contribution of each input to output growth as measured by its share of national income ($0 \le s_i \le 1$ and $s_L + s_K + s_R = 1$). T. C. measures technological change.

(a) In the poorest developing countries, the share of capital is close to zero, the main resource is agricultural land (which is constant), and there is little technological change. Can you see why per capita output is likely to be stagnant or even to decline (i.e., $g_Q < g_L$)? Explain the Malthusian hypothesis in terms of this model.

(b) In advanced industrial economies, the share of land resources drops to virtually zero. Why does the generalized growth-account equation then become identical to that given in Chapter 12? Can you explain the failure of the Malthusian hypothesis in terms of this equation?

(c) According to economists who are pessimistic about future prospects (including a group known as "neo-Malthusians"), T. C. is close to zero, the available supply of natural resources is declining, and the share of resources is large and rising. Does this explain why the future of industrial societies might be bleak? What assumptions of the neo-Malthusians might you question?

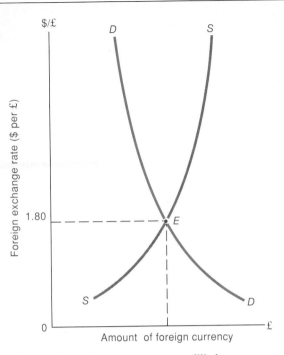

Figure 21-1.   Exchange-rate equilibrium

The market exchange rate comes when supply and demand for goods, services, and capital flows are in balance. Behind demand is the desire to import British goods, buy British securities, visit the Bard's grave, and so forth. Behind the supply of pounds to be traded for dollars is British desire for U.S. goods, services, and capital. If the rate were above *E*, there would be an excess supply of foreign currency; market forces would push the exchange rate back down to *E*, where the supply and demand for foreign currency are just in balance.

want to buy land in Britain or to purchase shares in British companies. In short, we demand foreign currencies when we purchase foreign goods, services, and assets. The demand curve shown in Figure 21-1 is represented by the downward-sloping *DD* curve, with the vertical axis representing the price of the British pound. The demand curve generally slopes downward to indicate that as the price of the British pound falls, foreigners tend to want to buy more British goods. For example, if the pound were to fall from $1.80/£ to $1.20/£, other things being equal, Americans would want to buy more British bicycles and spend more time visiting Britain.

What lies behind the supply of foreign currency

(represented in Figure 21-1 by the *SS* supply curve of British pounds)? The British supply their currency when they import goods, services, and assets. For example, when a British student buys an American book or takes a trip to the United States, she supplies the British pounds necessary for the expense. Or when the British government purchases an American supercomputer for weather forecasting, this increases the supply of British pounds. In short, the British supply pounds to pay for their purchases of foreign goods, services, and financial assets. The supply curve in Figure 21-1 slopes upward to indicate that as the pound's value rises (and the dollar therefore becomes less expensive) British residents will want to buy more foreign goods, services, and investments and will therefore generally supply more of their currency to the foreign exchange market.

The supply and demand for British pounds interact in the foreign exchange market. Market forces move the foreign exchange rate up or down to balance the inflows and outflows of pounds; the price will settle at the equilibrium foreign exchange rate at which the pounds willingly bought just equal the pounds willingly sold.

The balance of supply and demand for foreign exchange determines the foreign exchange rate of a currency. At the market exchange rate of $1.80 per £1, shown at point *E* in Figure 21-1, the exchange rate is in equilibrium and has no tendency to rise or fall.

We saw above that the exchange rate is a reciprocal relationship. Just as we sell a British pound for $1.80, we buy a dollar for £0.56. We could also have drawn the reciprocal demand-and-supply relationship by analyzing the demand and supply of U.S. dollars. In our simplified bilateral trading world, the British supply of pounds would translate into a demand for dollars, while the American demand for pounds would represent a supply of dollars. We could then draw the supply and demand for the dollar foreign exchange, and the equilibrium would come at £0.56/$ rather than $1.80/£.

Moreover, this supply and demand for foreign exchange exists for every currency. And in a world of many nations, it is the many-sided exchange and trade, with demands and supplies coming from all quarters, that determines the entire array of foreign exchange rates.

Effects of Changes in Trade. What would happen if there were changes in the volume of international trade? For example, what would happen if the United States withdrew its troops from Europe or decided to curb imports from Britain, or if we traveled less abroad?

In each of these cases, America's demand for foreign currencies would decrease. The result is shown in Figure 21-2 for the case where the shift affects Britain. The decline in purchases of goods, services, and investments decreases the demand for foreign currencies. This change is represented by a leftward shift in the demand curve. The result

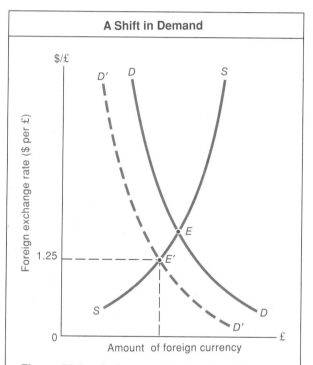

A Shift in Demand

Figure 21-2.   A decrease in American Imports leads to a higher dollar exchange rate

Suppose Americans travel less to Britain or decide to withdraw troops from Europe. This will lower the imports from Britain and decrease the demand for British pounds, shifting the *DD* curve to the left to *D'D'*. As a result, the exchange rate of the pound falls to $1.25 per £1 (similarly, the exchange rate of the dollar rises to £0.80/$). At the new exchange rate at *E'*, British exports are stimulated and American imports decline until the supply and demand for British pounds are once more in balance. (What would be the impact of a decision by the British government to stop buying American military equipment?)

will be a lower price of foreign currencies, that is, a lower exchange rate on the pound and a higher exchange rate on the dollar. How much will exchange rates change? Just enough so that British exports and capital flows to America are increased, and imports and capital flows from America to Britain are decreased, until supply and demand are again in balance. In the example shown in Figure 21-2, the pound has declined from $1.80 to $1.25 per £1.

Terminology for Exchange-Rate Changes

Foreign exchange markets have a special vocabulary. By definition, a fall in the price of one currency in terms of one or all others is called a "depreciation." A rise in the price of a currency in terms of another currency is called an "appreciation." In our example above, when the price of the pound went from $1.80 to $1.25, the pound depreciated and the dollar underwent an appreciation.

The term "devaluation" is often confused with the term "depreciation." Devaluation is confined to situations in which a country has officially pegged its exchange rate to another currency or to gold and in which the pegged rate or "parity" is changed by raising the price of the other currency or gold.

For example, in 1971 the United States changed the official price of gold from $35 to $38 per ounce, so we say the dollar was devalued. But when the dollar fell from 150 yen/$ to 120 yen/$ in the marketplace, the dollar depreciated.

When a country's foreign exchange rate declines relative to that of another country, we say that the domestic currency **depreciates** while the foreign currency **appreciates.**

When a country's official foreign exchange rate (relative to gold or other currencies) is lowered, we say that the currency has undergone a **devaluation,** while an increase in the official foreign exchange rate is called a **revaluation.**

Three Major Exchange-Rate Systems

Having reviewed the principles underlying the market determination of exchange rates, we can now turn to an analysis of the **exchange-rate system,** which denotes the set of rules, arrangements, and institutions under which payments are made and received for transactions reaching across national boundaries.

At the outset, we must ask why there is an exchange-rate system to regulate exchange rates, when there is no "lettuce system" to regulate lettuce prices or even a "machinery system" to affect the machinery market. The reason is that foreign exchange rates affect output, inflation, foreign trade, and many other central economic goals, so it is natural that governments will regulate exchange markets in an attempt to improve international economic performance.

The importance of the international monetary system was well described by economist Robert Solomon:

> Like the traffic lights in a city, the international monetary system is taken for granted until it begins to malfunction and to disrupt people's lives. . . . A well-functioning monetary system will facilitate international trade and investment and smooth adaptation to change. A monetary system that functions poorly may not only discourage the development of trade and investment among nations but subject their economies to disruptive shocks when necessary adjustments to change are prevented or delayed.[1]

There are three major exchange-rate systems:

- The gold standard
- A system of "pure" floating exchange rates, in which exchange rates fluctuate with private supply and demand so as to balance the exchange market
- A hybrid system of "managed" floating exchange rates, which involves some currencies whose values float freely, some currencies whose values are determined by a combination of government intervention and the market, and some that are pegged or fixed to one currency or a group of currencies

The Classical Gold Standard

Historically, one of the most important exchange-rate systems was the gold standard. This system held sway in its purest form during the period 1880–1913. In this system, countries defined their

currencies in terms of a fixed amount of gold, thereby establishing fixed exchange rates among the countries on the gold standard.

The functioning of the gold standard can be seen easily by a simplified example. Suppose people everywhere insisted on being paid in bits of pure gold metal. Then buying a bicycle in Britain would merely require payment in gold at a price expressed in ounces of gold. By definition there would be no foreign-exchange-rate problem. Gold would be the common world currency.

This example captures the essence of the gold standard. It became customary for each country to issue gold coins carrying the seal of the state to guarantee purity and weight. Once gold coins became the medium of exchange—money—foreign trade was no different from domestic trade; everything could be paid for in gold. Differences arose only if countries chose different *units* for their coins. Thus, Queen Victoria chose to make British coins about $\frac{1}{4}$ ounce of gold (the pound) and President McKinley chose to make the U.S. unit $\frac{1}{20}$ ounce of gold (the dollar). In that case, the British pound, being 5 times as heavy as the dollar, had an exchange rate of $5 to £1.

In the years before 1914, this was basically how the gold standard worked. Of course, countries tended to use their own coins. But anyone was free to melt down coins and sell them at the going price of gold. So, exchange rates were fixed for all countries on the gold standard; the rates of exchange (also called "par values" or "parities") for different currencies were determined by the gold content of their monetary units.

Only minor qualifications need be brought to the gold-standard example analyzed above. Because gold is quite inconvenient to carry around, governments inevitably issued paper certificates that were pledged to be redeemable in gold metal. People had the right to exchange gold for certificates and certificates for gold, and they often exercised that right. Also, in those days ocean transport was slow and costly, and there were in reality costs of melting and recoining. Therefore, exchange rates were not exactly fixed but fluctuated in a narrow band.

Hume's Gold-Flow Equilibrating Mechanism

Under the gold standard, what kept America from buying more British goods and services and lend-

---

[1] Robert Solomon, *The International Monetary System, 1945–1976: An Insider's View* (Harper & Row, New York, 1977), pp. 1, 7.

ing more capital to Britain than Britain bought from or lent to America? Put differently, what kept us from demanding more British pounds than Britain wanted to supply? We would have had to ship gold to Britain to pay for our trade deficit. Wouldn't we eventually lose all our gold?

Mercantilists fretted that there would be a drain of a country's gold and argued that the government should halt this drain by placing tariffs and quotas on imports, subsidizing exports, and invoking numerous other interferences.

Mercantilism came under attack from Adam Smith. But the clearest refutation of mercantile reasoning flowed from the pen of the British philosopher David Hume in 1752. His argument is as valid today as it was then for understanding how trade flows get balanced.

First of all, Hume pointed out, all countries could not be simultaneously losing gold. Where would it go, into the sea? And even if a single nation were to lose a good deal of its gold, that would be no tragedy if prices were to adjust as well. Suppose Britain lost half its gold. If at the same time all prices and incomes in Britain were exactly halved, then no one in the country would be any better or worse off. Even though people have only half as much gold, that smaller amount will buy the same quantity of goods and services. The *real* value of monetary gold (that is, the quantity of real commodities that the gold will buy) is unchanged. So, Hume argued, losing half or nine-tenths of a nation's gold is of no concern if the nation ends up with a balanced reduction of all prices and costs.

The second part of Hume's reasoning showed that there is an automatic mechanism that tends to keep international payments in balance under the gold standard. This explanation rested in part upon the quantity theory of prices outlined in Chapter 17, so we would do well to review the quantity theory here.

Gold and the Quantity Theory. Hume was, in fact, one of the earliest proponents of the quantity theory of prices. This doctrine holds that the overall price level in an economy is proportional to the supply of money. Under the gold standard, gold formed an important part of the money supply— either directly, in the form of gold coins, or indirectly when governments used gold as backing for paper money.

What would be the impact of a country's losing gold? First, the country's money supply would decline either because gold coins would be exported or because some of the gold backing for the currency would leave the country. Putting both these consequences together, we would find that a loss of gold leads to a reduction in the money supply. The next step, according to the quantity theory, is that prices and costs would change proportionally to the change in the money supply. If Britain loses 10 percent of its gold to pay for a trade deficit, the quantity theory predicts that Britain's prices, costs, and incomes would fall 10 percent. If gold discoveries in California increased gold supplies sharply, we would expect to see a proportional increase in the price level in the United States.

The Four-Pronged Mechanism. Now consider Hume's theory on international payments equilibrium. Suppose that America runs a large trade deficit and begins to lose gold. According to the quantity theory of prices, this loss of gold reduces America's money supply, driving down America's prices and costs.

As a result, (1) America decreases its imports of British and other foreign goods, which have become relatively expensive; (2) because America's domestically produced goods have become relatively inexpensive on world markets, America's exports increase. The opposite effect occurs in Britain and other foreign countries. When Britain's exports grow rapidly, it receives gold in return. Britain's money supply increases, driving up British prices and costs according to the quantity theory.

At this point, two more prongs of the Hume mechanism come into play: (3) British and other foreign exports have become more expensive, so the volume of goods exported to America declines; and (4) British citizens, faced with a higher domestic price level, now import more of America's low-priced goods.

The result of Hume's four-pronged gold-flow mechanism is to improve the balance of payments of the country losing gold and to worsen that of the country gaining the gold. In the end, an equilibrium of international trade and finance is reestablished at new relative prices, which keep trade and international lending in balance with no net gold flow. This equilibrium is a stable one and requires no tariffs or other government intervention.

Flexible Exchange Rates

Having seen how a gold standard works, we turn next to flexible exchange rates. A system of **flexible exchange rates** is one in which the foreign exchange rate is predominantly determined by the market forces of supply and demand. That is, in a flexible-exchange-rate system, the relative prices of currencies are determined by buying and selling among people, firms, and governments.

Under the gold standard, the dollar and the pound were tied in a $5-to-£1 relationship. But what would have happened in 1913 if the United States had decided not to define its dollar in terms of a fixed weight of gold? Would the dollar have sold for $4 per £1? Or $6 per £1? Since 1973, the world has learned that flexible exchange rates tend to fluctuate widely.

Within the class of flexible-exchange-rate systems, we can distinguish the two important subcases of a *free-floating* system and a *managed-floating* system. The difference between these two systems depends on the amount of government intervention. Government exchange-rate **intervention** occurs when the government buys or sells its own or foreign currencies to affect exchange rates. For example, the Japanese government on a given day might buy $1 billion worth of Japanese yen with U.S. dollars. This would cause a rise in value, or appreciation, of the yen. Governments generally tend to intervene heavily when they believe their country's foreign exchange rate is higher or lower than is desirable.

A **freely floating** exchange rate is one determined purely by supply and demand without any government intervention. In a **managed-floating** system, the government intervenes in exchange markets to affect the exchange rate.

Freely Floating Exchange Rates

The first case we examine is that of freely floating exchange rates. In a system of freely floating exchange rates, prices are determined by the forces of supply and demand, as was illustrated at the beginning of this chapter. Say that at an exchange rate of $1.50 per £1, Americans are importing many British goods, while the British are importing few American goods. This means that Americans will be de-

manding a large quantity of British pounds to buy British goods, but the British will be supplying few British pounds.

What will be the outcome? The excess demand for British pounds will bid up the price of pounds (or, equivalently, will bid down the price of the dollar).

How far will exchange rates move? Just far enough so that—at the new higher price of, say, $2 for the British pound—the foreign exchange market will be in equilibrium. The price of the pound must move up until the diminished quantity of British pounds demanded is equal to the increased supply of British pounds.

Two main steps are involved. (1) With the pound more expensive, it will cost more to import British goods, services, and investments, causing our demand for imports to fall off in the usual fashion. (2) With the dollar now cheaper, our goods will cost less to foreigners. They will want to purchase more of our export goods. (If we look at these two effects from the viewpoints of both countries, we have something much like the four-pronged mechanism of Hume.)

Managed Exchange Rates

In the freely floating exchange-rate system just described, the government is on the sidelines. It allows the foreign exchange market to determine the value of the dollar (just as it allows markets to determine the value of oats, GM stock, or copper).

Few countries, in reality, allow their currencies to float freely. Rather, they manage their exchange rates, intervening to prevent wide swings in exchange rates, or even to maintain a *parity* (an announced target exchange rate with other countries).

A particularly important example of a managed exchange-rate system, known as *pegged exchange rates*, prevailed during the period from World War II until 1971. Called the *Bretton Woods system*, it allowed countries to set fixed parities or pegged exchange rates with each other; the rates might be $2.40 per British pound, 4 German marks per $1, and so forth. Countries then took steps to defend the set of exchange rates. From time to time, when exchange rates deviated too far from the official rates, countries would adjust the official parities. The essence of the Bretton Woods system was that the exchange rates were fixed but adjustable—that is, fixed in the short run but adjustable in the long run.

Today, we see a variety of different exchange-rate systems coexisting. Western European countries have joined together in a system similar to the Bretton Woods system. But each of the three major currency areas—the U.S. dollar, the Japanese yen, and the European currencies—has floated more or less freely against the others since 1973. Many countries in Latin America peg their exchange rates to the U.S. dollar. In addition, almost all countries tend to intervene either (a) when markets become "disorderly" or (b) when exchange rates seem far out of line with the "fundamentals," that is, with exchange rates that are appropriate for existing price levels and trade flows. This system—with a mixture of different components—is called *managed floating*. We return to a full discussion of this system in the next section of this chapter.

B. Issues of International Economics

Now that we have analyzed the highlights of exchange rates and of the international monetary system, we will survey the history of international economic institutions along with current problems of the international economy.

Building International Institutions after World War II

After World War II, the United States emerged with its economy intact and was able to help rebuild the countries of allies and foes alike. The postwar international political system also responded to the needs of war-torn nations by constructing durable institutions within which the international economy could recover quickly. The four major economic institutions of the 1940s—the GATT (described in Chapter 19), the Bretton Woods exchange-rate system, the International Monetary Fund, and the World Bank—stand as monuments to wise and farsighted statecraft.

The Bretton Woods System

The economic and social turmoil of the 1930s deeply impressed economic thinkers of the 1940s. They were determined to avoid the economic chaos and competitive devaluations of the Great Depression.

In order to map out a new international economic order, the United States, Britain, and their major allies gathered in Bretton Woods, New Hampshire, in 1944. Under the intellectual leadership of J. M. Keynes and the American diplomat H. D. White, this landmark conference hammered out an agreement that led to the formation of the International Monetary Fund (IMF), the World Bank, and the Bretton Woods exchange-rate system. For the first time in history, nations agreed upon a system for regulating international financial transactions. Even though some of the rules have changed since 1944, the institutions established at Bretton Woods continue to play a vital role today.

The conference designed a framework for managing exchange rates that is known as the **Bretton Woods system.** Those who attended the Bretton Woods conference remembered well how the gold standard was too inflexible and served to deepen economic crises. To replace the gold standard, the Bretton Woods system established a parity for each currency in terms of both the U.S. dollar and gold. As the key or reserve currency, the parity of the dollar was pegged only in terms of gold, initially at $35 per ounce of gold. Other currencies were defined in terms of both gold and the dollar.

For example, the parity of the British pound was set at £12.5 per ounce of gold. Given the gold price of the dollar, this implied an official exchange rate between the dollar and the pound of $35/£12.5 = $2.80 per £1, which was thereby set as the official parity on the pound. Under the Bretton Woods system, therefore, because each currency's parity was

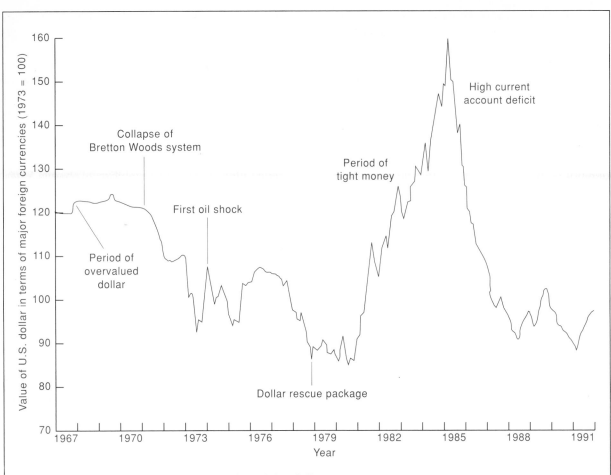

Figure 21-3.   The foreign exchange value of the dollar

The dollar has shown extreme instability under flexible exchange rates. Before the collapse of the Bretton Woods system, the dollar's value was stable in exchange markets. After 1971, the dollar first drifted down, next rose sharply during the high-interest-rate era of the early 1980s, then collapsed as U.S. interest rates fell and the U.S. trade deficit mounted. (Source: Federal Reserve System.)

tal Europe, along with political unrest and a debt crisis in many Latin American countries, led foreigners to ask in effect, "Why risk your nest egg in socialist France or in strife-torn Brazil when you can obtain a high real return on your funds in the safe dollar?"

Figure 21-3 shows the result: from 1979 to early 1985, the exchange rate on the dollar rose 80 percent. Indeed, the dollar soared to levels far above those attained just before the Bretton Woods system collapsed because of an "overvalued dollar" in 1971. Many economists and policymakers became convinced that the dollar was overvalued in 1985,

and a swift decline soon followed. Over the next 6 years, the dollar fell more than it had risen in the early 1980s.

Impacts of the Overvalued Dollar. Many economists believed that the dollar was "overvalued" in the early 1980s. An *overvalued currency* is one whose value is high relative to its long-run or sustainable level. What were the impacts of U.S. financial policies and the overvaluation of the dollar in the 1980s? The consequences were profound not only for the United States but for virtually the entire world economy.

The first results came as the high interest rates slowed economic growth in the United States and abroad. We learn in macroeconomics that high interest rates tend to reduce business and residential investment, thereby reducing aggregate spending, slowing economic activity, and raising unemployment. The United States experienced an economic slowdown beginning in 1980, with the trough of the recession coming in 1982.

In addition, the high U.S. interest rates pulled up the interest rates of other major countries. These high interest rates slowed investment in other industrial economies and triggered a sharp slowdown in overall economic activity in the industrial world. This slowdown began in 1981, and the European economies had not fully recovered from it by 1991. In addition, high interest rates increased debt-service burdens in poor and middle-income countries.

The next reaction came in exchange markets. As the dollar rose, American export prices increased and the prices of goods imported into the United States fell. As a result, America's exports declined while its imports mounted sharply. From 1980 to 1985, the prices of imported goods and services fell by 1 percent, while the prices of our exports in foreign currencies rose over 60 percent. In response, the volume of imports rose 42 percent while export volumes fell 5 percent.

The impact on the overall economy is measured by the changes in *real net exports*, which measure the trade balance in quantity terms; more precisely, real net exports are the quantity of exports minus the quantity of imports, where both are measured in constant dollars.

Figure 21-4 illustrates the dramatic effect of the rising exchange rate of the dollar on real net exports. From the peak in 1980 to the trough in 1986, real net exports declined by $216 billion, or 5.8 percent of 1986 GNP (all these figures are in 1982 prices).

What was the impact of the decline in real net exports upon the American economy? A drop in real net exports has a contractionary multiplier effect upon domestic output and employment. When foreigners spend less here and Americans spend more abroad, the demand for American goods and services declines, real GNP falls, and unemployment tends to rise. Economic studies indicate that the fall in real net exports was a major contributor to the deep recession in the early 1980s and tended

to retard the growth of real GNP during much of the first half of the 1980s.

Deindustrialization of America. The overvalued dollar produced severe economic hardships in many U.S. sectors exposed to international trade. Industries like automobiles, steel, textiles, and agriculture found the demand for their products withering as their prices rose relative to the prices of foreign competitors. Unemployment in the manufacturing heartland increased sharply as factories were closed and the midwest became known as the "rust belt."

The political response to the soaring trade deficit took many forms. Economists tended to emphasize macroeconomic forces such as the overvalued dollar, tight monetary policy, and growing fiscal deficit. They called for reducing the government deficit to force down the dollar's exchange rate and reduce the trade deficit.

Many non-economists interpreted U.S. trade problems as indicative of "America in decline." They sometimes advocated economic protection against stronger trading partners like Japan, Korea, and Western Europe. Some argued for "industrial policies," fiscal aid to beleaguered industries to help stem the "deindustrialization of America."

The Dollar's Decline. In early 1985, the dollar peaked and began a sharp decline. The reversal was caused in part by governments that intervened by selling dollars and buying other currencies, in part by speculators who believed that the dollar was overvalued, and in part by lower relative dollar interest rates. As can be seen in Figure 21-3, the dollar declined steadily for the next 6 years, and by 1991 it had lost all the ground gained between 1980 and 1985.

The recovery in U.S. net exports after 1985 was slow but steady, and Figure 21-4 shows that the current and trade accounts remained in deficit into 1991. What was the reason for the slow improvement after the dollar's decline? Trade flows react to exchange-rate changes with a substantial delay because both prices and quantities change slowly in response to exchange-rate movements. Prices react slowly because importers into the United States tend to keep their dollar prices stable and squeeze their profit margins rather than lower their market shares. When importers ultimately raise

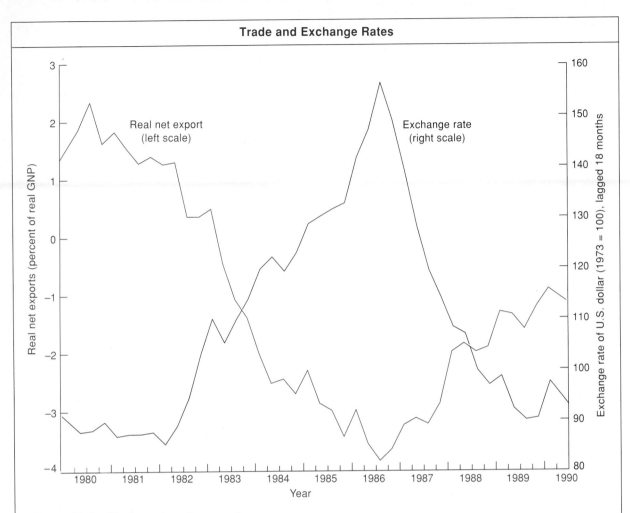

Figure 21-4.   Trade and exchange rates

Real net exports react to exchange-rate changes, but with a time lag. The rising real exchange rate of the dollar during the early 1980s increased U.S. export prices and reduced prices of goods imported into the United States. As a result, real net exports (that is, exports minus imports, both measured in constant 1982 prices) fell sharply. When the dollar started to fall in 1985, real net exports began to react only after a considerable time lag. (Source: Real exchange rate is trade-weighted exchange rate corrected for differences in national price levels, from Federal Reserve Board; real net exports from U.S. Department of Commerce.)

their prices, people substitute domestic for imported goods only after they have evaluated and selected new products: brand loyalties become entrenched, so that Toyotas and Canons may retain a substantial market share many years after these products have migrated to the high end of the price range. All these forces imply that the full reaction to the exchange-rate depreciation of 1985–1991 may not be felt until well into the 1990s. As a result, the United States may continue to experience deficits in its trade and current accounts and in its real net exports for a substantial period of time.

Assessment of Flexible Exchange Rates

The year 1991 marks two decades of experience with flexible exchange rates. How well have they functioned? Figure 21-3 tells the story of how a key currency, the U.S. dollar, evolved over the 1970s and 1980s. Note how much greater were the fluctuations after the flexible-rate regime began in 1973.

Many economists and policymakers, having lived through the violent ups and downs of the last two decades, have concluded something like the following:

We had high hopes that flexible exchange rates would allow our economies to adjust to changes in national economic conditions without unacceptable business cycles or currency fluctuations. But currencies left to free markets wander around like a bunch of drunken sailors. We must put some control over these wayward exchange rates by moving back toward the fixed or stable exchange rates of the Bretton Woods period.

The historical record reveals that flexible exchange rates have indeed performed less well than their advocates had hoped. Exchange rates have been extremely unstable, as the volatile dollar illustrates. Other countries, particularly Japan and those in Europe, also saw excessive fluctuations in their currencies.

Moreover, the sharp currency movements have had unwelcome macroeconomic effects. The dollar's rise caused a severe external deficit in the United States and turned the country into the world's largest debtor. The counterpart of the dollar's swings has left Japan and Germany with large trade surpluses. Thus, critics of flexible exchange rates argue that the exchange rate should not be left to the market but must be controlled by governments and central banks.

The EMS. Many countries have moved to curb exchange-market fluctuations. One early step was the creation in 1978 of a currency bloc known as the European Monetary System (or EMS). A group of West European countries, notably Germany, France, and Italy, designed this system along lines of the Bretton Woods regime; in the EMS, countries intervene to keep their relative exchange rates within narrow limits.

The EMS has some of the advantages of both worlds: The French and the Germans can conveniently transact with each other on quite predictable currency terms. At the same time, any fundamental change in world affairs, such as the major shift in American monetary policy in 1979 or the oil-price increases that have so often occurred, can be absorbed by allowing the EMS exchange rates to float flexibly upward or downward.

European countries agree that their experiment with a currency zone has been successful. Indeed, they are considering a plan to move beyond the EMS to a *common currency* under a blueprint known as the "Delors plan." Its objective is to replace the several central banks of Europe with a single European central bank (some call it the

"Eurofed"). With a unitary monetary policy in place, a common currency could be issued. Many Europeans believe that a single currency, like the one enjoyed by the United States, will unify the continent politically and economically and sustain economic growth for many years to come.

Floating Rates and Discipline. We saw that fixed exchange rates, such as the gold standard, impose very tight discipline on a nation. If domestic prices began to rise and a balance-of-payments deficit occurred, gold would leave the country, leading to monetary contraction and recession or worse. A similar (albeit somewhat less tight) chain of events would occur under the Bretton Woods system.

With a floating-rate system, these tight constraints are removed. Countries are free to use macroeconomic policies to determine their own domestic price levels—they can be high-inflation countries or low-inflation countries without automatically triggering a balance-of-payments crisis. But removing the old constraints leads to new ones. Freedom to choose price levels does not mean that a nation can have any *real* wage rate it chooses.

Suppose the United States raises money wage rates 50 percent overnight. Our costs are now high. Our exports can no longer compete. The dollar floats down to correct the imbalance. Imports (raw materials, etc.) become more expensive, so U.S. prices rise. In the end, our prices are likely to rise about as much as money wage rates rose.

The moral here is that floating exchange rates eliminate the discipline of the gold or dollar standard on the *nominal* price and wage levels. But nothing can remove the irreducible constraint of an economy's real productivity level. Flexible exchange rates remove one set of constraints (the straightjacket of gold) and impose another (the harsh verdict of markets about a currency's true value).

Improving International Cooperation

During the turbulent 1980s, the United States came of age as a mature partner in world economic affairs. It saw its domestic monetary and fiscal policies spill over to affect exchange rates and trade flows; the country even found its unemployment rate buffeted by the ups and downs of foreign trade. The central lesson of the 1980s is clear: In a world where economies are increasingly linked by trade and capital flows, interdependence is unavoidable. No walls can prevent domestic actions from spilling over territorial boundaries. National strengths can be leveraged in a global marketplace, while national weaknesses fall prey to intense foreign competitors. Isolationism is today no more feasible in economic affairs than it is in political or military affairs.

All this means that exchange with other nations is an integral part of domestic economic welfare. This fact is captured in the old saying, "When America sneezes, Europe catches cold." An updated adage might read, "When the global economy is sick, the contagion spreads everywhere."

Since World War II, international economic cooperation has entered the agenda of domestic economic policy. Here are the major issues:

• *Trade agreements.* Nations can take measures to protect their industries through tariffs and quotas. These steps would reduce trade deficits and at the same time increase domestic output and employment. But this cure would be a "beggar-thy-neighbor" policy, in a sense exporting trade deficits and unemployment. Having learned the dangers of protectionism in the 1930s, nations have banded together in multinational trade treaties and agreements to desist from imposing trade restrictions.

• *International monetary arrangements.* Foreign exchange rates necessarily affect many nations. In the past, nations would sometimes manipulate their exchange rates to attain domestic political objectives—forcing a depreciation of their currencies to increase net exports, output, and employment. At other times, nations allowed their domestic inflation to spill over to other regions. In an attempt to curtail undesirable manipulation of exchange rates, nations now gather periodically to oversee exchange-rate policies and to ensure that no nation engages in "competitive devaluations" that export its unemployment. The process of "exchange-rate surveillance" is overseen by the IMF.

• *Macroeconomic coordination.* The most recent and controversial of cooperative steps include attempts to coordinate macroeconomic policy. Suppose the world economy is in recession. No single nation is powerful enough to bring the

world economy back to its potential output. Moreover, if one small nation takes fiscal or monetary steps to increase its output, much of the stimulus spills over to other countries and, because open-economy multipliers are small, the home economy enjoys relatively less economic expansion. Even worse, if a small country expands on its own, not only will it find that much of the stimulus spills over its borders, but also it is likely to witness a turn in its trade account toward deficit.

To break out of this bind, economists and policymakers have sometimes proposed "coordinated expansion," wherein all countries would take expansionary steps simultaneously. A coordinated fiscal or monetary expansion would find each country both causing and enjoying expansionary spillovers. Moreover, because foreign countries would be expanding, a nation could hope that its exports (driven up by expansion abroad) would rise as much as its imports (driven up by expansion at home). Such coordinated macroeconomic policies could also be used to contract global economic activity if that were called for. Today, the major market economies regularly meet to discuss their macroeconomic policies, particularly monetary policy, and from time to time policy measures are coordinated to improve overall macroeconomic performance.

America in Decline?

As the millenium approached, many observers worried that the United States was traveling rapidly down the road to economic and political decline. They pointed to a variety of symptoms: a declining national savings rate, a persistent federal budget deficit, slow productivity growth, and a large external deficit, which was turning the United States into the world's largest debtor nation. At the same time, the country appeared to lack the political will to take forceful steps to reverse these trends.

Against this backdrop, Yale historian Paul Kennedy published a massive study of economic change and political conflict, *The Rise and Fall of the Great Powers.*[2] Kennedy argued that, because of

[2] Paul Kennedy, *The Rise and Fall of the Great Powers: Economic Change and Military Conflict from 1500 to 2000* (Random House, New York, 1987). See especially the introduction, Chap. 1, and Chap. 8.

underlying long-term economic trends, the United States was likely to suffer a significant decline in political and military power in the decades to come.

After reviewing five centuries of economic, political, and military history, Professor Kennedy puts forth the following theses:

1. "The historical record suggests that there is a very clear connection in the long run between an individual Great Power's economic rise and fall and its growth and decline as an important military power (or world empire). . . . Both wealth and power are always relative. . . . " He buttressed his argument by a thorough historical study of Spain, France, the British Empire, the Soviet Union, and the United States.

2. "The relative strengths of the leading nations in world affairs never remain constant, principally because of the uneven rate of growth among different societies and of the technological and organizational breakthroughs which bring a greater advantage to one society than to another." Economic and technological developments from the development of steam power to the introduction of nuclear weapons illustrate the way technology changes the economic and political fortunes of nations differently and unpredictably.

Kennedy then applies these lessons of history to contemporary economic and political affairs. He notes that the U.S. share of world GNP and manufacturing has declined significantly since its zenith in 1945; that many critical American industries and skills have declined, to be replaced by those of foreign countries; that the political consensus has become less favorable to economic growth; and that high defense spending and research and development (R&D) has sapped the nation's civilian economy. At the same time, other regions—particularly Japan and the European Community—are growing rapidly, producing an increasing share of world GNP and manufacturing, and possessing the potential of becoming "Great Powers." From these and other facts, Kennedy concludes:

> The only answer to the question . . . of whether the United States can preserve its existing [military and political] position is "no"—for it simply has not been given to any one society to remain permanently ahead of all the others, because that would imply a freezing of

the differentiated patterns of growth rates, technological advance, and military developments which has existed since time immemorial. . . . One is tempted to paraphrase Shaw's deadly serious quip and say, "Rome fell; Babylon fell; Scarsdale's turn will come."[3]

Kennedy's thesis provoked a storm of debate and criticism. Some argued that the lessons of Europe do not apply to a continental power like the U.S.; others believe that, as the exchange rate of the dollar falls and America gets its fiscal house in order, American industry will increase its share of world trade. Many point to U.S. victory in the Persian Gulf as proof that its economic problems are small and that its technological virtuosity is preeminent.

Perhaps the argument has greater weight for countries like the Soviet Union. Central planning, an overarching bureaucracy, lack of incentives, and militarization of science and technology proved a poor recipe for economic vigor. Although the Soviet Union was a military superpower, its economy fell further behind the market economies. The crumbling of the Soviet empire in the 1990s testifies to the growing importance of economic strength in national power today.

Epilogue: Affluence for What?

Whether America is on the path to decline or destined to be the economic superpower of the next century cannot now be foretold. The issues raised by Kennedy's bold hypothesis serve as a stern reminder of the continuing importance of productive efficiency and economic growth.

At a deeper level, we recognize in his words the age-old dilemma of choice, posed in a new form for wealthy societies: *affluence for what?* How shall we use the resources that have been made so productive by technological change? For guns or butter or machines? For guns to protect our oil lifeline abroad, ensuring energy supplies to the industrial world? Or for butter and other consumption goods, enjoying the fruits of our past investments with high consumption today and letting the future fend for itself? Or for machines and other forms of investment, in capital goods and education and research and environmental quality, all of which will ensure a higher standard of living for those who follow us?

[3] The quotes above are from Kennedy, ibid., pp. xxii, xv, and 533.

There are no right answers to these fundamental questions of economics. Each of us must reflect on our values and strive to work toward the greater good. We particularly like the observation of John F. Kennedy, who showed great wisdom in matters economic: "Now the trumpet summons us again— not as a call to bear arms [but in] a struggle against the common enemies of man: tyranny, poverty, disease, and war itself."

This plea might serve as a trumpet call for young economists as well. Even though market economies are many times wealthier than they were in the age of Adam Smith, the vitality of economics knows no diminishing returns. The catalogue of unsolved economic problems remains long. Yet we remain cautiously optimistic that the study of economics will enhance not only the gross national product but also those best things in life that are beyond the marketplace—freedom to criticize, freedom to change, and freedom to pursue one's own dreams.

SUMMARY

A. The Determination of Foreign Exchange Rates

1. International trade involves use of different national currencies, which are linked by relative prices called foreign exchange rates. When Americans import British goods, they ultimately need to pay in British pounds. In the foreign exchange market, British pounds might trade for $1.80 per £1 (or reciprocally, $1 would trade for £0.56).

2. In the foreign exchange market involving only two countries, the demand for British pounds comes from Americans who want to purchase goods, services, and investments from Britain; the supply of British pounds comes from Britons who want to import commodities or financial assets from America. The interaction of these supplies and demands determines the foreign exchange rate. More generally, foreign exchange rates are determined by the complex interplay of many countries buying and selling among themselves. When trade or capital flows change, supply and demand shift and the equilibrium exchange rate changes.

3. A fall in the market price of a currency is a depreciation; a rise in a currency's value is called an appreciation. In a system where governments announce official foreign exchange rates, a decrease in the official exchange rate is called a devaluation while an increase is a revaluation.

4. A well-functioning international economy requires a smoothly operating exchange-rate system, which denotes the rules and institutions that govern transactions among nations. Three important exchange-rate systems are: (a) the gold standard, in which countries define their currencies in terms of a given weight of gold and then buy and sell gold to balance their international payments; (b) a pure floating-exchange-rate system, in which a country's foreign exchange rate is entirely determined by market forces of supply and demand; and (c) a managed floating-exchange-rate system, in which government interventions and market forces interact to determine the level of exchange rates.

5. Classical economists like David Hume explained adjustments to trade imbalances by the gold-flow mechanism. Under this process, gold movements would change the money supply and the price level. For example, a trade deficit would lead to a gold outflow and a decline in domestic prices

that would (*a*) raise exports and (*b*) curb imports of the gold-losing country while (*c*) reducing exports and (*d*) raising imports of the gold-gaining country.

B. Issues of International Economics

6. After World War II, countries created a group of international economic institutions to organize international trade and finance. These included the International Monetary Fund (IMF), which oversees exchange-rate systems and helps countries with their balance of payments; the World Bank, which lends money to low-income countries; and the Bretton Woods exchange-rate system. Under the Bretton Woods system, countries "pegged" their currencies to the dollar and to gold, providing fixed but adjustable exchange rates. When official parities deviated too far from fundamentals, countries could adjust parities and achieve a new equilibrium without incurring the hardships of inflation or recession.

7. When the Bretton Woods system broke down in 1971, it was replaced by today's system of generally flexible exchange rates. Some large countries or regions allow their currencies to float independently; most small countries peg their currencies to the dollar or to other currencies; and most European countries adhere to the European Monetary System (EMS), which resembles closely the Bretton Woods system. Governments often intervene when their currencies get too far out of line with fundamentals or when exchange markets become disorderly.

8. The most dramatic development of the last two decades has been the rise and fall of the dollar. The dollar surged in 1980, and this appreciation led to a sharp fall in real net exports, exacerbating the 1980–1982 recession. The fall in the dollar after 1985 has gradually begun to cure the huge trade deficit of the United States.

9. Floating exchange rates appear to remove the automatic discipline of the earlier gold or dollar standards—allowing countries to pursue their own inflationary or non-inflationary policies. But in fact a new discipline emerges—that of markets which move exchange rates in response to divergent relative price levels or interest rates, or even to people's expectations about prices or interest rates.

10. Because of the increasing interdependence of national economies, countries often attempt to coordinate their economic policies. Important policy issues are:
    (a) National trade policies will affect the output and employment of other countries. A policy of protecting one's own industries by trade barriers is a "beggar-thy-neighbor" approach, in essence exporting unemployment and trade deficits.
    (b) Foreign exchange rates can affect relative prices and net exports. A rise in a nation's foreign exchange rate will depress that nation's net exports and output, while a fall in a nation's foreign exchange rate will increase net exports and output. Because of the significant impact of exchange rates on national economies, countries have entered into agreements on international monetary arrangements.

(c) In recent years, countries have often coordinated their macroeconomic policies, simultaneously trying to increase their national outputs or to lower their national inflation rates. By cooperating in fiscal or monetary policies, countries can take advantage of the expansionary or contractionary impacts that inevitably spill over the borders when output changes.

CONCEPTS FOR REVIEW

The international financial system
foreign exchange rate
supply of and demand for foreign currencies
currency: appreciation and depreciation; revaluation and devaluation

exchange-rate systems: gold standard, freely floating, managed floating
intervention
Hume's four-pronged gold-flow mechanism
fixed exchange rates; pegged parities

Current issues of international economics
World Bank and IMF
Bretton Woods system and its breakdown, EMS
volatility of flexible exchange rates
international economic cooperation
America in decline?

QUESTIONS FOR DISCUSSION

1. Define the following and explain the significance of each: foreign exchange rate, gold standard, Bretton Woods system, and freely floating exchange rate.
2. The following table shows some foreign exchange rates (in dollars per unit of foreign currency) as of mid-1991:

	Price	
Currency	Dollars per unit of foreign currency	Foreign currency per $1
Pound (Britain)	1.6325 ($/pound)	_____
Franc (France)	0.1637 ($/franc)	_____
Yen (Japan)	0.00726 ($/yen)	_____
Won (South Korea)	0.00138 ($/won)	_____
Mark (Germany)	0.5565 ($/DM)	_____

Fill in the last column of the table with the reciprocal price of the dollar in terms of foreign currencies, being especially careful to write down the relevant units.
3. Figure 21-1 shows the demand and supply for British pounds in an example in which Britain and the United States trade only with each other. Describe the reciprocal supply and demand schedules for U.S. dollars. Explain why the supply of pounds is equivalent to the demand for dollars. Also explain the schedule that corresponds to the demand for pounds. Find the equilibrium price of dollars in this new diagram and relate it to the equilibrium in Figure 21-1.
4. James Tobin has written, "A great teacher of mine, Joseph Schumpeter, used to find puzzling irony in the fact that liberal devotees of the free market were unwilling to let the market determine the prices of foreign currencies. . . . " [*National Economic Policy* (Yale University Press, New Haven, Conn., 1966), p. 161]. For what reasons might economists allow the foreign exchange market to be an exception to a general inclination toward free markets?
5. Show an initial equilibrium in the foreign exchange market for Japanese yen (similar to that for pounds in Figure 21-1). Let the initial equilibrium be 150 yen to the dollar and consider the impact on the market equilibrium of the following:
   (a) The Japanese government decides to sell very large quantities of yen at 160 yen to the dollar.
   (b) Higher interest rates in New York lower the demand for yen.
   (c) The demand for Toyotas and Hondas by Americans increase sharply.

(d) Japan pays the United States in dollars for American forces in the Far East.

6. In the Louvre accord in 1987, major countries agreed to keep their currencies within "reference zones." Say that the United States and Germany agree to keep the German mark in the range of 1.60 to 1.80 marks to the dollar. Show with the help of a supply-and-demand diagram how the governments could implement this policy.

7. Figure 21-5 shows a proposal for a "gliding parity" or "crawling peg" for the exchange rate between the dollar and the German deutsche mark (DM). Such a system lets an exchange rate change a few percent per year. What are its pros and cons relative to fixed exchange rates or freely floating rates?

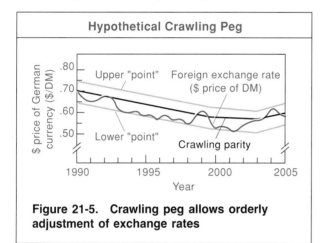

Figure 21-5. Crawling peg allows orderly adjustment of exchange rates

8. Suppose a country discovers oil, but it takes a decade to exploit the new find. What would happen to the country's trade balance after oil began to flow onto world markets? What might happen to the nation's freely floating currency once people realized that the trade balance would soon move into surplus? Why would the trade balance thus go into deficit in the period before the oil is actually recovered?

9. Consider the following three exchange-rate systems: classical gold standard, freely floating exchange rates, and Bretton Woods system. Compare and contrast the three systems with respect to the following characteristics:
   (a) Role of government vs. that of market in determining exchange rates
   (b) Degree of exchange-rate volatility
   (c) Method of adjustment of relative prices across countries
   (d) Need for international cooperation and consultation in determining exchange rates
   (e) Potential for establishment and maintenance of severe exchange-rate misalignment

10. The 1984 *Economic Report of the President* states:

    In the long run, the exchange rate tends to follow the differential trend in the domestic and foreign price level. If one country's price level gets too far out of line with prices in other countries, there will eventually be a fall in demand for its goods, which will lead to a real depreciation of its currency.

    The first sentence espouses the "purchasing-power parity" or "PPP" theory of exchange rates. The PPP theory, which was proposed by David Ricardo in 1817 and by Sweden's Gustav Cassel around 1916, holds that floating exchange rates will move in proportion to relative prices in different countries; that is, if prices in the United States are rising 7 percent annually while those in Germany are rising 3 percent annually, the PPP theory holds that the U.S. dollar will tend to depreciate about 4 percent annually relative to the German mark. Explain the reasoning behind the PPP theory of exchange rates. In addition, using a supply-and-demand diagram like that of Figure 21-1, explain the sequence of events, described in the second sentence of the quotation, whereby a country whose price level is relatively high will find that its exchange rate depreciates.

11. Suppose America is running a trade deficit with output at the desired level, while Europe has a trade surplus with excessively high unemployment. What combination of coordinated exchange-rate changes and fiscal policies could move trade positions toward balance and output toward the desired levels?

GLOSSARY OF TERMS[1]

Ability-to-pay principle (of taxation). The principle that one's tax burden should depend upon the ability to pay as measured by income or wealth. This principle does not specify *how much* more those who are better off should pay.

Absolute advantage (in international trade). The ability of Country A to produce a commodity more efficiently (i.e., with greater output per unit of input) than Country B. Possession of such an absolute advantage does not necessarily mean that A can export this commodity to B successfully. Country B may still have the comparative advantage.

Actual, cyclical, and **structural budget.** The **actual budget** deficit or surplus is the amount recorded in a given year. This is composed of the **structural budget,** which calculates what government revenues, expenditures, and deficits would be if the economy were operating at potential output; and the **cyclical budget,** which measures the

[1] Words in bold type within definitions appear as separate entries in the glossary. For a more detailed discussion of particular terms, the text will provide a useful starting point. More complete discussions are contained in Douglas Greenwald, ed., *Encyclopedia of Economics* (McGraw-Hill, New York, 1983); David W. Pearce, *The Dictionary of Modern Economics,* rev. ed. (MIT Press, Cambridge, Mass., 1983); *International Encyclopedia of the Social Sciences* (Collier and Macmillan, New York, 1968); and John Eatwell, Murray Milgate, and Peter Newman, *The New Palgrave: A Dictionary of Economics* (Macmillan, London, 1987), four volumes.

effect of the business cycle on the budget.

Adaptive expectations. See **expectations.**

Adjustable peg. An exchange-rate system in which countries maintain a fixed or "pegged" exchange rate with respect to other currencies. This exchange rate is subject to periodic adjustment, however, when it becomes too far out of line with fundamental forces. This system was used for major currencies during the Bretton Woods period from 1944 to 1971 and is called the **Bretton Woods system.**

Administered (or **inflexible**) **prices.** A term referring to prices which are set and kept constant for a period of time and over a series of transactions. (In contrast, refer to **price flexibility.**)

Aggregate demand. Total planned or desired spending in the economy during a given period. It is determined by the aggregate price level and influenced by domestic investment, net exports, government spending, the consumption function, and the money supply.

Aggregate demand (*AD*) curve. The curve showing the relationship between the quantity of goods and services that people are willing to buy and the aggregate price level, other things equal. As with any demand curve, important variables lie behind the aggregate demand curve, e.g., government spending, exports, and the money supply.

Aggregate supply. The total value of goods and services that firms would willingly produce in a given time period. Aggregate supply is a function of available inputs, technology, and the price level.

Aggregate supply (*AS*) curve. The curve showing the relationship between the output firms would willingly supply and the aggregate price level, other things equal. The *AS* curve tends to be vertical at potential output in the very long run but may be relatively flat in the short run.

Allocative efficiency. A situation in which no reorganization or trade could raise the utility or satisfaction of one individual without lowering the utility or satisfaction of another individual. Under certain limited conditions, perfect competition leads to allocative efficiency. Also called **Pareto efficiency.**

Antitrust legislation. Laws prohibiting monopolization, restraints of trade, and collusion among firms to raise prices or inhibit competition.

Appreciation (of a currency). See **depreciation** (of a currency).

Arbitrage. Speculation without risk. The act of buying a currency or a commodity in one market and simultaneously selling it for a profit in another market. Arbitrage is an important force in eliminating price discrepancies, thereby making markets function more efficiently.

Asset. A physical property or intangible right that has economic value. Important examples are plant, equipment, land, patents, copyrights, and financial instruments such as money or bonds.

Asset demand for money. See **demand for money.**

Automatic (or **built-in**) **stabilizers.** The property of a government tax and spending system that cushions income changes in the private sector. Examples include unemployment compensation and progressive income taxes.

Average cost. Refer to **cost, average.**

Average cost curve, long-run (LRAC, or LAC) The graph of the minimum average cost of producing a commodity for each level of output, assuming that technology and input prices are given but that the producer is free to choose the optimal size of plants.

Average cost curve, short-run (SRAC, or SAC). The graph of the minimum average cost of producing a commodity, for each level of output, using the given state of technology, input prices, and existing plant.

Average product. Total product or output divided by the quantity of one of the inputs. Hence, the average product of labor is defined as total product divided by the amount of labor input, and similarly for other inputs.

Average propensity to consume. See **marginal propensity to consume.**

Average revenue. Total revenue divided by total number of units sold—i.e., revenue per unit. Average revenue is generally equal to price.

Average variable cost. Refer to **cost, average variable.**

Balance of international payments. A statement showing all a nation's transactions with the rest of the world for a given period. It includes purchases and sales of goods and services, gifts, government transactions, and capital movements.

Balance of trade. The part of a nation's balance of payments that deals with merchandise (or visible) imports or exports. When "invisibles," or services, are included, the total accounting for imports and exports of goods and services is called the **balance on current account.**

Balance on current account. See **balance of trade.**

Balance sheet. A statement of a firm's financial position as of a given date, listing **assets** in one column, **liabilities** plus **net worth** in the other. Each item is listed at its actual or estimated money value. Totals of the two columns must balance because net worth is defined as assets minus liabilities.

Balanced budget. See **budget, balanced.**

Bank, commercial. A financial intermediary whose prime distinguishing feature until recently was that it accepts checking deposits. Also it holds savings or time deposits and money market deposit accounts; sells traveler's checks and performs other financial services; and lends to individuals and firms. Since 1980, savings banks and other depository institutions have been allowed to accept checking accounts and are thus becoming more like commercial banks.

Bank money. Money created by banks, particularly the checking accounts (part of M_1) that are generated by a multiple expansion of bank reserves.

Bank reserves. Refer to **reserves, bank.**

Barriers to competition. Factors that reduce the amount of competition or the number of producers in an industry, allowing greater economic concentration to occur. Important examples are legal barriers, regulation, and product differentiation.

Barter. The direct exchange of one good for another without using anything as money or as a medium of exchange.

Benefit principle (of taxation). The principle that people should be taxed in proportion to the benefits they receive from government programs.

Bond. An interest-bearing certificate issued by a government or corporation, promising to repay a sum of money (the principal) plus interest at specified dates in the future.

Break-even point (in macroeconomics). For an individual, family, or community, that level of income at which 100 percent is spent on consumption (i.e., the point where there is neither saving nor dissaving). Positive saving begins at higher income levels.

Break-even price or **level,** or **point** (in microeconomics). For a business firm, that level of price at which the firm breaks even, covering all costs but earning zero profit.

Bretton Woods system. See **adjustable peg.**

Budget, balanced. A budget in which total expenditures just equal total receipts (excluding any receipts from borrowing).

Budget constraint. See **budget line.**

Budget deficit. For a government, the excess of total expenditures over total receipts, with borrowing not included among receipts. This difference (the deficit) is ordinarily financed by borrowing.

Budget, government. A statement showing, for the government in question, planned expenditures and revenues for some period (typically 1 year).

Budget line. A line indicating the combination of commodities that a consumer can buy with a given income at a given set of prices. If the graph shows food and clothing, then each point on the line represents a combination of food and clothing that can be bought for a certain income level and with a given set of prices for the two goods. Also sometimes called the **budget constraint.**

Budget surplus. Excess of government revenues over government spending; the opposite of **budget deficit.**

Built-in stabilizers. See **automatic stabilizers.**

Business cycles. Fluctuations in total national output, income, and employment, usually lasting for a period of 2 to 10 years, marked by widespread and simultaneous expansion or contraction in many sectors of the economy. In modern macroeconomics, business cycles are said to occur when actual GNP rises relative to potential GNP (expansion) or falls relative to potential GNP (contraction or recession).

$C + I$, $C + I + G$, or **$C + I + G + X$ schedule.** A schedule showing the planned or desired levels of aggregate demand for each level of GNP, or the graph on which this schedule is depicted. The schedule includes consumption (C), investment (I), government spending on goods and services (G), and net exports (X).

Capital (capital goods, capital equipment). (1) In economic theory, one of the triad of productive inputs (land, labor, and capital). Capital consists of durable produced goods that are in turn used in production. The major components of capital are equipment, structures, and inventory. When signifying capital goods, reference is also made to real capital. (2) In accounting and finance, "capital" means the total amount of money subscribed by the shareholder-owners of a corporation, in return for which they receive shares of the company's stock.

Capital consumption allowance. See **depreciation** (of an asset).

Capital deepening. In economic-growth theory, an increase in the capital-labor ratio. (Contrast with **capital widening.**)

Capital gains. The rise in value of a capital asset, such as land or common stocks, the gain being the difference between the sales price and the purchase price of the asset.

Capital markets. Markets in which financial resources (money, bonds, stocks) are traded. These, along with **financial intermediaries,** are institutions through which savings in the economy are transferred to investors.

Capital-output ratio. In economic-growth theory, the ratio of the total capital stock to annual GNP.

Capital widening. A rate of growth in real capital stock just equal to the growth of the labor force (or of population), so that the ratio between total capital and total labor remains unchanged. (Contrast with **capital deepening.**)

Capitalism. An economic system in which most property (land and capital) is privately owned. In such an economy, private markets are the primary vehicles used to allocate resources and generate incomes.

Cartel. An organization of independent firms producing similar products that work together to raise prices and restrict output. Cartels are illegal under U.S. antitrust laws.

Central bank. A government-established agency (in the United States, the Federal Reserve System) responsible for controlling the nation's money supply and credit conditions and for supervising the financial system, especially commercial banks.

Change in demand vs. change in quantity demanded. A change in the quantity buyers want to purchase, prompted by any reason other than a change in price (e.g., increase in income, change in tastes, etc.), is a "change in demand." (In graphical terms, it is a shift of the demand curve.) If, in contrast, the decision to buy more or less is prompted by a change in the good's price, then it is a "change in quantity demanded." (In graphical terms, a change in quantity demanded is a movement along an unchanging demand curve.)

Change in supply vs. change in quantity supplied. This distinction is the same for supply as for demand, so see **change in demand vs. change in quantity demanded.**

Checking accounts (or **bank money**). A deposit in a commercial bank or other financial intermediary upon which checks can be written and which is therefore transactions money (or M_1). The major kinds of checking accounts are demand deposits (which can be withdrawn without notice and do not bear interest) and **NOW accounts** (which are indistinguishable from traditional demand deposits except that they earn interest). Checking accounts are the largest component of M_1.

Chicago School of Economics. A group of economists (among whom Henry Simons, F. A. von Hayek, and Milton Friedman have been the most prominent) who believe that competitive markets free of government intervention will lead to the most efficient operation of the economy.

Classical economics. The predominant school of economic thought prior to the appearance of Keynes' work; founded by Adam Smith in 1776. Other major figures who followed him include David Ricardo, Thomas Malthus, and John Stuart Mill. By and large, this school believed that economic laws (particularly individual self-interest and competition) determine prices and factor rewards and that the price system is the best possible device for resource allocation. Their macroeconomic theory rests on **Say's Law of markets.**

Classical theories (in macroeconomics). Theories emphasizing the self-correcting forces in the economy. In the classical approach, there is generally full employment and policies to stimulate aggregate demand have no impact upon output.

Clearing market. A market in which prices are sufficiently flexible to equilibrate supply and demand very quickly. In markets that clear, there is no rationing, unemployed resources, or excess demand or supply. In practice, this is thought to apply to many commodity and financial markets but not to labor or many product markets.

Closed economy. See **open economy.**

Coase theorem. A view (not actually a theorem) put forth by Ronald Coase that externalities or economic inefficiencies will under certain conditions be corrected by bargaining between the affected parties.

Collective bargaining. The process of negotiations between a group of workers (usually a union) and their employer. Such bargaining leads to an agreement about wages, fringe benefits, and working conditions.

Collusion. Agreement between different firms to cooperate by raising prices, dividing markets, or otherwise restraining competition.

Collusive oligopoly. A market structure in which a small number of firms (i.e., a few oligopolists) collude and jointly make their decisions. When they succeed in maximizing their joint profits, the price and quantity in the market closely approach those prevailing under monopoly.

Command economy. A mode of economic organization in which the key economic functions—*what*, *how*, and *for whom*—are principally determined by government directive. Sometimes called a "centrally planned economy."

Commodity money. Money with **intrinsic value;** also, the use of some commodity (cattle, beads, etc.) as money.

Common stock. The financial instrument representing ownership and, generally, voting rights in a corporation. A certain share of a company's stock gives the owner title to that fraction of the votes, net earnings, and assets of the corporation.

Communism. At the same time (1) an ideology, (2) a set of political parties, and (3) an economic system. A communist economic system is one in which private ownership of the means of production, particularly industrial capital, is prohibited (for such ownership of capital goods is believed to result in exploitation of workers). In addition, communism holds that income should be distributed equally, or, more ideally, according to "need." In today's communist countries, most capital and land are owned by the state. These countries are also characterized by extensive central planning, with the state setting many prices, output levels, and other important economic variables.

Comparative advantage (in international trade). The law of comparative advantage says that a nation should specialize in producing and exporting those commodities which it can produce at *relatively* lower costs, and that it should import those goods for which it is a *relatively* high-cost producer. Thus it is a comparative advantage, not an absolute advantage, that should dictate trade patterns.

Compensating differentials. Differences in wage rates among jobs that serve to offset or compensate for the nonmonetary differences of the jobs. For example, unpleasant jobs that require isolation for many months in Alaska pay wages much higher than those for similar jobs nearer to civilization.

Competition, imperfect. Refers to markets in which perfect competition does not hold because at least one seller (or buyer) is large enough to affect the market price and therefore faces a downward-sloping demand curve (or supply). Imperfect competition refers to any kind of imperfection—pure **monopoly, oligopoly,** or **monopolistic competition.**

Competition, perfect. Refers to markets in which no firm or consumer is large enough to affect the market price. This situation arises where (1) the number of sellers and buyers is very large and (2) the products offered by sellers are homogeneous (or indistinguishable). Under such conditions, each firm faces a horizontal (or perfectly elastic) demand curve.

Competitive equilibrium. The balancing of supply and demand in a market or economy characterized by **perfect competition.** Because perfectly competitive sellers and buyers individually have no power to influence the market, price will move to the point at which price equals both marginal cost and marginal utility.

Competitive market. See **competition, perfect.**

Complements. Two goods which "go together" in the eyes of consumers (e.g., left shoes and right shoes). Goods are **substitutes** when they compete with each other (as do gloves and mittens).

Compound interest. Interest computed on the sum of all past interest earned as well as on the principal. For example, suppose $100 (the principal) is deposited in an account earning 10 percent interest compounded annually. At the end of year 1, interest of $10 is earned. At the end of year 2, the interest payment is $11, $10 on the original principal and $1 on the interest—and so on in future years.

Concentration ratio. The percentage of an industry's total output accounted for by the largest firms. A typical measure is the **four-firm concentration ratio,** which is the fraction of output accounted for by the four largest firms.

Conglomerate. A large corporation producing and selling a variety of unrelated goods (e.g., some cigarette companies have expanded into such unrelated areas as liquor, car rental, and movie production).

Conglomerate merger. See **merger.**

Constant returns to scale. See **returns to scale.**

Consumer price index (CPI). A price index that measures the cost of a fixed basket of consumer goods in which the weight assigned to each commodity is the share of expenditures on that commodity by urban consumers in 1982–1984.

Consumer surplus. The difference between the amount that a consumer would be willing to pay for a commodity and the amount actually paid. This difference arises because the marginal utilities (in dollar terms) of all but the last unit exceed the price. Hence the monetary equivalent of the total utility of the commodity consumed may be well above the amount spent. Under rigorous assumptions, the money value of consumer surplus can be measured (using a demand-curve diagram) as the area under the demand curve but above the price line.

Consumption. In macroeconomics, the total spending, by individuals or a nation, on consumer goods during a given period. Strictly speaking, consumption should apply only to those goods totally used, enjoyed, or "eaten up" within that period. In practice, consumption expenditures include all consumer goods bought, many of which last well beyond the period in question—e.g., furniture, clothing, and automobiles.

Consumption function. A schedule relating total consumption to personal disposable income (*DI*). Total wealth and other variables are also frequently assumed to influence consumption.

Consumption-possibility line. Refer to **budget line.**

Cooperative equilibrium. In game theory, an outcome in which the parties act in unison to find strategies that will optimize their joint payoffs.

Corporate income tax. A tax levied on the annual net income of a corporation.

Corporation. The predominant form of business organization in modern capitalist economies. A corporation is a firm owned by individuals or other corporations. It has the same rights to buy, sell, and make contracts as a person would have. It is legally separate from those who own it and has "limited liability."

Correlation. The degree to which two variables are systematically associated with each other.

Cost, average. Total cost (refer to **cost, total**) divided by the number of units produced.

Cost, average fixed. Fixed cost divided by the number of units produced.

Cost, average variable. Total variable cost (refer to **cost, variable**) divided by the number of units produced.

Cost, fixed. The cost a firm would incur even if its output for the period in question were zero. Total fixed cost is made up of such individual contractual costs as interest payments, mortgage payments, and directors' fees.

Cost, marginal. The extra cost (or the increase in total cost) required to produce 1 extra unit of output (or the reduction in total cost from producing 1 unit less).

Cost, minimum. The lowest attainable cost per unit (whether average, variable, or marginal). Every point on an average cost curve is a minimum in the sense that it is the best the firm can do with respect to cost for the output which that point represents. Minimum average cost is the lowest point, or points, on that curve.

Cost-push inflation. Inflation originating on the supply side of markets from a sharp increase in costs. In the aggregate supply-and-demand framework, cost-push is illustrated as an upward shift of the *AS* curve. Also called **supply-shock** inflation.

Cost, total. The minimum attainable total cost, given a particular level of technology and set of input prices. Short-run total cost takes existing plant and other fixed costs as given. Long-run total cost is the cost that would be incurred if the firm had complete flexibility with respect to all inputs and decisions.

Cost, variable. A cost that varies with the level of output, such as raw materials, labor, and fuel costs. Variable costs equal total cost minus fixed cost.

Crawling (or **sliding**) **peg.** A technique for managing a nation's exchange rate that allows the exchange rate (or the bands around the rate) to "crawl" up or down by a small amount each day or week (say, 0.25 percent per week).

Credit. (1) In monetary theory, the use of someone else's funds in exchange for a promise to pay (usually with interest) at a later date. The major examples are short-term loans from a bank, credit extended by suppliers, or commercial paper. (2) In balance-of-payments accounting, an item such as exports that earns a country foreign currency.

Cross elasticity of demand. A measure of the influence of a change in one good's price on the demand for another good. More precisely, the cross elasticity of demand equals the percentage change in demand for good A when the price of good B changes by 1 percent, assuming other variables are held constant.

Crowding out. The proposition that government spending or government deficits reduce the amount of business investment.

Currency. Coins and paper money.

Currency appreciation (or **depreciation**). See **depreciation** (of a currency).

Current account. See **balance of trade.**

Cyclical budget. See **actual, cyclical, and structural budget.**

Cyclical unemployment. See **frictional unemployment.**

Deadweight loss. The loss in real income or consumer and producer surplus that arises because of monopoly, tariffs and quotas, taxes, or other distortions. For example, when a monopolist raises its price, the loss in consumer satisfaction is more than the gain in the monopolist's revenue—the difference being the deadweight loss to society due to monopoly.

Debit. (1) An accounting term signifying an increase in assets or decrease in liabilities. (2) In balance-of-payments accounting, a debit is an item such as imports that reduces a country's stock of foreign currencies.

Decreasing returns to scale. See **returns to scale.**

Deficit spending. Government expenditures on goods and services and transfer payments in excess of its receipts from taxation and other revenue sources. The difference must be financed by borrowing from the public.

Deflating (of economic data). The process of converting "nominal" or current-dollar variables into "real" terms. This is accomplished by dividing current-dollar variables by a price index.

Deflation. A fall in the general level of prices.

Demand curve (or **demand schedule**). A schedule or curve showing the quantity of a good that buyers would purchase at each price, other things equal. Normally a demand curve has price on the vertical or Y axis and quantity demanded on the horizontal or X axis. Also see **change in demand vs. change in quantity demanded.**

Demand for money. A summary term used by economists to explain why individuals and businesses hold money balances. The major motivations for holding money are (1) **transactions demand,** signifying that people need money to purchase things, and (2) **asset demand,** relating to the desire to hold a very liquid, risk-free asset.

Demand-pull inflation. Price inflation caused by an excess demand for goods in general, caused, for example, by a major increase in aggregate demand. Often contrasted with **cost-push inflation.**

Demography. The study of the behavior of a population.

Depreciation (of an asset). A decline in the value of an asset. In both business and national accounts, depreciation is the dollar estimate of the extent to which capital has been "used up" or worn out over the period in question. Also termed **capital consumption allowance** in national-income accounting.

Depreciation (of a currency). A nation's currency is said to depreciate when it declines relative to other currencies. For example, if the foreign exchange rate of the dollar falls from 6 to 4 French francs per U.S. dollar, the dollar's value has fallen, and the dollar has undergone a depreciation. The opposite of a depreciation is an **appreciation,** which occurs when the foreign exchange rate of a currency rises.

Depression. A prolonged period characterized by high unemployment, low output and investment, depressed business confidence, falling prices, and widespread business failures. A milder form of business downturn is a **recession,** which has many of the features of a depression to a lesser extent; the precise definition of a recession today is a period in which real GNP declines for at least two consecutive calendar quarters.

Derived demand. The demand for a factor of production that results (is "derived") from the demand for the final good to which it contributes. Thus the demand for tires is derived from the demand for automobile transportation.

Devaluation. A decrease in the official price of a nation's currency, as expressed in the currencies of other nations or in terms of gold.

Thus when the official price of the dollar was lowered with respect to gold in 1971, the dollar was devalued. The opposite of devaluation is called **revaluation,** which occurs when a nation raises its official foreign exchange rate relative to gold or other currencies.

Developing countries. See **less developed country.**

Diminishing marginal utility, law of. The law which says that, as more and more of any one commodity is consumed, its marginal utility declines.

Diminishing returns, law of. A law stating that the additional output from successive increases of one input will eventually diminish when other inputs are held constant. Technically, the law is equivalent to saying that the marginal product of the varying input declines after a point.

Direct taxes. Those levied directly on individuals or firms, including taxes on income, labor earnings, and profits. Direct taxes contrast with **indirect taxes,** which are those levied on goods and services and thus only indirectly on people, and which include sales taxes and taxes on property, alcohol, imports, and gasoline.

Discount rate. (1) The interest rate charged by a Federal Reserve Bank (the central bank) on a loan that it makes to a commercial bank. (2) The rate used to calculate the present value of some asset.

Discounting (of future income). The process of converting future income into an equivalent present value. This process takes a future dollar amount and reduces it by a discount factor that reflects the appropriate interest rate. For example, if someone promises you $121 in 2 years, and the appropriate interest rate or discount rate is 10 percent per year, then we can calculate the present value by discounting the $121 by a discount factor of $(1.10)^2$. The rate at which future incomes are discounted is called the **discount rate.**

Discrimination. Differences in earnings that arise because of personal characteristics that are unrelated to job performance, especially those related to gender, race, or religion.

Disequilibrium. The state in which an economy is not in **equilibrium.** This may arise when shocks (to income or prices) have shifted demand or supply schedules but the market price (or quantity) has not yet adjusted fully. In macroeconomics, unemployment is often thought to stem from market disequilibria.

Disinflation. The process of reducing a high inflation rate. For example, the deep recession of 1980–1983 led to a sharp disinflation over that period.

Disposable income (*DI*). Roughly, take-home pay, or that part of the total national income that is available to households for consumption or saving. More precisely, it is equal to GNP less all taxes, business saving, and depreciation *plus* government and other transfer payments and government interest payments.

Dissaving. Negative saving; spending more on consumption goods during a period than the disposable income available for that period (the difference being financed by borrowing or drawing on past saving).

Distribution. In economics, the manner in which total output and income is distributed among individuals or factors (e.g., the distribution of income between labor and capital).

Division of labor. A method of organizing production whereby each worker specializes in part of the productive process. Specialization of labor yields higher total output because labor can become more skilled at a particular task and because specialized machinery can be introduced to perform more carefully defined subtasks.

Dominant equilibrium. See **dominant strategy.**

Dominant strategy. In game theory, a situation where one player has a best strategy no matter what strategy the other player follows. When all players have a dominant strategy, we say that the outcome is a **dominant equilibrium.**

Downward-sloping demand, law of. The rule that says that when the price of some commodity falls, consumers will purchase more of that good when other things are held equal.

Duopoly. A market structure in which there are only two sellers. (Compare with **oligopoly.**)

Durable goods. Equipment or machines that are normally expected to last longer than 3 years, e.g., machine tools, trucks, and automobiles.

Easy-money policy. The central-bank policy of increasing the money supply to reduce interest rates. The purpose of such a policy is to increase investment, thereby raising GNP. (Contrast with **tight-money policy.**)

Econometrics. The branch of economics that uses the methods of statistics to measure and estimate quantitative economic relationships.

Economic good. A good that is scarce relative to the total amount of it that is desired. It must therefore be rationed, usually by charging a positive price.

Economic growth. An increase in the total output of a nation over time. Economic growth is usually measured as the annual rate of increase in a nation's real GNP (or real potential GNP).

Economic regulation. See **regulation.**

Economic rent. See **rent, economic.**

Economic surplus. A term denoting the excess in total satisfaction or utility over the costs of production. Equals the sum of consumer surplus (the excess of consumer satisfaction over total value of purchases) and producer surplus (the excess of producer revenues over costs).

Economies of scale. Increases in productivity, or decreases in average cost of production, that arise from increasing all the factors of production in the same proportion.

Economies of scope. Economies of producing multiple goods or services. Thus economies of scope exist if it is cheaper to produce both good X and good Y together rather than separately.

Efficiency. Absence of waste, or the use of economic resources that produces the maximum level of satisfaction possible with the given inputs and technology. A shorthand expression for **allocative efficiency.**

Efficient-market theory. See **random-walk theory** (of stock market prices).

Elasticity. A term widely used in economics to denote the responsiveness of one variable to changes in another. Thus the elasticity of X with respect to Y means the percentage change in X for every 1 percent change in Y. For especially important examples, see **price elasticity of demand** and **price elasticity of supply.**

Employed. According to official U.S. definitions, persons are employed if they perform any paid work, or if they hold jobs but are absent because of illness, strike, or vacations. Also see **unemployment.**

Equilibrium. The state in which an economic entity is at rest or in which the forces operating on the entity are in balance so that there is no tendency for change.

Equilibrium (for a business firm). That position or level of output in which the firm is maximizing its profit, subject to any constraints it may face, and therefore has no incentive to change its output or price level. In the standard theory of the firm, this means that the firm has chosen an output at which marginal revenue is just equal to marginal cost.

Equilibrium (for the individual consumer). That position in which the consumer is maximizing utility, i.e., has chosen the bundle of goods which, given income and prices, best satisfies the consumer's wants.

Equilibrium, competitive. See **competitive equilibrium.**

Equilibrium, general. See **general equilibrium.**

Equilibrium, macroeconomic. A GNP level at which intended aggregate demand equals intended aggregate supply. At the equilibrium, desired consumption (C), government expenditures (G), investment (I), and net exports (X) just equal the quantity that businesses wish to sell at the going price level.

Exchange rate. See **foreign exchange rate.**

Exchange-rate system. The set of rules, arrangements, and institutions under which payments are made among nations. Historically, the most important exchange rate systems have been the gold exchange standard, the Bretton Woods system, and today's flexible-exchange-rate system.

Excise tax vs. sales tax. An excise tax is one levied on the purchase of a specific commodity or group of commodities (e.g., on alcohol or tobacco). A **sales tax** is one levied on all commodities with only a few specific exclusions (e.g., on all purchases except food).

Exclusion principle. A criterion by which public goods are distinguished from private goods. When a producer sells a commodity to person A and can easily exclude B, C, D, etc., from enjoying the benefits of the commodity, the exclusion principle holds and the good is a private good. If, as in public health or national defense, people cannot easily be excluded from enjoying the benefits of the good's production, then the good has public-good characteristics.

Expectations. Views or beliefs about uncertain variables (such as future interest rates, prices, or tax rates). Expectations are said to be **rational** if they are not systematically wrong (or "biased") and use all available information. Expectations are said to be **adaptive** if people form their expectations on the basis of past behavior.

Expenditure multiplier. See **multiplier.**

Exports. Goods or services that are produced in the home country and sold to another country. These include merchandise trade (like cars) and services (like transportation or interest on loans and investments). **Imports** are simply flows in the opposite direction—into the home country from another country.

External diseconomies. Situations in which production or consumption imposes uncompensated costs on other parties. Steel factories that emit smoke and sulfurous fumes harm local property and public health, yet the injured parties are not paid for the damages. The pollution is an external diseconomy.

External economies. Situations in which production or consumption yields positive benefits to others without those others paying. A firm that hires a security guard scares thieves from the neighborhood, thus providing external security services. Together with external diseconomies, these are often referred to as **externalities.**

External vs. induced variables. External variables are those determined by conditions outside the economy. They are contrasted with **induced variables,** which are determined by the internal workings of the economic system. Changes in the weather are external; changes in consumption are often induced by changes in income.

Externalities. Activities that affect others for better or worse, without those others paying or being compensated for the activity. Externalities exist when private costs or benefits do not equal social costs or benefits. The two major species are **external economies** and **external diseconomies.**

Factors of production. Productive inputs, such as labor, land, and capital; the resources needed to produce goods and services. Also called **inputs.**

Fallacy of composition. The fallacy of assuming that what holds for individuals also holds for the group or the entire system.

Federal Reserve System. The **central bank** of the United States.

Fiat money. Money, like today's paper currency, without **intrinsic value** but decreed (by fiat) to be legal tender by the government. Fiat money is accepted only as long as people have confidence that it will be accepted.

Final good. A good that is produced for final use and not for resale or further manufacture. (Compare with **intermediate goods.**)

Financial intermediary. An institution that receives funds from savers and lends them to borrowers. These include depository institutions (such as commercial or savings banks) and non-depository institutions (such as money market mutual funds, brokerage houses, insurance companies, or pension funds).

Firm (business firm). The basic, private producing unit in a capitalist or mixed economy. It hires labor and buys other inputs in order to make and sell commodities.

Fiscal-monetary mix. Refers to the combination of fiscal and monetary policies used to influence macroeconomic activity. A tight monetary–loose fiscal policy will tend to encourage consumption and retard investment, while an easy monetary–tight fiscal policy will have the opposite effect.

Fiscal policy. A government's program with respect to (1) the purchase of goods and services and spending on transfer payments, and (2) the amount and type of taxes.

Fixed cost. Refer to **cost, fixed.**

Fixed exchange rate. See **foreign exchange rate.**

Flexible exchange rates. A system of foreign exchange rates among countries wherein the exchange rates are predominantly determined by private market forces (i.e., by supply and demand) without government's setting and maintaining a particular pattern of exchange rates. Also sometimes called **floating exchange rates.** When the government refrains from any intervention in exchange markets, the system is called a pure floating exchange-rate system.

Floating exchange rates. See **flexible exchange rates.**

Flow vs. stock. A flow variable is one that has a time dimension or flows over time (like the flow through a stream). A stock variable is one that measures a quantity at a point of time (like the water in a lake). Income represents dollars per year and is thus a flow. Wealth as of December 1992 is a stock.

Foreign exchange. Currency or other financial instruments that allow one country to settle amounts owed to other countries.

Foreign exchange rate. The rate, or price, at which one country's currency is exchanged for the currency of another country. For example, if one British pound costs $1.40, then the exchange rate for the pound is $1.40. A country has a **fixed exchange rate** if it pegs its currency at a given exchange rate and stands ready to defend that rate. An exchange rate which is not fixed is said to float. See also **flexible exchange rates.**

Four-firm concentration ratio. See **concentration ratio.**

Fractional-reserve banking. A regulation in modern banking systems whereby financial institutions are legally required to keep a specified fraction of their deposits in the form of deposits with the central bank (or in vault cash). In the United States today, large banks must keep 12 percent of checking deposits in reserves.

Free goods. Those goods that are not **economic goods.** Like air or seawater, they exist in such large quantities that they need not be rationed out among those wishing to use them. Thus, their market price is zero.

Free trade. A policy whereby the government does not intervene in trading between nations—by tariffs, quotas, or other means.

Frictional unemployment. Temporary unemployment caused by changes in individual markets. It takes time, for example, for new workers to search among different job possibilities; even experienced workers often spend a minimum period of unemployed time moving from one job to another. Frictional is thus distinct from **cyclical unemployment,** which results from a low level of aggregate demand in the context of sticky wages and prices.

Full employment. A term that is used in many senses. Historically, it was taken to be that level of employment at which no (or minimal) involuntary unemployment exists. Today, economists rely upon the concept of the **natural rate of unemployment** to indicate the highest sustainable level of employment over the long run.

Galloping inflation. See **inflation.**

Game theory. An analysis of situations involving two or more decision makers with at least partly conflicting interests. It can be applied to the interaction of oligopolistic markets as well as to bargaining situations such as strikes or to conflicts such as games and war.

General equilibrium. An equilibrium state for the economy as a whole in which the markets for all goods and services are simultaneously in equilibrium. Since at these prices producers want to supply exactly the amount of goods that consumers want to buy, there are no pressures encouraging any agent in the economy to change behavior. By contrast, **partial-equilibrium analysis** concerns the equilibrium in a single market.

GNP. See **gross national product.**

GNP deflator. The "price" of GNP, that is, the price index that measures the average price of the components in GNP relative to a base year.

GNP gap. The difference or gap between potential GNP and actual GNP.

Gold standard. A system under which a nation (1) declares its currency unit to be equivalent to some fixed weight of gold, (2) holds gold reserves and will buy or sell gold freely at the price so proclaimed, and (3) puts no restriction on the export or import of gold.

Government debt. The total of government obligations in the form of bonds and shorter-term borrowings. Government debt held by the public excludes bonds held by quasi-governmental agencies such as the central bank.

Graduated income tax. See **income tax, personal.**

Gresham's Law. A law first attributed to Sir Thomas Gresham, adviser to Queen Elizabeth I of England, who stated in 1558 that "bad money drives out good"—i.e., that if the public is suspicious of one component of the money supply, it will hoard the "good money" and try to pass off the "bad money" to someone else.

Gross domestic product (GDP). The total output produced inside a country during a given year. Contrasts with **GNP,** which is the output produced by factors owned by the country.

Gross national product, nominal (or **nominal GNP**). The value, at current market prices, of all final goods and services produced during a year by a nation.

Gross national product, real (or **real GNP**). Nominal GNP corrected for inflation, i.e., real GNP = nominal GNP/GNP deflator.

Growth accounting. A technique for estimating the contribution of different factors to economic growth. Using marginal-productivity theory, growth accounting decomposes the growth of output into the growth in labor, land, capital, education, technical knowledge, and other miscellaneous sources.

Hedging. A technique for avoiding a risk by making a counteracting transaction. For example, if a farmer produces wheat that will be harvested in the fall, the risk of price fluctuations can be offset, or hedged, by selling in the spring or summer the quantity of wheat that will be produced.

High-powered money. Same as **monetary base.**

Horizontal equity vs. vertical equity. Horizontal equity refers to the fairness or equity in treatment of persons in similar situations; the principle of horizontal equity states that those who are essentially equal should receive equal treatment. **Vertical equity** refers to the equitable treatment of those who are in different circumstances; there are no universally accepted practical applications of vertical equity, although some hold that vertical equity requires progressive taxation.

Horizontal integration. Refer to **integration, vertical vs. horizontal.**

Horizontal merger. See **merger.**

Human capital. The stock of technical knowledge and skill embodied in a nation's work force, resulting from investments in formal education and on-the-job training.

Hyperinflation. See **inflation.**

Imperfect competition. Refer to **competition, imperfect.**

Imperfect competitor. Any firm that buys or sells a good in large enough quantities to be able to affect the price of that good.

Implicit-cost elements. Costs that do not show up as explicit money costs but nevertheless should be counted as such. For example, if you run your own business, then in reckoning your profit you should include as one of your implicit costs the wage or salary you could have earned if you had worked elsewhere. Sometimes called **opportunity cost** although "opportunity cost" has a broader meaning.

Imports. See **exports.**

Inappropriability. The inability of firms to capture the full monetary value of their actions; particularly applicable to inventive activity.

Incidence (or **tax incidence**). The ultimate economic burden of a tax (as opposed to the legal requirement for payment). Thus a sales tax may be paid by a retailer, but it is likely that the incidence falls upon the consumer. The exact incidence of a tax depends on the price elasticities of supply and demand.

Income. The flow of wages, interest payments, dividends, and other receipts accruing to an individual or nation during a period of time (usually a year).

Income effect (of a price change). Change in the quantity demanded of a commodity because the change in its price has the effect of changing a consumer's real income. Thus it supplements the **substitution effect** of a price change.

Income elasticity of demand. The demand for any given good is influenced not only by the good's price but by buyers' incomes. Income elasticity measures this responsiveness. Its precise definition is percentage change in quantity demanded divided by percentage change in income. (Compare with **price elasticity of demand.**)

Income statement. A company's statement, covering a specified time period (usually a year), showing sales or revenue earned during that period, all costs properly charged against the goods sold, and the profit (net income) remaining after deduction of such costs. Also called a **profit-and-loss statement.**

Income tax, negative. Refer to **negative income tax.**

Income tax, personal. Tax levied on the income received by individuals, either in the form of wages and salaries or income from property, such as rents, dividends, or interest. In the United States, personal income tax is **graduated,** meaning that people with higher incomes pay taxes at a higher average rate than people with lower incomes.

Income velocity of money. Refer to **velocity of money.**

Incomes policy. A government policy that attempts directly to restrict wage and price changes in an effort to slow inflation. Such policies range from voluntary wage-price guidelines to outright legal control over wages, salaries, and prices.

Increasing returns to scale. See **returns to scale.**

Independent goods. Goods whose demands are relatively separate from one another. More precisely, goods A and B are independent when a change in the price of good A has no effect on the quantity demanded of good B, other things equal.

Indexing (or **indexation**). A mechanism by which wages, prices, and contracts are partially or wholly adjusted to compensate for changes in the general price level.

Indifference curve. A curve drawn on a graph whose two axes measure amounts of different goods consumed. Each point on one curve (indicating different combinations of the two goods) yields exactly the same level of satisfaction for a given consumer. That is, the consumer is indifferent between any two points on an indifference curve.

Indifference map. A graph showing a family of indifference curves for a consumer. In general, curves that lie farther northeast from the graph's origin represent higher levels of satisfaction.

Indirect taxes. See **direct taxes.**

Induced variables. See **external vs. induced variables.**

Industry. A group of firms producing similar or identical products.

Inertial inflation. A process of steady inflation that occurs when inflation is expected to persist and the ongoing rate of inflation is built into contracts and people's expectations.

Infant industry. In foreign-trade theory, an industry that has not had sufficient time to develop the experience or expertise to exploit the economies of scale needed to compete successfully with more mature industries producing the same commodity in other countries. Infant industries are often thought to need tariffs or quotas to protect them while they develop.

Inferior good. A good whose consumption goes down as income rises.

Inflation (or **inflation rate**). The inflation rate is the percentage annual increase in a general price level. **Hyperinflation** is inflation at extremely high rates (say, 1000, 1 million, or even 1 billion percent a year). **Galloping inflation** is a rate of 50 or 100 or 200 percent annually. **Moderate inflation** is a price-level rise that does not distort relative prices or incomes severely.

Innovation. A term particularly associated with Joseph Schumpeter, who meant by it (1) the bringing to market of a new and significantly different product, (2) the introduction of a new production technique, or (3) the opening up of a new market. (Contrast with **invention.**)

Inputs. See **factors of production.**

Insurance. A system by which individuals can reduce their exposure to risk of large losses by spreading the risks among a large number of persons.

Integration, vertical vs. horizontal. The production process is one of stages—e.g., iron ore into steel ingots, steel ingots into rolled steel sheets, rolled steel sheets into an automobile body. **Vertical integration** is the combination in a single firm of two or more different stages of this process (e.g., iron ore with steel ingots). **Horizontal integration** is the combination in a single firm of different units that operate at the same stage of production.

Interest. The return paid to those who lend money.

Interest rate. The price paid for borrowing money for a period of time, usually expressed as a percentage of the principal per year. Thus, if the interest rate is 10 percent per year, then $100 would be paid for a loan of $1000 for 1 year.

Intermediate goods. Goods that have undergone some manufacturing or processing but have not yet reached the stage of becoming final products. For example, steel and cotton yarn are intermediate goods.

Intervention. An activity in which a government buys or sells its currency in the foreign exchange market in order to affect its currency's exchange rate.

Intrinsic value (of money). The commodity value of a piece of money (e.g., the market value of the weight of copper in a copper coin).

Invention. The creation of a new product or discovery of a new production technique. (Distinguish from **innovation.**)

Investment. (1) Economic activity that forgoes consumption today with an eye to increasing output in the future. It includes tangible capital (structures, equipment, and inventories) and intangible investments (education or "human capital," research and development, and health). Net investment is the value of total investment after an allowance has been made for de-preciation. Gross investment is investment without allowance for depreciation. (2) In finance terms, investment has an altogether different meaning and denotes the purchase of a security, such as a stock or a bond.

Investment demand (or **investment demand curve**). The schedule showing the relationship between the level of investment and the cost of capital (or, more specifically, the real interest rate); also, the graph of that relationship.

Invisible hand. A concept introduced by Adam Smith in 1776 to describe the paradox of a laissez-faire market economy. The invisible-hand doctrine holds that, with each participant pursuing his or her own private interest, a market system nevertheless works to the benefit of all as though a benevolent invisible hand were directing the whole process.

Involuntary unemployment. See **unemployment.**

Iron law of wages. In the economic theories of Malthus and Marx, the theory that there is an inevitable tendency in capitalism for wages to be driven down to a subsistence level.

Keynesian economics. The body of thought developed by John Maynard Keynes holding that a capitalist system does not automatically tend toward a full-employment equilibrium. According to Keynes, the resulting underemployment equilibrium could be cured by fiscal or monetary policies to raise aggregate demand.

Labor force. In official U.S. statistics, that group of people 16 years of age and older who are either employed or unemployed.

Labor-force participation rate. Ratio of those in the labor force to the entire population 16 years of age or older.

Labor productivity. See **productivity.**

Labor supply. The number of workers (or, more generally, the number of labor-hours) available to an economy. The principal determinants of labor supply are population, real wages, and social traditions.

Labor theory of value. The view, often associated with Adam Smith and Karl Marx, that every commodity should be valued solely according to the quantity of labor required for its production.

Laissez-faire ("Leave us alone"). The view that government should interfere as little as possible in economic activity and leave decisions to the marketplace. As expressed by classical economists like Adam Smith, this view held that the role of government should be limited to (1) maintenance of law and order, (2) national defense, and (3) provision of certain public goods that private business would not undertake (e.g., public health and sanitation).

Land. In classical and neoclassical economics, one of the three basic factors of production (along with labor and capital). More generally, land is taken to include land used for agricultural or industrial purposes as well as natural resources taken from above or below the soil.

Least-cost rule (of production). The rule that the cost of producing a specific level of output is minimized when the ratio of the marginal revenue product of each input to the price of that input is the same for all inputs.

Legal tender. Money that by law must be accepted as payment for debts. All U.S. coins and currency are legal tender, but checks are not.

Less developed country (LDC). A country with a per capita income far below that of "developed" nations (the latter usually includes most nations of North America or Western Europe).

Liabilities. In accounting, debts or financial obligations owed to other firms or persons.

Libertarianism. An economic philosophy that emphasizes the importance of personal freedom in economic and political affairs; also sometimes called "liberalism." Libertarian writers, including Adam Smith in an earlier age and Milton Friedman and James Buchanan today, hold that people should be able to follow their own interests and desires and that government activities should be limited to guaranteeing contracts and to providing police and national defense, thereby allowing maximum personal freedom.

Limited liability. The restriction of an owner's loss in a business to the amount of capital that the owner has contributed to the company. Limited liability was an important factor in the rise of large corporations. By contrast, owners in partnerships and individual proprietorships generally have **unlimited liability** for the debts of those firms.

Long run. A term used to denote a period over which full adjustment to changes can take place. In microeconomics, it denotes the time over which firms can enter or leave an industry and the capital stock can be replaced. In macroeconomics, it is often used to mean the period over which all prices, wage contracts, tax rates, and expectations can fully adjust.

Long-run aggregate supply. The relationship between output and the price level after all price and wage adjustments have taken place, and the *AS* curve is therefore vertical.

Lorenz curve. A graph used to show the extent of inequality of income or wealth.

M_1, M_2. Refer to **money supply.**

Macroeconomics. Analysis dealing with the behavior of the economy as a whole with respect to output, income, the price level, foreign trade, unemployment, and other aggregate economic variables. (Contrast with **microeconomics.)**

Malthusian theory of population growth. The hypothesis, first expressed by Thomas Malthus, that the "natural" tendency of population is to grow more rapidly than the food supply. Per capita food production would thus decline over time, thereby putting a check on population. In general, a view that population tends to grow more rapidly as incomes or living standards of the population rise.

Managed float. The most prevalent exchange-rate system today. In this system, a country occasionally intervenes to stabilize its currency.

Marginal cost. Refer to **cost, marginal.**

Marginal principle. The fundamental notion that people will maximize their income or profits when the marginal costs and marginal benefits of their actions are equal.

Marginal product (*MP*). The extra output resulting from 1 extra unit of a specified input when all other inputs are held constant. Sometimes called marginal physical product.

Marginal product theory of distribution. A theory of the distribution of income proposed by John B. Clark, according to which each productive input is paid according to its **marginal product.**

Marginal propensity to consume (*MPC*). The extra amount that people consume when they receive an extra dollar of disposable income. To be distinguished from the **average propensity to consume,** which is the ratio of total consumption to total disposable income.

Marginal propensity to import (*MPm*). In macroeconomics, the increase in the dollar value of imports resulting from each dollar increase in the value of GNP.

Marginal propensity to save (*MPS*). That fraction of an additional dollar of disposable income that is saved. Note that, by definition, $MPC + MPS = 1$.

Marginal revenue (*MR*). The additional revenue a firm would earn if it sold 1 extra unit of output. In perfect competition, *MR* equals price. Under imperfect competition, *MR* is less than price because, in order to sell the extra unit, the price must be reduced on all prior units sold.

Marginal revenue product (*MRP*) (of an input). Marginal revenue multiplied by marginal product. It is the extra revenue that would be brought in if a firm were to buy 1 extra unit of an input, put it to work, and sell the extra product it produced.

Marginal tax rate. For an income tax, the percentage of the last dollar of income paid in taxes. If a tax system is progressive, the marginal tax rate is higher than the average tax rate.

Marginal utility (*MU*). The additional or extra satisfaction yielded from consuming 1 additional unit of a commodity, with amounts of all other goods consumed held constant.

Market. An arrangement whereby buyers and sellers interact to determine the prices and quantities of a commodity. Some markets (such as the stock market or a flea market) take place in physical locations; other markets are conducted over the telephone or are organized by computers.

Market economy. An economy in which the *what, how,* and *for whom* questions concerning resource allocation are primarily determined by supply and demand in markets. In this form of economic organization, firms, motivated by the desire to maximize profits, buy inputs and produce and sell outputs. Households, armed with their factor incomes, go to markets and determine the demand for commodities. The interaction of firms' supply and households' demand then determines the prices and quantities of goods.

Market equilibrium. Same as **competitive equilibrium.**

Market failure. An imperfection in a price system that prevents an efficient allocation of resources. Important examples are **externalities** and **imperfect competition.**

Market power. The degree of control that a firm or group of firms has over the price and production decisions in an industry. In a monopoly, the firm has a high degree of market power; firms in perfectly competitive industries have no market power. **Concentration ratios** are the most widely used measures of market power.

Market share. That fraction of an industry's output accounted for by an individual firm or group of firms.

Markup pricing. The pricing method used by many firms in situations of imperfect competition; under this method they estimate average cost and then add some fixed percentage to that cost in order to reach the price they charge.

Marxism. The set of social, political, and economic doctrines developed by Karl Marx in the nineteenth century. As an economic theory, Marxism predicted that capitalism would collapse as a result of its own internal contradictions, especially its tendency to exploit the working classes. The conviction that workers would inevitably be oppressed under capitalism was based on the **iron law of wages,** which holds that wages would decline to subsistence levels.

Mean. In statistics, the same thing as "average." Thus for the numbers 1, 3, 6, 10, 20, the mean is 8.

Median. In statistics, the figure exactly in the middle of a series of numbers ordered or ranked from lowest to highest (e.g., incomes or examination grades). Thus for the numbers 1, 3, 6, 10, 20, the median is 6.

Mercantilism. A political doctrine perhaps best known as the object of Adam Smith's attack in *The Wealth of Nations.* Mercantilists emphasized the importance of balance-of-payments surpluses as a device to accumulate gold. They therefore advocated tight government control of economic policies, believing that laissez-faire policies might lead to a loss of gold.

Merger. The acquisition of one corporation by another, which usually occurs when one firm buys the stock of another. Important examples are (1) **vertical mergers,** which occur when the two firms are at different stages of a production process (e.g., iron ore and steel), (2) **horizontal mergers,** which occur when the two firms produce in the same market (e.g., two automobile manufacturers), and (3) **conglomerate mergers,** which occur when the two firms operate in unrelated markets (e.g., shoelaces and oil refining).

Microeconomics. Analysis dealing with the behavior of individual elements in an economy—such as the determination of the price of a single product or the behavior of a single consumer or business firm. (Contrast with **macroeconomics.**)

Minimum cost. Refer to **cost, minimum.**

Mixed economy. The dominant form of economic organization in non-communist countries. Mixed economies rely primarily on the price system for their economic organization but use a variety of government interventions (such as taxes, spending, and regulation) to handle macroeconomic instability and market failures.

Model. A formal framework for representing the basic features of a complex system by a few central relationships. Models take the form of graphs, mathematical equations, and computer programs.

Moderate inflation. See **inflation.**

Momentary run. A period of time that is so short that production is fixed.

Monetarism. A school of thought

holding that changes in the money supply are the major cause of macroeconomic fluctuations. For the short run, this view holds that changes in the money supply are the primary determinant of changes in both real output and the price level. For the longer run, this holds that prices tend to move proportionally with the money supply. Monetarists often conclude that the best macroeconomic policy is one with a stable growth in the money supply.

Monetary base. The net monetary liabilities of the government that are held by the public. In the United States, the monetary base is equal to currency and bank reserves. Sometimes called **high-powered money.**

Monetary policy. The objectives of the central bank in exercising its control over money, interest rates, and credit conditions. The instruments of monetary policy are primarily open-market operations, reserve requirements, and the discount rate.

Money. The means of payment or medium of exchange. For the items constituting money, refer to **money supply.**

Money demand schedule. The relationship between holdings of money and interest rates. As interest rates rise, bonds and other securities become more attractive, lowering the quantity of money demanded. See also **demand for money.**

Money funds. Shorthand expression for very liquid short-term financial instruments whose interest rates are not regulated. The major examples are money market mutual funds and commercial bank money market deposit accounts.

Money market. A term denoting the set of institutions that handle the purchase or sale of short-term credit instruments like Treasury bills and commercial paper.

Money supply. The narrowly defined money supply (M_1) consists of coins, paper currency, plus all demand or checking deposits; this is narrow, or transactions, money. The broadly defined supply (M_2) includes all items in M_1 plus certain liquid assets or near-monies— savings deposits, money market funds, and the like.

Money-supply effect. The relationship whereby a price rise operating on a fixed nominal money supply produces tight money and lowers aggregate spending.

Money-supply multiplier. The ratio of the increase in the money supply (or in deposits) to the increase in bank reserves. Generally, the money-supply multiplier is equal to the inverse of the required reserve ratio. For example, if the required reserve ratio is 0.125, then the money-supply multiplier is 8.

Money, velocity of. See **velocity of money.**

Monopolistic competition. A market structure in which there are many sellers who are supplying goods that are close, but not perfect, substitutes. In such a market, each firm can exercise some effect on its product's price.

Monopoly. A market structure in which a commodity is supplied by a single firm. Also see **natural monopoly.**

Monopsony. The mirror image of monopoly: a market in which there is a single buyer; a "buyer's monopoly."

MPC. See **marginal propensity to consume.**

MPS. See **marginal propensity to save.**

Multiplier. A term in macroeconomics denoting the change in an induced variable (such as GNP or money supply) per unit of change in an external variable (such as government spending or bank reserves). The **expenditure multiplier** refers to the increase in GNP that would result from a $1 increase in expenditure (say on investment).

Multiplier model. In macroeconomics, a theory developed by J. M. Keynes that emphasizes the importance of changes in autonomous expenditures (especially investment, government spending, and net exports) in determining changes in output and employment. Also see **multiplier.**

Nash equilibrium. In game theory, a set of strategies for the players where no player can improve his or her payoff given the other player's strategy. That is, given player A's strategy, player B can do no better, and given B's strategy A can do no better. The Nash equilibrium is also sometimes called the **noncooperative equilibrium.**

National debt. Same as **government debt.**

National-income and -product accounting. A set of accounts that measures the spending, income, and output of the entire nation for a quarter or a year.

Natural monopoly. A firm or industry whose average cost per unit of production falls sharply over the entire range of its output, as for example in local electricity distribution. Thus a single firm, a monopoly, can supply the industry output more efficiently than can multiple firms.

Natural rate of unemployment. The unemployment rate at which upward and downward pressures on wage and price inflation are in balance, so that inflation neither rises nor falls. Equivalently, the unemployment rate at which the long-run **Phillips curve** is vertical.

"Near-money." Financial assets that are risk-free and so readily convertible into money that they are close to actually being money. Examples are money funds and Treasury bills.

Negative income tax. A plan for replacing current income-support programs (welfare, food stamps, etc.) with a unified program. Under such a plan, poor families would receive an income supplement and would have benefits reduced as their earnings increase.

Neoclassical growth model. A theory or model used to explain long-term trends in economic growth of industrial economies. This model emphasizes the importance of capital deepening (i.e., a growing capital-labor ratio) and technological change in explaining the growth of potential real GNP.

Net economic welfare (NEW). A measure of national output that corrects several limitations of the GNP measure.

Net exports. In the national product accounts, the value of exports of goods and services minus the value of imports of goods and services.

Net investment. Gross investment minus depreciation of capital goods.

Net national product (NNP). GNP less an allowance for depreciation of capital goods.

Net worth. In accounting, total assets minus total liabilities.

NNP. See **net national product.**

Nominal GNP. See **gross national product, nominal.**

Nominal (or **money**) **interest rate.** The **interest rate** paid on different assets. This represents a dollar return per year per dollar invested. Compare with the **real interest rate,** which represents the return per year in goods per unit of goods invested.

Noncooperative equilibrium. See **Nash equilibrium.**

Normative vs. positive economics. Normative economics considers "what ought to be"—value judgments, or goals, of public policy. **Positive economics,** by contrast, is the analysis of facts and behavior in an economy, or "the way things are."

NOW (negotiable order of withdrawal) account. An interest-bearing checking account. See also **checking accounts.**

Okun's Law. The empirical relationship, discovered by Arthur Okun, between cyclical movements in GNP and unemployment. The law states that when actual GNP declines 2 percent relative to potential GNP, the unemployment rate increases by about 1 percentage point. (Earlier estimates placed the ratio at 3 to 1.)

Oligopoly. A situation of imperfect competition in which an industry is dominated by a small number of suppliers.

Open economy. An economy that engages in international trade (i.e., imports and exports) of goods and capital with other countries. A **closed economy** is one that has no imports or exports.

Open-economy multiplier. In an open economy, income leaks into imports as well as into saving. Therefore, the open-economy multiplier for investment or government expenditure is given by

$$\frac{\text{Open-economy}}{\text{multiplier}} = \frac{1}{MPS + MPm}$$

where MPS = marginal propensity to save and MPm = marginal propensity to import.

Open-market operations. The activity of a central bank in buying or selling government bonds to influence bank reserves, the money supply, and interest rates. If securities are bought, the money paid out by the central bank increases commercial-bank reserves, and the money supply increases. If securities are sold, the money supply contracts.

Opportunity cost. The value of the next best use (or opportunity) for an economic good, or the value of the sacrificed alternative. Thus, say that the best alternative use of the inputs employed to mine a ton of coal was to grow 10 bushels of wheat. The opportunity cost of a ton of coal is thus the 10 bushels of wheat that *could* have been produced but were not. Opportunity cost is particularly useful for valu-

ing nonmarketed goods such as environmental health or safety.

Other things equal. A phrase that signifies that a factor under consideration is changed while all other factors are held equal or constant. For example, a downward-sloping demand curve shows that the quantity demanded will decline as the price rises, as long as other things (such as incomes) are held equal.

Output. See **total product.**

Paradox of value. The paradox that many necessities of life (e.g., water) have a low "market" value, while many luxuries (e.g., diamonds) with little "use" value have a high market price. It is explained by the fact that a price does not reflect the total utility of a commodity but its marginal utility.

Pareto efficiency (or **Pareto optimality**). See **allocative efficiency.**

Partial-equilibrium analysis. Analysis concentrating on the effect of changes in an individual market, holding other things equal (e.g., disregarding changes in income).

Partnership. An association of two or more persons to conduct a business which is not in corporate form and does not enjoy limited liability.

Patent. An exclusive right granted to an inventor to control the use of an invention for, in the United States, a period of 17 years. Patents create temporary monopolies as a way of rewarding inventive activity and are the principal tool for promoting invention among individuals or small firms.

Payoff table. In game theory, a table used to describe the strategies and payoffs of a game with two or more players. The profits or utilities of the different players are the **payoffs.**

Payoffs. See **payoff table.**

Perfect competition. Refer to **competition, perfect.**

Personal savings rate. The ratio of personal saving to personal disposable income, in percent.

Phillips curve. A graph first devised by A. W. Phillips, showing the tradeoff between unemployment and inflation. In modern mainstream macroeconomics, the downward-sloping "tradeoff" Phillips curve is generally held to be valid only in the short run; in the long run, the Phillips curve is usually thought to be vertical at the natural rate of unemployment.

Portfolio theory. An economic theory that describes how rational investors allocate their wealth among different financial assets—that is, how they put their wealth into a "portfolio."

Positive economics. Refer to **normative vs. positive economics.**

Post hoc fallacy. From the Latin, *post hoc, ergo propter hoc*, which translates as "after this, therefore because of this." This fallacy arises when it is assumed that because event A precedes event B, it follows that A *causes* B.

Potential GNP. High-employment GNP; more precisely, the maximum level of GNP that can be sustained with a given state of technology and population size without accelerating inflation. Today, it is generally taken to be equivalent to the level of output corresponding to the natural rate of unemployment.

Potential output. Same as **potential GNP.**

Poverty. Today, the U.S. government defines the "poverty line" to be the minimum adequate standard of living.

PPF. See **production-possibility frontier.**

Present value (of an asset). Today's value for an asset that yields a stream of income over time. Valuation of such time streams of returns requires calculating the present worth of each component of the income, which is done by applying a discount rate (or interest rate) to future incomes.

Price-elastic demand (or elastic demand). The situation in which price elasticity of demand exceeds 1 in absolute value. This signifies that the percentage change in quantity demanded is greater than the percentage change in price. In addition, elastic demand implies that total revenue (price times quantity) rises when price falls because the increase in quantity demanded is so large. (Contrast with **price-inelastic demand.**)

Price elasticity of demand. A measure of the extent to which quantity demanded responds to a price change. The elasticity coefficient (price elasticity of demand = E_D) is percentage change in quantity demanded divided by percentage change in price. In figuring percentages, use the averages of old and new quantities in the numerator and of old and new prices in the denominator; disregard the minus sign. Refer also to **price-elastic demand, price-inelastic demand, unit-elastic demand.**

Price elasticity of supply. Conceptually similar to **price elasticity of demand,** except that it measures the supply responsiveness to a price change. More precisely, the price elasticity of supply measures the percentage change in quantity supplied divided by the percentage change in price. Supply elasticities are most useful in perfect competition.

Price flexibility. Price behavior in "auction" markets (e.g., for many raw commodities or the stock market), in which prices immediately respond to changes in demand or in supply. (In contrast, refer to **administered prices.**)

Price index. An index number that shows how the average price of a bundle of goods has changed over a period of time. In computing the average, the prices of the different goods are generally weighted by their economic importance (e.g., by each commodity's share of total consumer expenditures in the **consumer price index**).

Price-inelastic demand (or inelastic demand). The situation in which price elasticity of demand is below 1 in absolute value. In this case, when price declines, total revenue declines, and when price is increased, total revenue goes up. Perfectly inelastic demand means that there is no change at all in quantity demanded when price goes up or goes down. (Contrast with **price-elastic demand** and **unit-elastic demand.**)

Private good. See **public good.**

Producer price index. The **price index** of goods sold at the wholesale level (such as steel, wheat, oil).

Product, average. See **average product.**

Product differentiation. The existence of characteristics that make similar goods less-than-perfect substitutes. Thus locational differences make similar types of gasoline sold at separate points imperfect substitutes. Firms enjoying product differentiation face a downward-sloping demand curve instead of the horizontal demand curve of the perfect competitor.

Product, marginal. See **marginal product.**

Production function. A relation (or mathematical function) specifying the maximum output that can be produced with given inputs for a given level of technology. Applies to a firm or, as an aggregate production function, to the economy as a whole.

Production-possibility frontier (PPF). A graph showing the menu of goods that can be produced by an economy. In a frequently cited case, the choice is reduced to two goods, guns and butter. Points outside the *PPF* (to the northeast of it) are unattainable. Points inside it are inefficient since resources are not being fully employed, resources are not being used properly, or outdated production techniques are being utilized.

Productivity. A term referring to the ratio of output to inputs (total output divided by labor inputs is **labor productivity**). Productivity increases if the same quantity of inputs produces more output. Labor productivity increases because of improved technology, improvements in labor skills, or capital deepening.

Productivity growth. The rate of increase in **productivity** from one period to another. For example, if an index of labor productivity is 100 in 1990 and 101.7 in 1991, the rate of productivity growth is 1.7 percent per year for 1991 over 1990.

Productivity of capital, net. Refer to **rate of return.**

Profit. (1) In accounting terms, total revenue minus costs properly chargeable against the goods sold (refer to **income statement**). (2) In economic theory, the difference between sales revenue and the full opportunity cost of resources involved in producing the goods.

Profit-and-loss statement. Refer to **income statement.**

Progressive, proportional, and **regressive taxes.** A progressive tax weighs more heavily upon the rich; a regressive tax does the opposite. More precisely, a tax is progressive if the average tax rate (i.e., taxes divided by income) is higher for those with higher incomes; it is a regressive tax if the average tax rate declines with higher incomes; it is a proportional tax if the average tax rate is equal at all income levels.

Property rights. Property rights define the ability of individuals or firms to own, buy, sell, and use the capital goods and other property in a market economy.

Proportional tax. Refer to **progressive, proportional,** and **regressive taxes.**

Proprietorship, individual. A business firm owned and operated by one person.

Protectionism. Any policy adopted by a country to protect domestic industries against competition from imports (most commonly, a tariff or quota imposed on such imports).

Public choice (also **public-choice theory**). Branch of economics and political science dealing with the way that governments make choices and direct the economy. This theory differs from the theory of markets in emphasizing the influence of vote maximizing for politicians, which contrasts to profit maximizing by firms.

Public debt. See **government debt.**

Public good. A commodity whose benefits are indivisibly spread among the entire community, whether or not particular individuals desire to consume the public good. For example, a public-health measure that eradicates smallpox protects all, not just those paying for the vaccinations. To be contrasted with **private goods,** such as bread, which, if consumed by one person, cannot be consumed by another person.

Pure economic rent. See **rent, economic.**

Quantity demanded. See **change in demand vs. change in quantity demanded.**

Quantity equation of exchange. A tautology, $MV \equiv PQ$, where M is the money supply, V is the income velocity of money, and PQ (price times quantity) is the money value of total output (nominal GNP). The equation must always hold exactly since V is defined as PQ/M.

Quantity supplied. See **change in supply vs. change in quantity supplied.**

Quantity theory of prices. A theory of the determination of output and the overall price level holding that prices move proportionately with the money supply. A more cautious approach put forth by monetarists holds that the money supply is the most important determinant of changes in nominal GNP (see **monetarism**).

Quota. A form of import protectionism in which the total quantity of imports of a particular commodity (e.g., sugar or cars) during a given period is limited.

Random-walk theory (of stock market prices). Increasingly called the **efficient-market theory.** A view that holds that all currently available information is already incorporated into the price of common stocks (or other assets). Consequently, the stock market offers no bargains that can be found by looking at old or "stale" information or at easily available information (like recent price movements). Stock prices do change, however—on the basis of *new* information. If we assume that the chances of good news and of bad are 50:50, then stock prices will follow a "random walk," i.e., they are equally likely to move up or down.

Rate of inflation. See **inflation.**

Rate of return (or **return**) on capital. The yield on an investment or on a capital good. Thus, an investment costing $100 and yielding $12 annually has a rate of return of 12 percent per year.

Rational expectations. (1) For the narrow definition, see **expectations.** (2) More generally, part of a view of the economy held by proponents of **rational-expectations macroeconomics.**

Rational-expectations macroeconomics. A school, led by Robert Lucas and Thomas Sargent, holding that markets clear quickly and that expectations are rational. Under these and other conditions it can be shown that predictable macroeconomic policies have no effect on real output or unemployment. Sometimes called new classical macroeconomics.

Real GNP. GNP adjusted for price change. Real GNP equals nominal GNP divided by the GNP deflator. See **gross national product, real.**

Real interest rate. The interest rate measured in terms of goods rather than money. It is thus equal to the money (or nominal) interest rate less the rate of inflation.

Real wages. The purchasing power of a worker's wages in terms of goods and services. It is measured by the ratio of the money wage rate to the consumer price index.

Recession. A downturn in real GNP for two or more successive quarters. See also **depression.**

Regressive tax. Refer to **progressive, proportional,** and **regres-**... **sive taxes.**

Regulation. Government laws or rules designed to control the behavior of firms. The major kinds are **economic regulation** (which affects the prices, entry, or service of a single industry, such as telephone service) and **social regulation** (which attempts to correct externalities that prevail across a number of industries, such as air or water pollution).

Rent, economic (or **pure economic rent**). This term was applied by nineteenth-century British economists to income earned from land. The total supply of land available is (with minor qualifications) fixed, and the return paid to the landowner is rent. The term is often extended to the return paid to any factor in fixed supply—i.e., to any input having a perfectly inelastic or vertical supply curve.

Required reserves. See **reserves, bank.**

Reserves, bank. That portion of deposits that a bank sets aside in the form of vault cash or non-interest-earning deposits with Federal Reserve Banks. In the United States, banks are required to hold 12 percent of checking deposits (or transactions accounts) in the form of reserves.

Reserves, international. Every nation holds at least some reserves, in such forms as gold, currencies of other nations, and special drawing rights. International reserves serve as "international money," to be used when a country encounters balance-of-payments difficulties. If a nation were prepared to allow its exchange rate to float freely, it would need no reserves.

Resource allocation. The manner in which an economy distributes its resources (its factors of production) among the potential uses so as to produce a particular set of final goods.

Returns to scale. The rate at which output increases when all inputs are increased proportionately. For example, if all the inputs double and output is exactly doubled, that process is said to exhibit **constant returns to scale.** If, however, output grows by less than 100 percent when all inputs are doubled, the process shows **decreasing returns to scale;** if output more than doubles, the process demonstrates **increasing returns to scale.**

Revaluation. An increase in the official foreign exchange rate of a currency. See also **devaluation.**

Revenue, average. Refer to **average revenue.**

Revenue, marginal. Refer to **marginal revenue.**

Revenue, total. Refer to **total revenue.**

Risk averse. A person is risk-averse when, faced with an uncertain situation, the displeasure from losing a given amount of income is greater than the pleasure from gaining the same amount of income.

Risk spreading. The process of taking large risks and spreading them around so that they are but small risks for a large number of people. The major form of risk spreading is **insurance,** which is a kind of gambling in reverse.

Sales tax. See **excise tax vs. sales tax.**

Saving. That part of income which is not consumed; in other words, the difference between disposable income and consumption.

Savings function. The schedule showing the amount of saving that households or a nation will undertake at each level of income.

Say's Law of markets. The theory that "supply creates its own demand." J. B. Say argued in 1803 that, because total purchasing power is exactly equal to total incomes and outputs, excess demand or supply is impossible. Keynes attacked Say's Law, pointing out that an extra dollar of income need not be entirely spent (i.e., the marginal propensity to consume is not necessarily unity).

Scarcity, law of. The principle that most things that people want are available only in limited supply (the exception being **free goods**). Thus goods are generally scarce and must somehow be rationed, whether by price or some other means.

Securities. A term used to designate a wide variety of financial assets, such as stocks, bonds, options, and notes; more precisely, the document used to establish ownership of these assets.

Short run. A period in which all factors cannot adjust fully. In microeconomics, the capital stock and other "fixed" inputs cannot be adjusted and entry is not free in the short run. In macroeconomics, prices, wage contracts, tax rates, and expectations may not fully adjust in the short run.

Short-run aggregate supply. The relationship between output and prices in the short run wherein changes in aggregate demand can affect output. Also represented by an upward-sloping or horizontal AS curve.

Shutdown price (or **point,** or **rule**). In the theory of the firm, the shutdown point comes at that point where the market price is just sufficient to cover average variable cost and no more. Hence, the firm's losses per period just equal its fixed costs; it might as well shut down.

Single-tax movement. A nineteenth-century movement, originated by Henry George, holding that continued poverty in the midst of steady economic progress was attributable to the scarcity of land and the large rents flowing to landowners. The "single tax" was to be a tax on economic rent earned from landownership.

Slope. In a graph, the change in the variable on the vertical axis per unit of change in the variable on the horizontal axis. Upward-sloping lines have positive slopes, downward-sloping curves (like demand curves) have negative slopes, and horizontal lines have slopes of zero.

Social overhead capital. The essential investments on which economic development depends, particularly for transportation, power, and communications. Sometimes called "infrastructure."

Social regulation. See **regulation.**

Socialism. A political theory that holds that all (or almost all) the means of production, other than labor, should be owned by the community. This allows the return on capital to be shared more equally than under capitalism.

Speculator. Someone engaged in speculation, i.e., who buys (or sells) a commodity or financial asset with the aim of profiting from later selling (or buying) the item at a higher (or lower) price.

Spillovers. Same as **externalities.**

Stagflation. A term, coined in the early 1970s, describing the coexistence of high unemployment, or *stagnation*, with persistent *inflation*. Its explanation lies primarily in the inertial nature of the inflationary process.

Stock, common. Refer to **common stock.**

Stock market. An organized marketplace in which common stocks are traded. In the United States, the largest stock market is the New York Stock Exchange, on which are traded the largest American companies.

Stock vs. flow. See **flow vs. stock.**

Strategic interaction. A situation in oligopolistic markets in which each firm's business strategies depend upon its rivals' plans. A formal analysis of strategic interaction is given in **game theory.**

Structural budget. See **actual, cyclical,** and **structural budget.**

Structural unemployment. Unemployment resulting because the regional or occupational pattern of job vacancies does not match the pattern of worker availability. There may be jobs available, but unemployed workers may not have the required skill; or the jobs may be in different regions from where the unemployed workers live.

Subsidy. A payment by a government to a firm or household that provides or consumes a commodity. For example, governments often subsidize food by paying for part of the food expenditures of low-income households.

Substitutes. Goods that compete with each other (as do gloves and mittens). By contrast, goods that go together in the eyes of consumers (such as left shoes and right shoes) are complements.

Substitution effect (of a price change). The tendency of consumers is to consume more of a good when its relative price falls (to "substitute" in favor of that good), and to consume less of the good when its relative price increases (to "substitute" away from that good). This substitution effect of a price change leads to a downward-sloping demand curve. (Compare with **income effect.**)

Supply curve (or **supply schedule**). A schedule showing the quantity of a good that suppliers in a given market desire to sell at each price, holding other things equal.

Supply shock. In macroeconomics, a sudden change in production costs or productivity that has a large and unexpected impact upon aggregate supply. As a result of a supply shock, real GNP and the price level change unexpectedly.

Supply-side economics. A view emphasizing policy measures to affect aggregate supply or potential output. This approach holds that high marginal tax rates on labor and capital incomes reduce work effort and saving.

Tariff. A levy or tax imposed upon each unit of a commodity imported into a country.

Tax incidence. See **incidence.**

Technological change. A change in the process of production or introduction of new products such that more or improved output can be obtained from the same bundle of inputs. It results in an outward shift in the production-possibility curve.

Technological progress. Same as **technological change.**

Terms of trade (in international trade). The "real" terms at which a nation sells its export products and buys its import products. It equals the ratio of an index of export prices to an index of import prices.

Tight-money policy. A central-bank policy of restraining or reducing the money supply and of raising interest rates. This policy has the effect of slowing the growth of real GNP, reducing the rate of inflation, or raising the nation's foreign exchange rate. (Contrast with **easy-money policy.**)

Time deposit. Funds, held in a bank, that have a minimum "time of withdrawal." Included in broad money (M_2) but not in M_1 because they are not accepted as a means of payment.

Token money. Money with little or no intrinsic value.

Total cost. Refer to **cost, total.**

Total factor productivity. An index of productivity that measures total output per unit of total input. The numerator of the index is total output (say GNP), while the denominator is a weighted average of inputs of capital, labor, and resources. The growth of total factor productivity is often taken as an index of the rate of technological progress.

Total product (or **output**). The total amount of a commodity produced, measured in physical units such as bushels of wheat, tons of steel, or number of haircuts.

Total revenue. Price times quantity, or total sales.

Trade balance. See **balance of trade.**

Trade barrier. Any of a number of protectionist devices by which nations discourage imports. Tariffs and quotas are the most visible barriers, but in recent years non-tariff barriers (or NTBs), such as burdensome regulatory proceedings, have replaced more traditional measures.

Transactions demand for money. See **demand for money.**

Transfer payments, government. Payments made by a government to individuals, for which the individual performs no current service in return. Examples are social security payments and unemployment insurance.

Treasury bills (T-bills). Short-term bonds or securities issued by the federal government.

Underground economy. Unreported economic activity. The underground economy includes otherwise legal activities not reported to the taxing authorities (such as garage sales or services "bartered" among friends) and illegal activities (such as the drug trade, gambling, and prostitution).

Unemployment. (1) In economic terms, **involuntary unemployment** occurs if there are qualified workers who would be willing to work at prevailing wages but cannot find jobs. (2) In the official (U.S. Bureau of Labor Statistics) definition, a worker is unemployed if he or she (a) is not working and (b) either is waiting for recall from layoff or has actively looked for work in the last 4 weeks.

Unemployment, frictional. See **frictional unemployment.**

Unemployment rate. The percentage of the labor force that is unemployed.

Unemployment, structural. See **structural unemployment.**

Unit-elastic demand. The situation, between **price-elastic demand** and **price-inelastic demand,** in which price elasticity is just equal to 1 in absolute value. See also **price elasticity of demand.**

Unlimited liability. See **limited liability.**

Usury. The charging of an interest rate above a legal maximum on borrowed money.

Utility (also **total utility**). The total satisfaction derived from the consumption of goods or services. To be contrasted with **marginal utility,** which is the additional utility arising from consumption of an additional unit of the commodity.

Utility-possibility frontier. Analogous to the **production-possibility frontier;** a graph showing the utility or satisfaction of two consumers (or groups), one on each axis. It is downward-sloping to indicate that redistributing income from A to B will lower the utility of A and raise that of B. Points on the utility-possibility frontier display **allocative** (or **Pareto**) **efficiency.** For the allocation implied by these points, it is impossible to devise feasible outcomes that would make one party better off without making someone else worse off.

Value added. The difference between the value of goods produced and the cost of materials and supplies used in producing them. In a $1 loaf of bread embodying $0.60 worth of wheat and other materials, the value added is $0.40. Value added consists of the wages, interest, and profit components added to the output by a firm or industry.

Value-added tax (or **VAT**). A tax levied upon a firm as a percentage of its value added.

Value, paradox of. See **paradox of value.**

Variable. A magnitude of interest that can be defined and measured. Important variables in economics include prices, quantities, interest rates, exchange rates, dollars of wealth, and so forth.

Variable cost. Refer to **cost, variable.**

Velocity of money. In serving its function as a medium of exchange, money moves from buyer to seller to new buyer and so on. Its "velocity" refers to the "speed" of this movement. The **income velocity of money** is defined as nominal GNP divided by the total money supply for the period in question, or $V \equiv P \times Q/M \equiv \text{GNP}/M$.

Vertical equity. See **horizontal equity vs. vertical equity.**

Vertical integration. Refer to **integration, vertical vs. horizontal.**

Vertical merger. See **merger.**

Voluntary unemployment. The unemployment that occurs when an individual perceives the value of wages to be less than the opportunity use of time, say in leisure.

Wealth. The net value of tangible and financial items owned by a nation or person at a point of time. It equals all assets less all liabilities.

Welfare economics. The normative analysis of economic systems, i.e., the study of what is "wrong" or "right" about the economy's functioning.

Welfare state. A practice whereby the government of a mixed economy uses its fiscal and regulatory policies to modify the market distribution of income and to provide service to the population.

What, how, and for whom. The three fundamental problems of economic organization. *What* is the problem of how much of each possible good and service will be produced with the society's limited stock of resources or inputs. *How* is the choice of the particular technique by which each good of the *what* shall be produced. *For whom* refers to the distribution of consumption goods among the members of that society.

Yield. Same as the **interest rate** or **rate of return** on an asset.

INDEX

Page references in **boldface** indicate Glossary terms.